FRANCES BURNEY

FRANCES BURNEY
The Life in the Works

MARGARET ANNE DOODY

Rutgers University Press
NEW BRUNSWICK, NEW JERSEY

Library of Congress Cataloging-in-Publication Data

Doody, Margaret Anne.
    Frances Burney : the life in the works

    Bibliography: p.
    Includes index.
    1. Burney, Fanny, 1752–1840.   2. Novelists,
English—18th century—Biography.   I. Title.
PR3316.A4Z63   1988   823'.6 [B]   88-1921
ISBN 0-8135-1309-X
ISBN 0-8135-1355-3 (pbk.)

Frontispiece. Frances Burney, 1782, by Edward Francesco
Burney (Parham Park, Sussex)

Contents

List of Illustrations   vii

Acknowledgments   xi

Abbreviations and Short Titles   xiv

A Burney Family Tree   xvi

Introduction   1

1   Frances; or, A Young Lady's Entrance into Life   9

2   *Evelina; or, A Young Lady's Entrance into the World*   35

3   *The Witlings:* The Finished Comedy   66

4   *Cecilia; or, Memoirs of an Heiress*   99

5   Love, Loss, and Imprisonment: The Windsor and Kew Tragedies   150

6   Marriage, "Clarinda," and *Camilla; or, A Picture of Youth*   199

7   *Camilla:* Mysteries, Clues, and Guilty Characters   239

8   Incest, Bereavement, and the Late Comic Plays   274

9   *The Wanderer; or, Female Difficulties:* Revolution, the Rights of Woman, and "The Wild Edifice"   313

vi • Contents

10 End of Story   369

    Conclusion   385

    Notes   391

    Index   427

    Index of Works   438

Illustrations

(between pages 98 and 99)

1. Charles Burney, Mus. D., by Sir Joshua Reynolds
   (National Portrait Gallery, London)

2. Esther Sleepe Burney, Frances's mother, by Gervase Spencer
   (Paula Peyraud)

3. Esther Sleepe's sampler
   (Parham Park, Sussex)

4. Esther ("Hetty") Burney, Frances's elder sister, by an unknown artist
   (National Portrait Gallery, London)

5. Susanna Burney (Mrs. Molesworth Phillips), by Edward Francesco Burney
   (National Portrait Gallery, London)

6. Charles Burney, Frances's younger brother, by Daniel Gardner
   (National Portrait Gallery, London)

7. Samuel ("Daddy") Crisp, by Edward Francesco Burney
   (National Portrait Gallery, London)

8. Frontispiece to the 1779 edition of *Evelina*, by Mortimer and Walker
   (Princeton University Library)

9. Frontispiece to volume II of *Evelina*, by Mortimer and Walker
   (Princeton University Library)

10. Edward Francesco Burney, "The Practical Joker"
    (Trustees of the British Museum)

11. Samuel Johnson, by Thomas Trotter, 1782
    (Henry W. and Albert A. Berg Collection, The New York Public
    Library, Astor, Lenox and Tilden Foundations)

12. Hester Thrale, by an unknown artist, c. 1785
    (National Portrait Gallery, London)

13. "Mrs. Philips' Minuet," by Dr. Charles Burney
    (British Library)

14. Mrs. Thrale, silhouette, by an unknown artist
    (Henry W. and Albert A. Berg Collection, The New York Public
    Library, Astor, Lenox and Tilden Foundations)

15. Illustration to *Cecilia* by E. F. Burney and Walker, in *Norfolk Ladies
    Pocket Book*
    (Henry W. and Albert A. Berg Collection, The New York Public
    Library, Astor, Lenox and Tilden Foundations)

16. Frontispiece to German edition of *Cecilia*
    (Princeton University Library)

17. Miniature of Frances Burney, by John Bogle, 1783
    (Paula Peyraud)

18. Frances Burney, by Edward Francesco Burney, c. 1784–85
    (National Portrait Gallery, London)

19. Caricature (1784) referring to dramatic "Epilogue" by Miles Andrews,
    based on *Cecilia*
    (Trustees of the British Museum)

20. George Owen Cambridge, by an unknown artist
    (National Portrait Gallery, London)

21. Mary Delany, silhouette by Lady Elizabeth Templetown
    (Henry W. and Albert A. Berg Collection, The New York Public
    Library, Astor, Lenox and Tilden Foundations)

22. Juliana Schwellenberg and Queen Charlotte in Thomas Rowlandson's
    "The Prospect Before Us," 1788
    (Trustees of the British Museum)

23. Detail: Mrs. Schwellenberg as toad-eater in James Gillray's "The Of-
    fering to Liberty"
    (Trustees of the British Museum)

24. General d'Arblay, by Carle and Horace Vernet, 1817
(Parham Park, Sussex)

25. Manuscript page of "Clarinda" story, an earlier form of *Camilla*
(British Library)

26. Alex at three years old, silhouettes by Amelia Locke
(Henry W. and Albert A. Berg Collection, The New York Public
Library, Astor, Lenox and Tilden Foundations)

27. "Camilla Cottage," drawing presumably by General Alexandre
d'Arblay
(National Portrait Gallery, London)

28. Captain (later Admiral) James Burney, silhouette by an unknown artist
(National Portrait Gallery, London)

29. Portrait by John Hoppner of a woman presumed to be Sarah Harriet
Burney
(National Portrait Gallery, London)

30. "À Maman, Juvenile Birthday Verses from Alex d'Arblay to his Mother"
(Henry W. and Albert A. Berg Collection, The New York Public Library, Astor, Lenox and Tilden Foundations)

31. James Gillray, "The Storm rising;—or—the Republican Flotilla in
danger," February 1798
(Princeton University Library)

32. Stonehenge, drawing by Thomas Hearne, engraving by W. Byrne and
T. Medland, 1786
(National Portrait Gallery, London)

Acknowledgments

In the production of any book, a number of people and influences are at work. The chief influence upon this book has been Frances Burney herself; I am glad I discovered her novels in my youth and read them for pleasure before I knew that I was going to write about them. I am grateful to the Guggenheim Foundation for awarding me a Fellowship that allowed me to read the unpublished works of Burney in the Henry W. and Albert A. Berg Collection of the New York Public Library in 1979. I have a particular debt of longstanding personal gratitude to Catherine M. Ing who as my tutor in undergraduate days at Oxford always encouraged the lively reading of eighteenth-century novels; Catherine Ing, who became a permanent friend, always encouraged the work on Burney, and left me a legacy that allowed me to buy a Burney letter, printed in this book for the first time. My gratitude for that gift is counterbalanced by the sense of loss, and the sad knowledge that Catherine will never see the book she knew I was working on, parts of which I wrote at her house in Oxford.

The Princeton Committee for Research in the Humanities gave me a grant that permitted me to return to England and read Burney material in the British collections; Princeton also assisted me in paying for the typing and indexing of the manuscript. Librarians have been very helpful. I should like to thank the archival staff of the Huntington Library, San Marino, California, and Shelley Bennet of the Prints and Drawings Collection at that Library. I should also thank the staff of the John Rylands Library, Manchester; the Bodleian Library, Oxford; the Manuscript Room of the British Library and the Print Collections of the British Museum, especially Duncan Smith of the British Museum Print Room and Chris Rawlings of the British Library for their help in assisting me to obtain illustrations; the Osborn Collection, Yale University Library; the curators of manuscripts at the Houghton Library, Harvard University; the Librarian and curator of the library of Trinity College, Cambridge; and the librarian and archivist of the Dunedin Library, Dunedin, New Zealand. I should render special thanks for perpetual help to the staff of the Rare Books and Manuscripts Collections of the Firestone Library, Princeton University. A very particular debt of gratitude is owed to Dr. Lola Szladits, curator of the Henry W. and Albert A. Berg Collection, Astor, Lenox and Tilden Foundations of the New York Public Library, a zealous but sympathetic guardian of the Burney treasure. The Library has given kind permission to quote here from Burney texts. I am glad to have the opportunity to express personal thanks also to Sarah Wimbush of the National Portrait Gallery Archive, London, for kindness in helping me to find and to reproduce Burney material. I am grateful, as well, to Lindy Jordan for providing transport to Parham Park, and a happy and fruitful afternoon.

I wish to express heartfelt thanks for both general encouragement and particular response to queries offered by colleagues at the institutions where I have taught and elsewhere, particularly the following: Paula Backscheider, James Basker, Edward A. and Lillian D. Bloom, Zelda Boyd, Marilyn Butler, Patricia Dahlman Crown, Julia Epstein, Jan Fergus, Joyce Hemlow, Claudia Johnson, Thomas Keymer, Ulrich C. Knoepflmacher, Leonard Michaels, David Miller, Felicity Nussbaum, Ruth Perry, Clark Piper, Thomas P. Roche, Jr., Robert Spoo, John Worthen. My colleague Richard Kroll is a perpetual fountain of good sense and knowledge and a generous and forthright monitor of the good. Lars Troide at the Burney Project at McGill University has been unfailingly kind and helpful in answering queries and sharing knowledge, as has Alvaro Ribeiro, editor of Charles Burney's *Letters*. Paula Peyraud has been wonderfully kind in sharing material, knowledge, and enthusiasm.

Those who have taught will know how much I owe to my students over many years and in many classes. But I should like to make special reference to graduate students in eighteenth-century studies at Princeton in recent years who have been a powerful source of encouragement and stimulation: Carol Barash, Aileen Douglas, Fraser Easton, Melinda Finberg, Siobhàn Kilfeather, David Kramer, Jayne Lewis, Marie McAllister, Robert Mack, Julie Peters. Jayne Lewis is owed particular thanks for wrestling the manuscript onto a word processor during the long hot summer of 1987.

My expression of deepest thanks is owed to two people outside my own institution whom I yet count among my closest colleagues, and with whom I am collaborating in separate ventures. Peter Sabor of Queen's University, Kingston, Ontario, is an inspiration to sound scholarship; I value both the witty friend and the acute judge who patiently and thoroughly read chapters as they emerged. Florian Stuber, of the Fashion Institute of Technology,

New York City, is a deeply valued friend who possesses an illuminating understanding of the eighteenth century. I like to think that I introduced him to Burney, but Florian, with his superb capacity for detailed analytical reading, has brought out many points in the novels. Florian has also read my chapters as they emerged—not once but twice, in the old version and the new. It is scarcely necessary to add that while much that is good is owing to Peter Sabor and Florian Stuber, any errors or infelicities that remain are entirely my own responsibility.

It would not seem right to send this book on its way without expressing thanks to two editors. Andrew Brown of Cambridge University Press has been a helpful and tough-minded encourager of the project for several years, who has taken trouble over it when it was in a less complete state. I am truly happy also to express here my gratitude to Leslie Mitchner of Rutgers University Press, whose belief in the book has been an inspiration, and a decided stimulus to its completion.

Princeton, N.J.
October 1987

Abbreviations and Short Titles

Works by Frances Burney

A Busy Day	*A Busy Day*. Edited by Tara Ghoshal Wallace. New Brunswick, N.J.: Rutgers University Press, 1984. (Cloth edition; paperback edition lacks important materials.)
Camilla	*Camilla; or, A Picture of Youth*. Edited with an introduction by Edward A. Bloom and Lillian D. Bloom. 5 vols. in 1. London: Oxford University Press, 1972.
Cecilia	*Cecilia; or, Memoirs of an Heiress*. Edited by Peter Sabor and Margaret Anne Doody, with an introduction by Margaret Anne Doody. 5 vols. in 1. London: Oxford University Press, 1988.
D&L	*The Diary and Letters of Madame d'Arblay*. Edited by her Niece [Charlotte Barrett]. 7 vols. 1842–1847; new ed. London: Henry Colburn, 1854.
ED	*The Early Diary of Frances Burney, 1768–1778*. Edited by Annie Raine Ellis. 2 vols. 1889; rev. ed. London: George Bell and Sons, 1907.
Evelina	*Evelina; or, The History of a Young Lady's Entrance into the World*. Edited with an introduction by Edward A. Bloom. 3 vols. in 1. Oxford: Oxford University Press, 1970.
J&L	*The Journals and Letters of Fanny Burney (Madame d'Arblay), 1791–1840*. Edited by Joyce Hemlow et al. 12 vols. Oxford: Clarendon Press, 1972–1984.

Memoirs	*Memoirs of Doctor Burney, arranged from his own Manuscripts, from Family Papers, and from Personal Recollections.* By his Daughter, Madame d'Arblay. 3 vols. London: Edward Moxon, 1832.
The Wanderer	*The Wanderer; or, Female Difficulties.* 5 vols. London: Longman, Hurst, Rees, Orme, and Brown, 1814.

Manuscript Collections

Berg MS	The Henry W. and Albert A. Berg Collection, The New York Public Library, Astor, Lenox, and Tilden Foundations, New York
BL Egerton MS	Egerton manuscripts (originally in the Barrett Collection), British Library, London
Rylands MS	English manuscript collection, John Rylands University Library, Manchester

Other Sources

Hemlow	Joyce Hemlow, *The History of Fanny Burney.* Oxford: Clarendon Press, 1958.
Lonsdale	Roger Lonsdale, *Dr. Charles Burney: A Literary Biography.* Oxford: Clarendon Press, 1965.
Thraliana	*Thraliana: The Diary of Mrs. Hester Lynch Thrale (Later Mrs. Piozzi), 1776–1809.* Edited by Katharine C. Balderston. 2 vols. (paged continuously). 2nd ed. Oxford: Clarendon Press, 1951.

A Burney Family Tree

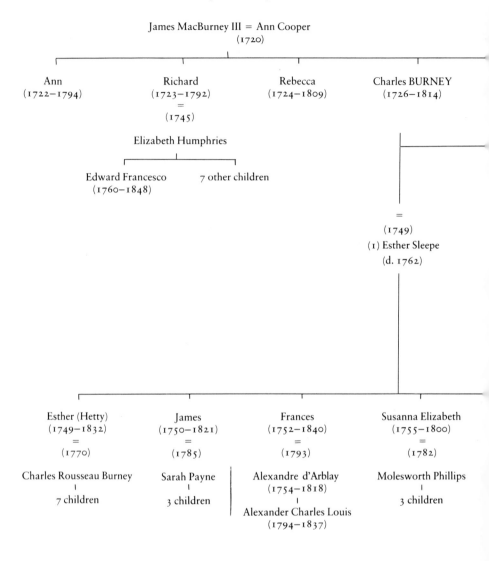

James MacBurney III = Ann Cooper
(1720)

Ann
(1722–1794)

Richard
(1723–1792)
=
(1745)
Elizabeth Humphries

Rebecca
(1724–1809)

Charles BURNEY
(1726–1814)

Edward Francesco
(1760–1848)

7 other children

=
(1749)
(1) Esther Sleepe
(d. 1762)

Esther (Hetty)
(1749–1832)
=
(1770)
Charles Rousseau Burney
|
7 children

James
(1750–1821)
=
(1785)
Sarah Payne
|
3 children

Frances
(1752–1840)
=
(1793)
Alexandre d'Arblay
(1754–1818)
|
Alexander Charles Louis
(1794–1837)

Susanna Elizabeth
(1755–1800)
=
(1782)
Molesworth Phillips
|
3 children

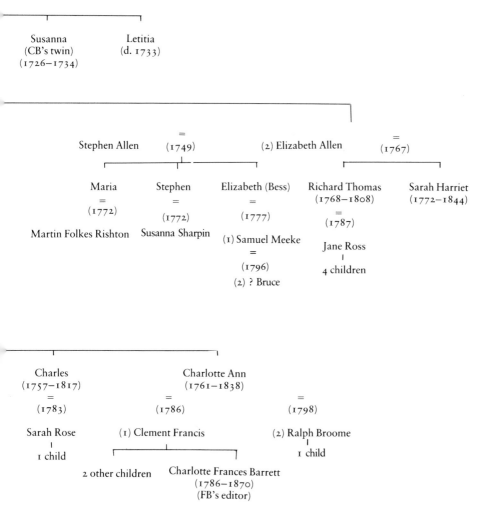

Susanna
(CB's twin)
(1726–1734)

Letitia
(d. 1733)

Stephen Allen = (1749) (2) Elizabeth Allen = (1767)

Maria
=
(1772)
Martin Folkes Rishton

Stephen
=
(1772)
Susanna Sharpin

Elizabeth (Bess)
=
(1777)
(1) Samuel Meeke
=
(1796)
(2) ? Bruce

Richard Thomas
(1768–1808)
=
(1787)
Jane Ross
|
4 children

Sarah Harriet
(1772–1844)

Charles
(1757–1817)
=
(1783)
Sarah Rose
|
1 child

Charlotte Ann
(1761–1838)
=
(1786)
(1) Clement Francis

=
(1798)
(2) Ralph Broome
|
1 child

2 other children

Charlotte Frances Barrett
(1786–1870)
(FB's editor)

NOTE: This family tree has been simplified to eliminate children who did not survive to grow up and relatives beyond FB's immediate family who are not important to this biography.

FRANCES BURNEY

Introduction

Frances Burney has long enjoyed a reputation, but it is an obscured reputation. Her name (or one of her names) appears, at least for a condescending sentence or two, in any history of the English novel. To F. R. Leavis, for instance, she represents an early phase of the English fictional tradition, before the truly Great Tradition of the English novel began. Yet, in the twentieth century Burney's fame has been to a large extent that not of a novelist but of a diarist. The publication of her *Diary and Letters* begun in 1843 (only three years after her death) was intended by the editor, her niece Charlotte Barrett, as an admiring tribute. The new volumes were read with interest by the Victorian public; their effect was to begin to displace the novelist by the diarist, initiating a steady decline in her reputation as a writer of fiction. Austin Dobson was to wonder why Macaulay, an early reviewer who praised the *Diary,* did not "place it high above Mme D'Arblay's efforts as a novelist," since the *Diary* has "the charm of the best passages in *Evelina"* with "the further advantage that it is true; and that it deals with real people."[1] It is rather hard on the novelist's art in general to decide that as reading matter "real people" and true events should be essentially preferable to fictional ones. The antifictional prejudice set one aspect of Burney's writing career against another. Burney's identity as a diarist who happened to write some fiction was hardened by the publication of the *Early Diary* (1889) and in our time by Joyce Hemlow's edition of the *Journal and Letters* (1972–1984). No one interested in Frances Burney can disregard these (nor the corrected and amplified *Diary* forthcoming, edited by Lars Troide).[2] Yet if Frances Burney had not been one of England's great diarists, she might have held her place as a novelist more tenaciously. In any case, the Victorians' condescending attitude to both the fiction of the previous century in general and to the work of the early female novelists in particular was bound to injure the estimation of Burney's novels. Certain hackneyed views of Frances Burney's fiction were built into the critical orthodoxy by the end of the last century and carried over into our own: *Evelina* is charming save for certain passages of horseplay, *Cecilia* is written in Johnsonese, the late novels are sad fallings-off from the charming *Evelina*, and so on. Such complacent received opinions are customarily corrected by time. (Consider the Victorians' truisms about Fielding and Smollett, and the early twentieth-century opinions of Dickens's vulgarity and lack of moral subtlety.) In Burney's case, however, the process of rehabilitation has been retarded both by the popularity of the diary material and by a persistent tendency to compare Burney only with Austen and only to Burney's detriment. The novels, when they are not being viewed as less successful diaries of a slightly odd kind, are seen as pale forerunners of Austen's work, or useful examples of failure to set against Austen's success. Even Burney's first and most widely read novel, *Evelina* (1778), is not accorded a very high place by its recent modern editor, who concludes his "Introduction" by pointing to a "line of influence" that "culminates superbly in Jane Austen," adding that "with her superior comic vision, acute psychological understanding, and sheer craftsmanship, Jane has overshadowed her predecessor."[3] Burney, the winsome but inferior author of *Evelina*, is almost essential to critics who want to point out the acceptable, canonized, and safe Jane Austen ("Jane" indeed!) as the model for ladies' writing. It is as if there were a quota for female fiction writers, preferably no more than one per century or at most per half-century. We have one already in Austen, the position is filled—and Austen is so safe, so unabrasive. (Recent reprintings of a number of eighteenth-century and early nineteenth-century novels by women elicited this familiar and predictable reaction from male reviewers for the *TLS*, the *London Review,* and *The New York Review of Books*.) The terms of the implied argument are really debatable if Austen and Burney are fairly considered. Austen may or may not have "superior" comic vision—it depends partly on one's feelings about violence in comedy. Burney's comedy is much more violent and disturbing than Austen's—I happen to prefer that, or at least I do half the time.

The important thing, however, is that Austen and Burney are very *different* writers. When they are both at their best and most characteristic, they are most unlike. Should we readily assume that it is easy to make comparisons between a realistic novelist who employs mannered and unbroken comedy, and an expressionistic novelist who mingles the pathetic and the comic, the grotesque and the farcical? Nobody would now say that Dickens should have written like Trollope, or like Henry James. We can have all of these—why cannot we have a number of different kinds of women writers? Austen's reputation needs none of such help as can be gained by snubbing a predecessor and contemporary whom she admired. In my own study I have largely, if not entirely, resisted making allusions to Austen's novels in relation to Burney's, feeling that that kind of thing has been overdone, and has contributed to some very poor criticism of both.

What Frances Burney did attempt to do, and precisely where her greatest strength lies, can be considered only in an examination of all her novels—not merely *Evelina*. The stale old assessments have omitted to remark that Burney is a large-scale novelist, an ambitious novelist. Rather than satirizing individual follies, or offering paragon heroines in conventional love stories, the author uses satire of follies, the adventures of a heroine, and the frame of a love story (more and more strangely treated in each novel) for her own purposes. Burney offers not a reflection but an examination of her society in its structure, functions, and beliefs. Much more like Dickens than Austen, she attacks her society's principles. She writes well about money and work, and extremely well about social class. She is not content with illustrating comic individual aberration from the norm; she sees in her characters the grotesque and macabre symptoms of society's own perverseness, and of the wildness in the human psyche that leads to the creation of such strange structures as society itself.

It is her insight into her society that makes Burney's comedy so telling—and she is a very good comic writer. Understanding her world, she also understands how to experiment with the novel as a form. After the effective and subtle use of apparently artless epistolary narration in *Evelina*, in *Cecilia* (1782) she employed the third person, with a wide variety of effects. In *Camilla* (1796) she plays with mystery, intertextuality, and bizarre metaphor; she also experiments with *style indirect libre*.[4] *The Wanderer* (1814), with its inset narratives, its mystery and fragmentation (indicated in the Stonehenge sequence), is a unique Romantic novel, drawing upon the feminist and Gothic traditions, engaging in conversation with Burney's own successors (such as Charlotte Smith and Ann Radcliffe) who had themselves been influenced by her earlier works.

All of Burney's novels are violent. She is a student of aggression and obsession; one of her major motifs is suicide. She is masterly at depicting emotional blackmail. The forms of her novels are designed to express tension; each plot is an image of anxiety. She developed characteristic methods of making farcical, grotesque, or macabre images serve thematic complexity. She is not a "realistic" novelist, but then few novelists are; "realism" is an ingredient novelists use. Burney is further away from an imaginary realistic meridian than Jane Austen —much further, along with Smollett, Dickens, and Joyce. A reading of her novels as if they were diaries (rather than vice versa) is fundamentally mistaken. Burney's works have long suffered from a lack of literary reading. The novels simply need to be read as if they mattered, and as if they were novels.

There are encouraging signs that the tide may even now be turning in Burney's favor, that the process of rehabilitation may have begun. Articles and comments by Patricia Spacks, Janet Todd, Jan Fergus, and Julia Epstein all cast some new light on Burney's written work.[5] John J. Richetti has some interesting things to say about the narrative mode of *Evelina*, and J. N. Waddell in his studies of Burney's language has given us a glimpse of a woman writer as a linguistic innovator, a language-maker (welcome indeed in an era when theories promote the notion of woman's lack of claim to language).[6] The recent short books by Judy Simons and D. D. Devlin provide occasional interesting insights and despite their hesitancies, insecurities, and qualifications are symptomatic of a growing tendency to take Burney's work (and her life) seriously, a tendency the more marked in Kristina Straub's longer and more thoughtful study *Divided Fictions: Fanny Burney and the Feminine Strategy.*[7] The forthcoming book by Julia Epstein, an important and serious study of Burney, will mark a major step in her rehabilitation.

Even more heartening is the republication of Burney's works. *Evelina, Cecilia,* and *Camilla* are now available as World's Classics paperbacks. *Cecilia* appeared as a Virago paperback in 1985.[8] Pandora promises a reissue of *The Wanderer,* and the World's Classics will provide a paperback edition, fully annotated. Never republished since 1814, this last novel will soon be available in competing editions. One of Burney's plays, her comedy *A Busy Day,* was given its first printing in 1984, in a Rutgers University Press edition edited by Tara G. Wallace. There are reasons to hope that others of the manuscript plays will be edited and printed. Nothing can do more good to Burney's reputation than her fictions' being available.

When I began my own work on Burney in the middle of the last decade, the atmosphere was very different. After my offer to edit either *Cecilia* or *The Wanderer* was turned down by publishers, I felt I ought to try to create a wider appreciation of Burney's novels. This project began as a short critical book on the novels. I soon realized, however, that I could not rewrite the literary estimate of Burney's work as it really needed to be rewritten without looking at important manuscripts, particularly those in the Berg Collection in New York. It was not until I had taken employment on the American side of the Atlantic that I was able to look at these manuscripts. The generosity of the Guggenheim Foundation enabled me to travel from California to do extensive research in New York and London in 1979. Meanwhile, old negative critical judgments of Burney's novels were perforce carried about in my luggage, and encountered in every library, to be stumbled upon almost every time I looked up a reference. The stimulus of anger helped to drive me on during the time that I read the manuscripts and realized that the critical work as originally envisaged would now be impossible for me to write. The manuscripts of the plays, especially, not only served to illuminate the novels but also demanded a couple of chapters to themselves. The topography of an imaginative and emotional literary world could at last be seen. But commentary on Burney's late comedies dealing with the family romance, or on the dramatic tragedies Burney wrote during her agony at the court of King George III, could not be comprehended by any reader without the reader's knowing the story of Burney's own life and inner conflicts. I therefore decided that the author's work as a whole should be given its biographical setting, and that my discussion should include as thematic narrative the story of the author's life and its deepest sources of pain and self-division.

The story of the author's life as it is here set out is not the whole story. Indeed, I have had to exclude some amusing anecdotes, and the account of many major events is pared down. Nor do I carry out the story in detail beyond the term of Burney's career as a publishing writer of fiction. Frances Burney's own life is here presented as subordinate to her activity as a writer. It may be objected that I have made Dr. Charles Burney the villain of the piece, but that would be a misinterpretation of my intention. Charles Burney's own difficulties are sympathetically considered. The "blame" for much unhappiness, if "blame" there must be, rests partly on the culture of the Burneys' time. In any case, the great musicologist has had his own biographers and defenders, and will have them again. It is simply not my business here to veil Charles Burney's defects at Frances Burney's expense. What is said of Charles here is included only for the sake of illuminating Frances Burney's life and works—although she, who so much wanted to shield and glorify her father, would not be totally happy at such an exposure.

The literary biographer, it must be admitted, is engaged in a strange and perhaps unholy task, both unravelling what is woven together (the texture of the subject's own writings) and making a new fabric or fabrication. This new fabric is a tissue of odds and ends, scraps, clues; it takes threads of connection that the subject in some sense tried to conceal and makes them into figures in the carpet. The old New Criticism, under whose dispensation I came of age (the only alternative aesthetic being the cool generic taxonomies of the Chicago School) taught us that it is wrong, ignoble, anti-intellectual to suggest a connection between an author's lived life and the printed oeuvre. Only the vulgar connect Life and Art. The new dispensation of the *new* new criticism, the refined aestheticism of structuralism and deconstruction, enjoins us to eschew any notion of the author's having any importance whatsoever. The Language—under social pressure—writes the text, and the writer is nowhere. This vaticide at least puts all writers on a level (as nonentities), but of course denies any interest in biography. It remains, however, a stubborn fact that those novelists whose novels have been most talked of have had a number of biographies written about them. By contributing my literary biography, I may put Burney in a position to be the more prized by my successors, who, decrying the need for any biography at all, will deal solely with her fiction. She will thus at length arrive at that bourne of aesthetic purity so much to be prized, and so likely to be granted to the famous. Meanwhile, I wish to stress that I genuinely believe Burney to be a true artist who made something handsome and lasting out of her discontents. All novelists have their blacking factory somewhere. My pursuit is born out of sympathy; the biography is not an attempt to find faults or to look pityingly down or to condescend to the past, but to examine the effort and pain that goes into human art and human life.

Frances Burney is a sufficiently complex subject to raise interesting problems for the biographer. The first and most immediately pressing is—what to call her? She published in later life as Madame D'Arblay—but this formal-sounding Frenchwoman is not the author of *Evelina* or *Cecilia*. Any marital title militates against female success in gaining literary esteem, but "Madame" particularly will not do. No, she must have simply a first name and a last name. But the last name is so varied that she may turn up in a library filed and shelved under "B" or "A" or even "D." Her last name after her marriage was "d'Arblay," but she never relinquished the maiden name entirely; before marrying she often signs letters with the initials "F.B." and after marriage as "F.B.d'A." Let "Burney" remain—but her first name is as troublesome a matter. For nearly a century we have been calling the author "Fanny"—a familiarity assumed after the Diaries were published, and really cemented by Austin Dobson's *Fanny Burney* in 1903. Yet we are not, after all, among her intimates; the nickname should not be put on book covers and title pages, any more than Boswell's *Life of Johnson* should be presented as by "Jemmy" Boswell. "Fanny" is a patronizing diminutive. It makes the author sound the harmless, childish, priggish girl-woman that many critics want her to be—as if the heroine of *Mansfield Park* had set up as novelist. Let her have an adult full name. That this would be her wish is clear from the fact that it is her own practice: she refers to herself as "Frances" throughout the *Memoirs of Doctor Burney*. The Victorian editor of the *Early Diary* refers to her subject very properly as "Frances Burney." I shall follow suit, despite long precedent in this century. The central character in my story is "Frances Burney"; the only reasonable alternative would be "Frances Burney d'Arblay." "Frances Burney" in my narrative refers to the human woman who was born and died, and wrote and read, and had the experiences that she put to use in her writing. As the author, she is referred to only as "Burney." There is strong eighteenth-century precedent for referring to the author of *Evelina* and *Cecilia* in that form. The author was "Miss Burney" or simply "Burney" to her public, as when she was cited in 1783 in Samuel Hoole's poem *Aurelia:* "I stood a favouring Muse, at BURNEY's side."[9] The old nickname still slips in at times, but "Fanny" is now reserved for the human person in her roles as daughter and sister and intimate friend—with some of the implicit anxieties the diminutive itself expresses. Burney herself would never have signed her public and published work as "Fanny" and I think she would approve my method—she who had such a number of names and at the end of at least one letter signed herself jovially "Francesca Scriblerus."[10] She understood the importance of *persona*, and the fact that it is itself a creation. There is a nice irony in all this ado about her name, for she herself is extremely conscious of the significance of names. Almost every one of her novels or plays deals with the name problem as it affects a woman. Indeed, a woman's problematic relation to society is signified by her name, and her name is part of a woman's problem. Who a woman is does not square with what she is called.

That being so, it is perhaps in vain to wish that the libraries of the world would reach a concord in their catalogue entries concerning this author. It is fortunately a more reasonable hope that soon the catalogues of public libraries will refer readers to modern reprints of Burney's novels, that bookstores will offer them for sale on paperback shelves, and that the process of re-reading Frances Burney will have begun.

Frances; or, A Young Lady's Entrance into Life

The works of any artist represent the meeting of three histories: the life of the individual, the cultural life of the surrounding society, and the tradition of the chosen art. Frances Burney's works reflected upon as well as reflected the world she knew, and she contributed something new to the genre in which she worked. For these reasons her works merit our attention. The story of Frances Burney's works is deeply involved also with the story of her life. We cannot fully appreciate what she achieved until we have some idea of what she experienced. She often draws upon private psychological material, and upon the allegories suggested by intricate family relationships, even when such material is not only creatively disguised but transcended in the art of her fiction.

By now it is surely possible to rid ourselves of the notion that any person (let alone one who produces a number of fictions dealing extensively with obsession, blackmail, suicide) can be comfortably dismissed as "a singularly uncomplicated personality," as one of Burney's modern critics has described her. It is not only unreasonably patronizing but a fudging of the facts to refer to her first novel as emerging "from the orderly pattern of a tranquil existence."[1] Perhaps such things have been said because of a quasi-belief since the nineteenth century that eighteenth-century people were amusing characters, not quite serious human beings (see Macaulay's Johnson). Even in the twentieth century this attitude has tended to linger, though Johnson, Swift, and Pope have escaped. Richardson, Fielding, and Smollet (despite biographies) have not yet received the same kind of attention as Dickens or George Eliot; personal experience, psychic pain, creative struggle are not thought of as animating their writings. In Burney's case even her justly admired biographer, Joyce Hemlow (to whose massive research I am deeply indebted) sees no deep connection between the life and the writings. Roger Lonsdale in his literary biography of Charles Burney (1965) comes to the conclusion that his subject was interesting because of his work and his friendships, but was "not a profound personality."[2] We do our subjects an injustice if we avoid clues to their complexities. Acknowledgment of the complexities, of course, also means that we shall not like everything that we see.

In my study of Frances Burney's life and works I have become, though almost unwillingly, increasingly impressed by the vital importance to her—both in her life and her writings—of her relationship with her father. That relationship, in its many complications, has become a major strand in my story of her writing life and the life of her works. In that story Charles Burney is the major secondary character, as he was in her life. In her *Memoirs of Doctor Burney* (1832), published when Frances was eighty, she makes herself into the second most important character in *his* life, as some critics have noted unfavorably. The only way she could bring herself to tell her own story in public was to tell the story of her father, and in doing so glorified both almost out of recognition. She re-creates Dr. Burney as the perfect gentleman, urbane and courtly (not quite what he was, but what he wanted to be). In her inexcusable tampering with his own journals and other documents she insists on presenting herself as his favorite and most admired child, suppressing reality in order to give herself the satisfaction she craved and was always partially denied. There is a great deal of psychological evidence in this biography (or autobiography), and the points at which awkwardness of style markedly increases usually indicate that important material is struggling to get through and being suppressed. For one thing, in the *Memoirs* Frances Burney was walking cautiously over the family plot, trying not to disturb any of the skeletons. She knew where the bodies were buried— there are a number of smothered facts (discord, illegitimacy, incest). And she is walking not only through the family boneyard, but through her own and what she guesses to be her father's.

Frances Burney was hampered in writing the *Memoirs* by the felt need to justify herself to the dead father still living in her mind, and also by that singular desire (not uncommon in familial biographers) to exonerate the subject from faults that he himself did not recognize, or recognize as defects. The moments at which Frances almost dares to become critical are the moments of greatest effort at exculpation, for she did have grudges against—or conflicts with—her father which she could not allow herself to acknowledge. The daughter officially refuses to allow any faults at all in her subject. At the end of her biography she acknowledges that in biographies it is customary "to delineate the character of him whom it has brought to view, with its FAILINGS as well as its EXCELLENCIES," but goes on to say defiantly that though "Impartiality" and "Truth" demand this contrast, it is impossible in her case, as her subject had no failings whatsoever.[3] By making her father publicly perfect, embalming him as a faultless hero, Frances made herself into the faultless daughter, to whom no blame or guilt could attach, and in this way proved herself at last worthy of his love. To accomplish this feat she was willing to censor and even ruthlessly destroy Burney's own manuscript *Memoir*—thus getting an unconscious revenge, too, on the father who had formerly censored her writings. The *Memoirs of Doctor Burney* is the inadvertently explicit record of the tensions between father and daughter. In that book we can clearly trace, even against the writer's wishes, the ways in which the psychic paths of both met and crossed and intertwined. A full discussion of Frances Burney's own history, then, must include the story of Charles Burney.

Charles Burney, born in 1726, was the son of James Macburney, dancer, musician, and portrait painter. (In Charles's generation the "Mac" was dropped —Scottish names were not assets.) James's multifarious talents are typical of the Burney family. He also displayed what one might call the Burney family habit of making misalliances and indulging in elopements; Charles Burney's account of James's first marriage survives:

> Early in his life, my father lost the favour of his sire, by eloping, from home, to marry a young actress of Goodman's-Fields' theatre, by whom he had a very large family. My grandfather's affection was completely alienated by this marriage. . . . To the usual obduracy of old age, he afterwards added a far more than similar indiscretion himself, by marrying a female domestic, to whom, and to a son . . . of that marriage, he bequeathed all his possessions.[4]

The Burney ability to cut off affection and connection is here first illustrated. Charles, though an innocent sufferer through this disinheritance, may ironically have inherited the notion that such acts of total parental displeasure were manly and admirable.

Charles was not the offspring of the young actress, Rebecca Ellis, but of James's second wife, Anne Cooper of Shrewsbury. James moved among dancers, actors, painters, and musicians (riff-raff, according to the social standards of the day), earning little and giving little thought to the future. There were other children. Charles was born with a twin, his sister Susanna, who died when they were age eight. The loss of that twin sister must have left Charles with a sense of irremediable absence, and may help to explain his lifelong need of company, especially feminine company, and his attraction to and for women in friendly relationships. He never forgot that sister "for whom he cherished a peculiar fondness that he seemed tenderly to transmit to the beloved and meritorious daughter to whom he gave her name," as Frances acknowledges at one point in the *Memoirs*.[5] It was always Susanna, not Frances, who was the favorite daughter. In relations with all of his daughters—unusually kind, friendly, and familiar for his period—Charles Burney can be seen as recapturing that early lost relationship.

We know little about Charles's parents; Frances suppressed everything she discovered:

> What respected his family . . . was utterly unpleasant—& quite useless to be kept alive. The dissipated facility & negligence of his Witty . . . but careless Father; the niggardly unfeelingness of his nearly unnatural Mother . . . furnish matter . . . unnecessary . . . opening to the publick view a species of Family degradation to which the Name of Burney Now gives no similitude.[6]

If the father was feckless and the mother cold and mean, it is probable that the "Family degradation" included severe marital discord. Charles always had to believe that his father loved him; it is evidently his mother he blames for what happened to him.[7] At the time of his twin's death, Charles and his brother Richard were banished from home. For whatever reason (poverty must have been a large factor), the parents parked the two boys in a dame-school (or baby farm) in the village of Condover, under the care of one nurse Ball. There they stayed, for five years or more, neglected and apparently forgotten. (It is only speculation, but the spendthrift father might have been sent to debtor's prison for a while—"degradation.") Frances speaks of her father's career as "the progress of a nearly abandoned Child, from a small village of Shropshire, to a Man . . . elevated to an intellectual rank in society, as a Man of Letters."[8] But the Child is father of the Man. The progress of Dr. Burney was always motivated by a deep desire for recognition, for an identity, for an assured place that no one could take from him. Genius and drive helped him to raise his status (and with it, that of other musicians), and enabled him practically to invent musicology as a serious study for the English-speaking world. As Lonsdale recognizes, he wanted to be a "man of letters" because men of letters were given a place in society denied to the music teacher or musician. His ambition—and snobbishness—had deep roots. His relation to society could be managed, whereas childhood relations with the parents could not. He could make his world accept him, take him in, offer him prizes for good behavior. The emotional content of social praise and awards was evidently very great for Charles Burney, as is seen in his delight in his Oxford doctorate (1769) and his insistence on being portrayed by Reynolds in his doctoral robes, despite Johnson's objection. (See Fig. 1.) His fear of any kind of censure is noticeable, particulary in his somewhat underhanded arrangements that reviews of his books should be done by friends in consultation with himself.[9]

Charles Burney was always afraid of being again abandoned, and some of his occasional harshness to his children can be seen as an effort to forestall being abandoned by them. Otherwise, he was grateful to anyone who was kind to him, and enormously careful not to give offense. He kept friends well, and made new friends easily. No one more enjoyed being included in any social group. He went out of his way to charm, to flatter, to sustain others' favorable feelings in his absence as in his presence. He wrote amusing letters, and sent little rhymed tetrameter verses at the drop of a hat. If there were any kind of disagreement, he felt it—almost literally. He writes to Mrs. Thrale in November 1777, after some argument with Mr. Thrale, "I know not how it is, but I feel less sore after a beating from him than anyone else who can hit hard." Verbal blows are "a beating." To prevent further blows he placates with sweets, in an image unconsciously telling:

> When I put Comp^{ts}. to my Master into your hands, who knows how dearly he loves them, I need not fear his being over-dosed. Pray administer to him just as many as you can get him to swallow without Nausea.[10]

Charles Burney was willing to compliment people to satiety and beyond. Flattery was a vital activity; some of his own family in the fallout of these showers of well-directed sweets may have felt overdosed or feared "Nausea." Frances was always suspicious of public compliments.

Charles Burney never willingly made an enemy. The one exception to this perpetual agreeableness is his intense hostility to Sir John Hawkins, the rival historian of music. That hostility, even to the point of mean behavior, is explicable if one imagines the deeper significance of that rivalry: the fear that he might be abandoned by the world in favor of the cuckoo-sibling. Yet the attacks upon Hawkins were conducted behind the scenes. Charles Burney was almost incapable of getting angry with anyone to his face. Quarrelling in the strict sense, involving dispute between two people both present and empowered to speak, was difficult, even impossible, for Charles Burney, and for his children. The Burney method in anger was to take evasive action, or to retreat behind a barrier, pretending that the offender was erased from the cosmos. In his own *History of Music* (1776–1789), Burney never mentions Hawkins's name. But as long as other people did deserve to exist, they could be charmed.

Charles's early education incessantly taught him that charm could work wonders, and that ambition and talents need charm to win love and status. After some schooling, and some training in music by his elder half-brother, he was apprenticed in his teens to Thomas Arne, the celebrated musician, and went to London. Arne proved an unappreciative taskmaster, somewhat jealous of outstandingly talented pupils. From a life of drudgery Charles was rescued through his friendship with Fulke Greville. The aristocratic Greville, a sophisticated man about town, had complained to his harpsichord maker that though he wished to learn music, he required someone with "mind and cultivation" as a teacher. Greville expressed doubt that any musician existed who was "fit company for a gentleman." He was surprised and pleased when Kirkman arranged an interview with young Burney, without the candidate's knowing he was being vetted: "he saw a character full of talents, yet without guile; and conceived, from that moment, an idea that it was one he might personally attach."[11] He invited Charles for long visits and took him about with him, introducing the young man to gambling dens and other fashionable haunts. Eventually, Greville paid Arne three hundred pounds for Burney's remaining three years of apprenticeship (technically the transaction made Charles into Greville's apprentice). Greville had bought himself a companion, and Charles had pulled off his first feat in convincing the world that a musician could possess "mind and cultivation" and be "fit company for a gentleman."

There is something strangely freakish about this episode.[12] For one thing, three hundred pounds was a very solid sum, though Greville could spend or lose much more on his pleasures in an evening. Greville was twenty-nine when Charles first met him; the young musician was seventeen. No one has suggested any sexual content in this association, but a homosexual attraction, if only latent, and if only on Greville's side, does not seem impossible, even though Greville was engaged in courtship and marriage at that time. One can see that for Charles Burney Greville was a substitute father—is not *patronus* a *pater?* Charles enjoyed the sunshine and luxury of Wilbury House, and especially the luxury of belonging, of being included in a family.

Before the articles with Arne were signed, Greville had eloped with the beautiful Frances Macartney; Charles Burney gave the bride away at the secret wedding, and later stood proxy godfather to Frances Anne Greville (later Mrs. Crewe, a lifelong friend of Dr. Burney and his Fanny). Indeed, Charles was later to name his second daughter Frances after Mrs. Greville (née Macartney) and her child. In Charles's youth, his inferior position in his new family did not bother him. Many years later he remembered happily in a letter to Mrs. Crewe that the Grevilles had treated him kindly, never sending him to the second table, and that Mrs. Greville was always tactful: "I was called the *Youth*. . . . My *lady* gave me that appellation, to steer clear of the too high title of young Gentleman, or too degrading address of boy, or young man."[13] A man of stronger pride (Johnson, for instance) would have chafed at both the thing itself and the recollection. Charles Burney never worried about inferiority in rank, as long as his superiors were acknowledged superior by the world. He was (unlike his daughter) one of those to whom gradations of rank and status readily make sense. He had no dislike of offering adulation and no objection to being patronized. People in power made him feel better. Charles Burney had a very strong will, and more than adequate vanity, but his need for acceptance and approval was too strong to be checked by pride. He liked public signs (such as rank) which certified the value of approval and praise, and he could never really understand why his Fanny minded being patronized, or even that she did mind. Frances Burney's peculiar stiffness about public notice, her shyness at being loudly praised (qualities which have annoyed critics of her *Diaries*) can be seen as a reaction to her father's praise-seeking, and his almost abject, if graceful, submission to any patronage.

In the *Memoirs,* Frances is evidently somewhat worried by the Greville episode, though she stresses the artlessness and ingenuousness of Charles's winning behavior, so that it will not be thought that he was selling his personality. She emphasizes an essential equality in the "friendship." Yet the episode occasions one of her rare near-criticisms of her father: she says that when Charles desired to marry "it was then he appreciated the high male value of self-dependence."[14] And she stresses that, once he was married, he exhibited "the ardour of his desire to obtain self-dependence."[15] "Self-dependence"—and not only for males—is a perpetual moral issue in Burney's works.

She includes in the *Memoirs* one particularly revealing anecdote regarding Charles's marriage. When he wanted to marry Esther Sleepe, the youth felt hamstrung by his commitment to Fulke Greville, who had bought his time— and in effect himself—for some years. Charles said nothing directly to the Grevilles about his situation or desires but, as Frances puts it, consented "to be passive only while awaiting some happy turn for propitiating his efforts to escape."[16] Passive efforts to escape characterized both Charles and his children whenever they were caught in tight situations involving the will of some other party. The secret engagement was developing into a crisis; the Grevilles announced their intention of going to Italy and taking Charles with them. He waited for the right moment, and then showed his patrons Esther's picture:

> It was instantly and eagerly snatched from hand to hand by the gay couple; and young Burney had the unspeakable relief of perceiving that this impulsive trial was successful. . . .
>
> As a statute he stood fixed before them; a smiling one, indeed; a happy one; but as breathless, as speechless, as motionless.
>
> Mr. Greville then, with a laugh, exclaimed, "But why, Burney, why don't you marry her?"
>
> Whether this were uttered sportively, inadvertently, or seriously, young Burney took neither time nor reflection to weigh; but, starting forward with ingenuous transport, called out, "May I?"
>
> No negative could immediately follow an interrogatory that had thus been invited; and to have pronounced one in another minute would have been too late; for the enraptured . . . young lover, hastily construing a short pause into an affirmative, blithely left them to the enjoyment of their palpable amusement at his precipitancy.[17]

Charles Burney's own account (still extant in a fragment of his *Memoirs*) is quite unabashed about the incident, and offers none of the explanation, the atmosphere, or exculpatory adjectives ("impulsive," "ingenuous") that qualify Frances's account. She could feel something wrong in this; he never did. Charles was pleased that all had turned out so well, as he says, "without my hinting a wish to complete our union till the full time of my apprenticeship was expired."[18]

He does not pause to wonder how seriously Greville meant the question. The display of ingenuousness veiled some cunning; Charles Burney got his own way, without offense, without confrontation. The incident reminds one of a child, coaxingly surprising an unserious or equivocal consent from its elders. The Burney children likewise learned to be expert in the strategies of inexpressible requests, and the technicalities of consent.

Charles Burney's "May I?" expresses many of his most deeply typical qualities. Though he might elicit a merely technical consent, he always found difficulty in acting without permission—the permission of his superiors (intellectual or social), or society at large. In the Greville case, of course, Charles would technically have been subject to legal penalties had he actually married without his guardian's consent, but the obvious way out was for Burney to talk frankly to Greville about his problem—and there were pressing reasons for doing so. But he had not received permission to engage in this kind of talk. There was a kind of deep inner taboo against offending substitute parents, and the formalities of permission marked the safe zones of inoffensiveness. Charles was to inculcate in his children the pervasive dread of offending someone whose permission should be asked, and he indicates some unwitting enjoyment of being the person who had power to give or withhold permission from his children, the only group to whom he could give it and to whom he need not apply for it. Basically, he was anxious over all social observances, wishing his children to stay with him safely inside the boundaries of the permissible. The issue of "permission" figures very large in the Burneys' life and history. Was Frances permitted to publish her novel? Could she be permitted to have a play produced? Was it permissible for her to leave Queen Charlotte's court? Could Susy be permitted to live separate from her husband? Was it permissible for Frances to marry an émigré? The attitudes affected their views toward other people as well: had Mrs. Thrale behaved impermissibly in marrying Piozzi? One can see why the French Revolution caused Charles Burney such particularly enormous upset that he could not agree that any movement to reform had been needed. The Revolution did away with the parental boundaries between the permissible and the impermissible.

There were good reasons why Charles Burney and Esther Sleepe should not have pursued a policy of watchful waiting for "some happy turn." As Frances Burney very well knew (and as Joyce Hemlow discovered), Charles Burney and Esther Sleepe were already parents of a daughter, a baby born in May 1749, one month before the rushed wedding.[19] They had forgotten to ask "May I?" of Church or State before consummating their love, and little Esther (or Hester) was the result. Charles was no seducer; he was given to personal attachments, and observation of Arne's slovenly and neurotic lechery seems to have increased his fastidiousness. He was only twenty-one when he met Esther, who was three years older than he, the beautiful and talented daughter of a "Cit" of Foster Lane. Frances remarks that her mother's birth "had nothing to boast from parental dignity, parental opulence, nor—strange, and stranger yet to tell—parental worth." But she goes on to explain that parental worthlessness applied only to the father, "since the Male parent was not more wanting in goodness, probity, and conduct, than the Female was perfect in all."[20] In what ways the lack of probity and conduct was manifest in this detestable father (Frances's maternal grandfather) we do not know. Frances's strong impression of James Sleepe's defectiveness can have been derived only from her mother and grandmother. Esther evidently came from an inwardly broken home—as Charles Burney seems to have done. Each of the partners felt sundered from the parent of the opposite sex—Charles from his "unfeeling unnatural mother," Esther from her bad father.

The misconduct of the father (whatever it was) may well have hindered Esther's marriage prospects, though her family's lack of money also could have discouraged suitors, and her mother's Frenchness and Catholicism would not generally have been seen as advantages. Esther was a trifle old for a bride; she married at twenty-six, an age at which a woman of that time was thought well on the way to being an old maid—though the term could not strictly apply to Esther after the fall of 1748. Her beauty is well attested by her portrait (Fig. 2), and various sources pay tribute to her talents and sweet temper. In Esther Charles found an ideal combination, a woman whose social and familial background would not make his seem inferior, who at the same time had talents and disposition to make her "fit company" for gentlemen and ladies. Her gentleness could offer him the mothering he had missed—even the age discrepancy could be an advantage. On her side, she found a lively young man (they met at a dance) whose sparkle and ambition promised a way out of Foster Lane—though she was too uncalculating about holding out for marriage. Charles's love for her was real; he did not take advantage of the eighteenth-century code that encouraged a man to despise and abandon a woman who had let him sleep with her—marrying a girl who had done so was harshly spoken of as "marrying your whore."[21] In real life, attitudes to sexual relations seem kinder than those invoked in fiction, but the double standard was certainly applied in real life. Of course, Charles and Esther did not belong to the land-owning or trading classes among whom arguments about inheritance enforced the crueler standards. Charles was only too anxious to get married, ludicrously so, many would have felt, in view of his youth, lack of a job, and total want of prospects. He was offered what some men would have seen as the perfect way out (the trip to Italy). But to have abandoned Esther would have meant being himself abandoned by his own new family. Yet Charles let his beloved suffer in anxiety and suspense—to the point where the wedding cannot even be called a shotgun wedding—while he procrastinated about dealing with the Grevilles. In matters of work and business Charles never procrastinated; he was industrious and persevering in anything that depended on his own efforts. But he was a moral Micawber in approaching any matter that involved confronting and changing the mind of some other person, especially a superior. In trying not to offend, he hurt those close to him. If we imagine Esther's anxiety during those long months of pregnancy with no progress made toward a change in her status, we can see that her situation anticipates Frances's long suspense in 1790–1791 when her father was psychically paralyzed about effecting her removal from court.

It is a fact that Hester Burney, the novelist's elder sister, was technically illegitimate, and equally a fact that Frances hushes the matter up entirely in the biography. Even when she penned the praises of her mother's sweetness, goodness, and rectitude she knew inwardly, as she must have done most of her life, that her adored mother had made a puzzling and consequential slip. The circumstances of the first child's birth were among the family secrets. In the *Memoirs* Frances Burney deliberately omits all early dates (of the marriage, of the children's births), a piece of discretion which has led to her being accused by critics from Croker in 1833 to Lonsdale in 1965 of having fudged the matter in order to perpetuate (for vanity's sake) the myth that *Evelina* was published when its author was seventeen. "Fanny's obfuscation of dates can have no other explanation."[22] There *is* another explanation.

After his marriage in June 1749, Charles Burney settled down to self-dependence with a vengeance. Self-dependence involved enormously long hours of teaching (he did not give up work as a music teacher until 1804). It was not only he who depended upon himself, but a wife and child, and soon a number of children: James (1750), Frances (1752), Susanna (1755), Charles (1757), Charlotte (1761). (Three boys died in infancy.) Not content with the labor and slender rewards of teaching, Charles continued composing in his scant spare time. Eventually he made his claims to fame through his musical *Tours* of France and Italy, and of Germany (1771; 1773), and through his monumental and carefully researched *History of Music* (1776–1789).[23]

There was a hard core to Charles Burney, a toughness capable of great perseverance. He was not going to be a failure like his father, he was going to be somebody. And he succeeded. There was perhaps at the back of his mind since the Greville episode a desire to recapture for himself and by his own efforts the elegance and high style (intellectual as well as material) of Wilbury House. He had once seen the glamor, and been a part of it. He was always to be affected by glamor, even in his seventies when he was so appreciative of the Duke of Portland's invitations to the delights of Bulstrode. As Macaulay caustically remarked about his attitude to Frances's court appointment, "Dr. Burney was an amiable man, a man of good abilities, a man who had seen much of the world. But he seems to have thought that going to court was like going to heaven."[24] He did feel like that.

There was one interruption to Charles Burney's early pursuit of success. After a period of particularly hard work, including writing music for a pantomime and an opera, he fell ill for three months. As he had a cough and night sweats, tubercular consumption was suspected, and to save his health he took a post as organist at St. Margaret's Church in King's Lynn, Norfolk. It was in King's

Lynn that Frances was born (13 June) and baptized (7 July 1752). She spent her first eight years in Norfolk. Charles Burney's illness can be seen as induced not only by too strenuous work, but also by the extra burden of mental stress under which he labored, a young man of twenty-five trying to storm London. Throughout his life he suffered occasional fits of illness, including enigmatic fits of "rheumatism" from which, until old age, he would recover completely. His essential health was very good, his constitution elastic, and he remained spry until near the end. Illness allowed him his only holidays. Frances inherited both his delicacy and his elasticity.

Charles returned from his provincial sojourn ready to take London on again. But then his wife fell ill. Her sudden sickness was not amenable to treatment, though a trip to Bath and Bristol Hot Wells was tried. Esther died in September 1762, three months after Frances's tenth birthday. (The fatal malady was thought to be tuberculosis, though from the symptoms it may have been cancer.) Charles was plunged into deep grief, though he found some solace in writing melancholy verses to his wife's memory—a therapeutic occupation suggested by Esther herself. Frances Burney believed that that great bereavement caused her father's subsequent determination to remain blind to any forthcoming affliction:

> His heart, during the ardent passions of glowing early manhood, had been rived by a deprivation that had nearly assailed his reason; and ever since that baleful period, he had recoiled from the approach of excessive affliction with a horror of its power over his mind, that made him shut his ears, and close his eyes, on the menace of every sorrow.[25]

She offers this explanation (or excuse) for what was really (though she does not put it so harshly) a strange optimism in the face of the fatal illness of his daughter Susanna (d. January 1800); "he had sedulously turned aside" from the menace of this sorrow, just as, during Frances's illness of the latter court years, he preferred not to think anything could be seriously wrong. Frances says that the death of Esther "nearly assailed his reason"; if Charles felt inwardly that his mind could become unbalanced under sorrow, that would explain much of his persistent repelling of unhappiness. Even before the death of his wife there were occasional spells of depression, and there is a pattern of depressed periods throughout his life. Bereavement hit Charles especially hard; it meant being abandoned again. Depression frightened him; he could not learn from it. He could acknowledge only two states, cheerfulness (which he regarded as normal) and depression, which he felt to be abnormal, foreign to his nature, something that must be driven away by business or society. His children were early taught to consider his feelings first; it was their duty to beguile the low spirits he dreaded.

Charles Burney was never self-analytical; he could not acknowledge more than the slightest speck of imperfection in himself, and to his own defects, as well as to his fears, he devoutly shut his eyes. Every bereavement has about it a residue of guilt. In his daughter Susanna's case later, there were to be some real reasons for Charles to feel guilty because he had not taken the decisive action that might have prolonged her life, and would certainly have spared her great misery (see below, Chapter Eight). Guilt in any form was something Charles Burney could not cope with. The injuries he had suffered in childhood do much to explain this. Any "abandoned child" wonders if something acutely awful and repellent in her/himself caused the parents' rejection. The child can save self-respect and identity only by repelling that suggestion of worthlessness whenever it makes itself felt. Charles sustained his sense of worth by observing society's parental rules, by striving for success and honoring the permissible. He had high standards but no self-criticism. Guilt was too psychically expensive for him to honor any demand upon it.

His reaction when any of his children went wrong was to say, in effect, "Look what you've done to me!" and never to wonder "How might I have contributed to this?" And some of his children did go wrong. The boys in particular, shared an urge to rebel, to offend against the permissible. Charles, the younger son of the first marriage, was expelled from Caius College, Cambridge, in 1777 for stealing books from the University Library—a stupid and obvious theft almost designed to be detected. One can see in the action not only an effort to mimic his admired father in this "Mad rage for possessing a library,"[26] but also an unconscious statement that the father had stolen something from him. Dr. Burney, wrapped in his production of the *History,* had not given him time and affection, and now the son needed something. This piece of misconduct met with an unusually harsh reaction. Charles Burney Senior would not even see his son, who was sent off to live in penitent disgrace in the country. The father, full of self-pity, proclaimed he would never see the boy again. Young Charles should change his name, should go to another country. Friends and family, who took a saner view of the matter, managed to pull him round (and he must have wished to be pulled round). In or about 1785 his youngest son Richard (born in 1768 of the second marriage) was involved in some crime or scandal, and was packed off to India, for life. Family documents relating to this matter have been censored (especially by Frances) so that what actually happened is not known. Although Charles did correspond with Richard, he also considered him a perpetual disgrace, though the offense was committed while the boy was still in his teens.[27] The even more shameful delinquency of his eldest son and youngest daughter in running away together (in 1798) met a similar response of denial and repudiation (see below, Chapter Eight).

Charles Burney's children were supposed to assist him in his campaign for public acceptance, for success. They were supposed to succeed. This had its good side; the father provided education and stimulus, and was delighted with their talents. Mrs. Thrale noted of the Burney family "their Esteem and fondness for the Dr. seems to inspire them all with a Desire not to disgrace him; & so every individual of it must write and read & be literary."[28] The bad side was that the "desire not to disgrace him" could become obsessive, or even turn into a perverse desire to do the disgraceful—upon which the father would turn off his love, cast the transgressor from him. Frances's fear of losing her father's affection if she offended him was not ill-founded.

Frances, the third child in that first family of six children, seemed at first middling in all respects, not likely to contribute much to the family pool of genius and success. Her father said, "She was wholly unnoticed in the nursery for any talents, or quickness of study."[29] The novelist says of herself

> Frances . . . was during her childhood the most backward of all his family in the faculty of receiving instruction. At eight years of age she was ignorant of the letters of the alphabet; though at ten, she began scribbling, almost incessantly, little works of invention; but always in private.[30]

Frances observed the education of her older sister Hester by the much admired mother, and when nearly seventy could still remind the older sister of this time:

> . . . she [their mother] very early indeed began to form your taste for reading, & delighted to find time . . . to guide you, in your most tender years, to the best authours; & to read them with you . . . I perfectly recollect, Child as I was, & never of the party, this part of your education. . . . I . . . was so peculiarly backward that even our Susan stood before me. She could read when I knew not my Letters. But though so sluggish to learn, I was always observant. . . . Well I recollect your reading with our dear Mother all Pope's Works, & Pitt's Aeneid. I recollect, also, your spouting passages from Pope, that I learnt from hearing you recite them.[31]

Hester cannot have been more than ten at the time Burney recollects, and Frances herself six or seven years of age. The scenes recalled give some insight into the mother's high literary taste, and some idea of what was involved in the idea of reading in the Burney family. To be able to read was to be able to read Pope. Burney offers no explanation for her being so "sluggish to learn";[32] diffidence may have been a large part of the reason, but perhaps too her own quick and entertaining imagination made her impatient of the laborious steps toward the Parnassus formed by other people's words and ideas. In Burney's late comic play, *The Woman-Hater,* the heroine Joyce questions the business of reading: "I wonder what's the use of Books, Nurse? If Papa had as many words of his own as I have, he would not be always wanting to be poring over other people's so."[33] Whatever the reason, little Fanny was slow in learning to read; she remembered gratefully that her mother refused to take up the suggestion that "the little dunce" be whipped for her dullness; Esther only replied, "No—no—I am not uneasy about her!"

But alas! the soft music of those encouraging accents had already ceased to vibrate on human ears, before these scrambling pot-hooks had begun their operation of converting into Elegies, Odes, Plays, Songs, Stories, Farces,—nay, Tragedies and Epic Poems, every scrap of white paper that could be seized upon without question or notice; for she grew up, probably through the vanity-annihilating circumstances of this conscious intellectual disgrace, with so affrighted a persuasion that what she scribbled, if seen, would but expose her to ridicule, that her pen, though her greatest, was only her clandestine delight.[34]

There seems to be a connection between Frances's first great spurt of writing and the death of her mother when the child was ten. In turning to writing as a solace she was imitating the admired father. But her own activities were associated with her sense of "conscious intellectual *disgrace*"—an ominous word in the Burney family vocabulary. In her undistinguished nursery career she had not succeeded at all in attracting her father's attention or admiration. Esther ("Hetty"), the eldest, shared her father's musical talent; James and Charles were the boys (and Charles, "Carlos," was a promising scholar), Susanna was the favorite beautiful child, and Charlotte was the baby. Fanny's place in the family was a humble one. In 1764 Charles took Esther (age fifteen) and Susanna (age nine) off to France to attend school and perfect their French. Untalented Frances was left out; she was also, not quite two years after her mother's death, deprived of a natural mother-substitute in her elder sister, and of her dearest friend and favorite playmate in the younger Susanna.

There is every reason to believe little Frances was hit hard by her mother's death. At the end of Esther's illness, in the last week of September, the smaller children—Frances, Susan, and Charles—were placed in Mrs. Sheeles's boarding school in Queen Square, where Charles Burney taught music. It was there that little Fanny heard the terrible news. A neighbor, Mrs. Pringle, told Frances in 1775 that she remembered hearing of the child's sorrow before meeting the child:

> "*You,*" said she, "was a particular favourite with me before ever I saw you; for I had heard of you from M^rs. Sheele [*sic*] whose House you were at, when a Child, when you lost your Mother;—& she told me that of the Hundred Children she had had the care of, she never saw such affliction in one before—that you would take no Comfort—& was almost killed with Crying."[35]

Despite the relief such outward signs of grief are supposed to bring, little Frances may have been more wounded than anyone around her quite realized. Many years later she was to tell her elder sister, "if praying for the Dead make a

Roman Catholic, I have been one all my life. . . . Well, well I remember, never getting into Bed without praying for my dear Mamma, & that I might be good enough to join her."[36] She evidently tried to conjure up memories of her mother, in which she was perhaps helped by one talisman, her mother's old sampler, worked by Esther in childhood and give to her daughter Frances, who was to treasure it all her life.[37] It can still be seen, with the label inscribed by Frances, "Sampler of my own dearest Mother. Given to me by her precious Self, when I was 8 years of age" (Fig.3).

What particular household arrangements were made in the years until 1767 is not clear; there must have been some kind of housekeeper as well as servants. Both grandmothers helped, though they remained in their own residences. Frances spent a great deal of her time with her grandmother Sleepe (née Dubois) whom she deeply loved; later, her affection for the elderly Mrs. Delany was founded on seeing a resemblance to the cherished grandmother. Mrs. Sleepe was of French extraction and from her, Frances—like her mother before her —might learn some French, although Frances regarded herself as self-taught in that language, and was shy of speaking French in public.[38] Mrs. Sleepe was also a pious Roman Catholic; Charles pretended to think that one good reason for his not taking Frances to France was her already too great fondness for Catholicism.[39] Roman Catholicism was not only a despised persuasion in England; it was still officially proscribed, and those who practiced it were subject to special disabilities in law. Having a Roman Catholic grandmother posed problems about the relation to the permissible; could society and the law be right in frowning on the religion of someone as gentle, virtuous, and tolerant as Mrs. Sleepe? Her affection for her grandmother was Frances Burney's first unconscious lesson against bigotry, intolerance, and snobbishness. The relationship also gave her a sense of her dual heritage; Frances was not perfectly English, or rather British, like the Scots-descended (Mac)Burneys, for on her mother's side she was partly French. Her novels from *Evelina* to *The Wanderer* —particularly those, the first and last—exhibit her interest in exploring multiple heritages. Frances's eventual marriage to a Roman Catholic Frenchman was not an anomaly. She was reenforcing one aspect of her own identity, collecting one part of her inheritance. She had learned in her childhood to associate dignity, virtue, and the power of loving with a French Roman Catholic—even though common English opinion assigned levity, amorality, and fickleness to "frogs" and "papists."

Frances was hit hard by her mother's death, but her brothers and sisters suffered too. What permanent scars the sudden loss left on James (age twelve) can only be guessed; he was away from home at the time, already serving as a midshipman as he had done since he was ten. Some of his peculiar behavior in relation to his sister Sarah many years later could be related to that early loss with its accompanying circumstances, in his case, of mystery, of guilt, and of anger at the father for somehow making away with the mother. Incest with his sister could have provided a means of symbolic reengagement with the mother, taking her illicitly away from the father.

When a child's parent dies (a distinct type of bereavement now receiving special attention from psychologists),[40] the child suffers not only from great longing, but from some (often unacknowledgeable) anger at the dead parent for having departed. The child whose parent has thus "gone" feels abandoned. There may also be some irrational tendency to blame the surviving parent for what has happened, or, equally irrationally, to blame the self. At the same time the child is thrown back upon love for the surviving parent; the need for that parent's love and reassurance is especially strong. Frances intensely needed her father's love, but felt handicapped at the time of greatest need because of her recollection of infant "intellectual disgrace." All the Burney children made a kind of religion of their father—he was to be venerated, he was not only a genius but faultless, the best of fathers. This adoration, from which all criticism was to be suppressed, not only pleased Charles (it saved him from critics on the hearth, and he could not bear criticism) but also assured the children of an identity (they had a wonderful father, so they were important, too). And, as long as they did not allow this adoration to fail, they would be assured of love and approval in compensation. But if they faltered in his service, affection could be withdrawn. This shared complex, this dependence on the family myth of the perfect father, was enforced by eighteenth-century emphasis on filial piety, especially daughterly piety.

Filial piety was not a new virtue; earlier periods had of course enforced it. But in the sixteenth and seventeenth centuries, filial duty and obedience were viewed largely as aspects of a structural relation, related to hierarchies and authority. It took the eighteenth century (when in fact the old structures were crumbling, and kings and fathers actually had less authority than previously) to insist on the high emotive content of parental-filial relations. The child (especially a daughter) should not only *be* obedient, but *feel* the oozy luxury of obedience; and the father, while making demands, could (especially to a daughter) give expression to soft, tender (not to say gushing) emotion. Close relations between father and daughter were insisted on as never before, even to the point where we can question the emotional health of the culture whose literature gave rise to such elaborate representations of those feelings as we find in England in the eighteenth century, particularly in the drama. Perhaps the increasing emphasis on father-daughter relations in the eighteenth century can be seen as symptomatic of the effort of eighteenth-century men to become less aggressive, more "feminine," more gentle (in the modern sense) in a feminizing process which Jean Hagstrum thinks has been taking place in the last three centuries.[41] If the daughter is charmingly childlike in trust, devotion, submissiveness, the father is also permitted to be familiar, soft, and tender. In fact, the father is to gain authority (even authority to destroy) through tenderness; a sort of emotional blackmail is substituted for more straightforward authoritarianism.

Personal difficulties are increased when an individual's unbalanced tendencies fit in with a general cultural neurosis or communal obsession—as happened in Frances's case (and indeed, that of all the Burney children) over the issue of filial piety. Mary Shelley, daughter of William Godwin and Mary Wollestonecraft, was to suffer similar personal difficulties when, a motherless child, she grew up trying to please her father, and felt perpetually undervalued and unsupported. Shelley speaks of a "state of loneliness" never endured by any other person "except Robinson Crusoe."[42] Frances Burney, like Mary Shelley, had difficulty putting herself forward. She too understood loneliness; her last heroine, Juliet in *The Wanderer,* is "a female Robinson Crusoe."[43] Frances Burney obtained much more support from her father than Mary Shelley did from Godwin—though at a price. Throughout her youth Frances kept each matter of importance secret from her father; she was terrified of his disapproval of her writings. She did not elope, but her publication of *Evelina* can be seen as a kind of elopement—she went into the world without her father's knowledge. And her marriage, in 1793, though not clandestine, took place without her father's approval or presence. By that time there were plenty of examples of elopement in the revised Burney family unit.

The first and most comic was Charles Burney's own elopement in October 1767 with Mrs. Stephen Allen, a handsome widow. The Burneys had known her since their Norfolk days, when she seems to have been the bright particular star of the provincial reading circle of King's Lynn. Mr. Burney proposed to her in 1764, only a year after she lost her husband; he was rebuffed then, but the courtship proceeded later, against the decided wishes of the lady's mother and brother. Mrs. Allen had been left a fortune of forty thousand pounds; no wonder her relatives regarded Burney as a fortune-hunter. Ironically, she lost her money in a bad speculation during the latter part of their courtship, but the disapproval of Elizabeth Allen's family did not abate. The couple, after much "mystery and intrigue," as Charles admitted,[44] eloped in a secret wedding followed by a short honeymoon, without the knowledge of her family or his —including the children on both sides. In effect, they both eloped from their children. The Allen children and the Burney children were, however, acquainted with the prospective stepparent, and must have known the marriage was in the wind, though they did not know when it happened. Frances Burney gives a very strained and guarded account of the marriage, as of the stepmother, in the *Memoirs.* The tone is of a scrupulous and hard-wrung endeavor to be just. Although she finds words in which to praise her stepmother's beauty, wit, and hospitality, the difference between such commendation and the warmer language in which she refers to her stepsister ("the very amiable Miss Allen") is noticeable. In the *Memoirs* Frances excuses (over-excuses) her father from infidelity to Esther's memory and defends second marriages (with an overt tolerance she denied to Mrs. Thrale) but the language in which she discusses the courtship is suspect:

Mrs. Allen saw him with daily increasing interest, Mr. Burney was not less moved by her commiseration, nor less penetrated by her sympathy; and insensibly he became solaced, while involuntarily she grew grateful, upon observing her rising influence over his spirits.

To the tender sentiments of the heart, the avenues are as infinite for entrance as they are difficult for escape; but there are none so direct, and, consequently, none so common, as those through whose gentle mazes soft pity encounters soothing sensibility.[45]

Within this very stiff public language, the soft alliterations (and what seem to be sexual puns—"rising influence over his spirits") mock the sensibility they describe. Frances certainly thought Mr. Burney oversusceptible; one may read beneath such language an involuntary scorn for her father, in having been so easily caught, and a wish that he had escaped the "mazes" of the "tender sentiments." If such were her feelings at the age of eighty—when she could not yet bring herself to say that Elizabeth Allen Burney was "amiable"—one can imagine her feelings at fifteen, when her father ran off to an unwelcome stepmother, and then insisted on bringing this rival (to Esther Sleepe Burney, and to his daughter) into the family.

The threatening advent of the unwanted stepmother cemented the already close relation between Frances and her best-loved sister Susanna, her lifelong dearest friend and confidante (Fig. 5). Frances Burney's diary was to become a series of journal-letters to Susanna whenever the two were separated. Susanna is the recipient or addressee of many of the few surviving works written before the publication of *Evelina*, including the set of verses written 23 May 1776, "To Sue on her recovery From the Jaundice." This comic piece begins with a compliment to yellowness: "When the Crocus & Snow-drop their *white* have display'd/ Come the Primrose & Cowslip, in *Yellow* array'd." The "Belles in the Street & the Park" wear spring finery of the same color, "& all, like my Susan, in *Jaundice* appear."[46] This is one of Burney's very few references to flowers; she was never given to describing prettiness. It is typical of her in that she connects the natural with the social, and, in a turn of Augustan wit, the pretty with the ugly, spring flowers with disease. Susanna could be counted on to appreciate the comedy. Susanna was always to be counted on to understand, and her letters in reply to her Fanny, whenever the sisters were separated, are full, affectionate, and detailed.

If one sister became an ever-closer companion, another valued sister was removed. As well as adjusting to an unwanted mother, and accommodating unwished-for new siblings, Frances soon had to undergo the first loss in the family since the death of her mother. She lost to marriage her loved elder sister (and sometime substitute mother), Esther Burney (Fig. 4). Spurred on apparently by the desire to depart from her stepmother's jurisdiction, Esther married her cousin, the harpsichordist Charles Rousseau Burney, in September 1770. Frances had earlier sympathized with her sister when Esther had hoped she was courted by the charming if elusive Alexander Seton of ambiguous intentions, but Frances was not overly pleased at Hetty's marriage. She worried about the eternal poverty into which her sister was plunged, and thought that Hetty was worn out by having too many children. Yet at least Hetty, the buoyant and cheerful, now had a home to which Frances could sometimes escape when life at home with her stepmother became too burdensome.

It is a fact that all the children of Charles and Esther Burney hated their stepmother. Despite the later careful censorship of diaries and letters, surviving manuscripts testify to a remarkably enduring detestation. Mrs. Allen did not much care for the Burney children, and accused them, not without reason, of caballing against her. The two families did not unite under one roof until 1770, so the children had a period for some adjustments, but relations with the father's new wife, bad before, grew even worse in the shadow of her constant presence and authority. To the children she seemed gloomy, reproachful, bad-tempered, given to rude speeches and to quarreling.

To Charles Burney she seemed quite different; she loved him, and he thought her handsome and clever. Also (a fact Frances Burney stifles in the *Memoirs*) the second Mrs. Burney's remaining wealth was undoubtedly useful; without the financial support that she could give to the household, Charles Burney would not have been able to leave work for the extended Continental travels that provided material for the books that established his fame. When he left his family from June to December 1770, and again from July to November 1772, the children must have felt freshly deserted. Elizabeth Allen Burney was presumably not best pleased to find out how easily her adored husband could do without her while expecting her to look after his hostile children, but she loyally supported his endeavors and enthusiasms. Charles was happy and busy, and he had reason to think well of, and to treat well, the woman who had brought him the means to happiness and freedom. He had no time for squabbles, and an aversion to quarreling; it suited him to believe in family harmony. Hostility and family strain were exacerbated by the necessity of keeping them hidden from the husband and father. The Burney children's hatred of their "mama" was one of their secrets. Not quarrelsome, or capable of quarreling, they took evasive action, ganging up secretly to make fun of the stepparent behind her back, writing about her in unkind code as "the *Lady*," "Precious," "Madam."

Sympathetic persons outside the family could be drawn into this game. Samuel Crisp (Fig. 7), one of Charles Burney's friends from the Greville days, was fond of the Burney children (especially Fanny) and took their part against his friend's wife. Charlotte, the youngest, in particular seems to have provided him with material for deriding Mrs. Burney; Crisp was let into the codes and attitudes, as some scenes described by a delighted Charlotte make clear:

Yesterday fortnight my Father the Lady & self set off in a post *sha* for Chessington . . . Mr Crisp . . . soon espied *me* & I him, &

notwithstanding his *passionate message* that he had sent me respecting the Lady, he gave me a most cordial reception. . . .

As to the Lady to do him justice, he did not trouble her wth *too much* of his conversation, for the whole time we were there . . . he never spoke to, or took the least notice of her any more than he c^d.n't possibly avoid!—& was so excessively impudent to her, at the same time, that tho' I was ready to laugh, I was nevertheless in an almost continual fright, least he sh^d carry it too far.

While we were at Supper, she attacked him about his coming to Town, when *she* was out of it—

"When shall we see you in Town Mr. Crisp?"

"I don't know *Ma'am?"*—

"but I need not say *we* tho', for I see you are Determined not to come to Town while *I* am in it—[he sat chewing his pie & *never a word spoke he*] "Oh yes! I see that very plainly I suppose you always intend to come *croaking* up to Town when I am out of it?"—One w^d have imagined that he c^d.n't have forborne to say something or other, by Way of *Douceur* my father present & all—but the Duce a bit—there he sat without uttering a sillable, & every body at table expecting him to speak! . . . in short, nothing c^d. equal his impudence! I never saw anything like it!— Kitty Cooke said he told her, that she walked & dressed like a girl of fifteen—& all the way we came down stairs, he was diverting himself (not *me* I'm sure) with *taking her off!*—putting his hands behind him, & kicking his heels about![47]

This is funny, but very unpleasant. There is something distasteful in the idea of godfatherly or even grandfatherly Samuel Crisp (he was a good deal older than Charles Burney) insulting Frances's and Charlotte's stepmother, a guest at his own table, even *"taking her off"* secretly to win the girls' approbation. Crisp may not have liked Mrs. Burney, he may have wished that she would not visit him at his home at Chessington (where he lived in a sort of glorified boarding house kept by Mrs. Hamilton and her niece, the goodhearted naïve Kitty Cooke). But after all, this "Lady" was the beloved wife of a dear friend. Manners and morals would have dictated courtesy at least, and intelligent friendship for the Burney girls should have extended to helping them deal in a mature way with a difficult relationship. Crisp only joined in the childishness; he was never quite a grown-up himself. It is a pity that the Burney children never received any real help in dealing with their stepmother. Before outsiders they usually acted according to a forced decorum relieved by sly petulance and secret hostilities; those they trusted with the truth were enlisted as accomplices in their guerrilla games.

Elizabeth Allen Burney undoubtedly had a temper, and it was certainly tried. Perhaps the Burneys, male and female, tended to gravitate toward mates with a temper (as Charles did in his second marriage); fieriness and flarings-up provided a counterpoise to their own inability to express anger. The gentle Burneys were not, however, good at calculating the potential quality of rage, or at fighting back. Some Burneys made grievous mistakes in marrying bad-tempered mates. Susanna married Molesworth Phillips, who became a bully and a tyrant. Charlotte in her second marriage insisted on taking Ralph Broome, who proved a wretched husband, given to irrational fits of rage. James's wife fought with him, and he had already left her twice before he ran away with Sarah. When confronted by anger the Burneys found it difficult not to be at least superficially mild in response. They could not engage in open conflict, such warfare not being permissible. They were more likely to take evasive action, as James did in running away from his wife (to whom he was ultimately reconciled). Burney women became too passive. Susanna's sweetness and submission seem only to have stimulated her husband's irrational anger. She might have fared a bit better had she been able to fight back. Her own anger remained secret, conveyed only in writings to and from her siblings, with their references to her husband as "the Weather," "the Thunder." Frances's references to her crude superior, Mrs. Schwellenberg, during her service at court, reflect a similar resort to codes of hatred.

The second Mrs. Burney also might have been better off with a stepfamily less sweet, more vigorous in reply, more willing to be a bit "vulgar." But the Burney children were not innately dislikable; the fault was certainly not all on their side. Elizabeth Allen Burney was jealous, and at times vindictive. Her eldest daughter, Maria Allen (sixteen at the time of her mother's marriage) fell in love with her stepfather and delighted in her new sisters. A particular favorite of the dashing and witty Maria, Frances herself was lively and witty; it was among her siblings and schoolmates, not her elders, that she displayed her real liveliness and talent. She was a mimic, and full of invention; as a playmate remembered the juvenile Frances, "*you* were always so merry, so gay, so droll, & had such imagination in making plays; always something new, something of your own contrivance."[48] It was her father who called the child Frances "The Old Lady," thinking her comically solemn, and she was shy with him and before strangers, especially in his presence. In Maria Frances found a congenial friend and sister who appreciated and brought out the qualities of merriment and drollery. Maria was a plus (nearly the only one) of this new marriage. Stephen Allen seems to have remained close to his mother, and to have taken her part, while Bessy, the third Allen child (age six in 1767), did not get along very well with her mother or with the other Allen or Burney children.

The Allen children were to create new problems, bringing their own fears, resentments, desires, and elopements into the enlarged family. In 1770 Maria was sent to the Continent and there conducted a courtship with Martin Folkes Rishton, against the wishes of both their families. She married Rishton secretly in Ypres in 1772 and then traveled back to England pretending to be single. The secret was dramatically let out, to the horror of the elders, though Frances and the other girls had known about the marriage. "Good Heaven! what a romantic life has this beloved friend lived! . . . What scenes we shall have!"[49] Frances wrote in her diary. In 1777 Bessy Allen, sent abroad to complete her education, followed suit by eloping with the misnamed Mr. Meeke. Neither of these bold ventures turned out well; Bessy's relationship with Meeke seems to have been peculiarly disastrous, and Maria was eventually to leave her husband.

The family, with its shared progeny, was also complicated by the arrival of two offspring of Elizabeth and Charles. Richard, a handsome boy ("gai, spirituel, comique, et beau comme un Ange" as Frances later remembered him),[50] became a family disgrace. Sarah Harriet (b. 1772), the youngest child, was always thought difficult, and was eventually to add to the family "disgrace" by running away with her half brother, James. Charles Burney's marriage to Elizabeth Allen introduced a great deal of jangling emotion into his children's lives forever after.

For Frances, her father's marriage meant a betrayal. The emotional pattern which originated in the first childhood bereavement was unfortunately repeated in her later life. Each time she was bereaved, and especially when she lost a mother-substitute, she was, as in childhood after her mother died, thrown back upon emotional reliance on her father, and into painful devotion to his wishes, accompanied by the inner fear that he would betray her again, as he had (in her eyes) when he handed her and her sisters over to the chaperonage and care of the second wife. The abandonment by the "good mother" was also recurrent. From Frances's emotional point of view, the good mothers tended to leave her, unsupported, to her fate. Esther, Mrs. Sleepe, Mrs. Thrale, Mrs. Delany—each in various ways left her. One reason for Frances Burney's unkindness to Hester Thrale over the marriage with Piozzi is an instinctive irrational identification of herself with the daughters, abandoned (as she saw it) by a willful mother. Hester Thrale had not seen into Frances's character very deeply, and made the mistake of trying to treat the thirty-one-year-old Frances Burney as a contemporary, not realizing that Frances, however wise as a novelist, still clung to girlhood and was haunted by the events of her youth. Frances's disapproval was urged on by her father who was "shocked" that Mrs. Thrale "should thus fling away her talents, situation in life, & character;—for thus to quit all her maternal duties is a blot upon it."[51] Charles Burney condemned Mrs. Thrale for throwing herself away on a penniless musician—which is just what Mrs. Allen had done, to the equal disapproval of her family and friends. Charles's total refusal to think of that obvious comparison reveals his desire to obscure from himself the social view that he and his wife had done the impermissible. He found severe fault with the Thrale-Piozzi union not in spite of, but largely because of, the strong similarity to his own case.[52] He delighted in standing for the proprieties, aggrandizing the difference between himself and Piozzi, the musician whom he could regard as having been his own protégé.

If the "good mothers" tended to desert their Frances, and to seem, while present, rather fragile, the "bad mothers" seemed only too hardy. In early life Frances had to deal with her unpleasantly real stepmother. Throughout her early life (which in her case includes her thirties), she can be seen turning to her father and away from him. She sought substitute fathers, and was favored in this search by Samuel Crisp, gentleman, connoisseur, failed dramatist, and near-recluse who was one of Charles's oldest friends from the Greville days. "Daddy" Crisp encouraged young Frances (or "Fannikin") in her teens; he praised her lively familiar letters, instituting a correspondence that lasted all his life. He was later to encourage her novel-writing; she wrote much of *Cecilia* at his home at Chessington. In Frances Burney's relationship with Dr. Johnson we can see some elements of a substitute father/substitute daughter relation, though that is not all there was to the friendship. We have little record of that friendship, however, as Frances refused to give Boswell any of Johnson's letters to her, and, with true filial devotion and exclusiveness, destroyed them.

Frances turned to father-substitutes to try to take some of the pressure out of the intense and demanding relationship with her father. She loved Charles and needed him. She also did not always approve of him in her heart of hearts, but could not tell him so—could scarcely admit her disapproval openly to herself, so great was the inhibiting fear of criticizing nourished in the Burney family, and so deep was her inculcated need to revere him. The father and daughter were both "abandoned Children," each with urgent needs that the other could not totally meet. Charles required uncritical adulation, reassurance, submission to his worth; Frances needed praise, independence, and the license to justify herself by criticizing her father. Her efforts at expressing her own worth—in her writing—seemed, in her everyday life, like attempts to attack or criticize (if only by making herself an equal through the power of the pen). Her writing ought to be private, ought to be acknowledged as inferior. Even as an adult she had to reiterate protestations of placatory humility. The poem prefixed to *Evelina* exactly illustrates the problem:

To ——— ———

Oh author of my being!—far more dear
    To me than light, than nourishment, or rest,
Hygieia's blessings, Rapture's burning tear,
    Or the life blood that mantles in my breast!

If in my heart the love of Virtue glows,
    'Twas planted there by an unerring rule;
From thy example the pure flame arose,
    Thy life, my precept—thy good works, my school.

Could my weak pow'rs thy num'rous virtues trace
    By filial love each fear should be repress'd;
The blush of Incapacity I'd chace
    And stand, recorder of thy worth, confess'd:

But since my niggard stars that gift refuse,
   Concealment is the only boon I claim;
Obscure be still the unsuccessful Muse,
   Who cannot raise, but would not sink, thy fame.

Oh! of my life at once the source and joy!
   If e'er thy eyes these feeble lines survey,
Let not their folly their intent destroy;
   Accept the tribute—but forget the lay.[53]

This set of verses is an odd riddle; it is prefixed to the first edition of *Evelina*, published anonymously. Charles Burney is only "———— ————," and his daughter hoped, when he first read the novel (including the prefatory verses) he would not know who had written the book, nor that his name should fill the blanks. So Frances Burney had it both ways, producing a novel without her father's knowledge, and then dedicating it to him with the most profuse claims to filial humility. Paradoxically, verses three and four say she should openly praise him, naming herself and thus naming him, if only her "weak pow'rs" could trace his "virtues." Why does she not do that then? She claims "Incapacity" would not in that case stand in her way. But "since [her] niggard stars that gift refuse" she will be nameless. What Frances is saying in these doubly obscure verses is that she apologizes for doing something on her own; she apologizes for being an author. The potential offense of authorship can be cancelled out by calling her secret addressee the "author of my being"—primary authorship, authority in all senses, is yielded to him. And if the work is inferior, unsuccessful, he can disclaim it in advance—more than disclaim it, as he will never know about it, and his name will never appear to fill in the blanks of the tribute. The unnamed Charles is the Super-Author, the author of the author.

The frontispiece prefixed to Volume I of *Evelina* illustrates, not, as in the other two volumes, an incident in the story but the poem, and that may have been Frances's choice. In that frontispiece (Fig. 8), a large figure in vaguely classical garb, feminine (though somewhat heavily male in contour and with anatomically impossible legs) gazes at, and reaches toward, a monument. The figure is not Evelina, and certainly not a portrait of Frances Burney; it is the Muse ("the unsuccessful Muse"?), representing the aspect of Frances that wrote the book, and the spirit of the novel. Of the inscription on the tomb we can read only the last word: "Belmont." In the story, Sir John Belmont had deserted the heroine's mother (the real Lady Belmont) who is dead when the story opens; the father acknowledges the daughter only in the last volume. The picture represents a conflation of external world (author, Muse) with the internal world of the tale—the story of the Belmonts. If—as makes sense within the context of the story—the tomb is the mother's, at last properly acknowledged with her name on it, then the first two lines of the verse which appear underneath refer not to the idea of father, but to the idea of *mother*. ("Oh author of my being!") The mother, the feminine side, the female author's muse, must be acknowledged, and that which has been buried (like the author's real name) should be honored by being named aright. The father, as in the Belmont story which gives rise to Evelina's story, should recognize the daughter, permitting her at once both her relation to him, and her true identity.

Though there were to be other dedicatees, all of Frances Burney's novels were really addressed "To ——— ———." They were all messages she was trying to communicate to her father. That is not all they are, but they are that. He never got her messages. He was delighted with the books' success, but he did not want to hear what the novels really said. A contemporary reader of the *Memoirs* of 1832 commented with displeasure, "she must fancy that she was *writing a novel*";[54] and in the glorification of herself and her father in the *Memoirs* there is certainly a large element of fiction. But in her real novels Frances Burney deals with precisely those things—lowly origins, vulgar relatives, embarrassments and awkwardness, conflict between parent and child—which she suppresses in the fantasy *Memoirs*. In the novels, the effect of relationships with parents or parent-substitutes is to make a heroine learn to stand on her own feet rather than rely on her elders. In her presentation of society, Frances questions the very entities and values that made Charles Burney feel safe. She had a very sharp, critical mind, and a moral insight that made her a social critic. She also possesses a wild and disturbing sense of the comic.

For plots and situations she drew, as authors do, upon the material her life supplied her with, and upon the conventions of fiction in her time. But the conventions of fictional plots found in the literature of any period are popular precisely because they are felt to be important in the common experience of that place and time. Something has been noticed because it has bitten deep. It is a mistake to assume that a writer is influenced only by something dry, called "literary convention," which has nothing to do with the sensations of living. To assert that, in *Cecilia* for instance, the writer merely turned to stage melodrama and the "she-tragedies of the age,"[55] and did so from a kind of literary tic is to misconstrue the nature of popular images and the emotional and imaginative reasons why writers choose them. The conventional themes and situations in literature are reflections (symbolic or naturalistic) of what happens in life. There are orphans in novels because parents do die. The Burney family history supplied examples of ill-sorted matches, elopements, disinheritances, filial difficulties—and was even to produce a case of fraternal incest. There are so many elopements in the Burneys' story that a novelist would condemn them as excessive. Burney took up the material and interest that her life, her observation, and the literary conventions supplied her with, and worked on them in her own way. She was to make her own kind of novel, contributing something to the change in the genre that marks the difference between mid-eighteenth-century novels and Victorian novels. Her courage emerges more in her works than in her life—as one might expect. But there is a connection between what interests her most in her novels—the search for identity, egotism, embarrassment, self-destruction, emotional blackmail—and her life. Even faults and self-divisions may help an artist discover certain truths.

But a young person with as fine a set of traumas as one may hope to see may be a total failure as a novelist. That Frances Burney's life had more perturbation in it than has often been perceived is not an argument for her as a writer. A young man may have a youthful experience of debtor's prison, and yet not be Dickens. Observation of Burney's life can, however, tell us that the novels are not the product of an "uncomplicated personality" and a "tranquil" existence, and that certain recurring themes and anxious situations may have been vividly imagined because deeply felt.

It is to Frances Burney's credit that we can say that the novels are not directly autobiographical. As a good artist she was not interested in that kind of self-indulgence. When she wrote her "tragedies" at court she was not a good artist, not in control, though those works have a great deal to tell us of her anxieties, conflicts, and breaking points. As a novelist, she had artistic consciousness and technical control. A good writer is capable of universalizing experience, of finding in his or her single existence some clues about life's diversity. We can ask if Frances Burney has done this, but we should never make the mistake of thinking she had little inner life, that she lived on detached observation. Some critics have made her a mere impersonal machine; she has been compared to a camera obscura and a tape recorder.[56] Her novels are not automatic transmissions from eighteenth-century drawing rooms. They are the creative products of an actively intelligent, witty, and passionate human being, drawing on an experience of considerable tension and complexity, who thought she had something to say which could only be said imaginatively.

Evelina; or, A Young Lady's Entrance into the World

"How came you—how happened it—what?—what?"

"I—I only wrote, sir, for my own amusement,—only in some odd idle hours."

"But your publishing—your printing,—how was that?"

"That was only, sir,—only because—"

I hesitated most abominably, not knowing how to tell him a long story . . . I was really hardly able to keep my countenance.

The *What!* was then repeated, with so earnest a look, that, forced to say something, I stammeringly answered—

"I thought—sir—it would look very well in print!"

I do really flatter myself this is the silliest speech I ever made!

(Dialogue between King George III and Frances Burney in 1785)[1]

The story that Frances Burney did not know how to tell the king was indeed "a long story." *Evelina* was not the author's first novel, but a sequel to an earlier work. The author was to tell the public in the "Dedication" to *The Wanderer* how that first novel was destroyed. More important, she was then telling her father, the addressee of that dedication, that on her fifteenth birthday (13 June 1767) she burned all her writings, including at least one complete work of fiction, *The History of Caroline Evelyn:*

So early was I impressed myself with ideas that fastened degradation to this class of composition, that at the age of adolescence, I struggled against the propensity which, even in childhood, even from the moment I could hold a pen, had impelled me into its toils; and on my fifteenth birth-day, I made so resolute a conquest over an inclination at which I blushed, and that I had always kept secret, that I committed to the flames whatever, up to that moment, I had committed to paper. And so enormous was the pile, that I thought it prudent to consume it in the garden.

You, dear Sir, knew nothing of its extinction, for you had never known of its existence. Our darling Susanna, to whom alone I had ever ventured to read its contents, alone witnessed the conflagration: and—well I remember!—wept, with tender partiality, over the imaginary ashes of Caroline Evelyn, the mother of Evelina.

The passion, however, though resisted, was not annihilated: my bureau was cleared; but my head was not emptied; and, in defiance of every self-effort, Evelina struggled herself into life.[2]

Frances Burney's fifteenth birthday was four months before the wedding of Mr. Burney and Mrs. Allen. The writing of *The History of Caroline Evelyn* would have gone on during the parental courtship. Perhaps in the summer before his marriage Charles Burney told the known journalizers, his Fanny and Susy, that unladylike and unsociable scribbling would vex Mrs. Allen. In her reminiscences Frances is vague about the precipitating cause of the conflagration. She exonerates her father while accusing him.

Dramatically, Frances at fifteen sought release of emotional tension in outward and visible fiery sign. She says she set fire to her manuscripts because she felt the writing of fiction to be shameful. In the ostensibly formal "Dedication," supposedly designed to soothe and praise Dr. Burney, there is a language of excitement and fear, a physical language, suggesting pleasurable instinct in conflict with moral notions. The phrases employed ("an inclination at which I blushed," "in defiance of every self-effort") suggest a more common vice indulged at "the age of adolescence." The secret "degradation" is both timidly hidden and angrily flaunted, just as the bonfire both censors the products of sin and momentarily makes a blazing display of them.

Self-dramatizingly, Frances tried to be "good," to cast off what would displease her father: "I felt ashamed of appearing to be a votary to a species of writing that by you, Sir, liberal as I knew you to be, I thought condemned." Why did she think it condemned? In this 1814 "Dedication," Burney claims that her father's library "contained only one work of that class" (i.e., novels), Fielding's *Amelia*. But the "library" of a man of letters does not include all the books in the house. All of the Burneys were great novel-readers, including Dr. Charles Burney.[3] Frances at seventeen observes that she is about "to *charm* myself for the third time with poor Sterne's 'Sentimental Journey.'"[4] The early pages of the surviving Diary exhibit reiterated imitation of Laurence Sterne's style, indicating that at sixteen Burney knew *Tristram Shandy* as well as *A Sentimental Journey*.[5] Most conduct-book writers would have considered both of Sterne's novels too indelicate for a lady's perusal. At the same time as she was entertaining herself with a variety of novels,[6] Burney was putting herself through an energetic course of solid reading, including Homer (in Pope's translation) and various histories of the ancient and modern world, as well as the works of major modern poets.[7] Such ambitious self-education might not have been encouraged or even allowed had Frances had a more ladylike upbringing. She was indeed fortunate that her reading was not censored, although she must always have been aware of how short her interests and acquirements fell of the grand masculine intellectual ideal. Novel reading and novel writing were officially considered below the sphere of the truly serious man of letters; in saying that her father did not possess novels his daughter is giving him credit for gentlemanly attitudes. But the supposed inferiority of fiction on the literary scale seems never to have bothered Frances herself, nor can she have believed that the Burney men did not read novels. The true cause of her concern and guilt seems to be the independence of the compulsion to write, to engage in a private and self-sustaining activity.

Reliving publicly the perturbations of her teens, Frances Burney relives the fear (or the pretense of fear) that the irresistible drive to write was merely masturbatory, a pleasure-giving perversion of the true feminine function. In 1814 Frances can remind her father that such shame was absurd, and that her productions were ultimately validated—as they were not in 1767, when "the mother of Evelina" and *Evelina*'s mother-novel were placed on a pyre like Hindi widows. Was the bonfire perhaps an unconscious piece of magic, the expression of an unrecognized hope that if Fanny were "good" enough and sacrificed the "good mother" Caroline Evelyn, her father in reciprocation would sacrifice Mrs. Allen? Whatever the circumstances, the episode aroused a good deal of passion in the author, even when she was sixty years old. She remembered Charles Burney's censorship, which she had dramatized into a book-burning, and she proudly remembered that she had not finally capitulated. In *The Wanderer* Burney tried to tell her father, for the last time, that her own creative instincts were healthy and trustworthy, and that the real author of *Evelina*'s being (and that of her other novels) was Frances herself, however much credit Dr. Burney might take upon himself for her success.

Yet, when she published *Evelina* Frances Burney's guilt led her to write the strange riddling verses "To ——— ———." On the back of what seems to be the first draft of this "Ode," Frances pencilled "4 in the Morn[g]"; she claimed she wrote it in a fit of inspiration in the middle of the night[8] The opening line was originally "Friend of my Soul, & Parent of my Heart," which was changed to the more awesome and weighted "Author of my Being!" Significantly, the penultimate line of the last verse, which became "Let not their folly their intent destroy," is in this draft "The folly pardon, the attempt destroy,"—a more violently propitiatory invitation to the unnamed father to obliterate his child's work. Burney evidently later saw the absurdity of this (her father could not really destroy her novel). But whenever she thought of her father getting too close to her work she (or part of her mind) immediately thought of destruction.

The History of Caroline Evelyn, which we know from the first letters of *Evelina,* is the story of how a woman comes to be a mother and is destroyed. Caroline's father, an English gentleman who had made a misalliance with a barmaid, dies in her infancy, and his daughter is brought up by her guardian, Mr. Villars, her father's tutor. At the age of eighteen, Caroline is taken in charge by her mother, who has married a Frenchman. The mother summons the daughter to Paris, where the girl is tyrannically treated and threatened with a degrading match. To escape this, she consents to a secret marriage with Sir John Belmont, an unscrupulous nobleman who later burns the marriage certificate and repudiates his child. Caroline, rejected, makes her way back to England and the home of her guardian. She dies, either in childbirth or soon after the birth of the daughter whom she bequeaths to the care of the elderly Mr. Villars.

If after the destruction of this first novel Frances went on almost at once with *Evelina,* writing and rewriting the new novel occupied her for years. Her sister Susanna and her brother Charles shared the secret, and young Charles, disguised, acted as Frances's agent in taking the manuscript to a bookseller. She was not deterred when the first publisher rejected her book; unlike her father, Frances Burney was never unduly upset by mere practical and professional setbacks. Lowndes was offered the first two volumes and expressed interest, but would not contract to publish until he saw the whole work. It was when she was finishing the third volume that the author was suddenly smitten with an attack of conscience. According to her recollections in the *Memoirs,* she asked herself "whether it were right to allow herself such an amusement . . . unknown to her father? She had never taken any step without the sanction of his permission." She "seized a happy moment" to avow "her secret little work and her odd inclination to see it in print." She added that her brother would transact the business "with a distant bookseller, who should never know her name." Dr. Burney's reaction was "amazement . . . surpassed by his amusement"; "his laugh was so gay, that . . . she . . . heartily joined in it."[9] The episode is remarkably like Charles gaining the Grevilles' "consent" to his marriage; an (understood) petition was "tacitly granted." Ingenuous Frances did not tell the whole truth; did she even say what genre the "little work" was? Lowndes was not a *distant* bookseller. Frances most probably in an odd moment mumbled something about how she would like to publish some writing sometime, and her father thought the idea amusing. His laughter was most probably the reaction his daughter wanted, "though somewhat at the expence of her new author-like dignity."[10] She could always say "but I did tell you"; all children know there are ways of "telling" an adult something so the person told does not take the truth in. Fanny had "permission." The proclaimed filial dutifulness only lightly conceals self-will, determination, a design.

Despite her artificial "May I?" Frances Burney had lined up a publisher and made all her arrangements. She had considered all the practicalities, copying the manuscripts "in a feigned hand" because, as she was Dr. Burney's amanuensis, her "common writing" could be identified by any compositor who had set the *History of Music*.[11] It is a mistake to think of Frances as a leisured young lady during her early years as a novelist; she worked steadily and devotedly as her father's secretary and copyist, sometimes laboring into the small hours. She was a working woman, if an unpaid one. Doubtless Dr. Burney diagnosed his bashful girl's wish to publish something someday too as a childlike desire to imitate his successful writing, in which she figured in a subordinate role. *Evelina* was Frances's elopement, her rebellion, her declaration of independence.

It was, however, a secret declaration of independence. The identity of the new novel's author was concealed well after publication. *Evelina* came out in January 1778, in true anonymity, and was received with almost universal admiration. Dr. Burney was not informed of the author's identity until June (when one of the author's sisters told him). By then, the book's success was certain. Frances Burney's fame was such that Dr. Burney could draw her after him into the public world of fashion (social and intellectual) in which he himself so much desired to shine. She could be taken to the Thrales' home at Streatham, and be introduced to Dr. Johnson, to Edmund Burke, and to Sir Joshua Reynolds. *Evelina* did indeed "look well in print" and its author was now a somebody. Charles was, of course, magnanimous about the secret when it was a secret of success. According to his account, which differs slightly from his daughter's, he did not read the book until he knew Frances had written it.

> I perused the first Vol. with fear & trembling, not supposing she w^d. disgrace her parentage, but not having the least idea that without . . . knowledge of the world, she c^d. write a book worth reading. The dedication to myself, however, brought tears in my eyes, and . . . [I] found so much good sense & good writing in the Letters of M^r. Villers [*sic*], that I was struck . . . when I saw her next. . . . [I] thought she w^d. have fainted; but I hasten'd to take her by the hand, & tell her that I had read part of her book with such pleasure, that instead of being angry, I congratulated her on being able to write so well; this kindnesss affected her so much that she threw herself in my arms, & cried *à chaudes larmes*, till she sobbed. The poor humble author I believe never was happier in her life.[12]

The scene, recorded by both father and daughter, is a strange scene of tears and smiles, of forgiveness without fault and reconciliation without breach. Frances had not disgraced her parentage, and the author of her being could shed pleasant and, as it were, forgiving tears over the ode to himself. After this, Charles was extremely encouraging about his daughter's writing—at least, her novels. Plays were to be another matter. Would he have been as encouraging about her fiction if *Evelina* has been a failure? Or even if it had had only partial success and mixed reviews? Frances was wise in maintaining anonymity until success was unequivocal.

An older school of critics of *Evelina* tended to treat the novel as an attempt to exhibit a variety of manners, with a frame story added to make a plot and to allow these manners to be happily exhibited. Recent critics, especially feminists, have seen that the novel's plot, involving the story of the dead mother and the absent father, has its own importance. These critics have tended, however, to see Evelina herself as somewhat two-faced, thus reflecting back on Burney the old charge of slyness. Evelina, it is indicated, acquiesces too readily in the ways of a snobbish, conventional, and misogynistic society.[13] And she is slavishly filial, not only toward her paternalistic guardian, but also toward her absconding father, Sir John Belmont.[14] Some of these charges can be lightened if we see *Evelina* against the background of *Caroline Evelyn*. The subtitle of the new novel is "A Young Lady's Entrance into the World," but the heroine is not an ordinary young lady of fashion, perhaps not a "young lady" at all. In the eyes of any inquisitive stranger, Evelina, "this deserted child" as Villars calls her (I:19), must be identified as a bastard. And she has no financial expectations to mend her status. The reader is expected to see the social implications of these facts more clearly than Evelina does. The social destiny of such an attractive, well-bred female bastard would seem inevitably to be some upper-class man's kept mistress, as Sir Clement Willoughby implicitly believes.

Evelina is unplaced in society, unclassified. Her name is a crucial problem. Her name really is "Evelina Belmont." Her father has, however, refused to admit her right to that important last name which identifies *gens* and status. She is unfathered and unauthorized. Her mother's maiden name has been given to her as first name. Both her mother and Mr. Villars were determined that Evelina should not use her mother's surname—that would admit illegitimacy. She is called "Evelina Anville"; the last is a made-up name, an anagram of the first. So the heroine's names are doubly private, doubly feminine. She has a matriarchal identity which is weakness, and no named place in the patriarchy which is strength. Her two names are unfixed, like two adjectives looking for a substantive.

The hint or clue of an anagram is inviting. "Evelina Anville" is "Eve in a Veil"—Woman not known, Woman obscured. But her name is also "Elle in Alive"—Woman persisting in living. "Evelina struggled herself into life." The original subtitle of the novel was not "A Young Lady's Entrance into the World" but "A Young Lady's Entrance into *Life*." Evelina the character, like the novel, insists on existing against the will of a father (Sir John Belmont within the story) who insists she has no being. She comes into life despite all efforts to annihilate or suppress this Eve. It is noticeable that a multitude of Burney's female characters have that hidden "elle" or "ella," that supportive "she" in their names: Camilla, Elgiva, Adela, Eleanora, Elinor, Eliza. The pseudonym of the last heroine, the central character of *The Wanderer*, is "Ellis"—"Elle is."

That is what Burney is trying to convey in all her novels, that "elle" is alive, that "elle" *is.*

If Evelina the hidden Eve is happily alive, she is also on the anvil of the world. Coming into consciousness means being conscious of her nameless state. Her first letter to Mr. Villars (and that she writes to him shows they are now separate) is signed

> Your
>
> *EVELINA*——— ———
>
> I cannot to *you* sign *Anville,* and what other name may I claim?

(I:24)

Through the sign of the dash she is allied to "——— ———," the unknown dedicatee of the sacred ineffable name. Evelina begins to notice the symptoms of her lack of social identity. At her first ball she is upset by the notion that Lord Orville's apparent boredom with her might be explained by his having discovered her nonentity: "I fancied, he has been inquiring *who I was*" (I:34). The fop Lovel maliciously complains of her to Lord Orville: "for a person who is nobody, to give herself such airs" (I:35). The remark rankles; Evelina recollects it much later: "Since I, as Mr. Lovel says, am *Nobody*, I seated myself quietly . . . not very near to any body" (III:289).

In March 1768, Frances Burney had begun a journal and addressed it to "Nobody" because

> to *whom* dare I reveal my private opinions of my nearest relations? my secret thoughts of my dearest friends? my own hopes, fears, reflections, and dislikes—Nobody!
>
> To Nobody, then, will I write my Journal! . . . No secret *can* I conceal from Nobody. . . . From Nobody I have nothing to fear. . . .
>
> I will suppose you, then, to be my best friend (tho' God forbid you ever should!) my dearest companion—and a romantick girl. . . . From this moment, then, my dear girl—but why, permit me to ask, must a *female* be made Nobody? Ah! my dear, what were this world good for, *were* Nobody a female?[15]

In her novel, Burney explores the universal adolescent experience of making an entrance into the world as "nobody," without an established personality or fixed social self. But Burney explores that experience from the female point of view, asking "why must a *female* be made Nobody?" throughout her presentation of her Eve-Nobody.

Evelina is pretty, charming, and naïve; she seems (much more than any of Burney's subsequent heroines) exactly what the men want. But we see that pretty person from within, and thus as a person, not as a prettiness. "Behind that lovely face Evelina is busy *worrying,*" says Anthea Zeman;[16] it would be truer to say that she is busy *observing.* Burney is influenced by the Richardson of *Sir Charles Grandison* (1753), whose heroine Harriet Byron, fresh from the country, makes pointed observations on town society. But Harriet is twenty-one, polished, self-assured. Evelina in her unsocialized innocence can unalarmingly voice basic female criticism of social arrangements. Her first ball is not a Cinderella's triumph (though her beauty attracts wide attention) but the beginning of trouble and wisdom. In a brilliantly fluid comic sequence, which must remind almost every female reader of her youth, the author shows us Evelina floundering along. She notices straightaway that the men flaunt their right of choice of partner: "they sauntered about, in a careless indolent manner, as if with a view to keep us in suspense" (I:28). She is chosen as a partner by "a young man, who had for some time looked at us with a kind of negligent impertinence." She wonders at him: "his dress was so foppish, that I really believe he even wished to be stared at; and yet he was very ugly" (I:29). Evelina not only refuses him, but "could scarce forbear laughing"; later, when he pursues her, she laughs in his face. Much more strongly than Harriet Byron's commenting on Sir Hargrave's goggling eyes, Evelina's free laugh illustrates women's right to look on men in their turn as sexual objects. This primitive right is not, however, a social right accorded to women, and the infuriated Lovel, a wealthy gentleman and a member of Parliament, repays Evelina with constant petty malice.

Frances Burney's own experience when a Mr. Thomas Barlow proposed to her in 1775 has been taken by at least one recent critic as signaling Burney's unhappy education in male control of the marriage market, an education that influenced *Evelina.*[17] But *The History of Caroline Evelyn* had evidently already dealt with the trials of the marriage market, and male control over marriage as both legal act and status. The *Early Diary* entries indicate rather that Burney was not utterly displeased with the novelistic situation of Barlow's unwanted courtship, partly because she felt herself essentially safe. True, Daddy Crisp distressed her by urging her not to neglect a good chance: "Consider the situation of an unprotected, unprovided woman!"[18] And she wept when her father urged her not to be *"peremptory"* in refusal of Barlow.[19] Charles Burney then cheered his daughter by promising "Thou shalt live with me for ever, if thee wilt! . . . I wish not to part with my girls!"[20] But Frances really knew that it would take a much bigger inducement than Mr. Barlow's modest status to induce Dr. Burney to part with his Fanny, for she was deeply engaged in assisting him with the *General History of Music,* the first volume of which was to come out in the next year. He would not want to lose his valuable assistant.

Her employment gave Frances a sense of security, which allowed her to treat Barlow throughout her Journal as a comic character. After one evening's acquaintance, at a party at her grandmother Burney's, Barlow had sent a letter declaring that "the Affability, Sweetness, and Sensibility, which shone in your every Action, lead me irresistibly to Love and Admire."[21] She found the epistle absurd, and its author dull (and also short). She gives them a splendid comic (and novelistic) dialogue. Barlow, the naïve male, is sentimental about marriage; his interlocutor is not:

> ". . . but is it possible that you can have so bad an opinion of the Married State? It seems to me the *only* state for happiness!"
>
> "Well, Sir, *you* are attracted to the married life—I am to the single— therefore *every man in his humour*—do *you* follow *your* opinion—and let *me* follow *mine.*"
>
> . . .
>
> "What—what can I do?" cried he very sorrowfully.
>
> "Why—go and *ponder* upon this affair for about half an hour. Then say—what an odd, queer, strange creature she is—and then—think of something else."[22]

Burney was able to write very firmly to Crisp, "I AM QUITE FIXED." She made it plain that even his injunctions and emotive threats could not prevail in this case, and was strong enough to make his threats and her firmness into a comical matter:

> And so it is all over with me!—and I am to be given up—to forfeit your blessing—to lose your good opinion—to be doomed to regret and the horrors—*because*—I have not a mind to be married.[23]

In her early twenties Frances had no "mind to be married." When she was sixteen, the sight of a wedding had seemed rather sinister: "O how short a time does it take to put an eternal end to a woman's liberty!"[24] The life of an old maid was visibly preferable to the lot of most wives. She allowed, as most of us do, a reservation in the case of true love. But she was basically heart-whole, and did not think of herself as on the marriage market. The secure wholeness of heart was not to last forever; at thirty she would be lacerated by unrequited love. But the heart-whole courage of her earlier years gave her the freedom to write *Evelina* and to criticize the society that puts women in such preposterous situations. Her heroine might have the qualities of "Affability, Sweetness, and Sensibility" that men (like Thomas Barlow) prize in women. But even Evelina has a dash of lemon as well as sweetness, and the author is using the sweet innocent heroine as the implement of the satirist.

One of the first things Burney makes us notice in the novel is the artificiality of the language with which men address women. The fop's silly speech, "Al-low me, Madam . . . the honour and happiness . . . to have the happiness and honour—," is made up of dance-floor fragments of an old and suspect *Frauendienst*. Evelina notices the same absence of meaning in the language of Lord Orville when he accosts her: "but these sort of expressions, I find, are used as words of course" (I:29). The gentlemen who have chosen this language of courtesy and have always the right to be first speakers, manipulate the moribund chivalry so as to make their superiority clear; the soft cover of language permits no lady to contradict or resent. Lord Orville is accustomed to dazzling others through correct use of language. In the face of such banal fluency, Evelina becomes more and more tongue-tied. She suspects that Lord Orville is playing with her, as she mutely hears him going from topic to topic. "It now struck me, that he was resolved to try whether or not I was capable of talking upon *any* subject" (I:32).

Too much, I think, has been made of Lord Orville's intended perfection: critics have called him a stick, "a young girl's dream of a nobleman," a Mentor, a model of cold courtesy as dead as Launcelot and Gawain.[25] Launcelot and Gawain, however, had their defects, and so does Lord Orville. He is cast in the role of romantic hero, but he is, after all, a fount of Evelina's woes, as well as her eventual reward. His conversation about her among the men is not very sweet or chivalrous:

> "Why, my Lord, what have you done with your lovely partner!"
> *"Nothing!"* answered Lord Orville, with a smile and a shrug.
> "By Jove," cried the man, "she is the most beautiful creature I ever saw in my life!"
> Lord Orville, as well as he might, laughed, but answered, "Yes, a pretty modest-looking girl."
> "O my Lord!" cried the madman, "she is an angel!"
> "A *silent* one," returned he.
> . . .
> "A poor weak girl!" answered Lord Orville, shaking his head.
>
> (I:35)

Lord Orville's disdainful view of Evelina as an unimportant object is more apparent in the draft, where, to Sir Clement's exclamation, "she is the most beautiful Creature I ever saw!" Lord Orville responds "Yes—a pretty Modest looking Thing."[26] The final speech in this published version of the fraternal conversation expresses Orville's mixture of pique and contempt. His vanity has been put out by Evelina's "most immoveable gravity" in the face of his efforts: "I have really fatigued myself with fruitless efforts to entertain her" (I:36). Shyness cannot be the explanation, he thinks, as he has seen the girl, whom he refers to as "your [i.e., Sir Clement's] Helen" acting brazenly. She laughed at Lovel, "first affronting the poor beau, and then enjoying his mortification." Lord Orville's remarks are addressed to Sir Clement, to whom he appears to give this "Modest looking Thing," this "Helen." Burney had been uncomfortably impressed by Homer's depiction of Helen:

> Thus has Homer proved his opinion of our poor sex—that the love of beauty is our most prevailing passion. It really grieves me to think that there certainly must be some reason for this insignificant opinion the greatest men have of women—at least I fear there must. But I don't in fact believe it.[27]

In this first male conversation in *Evelina*, Burney registers the "insignificant opinion" even the best of men may have of women, and protests against the power and prejudice that categorize a "Helen" and make her beauty the property of some man or other. Sir Clement Willoughby, a rakish would-be Paris who will try to take this Helen from the man who first possessed her, is struck by the description of the "poor weak girl" and decides to pursue this foolish nobody who would probably be an easy conquest. Near the end of the novel Sir Clement, not without justice, defends himself by throwing this early conversation back in Lord Orville's teeth (I:346–347).

Evelina is wrongly identified because she cannot yet arrange a social personality, a mask that will project the self she both is and wants to be. The struggle toward identity is complicated because identity cannot be acquired on Evelina's own terms. No individual is free to choose the means by which we are both formed and represented. Language, to use Lacanian terms, is imposed by "the Other," and "the Other" defines the self before the self is formed. Women are indeed defined by the Other, for the other sex creates all the laws, economic arrangements, and social connections which give or withhold status. Evelina's mother, not able to *prove* she was married, was in some sense not married. Evelina is a bastard as long as her father denies her legitimacy. Once Lord Orville says she is "a poor weak girl," that is what she signifies to Sir Clement. Evelina has to begin to understand these distressing circumstances, while at the same time learning that she cannot resort to instinctive natural responses (laughter, tears, running away) as social solutions. The novel shows Evelina growing up, coming into adult life.

To the extent that the novel is "about" Evelina's growing up it may be termed a *Bildungsroman*, and we may remember that a *Bildungsroman* about a woman is still relatively rare in the eighteenth century. A virtuous heroine cannot be a good-hearted picaro, and the scope for exhibiting learning and formation is limited. Usually the Augustan solution to showing a heroine's formation and development is to show her making some giant mistake and learning to repent of it—as is the case with Lennox's Arabella (the Female Quixote), with Haywood's Betsy Thoughtless, with Sheridan's Sidney Bidulph, and with Catherine Morland, Marianne Dashwood, or even Emma Woodhouse. Heroines who are not paragons have a story because they commit errors.

Evelina is no paragon, but the story of her coming-to-be does not rely on her mistakes. Rather, the trials of her growing up reflect the errors in her society rather than herself. Evelina's letters show her increasingly acquiring maturity. In the very first part of the story she is beginning to recognize the sad truth of her familyless situation, and to come to terms with it. At first she calls Mr. Villars "my . . . most beloved father" and asks rhetorically "by what other name can I call you?" (I:24). But she is soon to accept the fact that the rejecting absent parent is the real "father." In a less intense fashion, she tries to perform a similar work of denial and adoption in claiming her friends Lady Howard, Mrs. Mirvan, and Maria as a new family—a fantasy encouraged by these kindly women. Evelina proudly refers to "My mamma Mirvan, for she always calls me her child" (I:28). Evelina happily indulges this pleasant familial fiction, believing also the fiction (most assiduously if guardedly attended to by Mrs. Mirvan's mother, Lady Howard) that the coming reunion with Mrs. Mirvan's husband and Maria's father must be an occasion of great joy. Evelina says "their domestic happiness will be so great,—it is natural to wish to partake of it" (I:24). But she refuses to carry on this fantasy further once she encounters the reality of Captain Mirvan: "that kind and sweet-tempered woman, Mrs. Mirvan, deserved a better lot. I am amazed she would marry him" (I:38). Evelina expresses her true feelings of dislike and distrust, and a sharp sense of disappointment— not only in the brutal captain but in the woman who would marry him. Quietly, Evelina desists from claiming family relationship to the Mirvans anymore; we hear no more of "mamma Mirvan." We may realize that Lady Howard, who evidently pushed Mrs. Mirvan into this unsuitable match, is not much better as a mother and grandmother than the Madame Duval whom Lady Howard, in the seventh letter of the novel, dismisses so readily. (Lady Howard, too, has a rather disturbing manner of speaking of Evelina, not by her name but by listing salable attributes: "a little angel," "so perfect a face" [I:21].) Evelina has seen through one family romance at least; her first true manifestation of "excellent understanding" and good sense involves the quiet repudiation of both masculine superiority and polite and subservient female fictions about males, marriage and "domestic happiness."

In the last volume of the novel, Evelina's chaperone and companion is the independent-minded Mrs. Selwyn, who makes no claims on the young woman based on real or fictitious relationship. Mrs. Selwyn accompanies Evelina in her excursion to Bristol Hot Wells—the place where Burney's own mother had gone in a futile effort to recover strength. In this place (privately associated by the author with the mother), Mrs. Selwyn and Evelina both exhibit strength. In contrast to Lady Howard and Mrs. Mirvan, Mrs. Selwyn says what she feels like saying. Evelina notes "her understanding . . . may be called *masculine;* but, unfortunately, her manners deserve the same epithet" (II:268). Mrs. Selwyn's masculine "want of gentleness" can be hurtful, and Mr. Villars is not the only gentleman often "disgusted at her unmerciful propensity to satire" (II:269).

There is a high social tax on female aggression, a tax that the young single woman cannot afford, and, besides, may not something be truly lost in trading the "feminine" for the "masculine"? Yet if officially and at one level of the novel Mrs. Selwyn represents another bad alternative, an extreme to be avoided, we notice that this lady is associated with the heroine once the girl has begun to learn to stand on her own feet, and that Evelina's own responses in her letters have always shown a propensity to satire and judgment. Elderly Mrs. Selwyn's qualities are those that Frances at nineteen had noted as characteristic of her twenty-year-old stepsister Maria Allen: "she is too sincere; she pays too little regard to the world; and indulges herself with too much freedom of raillery . . . towards those whose vices and follies offend her." Yet Frances herself quickly comes to the defense of such female outspokenness: "I am unjust to my own opinion in censuring the first who shall venture, in a good cause, to break through the confinement of custom, and at least shew the way to a new and open path."[28]

As satiric writer, Frances Burney, like Maria Allen, is showing the way to a new and open path of speaking out. Evelina's own language is clear and outward looking; she is not egotistical or self-dramatizing (or self-knowing). She says what she thinks in her letters as not in public rooms, and at the outset she does not think ahead; when she begins a paragraph she does not know how it will continue. Mr. Villars, in contrast, structures his sentences and paragraphs, building them with the large pale bricks supplied by the eighteenth-century high middle style. He fears for the future, and tries to control his ward's life as he tries to control his sentences. Evelina with overt innocence evades that control, and pretty largely evades Villars's style of language. Her public and enjoined timidity is a veil for the vivid observation, sincere reaction, and shrewd judgment we accept in her letters.

The novel shows us how the restrictions upon women's speaking create a certain degree of doubleness in most women. The affected Lady Louisa Larpent in effect parodies the silencing of women by delicately "speaking so softly she could hardly be heard" (III:279), thus making her auditors strain to hear her —and so gaining power over them. In the Mirvan household, absolute restrictions upon women's speaking underwrite the code of marriage, and enforce the unhappy nervous silences and the abused hypocrisies of Captain Mirvan's women—hypocrisies Evelina sincerely rejects. ("I am amazed she would marry him"). Such force and decisiveness make her a valiant if unpolished heroine. Evelina is consistently heroic in never quite falling for the absurd terms of her world, though she is often as puzzled as Alice in Wonderland, and has only slender resources to pit against her society's certainties.

At the beginning, the heroine has a noticeably underdeveloped ego, and is thrust among a crowd of warring egotists. "Egotist" and "egotism" are among Burney's favorite terms. She uses the relatively new word "egotism" in the "Dedication" of *Evelina* in which she mocks the egotism of both the author and the reviewers to whom she dedicates the novel. Johnson's *Dictionary* defines "egotism" as a tendency to talk about oneself. In the mock-Dedication the word has that sense, but in general Burney's use of the word in her works does much to establish the modern meaning, a faithful self-love with accompanying disregard of others, of which talking about the self may or may not be a symptom.

Burney believes that we are all egotists, and her minor characters in *Evelina* show what this means by exhibiting unbridled egotism at play. These characters are busy presenting themselves to their outer world, and they are the outer world the heroine enters. Unlike Richardson, Burney is not much interested in examining creatures of the deep; she looks to the point where the ripples break. Perhaps because she felt herself so much submerged, so often frightened at the social outer air, Frances Burney was fascinated by the large amphibians moving gracefully (or so they think) in the social element. Her grotesque characters are not a gallery of funny pieces, but inherent aspects of the novel's fable of identity. As soon as Evelina has discoverd her handicaps in the world she must live in, the novel explodes into comic activity. The violent farcical actions and characters in *Evelina* are images of what the comedy is about. An older generation of critics was puzzled and offended, tending to treat the material either as an allusion to Smollett, or as a sign of the novelist's incompetence or inexperience. Austin Dobson complained of a lack of "a touch of tenderness" in the author's treatment of Madame Duval, and lamented the excess of "horseplay."[29] It has been a serious misreading of the novel to see it as a semi-sentimental comedy of manners that has interludes of "horseplay" scattered about in it.

Burney is truly innovative in doing what no English woman novelist before her had done—writing not only a novelistic comedy (like the works of, e.g., Charlotte Lennox) but employing sustained emphatic and expressionistic farce. In the English theatrical world at large, traditional five-act comedy during the eighteenth century had become increasingly more controled, timid, and formulaic; farces and burlesques were the last resort of satire and sustained the real tradition of English comic writing. Burney's fiction reflects this dramatic situation. She seizes a "masculine" mode of comedy, largely derived from the public medium of the stage, wraps it up in the "feminine" epistolary mode, and uses the combination for her own purposes.

Burney was always drawn to farce; it is a mode of demonstrating the absurdities within the permissible and customary. In a conversation of 1774, Burney pretended to Crisp and some impressionable women that she was to write a book on etiquette:

> "Will it be like Swift's 'Polite Conversation'?" said Mr. Crisp.
> "I intend to dedicate it to Miss Notable," answered I; "it will contain all the *newest fashioned* regulations. In the first place, you are never again to *cough* . . . it is as much a mark of ill breeding, as it is to *laugh;* which is a thing that Lord Chesterfield has stigmatized. . . . You may *smile* . . . but

to *laugh* is quite abominable; though not quite so bad as *sneezing*, or *blowing the nose*."

"Why, if you don't blow it," cried Kitty, [taking me literally,] "what *are* you to do with it, don't you think it nastier to let it run, out of politeness?"

I pretended to be too much shocked to answer her.

"But pray, is it permitted," said Mr. Crisp, very drily, "to *breathe?*"

"*That* is not yet, I believe, quite exploded," answered I; "but I shall be more exact about it in my book."[30]

Evelina is in some sense that ironic book on etiquette. The conversation, which displays Burney's responsiveness to Swift, is a verbal farce exploding the repressive elements of a politeness that would deny the physical self. In turning to farce Burney repudiates the restrictions of being "the proper lady" and implicitly rebels against the *convenances* that meant so much to Dr. Charles Burney. Her comedy is, as Jane Austen's never is, insistently physical, always bursting through restrictions and taking strange turns. The text of *Evelina* itself insists, in rather a Sternean fashion, that straight lines and enclosures, like the disagreeable Mall, "a long straight walk, of dirty gravel" (I:26), or the "strait walks" of Vauxhall (II: 193) are dull and dangerous—like the blank straight line which is Evelina's last name. In the stylistic management of the novel, farce happily perverts the narrative straightness, the decorous dull walk from beginning to end, which is the formula for a woman's life.

The novel's connection with stage farce is pointed out in the references to Colman's *The Deuce Is in Him* (1763) and to two plays by Samuel Foote, *The Minor* (1760) and *The Commissary* (1765). Evelina goes to Foote's theater in the Haymarket in company with her loud grandmother Madame Duval, and her embarrassing newfound cousins, the Branghtons (the vulgar family of a silversmith of Snow Hill), and their smart City friend Mr. Smith. The party bear a marked resemblance to characters in the plays. *The Minor's* hero is the son of a mercantile family trying to forget his origins. The old merchant complains, "Our modern lads . . . have their gaming clubs in the Garden, their little lodgings, the snug depositories of their rusty swords."[31] *The Commissary* exhibits a war profiteer now trying to become a fine gentleman. In both plays there is the character of a raddled old bawd, customarily played by a man (they were Foote's own roles).

Burney was fond of Foote's plays; in 1789, upon seeing a performance of *The Commissary* at Weymouth, she remarks that the play is "comic to convulsion."[32] The reference in *Evelina* to Foote's plays may be seen as a tribute not only to his plays but to Foote himself (recently deceased) and his achievement as both dramatist and actor. Foote was an exponent of a highly physical kind of comedy, the more physical after he wore a wooden leg and incorporated it into the laugh-getting business. An accomplished mimic, Foote was famous for "taking off" well-known members of society. His kind of theater is a theater of exhibition and embarrassment. As a dramatist, Foote recognized the possibilities of nonsense statements uttered in lively comic language. In *Taste* (1752), Lady Pentweazel ("from *Blowbladder-Street*") happily gushes to Mr. Carmine as he paints her portrait:

> I have heard, good Sir, that every Body has a more betterer, and more worserer Side of the Face than the other—now which will you chuse?
> . . .
> Why all my Family by the Mother's Side were famous for their Eyes: I have a great Aunt among the Beauties at Windsor; she has a Sister at *Hampton-Court,* a *perdigious* [*sic*] fine Woman—she had but one Eye indeed, but that was a Piercer.[33]

Like the other heavy female roles in Foote's plays, the part of Lady Pentweazel was taken by a male actor; it became "one of Foote's most popular roles."[34]

Transvestism is a feature of eighteenth-century theater, leading to the pantomime dame role as we know it. In private theatricals gentlemen could take on such a role, as young James did in the family production of *Tom Thumb* in 1777, when Frances played Huncamunca and he played the giantess Glumdalca:

> James was dressed in a strait body with long sleeves . . . he had a fan in his hand, a large hoop on, and a cap made of every thing that could be devised, that was gaudy and extravagant, feathers of an immense height . . . streamers of ribbons of all colours. . . . His face was very delicately *rouged.* . . . You cannot imagine how impossible it was to look at him, thus transformed, without laughing,—unless you recollect our infinite grinning, when we saw aunt Nanny in Dr. Prattle.[35]

As that last sentence indicates, comic male roles could be taken on by women; transvestism could go both ways. What is, however, noticeable in eighteenth-century memoirs is the number of festive occasions among both high and low when men dressed as women. Such acting is a joke about the social boundaries and rules that apply to sex roles, but the travesty also expresses and relieves fears about sexual identity.

Frances Burney uses this contemporary convention to explode and express the tensions involved in playing the female role in the eighteenth century. Madame Duval—vain, overdressed, highly painted, simpering, and rude—has all the traditional larger-than-life qualities of the stage dame. Burney's contemporaries presumably understood that intuitively. Her family certainly saw the transvestite role that is Madame Duval's part in the novel. A letter from Susanna to Frances in the summer of 1779 gives an account of a surprising moment of spontaneous private theater at Chessington:

> Monday Night after Supper we were all made very merry by M^r. Crisp's suffering his wig to be turn'd the hind part before, & my Cap put over it—Hetty's Cloak—& M^rs. Gast's Apron & Ruffles—in this ridiculous trim he danced a Minuet wth Hetty, personifying *Mad^e Duval*, while she acted *M^r. Smith* at the Long Room Hampstead!—the Maids were call'd in.[36]

If we think of Madame Duval in terms of the tradition of the pantomime dame, we may more readily understand the author's willingness to involve her in brutally physical comic circumstances; such violence is traditionally the lot of the female character devised for representation by a man. Or rather, creating this dame-ish character allowed Burney to express astonishment and anger at the violence with which women really are treated while apparently going along with a jest. Madame Duval is the focus for everything that makes female life seem hopeless or depressing; she has only "feminine" interests (dress, parties, gossip), and she is a compound of "feminine" affectations. But she is also old, past her time as a sexual object, and therefore superfluous. She represents the lowering fate of womankind. She is Evelina's blood grandmother—she represents maternal inheritance, matriarchal principle—and the inheritance of woman is no good, no inheritance at all.

The discovery of the mother, of the inevitable female descent and fate, is very bad news. The published version of the novel is emphatic; Evelina is "amazed, frightened, and unspeakably shocked" at the discovery of Madame Duval, and "more dead than alive I sunk into Mrs. Mirvan's arms" (I:52). But the draft expresses even greater emotional agitation: "I heard no more—seized with unspeakable horror,—my Blood chill'd—my Heart sunk—I gasp'd for Breath—& more *Dead* than alive, I fell into M^rs. Mirvan's arms."[37] To look upon the embarrassing, absurd, pathetic female ancestry is an occasion for registering "unspeakable horror." The revelation of the Mother, the buried author of one's being, who should remain decently hidden but who insistently makes her powerless presence felt, is a Gothic moment. Surrounded by mothers (Madame Duval and the encircling Mrs. Mirvan), Evelina undergoes her most truly terrible experience. This is her *Scheintod*, to be followed by a rebirth as the child of the female, recognizing her feminine typing and destiny. That Madame Duval represents something important to Frances Burney may be guessed from the fact that like the author's own grandmother Sleepe (née Dubois) Madame Duval is apparently half-French. And her cicisbeo, M. Dubois, bears the maiden name of that loved grandmother.

Madame Duval the absurd is a magnificent egotist with a defective social mask that she believes effective. She has forgotten that she is not really French; as a tavernmaid who married a Frenchman she has found her assumed national- ity a useful camouflage for her errors in English. Rationality has, however, been transcended; she believes the assumed identity is the true, just as she assumes her rouge makes her young. Her public egotism has shaky foundations, but her refusal to admit that she is ludicrous makes her comically invincible. Even when she has been bound and thrown in a ditch, covered with weeds and dirt and robbed of her wig, she maintains assurance, rejecting one of Lady Howard's caps with scorn: "Lady Howard, indeed! why, do you think I'd wear one of her dowdies?" (II:151). She is ignorant of the subtleties of shame.

The absurd woman (super-"feminine" and not quite female at all) meets her match in the boorish Captain Mirvan who is so ultra-"masculine" as to be unmanly, inhumane, not quite human. His sources of pride are simpler and less illusory than Madame Duval's. He is proud of being English and male—two qualities none can dispute. He constitutes himself the punisher of Madame Duval because as a true male he despises old women, and as a loyal English- man hates the French. His cruelty resembles that of another of Foote's charac- ters (also acted by Foote), Buck in *The Englishman in Paris* (1753), who thus describes a pleasant jest committed in a French theater:

> . . . presently they had a Dance; and one of the young Women with long Hair trailing behind her, stood with her Back to a Rail, just by me: Ecod what does me! for nothing in the World but a Joke, as I hope for Mercy, but ties her Locks to the Rail; so when 'twas her turn to figure out, souse she flapp'd on her Back; 'twas devilish comical, but they set up such an Uproar, one whey-fac'd Son of a Bitch, that came to loose the Woman, turn'd up his Nose, and called me *Bête;* Ecod, I lent him a Lick in his Lanthorn Jaws, that will make him remember the Spawn of old *Marlborough.*[38]

In the conflicts between Captain Mirvan and Madame Duval all the unmen- tionables are tossed up—rank, nationality, age, looks, religion. They do what we have been told since childhood we should not do—they make personal remarks. The captain not only compares Madame Duval to Lady Howard's "wash-woman" but descends to personal violence: " 'Dirty fellow!' (exclaimed the Captain, seizing both her wrists) 'hark you, Mrs. Frog, you'd best hold your tongue . . . if you don't . . . I shall make no ceremony of tripping you out of the window' " (I:51). Like Foote's Englishman, Mirvan regards physical assault on a woman under the guise of jest as a sublime source of social pleasure. He wants to add injury to insult—literal injury. Through Mirvan's grimly sportive pres- ence we are made to see that the infliction of psychological pain manifests the same cruelty as that which inflicts physical pain. In what is called the practical joke, the two unite.

Hoodwinking Madame Duval with the story that M. Dubois has been sent to the Tower, so that she sets out for London in a fright, taking Evelina with her, Captain Mirvan and his servants hold up her coach. In the guise of a highwayman, he orders the older woman tied and thrown into a ditch. His language ("I've done for her!—the old buck is safe;—but we must sheer off directly" [II:147]) is at a far remove from the debased language of chivalry employed in the ballroom ("the honour, Madam, the pleasure"). Madame Duval is deprived of gender and social identity. The effect can be seen in the illustration designed by Mortimer and Walker that serves as frontispiece to the second volume (Fig. 9). The wigless head of the helpless victim is almost male, in grotesque contrast to her remaining feminine draperies. Here is an illustration of a "virago," as Sir Clement calls Madame Duval (III:343)—a virago mortified in the eyes of a superior grinning male above.

Madame Duval enraged in a ditch is a wild illustration of feminine helplessness. The ditch itself seems an image of the female sexual organ, and Madame Duval's name indicates the value of femaleness, the humility of the female estate, in contrast to the proud erection of mountain in the name of the father Bel*mont*. Madame Du*val* brings Evelina socially low in introducing her to her cousins, the untaught and uncivil Branghtons. She seems to intend marrying Evelina to one of these vulgar relatives, repeating the mistake she made with Caroline.

The elder Branghton is content with his wealth and the old ways, but his son and daughters are ambitiously on the move. The daughters force the family to attend the Opera, even though they have no idea of this form of entertainment: "young Mr Branghton said, 'It's my belief that that fellow's going to sing another song!'" (I:93). Most of the family are still below the level of social hypocrisy; only one of the daughters has developed the instinct for imitating the tastes of those on a higher social level. But they have a marked sense of expanding, of moving forward. They make territorial moves, as seen in their constant grabbing of seats, and in their commandeering Lord Orville's coach, using Evelina's name. Evelina, illegitimate though they believe her to be, has connections and beauty, and they wish to use her in their corporate progress.

Mr. Smith, the Holborn beau, is admired by the Branghtons, as he is just within their range. He knows the town, and has acquired the habit of impertinent compliment that seems to them sophisticated: "don't be severe upon the ladies . . . you know I always take their part" (II:186). He is forming himself attentively, and has begun to learn the debased language of chivalry that marks the gentleman. He has discovered what the Branghtons don't yet know: that formulas of politeness can enable him to get his own way, to have both power and approval together. Unlike the cruder egos, he is vulnerable because he knows opinion matters. There is a sense of duty in his smartness; he models himself on something outside himself, acknowledges the role of the Other in social affairs. He puts himself under some strain: "such a struggle to appear a gentleman!" as Dr. Johnson said of him.[39] Johnson often mimicked Smith, his favorite character in *Evelina*—perhaps because Johnson was conscious, as most of us must be, of a lurking Smith within. The comical Smith is not altogether unsympathetic in his absurdity, as when he tries to appear a connoisseur of art by explaining the paintings in the Rotunda at Vauxhall:

> 'I think a pretty picture is a—a very—is really a very—is something very pretty.—'
> 'So do I too,' said Madame Duval, 'but pray now, Sir, tell us who that is meant for,' pointing to a figure of Neptune.
> 'That!—why that, Ma'am, is,—Lord bless me, I can't think how I come to be so stupid, but really I have forgot his name,—and yet, I know it as well as my own, too,—however, he's a *general*, Ma'am, they are all generals.'
>
> (II:202–203)

Mr. Smith the lowborn is in the feminine position of not knowing the classical lore, having no share in the great Western tradition. In that he resembles Madame Duval, though Evelina may join Sir Clement in biting her lips to keep back a laugh, since, through the courtesy and care of Mr. Villars, she has learned some of this lore, if at second hand. Gender conflicts here with class. But Smith is in the main in possession of the upper hand, acting as superior male. His wit is largely censure of female behavior, and jokes against marriage: " 'I would go any where with you, Ma'am,' (to me) 'unless indeed it were to *church* . . . but, really, I never could conquer my fear of a parson;—ha, ha, ha.' " (II:190–191). Smith insists upon believing that he is consummately eligible and that all young women are living in a state of anxiety for marriage. This view Frances Burney herself detested. "Well, Sir, you are attracted to the married life—I am to the single—therefore *every man in his humour,*" as she airily told Mr. Barlow.

Germaine Greer has said, "Women have very little idea of how much men hate them."[40] That may be true, but misogynistic literature by writers from Juvenal to Kingsley Amis has given women some insight into this hatred, and a few women writers, of whom Burney is one, have explored and expressed it. Captain Mirvan, whose foulmouthed contempt for all females is constantly in evidence, supplies a fully committed and unignorable expression of that hatred, unadorned. Evelina does attempt both to resist and reason with the captain, but she cannot make any impression, save to stimulate him to further threats. In not telling her grandmother the full truth about the fake highway robbery, the girl becomes an unwilling accomplice in the trick. Evelina has her own reasons for disliking Madame Duval, whose assumption of power over her she resents. The older woman is an unwanted mother-figure, whose presence at every moment reminds the heroine of the imbecilities of the female position and the inadequacies of women's breeding, education, and inheritance. By a sleight-of-mind,

Frances Burney has conflated the dead mother, the loved grandmother Mrs. Sleepe (née Dubois), and the detested stepmother Mrs. Allen, "precious," "the *Lady.*" Captain Mirvan's wicked joking must surely have had some root in the good Daddy Crisp's mockery of his friend's wife, as when, dressed like a girl of fifteen, the second Mrs. Burney paid him a visit and all the way downstairs Crisp "was diverting himself . . . with *taking her off!*—putting his hands behind him, and kicking his heels about!" Frances Burney herself had been a not-unwilling accomplice in the mockery of the unwanted mother-figure in her life. Ambivalences emerge in her treatment of Madame Duval. While imaginatively releasing her own hatred of her stepmother, Burney points out that women's hatred of other women is useful to the most antipathetic concerns and desires of males. A woman condemning any other woman may reflect male hatred and support masculine irrational control over all womankind.

Having alerted us unmistakably to masculine contempt of and control over women in the captain, Burney is then able to make a case for the absurdity of such contempt and control by showing their manifestation in all classes of men, though not equally in all males. The elegant Sir Clement, who thinks Mirvan "gross" and yet assists him in the highwayman prank, is a tough tormentor. Disregarding the elder lady's shrieks and Evelina's terrified anger, he forces his attentions on the girl: "'suffer me now, my adored Miss Anville, to take the only opportunity that is allowed me, to speak upon another, a much dearer, much sweeter subject'" (II:145). It is no wonder that Evelina impatiently cries, "O Sir, this is no time for such language" (II:146), but the language is the instrument of Sir Clement's inclement control. Lord Merton, forcing himself to wed the languorous affected Lady Louisa, Lord Orville's sister, can barely sustain the affectation of gallantry through the courtship: "'You have been, as you always are,' said he, twisting his whip with his fingers, 'all sweetness'" (III:280). He consoles himself in Evelina's hearing with the thought that after his marriage to Lady Louisa the courtship pretense of her power will vanish: "'She gives me a charming foretaste of the pleasures of a wife! however, it won't last long'" (III:311).

It is Lord Merton who, in annoyance at the sarcastic and independent Mrs. Selwyn, says to Evelina, "'I don't know what the devil a woman lives for after thirty: she is only in other folks way'" (III:275). This casual speech nakedly expresses the masculine contempt for women which Mirvan's brutal "trick" on the elderly Madame Duval enacts. Nothing could be more shocking and depressing for a young girl to hear than that she need not engage in the preposterous struggle to grow up and achieve an identity. Her maturity (achieving the age of thirty) will mean only that she ought to be erased. Her living is not desired by half the population. This is an extremely ironic remark within a *Bildungsroman*, for it indicates that the *Bildung* is completely unnecessary. A woman is not meant to develop and become formed, but to bloom rapidly, and then to die or disappear soon from the scheme of things.

The cruel implications of Lord Merton's speech and the meaning of the constant use of the phrase "old woman" as a term of abuse are brought out in the grotesque and brutal scene of the old women's footrace. Mr. Coverley and Lord Merton, to settle a wager, make two poor old women ("both of them proved to be more than eighty") run a footrace. The poor women at first setting out collide and fall down on the gravel, but the competing gentlemen insist that they must continue.

> Again, therefore, they set off, and hobbled along, nearly even with each other, for some time, yet frequently, and to the inexpressible diversion of the company, they stumbled and tottered: and the confused hallowing of *'Now Coverley!'* *'Now Merton!'* rung from side to side during the whole affair.
>
> Not long after, a foot of one of the poor women slipt, and, with great force, she came again to the ground. Involuntarily, I sprung forward to assist her, but Lord Merton, to whom she did not belong, stopped me, calling out 'No foul play! No foul play!'
>
> (III:312)

Unlike the scene of the assault on Madame Duval, the brutality here has no pretense of appropriate punishment. The action spills over the boundary lines of comic acceptability. It adds to the disturbance within the scene that no one save Evelina and the reader seems upset for the right reasons. Kristina Straub points out that Lord Orville voices concern only over the wastefulness of gambling.[41] Women have no defender—so much for chivalry. The two old creatures are poor in being poverty-stricken, so the gentlemen can buy them for this inhumane purpose. They are temporarily enslaved; each must "belong" to a gentleman. They are also poor in being women and in being old. Part of the unspoken excitement for the spectators is that one of the racers may die on the spot. This scene is Frances Burney's version of the fall of woman, of woman's well-known tendency to make a slip. The author here retorts upon men who so often remind woman of her weakness and grin maliciously over her falling. In fiction, literal falling had been used for lubricious gloating, as when Fielding twice makes his Sophia fall off her horse, once exposing the "beauties" (of her backside) to the view of a giggling male audience.[42] Here in the old women's forced race is weakness falling indeed. Let us get any laughter or lubricity out of that.

Burney uses farce and the license farce gives to develop scenes of expressive violence. The odds are steadily raised until the laughing reader notices discomfort, protests that things have gone, as we say, beyond a joke. In all her novels she creates characters who are practical jokers, who are instrumental in pushing matters beyond the civil limits. She was interested in the personality of the practical joker, as well as in his (or her—not all are male) use of power. This interest Burney shared with her cousin, the artist Edward Francesco Burney, the illustrator who also drew caricatures. His sketch "The Practical Joker" (Fig. 10), although it illustrates no one scene in Burney's novels, might stand as an illustration of an aspect of all her work, if we consider the picture's expansive figure and strong suggestion of pain.[43] A practical joker is a pain-bringer. The most hostile and predatory actions of Burney's characters have some flavor of the practical joke about them, and the comic joke in her novels often moves quickly into belligerent action. The French Revolution as presented in *The Wanderer* resembles an ultimate practical joke in which numbers can join in the pleasure of exposing and slicing up a victim.

The society of the practical joker makes us all warily conscious of both the coercive nature of ordinary social controls and the ease with which those controls can be set at naught. The practical joker for a moment seizes all the power present in the group, and shows us in extreme form the part played by aggression in social relationships. Captain Mirvan is an invaluable exponent of what Burney finds the true nature of social life, the aggressive search for power. Captain Mirvan is a social buccaneer and the most extreme representative of one group of characters in the novel—the uninhibited social aggressors—to which Madame Duval, Lord Merton, and the sarcastic Mrs. Selwyn also belongs. Each of these displays ignorance or impudence in a different way and from different motives, but all disregard social laws and the comfort of others. They are the egotists outright. Those in the second group have found that manipulating social forms is an effective method of getting one's own way without paying in loss of popularity. Members of this second set are self-conscious, aware of the mask. Mr. Smith and Sir Clement Willoughby are brothers under the skin.

All members of both groups seek power to a greater or lesser degree. The few characters who, like poor Mrs. Mirvan, manifest neither form of egotism are in a most unenviable position. Even Evelina musters enough strength to become at times an effective manipulator of social convention—she shows this when she prevents Mr. Smith from dancing with her at the Hampstead assembly. Since she first wished for "a book, of the laws and customs *à-la-mode*" (I:83), Evelina has become fairly expert in using the proprieties for her own purposes, if only defensively. Those who know the rules have the advantage over the overt rule-breakers in that they can sustain others' amity and approval—but only if those they are dealing with themselves obey the rules. Even the smoothest of insiders who work by the rules may be disconcerted by someone who breaks the laws on which he relies. So Sir Clement Willoughby is disconcerted and even routed in a wonderful comic scene when he calls upon Madame Duval. She has just been airing her grievance over the part she (rightly) suspects him to have played in the mock highway robbery: he has overheard her, but he does not care what she may think. The Branghtons are too impressed by the splendid Sir Clement to say anything to him: "with looks of guilty confusion . . . they scrambled for chairs, and, in a moment, were all formally seated" (II:208). Sir Clement, thinking himself in control, thrusts Madame Duval into the role of hostess and oozes into chit-chat and compliment, apparently master of the scene. But Madame Duval bursts out:

> " 'you'll be a wanting of somebody to make your game of . . . but' . . . , raising her voice 'I've found you out . . . so if ever you go to play your tricks upon me again, I'll . . . go directly to a justice of peace.' "
>
> (II:209)

Sir Clement is "evidently embarrassed at this attack." Trying to turn it off, he meets more well-merited abuse: "O Sir, you're vastly polite, all of a sudden! but I know what it's all for;—it's only for what you can get!—" (II:209–210).

Sir Clement loses his footing, unable to muster an appropriate response. Expressing similar anger would only damage the image of himself as fine gentleman, already diminished as the Branghtons and Smith show in regaining their ease: "every one who, before, seemed at a loss how, or if at all, to occupy a chair, now filled it with the most easy composure" (II:210). Sir Clement, dismayed, is caught between potential forms of behavior, and subjected to a dreaded social punishment to which he is totally unaccustomed:

> Young Branghton . . . was again himself, rude and familiar; while his mouth was wide distended into a broad grin, at hearing *his aunt give the beau such a trimming.*
>
> . . .
>
> The ha, ha, ha's and he, he, he's grew more and more uncontroulable, as if the restraint from which they had burst, had added to their violence. Sir Clement could no longer endure being the object who excited them, and . . . he hastily stalked towards Mr. Smith and young Branghton, and sternly demanded what they laughed at?
>
> (II:210–212)

After quenching their merriment, at the sacrifice of cool gentility, Sir Clement gathers the shreds of his charm about him in saying his adieux to Evelina, and makes an awkward escape.

The scene typifies Burney's comedy, and her interest in physical, psychological, and social reactions during a social exchange. She traces currents, undertows, quick pressures. The Branghtons and Smith note every twitch in the person who is at once an object of imitative devotion and an antagonist. At each slip on his part into confusion, Sir Clement loses the attributes that inspire awe. When he loses his glamor and becomes an embarrassed man, given *"such a trimming"* (the phrase is Evelina's own version of what young Branghton thought) the Branghtons spontaneously turn upon him. They expand with the same social force that he is losing, grow as he shrinks. In the natural history of human beings, Burney suggests, what one social identity possesses is held at the expense of others. Superiority and control can be lost during any encounter, but the loss means an exchange. The totality of social power in the room is neither added to nor diminished, but only transferred from one person to another. The Branghtons' increasing laughter expresses the involuntary flow of power from Sir Clement into them; pressure builds up until laughter explodes. The interchange suggests an inevitable and frightening reciprocity, like the principles of Henry James's *The Sacred Fount;* the vitality of one is depleted in order to nourish the vitality of another. In all of Burney's fiction she suggests that in most social encounters—including those between lovers—something of this exchange takes place, whether parties consciously will it or no.

Burney is an acute observer of embarrassment, which is both a response to social law and an immediate manifestation of a flux of social power. Embarrassment is a signal example of an inner emotion that also *is* its outward and visible sign. Shame may be private and spiritual, but embarrassment is public and social. Embarrassment is a point of interface between the individual as known from within and social identity as known from without—and it represents the inner person's knowledge of his/her outer *persona.* The narrative form of *Evelina,* combining private letter with public farcical scenes, is perfectly designed to exhibit embarrassment—it is embarrassment's objective correlative.

Frances Burney herself was shy of entering a roomful of people. There was a Prufrockian quality in her nature; she feared the eyes that fix you with a formulated phrase. Mrs. Thrale's first recorded private remarks about Burney illustrate what we have to dread in others' observation of us. After commenting on Dr. Burney, "if he has any Fault it is too much Obsequiousness," she turns to Frances:

> his Daughter is a graceful looking Girl, but 'tis the Grace of an Actress not a Woman of Fashion—how should it? Her Conversation would be more pleasing if She thought less of herself; but her early Reputation embarrasses her Talk, & clouds her Mind with scruples about Elegancies which either come uncalled for or will not come at all.[44]

The public behavior exhibits a Smith within—such a struggle to appear a Woman of Fashion! Frances's stilted behavior was at least in part a reaction against the very "Obsequiousness" in her father that Mrs. Thrale noticed so sharply. The contrast in the social techniques of father and daughter indicates that he must often have secretly embarrassed her. Her diaries, like the *Memoirs,* show her trying to give him a dignity which she evidently thought him too willing to forgo in favor of ingratiation.

"Her early Reputation embarrasses her Talk": Mrs. Thrale uses the word in its older sense. In its primary meaning, an "embarrassment" is something in the way, an encumbrance weighing one down or an impediment tripping one up —the major possibilities of farce are in the metaphor. The later meaning still carries some of its original possibilities. Burney, who shows characters stumbling, sinking, sprawling, is one of the first writers to use "embarrassed," "embarrassing," and "embarrassment" in their modern, more psychological sense. Christopher Ricks has contended that in the Romantic period (and throughout the nineteenth century) "blushing and embarrassment came to be thought of as crucial to a great many social and moral matters."[45] If Ricks is right, then Burney is one of the first Romantics. Blushing and embarrassment are subjects she develops.

Evelina's entrance into the world is a series of blushes—she has no social mask, so her reactions are instantly visible, in contrast to those who cannot blush at all, like Captain Mirvan, or who can hide their blushes, like the rouged Madame Duval. The several discussions of blushing in the novel not only point out Evelina's naïveté and her presence as an erotic object—both matters discussed by other characters—but also make us aware that we should inquire into the meaning of such a manifestation, and of similar manifestations. The blush fascinates as an erotic expression of involuntary feeling. But there are less erotic and more disturbing expressions of such feeling, as threats to identity are registered in a number of motions that themselves threaten identity further. Smith, for instance, depressed by Sir Clement's genius, "seemed himself, with conscious inferiority, to shrink into nothing" (II:202). Evelina at one of her first parties is "ready to die with shame" (I:33). Experiences are "mortifying," that is, they threaten a death of identity.

The moments of greatest violence in the novel stress the closeness of psychological to physical terror by fusing causes and effects. A person's nerve breaks; he or she may blush, cry, bite the nails or lips, shrink, sink, cry out. We wait to see somebody go to pieces. We wait to see somebody "die"—a thrill sought by the gentlemen who make the old ladies run that trebly embarrassing race. The fun of the social game is spiced with the possibility that someone's nerve will break for good.

Suicide is the most extreme example of nerve giving way, the final term in the sequence of self-wounding release which begins in nail-biting, blushes, and tears. The novel apparently proposes an example of suicide—and suicide appears in all of Burney's novels. Evelina has seen and pitied the poor young lodger insulted by the Branghtons. The young Scotsman goes about like a stage Hamlet in deep gloom, with downcast eyes. Upon seeing this young man rush up to his room with a pair of pistols, Evelina bravely rushes after him to save him from suicide. She does the right thing, placing humanity ahead of the proprieties. Macartney is quite happy at being thus "saved"; he readily accepts Evelina's consolation, advice, and monetary loan. His action appears to have been what our contemporaries say attempted suicide often is, a "call for help." Even at first reading of the scene (II:181–184), however, the reader may wonder if the young Scot is truly bent on self-destruction. Why does he rush busily through the house with a pistol noticeably protruding from his pocket?

As we pursue the matter, ambiguity and irony increase. It is hard for the reader not to retain Evelina's own vivid first impression—that young Macartney was about to attempt suicide. Yet in a letter to her, Macartney explains that he was really going to rob on the highway, and his pistols were loaded "to *frighten* the passengers I should assault" (II:230). He would have killed himself, he says, only if he were taken by the law. The scheme lacks good sense, and the reader is always unsure to what extent Macartney is to be believed. What is clear is that he does not want to be seen as humble and fragile. This confused young man has a deal of aggression in him. His progress illustrates our modern notion that nobody commits suicide without having wished to kill someone else first.

Macartney *has* nearly killed someone else. Like Don Giovanni, he has fought with the father of a girl he was wooing when that man caught him in his "clandestine affair" and used "abusive language" (II:227). It was after this rencounter that Macartney was told the truth by his mother: "My son . . . you have then murdered your father!" (II:228). A few other English novelists of the eighteenth century had flirted with the Oedipal theme of the son's aggression toward the father, but shrank from developing it.[46] Burney explores this theme. Macartney nearly achieves what Freud tells us is every son's dream. And at the same moment he learns of his patricide, Macartney learns that the girl he loves is his sister. Murder and incest dog his steps, and his new knowledge of family relations entails also his learning of his own illegitimacy.

Mrs. Thrale in her diary repeats a piece of gossip that she got from Mrs. Crewe (daughter of Frances's godmother); she was told "Macartney's going to shoot himself actually did happen to her [Frances's] own Brother Charles Burney, who having been expelled the University & forbidden his Fathers house was actually discovered by his Sister Fanny in the desperate state mentioned."[47] With Branghtonian curiosity, Mrs. Thrale even probed Dr. Burney on the subject. Despite the source, it is highly unlikely that this story is strictly true. For one thing, by October 1777, when young Charles was expelled, Frances had finished the first two volumes of her novel. It seems rather more likely that literature anticipated life—for Charles undoubtedly was in a state of despair after his expulsion.[48] Yet it is true that the novel does tease us with the intense tangle of family romance, and echoes of the private life. "Macartney" is the maiden name of Frances's own godmother and namesake, Frances Greville (mother of Frances Anne Crewe, who is thus another Macartney). In some sense, Macartney's sister's name "should" be Frances. The woman the Scotsman thinks is his sister, his beloved, is Polly Green, the innocent daughter of the nurse and "wash-woman" (shades of Madame Duval) who has been palmed off on Sir John Belmont as the daughter of Caroline Evelyn. When Evelina regains her rightful place, legitimated, it is she who is Macartney's sister, but the brother, whose illegitimate status does not alter, is no heir and has no inheritance. He may marry the displaced Miss Belmont without incest. The incest openly alluded to within the plot is the supposed incestuous love between Polly and Macartney.

But Macartney's feelings toward Evelina at first seem (to other characters as well as to the reader) to have some erotic content, and incest is thus suggested in the flavor of feeling between this brother and this sister—even though the brother is undoubtedly also a responsibility and an impediment to the young woman.

Macartney is Evelina's male counterpart. Both are apparently illegitimate, both adolescent, both without fixed social identity. Macartney has the apparent advantages of masculinity—he can be adventurous, he can display aggression. But his story tells us that the male lot is not necessarily better than that of the female; adventure and aggressiveness may be not only destructive but also absurd. Macartney could be a sympathetic character if he would cast himself only as the tender victim of the Branghtons' crassness. But as soon as he talks for himself we see a large ego with a great deal of self-pity and self-regard. He is a little bourgeois imitation Hamlet, with a personality smaller than his story, and an ego bigger than his ideas. Thinking himself a man of learning and a poet, Macartney expects patronage and wants important friends. His immediate successors in Burney's fiction are Dabler in *The Witlings*, who is tinier and more conceited, and Belfield in *Cecilia*, who has the originality and nobleness of soul that Macartney conspicuously lacks.

It is in the relation with Macartney the troublesome rather than with the admired Lord Orville that Evelina develops as a person and a character. At one level of the fable, Macartney represents, as it were, the masculine competitor disqualified, and the story is a feminist fantasy in which the masculine, the male heir, is set aside as illegitimate and the female is legitimated. At another symbolic and psychological level of the story, Macartney is merely another aspect of Evelina herself, and this brother-self, alter ego or *animus*, has done her a favor by actively punishing the obstructive and rejecting father. The deeper psychological elements are, however, largely contained within the story Macartney tells; his present action in the story of Evelina engages him as a character on the social level. He becomes an insistent and often unwelcome presence in Evelina's life, while her position as benefactress both pleases and embarrasses him. He needs to regain his position, to recapture superiority. He does so in an apparent tribute, writing a set of verses on the beauties of Bristol Hot Wells, and giving the palm to Evelina, whom he celebrates poetically:

> SEE last advance, with bashful grace,
>   Downcast eye, and blushing cheek,
> Timid air, and beauteous face,
>   Anville,—whom the Graces seek.

(III:333)

His poetic pseudo-praise carefully eliminates the courage and decisiveness in Evelina which made her effectively spring to his rescue. He is equally blind to the sense of humor she so often displays. Macartney insists on re-feminizing

Evelina, making her an altogether unsuitable heir to the great tradition of courage and gallantry and wit. She becomes all blushing cheek, like Podsnap's Young Person. Macartney's glib little verses have the effect of drawing power back to himself, away from her—an effect that operates even when he is not present. Curious sauntering gentlemen crowd about Evelina in the street, identifying her through the lines she as yet does not know: "'tis certainly she!—mark but her *blushing cheek!*'" (III:326). These rude gentlemen press upon her so that she stumbles and falls on the rain-wet pavement. Macartney had once thought of assaulting people as a highway robber; his verses are suitably aggressive, though their aggression is concealed. He manages to assault Evelina by proxy so that, like the poor old women, embarrassed in all senses, she falls down.

Macartney as literary man attempts to usurp the authorial role and prerogative. His attempt offers Burney the chance to parody the language men use of women. (This *"blushing cheek"* sort of thing is harder to take than any amount of Juvenal.) We hear again the old hackneyed terms of the ballroom, the language of Lovel, Sir Clement, Smith, even of Lord Orville. Resorting to such stuff is the more unhandsome in Macartney because Evelina for his sake has fought off the temptations of bashful docility and found another language. When Lord Orville finds Evelina at the garden gate with Macartney, and overhears her making another appointment to meet him, he is shocked. (Unacknowledged jealousy strengthens disapproval.) Evelina impulsively offers to give up the meeting and to explain all circumstances. Lord Orville is glad to accept this docile offer.

> 'The sweetness of Miss Anville's disposition,' said he in a softened voice, 'I have long admired, and the offer of a communication which does me so much honour, is too grateful to me not to be eagerly caught at.'
>
> (III:300)

When men talk of "sweetness" in a woman they are dangerous—there is an uncomfortable echo here of Sir Clement Willoughby glozing on while Madame Duval is screaming. They are also a little absurd—like Mr. Barlow praising Frances's "Affability, Sweetness and Sensibility, which shone in your every Action." Once she is alone, Evelina begins to feel she should not yield to timidity, that the desire to please Lord Orville is a temptation: "I could not help asking myself what *right* I had to communicate the affairs of Mr. Macartney" (III:301). Her absent guardian, Mr. Villars, cannot answer in time, and her present chaperone, Mrs. Selwyn, thinks Macartney "an impostor" who merits no consideration (indeed, he is not worthy of it). Evelina makes her own decision. Realizing "the utter impropriety, nay treachery, of . . . publishing the misfortunes and poverty of Mr. Macartney," she decides: "I ought not to betray Mr. Macartney." He would not have placed confidence in her "but from a reliance upon my honour which I should blush to find myself unworthy of" (III:302). "Impropriety" has become, not a matter of etiquette, or of pretty femininity; it has been redefined as bearing a moral meaning. There are higher values than conformity to a code of feminine conduct. "Sweetness" must give place to integrity.

Evelina speaks of "honour." This word is commonly a masculine expression of masculine values, and it is often abused. In its higher sense it stands for a private nobility in all relationships, an integrity that does not give way to convenience or group pressures. In refusing to gain social power at the expense of another's loss, Evelina also breaks the novel's chain of farcical repetition and egoism. Her decision really does cost her something, for the interview with Lord Orville, when she has to disappoint him, is difficult. Lord Orville represents the strongest pressure that can be exerted on Evelina. He is her temptation, her challenge, not her Mentor. In refusing to do him "so much honour" at the expense of her own "honour" Evelina shows herself capable of resisting the world's attempts to feminize her unduly. She is to be seen as attractively feminine, but not refeminized by the social language Lovel, Willoughby, Smith, Macartney, and Orville have applied to her. It is her resistance, not her "sweetness," that makes Evelina a heroic heroine. Evelina has now truly entered life, as a person capable of moral decision. It is this maturity that is rewarded by paternal acknowledgment—when she no longer need live with Father. The name she sought is not one she will ever bear. From "Anville" she becomes "Orville," entering a golden city of civility composed of herself, Lord Orville, and Mr. Villars. (But "An-ville" and "Or-ville" are *ifs* and *an*s, possibilities, "if" cities.)

The last big scene of the novel, however, is not romantic or sentimental. The unpunishable Mirvan punishes Lovel by bringing into his presence a monkey "full dressed, and extravagantly *à-la-mode*!" (III:400). Lovel, angry at being confronted by his semblance but too cowardly to strike the captain with his raised cane (as we wish he would), vents his rage "by giving a furious blow to the monkey" which promptly revenges itself by biting his assailant's ear:

> Mr. Lovel was now a dreadful object; his face was besmeared with tears, the blood from his ear ran trickling down his cloaths, and he sunk upon the floor, crying out, 'Oh I shall die, I shall die!—Oh I'm bit to death!'
>
> (III:401)

This monkey finale serves a number of purposes. Burney is picking up an image common in Restoration and early eighteenth-century literature, expressing the low nature of man. A number of female speakers, including Artemisia's visitor in Rochester's poem, Susannah Centlivre's Miranda in *The Busy-Body*, and Richardson's Charlotte Grandison had taken the curious grimacing creature as the express image of Man as Male. Under the cover of Mirvan's brutality and Evelina's innocence, Burney is perpetrating an antimasculinist satire. She jokingly pays off the men for their demeaning language about women, and all that stuff about *"blushing cheek."* Lovel, who had tried to make Evelina blush and had gibed at her blushes, now himself blushes indeed, the flowing blood external and unusually visible. This is the only such violent scene in *Evelina* where the object is male, and the only one of such scenes in which the victim must be felt to deserve his fate. The scene no sooner entertains us with the comforts of its justice, however, than it reminds us of our guilt in participating in such satisfactions, which lower us to the level of Mirvan and the monkey. The cycle of revenge is itself an animal impulse cruelly refined by social ambition. The social game may entail constant losses, mortifications, pain—but that social world of power, ego, and embarrassment is an amoral world. Learning to conform to its ways too much is a mistake. To enter it is to become embarrassed. Yet the embarrassments need not and should not keep anyone back. A woman has to leave the paternal protection, the tender burial of a Berry (or Bury) Hill. Without stepping out into life and the world there is no identity. This is the meaning of the often violent and strange tale that Frances Burney addressed "To ⸺⸺." Through her novel, Burney did make an "entrance into the world."

The Witlings:
The Finished Comedy

Evelina made Frances Burney famous, although this was a blessing about which she had some reservations. Fame, however, also brought her new friends whom she valued without any reservation at all. Charles Burney was now pleased to take his daughter with him to the gatherings at Streatham, home of Henry Thrale the brewer and his vivacious wife, where the chief luminary was Dr. Samuel Johnson. Dr. Johnson (Fig. 11) now became Frances Burney's friend, and this friendship grew on its own, independent of Johnson's relationship with Dr. Burney. The great author of *The Rambler,* "The Vanity of Human Wishes," and *Rasselas* offered her personal affection, and encouragement in writing. Frances Burney also enjoyed his animated, profound, and humorous conversation, and was soon to become one of his correspondents. She valued this friendship so highly and guarded it so jealously that she was later to refuse to let Boswell see any of her letters from Johnson.

The young author Frances Burney was no longer to be seen as the shy girl who made part of the audience in Dr. Burney's music room. Hester Lynch Thrale, who had not noticed her on their first encounter, noticed her now.[1] The relationship with this aristocratic and intelligent woman (older than herself by eleven years) was an important feature of Frances's new life. The success of Streatham as a center for informal gatherings and lively conversation was largely owing to the qualities of Hester Lynch Thrale (Fig. 12), who sustained kindness and vivacity despite maternal griefs and constant marital unhappiness—and also despite the demands made upon her by Johnson's need for assistance in his battle with melancholia. Her home became in effect a kind of salon, the party varying from day to day but including such constant visitors as Edmund Burke and the dramatists Arthur Murphy and Richard Brinsley Sheridan.

Charles Burney had long been a happy member of the Streatham circle. He recognized the function of Mrs. Thrale as a social center of the Johnson group, and saw her as an important protectress. He wrote her charming little letters, not disdaining to quote foreign languages—even Latin phrases—to this learned lady. Mrs. Thrale in turn gave generously. One of Charles Burney's letters, sent from Turnham Green in March 1778, begins enthusiastically, "Why, what a Lady Bountiful you are!" and continues in the same strain:

> . . . most People content themselves & others by giving *Boxes* & *Turkies* at Xmas;—but you are an endless Giver.—never waiting for Times, Seasons, or Occasions, but making them at your pleasure. . . . The few paltry Sprigs of Lawrel I sometimes fancied I saw trembling before me in some degree of Verdure, have pined, shrivelled, & withered so much of late that I came hither to *Turn 'em Green*—but alas! in vain, as I shall shew you over the Leaf.

The composition over the leaf, introduced with such an excruciating pun, is a verse epistle in iambic tetrameter, "To Mrs. Thrale":

> Not more the hungry pilf'ring wretch
> His brain can sack, or fancy stretch
> How best his neighbour's Goods to seize
> Than you, your Friends to save & please.
> Forever on the watch to find
> New ways, & means their hearts to bind
> You eager seek with Argus' pry
> Each wish to know, & want supply.
>   When Wealth is lodged in hands like yours
> With patience Envy's self endures
> The Serpents which her heart devour
> At sight of such superior pow'r.
> Humiliation ne'er corrodes
> The Mind of those your bounty loads.
> . . . .
>
> While some, to whom Fate grants the purse
> Contrive to make each gift a curse;
> And Conflicts raise in ev'ry breast
> Whether to love or to detest
> The Cold, ungraceful, clumsy hand
> Which Pride & Insolence expand.

> Insolvent, yet I ne'er repine
> At Favours heap'd on me & mine,
> And though both numerous & great
> They no remorse or shame create
> For, by the Manner you bestow
> The Hearts acquire so warm a glow
> Of all who benefits receive
> As makes them feel like those who give.[2]

This tribute, an unwittingly frank exposition of the beneficiary's feelings, shows that Dr. Burney did know the serpentine envy of those with "superior pow'r," that is, superior wealth, and did feel some shame at his position as an "insolvent" taker. Yet he eagerly professes his readiness to go on taking. In some sense Charles is the "hungry pilf'ring wretch," sacking his brain to contrive means of getting his neighbor's goods; his wit is put to work to create compliments operative in securing endless supplies from this "endless Giver." Such feelings and such activity seem to have been stirred by more than a few "*Turkies*"; it is evident that Mrs. Thrale had given substantial money gifts privately to Charles Burney. She is the one to whom "Fate grants the purse" and wealth "lodg'd" in her hands has made its way to his.

If Charles Burney was receiving secret money donations from Hester Thrale, Frances, at least at this point, presumably did not know it. She was to surprise Mrs. Thrale by standing on her dignity and refusing some manifestations of bounty. At first offended, Hester came to admire: "I adore her for the Pride which once revolted me. There is no true Affection, no Friendship in the sneakers & Fawners."[3] Charles apparently felt a certain amount of charmful fawning to be appropriate conduct toward those whose money or rank made them suitable patrons. Hester was understandably surprised by Frances's "Pride," for the father's behavior had not prepared her for such dignity in a Burney; Mrs. Thrale seems to have expected them all to have their hands out.

Hester Thrale took Miss Burney in, and made much of her. The stiltedness, the Lady Louisa qualities of Frances's conversation that Mrs. Thrale first noticed, were the result of that resistant dignity which melted under the warmth of a true friendship. This friendship, which can be traced in their letters and the pages of their separate journals, is a story in itself, progressing from cautious beginnings through admiring intimacy to unfortunate strain and hostility. But the break was far from the thoughts of either when Frances started paying long visits to Mrs. Thrale and living part of her life among the "Streathamites."

At Streatham, Frances Burney was drawn out, encouraged to talk as well as to listen. She joined in the various *jeux d'esprit*, like the personality games invented by Mrs. Thrale, in which acquaintances were compared to some food, to some color and kind of silk, to a flower, to an animal. Frances was "a Woodcock," "a lilac Tabby," "the Ranunculus," "Doe, or Antelope." (Dr. Burney was "a dish of fine Green Tea," while Dr. Johnson came off as a "Haunch of Venison," "Marone" silk, and "Elephant.")[4] In March 1779, Hester Thrale and Frances Burney joined in writing a mock periodical, "A Weekly Paper," as Hester Thrale reports: "What says I shall we call our Paper? Oh the Flasher to be sure says She—we have a Hack Phrase here at Streatham of calling ev'ry thing *Flash* which we want other folks to call *Wit*." Burney wrote the editorial "introductory paper": "And let no Man be dissatisfied with the futilities of this paper, when he hears that it's (*sic*) writer and nomenclator contentedly adopts the definition of a Flasher given by D^r. Johnson in the following Words—A Man without any real power of Wit; or solidity of Thought."[5] There were many occasions of Streatham "*Flash.*" One evening in 1781, Burney records, "we made an extempore Elegy, Dr. Johnson, Mrs. Thrale & myself *spouting* it out alternately."

I

Here's a Woman of the Town,
Lies as Dead as any Nail!
She was once of high renown—
And so here begins my Tale.

II

She was once as cherry plump
Red her Cheek as Cath'rine Pear,
Toss'd her Nose, & shook her Rump,
Till she made her Neighbours stare.

III

But there came a Country 'Squire
He was a seducing Pug!
Took her from her friends & sire,
To his own House her did Lug.

IIII

There she soon became a Jilt,
Rambling often to & fro',
All her life was naught but guilt,
Till Purse & Carcase both were low.

V

Black her eye with many a Blow,
Hot her breath with many a Dram,

Now she lies exceeding low,
And as quiet as a Lamb.

So if any 3 people can do worse—let them!⁶

The extemporary composition of slightly ribald verse is not usually thought of as one of the accomplishments of the author of *Evelina*. Frances was now among the wits. Mrs. Thrale had warned her of the dangers: "you must be more careful than ever of not being thought bookish, for now you are known for a wit and a *bel esprit,* you will be watched," but Johnson said, "now it is too late. You may read as much as you will now, for you are in for it—."⁷ Johnson teased "little Burney" about her new status, telling her Dr. Jebb was right to forbid her wine: "he knows how apt wits are to transgress that way." Frances commented, "In this sort of ridiculous manner he *wits* me eternally."⁸

To call Frances "a wit" was to tease her; friends knew she disliked being identified with learned ladies, and did not wish to vie with the formidable Mrs. Montagu and her set of bluestockings, "the Blues." That Frances was "a wit and a *bel esprit*" was a jest, but there was truth in the jest. Given her introduction to circles of acknowledged "wits" it is no wonder that Frances Burney should choose as a topic for her next comic work the intellectual self-consciousness of would-be wits.

A number of admirers of *Evelina*, especially the new friends at Streatham, suggested that Burney should next write a comic play. The relation of scenes in the novel to theatrical pieces had not gone unnoticed. A successful play could make real money, in the hundreds of pounds, for its author (Burney had received only twenty guineas from Lowndes for *Evelina*). Also, dramatic works were supposed to belong to a higher species of literature than the novel. If, as was eventually planned at Streatham, Murphy were to advise Frances about the construction and style of the piece and Johnson were to write a prologue for the production, fame, fortune, and success (both literary and popular) seemed assured.

Mr. Samuel Crisp, the author's elderly friend and "Daddy," crudely advised Fanny to make her hay while the sun shone:

Your kind and judicious friends are certainly in the right in wishing you to make your talents turn to something more solid than empty praise. When you come to know the world half so well as I do, and what yahoos mankind are, you will then be convinced that a state of independence is the only basis on which to rest your future ease and comfort. You are now young, lively, gay. You please, and the world smiles upon you—this is your time. Years and wrinkles in their due season . . . will succeed. You will then be no longer the same Fanny of 1778, feasted, caressed, admired, with all the soothing circumstances of your present situation. The Thrales, the Johnsons, the Sewards, Cholmondeleys, &c. &c., who are now so high in fashion, and might be such powerful protectors as almost to insure success to anything that is tolerable, may then themselves be moved off the stage. I will no longer dwell on so disagreeable a change of the scene; let me only earnestly urge you to act vigorously . . . a distinguished part in the present one.

The "something more solid" Crisp wishes Frances to acquire is, of course, money. In order to secure financial independence she is encouraged to make use of her friends as patrons and supporters. In his own mind, Crisp seems to confuse his Fanny's writing with coquetting and being agreeable, as if the words she wrote had some intimate connection with the other kind of pleasing expected from a young woman. There is sense in Crisp's admonitions that Frances Burney should keep writing and now try to make some money; the girl was getting on a bit (twenty-six in June 1778) and if she remained unmarried there was no financial provision for her future. The good sense is oddly blurred by the moral atmosphere. Crisp, like the men in *Evelina*, seems dubious about the value of a female who survives to middle age. He urges upon Frances the very Burneyesque tactics of winsome charm—"obsequiousness"—that she was trying to escape. The letter is full of the kind of mixed signals Frances was always receiving: achieve independence by seeking patronage, be vigorous by being ever-charming.

Crisp does advise independence in the work itself:

> Let it be all your own till it is finished entirely in your own way; it will be time enough then to consult such friends as you think capable of judging and advising. If you suffer any one to interfere till then, 'tis ten to one 'tis the worse for it—it won't be all of a piece. In these cases . . . the more cooks the worse broth.[9]

Crisp's comments here are deeply felt. He himself was a failed playwright, having never fully recovered from the delay in producing his tragedy *Virginia* (1754) nor from its less than mediocre success. His play, incidentally, portrays a father who procrastinates about a problem until the only solution is to kill off his obedient daughter; it presents some odd attitudes to filial-parental relationships which Crisp might unconsciously have carried into the pseudo-father-daughter connection with Frances. (See also Chapter Five.) Crisp himself enormously resented advice and alterations, and had never forgiven Garrick—"his soul was little!"[10]

It is interesting that Burney did not take Crisp's advice; she showed the play in progress to readers, particularly to Murphy, for she was really interested in professional competence. Crisp's instructions spring partly from his own wounded egotism, which fostered a pudency about the horrid crudity of live theater. It was inevitable that in the end he would withdraw approval altogether.

He would never care for his "Fannikin's" power of pleasing being subjected to such molestation—or, to put it another way, arriving at literary consummation. Crisp was in the end one of the two cooks who spoiled her broth. He interfered, so as to prevent stage performance—the very fate he had most dreaded for himself during the years he had waited for the production of *Virginia*.

But in the autumn of 1778 Frances Burney was urged to "act vigorously" to try her wings. In her diary she describes her encounter with Sheridan and his flattering encouragement: "I think, and say, she should write a comedy." Sir Joshua Reynolds good-naturedly pushed the question: "And you (to Mr. Sheridan) would take anything of hers, would you not?—unsight, unseen?" Frances's shyness was well under control: "I was never so much astonished, and seldom have been so much delighted, as by this attack of Mr. Sheridan." She obviously believed Sheridan, who had the tact to make, immediately, a similar application to Dr. Burney: "Afterwards he took my father aside, and formally repeated his opinion that I should write for the stage, and his desire to see my play."[11] Asking a young lady to write a play seems almost like making a proposal of marriage, necessitating a formal application to the paternal parent. For a well-bred and marriageable young lady to write for the stage was unusual, so daring as almost to rank with sexual activity—it needed sanctions, the approval of the masculine guardian, to make it licit. At the time, Charles Burney was flattered by all the incense wafting about the family name and by the novelty of having someone like Sheridan ask something of him that was in his power to bestow. For a while he remained well-disposed to the project. There is no reason to doubt Sheridan's sincerity. He kept on hoping for the play, and inquiring after it years after the piece had been put aside.

Burney's present friends and supporters were unaware that "Farces and Tragedies" had been included in the collected works that fueled the bonfire of her fifteenth birthday. Now, as the author turned her adult attention to theatrical writing, she had to realize that in some ways she was more hampered than when using the more accommodating and private form of the novel. Her friends agreed that her forte was comedy—but how was a lady to write comic drama and remain a lady? The basis of comic drama was sexual escapades or difficulties within courtship and marriage, overtly signified in appropriate stage scenes. *Evelina* of course deals in its own way with sexual tensions and sexual identity, but the reader can choose to ignore these themes. If, however, some of the scenes from *Evelina* were put on stage (the overthrow of Madame Duval, for instance) they could no longer pretend to be innocuous. The narrative manner of *Evelina*, the epistolary mode supplying a gentle, ignorant, and unpresuming voice, offered a cover which would be blown away by the force of direct mimesis.

A good, well-bred woman should not be too forceful, nor should an unmarried virgin seem to know too much, though as a member of the audience she was permitted to laugh at sexual escapades. Crisp gloomily pointed out the difficulty, though he saw it (rather confusedly) only in terms of language:

> I need not observe to you, that in most of our successful comedies, there are frequent lively freedoms (and waggeries that cannot be called licentious, neither) that give a strange animation and vigour to the style, and of which if it were to be deprived it would lose wonderfully of its salt and spirit. I mean such freedoms as ladies of the strictest character would make no scruple, openly, to laugh at, but at the same time, especially if they were prudes (and you know you are one), perhaps would shy at being known to be the authors of.[12]

Having frightened his friend, so that she responded with the expected alarm ("I would a thousand times rather forfeit my character as a writer, than risk ridicule or censure as a female"), Crisp then soothed:

> A great deal of management and dexterity will certainly be requisite to preserve spirit and salt, and yet keep up delicacy; but it may be done, and you can do it if anybody. Do you remember, about a dozen years ago, how you used to dance Nancy Dawson on the grass-plot, with your cap on the ground, and your long hair streaming down your back, one shoe off, and throwing about your head like a mad thing? Now you are to dance Nancy Dawson with fetters on; there is the difference.[13]

The girl may caper with abandon, "like a mad thing"; the woman grown must consent to be chained. If we wonder what made Frances "a prude," Crisp's warning letter can tell us much. She was always given confused instructions, told to exert herself and yet be delicate, never to transgress into the impermissible.

Crisp's gloomy remarks also indicate something of the problems of the theater at the time. Frances Burney was not the only dramatist dancing in fetters. A reading of English stage comedies of the later eighteenth century is likely to leave a general impression of flat monotony, despite many good lines and witty wisecracks. The authors responded to an audience that they did not quite know by persistently "writing down" to them. Morality was to be clearly enunciated, and there should not be more than one side to the question. Irony became increasingly distrusted. As Paul Hunter has suggested, Augustan irony was an often unwilling strategy of toleration.[14] By the reign of George III, toleration itself had become enshrined as a paramount virtue. Love, equality, and freedom (within inoffensive limits) were to be the basis of the new society. Thus, we find in drama pleas for fair treatment of the traditional butts of English aristocratic satire—the tradesman, the lawyer, the foreigner. Colman gives us good bankers in *The Man of Business* (1774); Kelly supplies a virtuous lawyer in *The School for Wives* (1774). Cumberland ends *The Fashionable Lover* (1772) with a plea for an end to prejudice against the Scots. Kelly gives us a good and benevolent Irish clerk in Connolly in *The School for Wives*: "nobody's eye looks ever half so well, as when it is disfigured by a tear of humanity."[15]

For the sake of moral clarity, dramatists smooth out ambiguities, minimizing ironic pleasure to make sure we get the point. No character should stray too far from his description (e.g., "faithful, noble-hearted creature," or "Money is the spring of all his actions").[16] The characters must also display their particular foibles incessantly, and be ready to utter a "sentiment" when one is wanted. As a result the characters do not seem truly relaxed, truly themselves. Only two dramatists—Sheridan and Goldsmith—escape the devitalizing effects of such a scheme. Sheridan, however, never wishes to give offense. Even though in *The School for Scandal* (1773) he invents Joseph Surface to send up the constant uttering of "sentiments," Charles Surface and his uncle merely provide the right sentiments, the correct moral. And we are always aware that each character is blatantly busy exhibiting his particular folly. Mrs. Malaprop is remembered as Sheridan's funniest character because, in the farcical play with the absurdity of language, we seem free from the pressures of strict meaning. Goldsmith alone solved the problems and in only one play. In *She Stoops to Conquer* (1773) his young man who can talk to barmaids but is tongue-tied in the presence of a lady suggests real sexual and social conflict. Marlow's inability to speak in the feminine and feminized modern environment is a refreshing change: it can be taken as a commentary in itself on the difficulties of writing for a drama which has been stammering in its new ladylikeness and yet will have to come to terms somehow with the new forms of civilization. Young Marlow also wants to believe that he is at an inn—that is, somewhere where he can relax and be himself, without the formal labors of the drawing room or moral manner—like the manner of the new instructive plays. Characters' lack of ease is often indicated within the texts of the plays themselves. Various personages utter a desire to find a place where they can be comfortable, almost as if they wanted to get off the stage and out of the labor of sustaining a play. Hannah Cowley's *The Runaway* (1776) begins with George's line, "Oh, for the luxury of a night-gown and slippers!"[17] but of course we never see George in such dishabille.

If the chains the writers danced in were the chains of a new liberal morality (the importance of being earnest, and unironic), the dramatists were also hampered by a confusion about their liberalism. They were certain about some social ends, but not at all clear about means. This too applies whether the works are "crying" comedies or "laughing" comedies—the differences, even though Goldsmith talked about them, are barely visible in the 1770s.[18] Dramatists chipped away at the authority of fathers, or aristocrats, but were still searching for the acceptable face of paternalism. The eighteenth-century plays are full of benevolent older men, a bit cranky but good-natured, who will make everything all right (by giving permission to marry or bags of money). A kind, rich capitalist father or long-lost uncle is the best prize—like Stockwell in Cumberland's *The West Indian (1771)* or Mr. Tyrrel in *The Fashionable Lover* or Uncle Oliver in *The School for Scandal*. The old codgers have the money; they are also unthreatening, uncompetitive, past sexuality. Capitalism has a soft, kindly face. The men who have the money are rarely, if ever, shown actually engaged in making it (though Colman made a good attempt to use the terms of business and the Stock Exchange in *The Man of Business* [1774]). Generally, the good merchant must show that he has parlor manners as well as moral tone. There is nothing much left for the other characters to do. The author may use tired Restoration stage situations, now robbed of content, invent a few paper hoops for the young couples to jump through, but all the characters are *waiting*— waiting for permission to marry, or for Old Moneybags to come and bail someone out. What these plays show us is liberalism waiting on authority.

Crisp's worries about indelicate language were somewhat inappropriate in relation to the new delicate comedy. (Crisp had not been to the theater for some years.) This period saw a number of female dramatists in England: Frances Brooke, Elizabeth Griffith, Frances Sheridan, Hannah Cowley, Hannah More —and later Elizabeth Inchbald and Harriet Lee. But although by the 1770s women seemed to be about to come into their own as dramatists, there were difficulties confronting them. What they were doing was still thought odd. They still felt—or were required to feel—self-conscious, as Garrick's Prologue for Hannah More's tragedy *Percy* (1778) indicates:

> Though I'm a female, and the rule is ever
> For us, in Epilogue, to beg your favour,
>
> . . . .
>
> No little jealousies my mind perplex,
> I come, the friend and champion of my sex:
>
> . . . .
>
> The men, who grant not much, allow us charms—
> Are eyes, shapes, dimples, then our only arms?
>
> . . . .
>
> If joy from sense and matchless grace arise,
> With your own treasure, Britons, bless your eyes.
> If such there are—sure, in an humbler way,
> The sex, without much guilt, may write a play.
> That they've done nobler things, there's no denial;
> With all your judgment, then, prepare for trial—

> Summon your critic pow'rs, your manhood
>   summon,
> A brave man will protect, not hurt, a woman;
> Let us wish modestly to share with men,
> If not the force, the feather of the pen.[19]

Garrick had earlier writter the customary favor-begging Epilogue for More's play *The Inflexible Captive* (1774); in this he had felt compelled to argue against the views of such as Chesterfield:

> "How!" cries a sucking fop, thus lounging, straddling,
> (Whose head shews want of ballast by its noddling)
> "A woman write? Learn, madam, of your betters,
> "And read a noble lord's posthumous letters.
> "There you will learn the sex may merit praise
> "By making puddings—not by making plays;
> "They can make tea and mischief, dance and sing;
> "Their heads, though full of feathers, can't take wing."[20]

The possibility of "guilt" and of incapacity must be raised, if only to be exorcised. Garrick, who encouraged and helped a number of women dramatists, did not invent the attitudes he was trying to vanquish. A play by a woman still demanded particular apology. When Harriet Lee published her comedy *The New Peerage* (1787) she prefaced it with an "Advertisement" almost Heepishly humble:

> The Apprehensions that must ever attend a Woman on making a first Effort in the Drama, become justly heightened when she thinks of committing it to the Press. Precluded, by Sex, from the deep Observation of Life, which gives Strength to Character, or Poignancy to Expression, it will be difficult, even in her own Opinion, to supply the Deficiency; and it is from the Indulgence of the Publick only that she can hope, what she dares not expect, from their Judgment.[21]

What is the good of a comedy without "Observation of Life" or "Poignancy" of "Expression"? Harriet Lee presumably did not really mean it; she was trying to placate, through elaborate modesty, an audience and readership that had to be wooed. Even the more tolerant might believe that a woman was "Precluded, by Sex, from the deep Observation of Life" and should not presume upon the noble form of literature that since antiquity has been honored for its ability to hold a mirror up to the world. Comedy in particular was thought to require an unabashed knowledge of life and manners which it would ill become a lady to assume—it is a *bold* form. Even in her more dashing days, Hannah More never perpetrated a comedy.

Frances Burney was daring enough to attempt not only the writing of a play, but of a comic play. Full of confidence, she thought she might manage it, though she heeded the warnings and inhibitions, and shunned explicitly sexual situations, or even a very emphatic love-plot. But the attempt itself was a daring step, and her play, *The Witlings*, is a real achievement, though it was doomed to mournful seclusion, coming to posterity only as a pile of handwritten sheets in a library. A reading of the play shows that, despite the limitations under which she was working, she did find some real solutions to the problems besetting theatrical comedy in her time. If Burney had been able to produce her play in 1780, she might have made a career as a dramatist. She wanted to make people laugh; she believed that she could be funny, despite being a lady. She *was* funny—and that wrecked her dramatic prospects more thoroughly than anything else could have done.

The
Witlings
A
Comedy.
By
A Sister of the Order
Act I
Scene, a Milliner's Shop.
A Counter is spread with Caps, Ribbons, Fans & Band Boxes.
Miss Jenny & several young Women at Work.[22]

It is hard to convey to the reader unversed in late eighteenth-century comedy the freshness of surprise at coming upon an opening like this—the setting is so entirely different from the usual sort. Burney's play is a five-act comedy, and has "serious" lovers, so it is not what her contemporaries would have meant by a farce, but it operates on the basis of farce, employing varied and unglamorous settings and "low" characters, without suffering from the pressing necessity of offering liberal statement and advice. Burney, like Sheridan and Goldsmith, saw what modern farce could offer its elegant and pinched sister, Comedy. The comic world is widened to allow a view of commonplace life removed from the tribulations of the well-born Mr. X or beautiful Lady Y. Burney sees a connection between the lives of her obligatory frustrated couple and the bustling work-a-day world around them, the real world of making, buying, selling. This active, rather heartless, *full* world outside the drawing-room door was to interest her in all her works from *The Witlings* to *The Wanderer*—and in that last novel, the heroine herself works in a milliner's shop. Here in *The Witlings*, the first persons we see are Mrs. Wheedle and her troop of milliners, ordinary working women in a working world.

The secrets of their trade in frippery are given offhandedly:

> *Footman.* Is Lady Whirligig's Cloak ready? . . .
> *Mrs. Wheedle.* Sir, it's just done, & I'll take care to let her Ladyship have it directly. *Exit Footman.*
> *Miss Jenny.* I don't think it's cut out yet.
> *Mrs. Wheedle.* I know it i'n't.
>
> (Act I)

The reader must imagine the actresses playing the milliners actually "making" articles before the audience's eyes:

> *Mrs. Wheedle.* . . . Why, Miss Polly, for goodness' sake what are you doing?
> *Miss Polly.* Making a Tippet, Ma'am, for Miss Lollop.
> *Mrs. Wheedle.* Miss Lollop would as soon wear a Halter: 'twill be fit for nothing but the Window, & there the Miss Notables who Work for themselves may look at it for a Pattern.
>
> (Act I)

Having the actors thus "make" things is a striking piece of stage naturalism for the period—I can think of no other instance. The entertainment provided by watching people make and sell things is acknowledged on stage by the talkative neighbor, Mrs. Voluble: "there are so many pretty things to look at in your Shop, that one does not know which way to turn oneself. I declare it's the greatest treat in the World to me to spend an Hour or two here in a morning" (Act I). Exposition of the situation of the "high" characters in the play comes in conversation in the shop. The milliners are working on the wedding clothes for the orphan heiress Cecilia, soon to be married to Beaufort, Lady Smatter's nephew and heir. Mrs. Voluble's lodger is Mr. Dabler the poet, whose works are admired by Lady Smatter and Mrs. Sapient—and by Mrs. Voluble, who praises his "monody on the Birth of Miss Dawdle's Lap Dog . . . a Monody, or Elegy, I don't exactly know which you call it."

The *jeune premier* Beaufort comes into the shop fairly early in the scene, dragging with him his unwilling friend, the plain-speaking bachelor, Censor. Beaufort has been asked by Cecilia to meet her there, but he feels the need of male companionship in this very feminine place. The opportunity for stage business and for the use of millinery articles as comic props is suggested by Censor's speech as he tries to get away: "will you inthrall me in a Net of Brussels Lace? . . . Will you Fire at me a Broad Side of Pompoons?" The two men, uneasy in this foreign environment, keep on waiting for Cecilia as various customers come in, including Mrs. Sapient who utters her would-be original pronouncements, for example, "in *my* opinion, nothing can be really elegant that is Tawdry." Mrs. Sapient's opinions flutter dully along as she tries on a cap, is persuaded it is not too young for her, takes it, intends to run from further "temptation," yields ("as I *am* here"), buys a cloak, and orders a hat.

It is not only females who are tempted by these vanities. Beaufort's harum-scarum half-brother, always rushing around town "in monstrous haste" and perpetually accident-prone, is tempted to look over some ruffles. Mrs. Wheedle has cause to regret her salesmanship:

> but, dear Sir, pray don't put your Switch upon the Caps! I hope you'll excuse me, Sir, but the set is all in all in these little tasty things.
>
> (Act I)

Jack rushes away, leaving the goods in disorder. Eventually Jack returns to the embarrassed Beaufort, now deserted by Censor, to deliver the message he forgot to give before—that Cecilia could not come. Beaufort disconsolately leaves. The milliners straighten out their wares. Mrs. Voluble remarks placidly, "I'm sure you've a pleasant life of it here," but her time-wasting is interrupted by her son Bob, who comes looking for her: "you've been out all the Morning, & never told Betty what was for Dinner." The act concludes with Mrs. Voluble, unrepentant, scolding the neglected hobbledehoy as she moves off.

The whole act provides an examination of waste of time, but the author does not spell this out. There are some fairly obvious comic moral moments, as in Mrs. Sapient's self-contradictions, but time provides a subtle motif. The whole act might be called "Waiting for Cecilia." Burney has made a clever dramatic structure on the basis of things *not* happening. Early in the scene a young girl enters, one of the despised customers who don't come in a coach. Throughout the first half of the act she keeps on waiting, patiently, asking from time to time if she could look at some "Ribands." The assistants constantly respond "presently" and never attend to her. Eventually she leaves unnoticed, without having seen any ribbons. The cloak that hasn't been made, the tippet that won't get sold, the ruffles that aren't bought, the girl who never gets served, the dinner that hasn't been ordered—all these tie in with the lover's not meeting his lady, combining to create a comic effect of frustration, incompleteness, and anticlimax. Burney uses some formal devices learned from Sheridan, but the characters seem much more relaxed than any in *The School for Scandal*. Except for Censor, with his surly self-consciousness, the people in the play seem very much at ease. They seem to be talking to each other, just as they please, not talking at the audience and working at making a play. The action (or lack of it) as designed by the author is casual to the point of comic irritation. Nothing seems to be happening by contrivance or design—except the making of caps. There is no point in worrying about whether Mrs. Wheedle is basically avaricious, or basically benevolent. Other dramatists show they feel the need to define mercantile characters as one or the other; Frances Burney wants to show the shop itself. By changing the customary setting and giving her characters something to do (making, selling, buying), Frances Burney has got rid of the stilted quality of much late eighteenth-century drama, and she incorporates the real essential *waiting* of late eighteenth-century comedy in the structure of the play.

Act I characterizes the play, and the ease of the characters and action spreads into the next act, so that we see Lady Smatter and her friends on the same terms. As in *Evelina* there is no real difference between the "low" and the "high" characters. The members of what Mrs. Voluble called the "'Sprit Party" (Esprit Party) are in their intellectual trifling and vanity involved in another wilderness of frippery, though happily this is not spelled out by the author. In the preceding scene, characters were concerned with ribbons, laces, and caps, wishing to handle them, exchange them, or palm them off. Among this other group, the pseudo-currency is words; they are handled, tried on, palmed off, and advertised. They are even made, like the caps, in full view of the audience. The endeavors of the stupid patroness Lady Smatter and her pet poet Dabler produce less than the efforts of Mrs. Wheedle which result in "those little tasty things" (Act I), although there is hard work involved:

> *Lady Smatter.* O, I am among the Critics. I love criticism passionately, though it is really laborious Work, for it obliges me to read with a vast deal of attention. I declare I am sometimes so immensely fatigued with the toil of studying for faults & objections, that I am ready to fling all my Books behind the Fire.
>
> (Act II)

Like the milliners' art, this work endeavors to disguise or remodel nature. Lady Smatter triumphs over her past self overcome: "I had from Nature quite an aversion to reading." Her labors are undertaken to gain the applause of a public which would not exist if the group had not made a confederacy of mutual flattery. To Cecilia's very proper feminine stand, "My pursuits, whatever they may be, are too unimportant to deserve being made public," Lady Smatter replies indignantly,

> I declare, if my pursuits were not made public, I should not have any at all, for where can be the pleasure of reading Books . . . if one is not to have the credit of talking of them?

It is absolutely true that Burney's portrait of her witlings is indebted to Molière's *Les femmes savantes* (1672). So Dr. Burney and Samuel Crisp told her when they were trumping up charges against *The Witlings*. Frances protested that she had never read the play (which seems odd). In any case she had read or seen a number of English plays that borrowed from *Les précieuses ridicules* and

Les femmes savantes. Lady Smatter and Dabler owe their literary existence not only to Philaminte and Trissotin but also to a number of silly would-be intellectual ladies and pseudo-writers in English comedy. They belong to a tradition which includes Congreve's Lady Froth and Brisk in *The Double Dealer* (1693) and Gay's and Pope's Phoebe Clinket in *Three Hours after Marriage* (1717). Kelly in *The School for Wives* (a Molière title; 1774) presents Lady Rachel Mildew, an old-maid author who takes down the speeches of other characters when they utter something striking. George Colman in *The English Merchant* (1767) had created Spatter, a hack writer and dealer in scandal, and his patroness Lady Alton. That a dramatist took some ideas from Molière had never been a fault, let alone a reason for chasing a play from the English stage. It was inevitable that playwrights would be inspired by Molière, the first truly modern dramatist who identified so many of the qualities, pursuits, and obsessions of middle-class modern life. Each era requires or creates its own versions of *Les femmes savantes.*

Burney provides a version of the idea suited to the late 1770s. The distinctive qualities of her witlings are late eighteenth-century qualities. We have a new milieu, a prosperously dull English middle class, undereducated and bored. We see clearly that in this vulgar little set, the "'Sprit Party," are victims of a social and intellectual change which not only requires a higher level of culture in well-to-do persons than formerly, but also demands (as it still demands) that new vague something we call "originality." It is that modern, ur-Romantic quality that is pursued so heartily by Mrs. Sapient (in opinions), Dabler (in poems), and Lady Smatter (in criticism). (It is an irony that Dr. Burney in effect accused Fances Burney, who had her own originality, of plagiarizing—that must have hurt.)

By contrast, one member of the Esprit company, who is endured rather than invited, has not yet risen to the new ideas. Old Codger, Beaufort's stepfather, excels in pompousness and prosiness of an old-fashioned kind. Like a masculine and less amiable Miss Bates, he feels he should repeat to the company the entire unexciting contents of a letter from a sister in Yorkshire, including the exact dimensions of a new barn, and tidings of the parsonage dog kennel. It takes Codger half an hour to recollect his information, while the attention span of his auditors rarely exceeds half a minute. Codger dislikes books, and has no notion of fiction, but he too relies on written materials to supply his deficiencies, making notes in his tablets. He loves pointless facts and tries to remember them, whereas the other members of the party are desperately conscious of the need to be original, which involves the need to forget the contributions of real writers.

> *Lady Smatter.* I was reading, the other Day, that the Memory of a Poet should be short, that his Works may be original. . . .
> *Dabler.* Why, Madam, 'tis my own thought! I've just finished an Epigram upon that very subject! . . .
> *reads.* Ye gentle Gods, O hear me plead,

And kindly grant this little loan;
   Make me forget whate'er I read
That what I write may be my own.

(Act II)

Forgetting is a central activity in the play. In Act I, Jack's message, Mrs. Voluble's dinner, the girl's request for ribbons are all forgotten. Forgetfulness is mockingly presented as a kind of talent, a mental habit made into a principle. The ability to forget errands, the desire to forget books, shades off into the convenient forgetting of friends. In Act II, Jack, after dashing in and out several times, at last remembers to tell Cecilia his news: Stipend, her guardian and banker, has gone quite bankrupt. Dabler welcomes the sensation provided by this news as an addition to his stock of poetic ideas. Lady Smatter, for once galvanized out of her references to Addison and Swift, speaks to Beaufort forcefully and crudely:

> Nothing is so difficult as disposing of a poor Girl of Fashion. . . . She has been brought up to nothing,—if she can make a Cap, 'tis as much as she can do,—&, in such a case, when a Girl is reduced to a Penny, what is to be done? . . . you can never suppose I shall consent to your marrying a Girl who has lost her Fortune.

That Lady Smatter thinks of Cecilia as a potential milliner provides another link between this act and the previous one. Lady Smatter's real vulgarity emerges when she speaks to Cecilia, treating her to polite platitudes, as if the bearing of affliction were a matter of sentiments culled from authors. With condescending false politeness she makes it quite clear that the girl is not to expect to have anything more to do with Beaufort, or herself. Throughout the play, "sentiments" are derided, as they are in *The School for Scandal*, in being uttered as grace notes by people who do not believe them.

In this play and elsewhere Frances Burney shows she does not believe in the power of literature to soften manners or instruct the heart. Literary or artistic attainments are often acquired by leisured people with the money to buy them, and are used for social display, for passing the cultural test. Despite her recent best-selling success, Burney gently mocks herself and her readership. *The Witlings* is "By a Sister of the Order." Dabler, the author inside the play, has some relationship to the author herself, as did Macartney inside *Evelina*, with his anger, his self-centeredness, his desire to be published. If Burney did not exactly make the notes of her own and other's words in company, as Dabler does, she, like Boswell, did something very close to it. And there are other Burney family resemblances as well; Charles Burney was in the habit of making up little verses to ingratiate himself with friends, especially his friends in high life. And sometimes these little verses were a trifle imperfect: "You eager seek with Argus' pry / Each wish to know, & want supply."

In Act III we see Dabler alone and at work in his chamber at Mrs. Voluble's house. He is surrounded by what his landlady calls his "*Miniscrips,*" and endeavors to work himself "into the true Spirit of Poetry" with the assistance of Bysshe's *Art of Poetry* to help with rhymes. Like his author, Dabler is secretive, guarding heaps of manuscripts which he devoutly wishes to keep hidden until perfected. He prides himself on his reputation for ready wit, which would be lost if anyone knew the trouble his spontaneous trifles cost him (cf. Frances writing *Evelina* in a garret or unheated bedroom for years, revising, polishing). Dabler is both ashamed and proud of his secret hoard, as if the papers were private parts; in this play papers assume an importance equivalent to the sexual. When he leaves, anxiously urging Mrs. Voluble to make sure that "no human Being" enters his room, "& don't let one of my Papers be touched or moved upon any account," there is good comic shock in what follows:

> *Mrs. Voluble.* Sir I shall lock the Door, & put the key in my Pocket. Nobody shall so much as know there's a paper in the House.
> *Exit Dabler*
> *Mrs. Voluble alone.*
> I believe it's almost a Week since I've had a good rummage of them myself. . . . Yes; & he won't come Home till very late, so I think I may as well give them a fair look over at once.
> *Seats herself at the Table.*
> (Act III)

Having her own papers pried into was, we know, something Frances Burney herself dreaded. Here she makes comic capital of the matter, as Mrs. Voluble makes herself easy, has "a good rummage," and reads. She invites Miss Jenny up to Dabler's room, urging the milliner to make herself comfortable. She offers Jenny various titles of Dabler's unpublished works (*"Elegy on the Slaughter of a Lamb," "A Dialogue between a Tear & a Sigh," "Epitaph on a Fly killed by a Spider"*) as if these rather sickly sounding pieces were slices of cake.

When Cecilia arrives, seeking lodgings and some help, she fails in her attempt to have a private interview with the landlady, as nobody else present has any concept of the confidential. Mrs. Voluble finds another pleasant distraction from boredom. The parallel between Lady Smatter and Mrs. Voluble is noticeable throughout, though not labored by the author, who never points it out. Both women are important in their own circles, bossy, and talkative. But Mrs. Voluble is hospitable if slovenly, kind in her way to all save her snubbed son and overworked maidservant. After all Cecilia's difficulties and Beaufort's anxiety, Act III ends in Mrs. Voluble's neatly bathetic remark, "I must get in a little bit of something nice for Supper." Mrs. Voluble's untidy, unprivate house has its attractiveness. The atmosphere within it counteracts any tendency to formality —or to sternly formal plotting being started up within the play. The principles of clutter and anticlimax keep on being victorious.

The characters in all circles live lives of such persistent coziness that any mild sensation is desirable. The author confronts the fact that literature (the writing and the reading of it) is often resorted to as the readiest means of relieving ennui without risk. Dabler's dull little life is given an illusion of progression by his continual search for material for his "poetry." His titles are often comically sensational. Females observed frequently supply stimulating material: *"Verses on a Young Lady's Fainting Away," "On a Young Lady Blinded by Lighting."* Literature seems to be a means of recycling life, picking out sensational elements while rendering them innocuous. Dabler's response to Cecilia's misfortune is implicitly an indictment of all writers, not just of bad ones: "'Tis a shocking circumstance indeed. I think it will make a pretty good Elegy, though! . . . 'Twill be the most pathetic thing I ever wrote!" (Act II). Properly managed, literature need make no moral impression at all; a young lady blinded by lightning, or bereft of her fortune, can serve as entertainment. The whole drab society is primarily conscious of a need to be entertained. Mrs. Voluble uses the word "entertain" in both senses (to offer hospitality and to offer amusement) in an excellently ridiculous line when, looking at the sobbing Cecilia, she remarks, "I don't know what to think of to entertain her" (Act III). Everyone wants little treats, social occasions, and unrigorous mental games. Mrs. Voluble's malaprop- ism, *"Miniscrips,"* for Dabler's writings seems very apt; these are mini-scripts, miniature writings, instantly forgettable. Lady Smatter tries to memorize a line by Dabler, but gets it wrong; it is no wonder she makes a mistake, for the adjec- tives are interchangeable (Act II). Dabler himself, when writing, forgets a line just formed (Act III). The characters prefer forgettable, consumable writings; in a world where that is so, the old regulated structure of the formal comedy is irrele- vant, absurd.

In Act IV again the principles of clutter and anticlimax prevail. The act starts out formally, on two levels: the audience will expect a formal exhibition of the witlings' follies, and the characters plan a ceremonious intellectual seminar. They gather in a consciously arranged group, *"Seated at a round Table covered with Books"* (Act IV). Lady Smatter sets up a topic for discussion. Reciting "Most Women have no Character at all," she asks, "if this was true in the Time of Pope, why People should complain so much of the depravity of the present Age?"[23] Her getting the line and attribution almost right is a result of her private labor for the spontaneous flow of wit; she said in Act III, "I have some Notes to prepare for our Esprit Party of to Night." But Lady Smatter has been preparing on her own; nobody but herself has got up her question, and the mistaken topic soon vanishes. Taking the wrong handle of a pun, Lady Smatter assumes "character" to mean not distinct identity but reputation for sexual virtue. As in *Evelina*, the idea of female identity is difficult for people to grasp. Dabler immediately says "it reminds me" and works in the recital of another poem by himself, after which conversation flows, unregulated, into other chan- nels. Only Codger keeps trying to work out the question, bringing it up again when others have forgotten it, and explaining to Lady Smatter that she is wrong about Pope's meaning—a piece of offensive information which she waves away.

Old-fashioned Censor, a conventional satiric type, comes in to make things happen—but the fun of the scene lies in the others' steady opposition to everything Censor stands for, including dramatic plots and forward progression. Censor arrives full of zeal for the lovers, but he is deflected from his original purpose by his desire to sabotage the party and show them up. He wants to uncover Dabler's incapacities as a wit, so the ladies will no longer patronize him. The poet's reputation rests largely on his supposed talent for impromptu verse; he writes out *impromptus* privately at home, and carries some about in his hat. When Censor tries to make him invent a verse on the spur of the moment on a topic not of Dabler's choosing, the poet is horrified. He wriggles out of a succession of topics, finding reasons for rejecting "self-sufficiency" and "war"; at last he finds himself at a stand for something on "the use of time" (a hitherto concealed theme of the play). Dabler is tormented, oppressed, ordered not to stir from the room. Burney in her play uses the kind of scene she is so fond of in her novels—a leading member of a little group is suddenly turned upon, embarrassed, forced to endure the pain of all eyes focusing upon his distress:

> *Dabler, holding his Hand before his Eyes, & walking about.*
> Not one thought, not one thought to save me from ruin!
>
> (Act IV)

Dabler's embarrassment is a more emphatic, theatrical representation of the reactions of Sir Clement Willoughby at a loss.

While the empty-headed Dabler is trying to think, Jack begins a story, a piece of a scandal about " the Miss Sippets"; we expect some entertaining narrative, but it soon trails off into pointlessness. Dabler recovers himself, saying he now has the lines in his head, but will not say them, as he has been so badly treated. He gets away. Censor's would-be triumph is unsatisfactory; Beaufort now arrives and accuses his friend of wasting time. In attacking the Esprit Party Censor really joined them; in accusing them of wasting time he wasted time himself, and his enterprise, instead of being a satiric blowing-up, is an anticlimax. During the arguments among the other characters at the end of the scene, Codger is prosing away in the background, unheard by the audience, while Jack steadily falls asleep. The audience expects that Codger must be giving his son some moral lecture, but when we switch into that conversation again, we find this is not so. Codger has been treating Jack to another recital of the news from Yorkshire, though he is as annoyed at his son's falling asleep as if he had been uttering moral truths: "did not you hear my Story about your Aunt Deborah's Poultry? . . . You don't deserve ever to hear me tell a story again." But he does tell it again, *da capo*, until the interruptions are too much for him. Censor tries to enlist the help of Jack and Codger in aiding Beaufort, but they break away from him. Censor, who like everybody else here really desires to talk, is left with no one to talk to.

The same principles are at work in Act IV as in Act I: interruption, incompleteness, anticlimax. Everything is retarded, deflected. Even Censor, who looks like the plot catalyst and the moralist of the play, is unable to arrange anything. The play seems to be eluding the "Censorship" of applied and earnest meaning. The plot of the play itself seems to be perversely frittered away, obstructed by the play's own characters, who prefer to go on being as they are—an effect contrived by the dramatist. Nothing finds form or completion. Everything that happens is funny, but the humor seems to defy traditional comic patterning. Characters refuse to engage in any logical game (including that of dramatic plot), although a number of games are begun, only to be abandoned. Lady Smatter's "question" is not discussed, Dabler's poem never gets composed; Jack's story about the Miss Sippets is never finished—he does not even seem to realize a punchline is necessary. Codger's story never gets finished—or even heard.

The characters live comfortably in this world of bathos. We could take as a key to the whole Dabler's all-too-mortal line in his poem on self-love (which resembles Frances Burney's remarks on egotism in the prose Dedication to *Evelina*):

> *Censor reading.* That Passion which we strongest feel
> We all agree to disapprove;
> Yet feebly, feebly we conceal—
> *Dabler pettishly.* Sir you read without any Spirit,—
> Yet feebly,—feebly we conceal
> You should drop Your Voice at the Second feebly, or you lose all the effect.
>
> (Act IV)

They all drop their voices at the second "feebly." The subtext of the play is based on anticlimax as principle. In her defiance of the logic and clarity and ostentatious meanings expected in comedies of her period, Burney has hit upon what seem peculiarly modern devices in creating the comedy of pointlessness.

The ensuing scene, the begining of Act V, is a counterpart to the scene of the Esprit Party, showing an equally self-satisfied if happier group entertaining themselves:

> Scene *a Parlour at Mrs. Voluble's*
> Mrs. Voluble, Mrs. Wheedle, Miss Jenny & Bob are seated at a round table at Supper;
> *Betty is waiting*
>
> (Act V)

The novelty of this setting and stage business is striking. It was not customary to show characters eating meals on stage, though characters might be seen taking chocolate or tea (as Frances had done in 1777 when she acted Murphy's Mrs. Lovemore).[24] In Burney's supper scene the fact of the characters' eating is suggested by the dialogue, with its faded gentilities, now vulgarisms (very much in the manner of Swift's *Polite Conversation*), and its stress on the actual food:

> *Mrs. Voluble.* My dear Mrs. Wheedle, you don't Eat; pray let me help you to a little Slice more. . . . There, that little bit can't hurt you, I'm sure. As to Miss Jenny, she's quite like a Crocodile, for she Lives upon Air. . . . Ay, ay that's the way with all the Young Ladies; they pinch for fine Shapes.
> . . .
> *Miss Jenny.* I'll give Master Bobby a piece of mine, if you please, Ma'am.
> *Mrs. Voluble.* No, no, he can't be very hungry, I'm sure, for he Eat a dinner to frighten a Horse. . . . I think this is the nicest cold Beef I ever Tasted,—You *must* eat a bit, or I shall take it quite ill.
> *Mrs. Wheedle.* Well it must be [a] *leetle* tiny Morsel, then.
> *Mrs. Voluble.* I shall cut you quite a *fox-hall* Slice.
>
> (Act V)

Mrs. Voluble's love of talking is equalled by her love of eating. And just as her son Bob is never allowed to get a word in, but is always accused of "prating," so he is stinted of food while being accused of greed. The author suggests—but does not feel bound to explain to us—a parallel between the party at Lady Smatter's and Mrs. Voluble's company around the beef. Like the earlier Augustans (especially Swift), Burney finds concrete physical expressions for abstract ideas, social attitudes, and psychological processes. Thus in *Evelina* we have the literal throwing-away of a woman into a ditch, the literal forced race between women, the fall. Implicit metaphors are made lively, become part of the action. Here in *The Witlings* the idea of nourishing the self, greedily feeding the ego, is expressed in incarnate metaphor.

All these expressions of self-love are related to money, a subject never far away from anyone's thoughts. The milliners would like to belong to the time-wasting class above them; the party imagine what they would do if they had money. While her new friends are wishing themselves upward, Cecilia is trying to adjust to a move downward. She left Lady Smatter's house as soon as her former friend's position became clear. She thinks (mistakenly) that her fiancé Beaufort acquiesces in Lady Smatter's view of her downfall, and she refuses to get in touch with him. Now she endeavors to think of how she can earn her living. Mrs. Voluble sympathetically tries to relate a story about the financial misfortunes of Miss Maggy Grease, daughter of a bankrupt butcher—the story is not completed. Cecilia moves about the room, distraught, searching for ink to write a letter—and is offered beef.

Mrs. Wheedle promises assistance in obtaining for Cecilia the post of companion to a Mrs. Hollis, who is going abroad. Cecilia accepts, although she can see that she will be exposed to the disagreeable condescension of a vulgar woman, and the post seems less and less pleasant with each additional duty that Mrs. Wheedle remembers. Mrs. Wheedle seems about to go directly to Mrs. Hollis; the author teases us with the sense of forward movement. Inertia soon resumes its sway. Mrs. Wheedle reenters to ask a question, and is easily persuaded to resume her place at the supper table. To Cecilia's frustration, the festive meal continues until Betty announces that a fine lady has come to see Mrs. Voluble. The flustered hostess (who has just spilt a bottle of wine) tries to clear away all indications of the vulgar meal. Bob, scolded, rises in awkward haste and overturns the table. A mass of broken crockery and meat is hastily tidied up, under the hostess's excited directions:

> *Mrs. Voluble.* . . . I declare I was never in such a pucker in my life. . . . Look here, if my China Bowl i'n't broke! I vow I've a great mind to make that looby Eat it for his Supper—Betty, why don't you get a Mop?—You're as helpless as a Child.—No, a Broom,—get a Broom, & sweep them all away at once—Why, you a'n't going empty Handed are you?—I declare you have not half the Head you was Born with.
>
> *Betty.* I'm sure I don't know what to do no more than the Dog.
>
> (Act V)

There is no other example among contemporary plays of the use of sweeping-up as part of stage business. Burney's detailed rendering of domestic scenes is novel.

The lady arriving is Mrs. Sapient, whom we last saw leaving the Esprit Party before it broke up. She has come in Dabler's absence to do a bit of rummaging herself among his papers, hoping to find—by discovering more versified compliments—that she, rather than Lady Smatter, is his favorite lady. When Dabler comes in unexpectedly early (having, as we know, been routed by Censor's attack) Mrs. Sapient runs to hide in the closet—the same closet that harbors the remains of the beef, and the broken crockery. Throughout the rest of the act, Mrs. Sapient keeps in her hiding place, until she is discovered by Jack at the very end. But she might as well have kept in the open, for Mrs. Voluble tells every comer, including Dabler, "Mrs. Sapient is now in the Closet! Be sure you don't tell anybody."

The scene is obviously Burney's equivalent of famous scenes of hiding and discovery in stage plays of the eighteenth century, such as the "screen scene" in *The School for Scandal* or the closet scene in Murphy's *All in the Wrong* (1761).[25] She felt, however, that she had to avoid sexual meaning or innuendo, so the closet device lacks the kind of tension with which it is customarily associated, and seems curiously tamed. The ladies' interest in Dabler, their private flattery-machine, is, however, not devoid of sexual interest. In this play, curiosity and pudency about papers take the place usually accorded to sexual intrigue. Although characters dislike listening to other people, they are stimulated by the idea of secret words. The existence of *hidden* words arouses a peculiar lust to know, as if the *"Miniscrips"* might contain the real meaning which so eludes most conversation. And a person who keeps words hidden away seems to have some source of interest, as if he enjoyed a secret erotic life.

Also, what is being "hidden" is social position, failure to live up to social aspiration, as we see in Mrs. Voluble's wishing not to be discovered at her meat supper. When Mrs. Sapient loses her head and runs into hiding, she vulgarizes herself so that she keeps fit company with the greasy broken hoard. At the end of the play, when all the characters have gathered in Mrs. Voluble's back parlor, Censor threatens Lady Smatter with embarrassment, exposure, and loss of social position. Censor has written a series of lampoons on her, which he threatens to have published all over town if Lady Smatter does not consent to the marriage of Beaufort with Cecilia. Lady Smatter undergoes embarrassment in the small gathering as Jack sings Censor's cruel ballad:

> This lady with Study has muddled her head;
> Sans meaning she talk'd, & sans knowledge she read,
> And gulp'd such a Dose of incongruous matter
> That Bedlam must soon hold the Carcase of Smatter.
>
> (Act V)

The threat is offset by Censor's offer of a reward as well as a punishment. If Lady Smatter does what she ought, then, Censor says, he will see that her praises are publicly sung: "You will be another Sacharissa, a Second Sapho [*sic*],—a tenth Muse."[26] Lady Smatter has no choice; of course she yields.

Lady Smatter is gaily threatened with things that were very horrible to her author. Frances Burney shrank even from public praise, and was embarrassed and annoyed when her name came up in published verse. In *Evelina* her heroine had suffered under the onslaught of Macartney's verses. A female exposed in public light verse is always open to ridicule. Here, the author seems to feel that Lady Smatter, with her rage for publicity, deserves what she gets. Blackmail—a perennial subject in Burney's works—is allowed moral triumph here, as it is not elsewhere. The sequence of Lady Smatter's torment seems partly a means for Burney to exorcise her doubts about female fame, piling the guilt upon another figure, and at the same time conquering her own fears of public mistreatment by fully imagining the ridicule and abuse. There is a fear that those who live by public words will be punished for them, and the humiliation is enacted through the persona of Lady Smatter. Lady Smatter, like Madame Duval, stands for the monstrous mother figure, the false mother, through whom Frances can most cheerfully present the feared humiliation of women. Lady Smatter is more genteel that Madame Duval (her role is not a dame part) but she can be subjected to abuse of the kind permitted by the drama's exploitation of farce.

Censor himself, the masculine punisher, is ambiguously seen throughout. He succeeds in "censoring" Lady Smatter's conduct, but only by proving himself a Witling of sorts, composing verses for his own purposes—and his verses will have to be suppressed, or censored too, after this private hearing. Literary satire, Burney suggests in her satiric play, has little power; Lady Smatter the absurd is always referring to Pope and Swift. The lampoon is the only written satiric form with force to change anyone's behavior, and then only in a limited way. The author is careful to show that Beaufort and Cecilia have already rebelled against authority, and have decided in favor of poverty and work rather than dependence. The heroine has been looking for a job. As Beaufort says at the end, uttering the usual moral given to a play, "Self-dependance is the first of Earthly Blessings" (Act V).

The moral here ties in with "self-sufficiency," the topic Censor proposed to Dabler. Indeed, one can see a clue of meaning running through Burney's sequence of those three suggested topics in Act IV. The right use of time means "war" against inanity, and war or conflict leads to self-sufficiency. "Self-dependence," and "self-sufficiency" meant a great deal to Frances Burney at the time (and later); they represent an ideal for which she was striving against difficulties. Self-sufficiency means not being a parasite socially, not cheating intellectually, but having a mind and life of one's own and being willing to "act vigorously," to use Crisp's words. But Burney sees how much we are all affected by cultural climate and commonplaceness, as are the Witlings, and even the "Sister of the Order." She has presented in her light comedy issues that have no solution. At the end of the play, nothing has really altered. The last scene is a sort of neat mess. No one has reformed. Nor is it possible to label each personage as bad or good. Mrs. Voluble cannot be labeled a benevolent woman, or a hardhearted mercenary wretch. The milliners want their money, aren't always strictly honest in trade, and they are gossipy and affected, but they are what they are. People go on as they do. It's a big world, full of shops and money and intellectual and social fashions, and nothing alters that big world.

The Witlings is an unpretentious but intelligent comedy, which truly accommodates female knowledge and experience. The introduction of homely scenes and settings is no mere feminine touch; it offers new modes of dramatic approach. Burney keeps away from topics notoriously dangerous for a lady, but she exploits private and cultural absurdity, and uses a kind of absurdist naturalism that implicitly defies elegant platitude. The presentation of the milliners is in itself new, and the presentation of them neither as angels of virtue nor demons of hypocrisy and frivolity but rather as working women—persons, albeit comic persons, in their own right—seems an impressive piece of understated liberalism. Burney's version of the modern liberal views throughout the play is much less stilted and less obvious than is usual in eighteenth-century comedy. There are elements of the problem play in *The Witlings*. We see that the author advocates self-dependence—and independence for women—but there are real doubts about the possibilities of achieving this. The reader cannot feel life is satisfactorily settled. Within the play there is no humane consensus, just blunder. Authority, stupid and rigid, responds only momentarily to personal attack.

The play's best achievement is in its construction, in the use of the stasis, the waiting, that inadvertently but truly characterize the drawing room comedies of the period. The constant tendency to anticlimax—on which the characters themselves do *not* comment—is brilliantly devised by the author who had no exact model for the solution she chose. The relaxed characters drift away from the center—from issues, actions, and sentiment—forgetting what they were going to do or say, and going on to something else. Burney found in drift, inconsequentiality, and anticlimax dramatic principles that can work without falsehood. Her little play is more expressive of the real state of the drama and of society in her time (in expressive hesitation, fatigued boredom with old modes, repetition without certain form) than many grander pieces by well-known playwrights of the time. She does away with the formal machinery of pattern, clarified points, and logical sequence. Instead of the hectoring tone we come to associate with utterances on the late eighteenth-century stage—the "Can-you-hear-me-at-the-back?" tone—the characters' speeches are tantalizingly subdued or incomplete. The characters do not hear each other. Halting circular speech and incomplete stories take the comic place of smart verbal packages. Burney's solutions to the dramatic problems of her day, in making hesitation and uncertainty central, seem surprisingly modern. She shows in *The Witlings* that she has a talent for theater of the absurd.

Her play could be put on now. Her play could have been put on the stage then; Murphy thought well of it. Alas—it was not put on. It is an irony that the dramatist who took as her theme "self-dependence" could not produce her play because her father wouldn't let her. On stage she could embarrass Lady Smatter, representative of stupid authority, but her own crisis of authority was not to be solved so readily. The fear of humiliation, the guilt she had associated with the would-be intellectual Lady Smatter, were in real life thrown upon her. She was browbeaten into compliance by her two Censors: "my two daddies put their heads together."[27]

The rejection seems to have come immediately after a play-reading of *The Witlings* at Chessington. Burney told Crisp that she preferred not to be there when he heard it:

> I should like that your first reading should have nothing to do with me
> —that you should go quick through it, or let my father read it to you
> —forgetting all the time, as much as you can, that Fannikin is the writer,

or even that it is a play in manuscript . . . and then, when you have done, I should like to have three lines, telling me, as nearly as you can trust my candour, its general effect. After that take it to your own desk, and lash it at your leisure.[28]

That is in a letter of 30 July 1779. An unpublished letter from Susanna to Frances, dated 3 August, gives an account of the occasion: on 2 August, Charles Burney at Chessington read the work aloud to a party which included Crisp, Crisp's sister Sophia Gast and the other Chessington ladies, and two of the Burney sisters. Susanna's description of the reading, far from throwing any new light on the matter, makes everything even more puzzling. Susanna thought the reading—and the play—a success, and sent Frances at once an account which is, if not utterly uncritical, both admiring and confident:

The Witlings—"Good" s^d. M^r. Crisp—"Good—I like the Name—the Dramatis Personae too pleased him, & the name of Codger occasion'd a general Grin . . . the Milliners Scene & indeed all the first act diverted us extremely all round—"It's funny—it's funny indeed"—s^d. M^r. C. who you know does not love to throw away praise—the Second Act I think much improved, & its being more compressed than when I first heard it gives to the whole more Zest—it did not flag at all in the reading.—The 3^d. is charming—& they all went off wth. great Spirit . . . the fourth act was upon the whole that wch. seemed least to exhilarate or interest the audience, tho' Charlotte laugh'd till she was almost black in the face at Codger's part, as I had done before her—The fifth was more generally felt—but to own the truth it did not meet all the advantages one could wish—My Father's voice, sight, & lungs were tired . . . & being entirely unacquainted wth. what was coming not withstanding all his good intentions, he did not always give the Expression you meant to be given—Yet he exerted himself . . . to give it force & Spirit—& except this Act, I believe only yourself w^d. have read the play better.

For my own part the Serious part seem'd even to improve upon me by this 2^d. hearing, & made me for to cry in 2 or 3 places—I wish there was more of this Sort—so does my Father—so, I believe, does M^r. Crisp—however their sentiments you are to hear fully from themselves, wch. will make me the less eager to write them—Codger & Jack too seem Characters which divert every body, & w^d. yet more I sh^d. imagine in a public Representation.[29]

Susanna thought, and believed her father and Crisp also thought, that the play ought to be more sentimental—which will strike the modern theatergoer as a very odd objection to a comedy. But otherwise, although perhaps the last two acts could do with some tightening, the play seemed to go very well, even when given by a reader who had not seen all of the work before. Susanna thought the piece entertaining; she believed that her father, Crisp, and Sophia Gast had been entertained, and she was evidently assured that the "sentiments" that Dr. Burney and Crisp were going to send would be favorable. When the reading took place, Susanna had not the slightest idea that Crisp and Dr. Burney were about to join together to damn the piece utterly. Frances herself expected criticism in particulars (she would not have been upset if told that the last two acts needed a bit more work). But she could have no expectation that she would be told the piece was totally worthless and witless. Her sister's letter could certainly not have prepared her for the fatal stroke—though that indeed must have arrived almost at once. And since she possessed Susanna's account of the actual play-reading, she must have been the more inwardly puzzled, must have secretly suspected her two critics of bad faith.

Why did Charles Burney set his face against Frances's play? Not all of the correspondence or diary pages dealing with this matter seem to have come down to us; we are left to gather what the gentlemen said chiefly from two letters by Frances (one to Dr. Burney and one to Crisp) published in the *Diary and Letters*. From these emerge two reasons for the repudiation of *The Witlings*. One is the charge (coming first from Crisp) of the play's "resemblance to *Les Femmes Scavantes*[sic] and consequent immense inferiority."[30] The second and most serious reason offered by Dr. Burney for his antagonism to the piece was that it might offend real people, in particular Elizabeth Montagu, Queen of the Blues, and her circle. Certainly, any work about modern English *précieuses* would attract the comparison, and there are points of similarity between Lady Smatter and Mrs. Montagu, of whom Frances later wrote,

> . . . her reputation for wit seemed always in her thoughts. . . . No sudden start of talent urged forth any precarious opinion. . . . Her smile . . . was rarely gay; and her liveliest sallies had a something of anxiety rather than of hilarity—till their success was ascertained by applause.[31]

Dr. Burney heartily loathed the idea of ever offending the powerful, even in the slightest degree. He did not only loathe, he feared it; it took his supports away. Mocking the Branghtons was one thing; alienating Mrs. Montagu was another. He had no notion of the *debellare superbos*. After all, Lady Smatter is not a portrait of Mrs. Montagu, merely a representative of a generalized type well known in dramatic tradition. Lady Smatter's individualized faults of vulgarity and forgetfulness were not the particular defects of Mrs. Montagu. Hester Thrale saw another possible model for Lady Smatter: "I believe this rogue means me for *Lady Smatter*," she jokingly told Murphy, while bringing the play to Murphy's attention.[32] In her own journal she wrote, "I like it very well for my own part, though none of the scribbling Ladies have a Right to admire its general Tendency."[33] Yet her friend's comedy encouraged Hester Lynch Thrale to try something of the kind herself; "I cannot imagine why I should not write a Comedy," she wrote in her diary in May 1779, adding modestly "as I have not a Spark of Originality about me, I must take a French Model."[34] And thus she began her (uncompleted) play *The Humourist*. The "scribbling Lady" Hester Lynch Thrale continued to be supportive of *The Witlings* and of plans for its production. When she heard that Burney was giving up the play, Hester Thrale noted in her journal (18 August) that her friend was giving up "a Play likely to succeed." None of the readers outside the family thought the piece would not succeed.

Frances Burney was thus ill-prepared for the insistence of both her real and adoptive father that the play was an irremediable and humiliating failure. She was almost overwhelmed, and intensely surprised, at hearing from them that production must never be thought of:

> I expected many objections to be raised—a thousand errors to be pointed out—and a million of alterations to be proposed; but the suppression of the piece were words I did not expect; indeed, after the warm approbation of Mrs. Thrale, and the repeated commendations and flattery of Mr. Murphy, how could I?[35]

Frances might have added "and after your approbation," for Charles Burney apparently liked the beginning of the comedy when he read it in May. It appears to have been the last two acts, including the 'Sprit Party, Dabler's disgrace, and Mrs. Wheedle's supper party, that upset him; one can catch this in Susanna's account of the reading. It was these last two acts, the final one of which was completely new to him, that immediately sealed the play's fate.

Why did Charles suddenly (as it seemed to his daughter) turn against the piece? Was he at Chessington contaminated by Crisp's pessimism? Crisp had been in very low spirits in the summer of 1779, a state he attributed to the war with France and America, and the dreadful condition of England. He wrote Frances melancholy and reactionary letters on the "*Ugly Times*," saying he thought "an arbitrary Government mildly administered . . . is upon the whole the most permanent & eligible of all Forms."[36] Crisp was in a negative frame of mind, and his judgment of his Fannikin's play might have been given an extra edge by a little self-consciousness about Codger. But why, in any case, should Crisp's opinion *matter*? Why not take the judgment of Murphy, a successful dramatist? If Murphy liked the piece, it should have been offered to Sheridan. As Frances had told Dr. Johnson, if her play failed on stage, "I cannot do worse than Dr. Goldsmith, when his play failed,—go home and cry!"[37] She was willing to take her chance with the theater, but Dr. Burney was not. She was to have the tears without the excitement of staged performance.

Dr. Burney evidently did his best to check his daughter's developing hardihood about failure. It is hard not to feel that he used Crisp, and made the Chessington reading—and the letters fired off at once after it—into a dramatic final judgment. If Charles Burney had really desired his daughter's play to be staged, Crisp's negative could have been overcome. There was no reason to make that Daddy an arbiter. But if Dr. Burney had already been feeling uneasy about the piece, more than he had hitherto let on, then the Chessington reading both intensified the unease and provided the ideal moment of crisis. He also had the necessary cover, with Crisp performing part of the unpleasant task. Charles Burney dealt Frances a cruel blow, though in Burneyesque manner he both pretended to be kind, and charmingly appeared to soften the effects of the damage, once it was effectively done. In a letter in the British Library which seems to be an answer to one or more of his daughter's epistles during this tortured time, he plays with soothing hopes that she might write another play to come out that winter, salvaging some of her ideas and characters from *The Witlings*—a hope started by Frances herself. He appears to encourage but actually discourages any notion of a dramatic product:

> yours [i.e., letter] is rather serious, & requires Care in preaching an answer—I am glad the objections all fall on the [Blue] Stocking-Club-Party—as my chief & almost only quarrel was with its Members. As it is, not only the whole piece, but the *plot* had best be kept secret, from every body. As to finishing another upon a *new Story*, in a *hurry*, for next winter, I think it *may* be done, & w^d. be not only feasible but desirable at any other time than the present.—But public affairs are in such terrible Confusion, & there is so little likelihood of people having more money or more Spirits soon, that I own myself not eager for you to come out with any kind of Play *next Winter*. Many Scenes & Characters might otherwise be preserved, & perhaps save you time—though I am not sure of it—for the adjusting . . . & patching neatly is teadious work—. . .
>
> I believe you wondered at my taking no Notice of your new Project—indeed it was what at first struck me as the most feasible & desirable. But the Combined Fleets had not then frighted the whole Nation—But all this is no reason why you sh^d. not write—tho' it is one against doing anything of such Consequence to your Fame &c—in a *hurry*.[38]

This letter is a kind of double talk. Dr. Burney noticeably picks up Crisp's language about the state of the nation, as if that were a reason for not writing plays. (The war that followed the revolt in America, in fact, did not interfere with the theater; many new plays were produced from 1779 to 1783.) *The Witlings* must be buried, kept "secret, from every body."

In fact, Dr. Burney indicates at the conclusion of his letter, it would be better if his daughter were not to attempt to meet the demands of dramatic writing:

for the Stage, I w^d. have you very Careful, & very perfect—that is, as far
so as your own Efforts, & the best advice you can get, can make you. In
the Novel Way, there is no danger—& in that, *no Times* can affect
you.

Stage-writing demands a daunting perfection and must be put under the censorship of "the best advice." The emphasis on a paralyzing carefulness seems
designed to frighten his daughter back into the safety of writing prose fiction.
The novel is associated with safety, and the comedy with "danger."

Why was Charles Burney's reaction to *The Witlings* so intense, so absolute?
Frances was given the impression that "the general effect of the whole . . . has
so terribly failed, all petty criticisms would be needless."[39] One suspects more
than a rational prudence about offending Mrs. Montagu. Charles evidently had
not imagined that his Fanny's comedy would be satiric. He disliked anything in
her that seemed self-opinionated, too robust and bold. The very success with
which Frances had tackled the problems of writing good comedy without
explicit sex or "objectionable" material proved itself ultimately most objectionable—the result was too cynical, too freewheeling and alien. If Frances had
written a more sentimental comedy, with more of the "Serious part" that makes
one "for to cry," the objections might have been less. If she had written one of
the droopy tragedies of the time, like Hannah More's, preferably with a tender
plot involving a daughter's reunion with a father, Dr. Burney might not have
objected at all. As we shall see, Frances did write that sort of drama later—in a
period of desperation. The exhibition of a tragic piece by his Fanny did not
make Dr. Burney nervous, though he was always to start into fresh alarm at the
idea of her putting on a comedy.

It is most probable that for Dr. Burney there were in *The Witlings* private
points of unease. He may have been dimly aware that the unkindly treated Lady
Smatter bore a slight resemblance to his wife, as well as to Mrs. Montagu.
Certainly Lady Smatter is partly a reaction against "Precious," "the Lady"
whose conversational talents Frances was to describe in the *Memoirs* in ambiguous, even barbed, praise:

> The friends . . . were not slack in paying their devoirs to his new partner,
> whose vivacious society, set off by far more than the remains of uncom-
> mon beauty, failed not to attract various visitors . . . and whose love, or
> rather passion, for conversation and argument, were of that gay and
> brilliant sort, that offers too much entertainment to be ever left in the
> lurch for want of partakers.[40]

(The stress is on "*remains* of beauty," and "*passion* for argument," and what
kind of "entertainment" these offered is open to speculation.) As Dr. Burney
could not ever admit even to himself that the children did not get along splen-

didly with their stepmother, reading the play may have cost him extra efforts at repression. And did he unconsciously recognize himself in Dabler, with his obsequiousness, his desire for patronage, and his little poems to please the ladies? It was Act IV Charles found especially offensive, and in that it is not just the bluestocking ladies but the little toady, the would-be literary man and social climber, who is the target. The play's familiar treatment of vulgarity also might give rise to a public opinion that the Burneys were vulgar at home—after Charles had spent a lifetime rising into gentlemanliness. Whatever the reasons for Dr. Burney's intense dislike, he believed in his society and in himself, and suppressed the rebel.

Like Censor, Charles used blackmail, persuading his daughter that *he* would be the one hurt by criticism if she tried to have her unworthy play put on. He and Crisp joined in putting Fanny's play down; together they concocted what she refers to as "that hissing, groaning, catcalling epistle"[41] sent by the joint daddies. The rational thing would have been to say, in effect, "It is a funny play, and I laughed, but you know, people are going to think you're attacking Mrs. Montagu—so I wish you would not put it on, even though it is likely to succeed."[42] But Crisp and Dr. Burney had to persuade Fanny that her play was *bad*. No wonder if, after Murphy's approval (and after Susanna's innocent account of the reading), Frances Burney was puzzled at the vivid picture of theatrical disgrace they drew. Crisp was most likely drawing from memory of the fate of his own play. Dr. Burney had the tormenting recollection of the production of Garrick's version of *A Midsummer Night's Dream* in 1763, for which Charles Burney had written the music; that piece had failed completely, having an obstreperous audience during its one night, and terrible reviews.[43] The association of Charles's attempt in the comic theater with humiliation meant that the alarm-button was easy to press in his task of discouraging the writer who was, after all, only his Fanny.

In her letter replying to her father, an epistle of miserable obedience, Frances Burney takes care to make it clear to him that the only argument she recognized is *his* fear, and that it is for his sake rather than for her own that she agrees to suppression:

> I most solemnly declare, that upon your account any disgrace would mortify and afflict me more than upon my own; for whatever appears with your knowledge, will be naturally supposed to have met with your approbation . . . though all particular censure would fall where it ought —upon me—yet any general censure of the whole, and the plan, would . . . involve you in its severity.[44]

In thus spelling out the matter, she is obviously trying to make Dr. Burney change his mind; by making it so clear that his potential suffering was the major obstacle, she perhaps hoped still to elicit a magnanimous response. Perhaps he would say his back was broad enough, not to worry. Of course this was a hint he refused to take. He had suppressed the dreadful play for his daughter's sake. "You have finished it now in every sense of the word"; so she writes in this long, eloquent, and bitter letter.[45]

So much for humane liberal consensus; Authority (or "arbitrary Government mildly administered") was still alive and kicking. Dr. Burney's Fanny was not a rebel. She did not run away from home to have her play staged—that was not in her nature. The need for her father's approval was so strong that she had to persuade herself, even against her own opinion and Murphy's praise, that the play was bad. But there is no evidence that she ever really believed that.

If *The Witlings* had been staged, we would now remember Frances Burney as a predecessor of Pinero or Ayckbourn. Instead, it remains in neat manuscript, as copied out for the managers—a pile of papers in the Berg Collection. *The Witlings* has never been produced, nor even published (though surely this state of affairs will someday be altered). The daddies' censorship has been successful for two hundred years.

1. Charles Burney, Mus.D., Frances's father, by Sir Joshua Reynolds

2. Esther Sleepe Burney, Frances's mother, by Gervase Spencer

3. "Sampler of My own dearest Mother. Given to me by her precious Self, when I was 8 years of age." Gift of Esther Sleepe Burney to Frances.

4. Esther ("Hetty") Burney, Frances's elder sister

5. Susanna Burney (Mrs. Molesworth Phillips), Frances Burney's younger sister and dearest friend

6. Charles Burney, Frances's younger brother

7. Samuel ("Daddy") Crisp, by Edward Francesco Burney

8. "Oh author of my being!" frontispiece to the 1779 edition of *Evelina*

9. Mme. Duval in the ditch, frontispiece to volume II of *Evelina*

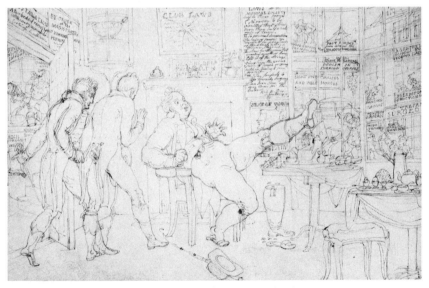

10. Edward Francesco Burney, "The Practical Joker"

11. Samuel Johnson, "Given to F.B. by Dr. Johnson, 1782"

12. Hester Thrale, c. 1785

13. "Mrs. Philips' Minuet," by Dr. Charles Burney

14. "Mrs. Thrale. Given by Herself to F.B."

15. Cecilia and Mrs. Hill, illustration by Edward Francesco Burney

16. Cecilia, overheard addressing Mortimer's dog Fidel, frontispiece to German edition of *Cecilia*

17. Miniature of Frances Burney, by John Bogle, 1783

18. Frances Burney, by Edward Francesco Burney, c. 1784–85

19. "Fore Gad that *Cecilia*'s a charming young Woman!": Caricature (1784) referring to dramatic "Epilogue" based on *Cecilia*.

20. George Owen Cambridge in middle age,
by an unknown artist

21. "My revered & dearest Mrs. Delany.
Cut by Lady Templetown for F.B."

22. Juliana Schwellenberg and Queen Charlotte in Thomas Rowlandson's "The Prospect Before Us," 1788

23. Detail: Mrs. Schwellenberg as toad-eater in James Gillray's "The Offering to Liberty"

24. General Alexandre d'Arblay, by Carle
and Horace Vernet, 1817

25. Manuscript page of "Clarinda" story, an
earlier form of *Camilla*

Alexander Charles Louis Piochard D'Arblay
Son of General & Madam D'Arblay Grandson of Dr Charles Burney.

"Alex three years old cut by sweet lovely dear Amine Lock"
1797

26. "Alex three years old cut by *sweet lovely dear* Amine Lock"

27. "Camilla Cottage," drawing presumably by General Alexandre d'Arblay

28. Captain (later Admiral) James Burney,
Frances's elder brother

29. Portrait by John Hoppner of a woman
presumed to be Frances's younger half-
sister, Sarah Harriet Burney

30. " 'A Maman': Juvenile Birthday Verses from Alex d'Arblay to his Mother. Written at 12 Years of Age"

31. James Gillray, "The Storm rising;—or—the Republican FLOTILLA in danger," February 1798

32. "The wild edifice": drawing of Stonehenge by Thomas Hearne, engraving by W. Bryne and T. Medland, 1786

Cecilia; or, Memoirs of an Heiress

Cecilia was written under entirely different circumstances from *Evelina*. Far from having to keep the new work a secret from her father, Frances Burney suffered from an undue impatience on his part that she should begin a new novel at once and finish it with rapidity. Charles Burney's anxiety that his daughter should begin a work of fiction ("in the Novel Way there is no danger") reflects his desire to get rid of both *The Witlings* and the guilt of having suppressed it. His urging on the completion was fired by his love of favorable publicity. He expected to bring out the second volume of his *History of Music* in 1781, and seems to have thought that his daughter's work appearing at the same time would make a bigger splash for both.[1] Frances Burney felt the pain of such pressure; she wrote to her sister Susanna: "he will expect me to have just *done*, when I am so behind hand as not even to see Land!—yet I have written a great deal,—but the Work will be a long one, & I cannot without ruining it make it otherwise."[2] Early in 1781, while visiting Crisp at Chessington where she had retired to write, Frances became ill with a "vile and irksome fever."[3] The work had to be slowed down; the illness seems typical of Burneyesque management, for after that she could go at her own pace with less argument.

Frances Burney herself was conscious of new public expectations. Her anonymity had gone. In January 1779 she had been annoyed to find herself referred to in a verse pamphlet called *Warley*: "Will it gain approbation from 'dear little Burney'?"[4] The phrase echoed Johnson's mode of referring to her; her private life was blown upon. Before the new novel appeared, she had another taste of publicity. Verses published in the *Morning Herald* in March 1782 bade the newspaper stop proclaiming "Naught of women but the *shame*" and to celebrate "Such as shine their sex's glory," including "Those of literary fame":

> Carter's piety and learning,
> Little Burney's quick discerning.[5]

The anonymous contributor, who writes very much in the style of Macartney (or Dabler), was Dr. Charles Burney, though his daughter did not know that. She did not care for this celebration, but Dr. Burney advertised his daughter (as *little* Burney) and her new work. He was also careful to scatter versified praise liberally among the crowd of female writers, including the "Blues" such as Mrs. Montagu and Hannah More, providing by flattery an antidote to any rumors about *The Witlings*.

Much of Burney's writing of *Cecilia* was done away from home, largely because consistent writing was difficult in the home of a querulous stepmother. As Burney acknowledged to Susanna, leaving Chessington for home would be bad for the book: "I know but too well the many interruptions from ill management, inconveniences, & ill nature I must meet with when I go, will retard me most cruelly, & keep me back."[6] The Thrales' home, for many reasons, was too distracting for an author. Yet her acquaintance with the Thrales had introduced Frances Burney to that wider fashionable world which plays such a part in *Cecilia*. In April 1780, Frances Burney journeyed with the Thrales to Bath, where they took a house in South Parade; assemblies and evening parties produced numbers of wits, bluestockings, fashionable characters, and oddities. This visit to Bath was interrupted in June by the Gordon Riots, so called because Lord George Gordon and his followers, in agitating for repeal of the Catholic Relief Act of 1778, whipped up popular feeling in the guise of staunch Protestantism. Burney's journal records the alarm, the coaches chalked over with "No Popery," the burning of the Roman Catholic chapel in Bath, both the chapel and the priest's house "burning with a fury that is dreadful," and the priest (her grandmother's co-religionist), "poor persecuted man . . . pelted, followed and very ill used."[7] The persecuted priest noted sympathetically in her diary for June 1780 prefigures the emigrant French clergy for whom Burney was willing to plead publicly in 1793. The Gordon Riots showed that social tranquillity is often illusory, that hostility may break out suddenly and violently—a vision very compatible with Burney's view of the truth about life.

The Thrales had reason for personal fear at the time, as rumors were being circulated that Henry Thrale was a "Papist."[8] The Thrales and Frances Burney left Bath quietly and traveled through the West Country byroads, pausing at Wilton to view the house and grounds before proceeding to Salisbury and then Brighton. The area traveled through prefigures the journey of Juliet, heroine of *The Wanderer*, the novel of revolution and violence; that heroine also visits Wilton strangely, during a flight full of anxiety. Frances Burney left the Thrales safely in Brighton and returned to London, presumably to start work on writing, though her departure was a disappointment to Hester Thrale.

Burney's new novel was undertaken and completed during the high noon of the friendship between Hester Lynch Thrale and Frances Burney. This was an important epoch in both their lives. Enough has already been said about the ill-advised efforts of Charles Burney to hurry on the novel, and some recent critics have wished to dismiss *Cecilia* as the mere work of industry, ground out at her father's bidding.[9] Nothing could be farther from the truth. Essentially, *Cecilia* is a "wanted" novel (as we speak of a "wanted" child), and incorporates at a very deep level the author's reaction not only to the suppression of *The Witlings* but to what that suppression means. It is a much more daring novel than *Evelina*, though some readers have lamented the loss of the "artlessness" of the earlier novel, which partly means its innocuousness, for *Evelina* is a book that, like its heroine, can be dismissed by the unwary as light and ingenuous. *Cecilia* has no artless ingénue narrator, but a sober, strong, and ironic third-person narrator, daring to speak out with authority about the nature of the people of the world and of the world itself. Female insight is raised to an authorial universal principle, not deprecatingly put into the words of a charming teenager. If we want to look at the positive circumstances surrounding this novel's composition, we may look at the relationship between Hester Lynch Thrale and the author.

Each woman found what was a novelty in her life—a friend of her own sex outside the home circle. So far, Frances Burney's only women friends had been her sisters, especially her dearest Susanna. Mrs. Thrale, miserably married off at the age of eighteen to a man for whom she was a convenience, and to whom she was a faithful helpmeet in a loveless marriage, had not been allowed to seek friendships outside the new home and the Thrale family (including sisters-in-law whom she despised).[10] Her husband's introduction of Johnson into their lives was of major importance, though Johnson's presence at Streatham was often a drain on her emotional resources. Worn out with childbearing, she garnered no sympathy for pregnancies or stillbirths. Her dearly loved son Harry died in 1776. Her mother, her only intimate female companion, had died in 1773. When Frances Burney was introduced to the Thrale circle as a new appendage of Johnson's all-male group, Mrs. Thrale was at first disposed to be somewhat supercilious, but fairly rapidly warmed to the stiff young author. Hester had too many gaps in the heart not to learn to value a kind, intelligent, witty, and appreciative friend.

Frances Burney had at first been fearful of being seen by Mrs. Thrale in the light of the creator of the Branghtons et al.: "I am afraid she will conclude I must have an innate vulgarity of ideas."[11] Her first visit to Streatham in July 1778 was something of an ordeal. As we have seen, Hester Thrale found her shy and stilted at first. The relationship slowly became deeper, more equal, visibly less dependent on the *grande dame* role on one side and that of the stiffly grateful newcomer on the other. Hester Thrale came to appreciate the wit of the young woman she learned to call "Fanny." She also admired Frances Burney's wholeness of heart. In some Shakespearean and mock-Shakespearean comments on various acquaintances, she wrote of "Fanny Burney":

> A fair Mark Coz: but she will not be hit
> By Cupid's Arrow—She hath Dian's Wit,
> And will not stay the Siege of loving Terms
> Nor bide th'encounter of assailing Eyes.

Her comments "of D^r. Burney" are not so flattering:

> What Reverence doth he throw away on Slaves,
> Seeming to dive into the dirtiest Hearts
> And woo them with familiar Courtesies![12]

Mrs. Thrale's chaste and witty friend proved a resource when Mr. Thrale threatened various kinds of breakdown (physical, emotional, and financial); after his first stroke in 1780 he stolidly persevered in his course of eating himself to death. If Hester Lynch Thrale supported Frances Burney through the entire episode of *The Witlings*, Frances Burney provided her with support and comfort during the last years of the difficult marriage to Henry Thrale. Eventually, Frances Burney admitted Mrs. Thrale into knowledge of the home difficulties regarding Mrs. Burney, and the pleasures of talking "Treason"; there are hints in some of their letters that something that might also be "Treason" was discussed concerning the difficulties of dealing with Henry Thrale. By 1781, when Frances was deep in the writing of her new novel, the women friends were on a level of mutual reliance and the kind of trust which permits the communication of very personal events and feelings. Henry Thrale, suffering from the aftereffects of his stroke (and having lost his campaign for election), decided to move to London early in 1781, for the pleasures of the season. Mrs. Thrale put a good face on the change, knowing that acquaintances would believe that gadding to town was her idea. To Frances Burney she confided her real anxieties:

> *My* Heroism consisted in not sending *for you home* when I was terrified into Agonies by my dear Master's uncontroulable Spirit, made violent by Illness which kept me in *such Terror!* & he would take Houses at 20, 30 Guineas p^r. Week, and he was *so Ill!* but 'tis all over now, and that's the Secret. I *knew* you w^d. come if I told you half what I suffered, & so I suppress'd it all . . . & wrote you even chearful Letters, that you might not suspect my Anxiety: now then love me as dearly, & come see me comfortably.[13]

Many of the barriers, the decorums which dictated what a wife should or should not say to others about a husband, are broken through—or barely maintained in the linguistic propriety of "my dear Master"—as Hester admits to her friend what she is undergoing in fear of her husband's "uncontroulable" temper, his tendencies to violence and to irrational manic fits. Frances Burney honored the honesty as well as the consideration of herself:

> . . . how shall I thank you in the midst of such cares & agonies for a kindness so affectionately considerate to *me!*—did not I once say, when we were Eating Strawberries & Cream with Sir Philip Clerke in his Library, that I knew not if you loved me *enough?*—what must I say now, when I find myself loved so much beyond all my pretensions, & all my knowing *the Why?*—yet don't you ask it, & love me any less, for I shall not tell how to bear that now. . . . I grieve, too, to think I could have been of the slightest use or comfort to you, & yet was not;—while I represent you to myself gay & happy, shining in Company, & flashing surrounding Friends, I am content enough to be away, if other avocations make it *right,*—but when I think I see you all care & watchfulness, apprehensive of every look, & disturbed by every speech—then I always think that were I with you I could help lighten the Burthen, or, at least, lend a shoulder towards supporting its weight.[14]

Care, concern, mutual support, the lightening of burdens—these were all involved now in a friendship that had gone far beyond the polite entertainments of Streatham's witty drawing room. Both women had a strong need for love, and each appeared to have found an invaluable affection in the other. One cannot miss the intensity and doubt in Frances Burney's wondering "if you loved me *enough*" and the intoxication and wonder of finding herself loved beyond desert or expectation. Frances Burney's trust in the love afforded by her family (and by the adoptive elder, Samuel Crisp) had presumably been shaken by the treatment of *The Witlings;* the new warm friendship outside the family would appear to have become increasingly important. In this female friendship, as never in literary friendships between men and women, the superiorities and hierarchies had dropped away and true intensity emerged. A good deal of intimacy is required even to voice the question whether the friend loves one enough; Burney's response "when I find myself loved so much" speaks an unusual openness, a clear-headed willingness to betray vulnerable feelings ("don't you . . . love me any less, for I shall not tell how to bear that now"). This high-water mark of feeling was reached by Burney when she was in the middle of *Cecilia;* near the end of this same epistle she tells Mrs. Thrale "I have finished the 3^d. Tom[e]— but the worst is, there must be another, & that I have merely *begun,* for I could not *squeeze* all I had to do in 3."[15]

The warmth and openness on Frances Burney's side was fully reciprocated by Hester Thrale. Although the busy wife, mother, and leader of fashion had many calls upon her emotional attention, her friend occupied increasingly a place near the center of her thoughts: "neither my Pleasure nor my Pains can be complete, without my Friend, my Fanny to participate."[16]

There were pleasures as well as pains. On 18 January 1781 Mrs. Thrale appeared at court in a wonderful dress of her own invention, inspired by the goods Captain James Burney had brought back from the last voyage with Captain Cook to the Pacific, from which he had returned in October 1780. Polynesian barkcloth, feather leis, and feather capes were the models for the gown, the material woven on a loom at Spitalfields according to the patterns from *"Owyhee"* (Hawaii); the dress was trimmed with grebe feathers and gold lace. The *Morning Herald*, puzzled but game, said, "Mrs. Thrale appeared in a striped sattin Otaheite pattern" and pronounced the effect "magnificent as well as singular."[17] Frances, too ill to come to London to see the dress, enjoyed reading about it:

> Lord, if you had seen how I smirked over the Account of your Dress in the News-papers!—I felt quite *proud* to see you so distinguished above the rest even in the *Ton Circle;* Why you have but to step forward, & be the First in *any* thing,—not only in the *tender* . . . the *refined,*—but as Mrs. Montagu will confess, in the *vulgar,* &, as the whole British Court will testify, in the *elegant!*[18]

Frances Burney, who had once worried that Mrs. Thrale would think her vulgar, had seen that her friend had a talent that way too, and could be first in the vulgar as well as the elegant. Hester Thrale's court appearance in the grand original gown not only marks her as the first introducer of Polynesian motifs into high fashion, but also signals a subdued impatience with local customs and constraints, a search for a wider world to live in. Hester took a certain pleasure in thinking of herself as "the O Why'hee Savage," although, or perhaps because, the Hawaiians, not the inhabitants of "Otaheite," had killed Captain Cook. (Did Hawaii signify violence and rebellion?) Polynesia also supplied a new word in their friendship; about this time, Frances Burney and Hester Thrale began to address each other as "Tyo," the word that James Burney had told them was used when each English sailor was adopted as a brother by a native Tahitian.[19] English decorum still demanded that Burney should address her older married friend as "Mrs. Thrale," though that friend could address her as "Fanny." As "Tyo" they were equal, and outside the rules of European language altogether.

In this era of warmest friendship, which might be called their "Polynesian days," Hester Thrale and Frances Burney sought symbols of union and special relationship. Mrs. Thrale's use of James Burney's travelers' tales and souvenirs for her court dress signifies a desire to express her connection to the Burneys.

Trying to cement the relationship into permanence, Hester Thrale urged her Fanny to consider marriage to Mr. Thrale's relative Henry Smith:

> do be well, & get some Flesh & Colour loveliest Burney, & come to Town & be my *Relation* as well as my *Friend*. I verily think *that* Scheme would take, & produce mutual Happiness: he is a good Boy, has 600£ a Year landed Estate & a Profession to keep him from idleness.[20]

Frances Burney refused to take the idea seriously:

> As to Harry Smith, I can only laugh—I know too little of him to think about him for a Moment—& I hope I have too warm a *Heart* to marry for the sake of warming my Hands!—Yet let me thank *you* again and again for this most sweet eagerness to prove to me in every way your true & *deep* affection.[21]

In 1781 and 1782 Hester Thrale also endeavored to promote a connection between her friend Burney and the mysterious Jeremiah Crutchley, whom Mrs. Thrale believed to be Mr. Thrale's illegitimate son. Crutchley's apparent attraction to Queeney Thrale was a source of anxiety; incestuous marriage between these two would have to be prevented, and Frances Burney would be well provided for if she married the master of the little estate at Sunning-hill Park. But neither of these principals would take an interest in the other.

If marriage would not do, there were other ways of cementing the relationship. In March 1781, racked with anxiety about her husband's failing health and odd behavior and full of apprehension regarding the tour to Italy that Henry Thrale appeared now to insist upon, Hester Thrale appointed Frances Burney as her surrogate and surviving self. A shocked Burney recorded in her diary the upshot of a conversation in Mrs. Thrale's dressing room in late March: "She would write to me . . . every post; leave me the keys of all she left of any value, and, in case of any evil to herself, make me her executrix!"[22] After this conversation, Hester Lynch Thrale repeated in a letter to Frances Burney her faith in her friend:

> Johnson best describes the Value of *her* Heart, wch. I now really believe does love me next her Family. Neither Spa nor Italy nor Conjugal Care shall in earnest divide us: my Letters shall give her constant Information of our Proceedings, & hers shall lie under my Pillow, when the Pillow is hard and disgusting of itself.[23]

The letters from the friend are to sweeten the "hard and disgusting" conjugal pillow. Henry Thrale, however, was dissuaded from the immediate European tour, to his wife's relief, but he continued to give dinner parties and suicidally overate himself into another and fatal fit of apoplexy. His daughter Queeney found him lying on the floor; "I chuse it," said Thrale, stubborn to the last, "I lie so o' purpose."[24] Stroke after stroke succeeded, and he died on 4 April 1781. "Conjugal Care" was now over. Much of the summer of 1781 was spent by Frances Burney in visiting and consoling the widowed Mrs. Thrale. The attachment to Piozzi growing within Mrs. Thrale's heart from the summer months of that year remained a secret yet from her friend and almost from herself. The rock upon which the friendship was to split still lay ahead during the writing of *Cecilia*. Visits to Mrs. Thrale often distracted Burney from her writing, but she set to again in deep earnest in November and wrote on through the winter.

In her youth Hester Thrale had always wanted to be (and thought of herself as) a writer. The presence of Frances Burney, a friend (not a "Blue") who was a dedicated writer helped renew Hester's confidence in the possibility of writing for a public. As we have seen, Burney's work on *The Witlings* prompted Hester Thrale to begin a comedy for the stage. Though this was not completed, in February 1781 Mrs. Thrale was asked by the Reverend John Delap to contribute a prologue to his tragedy *The Royal Suppliants*, produced at Drury Lane Theatre on 17 February. This prologue appeared in the *Gentleman's Magazine*, which explained that it was "suppos'd to be written by Mrs. Thr——le."[25] In the 1760s Mrs. Thrale had had several poems published, but the 1770s had been empty of public production. Now, in having her poem spoken on the stage, Hester Lynch achieved another sort of public voice. Frances Burney at Chessington, too ill to see the play, begged for a sight of the poem:

> But this Prologue—Oh how I die to see it!—I am *sure* it would come safe . . . besides, though your Name may be kept secret, the *Prologue* will appear in all the News Papers in a Week's Time. Do then, *Dear* Madam, suffer me to see it,—& some Time, I will shew you a most silly thing of that sort which *I* wrote, & which was spoken upon the Dublin theatre; No creature in all *England* has ever seen it: The story of the occasion is too long for a Letter, & the Composition is terribly feeble, but the less my reasons for vanity, the greater my power to shew confidence. Oh what would I give to be at the House to Night! & how much should I be tempted to *Clap* the Prologue myself!—pray let me know who spoke it, & how it was spoken.[26]

If Frances Burney was tantalized by Hester Thrale's new Prologue, she continues to tantalize us with this reference to her own prologue of the past; the "silly thing" once spoken in a Dublin theater has not come to light, and it is a pity from our point of view that she thought the story of the occasion too long for this letter. As Burney's own hopes of hearing words by herself spoken again in the live theater had been dashed with the banning of *The Witlings*, it was generous of her to support Mrs. Thrale's work. To be asked to write a prologue for Drury Lane was in itself flattering. (Mrs. Thrale knew that Delap had really hoped for Johnson, but enjoyed her opportunity nonetheless.) Hester Lynch Thrale Piozzi's most recent literary biographer has noted that her career was "interrupted" and describes it as "resumed" in 1784 after her second marriage, but concedes in passing that "even before Henry Thrale's death she had made her second appearance in print under her own name" with this prologue.[27] The encouraging influence of her friend Burney may well be taken into account. It can be suggested that the one lasting gift Burney gave to the woman who was once her dearest friend was the model of a writing career. At least, that was Burney's career during the 1770s and early 1780s. Burney was to be derailed just as the new Mrs. Piozzi started her writing career in earnest, an irony that also lay in the future.

At first Hester Lynch Thrale had some reservations about Burney's new writing project. She was inclined to be critical of Charles Burney, clearly seeing his desire to urge his daughter on with her book, and she remonstrated with him upon it:

> This Morning I talk'd very freely with D^r. Burney about Matters & Things, & told him that your anxious earnestness to oblige him had caused much of the Illness we lamented—why says he I did teize her to write while she was away so that the Book so long expected might at length be done. Very true, my Dear Sir quoth Saucebox, but whoever robs me of my *Friend*, & leaves me a *Book* in her Place, injures *me* grossly, tho' the Book were an *Iliad*.[28]

Hester Thrale could become a trifle jealous of whatever seemed to stand between herself and her friend. She was vexed at her Fanny's failure to become a constant companion at Streatham, a fact which she blamed on Charles Burney:

> What a Blockhead D^r. Burney is, to be always sending for his Daughter home so ! . . . is not She better and happier with me than She can be any where else? . . . I confess myself provoked excessively . . . . If I did not provide Fanny with every *Weare*able [sic], every *Wish*able indeed, it would not vex me to be served so.[29]

But Frances Burney did not like being the object of someone's bounty, provided with every "*Weare*able" and "*Wish*able." She was heartily vexed (although she promised Mrs. Thrale "to take it *like a man*") when in the spring of 1781 a newspaper announced knowingly that "Miss Burney, the sprightly writer of the elegant novel 'Evelina,' is now domesticated with Mrs. Thrale, in the same manner that Miss More is with Mrs. Garrick, and Mrs. Carter with Mrs. Montagu."[30] That false announcement turned Burney into another literary toady-cum-companion, a humble dependent. She disliked being patronized, playing the impoverished Cecilia Stanley to a more benevolent Lady Smatter. The real relation between the two "Tyos" required independence, female self-dependence, a matter that *Cecilia* tries to work out.

Once *Cecilia* had progressed far enough for Mrs. Thrale to be allowed to see it, the elder of the friends naturally became more engaged in its progress and turned into one of its warmest supporters. She was privileged to participate as a reader in the novel's creation. She was willing to play the game aright, to inquire after the characters by their names:

> Tell me how you go on, how the Harrels keep the Bailiffs at bay, how Belfield reconciles his pride & his poverty: where young Delvile is run to with his arrow in his Side—& when a Treaty of Marriage will commence between Miss Leeson & Mr. Meadows![31]

The author was grateful for this license to speak from her own world:

> A little chear-up from you, my dearest Madam, always new *Mans* me: & the Belfields, Harrels & Delviles will all profit from it. Even Mr. Meadows will animate, & even Miss Leeson be almost tempted to prate.[32]

Mrs. Thrale offered the kind of readings Burney, like Richardson, most valued, instant impressions before the entire novel had been read—or finished. "But poor Henrietta! some harm will come to her, I see. . . . I am just ready to order the coach . . . and fetch her away to Streatham, from that most inimitably painted mother, whom Queeney does so detest."[33] The praise of the ending was deeply gratifying:

> Such a novel! Indeed, I am seriously and sensibly touched by it, and am proud of her friendship who so knows the human heart. . . . If I had more virtue than "Cecilia," I should half fear the censures of such an insight into the deepest recesses of the mind. Since I have read this volume, I have seriously thanked Heaven that all the litter of mine was in sight; none hoarded in holes, nor hastily stuffed into closets. You have long known the worst of your admiring
> H.L.T.[34]

Novelists tend in the long run to be rather frightening friends; a certain ruthlessness goes into what we call the creation of "characters" and the observation of the human emotions. At this point, in early 1782, Mrs. Thrale was somewhat disingenuous in insisting that nothing was hidden in her mind's closet. The hidden love for Piozzi would emerge and wreck the friendship. But while *Cecilia* was being finished, the friendship was remarkably deep, consistent, and undisturbed.

Burney had the more need of Hester's friendship as the dearest friendship of her life sustained a shock. Susanna Burney at age twenty-six fell in love with handsome young Molesworth Phillips, an officer in the Marines, James's shipmate on Cook's voyages. James's "Tyo," Captain Phillips, as Frances noted, "played the fraternal part d'avance," coming to Chessington to see Frances and Mr. Crisp and delighting the latter especially with his ability to talk "Treason" against Mrs. Charles Burney.[35] At the first news of the engagement in January 1781 Frances protested against any idea of speedy marriage, and pointed out to Susanna the disadvantages of a wife's lot:

> Heaven be praised that Capt. P seems to have no mad schemes of entering into House Keeping before he is able!—indeed with such an example of the ill effects of precipitancy as our poor care-worn Hetty offers us, any of *her* sisters would be inexcusable for listening to such a plan.[36]

But Susanna was not to be discouraged by the example of her eldest sister. It is in this period, when she realized she was going to lose Susanna, that Burney became despondent; her illness coincides with the engagement, and the complaints about writing *Cecilia* belong almost entirely to this period. As she wrote to Susanna on 3 February 1781, it seemed a waste of time to be writing at Chessington, away from her sister, at this point:

> I begin, *somehow,* to grudge passing away so long a Time from Susy, now I consider that we are no longer destined to pursue our little snug Garret scheme & end our Lives 2 loving Maiden Cats.[37]

Frances Burney's vague plans for her own future had always included the dream of living with Susanna in middle and old age; now her idea of the future had to be changed, and a form of abandonment loomed. When she heard that Susanna and Molesworth Phillips were planning to marry soon, she tried to persuade them to postpone the evil day; her strange letter at this time indicates that she is in a kind of panic, imperfectly masquerading as jocularity:

> Capt. P. is quite right in saying I shall not be *selfish,* for no more I will, —but as to your decamping this Winter, I can by no means listen to it;—for I shall spend it all at Home, on purpose to live with you. . . .
> For the Spring, if Capt. P. wants a Second, to fight his Battles with the *Padre,* or with the *figlia* herself, I am his Man !—. . .
> April, I think, is an exceeding pretty month indeed—. . . Heaven bless me! if this vile Capt. P. a Traitor at last, to my puffing of his good Nature,

hauls you away in any of the gloomy preceding Months, I would at least advise him, for the Benefit of his own Conscience, to slyly cut down my Bed Posts !—neither, for Charlotte's sake, who is somewhat fonder of *floating* than *swinging,* would it be much amiss if he ordered the Bathing Tub in the Back Kitchen to be knocked in Pieces for Firing.[38]

The imagery in this passage is odd and sexually disturbed, picking up transvestism or sexual transformation ("I am his Man") and a kind of invitation to "Capt. P." to enter Frances's own bedroom, as well as a hint of nakedness in the idea of the "Bathing Tub." The picture composed is one of dramatic domestic disorder, with hyperbolically suicidal sisters busy in self-destruction about the house, one hanging from the bedpost, one drowned in the tub in the back kitchen. In her "joke" Burney makes a suicide threat, like one of the more unstable characters in her fiction.

More decorously, Frances could confess to Mrs. Thrale that she was not utterly rejoiced at the marriage:

> I am very *happy* about it in fact, *because* and *because*—but I am not very *merry,* for I shall miss her dreadfully,—my Heart was always big enough for You & Her too.[39]

Obliged to be conventionally happy that her sister had got her wish, Frances could not be truly merry at the prospect of the wedding, which took place in St. Martin-in-the-Fields on 10 January 1782. Charles Burney, who had at first been extremely enthusiastic about the engagement (because of oversanguine notions about the financial resources of Captain Phillips) had become more cautious on finding that the future son-in-law was less rich than he had supposed. (Hence the possibility of battles with "the *Padre.*") But Phillips had reasonable prospects, and Dr. Burney adopted an attitude of benign approval; he wrote verses to his daughter, presided over her marriage, and composed, as a wedding gift for Susanna, "Mrs. Phillips' Minuet" (Fig. 13). The somewhat suspicious promptness of the birth of the Phillipses' first child (5 October) perhaps allows us to wonder whether Susanna Burney and Molesworth Phillips had not anticipated their nuptials; if so, the matter would be of import only as showing that Susanna before her wedding had already separated from Frances in having a life secret from her, and perhaps as explaining some of Susanna's later feeling that she should stick by her marriage to expiate her sins (see Chapter Eight). At first, the Phillipses' marriage was very happy. Susanna was gone—into marriage and pregnancy and motherhood; the journal-letters and the love never abated, but the old perfect intimacy could never be recaptured. Mrs. Thrale's friendship proved a stabilizing force of great assistance to Frances Burney in 1781 and 1782. (The intimacy is expressed in Hester's gift of a silhouette of herself, a personal memento—see Fig. 14.)

The novel, published on 12 July 1782,[40] has as its heroine a beautiful young heiress. This rich orphan seems, unlike Evelina, to have only herself to please. As the story opens Cecilia Beverley has only nine months to wait before she comes into an inheritance of separate fortunes: she will have ten thousand pounds from her parents' bequest, and "an estate of 3000*l* per annum" from her uncle, passing to her "with no other restriction than that of annexing her name, if she married, to the disposal of her hand and her riches" (1:5).[41] The "condition" so casually mentioned at the end of a long sentence first seems, as it does to Cecilia herself, a minor and incidental matter. Ironically, no other restriction is needed to prevent happiness. But the reader, dazzled by the large sums of money, is led into complicity with the money-loving world around the girl.

The heroine, poised and well-educated with none of the juvenile disabilities of Evelina, does not know what the world she is entering is really like. She leaves her home in "Bury" (Bury St. Edmunds), the home of her youth, of the buried life (cf. "Berry Hill" in *Evelina*), for London, where she is to reside with one of her three guardians as her uncle's will directs. The natural choice of residence is with Mr. Harrel, who has married her old school-friend Priscilla. Cecilia "revived her spirits by plans of future happiness, dwelt upon the delight with which she should meet her young friend . . ." (1:7). Cecilia is setting out on her own search for happiness, that eighteenth-century quest. She is searching for friendship and for independence; she does not know (as the reader does) that she is searching for love, and in Cecilia's case, love will prove to be a bar to other hopes and plans. The novel has a number of subdued references to *The Merchant of Venice;* Cecilia resembles Portia of Belmont, Shakespeare's heiress, and like Portia could complain, "So is the will of a living daughter curbed by the will of a dead father"[42]—or uncle. The test provided by the dean's will is not, however, a test of a young man's virtue. Cecilia is an impeded Portia. She does not even know how many unworthy suitors seek her wealth.

Gifted with self-confidence and a sense of humor, as well as a sweet temper and candor, Cecilia has no developed judgment in emotional matters. From the very beginning, we see that friendship is a dangerous area for her. The first "friend" of Cecilia whom we see closely is her neighbor Mr. Monckton. Monckton is married to a woman many years his senior, and this ill-tempered old wife is rude to Cecilia. But the heroine has not seen into Monckton's secret history of greed and calculation, and the lethal wish at the center of his marriage to the blue-blooded Lady Margaret. The authorial voice, measured and ironic, tells us things which the young woman does not know: "Ten years, he had been married to her, yet her health was good . . . eagerly he had watched for her dissolution, yet his eagerness had injured no health but his own!" (I:7–8). Cecilia thinks of her old friend as a married man, her wise counselor, and has no idea of his plans concerning herself: "he had long looked upon her as his future property; as such he had indulged his admiration, and as such he had already appropriated her estate" (I:19). Monckton plans to marry her, but

Cecilia is in no sense stupid for not seeing what he keeps so well concealed beneath a suave and kind exterior; she cannot imagine that he could see her as "his property." In some sense, Monckton in this novel takes the place of Captain Mirvan in *Evelina*, as the heroine's chief male antagonist. Monckton, like Mirvan, contemns women, especially old women, and is not much troubled by scruples. In the moral scale of *Cecilia*, Monckton represents the lowest level of behavior in human relationships, as Mirvan did in *Evelina*. But this Mirvan is treated (mistakenly) by the heroine as a sort of Villars, paternal friend and prudent counselor (which casts an odd backward light on *Evelina*). Monckton is a much more formidable antagonist than Mirvan, as he is so truly acceptable socially. Monckton is decorous and influential; he plays his part as landed proprietor very well. He shows how a social pirate can be a pillar of the community, and makes one wonder about the nature of such a community. Like Sir Clement Willoughby, Monckton uses social conventions as stalking horses for private desire. He cannot admit to himself that he does anything unconscionable or out-of-the-way. Society permits gaining wealth through successive marriages, and encourages the exploitation of women as property. Our initial knowledge of Monckton should make us wonder about the value of conforming to such a society.

Cecilia, as we can see with the advantage of hindsight, is a novel of the new decade which was to end with the French Revolution. It raises the issues of that new era. The first conversation in the novel, at Monckton's house, is an unresolved debate upon the claims of conformity against the need for originality. Young Belfield, the poverty-stricken wit (who, we later find, is the son of a linen-draper, an intellectual risen from the tradesman's shop), argues that the "pitiful prevalence of general conformity extirpates genius, and murders originality; man is brought up, not as if he were 'the noblest work of God,' but as a mere ductile machine of human formation." Monckton argues that though an "excentric genius" like Belfield may complain about tedious custom, he would surely not wish "to see the world peopled with defiers of order." Belfield sticks to his guns: "I would have *all* men . . . whether philosophers or ideots [*sic*], act for themselves" (I:15–16). Belfield has complimented Cecilia on her intending "to be guided by the light of your own understanding," while Monckton holds that once a young person "mixes with the world" he soon finds "the necessity . . . of pursuing quietly the track that is already marked out." Belfield is appalled by such a tame and static view:

> "And why . . . but because your general rules . . . are but so many absurd arrangements to impede . . . the use of understanding? if man dared act for himself, if neither worldly views, contracted prejudices, eternal precepts nor compulsive examples, swayed his better reason and impelled his conduct, how noble indeed would he be!" (I:14–15)

The debate picks up issues raised more simply in *The Witlings:* "self-suffi-ciency," "self-dependence." Belfield is no pretentious Dabler; his talents and originality are real, but the world is not inclined to reward them, and the social and psychological costs of rising above one's original class are high—though Burney nowhere suggests that Belfield should have been kept down. Monckton's argument seems to accord with accepted eighteenth-century orthodoxy: individuals are limited, stability and law keep us from retrogression. Monckton sounds like a recognizable Augustan—but his life is a life of hypocrisy, greed, and exploitation. Might the "Augustan" attitudes and the exploitation be more intimately connected? There seems to be some connection between Monckton's proclaimed conformity, his anxious endeavors to protect the heroine from doing what she wants to do, and the cautious "protections" of Frances Burney by Charles Burney and Samuel Crisp, so anxious that she should not deviate from the track already marked out, should not be original or act for herself in the case of *The Witlings*. Monckton's style and terms were never very appealing to Frances Burney personally. She sounds more like Belfield in the passage in the *Early Diary* for 1771 when she praises "the first who shall venture, in a good cause, to break through the confinement of custom, and at least shew the way to a new and open path."[43] That diary entry, a paragraph anticipating the Belfield-Monckton debate in miniature, centers upon the nature and conduct of the admired female figure, Maria Allen. There is an added irony in the mascu-line pronouns used by the debaters in *Cecilia*. Although Belfield began by praising Cecilia, once the debate gets under way, he, like Monckton, does not deviate from the beaten track by including the female overtly within the terms ("If *man* dared act for himself"). The novel is sympathetic to many men; the position of the good man is often as hard as that of the good woman. Society respects boldness and power; some unlucky males feel the full discomfort of social arrangements. Belfield, handicapped by his origin in the wrong class, is robbed of his metaphorical riches (his talents and their full use) just as Cecilia is to be robbed of her literal fortune. The initial argument between conservative and radical, classical and romantic tempers supplies a major theme of the novel, and the questions raised here reverberate throughout. Should the individual be original, "act for himself"—or herself? What is independence? If the individual must conform, to what ought he—or she—to conform? To an ideal society? or to that which already exists?

This heroine's entrance into the world is the confrontation of the problem of when and how she should act for herself. Controlled still by another's will (liter-ally) she must accept her uncle the dean's three guardians: Mr. Delvile, a man of high birth (to see to respectability); Mr. Briggs, a City man (to look after the money); and Mr. Harrel, husband of her old school-friend (to offer company and friendship). The guardians refuse to remain in their allotted places; the guardian of birth can affect her friendship and affections, and the guardian for friendship's sake has a disastrous effect on the money. At first Cecilia finds few attractions, though many diversions, in London life. Her old school-friend, Priscilla Harrel, is a serious disappointment to her. The young matron pursues a round of amusements and money-spending, and has nothing serious to say, and no time to spend on the confidences and cares of friendship, which, indeed, she does not understand. Cecilia did not read her character very well when they were girls. The fashionable world to which Priscilla introduces her in perpetual partying is emotionally unsatisfactory. Cecilia "met with nobody for whom she could care" since politeness dictates amiability without intimacy; she observes "how ill the coldness of their hearts accorded with the warmth of their professions" (I:53).

The orphan heroine, oppressed by her sense of general coldheartedness, has a need for love, which makes her vulnerable, as well as a desire to do good in the world, which makes her difficult to satisfy. She is the more susceptible when she makes a real friend whom she can admire and in whom to some extent she can confide. Disgusted by her pompous blue-blooded guardian Mr. Delvile, so proud of his ancient name and lineage, Cecilia expects little better from Mrs. Delvile, but is agreeably surprised:

> all the unfavourable impressions with which she came into her presence immediately vanished, and that respect which the formalities of her introduction had failed to inspire, her air, figure, and countenance instantaneously excited. . . .
>
> Her carriage was lofty and commanding; but the dignity to which high birth and conscious superiority gave rise, was so judiciously regulated by good sense, and so happily blended with politeness, that though the world at large envied or hated her, the few for whom she had herself any regard, she was infallibly sure to captivate. (I:154–155)

Mrs. Delvile is "not more than fifty years of age"; that is, she is about the age of Mme. Duval. But this is no raddled, painted old woman: "the fine symmetry of her features, still uninjured by the siege of time . . . still laid claim to admiration in every beholder" (I:155). As in Hester Thrale, dignity, sense of high birth, and wit all coexist in Mrs. Delvile. The friendship between Cecilia and Mrs. Delvile is a full friendship, described in detail from its first inception through its progress. From the very beginning "each saw in the other an immediate prepossession in her favour." Partiality "quickly ripened into esteem by the charms of her [Mrs. Delvile's] conversation"; Cecilia

> found her sensible, well bred, and high spirited, gifted by nature with superior talents, and polished by education and study. . . . She saw in her, indeed, some portion of the pride she had been taught to expect; but it was so much softened by elegance, and so well tempered with kindness,

that it elevated her character, without rendering her manners offensive. (I:160)

As Cecilia's acquaintance with Mrs. Delvile matures, she is able to see some of the more subtle elements that go toward the composition of the older woman's leading qualities, such as the oft-attributed pride:

high spirited and fastidious, she was easily wearied and disgusted, she bore neither with frailty nor folly. . . .

In proportion, however, as she was thus at war with the world in general, the chosen few who were honoured with her favour, she loved with a zeal all her own. . . . She magnified their virtues till she thought them of an higher race of beings. (III:460–461)

All these qualities Burney had seen in Hester Thrale. Indeed, descriptions of Augusta Delvile may be compared with the description of Mrs. Thrale in Burney's *Memoirs:*

She had a sweetness of manner, and an activity of service for those she loved, that could ill be appreciated by others . . . she spoke of individuals in general with sarcasm; and of the world at large with sovereign contempt.[44]

And, like Mrs. Thrale when Frances Burney knew her best, Mrs. Delvile has had one deep and permanent source of unhappiness:

Her own youth had been passed in all the severity of affliction; she had been married to Mr. Delvile by her relations, without any consultation of her heart or her will. Her strong mind disdained useless complaints, yet her discontent, however private, was deep. Ardent in her disposition, and naturally violent in her passions, her feelings were extremely acute, and to curb them by reason and principle had been the chief and hard study of her life. The effort had calmed, though it had not made her happy. (III:461)

Augusta Delvile's affliction is the same as Mrs. Thrale's; the misery that Johnson could never bear to acknowledge was a misery and source of deep discontent in his friend's life. The growing friendship between two women as portrayed by Burney in her novel allows them to see into each other's private lives and emotions. No other novelist devoted so much time and attention to the development of a friendship between two women who are neither contemporaries nor relatives.

Of course, both characters have their limitations. Cecilia in her youthful egocentricity is likely to think of Mrs. Delvile primarily in relation to herself and her wishes. The original desire to please Mrs. Delvile sprang from the as yet unacknowledged attraction Cecilia felt to the son, Mortimer. Mrs. Delvile seems the ideal mother-in-law. The author also "cheats" us into believing that Mrs. Delvile's character is established, settled into reason and calm—unless we notice the constant clues to her still-living discontent, her "war with the world," her "violent" passions. We keep learning more and more about someone who is at once admirable and appalling, an affectionate and intelligent woman who can also become a tyrant and a blackmailer. It is the twenty-year-old Cecilia (and the reader) who can be tempted to suppose that well-bred older women no longer have any "story" left in them.

Cecilia has her own kind of pride, including a strong sense of what is her due; she makes allowances for others but is not at all likely to be discomposed or embarrassed as Evelina is. She has an active personality with a strong sense of her own future, her own story to come. She makes plans and tries to arrange her life. Discontented with her life at the Harrels, she designs her own "scheme of happiness":

> She purposed, for the basis of her plan, to become mistress of her own time, and with this view, to drop all idle and uninteresting acquaintance, who while they contribute neither to use nor pleasure, make so large a part of the community, that they may properly be called the underminers of existence: she could then shew some taste and discernment in her choice of friends, and she resolved to select such only as by their piety could elevate her mind, by their knowledge improve her understanding, or by their accomplishments and manners delight her affections. . . .
>
> Having thus, from her own estimation of human perfection, culled whatever was noblest for her society, and from her own ideas of sedentary enjoyments, arranged the occupations of her hours of solitude, she felt fully satisfied with the portion of happiness which her scheme promised to herself, and began next to consider what was due from her to the world. And not without trembling did she then look forward to the claims which the splendid income she was soon to possess would call upon her to discharge . . . her affluence she . . . considered as a debt contracted with the poor, and her independence, as a tie upon her liberality to pay it with interest.
>
> Many and various, then, soothing to her spirit and grateful to her sensibility, were the scenes which her fancy delineated; now she supported an orphan, now softened the sorrows of a widow, now snatched from iniquity the feeble trembler at poverty, and now rescued from shame the proud struggler with disgrace. The prospect at once exalted her hopes, and enraptured her imagination. (I:55–56)

Cecilia's "scheme of happiness" is ambitious, and takes for granted her own power to act as an independent agent. The authorial tone is sympathetic, blending with and endorsing the character's judgment of the "underminers of existence," but the author is also ironic about her character. Cecilia's assumption that she can "resolve to select" only the good, the wise, or delightful as friends is subtly absurd, and her perfect "scheme" may remind us of Swift's Gulliver dreaming of happiness and forming the "Scheme of Living" he would have adopted had he been born an immortal Struldbrugg.[45] Unlike Gulliver, Cecilia includes practical charity immediately in her dreams—but they are, despite her good will, merely soothing dreams. She at once realizes that she can carry out little of this plan at present: "these purposes demanded an house of her own, and the unlimited disposal of her fortune" (I:56).

Cecilia looks forward to her coming of age, and coming into her own, as a man would do. Her attention is not on the marriage market but on her own independence. When she does, however, come into her fortune, circumstances have altered. She is not as rich as she was, and she has experienced anxiety and unhappiness. On different occasions she tries to recapitulate "the scheme of happiness," but the friends she has around her are those to whom she is already attached by circumstance, like widowed and peevish Priscilla Harrel, or old soft-minded Mrs. Charlton. She does do some good in her neighborhood, and during one period of bitter disappointment is roused from sorrow by the exhortations of the crazy prophet Albany, who impresses her with the amount of human suffering that needs aid. At that point, "Any scheme of worldly happiness would have sickened and disgusted her; but her mind was just in the situation to be impressed with elevated piety, and to adopt any design in which virtue humoured melancholy" (IV:710–711). She literally dreams again:

In her sleep she bestowed riches, and poured plenty upon the land; she humbled the oppressor, she exalted the oppressed; slaves were raised to dignities, captives restored to liberty; beggars saw smiling abundance, and wretchedness was banished the world. From a cloud in which she was supported by angels, Cecilia beheld these wonders; and while enjoying the glorious illusion, she was awakened by her maid, with news that Mrs. Charlton was dying! (IV:711)

Cecilia is not a Saint Cecilia in the clouds supported by angels. The immediate pain, sorrow, and loss in the world mock the tendency to the grandiose. Cecilia's dream is an Augustan dream, like the male dreams of power that inspired, for instance, Pope's *Epistle to Burlington:* "These Honours, Peace to happy Britain brings, / These are Imperial Works, and worthy Kings."[46] Burney, like Pope, echoes Anchises' injunctions to Aeneas:

> But *Rome*, 'tis thine alone, with awful sway,
> To rule Mankind, and make the World obey,
> Disposing Peace, and War, thy own Majestick way;
> To tame the Proud, the fetter'd Slave to free:
> These are imperial Arts, and worthy thee.[47]

Dryden's translation changes *parcere subiectis et debellare superbos;* sparing the subjugated becomes freeing the slaves, an idea that Burney retains although she partly retains Virgil's idea also, with an added echo of the Magnificat: "Thou hast put down the mighty from their seats/And hast exalted the humble and meek." But Cecilia is quite Virgilian (and quite like Richardson's Lovelace, too)[48] in retaining the *debellare superbos,* desiring to tame the proud and oppressive. Her dreamed-of power is sufficiently aggressive. With a fine unconscious hubris, Cecilia puts herself in the Virgilian Augustan heroic center—her female self: "*she* humbled . . . *she* exalted."

The glorious illusion is just illusion. Cecilia has to wake up to the world of change and death. If that were all she were saying, Burney would be a minor moralist in the Johnsonian mode, but her onslaught upon Augustan assumptions is more ambitious and more far-reaching than that. Cecilia's dreams are neither common sense nor common folly. They have been shaped by her own situation, including immediate psychological needs, but her entire situation is not just her psychological state, or even her personal background. She is, however unwillingly, a participant in and a product of a society that profoundly affects her. Like other good characters in the novel, such as Belfield and young Delvile, she has dreams of retiring from the foolish world, but in each case we can see that the character is a product of the world and has blind spots about that world. Every character in *Cecilia* is affected by social circumstances more profound than he or she can grasp, and it is often the circumstances, not just the individual, that the novelist wishes us to focus upon. Burney is one of the first novelists to see that each person is the bearer or representative of what Marxist critics have taught us to call an "ideology." The burden of her characters' ideology is not just a set of political assumptions (like Squire Western's with his fulminations against "*Hanover* rats") but the basis of their view of what is decent, natural, possible, or desirable, the unspoken platform of their values. If her characters are "type characters" they are so in the sense that Scott's characters are so—they have gone far beyond the shallower typifications of contemporary drama, beyond Sneerwell, Sir Brilliant Fashion, and Joseph Surface. The dramatic comedies from Congreve to Sheridan operated in an acceptable framework of social assumptions that allowed individual aberrations to be noted, but gave increasingly less room for disturbing discussion of general defectiveness. *The Witlings* itself follows that comic model, though the acceptance of things as they are is in some subtle conflict there with the theme of "self-dependence." It is as if Burney in her comedy had written out the more superficial approach and was ready for bigger issues and a more independent design in *Cecilia.*

It takes the reader some while to see how far this novel is prepared to go in challenging society. The natural initial reaction to the first debate is to try to determine who is right and who is wrong, which team to side with. We can begin to see that the terms of the debate are being juggled by speakers who have some personal interest at stake. (It suits Monckton's secret designs better if everyone else behaves properly and predictably.) But it is perhaps not until we are finished with the novel or are reading it again that we can see that something is wrong with the society that poses this question, that the terms themselves miss out too much. A certain notion of conformity adhered to with a zealous fidelity may lead to behavior so bizarre as to be "original." Such is the case with Monckton, and with Mrs. Delvile, although they are two very different people with different objectives, different causes, and different modes of breaking out or breaking down. The free-spirited "original" may be exploitative and authoritarian—as is the case with Belfield even as he engages in that debate, though he is at first carelessly ignorant of the wrong he has done to his female relatives. Indeed, most human behavior in the world of *Cecilia*, whether that of the thoughtless or the principled conformist, the conscious or careless free spirit, tends toward the gratification of the desire for power. And the structure of society in which the personages operate, which gave them their notions of the "beaten track" or of "originality" in the first place, determines the forms that aggression and vanity may take, and creates its own platforms of value. Class and Money are the ruling powers, and nobody can escape their force; they dictate the original assumptions determining an individual's ideas as to his—or her—behavior, whether it is right or wrong, prudent or imprudent. People may act badly from sincere morality.

One of the symptoms of living under such puzzling pressures is madness. Many of the major characters in this novel become insane at some point in their career: the list includes the heroine as well as her lover Mortimer, Mrs. Delvile, Monckton, Belfield, and the scornful prophet Albany. This last character is the only one who has actually been incarcerated in a madhouse. With his tattered looks, his wild gestures and religious ejaculations, Albany seems reminiscent of Charles Burney's friend Christopher Smart, the poet who was twice incarcerated in a madhouse and died in King's Bench Prison. Frances Burney knew him in his latter years: "a man . . . endowed with talents, wit, and vivacity . . . whose unhappy loss of his senses was a public as well as private misfortune."[49] He once gave her a rose. She pays tribute to his memory in *Cecilia* by having Mortimer Delvile quote him. Scalded by hot tea (a fate from which he has saved Cecilia) in an accident at the Pantheon, Mortimer retires, jokingly saying, "Like a brave general after being beat / I'll exult and rejoice in a prudent retreat." Burney adds a footnote with the one-word attribution "Smart" (II:289). The piece quoted, an "Epilogue Spoken by Mrs. Midnight's Daughter, riding upon an Ass dressed in a great Tie-Wig" was first spoken in 1753, as a vulgar and surprising end to an odd variety show, "Mrs. Midnight's Oratory." Smart himself seems frequently to have played the part of "Mrs. Midnight" in this Monty Pythonish piece, and the "Epilogue," a satire upon Dr. John Hill (represented in the wigged ass), was presumably spoken by another male impersonator as "Miss Midnight."[50] Young Delvile's quotation of this odd piece by Smart links him momentarily with the mad originals of *Cecilia*, and suggests a cross-sexual theme (submerged here, and not open as in *Evelina*). The violent satiric capering upon an ass, engaged in and created by the poet of "talents, wit, and vivacity," is invoked as part of the disturbance of order. Young Belfield, that unhappy wit, the man of "talents, wit, and vivacity" who is trying to make his way by his talents and shows signs of increasing strain, is another Christopher Smart figure. Smart haunts the novel's background, a shade of human unsuccess and an inquistor of things as they are.

The heroine of *Cecilia; or, Memoirs of an Heiress* may have been designed to be a more original character-type than our Cecilia. At some point, the heroine of the new novel was apparently to be an "unbeautiful, clever heroine, beset all round for the sake of her great fortune."[51] An "unbeautiful" heroine may have seemed a novelty beyond her readers' capacities, but the intelligent heroine beset for her fortune remained. As Crisp said, the idea "presents a large field for unhackneyed characters, observations, subjects for satire and ridicule, and numberless advantages you'd meet with by walking in such an untrodden path." The heroine's name originally, as we know from what survives of the draft manuscripts, was "Albina Wyerley." If the last name connects her with Clarissa's most generous-minded suitor in Richardson's novel, the first name was probably inspired by that of Hannah Cowley's heroine in *Albina, Countess Raimond* (1779). "Albina" (meaning "white") connotes candor, clarity of mind as well as innocence; the heroine's lover originally had a counterpart last name, "Albany," a name eventually given to the old moralist when "Delvile" was allotted as the surname for the hero's entire family. (Burney originally thought of both "Egerton" and "Randolph" as first names for her hero, but "Mortimer" is an excellent choice, with its antique deathly ring.) The candid but wiry Albina Wyerley—or Cecilia Beverley—brings out the colors and absurdities of her surroundings. Cecilia's story is a means of making us see a number of other stories, and the significance of the characters she encounters. The novel offers an ambitious cross-section of English society from high to low, and different kinds of analysis are employed.

The edgy Mr. Gosport, whose name (that of a real town) is a pun ("Gosport"), acts as an amused cicerone of satire, initiating Cecilia into London ways. He points out and labels the Jargonists, the Supercilious, the Volubles, and we see these in action—or inaction. The silent Miss Leeson ("the SUPERCILIOUS") may have been based on Queeney Thrale, or at least Frances Burney's first impression of her, as Burney wrote to Crisp: "She is reckoned cold and proud . . . you . . . would have . . . called her a girl of fashion; for she was very silent . . . and never looked tired, though she never uttered a syllable."[52] Mr. Meadows, the blasé young man seen at every gathering displaying his imperturbable languor, has more interesting pretensions to maintain. He insults a young lady by asking if she doesn't dance and then leaves her dangling: "'O, do dance!' cried he, stretching himself and yawning, 'it always gives me spirits to see you'" (III:335). He lives to proclaim his boredom:

"No," said he, yawning, "one can tolerate nothing! one's patience is wholly exhausted by the total tediousness of every thing one sees, and every body one talks with. Don't you find it so, ma'am?"

"*Sometimes!*" said Cecilia, rather archly. (III:336)

In Mr. Meadows, we see the trouble taken among the affluent to erect a behavioral superstructure to decorate the imbecility of affluent life. Dramatized boredom is as useless and flimsy as the often elaborate constructions of the affluent—the Harrels' gallery for the dance band, their dessert table, summerhouse, and theater. Meadows goes everywhere to show off a boredom he probably does not feel; trying hard to be original, he is a dedicated conformist. Cecilia, who really does find much of fashionable life wearisome, is not really able to say so, since she has inhibitions about rudeness. She is not impressed or upset by the foolish socialites, however, and can even poke sly fun to their faces, as with her covert hint to Meadows that she finds him tedious. She is equally able to cope with Miss Larolles, the energetic absurd prattler who feels some attraction to Meadows and who is evidently aware of her duty to get a husband at the parties she frequents, though that husband-hunting is the one subject she does not allude to.

Miss Larolles, who would not have missed a private masquerade "for the whole universe" and traveled "in an agony" to get there, is perpetually uneasy. It is in the language of the verbose Miss Larolles (a name presumably suggested by Parolles) that we first hear clearly the undersong of restless unfixed hostility which pervades the language of *Cecilia's* characters, as if society's pressures were emerging in unconscious expression. Miss Larolles's egotistical discourse often plays upon the misfortunes, actual or imagined, of someone else, though she is rarely as malicious as she is about Mrs. Mears's red dress: "if there is not Mrs. Mears in her old red gown again! I begin to think she'll never have another. I wish she was to have an execution in her house, if it was only to get rid of it!" (II:286). Secret violence lurks under her gushing hyperboles, and her language interestingly confuses pleasure and pain: "It was the most elegant thing you ever saw in your life; every thing quite in a style. I was so monstrously fatigued . . . I really thought I should have dropt down dead" (II:285). Miss Larolles cannot believe in any experience that is not life-threatening (even a milliner is "dangerous"). She cannot speak her trivialities without touching on the brink of all we hate—shock, distress, bankruptcy, madness, death—all the things that afflict Cecilia herself in her "real life," the larger narrative. The flibbertigibbet Larolles is herself a survivor, and makes of her empty life a catalogue of dangers survived where others have faltered: "I can't imagine . . . what poor Lady Belgrade will do with herself; I hear the creditors have seized every thing" (I:31).

It is in the language of Miss Larolles that we first hear of crashes and auctions, and the pleasure of preying upon the goods (like Lady Belgrade's diamond shoe-buckles) of those who have lost the game. Auctions were indeed popular at the time, providing spectacle and the pleasures of shopping and scandal combined. The business was an advertising business, with private possessions held up for public scrutiny. *Cecilia* reminds us of the reality behind those faded bills. Bankruptcy is a form of social death in the novel, the result and cause of "embarrassment" in all senses of the word. There is something very disturbing in the oft-used phrase "an execution in the house" (a phase first emanating from Miss Larolles); it is as if the fatal headsman can irresistibly and suddenly enter the domestic dwelling to carry out the grisly task, as if loss of capital were indeed decapitation. Wealth governs this society, where the highest sin against manners is running out of money. Money rather than Law pronounces sentences, but Money's sentences (like Miss Larolles's sentences) are abrupt and arbitrary.

Miss Larolles is a character highly useful to Burney. She attaches the light satire to the major satiric theme. Not only does she in her folly introduce many of the novel's most serious themes (cost, execution), but her uneasy language prepares us insensibly to feel the meaning within the more forcibly drawn satiric characters, the males who control rather than flutter.

The three guardians—Harrel the Man of Fashion, Briggs the Man of Wealth, Compton Delvile the Man of Family—are three controlling males. The guardianship of these three male elders is the first trouble that arises out of the very first calamity that befell Cecilia—the will of her uncle. Dean Beverley, controlling Cecilia from beyond the grave by his "will," her false friend Monckton, and the three legal guardians make up a pressure group of five men who are all for different reasons determined to prevent Cecilia from acting for herself. In giving Cecilia her set of legal guardians, Burney may well have been influenced by Susanna Centlivre's still well-known and acted play, *A Bold Stroke for a Wife* (1718), in which the heroine is in the care of four representative cranks and fools, and suffers from her "ragout of guardians," none of whom approves of the others. Burney may also have been influenced by Cumberland's *The Fashionable Lover* (1772), whose orphan heroine is in care of a bad guardian who has mulcted her of her inheritance. Augusta Aubrey's father, however, suddenly returns, having not in fact been dead these eighteen years, so all is well. In *Cecilia* Burney could certainly not show a good daddy turning up at last. There are no good daddies anymore. Here all efforts at paternalism are afflicted and afflicting. The various guardians are representative of the guardians of society who perpetuate injustice and waste through customary and legal authority. Burney's vision of wrong, expressed in her fable of the guardians who strip the girl of her wealth, was probably stimulated by her sense that her guardians Burney and Crisp, her two daddies, had taken control of her own treasure, her talent, from her and had wasted it.

The three bad guardians are of course comic characters, and at first the reader may be lulled into seeing them as just other representatives of typical folly, of the same kind as the easily visible fools of the fashionable crowds. That is, the novel seduces us into thinking matters lighter than they are, and into believing that characters are easily typified by a very accessible kind of satire. Mr. Harrel, the dashing spendthrift with the party-going wife, seems at first unproblematic, if irritating. The most complex of the guardians, he is the most slowly developed in the narrative. Mr. Briggs, the City miser, rises upon us in full luster. Briggs has all the mad self-deprivation associated with miserliness. But Burney's imagination has seen in the squalid Briggs the possibilities of tremendous enjoyment of life; he has a buoyant assurance that makes him, in spite of the misery conventionally associated with misers, one of the happiest characters in the novel. Briggs is a strongly physical being, and makes a distinct impact even before we see him, when he is heard shouting to his child servant about his shaving rag: "exclaiming, in a furious passion, 'Dare say you've filched it for a dish-clout!'" (I:93). He comes to Cecilia in his dirt-disguising snuff-colored suit, bearing his wig in his hand. "Twinkling his little black eyes in her face," he advises her about sweethearts: "Take care of sharpers; don't trust shoe-buckles, nothing but Bristol stones!" He is confident of his ability to deal with her life and her suitors: "bring 'em to me. Won't be bamboozled. Know their tricks. . . . Ask for the rent-roll,—see how they'll look! stare like stuck pigs! got no such thing" (I:96).

Briggs speaks contemptuously of tinsel and glass beads, but admires everything that belongs to himself, including his sweaty bald head. He speaks with frank interest of accretions and evacuations others would not mention. He attends the Harrels' masquerade party with clothes and bag borrowed from a chimney sweep, and then complains about the provisions: "got a great lump of sweetmeat; found it as cold as a stone . . . forced to spit it out; believe it was nothing but a snowball . . ." (III:453). His bodily experiences fascinate him, and he enjoys the benefits of nature's compound accretions of dirt. No wonder he objects to soap as a useless luxury. Burney essentially sees the connection suggested by psychologists between the child's first interest in the self-manufactured treasure of the feces and the adult passion for accumulation of things and money. Briggs, his own treasure store, enjoys perpetual renewal of energy. His statements, with their perverse wit, move in clipped beats. He elaborates phrases in clichéd similes of objects: "smart as a carrot," "snug as a church." In contrast to such quick efforts of elaboration, his sentences themselves are pared down, deprived of prepositions, conjunctions, pronouns, even verbs. In the manuscript, one can see Burney discovering the implications of Briggs's speech as she went, removing pronouns and conjunctions to render more sharply a speech-world practically devoid of connectives. Briggs, in his speech, expresses what is true of the world around the heroine. This is a world of disconnection, full of things but unpeopled. Persons are left out of Briggs's sentences along with the pronouns. The central pronoun is also rarely pronounced, but that is because Briggs does not have to say "I," since all is "I." The rest is but disconnected material world —dirt—made real only through the magic of his body. Briggs's language reflects the two impulses, to retain and excrete, to save and to invest, in a contradictory terse volubility.

If Briggs represents the too-too sullied nature of the basic "I," and of Money considered at its dirty fundamental meaning, Mr. Delvile, the Man of Rank, illustrates the uncertain status of a proud social "I" resting on a fabric of lofty fiction. His claims are based on history and historical abstraction. Mr. Delvile receives Cecilia after the same kind of delay as preceded her interview with Briggs, and his opinion of their relation is the same as Briggs's ("Lucky you've me!"), though his offensiveness is different. He speaks to her with conscious superiority, a reproving condescension, and cannot divine that this irritates her:

> A display of importance so ostentatious made Cecilia already half repent her visit. . . .
>
> Mr. Delvile, still imputing to embarrassment, an inquietude of countenance that proceeded merely from disappointment, imagined her veneration was every moment encreasing; and therefore, pitying a timidity which both gratified and softened him, and equally pleased with himself for inspiring, and with her for feeling it, he abated more and more of his greatness, till he became, at length, so infinitely condescending . . . that he totally depressed her with mortification and chagrin. (I:97–98)

We can see in this last paragraph the usefulness for the author of the third-person narrator, whose ironic judgment and tone color the narrative. The narrator can give the views and sensations of both parties, in their ironic disparity; "he abated more and more of his greatness" seems like a quick touch of free indirect speech, satirically turned, the "greatness" of self and manner being all in Delvile's mind. Delvile enjoys Cecilia's supposed embarrassment, misinterpreting disappointment and annoyance. (The heroine of this novel suffers far less from simple embarrassment than Evelina, and feels more conscious anger.) Of course Mr. Delvile cannot see what anyone else thinks or feels, since he is so thoroughly engrossed in the work of maintaining a position (as he literally maintains a position in ungallantly refusing to rise from his chair to greet her). Throughout the novel, Mr. Delvile's rigidity (the opposite of Briggs's élan) is a function of his reverence for that abstraction which is himself as his Name, his Family, his Rank. In London, people cannot see that other embodiment of the family, the proud symbol, Delvile Castle, so he has all the work to do on his own. And he is on his own, always solitary. It is absurd of him to say, "At this time of day I am generally in a crowd"—we never see him in a crowd, and any conversation taxes his energies to the utmost. Whenever he has anything to do, even just to give some directions to his servants, he thinks himself "overwhelmed with business" (III:516). People and things come into mind not as concrete images (no shoe-buckles or carrots crowd his speech), but as abstractions, usually abstractions of inferiority. Work—even the idea of it—is abhorrent to him. He tactfully asks Cecilia, "Your father, I think . . . did nothing in that way himself?" (II:260). The anxious euphemism reflects the refined shudder from the crude idea. If he is to uphold the banner of his class, he must not let reality touch him, even to sully his tongue. At home in Delvile Castle, he has the drawbridge drawn up every night.[53]

Delvile seems to fortify himself against others and against the world, which always threatens to invade his solitude and invalidate his meaning. His own niece, Lady Honoria Pemberton, an impertinent rattle to whom the author delegates the work of uttering some truths more cutting than the heroine can utter, sees Delvile's weakness. She impudently repudiates the importance of his (and her) aristocratic position, refusing to believe in the dilapidated castle. She suggests "some capital alterations"; "it is only to take out these old windows and fix some thick iron grates in their place, and so turn the castle into a gaol for the county" (III:505). With the proceeds of the sale, he could run up "a mighty pretty neat little box somewhere near Richmond." Mr. Delvile is infuriated at her jest and at his own son's laughter—as well he might be, for if the younger generations of his own class refuse to acknowledge his values, then his values and himself will disappear.

Mr. Briggs may be beyond Delvile's myopic vision, but Briggs can see Delvile and feels free to comment, even to his face, upon the absurdity of his pretensions and their origins:

> "Come to a fair reckoning," continued Mr. Briggs; "suppose you were in my case, and had never a farthing but of your own getting; where would you be then? What would become of your fine coach and horses? you might stump your feet off before you'd ever get into one. Where would be all this fine crockery work for your breakfast? you might pop your head under a pump, or drink out of your own paw; What would you do for that fine jemmy tye? Where would you get a gold head to your stick? You might dig long enough in them cold vaults before any of your old grandfathers would pop out to give you one."
>
> Mr. Delvile, feeling more enraged than he thought suited his dignity, restrained himself from making any further answer, but going to the bell, rang it with great violence.
>
> "And as to ringing a bell," continued Mr. Briggs, "you'd never know what it was in your life, unless you could make interest to be a dust-man. . . . Ay, love it, don't you? suits your taste; why not one dust as well as another? Dust in a cart good as dust of a charnel-house; don't smell half so bad."
>
> (III:455–456)

Briggs throws Delvile off-balance by imagining what has not been conceivable—Delvile alone, the entity or animated body of Delvile with a paw and an appetite and no social and economic identity. Briggs's cartooning sketch, enlivened by visions of ancestors popping out of their graves, of Mr. Delvile with a dust-cart, embodies the visions of ruin and degradation that haunt so many characters in the novel.

Briggs's attack points out that the structure on which Delvile relies is a fantastic and dirty fiction. Noble birth is a fiction derived from the dead. Delvile has no counterbalance of concrete reality to point to—all his effort is continually engaged in keeping the fiction going. His nervous sense of threatened identity is revealed by tricks of speech when he does speak, in ponderous abstractions, abstract and collective nouns. He utters the "I" which, unlike Briggs, he cannot leave to take care of itself: an "I" marks off each pleat of his stiffly folded sentences.

Of course Briggs is right in pointing out that Delvile's notion of his aristocratic identity, his purity of social significance, is derived from the dead, and from dust and dirt. Briggs does not see the complementary nature of the dirt—mud and soot—into which he literally falls or crawls. We can see that Burney in her fiction was now openly and daringly questioning the very structures in which her father devoutly believed, and which he served too readily. Making fun of the power of Money as embodied in a dirty City miser, an uneducated man, was one thing. Making fun of aristocratic Mr. Delvile, the patron, the condescender, was quite another. Burney shows not only her dislike of condescension, but her deeper belief that it is useless to ask "May I?" of powers represented ultimately by Briggs and Delvile. Although the reader is at first encouraged to see Briggs and Delvile as opposites, we begin to realize that Rank and Money are alike—in dirty origins, in suppression of utterances, in callousness. Briggs and Delvile are alike in the two consecutive chapters where Cecilia goes to each in turn to request some money of her guardians for charitable purposes and to pay her bookseller. Both are scandalized at her pursuits. (Delvile says, "a lady should . . . never degrade herself by being put on a level with writers, and such sort of people," II:186.) And neither wishes to permit her to spend her money, on charity or books or anything else. Each considers it only proper that a husband be found as soon as possible, a real person to take care of that money. Cecilia's property is not hers in the manner she thinks. Mr. Harrel, the most obviously wicked of the guardians, is only carrying social assumptions to their furthest extent when he secretly makes a bargain with Sir Robert Floyer, his partner in gambling, that Floyer can marry his ward for a consideration. Before Cecilia's arrival in London, she had been in effect sold—as another's property. Her dreams of Augustan works, her plans for an independent life, are ludicrous in the ironic light of circumstances. Mr. Hobson, the fat, buttered-toast-eating merchant, a counterpart to the austere Briggs, thinks it a pity women can possess any money at all: "the fault is all in the law, for making no proviso against their having money in their own hands" (V:883). He puts the matter crudely, but Harrel and Floyer in the upper classes hold similar beliefs.

The antifeminism of Cecilia's world is satirically brought out by the harsh or condescending statements made about or to her. The satire around the guardian characters is tougher than the ridicule of the party-goers. We notice gradually that the guardians have victims. There are many victims other than Cecilia who suffer from society's crazy customs and the powers of the social guardians at large. Cecilia's story is woven through a number of other stories of mistakes and deprivation; the heroine's problems and even misery are yet only aspects of a complex and general experience of suffering.

The first of the victims whom we clearly see is Mrs. Hill, widow of a carpenter who became incurably ill after an accident while working on Mr. Harrel's new villa, the prettily named Violet Bank. The son of the family has just died, and the family has no resources after paying for a good funeral for Billy, "for we could not bear but bury him prettily, because it was the last we could do for him" (I:87). The family now has no income save what the wife and female children can earn. Mrs. Hill repeatedly comes to Mr. Harrel's door to collect the twenty-two pounds that gentleman owes Hill. Cecilia, hearing her story, assumes that Harrel will pay at once—but of course he does not. Cecilia meddles: her guardian thinks her a fool and a nuisance. Cecilia has to learn how gentlemen may respond to the poor, and to the female in distress, when there are no pretty young ladies present. Mr. Harrel's callousness is worthy of any Malthusian villain in Dickens: "when I told him I had no help now, for I had lost my Billy, he had the heart to say, so much the better, there's one less of you" (I:85).

Cecilia acts with practical and continuous kindness and sense in helping the Hill family. She looks into the facts, and is shocked at finding out the conditions in which the family lives. She pays for the doctor's care, and for various necessities. After Mr. Hill's death, she sets Mrs. Hill up with a job in a haberdasher's shop, and sees to the education of the children in a manner appropriate to their situation and prospects. Such practical, officious, and far-sighted charity belonged more properly to the masculine sphere of action in the eighteenth century; the word "philanthropist" applies to the male not the female, and it is men who are supposed to imitate Providence in a "God-like" way. Yet Richardson had shown Clarissa Harlowe setting up a charitable trust, and female writers before Burney had been interested in imagining what a female philanthropist might do. Sarah Scott, Elizabeth Montagu's sister, and her friend Barbara Montagu tried to develop a charitable community for women at their home near Bath. In *Millennium Hall* (1762), Scott invented a fictional female commune performing charitable works, and in *The History of Cornelia* (1750) she had depicted a heroine of managerial talents, capable of introducing "a manufacture" and benefiting an entire village.[54] In dealing with a single woman with money and a sense of responsibility to the community at large, *Cecilia* follows a largely female literary tradition that counteracts the assumptions of Harrel and Hobson. That the idea had a real attraction for women may be reflected in the fact that *The Norfolk Ladies Pocket Book* for 1787 has a frontispiece drawn by Frances Burney's cousin, Edward Francesco Burney, portraying the scene in which Cecilia promises Mrs. Hill she will take care of her family (Fig. 15). The idea of female benevolence keeps odd company here; the title page promises "a Beautiful Descriptive Plate, representing an Interesting Scene from Cecilia; Likewise Six of the most Fashionable Ladies Head Dresses." The jumble of ideas sounds like something we might hear from the lips of Miss Larolles, and reminds us how quick advertisers are to draw everything into their sphere, even the story which tries to counter feminine subjection to fashion with a sense of female responsibility.

In the Hill episode, Burney wants the reader to understand the truth of what Mrs. Hill says: "Oh madam! if you did but know what the poor go through!" (I:85). Cecilia shows not only compassion but an understanding not all Burney's readers would share. The heroine sympathizes with the Hills' desire to give poor Billy a good funeral, and passes no strictures, even inwardly, on that expense. Nor does she criticize Mr. Hill's desire to leave the hospital and die at home. Many middle-class people of the time, including some women writers, would have commented on the ingratitude or at least ignorance of the poor. Burney does not condescend in that way. Cecilia's notion of Christian stewardship includes a sense of relationship to the poor, which makes her guilty of singularity indeed.

Cecilia's sympathy draws her most strongly to women, as the people who need most help. Albany later takes her to a "miserable house in a court leading into Picccadilly" and to the third story where "a wretched woman" lies ill with rheumatic fever, surrounded by noisy and untended children. Cecilia is able to enlist the help of "the woman of the house, who kept a Green Grocer's shop on the ground floor" in buying provisions, hiring a nurse, and paying an apothecary (V:767–768). Later she takes poor Mrs. Matt to the country to convalesce, before setting her up as a clear-starcher and seamstress. And Mrs. Matt, who worked as a pew opener in the church where the heroine's wedding was interrupted, is able—once she sees the Monckton household—to throw light on that affair. Women can be useful to each other.

It is Albany, the intense and uncomfortable Jeremiah dogging the fashionable crowds, who introduces Cecilia to many of the objects of her charity, including Mrs. Matt. A strong male seems to be the initiator of the network, the guardian of Cecilia's morality. Albany's efforts inspire amusement and annoyance in some, and real anger in others, especially Briggs and Monckton who regard Cecilia's money as their charge, not to be given away. Briggs cannot even bear to hear of a beggar: "would not have 'em relieved; don't like 'em; hate a beggar; ought to be all whipt; live upon spunging" (V:749). Mr. Hobson announces, "as to a beggar . . . I take 'em all for cheats; for what I say is this, what a man earns, he earns" (V:749–750). Albany's fulminations against "the niggard cant of avarice" (V:750) can make no impression here, nor do the appeals that mean so much to Cecilia impress Monckton. Monckton speaks reasonably to Cecilia about the dangers of being "governed by Albany, whose insanity is but partially cured, and whose projects are so boundless, that the whole capital of the East India Company would not suffice to fulfil them" (V:770). But inwardly he is seething: "to see money thus sported away, which he had long considered as his own . . . excited a rage he could with difficulty conceal" (V:771). Monckton's general war against the poor makes it appropriate that Mrs. Matt, one of those unregarded poor women, should explode his career. Amid such oppressive variations of avarice, Albany seems impressively heroic, but the reader and the heroine undergo a shock at finding the basis of his insanity and his prophetic career.

Late in the novel, Albany tells his confessional tale to Cecilia: "Guilt is alone the basis of lasting unhappiness;—Guilt is the basis of mine, and therefore I am a wretch for ever!" (IV:704). Albany, born in the West Indies, was sent to university in England, where he fell in love with the fifteen-year-old daughter of a villager. He promised to marry her "in defiance of all worldly objections," but was recalled to Jamaica, came into his paternal inheritance, and forgot the girl, while he "revelled in licentiousness and vice." A fever incurred by intemperance brought on memory and remorse. Going back to England he found she had been seduced by another man; she implored forgiveness, but he spurned her, "barbarously struck her!—nor single was the blow!" (IV:706). He left her, then later repenting, went in search of her and, after two years, found her a street-walker dwelling in a brothel. He dragged her away to a house in the country, but the girl refused to take food, did not reply to him, "seemed deaf, mute, insensible . . . a settled despair fixed in her eyes" (IV:707). Only when she was actually dying did she acknowledge she had vowed "to live speechless and motionless, as a pennance [*sic*] for her offences!" Albany "kept her loved corpse till my own senses failed me," and has "lost all recollection" of the following three years (IV:708).

The story of Albany's girl seems a new commentary on the subject treated so lightheartedly in the ribald Streatham verses: "Black her eye with many a Blow . . . Now she lies exceeding low, / And as quiet as a Lamb." The girl's strange conduct at the end seems not simple penance, but a subtle revenge, as she caricatures what men seem to want of women—anorexia, silence, a decorous forgettableness here turned into the macabre unforgettable. It is not just Albany's desertion, or her seduction by another man, but Albany's physical cruelty that turned this unnamed girl into a prostitute. Albany at least is capable of remorse, knows that he has injured someone irreparably. Like the Ancient Mariner, he shot the albatross, and sometimes has to tell the tale of his own guilt. Once we see the guilt, however, we cannot take Albany simply as a clear satiric or prophetic voice; his injunctions are now subject to scrutiny. Ironically, this moral and spiritual guardian derived his spiritual capital from the injury done to a woman—just as Monckton has derived his financial and social capital from the injury done to Lady Margaret in marrying her, hoping for her quick death. (The opposite of the nameless young streetwalker, Lady Margaret torments her man by refusing to give up her life, instead of by refusing to live.) We begin to see by the time we get to Albany's tale that there is a general taint, that those men who advance themselves expect unconsciously to do so at the expense of women.

Even very attractive male characters may owe much more than they are aware of to the exploitation of women. Young Belfield is possibly the most attractive male character in the novel. He comes to the masquerade ball as Don Quixote, and tackles the world with some of Don Quixote's innocence. He believes in learning and wit, and is obviously well-read and witty, and kind and gracious. Yet he got his education at Eton and the university because his parents were willing to deny their daughters. Worse, since he has left the university he has been living among the aristocratic young men whose manners he affects, hoping vaguely for some place or position, having allowed the shop inherited from his father to go bankrupt. He is really sponging on his mother, and his sister Henrietta sees clearly what has gone wrong: Their mother "thinks all the rest of the world only made for his sake" and "used to deny both herself and me almost common necessaries, in order to save up money to make him presents" (II:222).

Henrietta loves her brother, but feels some justified resentment: "when we lived so hardly only to procure him luxuries he had no right to, I must own I used often to think it unfair" (II:225). Belfield never even noticed what the giving was costing the female household, but added to the injury by being ashamed of his relations. Cecilia is moved to sympathy for Henrietta, whom she finds in Belfield's lodging washing dishes—a lowly task rarely recorded in fiction of the time. But even Cecilia can forgive Belfield for not introducing his friends to his mother once she meets Mrs. Belfield; passionate and vulgar in her love of her son, she has muddled ambitions based on false premises: "But what is a daughter, madam, to such a son as mine? . . . Day after day I used to be counting for when he would come to tell me he'd got a place at court, or something of that sort" (II:315–317). Proud Mrs. Belfield assumes that the beautiful lady must wish to marry such a promising son, and hints loudly that all he needs to do is speak up. Mrs. Belfield is so used to exploiting herself and her daughter for her son's sake that she has no hesitation in sacrificing Cecilia and her fortune to that higher good. Cecilia tries to befriend Henrietta while keeping some distance between herself and Belfield, the more necessarily because her concern in the duel between him and Floyer has spread a rumor that Belfield and she have some kind of understanding. Belfield himself, who in fighting the duel proved his right to the title of gentleman at the cost of his health, has to face the reality of his position.

Belfield gives up his expensive law studies at the Temple and tries to find some other occupation, as he had already tried trade and the army. Provided by Mortimer with a job as a tutor-companion at Lord Vannelt's, he resents the patronizing disdain with which he is treated, "shaking off the base trammels of interest and subjection, I quitted the house . . . not chusing to remonstrate, where I desired not to be reconciled" (IV:661). Belfield's abrupt departure from Lord Vannelt seems very like Gabriel Piozzi's from the Duke of Ancaster in 1777; the musician found the post that Dr. Burney had obtained for him so disagreeable (he felt he was treated as a pet animal expected to "shew his tricks") that he fled, saying, "if he had left an eye behind him, he w^d. not go back to fetch it."[55] Burney's explicit sympathy with proud Belfield in his resentment of daily patronage as "oppression" illuminates her unease with the Greville episode in her father's life she comes to record in the *Memoirs*. After the experience among the great, Belfield drops out of polite society, insisting he can find "the true secret of happiness . . . Labour with Independence," as a day laborer (IV:659). His occupation in the fields lasts no longer than the others; he returns to London and becomes a hack writer, then exchanges this prostitution of his talents for the drudging mental work of an accountant.

Eighteenth-century literature has no better or fuller picture of the economic, social, and mental confusion that rising by the talents can involve than the portrait of Belfield in *Cecilia*. Education entails social rising, which is a hardship as well as a gain, requiring displacement; no visible assured place awaits the person who makes such a change. Belfield has partly shared Mrs. Belfield's greedy faith in the magic world of the great folks, but when he gets into trouble he has to realize he was only valued by his "friends" as an entertainer. In Belfield we see the social and psychological origins of apparent sycophancy, toadyism, snobbery. Burney makes amends for her characterization of Dabler in *The Witlings;* Belfield, the real "Man of Genius," can be dropped by affluent acquaintances as easily as the false poetaster. The problems of Belfield are the problems of the displaced risers Charles Burney and Frances Burney, ungentle geniuses who did not quite belong anywhere. In such conditions, it is very hard not to prostitute or misuse the talents to some degree. The defects of the individual are related to social causes; cultivation and talents (or the idea of "talents") exist in complex relation to social and financial status. At last acknowledging his own guilt toward his female relatives, Belfield still cannot bear to feel himself being looked down upon and mistreated.

Belfield is only one of many characters who are both exploiters and exploited. The most vivid example of such a character is Mr. Harrel, the modish trifler who seems at first a commonplace comic type. Harrel does not, like Briggs or Delvile, represent an essential value, like rank and money, but the effects of the reverence for these. His extravagance is all mediated desire; modish activities make him feel real to himself. Although he planned her sale to Floyer, the illegal desperate campaign by which Harrel personally swindles Cecilia of her fortune before she marries anyone was not designed by him from the beginning of his guardianship; it grows spontaneously from one extempore action to another. One of the novel's long movements is provided by the unfolding of

Harrel's constant criminality. The bold attrition of Cecilia's fortune begins in a fairly casual way. When Harrel is dunned for a tailor's bill, Cecilia herself offers to pay (thus making the first financial misstep) rather than have Priscilla's brother Arnott sell stock at a loss. Since her other guardians won't let her have the money, Harrel suggests recourse to a moneylender. He then gets another loan. Then, when creditors threaten Harrel with "three executions before night" (II:265), Mr. Harrel makes threatening gestures at his throat with a razor, declaring, "I will not outlive the seizure of my property" (II:266). An execution would be an execution indeed. Blackmailed at last into a wide promise to do anything necessary, Cecilia has let herself in for paying debts to the total of 7,500 pounds. After another visit to the usurer, she has parted with a total of 8,050 pounds, out of her liquid capital of 10,000 pounds, the only portion of her inheritance not subject to the restrictive clause in her uncle's will. Neither can parting with this enormous sum give her any of the pleasures of benevolence. In the next crisis, Cecilia is steeled (as she thinks) against Harrel and his tricks and melodramatic threats. Let him fly to the Continent. She takes a tough line with Harrel's brother-in-law, the gentle, worried Mr. Arnott, making him promise to get out of the way: "why should he be saved from it at all?" (III:378). In the draft of an earlier version, Burney made her heroine even more emphatically tough-minded:

> "I am both astonished & shocked at this acct.," said Albina, "& to find that yr. sister's connection with Mr. Harrel has been as unfortunate for you as for her. I am sorry to speak with severity of one so nearly allied to you, but the too great ascendant which he has gained over yr. soft & compassionate mind, will end in yr. utter ruin if you are not made sensible of yr. danger: be steady, therefore, in refusing to part with even an Inch of Land, for if there you once Waver, depend upon it, you are undone!"[56]

In the final version, the heroine's speeches are less emphatically harsh. Cecilia still takes a firm line to Mr. Arnott. Taking the firm line, however, Cecilia has underestimated the extent to which she herself can be moved. Under pressure of Priscilla Harrel's tearful requests, she begins to waver. Harrel appears to be out of his mind with rage, and poor Priscilla seems genuinely frightened: "I verily think . . . he will half murder me" (III:386). Harrel makes a bargain; he will fly to the Continent, but permit Mrs. Harrel to remain in England—*if* he is given one thousand pounds. Priscilla thus becomes a hostage. Cecilia, overcome, gives him the money; "perplexity and uneasiness, regret and resentment, accompanied the donation" (III:393). There seem to be no moral guidelines, no plain course free from guilt. As she says to Priscilla, "I know no longer what is kind or what is cruel, nor have I known for some time past right from wrong, nor good from evil!" (III:396)—a startling admission from an eighteenth-century heroine.

In what seems a feint to keep creditors from suspecting his flight, Mr. Harrel takes both women with him to Vauxhall, saying he will set out on his travels from there rather than from his home. Once in Vauxhall gardens he seems suddenly to be in a party mood, merrily collecting people and inviting them to supper. A miscellaneous and ill-matched party, including Meadows, fat Hobson, Sir Robert Floyer, and the toady, Morrice, become more and more flown with wine in a scene of comic disorder. This whole sequence is brilliantly turned. The Vauxhall scene is one of the best things in the English novel of the eighteenth century. In the middle of the tinselly and unreal place with its light, music, and crowds, we focus on the frantic gaiety of Harrel and his mad Champagne-party. The weird festivity is a fascinating and irritating superimposition upon real anxiety; the two women worry that Harrel may become too drunk to make his escape to the Channel, and keep hoping that he will make his departure. The episode illustrates Burney's use of counterclimax, frustration, and retardation; what should be urgent forward movement gets caught up in this wild eddy. The reader, like the heroine, does not know the occasion of his crazy last supper. The Vauxhall episode winds up the tension until the string breaks: "scarcely had Mr. Harrel quitted the box and their sight, before their ears were suddenly struck with the report of a pistol" (III:413). Mr. Harrel really was suicidal, after all.

Mr. Harrel tried to provide his own dramatic final climax, which the narrative refuses to acknowledge. His death is not even the end of the chapter. Exhausted Cecilia does not get away from Vauxhall until four o'clock in the morning, and we all go on with the business of making arrangements and assessing the damage—including the damage of miscalculation. Like Cecilia, we had thought Mr. Harrel's threats were all bluster, been persuaded that such a lightweight person could not do a heavy deed, that champagne never coincides with self-murder. Mr. Harrel himself has miscalculated. Nobody thinks him heroic. He has left behind him only a sheaf of bills labeled grandiosely *"To be all paid to-night with a* BULLET" (III:430). But a bullet does not pay bills. His death is an occasion for complaining comment, or grisly jokes, like Briggs's "a merry Vauxhalling, with pistols at all your noddles! . . . thought he'd tip the perch" (III:452). Harrel leaves others with loss; he has not only robbed Cecilia of 9,050 pounds but also foisted Mrs. Harrel upon her care. Yet, in his own way, Harrel has placated society by placing an absolute value upon the money that it honors. He had the lethal wish born of his obsession. Society itself has invented the concept of "ruin," the great communal sneer. With "an execution in the house" the public identity is annihilated. Characters in the novel cannot imagine enduring the pain of such rejection, being left with a shrinking person, left without the public mask, any more than Delvile can imagine himself drinking from his own paw under a parish pump. The annihilation of the loved identity is more inconceivable than death itself—Harrel literally cannot bear to disappear from the scene of the party. "One must live a little like other people"; not living like other people is to be a dead man. Harrel's pathetic villainy is the result of his frantic desire to belong, to conform, to tread the path marked out. He is a deluder and exploiter, but he is also truly a victim. A necessary sacrifice to the social delusions, he falls like a Spartan obeying the laws.

The public death of Harrel in the exact center of the novel supplies a mock "ending"—Harrel thought of it as *the* ending—and prepares us for breakdown, the collapse of smooth appearances and convenient pretenses. We have also by this time been taught that characters' behavior may not develop toward conclusions that look generically safe or aesthetically conventional. The Harrel story, which governs the first half of the novel, prepares us for the more complex developments of the story of Cecilia and the Delviles, the ironic "love story."

When she first meets him, Cecilia is unable to "conjecture" the identity of the teasing and agreeable young man at the masquerade. He is known to her only as "the white domino." That is, Mortimer Delvile, the white (*albus, Albinus*) appears to her first as a blank. He has not come under his own or any other name. The hero may be, as Terry Castle says, "clad in a chic (and morally impeccable)"[57] costume, whose significance he is anxious to spell out: "you will find me as inoffensive as the hue of the domino I wear" (I:116). But the allegory is not so simple. The white masquerade habit, which conceals without substituting another signifier, ironically has significance after all. It reveals Delvile's own unwitting obsessions—his desire to remain innocent, uncommitted, uncontaminated. In terms of the novel's themes, his blank appearance is a good indication of the young man's dependence on others to supply an identity for him, and of his inability to give himself away. The white domino is even a unisex costume and, as we have seen, Delvile's later quotation from Smart's Epilogue connects him fleetingly and in a hidden way with a disturbing and "carnivalesque" transvestite appearance. He is in his first appearance like most women (as Pope and Lady Smatter have it), in possessing "no Character at all." He teases the heroine to find out his character, but at a deeper level of the novel he is pleading to her to help him find an identity. In some ways, he badly needs rescuing.

The riddle of his identity is in one sense quickly answered. The hospitality offered at the Delviles' London house by Mortimer Delvile and his delightful mother makes amends for the pompous hauteur of Compton Delvile. At the death of Harrel, Cecilia is invited to stay at Delvile Castle, and friendship with Mortimer flourishes. Cecilia is a bit nervous that her friend Mrs. Delvile might intervene and try to accelerate her son's courtship. When offered a confidential conference, embarrassed Cecilia fears a promise of assistance which her pride must reject (III:498–501). But Mrs. Delvile's carefully tactful speech makes plain that she envisages Cecilia's future as having no possible connection with that of her son. "Undeceived in her expectations," Cecilia has to revise her notion of her relationship to this prospective ideal mother-in-law, while blaming "the haughty, impracticable father" (III:502) for whatever the puzzling obstacle may be. She and the reader concentrate on the conventions of courtship, and don't see the Delviles' reasons until Mortimer, with ungallant clarity, explains. The obstacle has been always present in his own mind—the name-clause: "barbarous and repulsive clause!" To marry under those conditions "would degrade me for ever!" (III:512). Cecilia's mixed feelings "between anger and disappointment, sorrow and pride" find relief in a private outburst:

> "Well, let him keep his name! since so wonderous its properties, so all-sufficient its preservation, what vanity, what presumption in me, to suppose myself an equivalent for its loss!"
>
> (III:514−515)

But Mortimer Delvile has been taught that his name has wondrous and magical properties. Without it, that magic cloak, he could not exist at all. He is, as he has been taught, his name. The only son and only child of a proud and foolish man dedicated to the cause of representing his ancient family which is its name, Mortimer cannot imagine stepping out of that system. The dean's will puts the man who marries Cecilia in a feminine position; it is the custom ("barbarous and repulsive"?) that women should change their surname upon marriage. Thus are genealogies and patriarchies established. Young Mortimer Delvile is confronted with a change of identity whereby he would be defined by the female Other. To betray the patriarchal line—and to such an extent—would be self-betrayal. Cecilia blames hereditary arrogance but forgets the arrogance of her uncle, the dean, in his mad attachment to his name.

Young Mortimer is bound to suffer once he is roused to a state of real longing and finds that what he longs for has an impermissible condition attached. To obey the impulse of love would be, according to his lights, committing a kind of suicide. Yet repressing his love proves self-destructive, and he falls ill. Mortimer is a very surprising hero in a love story—so likable, so nervous, so weak. Never was lover-hero more ruthlessly treated in his own novel. In the analysis of Mrs. Delvile the authorial narrator has already indicated some of the difficulties of Mortimer's position as son and only child:

> [Mrs. Delvile] rather idolised than loved him. . . . Whatever was great or good she expected him to perform; occasion alone she thought wanting to manifest him the first of human beings.
>
> (III:462)

Her attitude is very like that of vulgar Mrs. Belfield doting on her son.

The authorial irony is supported by Lady Honoria's directly sarcastic remarks, when she (like good Dr. Lyster) is amused at the parental fuss over Mortimer: "Why, this tender chicken caught cold . . . and not being put to bed by its mama, and nursed with white-wine whey, the poor thing has got a fever." Lord Ernolf replies that Mr. Delvile may be forgiven anxiety over a son who "is the last of so ancient a family," to which Honoria makes a strong retort: "That is his great misfortune . . . because it is the very reason they make such a puppet of him" (III:484). Mortimer's father "did not merely cherish but reverence him as his successor . . . without whose life and health the whole race would be extinct." Mr. Delvile consulted his son in all his affairs, "and expected the whole world to bow down before him" (III:462). Made into an idol and image, Mortimer has not been able to act for himself, and has been repeatedly enfeebled by parental spoiling. Lady Honoria openly thinks him babyish, and makes insulting jokes when she finds that Mortimer is not only being packed off to Bristol for his health, but must have his father accompany him:

> Lady Honoria . . . seized one of the napkins, and protested she would send it to Mortimer for a *slabbering-bib:* she therefore made it up in a parcel, and wrote upon the inside of the paper with which she envelloped it, "A *pin-a-fore* for Master Mortimer Delvile, lest he should daub his pappy when he is feeding him."
>
> (III:516)

The babied Mortimer is at this point still conforming, still trading the beaten track in obedience to the social and familial idea.

Mortimer as a character has a very important role as a special example of social victimization. Theoretically, Mortimer is at the top of the whole social pyramid. The young white male, the feudal inheritor with the world before him—and a world expected "to bow down before him"—is apparently the beneficiary for whom the whole arrangement of an empire has been designed. To procure goods for his drawing room and table, wealth and commerce flourish; to serve him at a humbler level, carpenters and haberdashers and greengrocers and clear-starchers perform their labors. For him the dead ancestors—now dust in vaults—have held their castle and their feudal honors, and his name and rank lend luster to all assemblies of wealth and fashion. He is the Heir—so different from the Heiress—the eldest son, the winner who takes all under the laws of primogeniture, the patriarch-to-be honored in that light by his father before him. But Burney shows that the apparent beneficiary is really another sufferer. Males can suffer as well as females from the imposition and constraints of an artificial system, and trying to live up to a theoretical position and an artificial identity robs nature of its strength and puzzles the will. Overloaded with external imperatives, young Delvile shrinks and weakens. His virility is ironically threatened by the very institutions which honor only males. Even his life is in danger. The novel shows there is a suicidal tendency in all fidelity to society's arrangements. In trying to preserve their sacred idea of Mortimer Delvile, the Delvile parents are willing to risk killing the real, physical individual, the human Mortimer.

Plucking up courage (once he is away from home), Mortimer returns to Cecilia. Finding she does love him, he conquers his aversion to the name-clause and declares himself willing to change his name. She consents to marry him in a clandestine wedding, and, after many changes of mind and retardations upon the way, Cecilia is persuaded that she must go through with the ceremony. The ceremony is, however, mysteriously interrupted—as in the later novels, Ann Radcliffe's *The Italian* (1797) and Charlotte Brontë's *Jane Eyre* (1847). Still unmarried, Cecilia goes home to live independently; she tries to keep herself busy in books and charities, to realize some of her original "scheme of happiness," but no longer has the freedom of heart to make her old scheme a pleasure. Nor can her establishment ever realize the old ideal: she has to house the bored Mrs. Harrel, and even sweet Henrietta Belfield, whom Cecilia has taken in, proves an unsatisfactory companion who has developed an inconvenient love for Mortimer. Her home is not Millennium Hall. Sisterhood, even when practiced, is not free from disappointments. Friendship has proved hard to find. And the woman formerly her closest female friend becomes her antagonist.

The aborted wedding gives Mrs. Delvile opportunity to encounter Cecilia and put a stop to relations between the girl and her son. Mrs. Delvile proves adroit in her maneuvers at each interview, taking advantage of the young woman's confusion to provoke her into usable statement, judiciously appealing to her, scolding her, flattering her. She cleverly equates Mortimer's loss "of the name he seemed born to make live" with a kind of murder. To make him lose his name would be "a crime." Renunciation is Cecilia's "duty" (IV:635–643). The argument itself is all about words, or about the meaning of the word "Delvile," a metonym made to function as if it were literally the entity "family." Mrs. Delvile is a cleverer blackmailer than Harrel, who took only the girl's money; Mrs. Delvile wants to take over her consciousness.

Cecilia has not really understood properly the pleasant woman who befriended her. Monckton was right, however, in saying that Mrs. Delvile is "the daughter of pride" (II:256). It is a good touch to make Mrs. Delvile Mr. Delvile's cousin, so that family pride is not something she adopted on her marriage but the only thing to make that enforced marriage reasonable and supportable. Surprisingly, this idea evidently came to Burney fairly late. In a manuscript draft (not a very early one, for the heroine is here "Cecilia" and not "Albina"), the heroine defends Mrs. Delvile (here "Mrs. Albany"):

> Cecilia . . . though she ventured not to name either the Son or the Father . . . vindicated Mrs. Albany herself with great spirit, justly observing that the hereditary Faults of the Family, whatever they might be, c^d. not possibly descend to one who was only connected with it by alliance.
>
> "She is therefore, but so much the worse," s^d. Mr. Monckton, "for she came herself from a race cruelly haughty, the Coverleys, & all the

insolence of her own Family she has engrafted into theirs, a Union which has expelled even the Shadow of decency from their arrogance."[58]

Added haughtiness and a new element of "insolence" from the Coverleys (an echo of Jack Coverley in *Evelina?*) came into the family attitudes. This explanation for Mrs. Delvile's passionate behavior must have come to seem unsatisfactory and even superficial. Burney found the perfect thematic solution, making both the senior Delviles serve one idea. That Mr. and Mrs. Delvile are cousins adds to the impression of them as enclosed, barricaded against the world. Mrs. Delvile herself apparently maintained identity in not changing her name upon her marriage—a reflection of what Cecilia is supposed to do in keeping hers. Serving the Family as an ideal, loving the abstraction of the family name because it justifies the sacrifices of her life, Mrs. Delvile is not going to be at all complaisant or agreeable when Cecilia threatens the purpose and meaning of her life. Cecilia cannot see how great is Mrs. Delvile's investment in the system to which she herself has been sacrificed, how ruthlessly far she is prepared to go. Young Delvile, at least, insists that he will not take his mother's word that Cecilia has renounced him; he must come to say good-bye. Mrs. Delvile supervises and orchestrates the short interview, but it gradually moves out of her control, and the room is charged with emotional currents.

Burney said this "conflict scene" in *Cecilia* is "the very scene for which I wrote the whole book." It is a three-way fight, with three different views in contention, but essentially this climactic scene in the novel is a struggle between the two women. The surviving draft shows that considerable rewriting was involved. In the earlier draft version the author makes the conflict between mother and son ("Egerton") over "Albina" more explicit from the outset of the interview. Mrs. Delvile loses control over her temper almost at once and appeals to her authority too soon, in tones of great anger and self-pity; her son defends himself too meekly, too slavishly:

> Mrs. Delvile, with an air calm though displeased, answered, "Who should have said to me but 2 Days ago, that I should live to know the bitter moment when my Son would brave my anger, & defy my authority,—who should have said this to me, & not have been Laughed to scorn, or pitied as insane?"
>
> "Reproach me not, Madam, I beseech you!" answered he, in a tone of the most submissive entreaty; "the Man lives not who loves, who reveres his Mother as I do! & hitherto to obey you has been my pride, pleasure, & first wish. To have spared you any pain, or given you any comfort, there is nothing I would not have sacrificed,—no not even Miss Beverley, though the peace of my life had flown wth. the resignation—but the Time is now past when that sacrifice is in my power—for scarce are you more my Mother, than I consider her as my Wife.—"[59]

In this draft, the son is crippled by Oedipal feelings: he admits that his mother is more important to him than his betrothed. The language used is inappropriate, in eighteenth-century terms, from a son to a mother. The statement "hitherto to obey you has been my pride, pleasure, & first wish" might be used by a dutiful son (like Wolfgang Amadeus Mozart) to a father, but it is even more appropriate to a *daughter* addressing a father. But neither in the draft nor in the published version does anyone present care about Mortimer's *father;* what Compton Delvile might feel is of concern to no one. In a novel that displays the patriarchal, the real emotional power and the only true acknowledged authority belong to the matriarchy. Burney cut out such excessive submission as is displayed in the draft's speech when she represented Mortimer trying cautiously to rebel, but she never thinks it ought to be easy for him to disregard his mother, even if he must rebel.

Mortimer had already rebelled more emphatically; earlier, when he was proposing a secret wedding to Cecilia, he asked, "is there no time for emancipation?" and reminded Cecilia that they were fortunate in "circumstances to relieve us from slavery" (IV:572). He had argued that his family were "Slaves . . . to habits, and dupes to appearances," who could not be rationally argued out of "notions that exist but by prejudice." The Delviles' ideas "have been cherished too long for rhetorick to remove them, they can only be expelled by all-powerful Necessity" (IV:564). This is Romantic and revolutionary rhetoric, with a vocabulary that sets up emancipation against slavery, reason against prejudice, Necessity against mere notions of things. We seem to be hearing Godwin's language eleven years before *Political Justice.* But when the big "conflict scene" takes place, there is no philosophical rhetoric at Mortimer's command. It is embarrassing to see that all he can do is waver, slowly. Mrs. Delvile resorts to threats and commands, and finally to the jeer direct: "How will the blood of your wronged ancestors rise . . . when wished joy upon your marriage by the name of *Mr. Beverley!*" (IV:677). This attack momentarily demoralizes Mortimer—the disappearance of the idea of himself is too much. He cries, "you have conquered!" and his mother cries, "Then you are my son!" But her triumph is an anticlimax—the scene changes when the young people escape her control simply by leaving the room. The flow of psychic power reverses, and Mortimer at length can assert, "I will not give her up!" (IV:680)

Mrs. Delvile comes to the end of her powers. Embarrassment and humiliation in the face of rebellion create unendurable feeling; the pressure within has been building during all her unhappy married life with its long study for self-control. Something has to burst. She rushes out of the room crying, "My brain is on fire!" (IV:680) and falls in an apoplectic fit. Burney may have taken satisfaction in visiting upon Mrs. Delvile the autocrat the same fate that befell the arbitrary Henry Thrale. Certainly some readers enjoyed it, like the Duchess of Portland who "called out 'I'm glad of it with all my heart!'"[60] But Burney also knows that the middle-aged, charming, aristocratic, and highly passionate Mrs.

Delvile has been a victim over a long period of time. "To love Mr. Delvile was impossible" (a good sentence, a clause beginning with passion and ending with frustration).

The marriage has cost Mrs. Delvile altogether too much; something has to give way. Mrs. Delvile's almost suicidal passion leads in fact to a revision of her life—the nearest thing to a reformation of character that Burney ever drew (she was no believer in reformation). Once she is weak instead of strong and successful, Mrs. Delvile begins to side with her son against her pompous and impossible husband. Husband and wife fight with each other, with Cecilia as an issue: "they parted without conviction, and so mutually irritated with each other, that they agreed to meet no more" (V:815). On recovering, Mrs. Delvile lives abroad, and her husband in England; the separation is evidently permanent. Burney's allowing Mrs. Delvile to separate from her husband is a quietly daring stroke on the author's part. Mrs. Delvile at last recognizes that she cannot accept the old terms of her existence. She had nearly cut off her life in the service of an outworn ideal. Burney was probably subconsciously moved to offer the Delviles (more particularly the wife) the relief of separation because of her intuition of the relief Henry Thrale's death had given his widow.

However derived, the separation of the Delviles represents a weakening of the class Compton Delvile has represented, once his wife is not present to underwrite his pretension by her attractive performance of aristocracy. The tacit divorce indicates a shift in class and values. An important image for antique class and values is Delvile Castle (Lady Honoria's "gaol"). The image is used in an interesting way by Mr. Gosport, who, suspecting Cecilia's attraction to young Delvile, teases her about the state of her heart. The fortress, "even in ruins," proves its old strength and teaches "the infallible power of time":

> "Many a fair structure have I seen, which like that now before me,"
> (looking with much significance at Cecilia), "has to the eye seemed . . .
> unhurt either by time or casualty, while within, some lurking evil, some
> latent injury, has secretly worked its way into her very *heart* of the edifice,
> where it has consumed its strength, and laid waste its powers, till, sinking
> deeper and deeper, it has sapped its very foundation, before the super-
> structure has exhibited any token of danger."
>
> (IV:598−599)

On the plot level, this allegorical metaphor points only to the state of Cecilia's heart, and the meaning is not, as Cecilia claims, "rather obscure." But on the thematic level of the novel the metaphor's energies point in the opposite way, and the figure of the castle so figuratively emphasized can bear other significations. Just as the heart (emotions, attitudes) of a person may change over time, so, too, may a social institution or set of public attitudes, signified by the castle partly ruined like the feudal past. The words "foundation" and "superstructure" leap out at us because Marxists have taught us how to employ them, but their use here seems anticipatory, not just coincidental. The superstructure of Cecilia's society may seem normal while the foundations are already sapped. *Cecilia* exhibits a social superstructure of money-getting, spending, party-giving, while also clearly indicating that social foundations are unsound and uneasy, that shifts and ruin and fragmentation (in all their revolutionary and romantic senses) may be expected. The Delvile marital separation is one of those shifts or fissures, a healthy ruination and sliding into fragments of what was before, while apparently "perfect in all its parts," a sickly and unstable whole.

The Delvile marriage repeats a central figure of the novel's plot—the high cost of marriage. The conflict of Cecilia and Mortimer's union arises over the predetermined cost to one of the parties of Cecilia's marriage (either the man's name or her property has to go). Cecilia falls in love with the wrong man, the very one least likely to accept the name-clause. Cecilia does fall in love, romantically, and has to admit that this is so. The first recognition by both lovers of their plight comes during a romantic storm. After the first rejection and separation Cecilia betakes herself to "a thick and unfrequented wood" where, "having now no part to act," she can give way to unrestrained weeping, consoled only by the affection of Delvile's dog, the emblematically named Fidel. The same dog is the only apparent addressee of her passionate soliloquy in the "romantic consolation" of apostrophizing (IV:546), in the summerhouse, an avowal of love overheard by Mortimer. The German edition of the novel (published in Dresden in 1790) presents this tender scene (with an eager hero in ambush, and the heroine at a disadvantage) in its only illustration (Fig. 16). These lyric scenes of delicate female passion have been favorites, particularly with male readers from Laclos to Pat Rogers.[61] But it is important to notice also that Cecilia in some degree resents her own feelings, and does not fall in love without putting up a good deal of resistance.

Nor does the novel itself unwaveringly end the love story, surrounded by so many ironies and parodic touches, including Lady Honoria's running commentary. Mortimer catches cold after the romantic storm, the sensibility lavished upon Fidel is paralleled by Miss Larolles's fuss over her unfortunate dog. The word "romantic" (in all its current senses) and the word "conflict" chase each other through the love-story scenes. Few of the conflicts are truly reconciled. The young couple do marry at last; once Mrs. Delvile agrees to give "separate consent" Cecilia feels that she can ignore Mr. Compton Delvile's opinion, and even his definite ban—a striking repudiation of paternal power and the necessity for permission. Cecilia treats Mr. Delvile's prohibition with disdain: "I will make him no promise; to Mrs. Delvile alone I hold myself bound; to him . . . I shall always hold myself free" (IV:692). Separating female right from male power, Cecilia defiantly joins the female side, refusing to enlist under the banner of patriarchy, and holding herself free of filial obedience to any father.

She—and the reader—are so caught up in the technicalities of permission, the hurry and anxiety over Monckton's machinations and the duel, that we subordinate the fact that Mortimer Delvile does not take Cecilia's surname when he marries her. They have forgotten that the instant she marries without her husband's name-change, she has lost the property. The next heirs are not so blind, and Cecilia is immediately expelled from her estate. Mortimer, in an overflourish of virility after long passivity, fights a duel with Monckton and seems to have killed him; Cecilia pursues her husband with frantic anxiety through the streets of London in a nightmarish sequence ending with her collapse in a pawnbroker's shop. Delirious, nearly penniless, she is advertised in the *Daily Advertiser* under the heading "MADNESS." Cecilia, who had thought she was not to be "set up for sale," becomes an object, advertised as a lost property. She is not a very valuable property: *Memoirs of an Heiress* proves an ironic title, as from an "Heiress" she is reduced to a Nobody, to that personal self almost bare of social identity: "Whereas a crazy young lady, tall, fair complexioned, with blue eyes and light hair, ran into the Three Blue Balls, . . . on Thursday night . . ." (V:901). Reduced to the thing itself, unaccommodated woman, Cecilia seems strange and mad, and her cries and struggles against the locked door only confirm the diagnosis. The landlady with kindly intentions brings her a bundle of straw, "having heard that mad people were fond of it"—perhaps the novel's most macabre illustration of received ideas and the usefulness of the beaten track.

Burney cannot leave her heroine in such a predicament, nor can she kill her off—though she teases us with a deathbed scene. Cecilia may go through some of Clarissa's experiences but the novel is not *Clarissa*, and there is certainly no need to deflect the satire by superimposing a tragic ending. Cecilia recovers from a state which reflects that of Albany's girl, "senseless, speechless, and motionless" (V:918). Found by Albany, claimed by Mortimer, even exciting some compunction in Compton Delvile, Cecilia returns from tragic fate to marriage and compromise. Mrs. Delvile's sister leaves her the legacy she once intended for Mortimer, in order that Cecilia should have something of her own, some slight share of "that power and independence" of which Mortimer himself knows "her generous and pure regard for himself had deprived her" (V:939). She can do some good, but nothing like that of her glorious Augustan dreams, which have now been shot through with Georgian realities. Cecilia may be a survivor after all, but she is not much of a success. The novel ends on a sober middle note in its closing words, the last description of Cecilia's life:

> yet human it was and as such imperfect! she knew that, at times, the whole family must murmur at her loss of fortune, and at times she murmured herself to be thus portionless, tho' an HEIRESS. Rationally, however, she surveyed the world at large, and finding that of the few who had any happiness, that there were none without some misery, she

checked the rising sigh . . . and . . . bore partial evil with chearfullest resignation.

(V:941)

The first edition of *Cecilia* was a large one for the time: two thousand copies. Even this event brought some partial evil; the author, who had received 250 pounds, was indignant, as she had expected a smaller first issue and further repayment on any reprinting. Crisp, however, thought she had done well: "if she can coin gold at such a Rate, as to sit by a warm Fire, and in 3 or 4 months . . . gain £ 250 by scribbling . . . only putting down . . . whatever comes into her own head . . . she need not want money."[62] The encouraging daddy underestimated her treasure and her labors.

Cecilia was not girlish "scribbling" but an attack upon the world, a judgment not mediated by the girlish naïvetés of an *Evelina*. And here Burney had taken up not the easy targets like bad-tempered sea captains, painted old coquettes, and cits but the great world itself; she had looked into society's, rather than her heroine's, embarrassments. At home, she was still "Fannikin" but in literature she was a force to be reckoned with. She did not shrink from public praise in Samuel Hoole's "Heroi-Comic Poem" *Aurelia* (1783), although that publicized her even more than *Warley* or the "Advice to the *Herald.*" In Hoole's poem, the guardian genius of womankind (or of "the wiser females of the world") says,

> I stood, a favouring muse, at BURNEY's side,
> To lash unfeeling Wealth and stubborn Pride,
> Soft Affectation, insolently vain,
> And wild Extravagance with all her sweeping train;
> Led her that modern Hydra to engage,
> And point a HARRELL to a mad'ning age:
> Then bade the moralist, admir'd and prais'd,
> Fly from the loud applause her talent rais'd.[63]

Frances Burney copied out this passage in her journal letters. She did not fly all applause. Patronizing as Hoole's poem may be in some ways, it was right on a central point. Let there be no more of "dear little Burney." This author is no longer to be treated as a naïve juvenile Evelina. A female author could administer the lash of satire, and that female was "BURNEY"—without the diminutives.

The immediate reviews were almost entirely favorable, and usually lengthy. Even the shortest and most condescending of these, in the *Gentleman's Magazine*, although surprised at the exhibition of "more knowledge of the world, or the *ton,* than could be expected from the years of the fair authoress," admits the "authoress" to the ranks of strong satirists: the novel "holds up a mirror to the gay and dissipated of both sexes in which they may see themselves and their deformities at full length."[64] Although critics were more interested in spelling out the satire upon the Harrels than in seizing the novel's troubling implications regarding the whole of society, they recognized the novelist as an author of significant power. The *English Review* and the *London Magazine* praised the novel's organization: "This novel is planned with great judgment, and executed with great skill and ingenuity" (*London Magazine*).[65] Reviewers incessantly praised the characters, "well drawn and well supported" *(Critical Review);*[66] "fairly purchased at the great work-shop of life and not the second-hand, vamped-up shreds and patches of the Monmouth-street of modern romance" *(English Review).*[67] The *English Review's* critic stresses the novel's truth to life, its realism: "No event takes place but what might have happened to any one," he says—surprisingly. He values unsentimental consistency of character: "No miraculous variety of disposition takes place which nature forbids"; he approves the unredeemable folly of Mrs. Harrel: "after all her misfortunes, we have her ready to begin again her course of futility." This reviewer raises only two objections. The first is an objection to the lack of physical description of the characters; evidently readers preferred to be able to visualize their heroes and heroines in detail. The second and stronger objection is to the conclusion:

> We shall conclude what we have to say on this excellent Novel with just hinting, that had the Eggleston family been represented as more worthy of their good fortune, or had a flaw in the Dean's will enabled Miss Beverley to enter again into possession of her estate, perhaps the conclusion would have left a more pleasing impression on the mind.[68]

Other readers and reviewers also pressed for heartier poetic distribution of rewards and punishments:

> Cecilia's conduct, in sacrificing so large a fortune to gratify the pride of the Delvile family, is an example which we would by no means wish to propose as an object of imitation for the fair sex, nor do we entirely approve of the conclusion, as we are of opinion that the pride and ostentation of old Delvile, ought, in justice, to have been punished; and the haughty slave convinced of his folly, by feeling in his own person the destructive consequences of his inhumanity.
>
> *(Critical Review)*[69]

It is amusing that reviewers who usually worried over the pernicious effects of idle love stories upon impressionable females could also worry about a novel's teaching members of "the fair sex" to despise money and neglect the duty to retain property. We can also see that Burney had broken a "rule" in an aesthetic derived from dramatic theory of the neoclassical school when she wrote her conclusion. She had not arranged totally exemplary fates for the characters, and deliberately ended her novel in a minor key, on the note of ironic "chearful

resignation." Many readers found this ending puzzling and objectionable—
Edmund Burke among them:

> He wished the conclusion either more happy or more miserable; "for in a
> work of imagination," said he, "there is no medium."
>
> I was not easy enough to answer him, or I have much . . . to say in
> defence of following life and nature as much in the conclusion as in the
> progress of a tale; and when is life and nature completely happy or
> miserable?[70]

Although she did not feel up to arguing with Edmund Burke in public on the
matter, Burney could and did defend the ending of her story to Crisp, who was
opposed to the loss of Cecilia's fortune, and tried to persuade the author to alter
the ending she wrote. She disagreed:

> I must frankly confess I shall think I have rather written a farce than a
> serious history, if the whole is to end, like the hack Italian operas, with a
> jolly chorus that makes all parties good and all parties happy! . . . Besides,
> I think the book, in its present conclusion, somewhat original, for the hero
> and heroine are neither plunged in the depths of misery, nor exalted to
> UNhuman happiness. Is not such a middle state more natural, more
> according to real life, and less resembling every other book of fiction? . . .
>
> You find, my dear daddy, I am prepared to fight a good battle here; but
> I have thought the matter much over, and if I am made to give up this
> point, my whole plan is rendered abortive, and the last page of any novel
> in Mr. Noble's circulating library may serve for the last page of mine,
> since a marriage, a reconciliation, and some sudden expedient for great
> riches, concludes them all alike.[71]

Samuel Crisp and Dr. Charles Burney tried hard to think of expedients that
would preserve Cecilia's estate for her and Mortimer—they were quite tender-
hearted at seeing the fictional girl robbed of her treasure. Charles Burney (of the
MacBurneys) could not really believe that anybody could prefer a mere name to
solid wealth. Frances Burney was very glad to be able to point out that Lord de
Ferrars "always says that old Delvile was in the right."[72] The issue of the *name*
struck out an ideal metaphor for the divisions and beliefs of her England.
Burney did "fight a good battle," as she said, in keeping her novel faithful to her
own design. She insisted on being herself, on being original, on thinking and
acting for herself as a creator. Burney also got her own way over her mixed
characters, although more readers than Crisp were puzzled by Mrs. Delvile.
Samuel Johnson appreciated her achievement in creating mixed characters;
according to Hester Thrale, Johnson told William Windham "Miss Burney's
new Novel" was "far superior to Fielding's" because "her Characters are nicer

discriminated, and less prominent, Fielding could describe a Horse or an Ass, but he never reached to a Mule."[73]

The most famous contemporary novelist to criticize *Cecilia* is Choderlos de Laclos, who published his epistolary novel of seduction and corruption, *Les liaisons dangereuses*, in the same year. It was Laclos's own idea to review the translation in three articles in the *Mercure de France* in 1784. Laclos had evidently not only read *Evelina* but drawn upon it for the epistolary portrayal of his naïve (and seduced) Cécile. His own mind running on seduction in relation to women, Laclos wishes that the female author could have shown a woman resisting a really attractive seducer (i.e., playing the other side of *Les liaisons*), and criticizes her for not creating any sexually attractive young men other than the hero. He thinks Belfield, however, one of the best conceived characters in the novel. Laclos admires the conduct of the love story, and the delicate strokes whereby it is developed. "Jamais l'amour ne fut pent sous des couleurs plus vraies." There are too many characters who do not contribute to the main action (the French neo-classical aesthetic is very evident in the desire for unity of action); although merely "épisodiques," the characters "forment une galerie de tableaux presque tous tracés de main de maître." The torment of Cecilia's encounter with the Harrels' old friends en route to her wedding provides a scene which would not have been disowned by Molière. The Vauxhall scene is also admirable, "la superbe scène . . . digne du talent le plus distingue."[74] Laclos rates Burney very high, placing *Cecilia* on a level below only *Clarissa*, Fielding's *Tom Jones*, and Rousseau's *La Nouvelle Héloise*. Aside from Diderot's *Eloge* at Richardson's death, the eighteenth century can produce little more generous criticism of one novelist by another, and nothing more seriously appreciative of a female novelist by a male.

Burney's oddest critic of this period is another novelist, William Godwin. Godwin in the next decade was to be England's leading radical philosopher, famous to us for his influence on Wordsworth and Shelley, and for his marrying Mary Wollstonecraft and fathering Mary Shelley, author of *Frankenstein*. In 1782 he had done none of these things, but was a twenty-six-year-old aspiring writer whose two earliest (short) novels came out a month or so after Burney's. In 1784 Godwin produced a small pamphlet, *The Herald of Literature*; this *jeu d'esprit* offered parodic reviews, accompanied by copious extracts, of imaginary works usually attributed to real writers, Burney among them. Godwin supplies "Miss Burney" with an imaginary forthcoming novel called *Louisa; or, Memoirs of a Woman of Quality*, explicitly compared to *Cecilia*: "The Principal story of Louisa, like that of Cecilia, is very simple, but adorned with a thousand beautiful episodes. As the greatest action of the latter is Cecilia's sacrifice of fortune to a virtuous and laudable attachment, so that of the former is the sacrifice of rank."[75] The language of the mock "reviewer" parodies that of the real reviewers of *Cecilia*: "The manner in which her gay and sportive character is supported in these scenes is beyond all commendation." The mimic "extracts" offer some shrewd hits at Burney's typical syntactic inversions: "she is yet capable, from singularity of thinking, of enterprises the most bold and unaccountable." The hero, Mr. Burchel, is ludicrously weak, even weaker than Mortimer, and is actually abducted by the "serious and romantic" Olivia. Godwin's parody shows that Burney might have been thought to sin against delicacy in showing Cecilia so much in love with Mortimer, so willing to think of expedients for the marriage despite opposition; the imaginary heroine is termed "as coming . . . as a milk-maid."[76] Evidently Godwin thought Cecilia "too coming," forthright in love to the point of sexual aggression. One could hardly gather Godwin's later sympathies for the feminists Mary Hays and Mary Wollstonecraft in *The Herald of Literature;* the mock review of Burney is male chauvinist enough. Yet Godwin's article reminds us that *Cecilia* anticipates issues to be brought up in the new feminist literature of the next decade, as also explicitly in Burney's own later novels—including the right of the woman to take the initiative in making a sexual choice.

Godwin's mock review, however, places Burney in good company, with Gibbon and others. Allotted one of the longest critiques, Burney is the sole female writer included in Godwin's gallery, and the only contemporary novelist individually treated. Godwin's parody shows to what extent she had "arrived." Godwin's own early novels may have been influenced by *Evelina;* reviewers of his works had compared them with hers,[77] a fact that probably sharpened his parody. Godwin's real tribute to Burney the novelist was to be made secretly, years later. When he was writing his powerful radical novel *Things as They Are* (1794) (better known as *Caleb Williams*), Godwin studied *Cecilia.*[78]

Mary Wollstonecraft, whose *Vindication of the Rights of Woman* (1792) and feminist fictions still lay in the future, was an admirer of *Cecilia* at the outset. She knew Burney's novel well enough to quote it almost by heart during the unhappy period when she was experiencing "high life" as a governess in Lord and Lady Kingsborough's household: "Miss Burney's account of high life is very just—I have seen the *supercilious* and been pestered to death by the *volubles.*"[79] The influence of *Cecilia* can be felt in the later fiction of Wollstonecraft, as it can in almost all the new fiction of the end of the '80s and the beginning of the '90s. *Cecilia* is the best English novel to appear in the two-decade period extending from the time of Smollett's last novel *Humphry Clinker* (1771) to the era of Gothic novels such as *The Mysteries of Udolpho* (1794) and the new "Jacobin" or democratic revolutionary fictions such as *Caleb Williams. Cecilia* can proleptically be termed the first of the "Jacobin" novels—not so much on account of its support of independence, or even rebellion, as because of its concerns with a large range of social and financial experience. It is—or it adumbrates—feminist "Jacobin" fiction, in its interest in women's work, in the cramped world of female haberdashers, greengrocers, clear-starchers. Yet, at the same time, it is one of the first novels to introduce Gothic symbolism, a violent expressionism to cut against the certainties of predictable Georgian moralizing. *Cecilia* speaks a figurative language of castle, ruin, gaol, gunshot, hallucination—language that predicts and supports a new Romanticism. It is a deeply moral novel that at the same time distrusts easy certainties. The most conscientious and intelligent of the novel's characters can be driven to say, "I know no longer what is kind nor what is cruel . . . right from wrong, nor good from evil." The beaten track is treacherous and there is no route "already marked out." Nice young ladies are supposed to find the good clearly distinguishable. But right and wrong, good or evil, can melt, frighteningly dissolve into a blur of questions.

Nobody who reads the novel can imagine this was a work ground out to please the author's father. Dr. Burney's deepest and most comforting beliefs are constantly questioned in this novel. There were many difficulties and delays in producing *Cecilia*, it is true; the writing was a long task because Burney kept revising and thought so carefully what she was about. At the end, of course, just copying out the manuscript in a fair hand was a huge chore which, unlike her father, she had to perform by herself. (In writing her next novel, she was to have valued aid in this labor.) Throughout the writing, Burney essentially kept her treasure safe against the advice of those who thought they knew better how to employ it. She produced something very important to her.

In an attempt at an "Introduction" to *Cecilia*, Burney began to investigate, if haltingly, some way of expressing publicly what really drove her to write.[80] In an awkward fable of Genius—"the Founder"—and Vanity—"the Patroness"— of "the School of Letters," Burney expresses her fear that the very genre she tries is, like herself, female and inferior, and thus far removed from real letters. At the same time, she tries to persuade herself and her reader out of that way of thinking. Every youthful author looks at "the Temple of Genius" with longing, but he or she may be wearied and settle for "the Temple of Vanity." Flattery entertains and gratifies authorial conceit. "Such is the fate of all those who mistake Inclination for Ability." Like other authors of best-sellers, Burney had already known flattery and success (if not financial reward); she resented being thought, even by herself, content to settle for that. Yet there are aspirants, not "blinded by self Love" but "fearfully & feelingly awake to the perils," who still are moved by the strange infatuation, the "enchantment" which draws them on. Burney speaks in warm emotional terms of the pilgrimage of the "youthful Author": "he wavers,—yet he proceeds; he repents,—but he never returns! . . . his accustomed ocupations [*sic*] become irksome, his former pleasures, insipid." The powerful urge to write is irresistible, though its sources are hard to determine—as she knows in her own case,

> whether the Spirit which moves me to write is a Being beneficent, who will countenance & protect me; or whether some malignant Daemon, delighting in mischief . . . I know not . . .

Reluctant though she must appear to claim genius, for only readers are entitled to decide whether an author's works show that divine quality, Burney still knows herself troubled by her spirit or demon, not just scribbling for applause. Her struggle with the language here shows how hard it was for a woman to claim kinship with the same deep motive power as forces the acknowledged genius forward. Yet for all the protestations of humility, that is what she does attempt. At least to herself, she begins to express it. Burney clings to the posture of a felt humility, but she rests nothing on pressure from external circumstances. She is driven by some psychic or spiritual urgency within. She knows it is never going to be possible to say *why* she wants so passionately to write:

> I will not, however, attempt a precise investigation of the interior move-
> ments by which I may be impelled: the intricacies of the human Heart are
> various as innumerable, & its feelings, upon all interesting occasions, are
> so minute & complex, as to baffle all the power of Language. What
> Addison has said of the Ways of Heaven, may with much more propriety
> & accuracy be applied to the Mind of Man, which, indeed, is
>
> Dark & Intricate,
> Filled with wild Mazes, & perplexed with *Error*.[81]

The connection between her writing and complex inner feelings is emphasized, though at the same time defined as inscrutable to examination. The writing, like the feelings, is associated with "Mazes" of inner "Error" (in the sense both of sin and of wanderings through the labyrinth). Language and rational analysis can never truly reach the inner depths of personality. Burney could never approach the sources of her need to write without guilt-shadowed thoughts, but the guilt itself relates writing to the deepest "interior movements" of the self, that spring of being which may be injured by others but can never be subjected to scrutiny and control. The intricacies of the human heart and its complex feelings are not in the end subject to daddying.

Love, Loss, and Imprisonment:
The Windsor and Kew Tragedies

Like the life of her heroine, Frances Burney's life was "human . . . and as such imperfect." Immediately after the publication of *Cecilia*, her life might seem to bloom in the brief roseate light of success. The novel was so well known that a dramatic Epilogue was written by Miles Andrews for the actress Mrs. Hobart to speak in the voice and manner of Miss Larolles, with reference also to other characters ("Old Delvile, Morrice, Lady Honoria, & Mr. Meadows"); this Epilogue seems to be alluded to in a caricature of 1784 (Fig. 19).[1] Burney herself was a celebrity; as she wrote to Susanna from Brighton in October 1782: "you would suppose me something dropt from the Skies. Even if Richardson or Fielding could rise from the Grave, I should bid fair for supplanting them in the *popular Eye*, for being a *fair female*, I am *accounted quelque chose extra-ordinaire.*"[2] A Brighton milliner begged for a sight of her, and stared, exclaiming, "It is quite a comfort to me, indeed! . . . O Ma'am! how sensible you must be!—it does my Heart good to see you!"[3] Mrs. Thrale teased her that she might "set up for a beauty," and Frances wryly noted that as she was not old, fat, or deformed, her looks were cried up by celebrity-hunters.[4] In the summer of 1782 Edward Francesco Burney painted her portrait (frontis). Burney worried that the picture was dishonest: "Never was Portrait so violently flattered . . . it really makes me uneasy to see a Face in which the smallest resemblance to my own can be traced looking almost *perfectly* handsome."[5] Edward Francesco's later, blander portrait of his cousin (Fig. 18) exhibits a more dignified (if agreeable) Burney: this is a woman suited to court office. The 1782 portrait, presenting a woman of introspective imagination combined with strength and humor, captured the look of the young Burney, the heart-whole and unshaken Burney, just before the most troubled period of her life. After the brilliant success of *Cecilia*, the decade of the 1780s was full of unhappy alteration. Resignation under the evils of life was to be severely tried. Frances Burney herself was to undergo an important emotional change. She had written about love in her novels, but had remained, as Hester Thrale noted, unhit by "Cupid's Arrow." Now at thirty she fell in love for the first time.

In December 1782 Frances Burney met Richard Owen Cambridge, a minor man of letters, and his son, the Reverend Mr. George Owen Cambridge, an ordained clergyman of the Church of England, some three years younger than Frances Burney. Richard Cambridge sought out Burney and made much of her, praising *Cecilia* and its author enthusiastically. The Cambridges were of a higher social position than the Burneys; Richard Cambridge had a villa and a small estate at Twickenham. Both father and son were rather old-fashioned—which does not always mean formal; Frances Burney praises the good breeding of both men, yet in her narrative accounts both are often bluff or abrupt, sometimes rather rude. Her first impression of Richard Cambridge was that he was "a little too precise in his manner, & rather prosing in his conversation." Her first impression of the son was likewise not altogether favorable: "There was something in his manner that, at first, I thought a little pedantic, but that notion entirely wears away upon further acquaintance," she wrote to Susanna on Boxing Day.[6] By 11 January 1783, she is able to say of Mr. George Cambridge, "I like him, indeed, extremely. He is *both* elegant & sensible, & almost all the other folks I meet, deserve, at best, but *one* of those epithets."[7] George Cambridge bore an impeccable character as to religion and morals, and also possessed the spirit and dry sense of humor that always delighted Burney. (For a drawing of this "elegant and sensible" man in later years, see Fig. 20.) Richard Cambridge invited Frances on family excursions; he and his son took to calling regularly (uninvited) at the Burneys' house. At moments, the elderly and married Richard Cambridge seemed problematically more interested himself in Frances than was quite comfortable. Yet most of his speeches and actions might justly be taken as indicating that the father was trying to promote the interest of the son, with the son's consent. In February 1783, Burney confided to Susanna that Mr. Cambridge senior "talked to me of *George* as of the only man to be compared with *my* Lord Orville, & told me of his temper, his sweetness, his rectitude of conduct, & dignity of mind."[8] Such a puff as this comparison with Burney's marriageable hero might well seem a broad and positive hint. Cambridge senior also gave Frances Burney a detailed account of his own courtship, when he had visited the Trenchards for three years "in love all the time with the Daughter, yet *honourably* forbearing ever to tell her so, because, not being rich enough to marry her, he chose to be at *liberty*."[9] Unable to marry, he had determined to go abroad when his uncle settled an estate upon him if he would give up the journey and marry—which he happily did. This story can easily be construed as offering the girl of George's choice a proleptic paradigm of the probable course of his affections; George could not marry until he was settled in life with a living and an income. Frances Burney disagreed with Mr. Cambridge's notion of the appropriate male behavior: "Miss Cambridge & I both agreed it would have been more *honourable*, to *our* thoughts, had he gone sooner." The woman suffers in such a case; the former Miss Trenchard had said that Richard's frequent visits had "caused every body else to regard him as her Lover, & she had so far given him her Heart, that she could never have been happy with any other Man." The woman would prefer a young man to declare himself or get out of the way. But Richard Cambridge had shown what Frances might expect in being courted by a male of the Cambridge family—assiduity without speaking until circumstances were propitious. Was Frances Burney to regard herself as being courted? Close friends like Mrs. Thrale thought that George Cambridge had serious intentions. Frances Burney, however, was only too strongly aware that a young (or not so young) woman looks ridiculous if she makes open her interest in a man who does not care for her. She took very seriously the social injunctions that a nice woman should not have any sexual feelings about a man until the man has spoken out. Her friendship with George Cambridge, at first largely a source of pleasure, became increasingly self-conscious and anxiety-ridden.

In early April 1783, Frances was seriously distressed by a newspaper paragraph, a gossip hint that coupled her name with that of George Cambridge. Highly uneasy at knowing they were being closely observed, Burney was proud of being able to speak to Mr. Cambridge "without any . . . alteration of manner, though so far removed from that inward gaiety which first made my conferences with him so pleasant."[10] Social embarrassment was taking a full toll: "Who *could write* that Paragraph?—What a never ceasing astonishment as well as grief & indignation does it give me!"[11] Burney decided upon the witling William Weller Pepys as the author, as he had been present "at the 2 striking Evenings of the Lozenges, & the almost riotous gaiety at Mrs. Montagu's." Frances Burney was, then, capable of "almost riotous gaiety." In deciding upon Mr. Pepys as the author of the hated paragraph, she may have erred; she had previously fixed upon him as the author of "Advice to the *Herald*" when the real author was Dr. Charles Burney. Could Dr. Burney have been the author of this piece as well? It came out at a time when both her father and stepmother were teasing their daughter about George Cambridge. Certainly, there is reason to imagine that whoever sent the paragraph into the newspaper did so in the hopes of pushing George Cambridge toward an honorable and open declaration. If that were the intention, the treatment did not take effect.

Frances Burney worried that she would soon be seen as dangling after Mr. Cambridge. She was acutely conscious that George might well expect to marry up rather than down. In her bitterer moments she gave Richard Cambridge, at least, full credit for worldliness: "as to his son,—his Heart's darling, his family's Pride, his model of perfection—I can never, 3 minutes following, think him so *humble* in his romantic singularity, as really to have in view the promotion of *so* disadvantageous a connection."[12] Frances Burney congratulated herself repeatedly that she was not at all to blame for the situation:

> I thank Heaven with my whole Heart that this is an affair in which I have been merely passive, however deeply concerned. What abundant reproach should I make myself for my own folly, & might the World make me for my own vanity, had I brought it on myself!—I believe, indeed, I *could* not have done it; Mr. G: C. is the last young man I ever saw in my life to be *drawn* in, & would be the first, I am certain, to detect the smallest impropriety, & to pay it with its due contempt. That, however can hardly be even *possible* to happen to one who has *no views* whatsoever, but who waits quietly till his own are devellop'd, before she will even ask *herself* what she *wishes* they should be. *Indeed,* this is true, & *indeed* I could not, if I would, at this moment tell *what* I should do, were all power in my own Hands. . . . I never before felt any real *hesitation* whether the married or single life would make me happiest. Upon the whole, however, I certainly think the latter.[13]

So she wrote to Susanna in April 1783, insisting, as she is to do again and again, upon her innocence of all views, designs, or even desires. It is true that Burney had serious doubts about marriage; her heart-free state during the whole of her twenties shows considerable resistance to the idea, and Mr. Barlow certainly had very short shrift. Marriage as she knew it and the life of the novelist were not compatible. She records Pacchierotti's suspicions of the oft-visiting Mr. Cambridge, and the singer's earnest injunction: "he then said he hoped for the sake of the Public I should never *marry*, as, if I kept single, I should be the first Genius of England!"[14] But the advice of a castrato about marriage may be taken with a grain of salt. Frances Burney had always intended not to marry, but since her old plan of herself and Susanna living together as "2 loving Maiden Cats" had had to be relinquished, she was the more inclined to consider a future life outside of her own family. And that family was in the process of changing. Her closest brother Charles married in June 1783; James was to marry in September 1785 and Charlotte in February 1786.

In the eventful spring of 1783 Burney again had her portrait painted, and it is tempting to try to see a reflection of her experience in her new image (Fig. 17). She notes on 28 June 1783: "I sat for the last Time to Mr Bogle, & my miniature is now improved into a flattered Picture."[15] John Bogle's miniature is an interesting contrast to the portrait by Edward Francesco Burney of the previous year. Burney's cousin emphasizes her strength; Bogle captures fragility, delicacy. The resemblance to Burney's mother as depicted by Spencer is visible about the mouth, and yet Frances looks strained, as Esther does not; there is a pinched quality about the lips. Perhaps some of the tensions and anxieties, the judgments and repressions of 1783 have had their effect upon the "flattered Picture." In any case, whatever artists might see or not see, the Frances Burney of 1783 was different from the young woman of 1782.

Frances Burney's original "inward gaiety" in conversing with George Cambridge in 1783 really meant the unsealing of sexual emotion. Frances was losing her heart even while she was proclaiming to the faithful confidante Susanna that she was not. Throughout the long drawn-out non-affair, Frances Burney insists with active passionate vehemence on her "passive" role, a passivity she equates with blamelessness. We can see the active self-protection brought into play, combined with an intense and sensitive fear of criticism from others, not least from "Mr. G: C." himself. A highly activated fear trembles through the unacknowledged sexuality of what rapidly becomes an obsession. To say she has no wishes until he has developed some intentions is highly disingenuous, as is the statement that she does not even ask herself what she wishes his views to be. By the time that statement is formulated, one has already asked the question. A self-reflexive play at spontaneous innocence is wretchedly at work here.

The bad faith is, of course, foisted on Frances Burney by the sexual and social mores of her time (and later), and in particular by the cruel position in which the Cambridges put her. It is hard at this distance to decide what George Cambridge was up to, if anything; the matter puzzled Burney's friends as well as herself. It would seem that George Cambridge was probably somewhat interested at first, and enjoyed talking to the novelist, but that the interest evaporated without his seeing the necessity for any dramatic gesture like going abroad. Mr. George Cambridge would not speak, nor would he go away. Frances would make good resolutions of reserve, and then some meeting at somebody's party would break the ice and the pair would start conversing in the old way. There was to be more of the "almost riotous gaiety" in 1783. One evening in November, at a party at Pepys's house, Frances Burney was sitting by elderly, ugly Mrs. Chapone when George Cambridge "braved all difficulties to talk with me, & stood facing me, & chatting all the night, & though Mrs. Chapone frequently offered to join in the discourse, we were both in too high spirits for her *seriousity*, & rattled away without minding her."[16] But Burney was always aware that she would pay for ignoring, even momentarily, such pillars of propriety as Hester Chapone, the author of a conduct book for young ladies, *Letters on the Improvement of the Mind* (1773).

Throughout 1783 Frances Burney anxiously records in her journals to Susanna every meeting with George Cambridge in enormous detail, the detail increasing as she tries to bring in every bit of evidence that could make for reassurance. In December 1783 she hopes that "Mr. G: C." is surprised when she leaves a party early: "I am *greatly* mistaken if he was pleased at seeing me thus decamping. . . . If you had seen with how irresolute an air he followed me in my retreat with his Eye, & turned entirely round to look after me, you *must* have concluded he was provoked at my departing in such a manner."[17] "You *must* have concluded . . ."; one feels the wistfulness, as Burney hopes it would be determined by an objective but close observer that George Cambridge has feelings for her even when he is perfectly silent. If Richard Cambridge's story of his taciturn courtship provides the paradigm of hope, Richardson's epistolary novel *Sir Charles Grandison* supplies the model for the modes of hoping and fearing. Burney's Richardsonian detail echoes the detailed description of the anxious heroine Harriet Byron, long uncertain as to whether or what Sir Charles feels for her. Like Harriet, Burney puts certain matters between hooks (i.e., in brackets) when writing letters to her confidante. She adopts Harriet's vocabulary, referring to "attacks" when someone taxes her with a relationship to Mr. Cambridge, just as Harriet refers to the Grandison sisters' "sudden attack" when they confront her in her dressing room and force her to confess that she is in love with Sir Charles. Sir Charles is not a speaker-out, and declares that "he should not, perhaps, were he in Love, be over-forward to declare his passion by words; but rather shew it by his assiduities and veneration, unless he saw, that the suspense was painful to the object."[18] But a lady of delicacy will not, of course, show that she is in suspense at all. Harriet Byron's anxious love, fearful of being unrequited, is finally rewarded. When the journal-letters to Susanna were written in 1783, and even in 1784 or later, Burney (for all her Harriet-like protestations of cessation of hope) did not know that her story would not end happily too. Burney's (non)courtship story provides a sad ironic *Grandison*, a tale told in letters in which the heroine does not get her man. Yet when the aged Frances Burney went through all these papers she did not destroy all the unhappy Journals of this period. She very successfully scored out paragraph after paragraph, but she left enough to let her reader (and she must have imagined a future reader) understand a great deal—perhaps a little more than she intended.

Burney's very acute recording of George Cambridge's every look, gesture, change of posture, tone of speech, kind of smile, etc. tells us that this is an observer passionately in love. The first time one is in love, one is an adolescent. When the two are in the same room, Frances Burney has extra antennae with which to monitor everything "Mr. G: C." may do or not do. And Burney is embarrassingly ready to read symptoms of hope into the smallest matters. At another party in December 1783, she is vexed at being taken possession of by Mrs. Montagu's nephew, so that she has no opportunity to speak to "Mr. G: C." Perhaps with kind intent, Mr. Montagu sticks close: "the more I endeavoured to have done, the more determined he grew to keep me engaged. What a Lesson & incitement to coquetry!"[19] But she does get a chance to talk to "Mr. G: C."; when she commiserates with him upon his cold, he moves into the place next to her and smiles: "His smile, indeed, had as much of pain as of pleasure in its expression;—what it meant, I can not tell, but it was a look of so much unaccountable consciousness as I cannot easily, if ever, forget." She is delighted to talk about unimportant Miss Baker; her teasing remark about the simple Miss Baker's being possibly misinterpreted as "deeper & deeper, & slyer & slyer" is really intended as a coded accusation of George as "deep" and "sly" which she hopes he has correctly interpreted. Frances Burney always hopes that she and Mr. Cambridge are talking in code, and that by writing down all his remarks (like his "O I am so glad you spoke to me! I would not but have had you for the world") she may recover satisfactory hidden meanings. At the end of this particular conversation, George Cambridge says, "But now—you must *always* come to me to confession—will you?—," delighting his interlocutor, who is busy at interpretation. She reads the remark to Susanna: "You see, at least, no design of *flight*—the repeated solicitation for confession seems to intend nothing less [i.e., anything but] . . . certainly his desire of my trust & communication are just what I should wish." She hopes for symptomatic gestures toward more intimacy, the promise of a future. Frances Burney lingers constantly over the social-sexual hermeneutics, puzzling herself—and us—with the idea of a look of "unaccountable consciousness." If only "Mr. G: C." would account for his consciousness in the satisfactory way! If only he were in love, but afraid to pursue the matter because of want of means on which to marry, and thus sad because talking to her is a painful reminder of what he still must forgo! Burney tries frantically to read a hopeful message under the peculiar text which is "Mr. G: C."

Such scenes as these give away all her hopes and desires, yet she is not able to admit how deep these hopes and desires are. She is always having to relinquish, to withdraw, to profess insensibility. By January 1784, she writes to Susanna that all emotion is over, that she can now rejoice that she has *"scarce any uneasiness, just now, in the World."*[20] There is nothing to hope for or wish, and Frances has never been so improper as to hope or wish. She finds her consolation in Susanna's praise of her behavior in this "various &, I own, *trying* business" that has consumed a large part of her attention. If her behavior has been "right," she admits, "it has not been so by *chance,* for enough, indeed, have I revolved all I could or should do or say in it."[21] She has not, she believes, ever let her guard down, through the paradoxically strenuous exercise of her wise passiveness: "I could not more passively have let it take its course. May I but go on with as little self-reproach." She is under compulsion to act "right," to be sure that neither she nor anybody else could find any fault in her behavior. The dictates of eighteenth-century propriety were designed to make young women cautious, anxiously self-monitoring, but in Frances Burney's case the generally inculcated feminine inhibitions were complicated by family traits. Charless Burney might be elaborately obsequious, but never frankly apologetic; he was strongly self-defensive. He always had to be right, and he passed on to his children a general inability to admit wrongdoing, or to accept that sometimes one is in the wrong. It is hard to catch any Burney saying openly "I'm sorry"—I do not think I have found Frances doing so. Reproach of any kind is more damaging than it ought to be to a Burney's sense of identity and self-esteem. The Burneys—perhaps especially Frances—became overattached to being right, overfearful of any kind of censure. Frances had conquered her fear of censure as a writer—and, in her willingness to face the public as a dramatist, she showed a willingness to risk failure and censure of the kind that frightened

Dr. Burney. But it was to take a personal cataclysm to shake her so that she could dare to take a step in her personal life of which others would disapprove.

At present, in 1783 and later, she was fearfully attached to a notion of herself as irreproachable, a notion that sometimes made her mask herself from herself and mock her true feelings. She had not entirely digested the moral of Richardson's *Grandison*. Richardson said that Harriet's problem was, "Was she to be honest, or not?"[22] and the novel defends honesty about feelings: "And why should you deny, that you *were* susceptible of a natural passion?"[23] Frances Burney could not imitate all Harriet Byron's openness as she did her epistolary technique—but then, Harriet was a beautiful fictional heiress of twenty, and not a real spinster, poor and past thirty. Frances was, however, aware that freedom from self-reproach is not the same as freedom from pain and self-divison: "I am sometimes dreadfully afraid for myself, from the *very* different behaviour which Nature calls for on one side, & the World on the other."[24] Love is a natural passion; in fighting off "the World" Burney is fighting her own nature—but if only Mr. Cambridge would declare himself, then Nature and the World together might be satisfied.

"Nature" steadily refuses to be denied. And the affair or non-affair tormentingly never seems to be over, for there are new "attacks" from friends, new reports of a forthcoming marriage which Burney must beg to have contradicted. In May 1784 Burney had a long argument with her friend Anna Ord, who assured her of a general report of her forthcoming marriage, which Mrs. Ord thought likely. Burney retorted with bitter worldliness, "it were much better to look for an alliance with the Archbishop of York."[25] Such a report—without foundation—stimulated something like anger in the wilfully passive Burney. She admitted to Susanna that, if the Cambridges were not suffering at present from a bereavement, "I do really believe I should feel an anger that would make me drive them all out of my Head!" She *does* reproach George Cambridge: "*some* thing must have been *very* wrong in *somebody's* management,—& I will not think it my own!—Neither, indeed, *could* it be my own;—were the rumour the effect of *my* behaviour, it could only be called a flirtation,—a coqueting,— &c.,—a *Marriage* is never settled but in consequence of conclusions from the *Man's* behaviour." Men have all the power, even in creating the important rumors. She must be guiltless, for had the attentions visibly come from her side alone, the matter would have been dismissed as a mere flirtation. She is both justified and calumniated at the same time.

Frances Burney had been incessantly anxious to escape the charge of flirting with Mr. Cambridge, leading him on. The reports which make her so embarrassed and miserable are his fault; he has looked meaningful while meaning nothing. She is indignantly helpless under constructions she cannot control. Yet, she cannot be quite angry, just as she cannot quite cease to hope that this silent method is Mr. Cambridge's mode of proceeding. There are to be many more encounters with "Mr. G: C." If she drove "them" out of her head, the departure would leave only a blank: "How I could ever fill it as well again I know not."[26] They—or rather "Mr. G: C."—continued to occupy Burney's mind and heart. By the end of 1785 all of Burney's friends felt certain that George Cambridge (though still unmarried) meant little or nothing. Frances Burney may have been secretly overaffected by Richard Cambridge's story of his three years of courtship. Not until the magic number of years was up could she truly begin to break the spell and really resign herself, and then only slowly.

The heroine of *Camilla*, the novel that came from hiding places ten years deep, was to undergo more successfully the ordeal that gave Frances Burney such pain. Camilla too is accused of wanting to draw a man in, learns lessons in coquetry, attempts reserves, and tries to read the baffling behavior of the man she loves. Only in *Camilla* would Frances Burney truly analyze the nature and meaning of that tortuous relation to "Mr. G: C.," going beyond the individual personalities to the social causes of such unhappiness. She retained some of the journal accounts of her personal unhappiness for posterity. More thorough than Frances Burney herself, her niece Charlotte Barrett censored all reference to this embarrassing heartbreak in her edition of the *Diary*. But the heartbreak was there. Burney's other diary-writing suffered during the period when her most extensive writing was this personal minute record. This infatuation, this obsession, this painful love occupied much of the center of Burney's life in the middle of the decade.

After the publication of *Cecilia*, Burney apparently wrote nothing aside from journals and letters for six years. That she could not write during the first part of her life at court in 1786–1787 is not surprising. But it is puzzling that she did not begin writing something earlier. In October 1783 the novelist and dramatist Frances Brooke, fresh from the triumph of her ballad-opera *Rosina* (1782), proposed to Frances Burney that the two successful women writers start a new periodical. Burney professed herself "much honoured by her very flattering proposition" but declined:

> I am at present so little disposed for writing, that I am certain I could produce nothing worth reading. I have bid adieu to my Pen since I finished Cecilia, not from *disgust*, nor *design*, but from having fairly *written all I had to write*: it was the same for 2 or 3 years after I had done with Evelina; & I am as unwilling now as I was then, to deal hardly with an empty Brain.[27]

In the throes of working on *Cecilia*, Burney had said to Susanna, "Whenever this Work is Done—if ever that Day arrives, I believe I shall not write another Word for 3 Years!"[28] But in her reply to Frances Brooke, Burney forgets that the interval between *Evelina* and the beginning of work on *Cecilia* had been largely filled in by work on *The Witlings*. Even so, it had not taken her three years from the publication of *Evelina* to *begin* a new novel. She may have wished to evade Frances Brooke (though a periodical by the two famous Franceses might have been interesting); Brooke's rather arch reply shows she only half believed her.[29] But the lack of inclination for writing is believable, given the entire absence of any kind of fictional writing by Burney in this period. The indisposition, and the "empty Brain," are not typical of the Frances Burney who had produced a novel, epic poems, and plays by the age of fifteen. Some particular factors must have caused what was to be a long silence.

Others were urging her to write. Mr. Crisp had been exhorting her to try again, almost from the very moment of *Cecilia*'s publication. If he invited her to Chessington, he told her in the summer of 1782, he would now expect her to write while she was there: "If you come here, come to Work—Work hard—Stick to it—this is the harvest time of your Life." He took almost too Briggs-like an interest in the financial reward: " '*Touch the yellow Boys*'— 'grow *Warm*'—make the Booksellers *come down handsomely*—*Count the ready*—*the Chink*—do but secure this one point, while it is in your Power, & *all Things else shall be added unto thee.*"[30] This somewhat blasphemous urgency might well have been disagreeable. And for all the emphasis on the profit motive, the money she earned from *Cecilia* did Burney no immediate good. It is something of a question what happened to the proceeds from the novel. The two daddies decided "that the ready should by Vested in the 3 per Cent Annuities";[31] as the money was in care of her father, Frances had no immediate access to it, and was no better off for current expenses. In September 1782 Hester Thrale, anxious to expedite Frances Burney's coming to Brighton, sent her some money:

> Your Mother when she was in Labour of you could alone long more to see you than does your H:L:T: accept the enclosed my Angel, & say nothing of it to any living Creature, it will save us a world of Diddle daddle, in paying Subscriptions Expenses &c. and unless you mean to *quite* break a Heart sadly cracked already, do not refuse me a piece of Friendship.[32]

Frances Burney indignantly returned the money, causing Hester to write repentantly, "I admire the Dignity I have offended and desire to embrace the '*little Morsel of a Lady*' whose Soul is so superior to common Mortals."[33] Yet it was true that Frances Burney had no money of her own, and this could cause difficulties about expenses, rather like the difficulties her heroine Camilla was to experience when visiting Tunbridge or Southampton. Camilla, however, is only seventeen, while Burney was now over thirty. In the autumn of 1783 Susanna sent her some money with which to visit Mrs. Thrale, although Burney could still boast, "I have, you know, in my Father's Hands a hoard of my own which I would exhaust upon this occasion with the utmost thankfulness."[34] Susanna evidently suspected that the "hoard" might not be readily at her disposal—as it proved, since her father did not now wish Frances Burney to visit Mrs. Thrale.

No freedom had come with the money. The financial reward so impressive to Crisp had brought no immediate gratification.

Yet, on the other hand, if Burney had wished to write, Crisp's home provided a sure refuge, and Crisp himself, however limited he may have been in some ways, believed in her abilities, her genius. But Crisp was not there to be a daddy at this unhappy juncture. Just after the matter of the newspaper paragraph, Samuel Crisp died, in April 1783. Crisp's death was a severe emotional blow to Frances Burney. One kind of home and a certain dependable encouragement had gone out of her life forever. The idea of writing was itself associated with Chessington and bereavement. Crisp's death is one of the factors that explains the long silence. It was also an important fact that home remained as difficult as ever, and the Streatham household was gone; there was no comfortable base from which to write.

In 1783, if Frances Burney felt that she might soon marry, she might well have felt it inappropriate to begin novel-writing again. A novel took her at least three years to complete, and the work took her out of circulation, away from the social scenes where she would meet Mr. Cambridge. Also, wives of upper-class clergymen do not scribble idle fiction (as for periodical writing, hack work, that is too low, beyond the pale). Novel-writing would not be a suitable occupation, for instance, for the lady of the Prebendary of Ely and the Archdeacon of Middlesex—which is what George Owen Cambridge eventually became. (In the latter position he was later to assist Frances in finding a position for her clergyman son Alex; strange are the uses of our old flames.) The pain of love despised but still suspenseful, the strain of passion acting as passivity, the sadness of a life haunted by the ghost of unreasonable hope, helps to explain why 1783, 1784, and 1785 are such unproductive years.

Something, too, may be attributed to the other prolonged emotional strain, the change in the relationship with Hester Thrale. During the period of *Cecilia's* appearance and just after, the friendship seemed to be upon its old footing, or only changed by Hester's increased admiration of her friend: "my Fondness is not half as disinterested as it was—Pride is got in, & swells it beyond bounds; This wonderful Girl they all talk of so is *my* Burney says I!"[35] The two friends spent time together, and traveled in the old manner. With Dr. Johnson, they were at Brighton in the autumn of 1782. At the last ball of the season in November, "The Room was very thin, & almost half the Ladies Danced with one another. . . . Some of the Ladies were in riding Habits, & *they* made admirable Men."[36] Both Hester Thrale and Frances Burney, unescorted and unattended, were "seized with a violent desire" to join the dancers. Hester "proposed, as so many Women Danced together, that we two should," but the prudent Frances refused. Soon after, Frances was pressed by "a flashy young officer" to dance, and declined, covering her refusal by saying, "I cannot, really, dance to night, for I have already refused a person"—thus putting to unexpected use the piece of ballroom etiquette that Evelina learns with such difficulty. Frances Burney had not turned down Mrs. Thrale's invitation to the dance out of want of inclination but from a sense of propriety: "nothing should I have liked so well; but I begged her to give up the Scheme, as that would have occasioned more fuss & observation than our Dancing with all the Men that ever were born." Neither was to dance "with all the Men that ever were born," but the interest of each in a man was soon to cause an unanticipated and unwelcome amount of "fuss & observation"—and to bring about the end of the friendship.

Before the time of *Cecilia*'s publication, Hester Thrale was already seriously interested in the Italian musician Gabriel Piozzi, but concealed her interest even from herself by engaging in an elaborate fantasy about their relationship. As Frances Burney later explains in annotating a mystifying reference to "these *loving Brothers*" in one of Mrs. Thrale's letters, "at that time, Mrs. Thrale had persuaded herself that Mr. Piozzi was the natural Son of her Father, Mr. Salusbury."[37] The fantasy could cover as fraternal love Hester's desire to converse with the musician, and act as a fragile barricade against sexual attraction. At the same time, incest itself has its attractions; the incest-fixated eighteenth century found in incest a complex symbolism for sexuality outside conventional social structures, and free of the hierarchies and estrangements of customary heterosexuality. Hester Thrale did not, however, rest long content with the consoling taboo fantasy. By September 1782 Hester was confessing her love for Piozzi openly, and from then on she made frequent demands on Burney to come and be confided in. During the Brighton visit in November, Mrs. Thrale determined to declare her intentions to marry Piozzi. She met terrific resistance from their daughters, from their guardians (executors of Henry Thrale's estate), and from Frances Burney—as she was later to meet opposition and ridicule from the English public at large. The first explosive phase of Hester Thrale's declared love coincided unhappily with the time in which Frances was just becoming involved with the Cambridges. Emotionally vulnerable herself, Frances Burney was for the first time required to act as confidante to another woman in an adult emotional crisis. Maria Allen's elopement with Rishton had been a fascinating entertainment enacted offstage in her teens. Her sisters Esther and Susanna had got engaged and married without her assistance. Now Frances had to face in another woman the force of female passion for a man, and that, too, in a woman to whom she was strongly attached. Being a confidante meant, among other things, learning to acknowledge that her own friendship was far from sufficient to give happiness to Mrs. Thrale. The feeling of indefinable abandonment made Frances vulnerable to the strong appeals of the Thrale daughters, particularly the tough-minded and resourceful Queeney who, never particularly interested in Burney before, realized by 1783 what an ally she might be.

This is the first occasion in which Frances Burney seriously took on the role of authority, of advice-giver. When she takes on that role, she takes on the voice of the world as mediated to her through her father's preferences and fears, and her own fears. What she became in the guise of sage counselor can be heard in the cruel letter she wrote to Hester Lynch Thrale in January 1783, after Mrs. Thrale had told her that she was about to give a final answer to Piozzi.

> oh, *think* a little before you utter it!—You will say you have been think-ing all this Time,—no, dear Madam, you have *never* thought,—you have distressed & horrified yourself not about *changing* your plan, but merely in a cruel anxiety to obtain *approbation* for it.
>
> That approbation will *forever* be with held! The Mother of 5 Children, 3 of them as Tall as herself, will never be forgiven for shewing so great an ascendance of passion over Reason. *Somebody,* you say, shall be made happy,—ah, that *somebody* will not be you!—the still small voice within will tell you, when all your contrasts are settled, & you are no longer struggling to obtain your immediate way, that you have wilfully deprived yourself of all hopes of happiness but One,—that one so uncertain! so *inadequate* to such a sacrifice. . . .
>
> Nothing should tear from me such words as these, but the greatness of your present danger, & my own firm conviction of your future repen-tance, but all is at stake—& for what?—a gratification that no one can *esteem,* not even he for whom you feel it, however gratefully or hon-ourably he may conduct himself.
>
> O reflect a little before this fatal final answer with which you terrify me is given!—
>
> *Children—Religion, Friends,*
>
> *Country, Character*—what on *Earth* can compensate the loss of all these?
>
> You will think this cruel,—it is nothing less,—my opinion has been uniform, & I have *said* all this repeatedly, at various Times,—but now, at last, I write it, that its last chance of being heeded may be tried. Heaven bless & direct you, ever dearest Madam,—my very Heart bleeds for your sufferings, when I think you *hesitate;*—when I see you *fixed,* my blame combats my sorrow!—We were not Born for ourselves, & I have regularly practiced, as far as occasion h[as] offered, the forbearance I recommend.[38]

"Dear Madam, you have *never* thought"—this is not the language to use to one's Tyo. Burney is undoubtedly sincere, but this is a histrionic sincerity; she cannot budge from her role. She cannot admit that sexual—and emotional—happiness might provide any adequate recompense for the "sacrifice" which she insists on demanding. Hester Thrale had no intention of giving up her Anglican religion, or her English nationality, nor did she desire to cast off her friends or her children—though she did think these should recognize her own needs and wishes. But Burney determines that the world *should* demand the loss of

"Children . . . Friends, Country, Character"—it is gratuitously assumed that Hester will lightly change her religion. Burney was by no means alone—Dr. Johnson thought in the same way. But Burney's own fear of the world's disapprobation, her own need for approval, for *permission*, her own personal tendency to conflate the "still small voice" of conscience and the big loud voice of public opinion are all too audible here. In her novels, Burney had excoriated the male social view of woman's sexual identity and function: "I don't know what the devil a woman lives for after thirty; she is only in other folks way." But in this official role as advisor, Burney is willing to collude in the coercive social lie that a woman ought to be sexually dead at forty. The tone of denunciation, the almost lip-smacking list of punishing losses may ultimately emanate from Charles Burney, while the real touches of pain are Frances Burney's own.

Frances Burney was later to annotate this epistle defensively, explaining that "FB wrote it in trembling haste, as a last chance of turning her poor infatuated—but Heart-dear Friend, from her astonishing purpose" but adds that "Mrs. Thrale brought it back herself to the Writer—almost instantly—& putting it into her hand, agitatedly said 'You charge me not to shew it—&, that I may not be tempted, I return it you—' She then ran out of the Room, & the House." That letter was not referred to again, but it probably played its part in deciding Mrs. Thrale's "final word" to Piozzi that January, when she said "No." Piozzi went to Italy, and Hester Thrale struggled on through the dull painful year, enduring the death of one child and racked with anxiety over the severe illness of another; throughout, she felt she would go mad or die without Piozzi.

Frances Burney sympathized with Hester in her pain, and was frightened when she thought she might die. In the autumn she was anxious to go to her, but still had to obtain "leave" and Dr. Burney did not wish to permit another visit. The brilliant generous wife of the successful brewer of former years was now a ridiculous object, a sick and infatuated widow, likely to get into trouble with her husband's executors and with society. In Dr. Burney's opinion, the widow who was about to misbehave herself was no proper friend for his Fanny anymore. Frances Burney never thought of her friend in this way. She continued to love Mrs. Thrale dearly, even if she withheld approval and understanding. Generously, on her side, Hester forgave the blame and valued the sincerity—but eventually she came to feel that Frances was not playing her fair, and had, in short, taken to talking "Treason" about her with her daughters. The record of that treason can be read in the letters to Queeney.[39]

In that letter of January 1783 Burney gave herself a full measure of approval for having always practiced "the forbearance I recommend." True, she had never directly opposed anyone else's direct commands or strong preferences; she practiced "forbearance" to her stepmother by obeying unreasonable behests and then complaining about them. This is the kind of "forbearance" she thinks Hester should practice with her daughters. But she is also recommending sexual forbearance—abstinence, inactivity—and she does not yet know what she is talking about. Burney did not know in January what she was to know by April—the force of sexual attraction and desire. Yet, as 1783 advanced, Burney's inescapable feeling for and attention to George Cambridge made her the less likely to say what Hester wished to hear. Obeying social injunctions not to make a fool of herself, Burney reined herself in very tightly, creating the desired "passivity" with violent checks; she could have little sympathy for Hester's overt emotion, her avowed desire to take what she wanted. Denied love and marriage herself, Burney would be the less willing that her friend's life should be enriched by that prize. Frances Burney had to believe, as her letter spells out, that no man is worth crossing the social rules for. Life was to teach her differently, though she was never able to admit that she was mistaken in her judgment upon Hester's grievous error in marrying Gabriel Piozzi.[40]

Her notion of the wisdom of maturity sadly handicapped, and herself suffering an acute emotional pain that sharpened and revived the old sense of abandonment, Frances increasingly took the Thrale daughters' side. She never intended a complete break with Hester, whom she never ceased loving. She thought that she could continue to love Hester while still pitying her and abominating the match with Piozzi. Once the marriage took place in July 1784, such an attitude was totally unacceptable to the new Mrs. Piozzi. Burney's reluctance to resign herself to offering congratulations and to taking up the friendship on its new basis may have partly been the result of secret guilt. She may in some corner of her soul have feared lest her portrait of the Delviles' sundered marriage was in some sense a support of Hester Thrale's break for freedom, and that she, Frances Burney, was an author of noxious moral examples. But, in any case, the influence of Charles Burney was paramount. He told Frances he was "shocked" that Mrs. Thrale "should thus fling away her talents, situation in life, & character"; he was opposed to further association with the lady who was falling from social grace, though he pretended a calm pity "& never speaks to me of the matter but with a sigh for the frailty of human nature!"[41] Charles Burney might well sigh for the frailty of human nature at the spectacle of himself reprobating his patroness for doing what his own second wife had done in marrying himself, then a mere penniless music master, against the wishes of her family.

Mrs. Thrale (Mrs. Piozzi after July 1784) felt deeply betrayed by Frances, recording in her own journal "She has played a false & cruel part towards me I find";[42] she did not at that point guess the full extent of Dr. Burney's treachery. Charles Burney encouraged his daughter to do all the dirty work of creating the breach, while he discreetly appeared nearly as polite as ever. At the time, Hester felt Charles was easier to deal with than his daughter—not knowing the jokes he made behind her back. Later, in a satiric poem, she was to include him among the crowds of her detractors: "And pliant Burney bows from Side to Side." Yet, with splendid magnanimity, Hester, who knew so many secrets of those who turned against her, never used her knowledge to attack them. Johnson's direst moments died with her—she never told all she knew. Neither did she tell the world what a sponge Charles Burney was, or how Frances and the other Burney children really felt about their stepmother. She never made fun of Frances Burney's unrequited love. There is something reliable about Hester's nobility which makes those around her look petty when they turn against her. At least Samuel Johnson and Frances Burney may be forgiven, for they both loved her and felt deeply wounded and betrayed when the wonderful woman in their lives left them for somebody else. Charles Burney's affections, on the other hand, rarely incommoded him. When she heard of Charles Burney's death in 1814, Hester Lynch Piozzi recorded in her Common Place Book her final opinion of the part played in her life by the man who once flattered the "Lady Bountiful" who was an "endless Giver":

> He *thought* himself my Friend once I believe, whilst he *thought* the World was so:—when the Stream turned against the *poor* Straw, he helped retard its Progress with his *Stick:* & made his Daughter do it with her *Fingers*—[43]

But it was "*my* Burney," "sweet Burney," "dear Tyo" whom Hester could not forgive.

The treachery to Hester, masquerading within Frances's own soul as good intentions (and there was a deal of good intention), was the worst act of Frances Burney's life. She was to suffer very sufficiently for it. When Hester went bitterly out of her life, Frances Burney lost a powerful support to her career as a writer, and the dearest friend she had ever had, aside her sister Susanna. Throughout her life, Frances was to be remarkably tenacious of friends and acquaintances; the sundering of relations was not at all her style. But Hester was too definite for compromise, and Burney had been manipulated—and had manipulated herself—into a position where a breach was inevitable. That did not prevent her missing Hester very much. Even in age, as she comments on past experience, she notes with intensity, "Ah! how I loved her!"[44]

In 1784 Burney entered a period of tension and privation. Even the best gifts that 1784 offered seemed to have their shadowed side. In some compensation for the loss of Mrs. Thrale, Frances Burney became acquainted with the Phillipses' neighbors, William Locke of Norbury Park and his wife Frederica. William Locke, a virtuoso and patron of the arts, liberal in his political views, was a model of all that was gentlemanly. Frederica Locke, the "dearest Fredy" of later letters, was two years older than Frances (and eighteen years younger than her husband); she had beauty, charm, and wit. Yet Frances knew that William Locke thought his wife overexcitable, and feared for her some sort of mental breakdown. In August 1784, while the two women were enjoying a country drive in the Lockes' chaise, they had an alarming conversation:

she [Frederica] told me, with an agitation that alarmed me, she had just had a Lecture from Mr Lock [*sic*], upon her want of *Moderation*,—that he had lessoned her with great earnestness upon the subject . . . & had repeatedly cautioned her against giving me an ill opinion of her, by her unguarded vehemence. I well understood he meant but to check what he considered as the remains of her late alarming nervousness, but she, believing it an attack upon her natural disposition, was wounded to the quick. O well do I know the justice he does her, & the motive which induces him to give her this counsel. He fears the return of that dreadful agitation which so strongly threatened her Reason, & he hopes, through her excessive fondness for her chosen Friend, to work upon her Mind to keep a constant curb upon the eagerness of her sensations.

Frances was put in a difficult position, for Frederica Locke's lack of *"Moderation"* was exhibited in expressions of fondness for Burney, expressions that had brought upon her the lecture from her husband. For Burney to be cool and rational in return for such ardor might seem snubbing. Frederica indeed felt that the vindication of her reason lay in assurances of Burney's reciprocal feeling:

she added, "I was forced, as he so much fears you cannot return my affection, to tell him I *knew* you *did* return it, to prevent his thinking me *mad*,—my Fanny, *mad!*— " This wholly overset me . . . & then it was the faintness came across me of which you saw the remains.[45]

Burney at this time was not given to fits of faintness; she reacts to the tension of being pulled two ways. William Locke wanted to use the women's friendship to teach Frederica the value of dampened enthusiasm, the decorous application of "a constant curb." Despite William Locke's reported praise of Burney, she cannot be sure he really does approve of her, since she affects his wife adversely, and the only way to earn his praise would be to withdraw to some extent from her friend. Burney in this situation is manipulated by the William of lectures and lessons, and the course of her affection for Frederica is rendered inhibited and self-conscious. The friendship did proceed, but was initially strained by anxiety; the threat of female madness hung over elegant Norbury Park.

At the end of 1784 Burney was undergoing a new grief. She visited Dr. Johnson on his deathbed. Two days before his death Johnson said, "I think I shall throw the ball at Fanny yet!" a remark that indicated a desire for her conversation, but Dr. Burney "decided, most tenderly, not to tell me this" until evening. Frances regretted that "the day was over before I knew he had said what I look upon as a call to me."[46] Dr. Burney's tender wisdom had kept her from seeing her old friend once more. Johnson's death on 13 December meant the loss of a real friend, and an end forever to the glory and "Flash" of the Streatham days. The loss of Johnson was the culmination of a miserable year in which Frances had been emotionally battered. She entered 1785 in a weary and depressed state.

There was one new friend of importance whose friendship was to cost Frances Burney dear. Early in 1783, Burney met Mary Delany (née Granville), the widow of Dr. Patrick Delany, Swift's friend. This dignified gentlewoman of eighty-three offered Frances what she seemed to need, even in her thirties—the stubstitute mother or grandmother (Fig. 21). To Charles Burney, Mrs. Delany was delightful because of her aristocratic lineage and connections. When Mary Delany's closest friend, Margaret Cavendish Harley, Dowager Duchess of Portland, died in 1785, Mary Delany fell ill, and Frances Burney offered care and companionship. The queen gave the aristocratic but impoverished old lady a house at Windsor, and the king supplied a three-hundred-pound annuity.

After the rupture with the new Mrs. Piozzi, Mary Delany in some sense took Hester's place, just as Frances, though so much younger, could help fill the gap made in Mrs. Delany's heart by the death of Margaret Cavendish. Mary Delany herself was sprightly and creative; in her seventies she had invented a new art form in her flower pieces, delicate and original collages that at once record botanical study and anticipate Georgia O'Keeffe.[47] Mourning the loss of this occupation through failing eyesight, Mrs. Delany had the more reason to feel grateful for Frances's companionship.

It had evidently not occurred to Frances Burney that her friends and relations might be actively worried about her situation. She mistakenly assumed that her lovelorn state was a purely private matter. But it must have seemed plain to those around her that she would marry no one if not George Cambridge, and that he was not going to propose. The Burney family saw an old maid, not a brilliant young novelist or potential dramatist whose best work might still be to come. Indeed, Burney seemed to have ceased to write. Had she had another novel about to come out, her friends would have held back, and certainly the queen would have been infinitely less disposed to take her on. The queen, making inquiries before having Frances Burney presented to her, was anxious to be assured that a report that Miss Burney had a new play coming out was untrue. Fortunately, from the point of view of both the queen and Mrs. Delany, it was untrue; they thought the blameless Burney had too high a reputation, a character "too delicate to suit with writing for the stage."[48] As she was not writing, Burney had no income, no prospects of any kind. It was reasonable for Dr. Burney to worry about the fate of the only unmarried daughter of his first marriage and to wish she could be provided for. Mary Delany also wanted to contrive some sort of secure future for her friend, and she was in a position to be helpful.

When Burney was first presented to the king and queen in December 1785, while she was visiting Mrs. Delany at Windsor, she took the matter with light-hearted curiosity. She respected King George III and Queen Charlotte, but they amused her, too. (Her account of her second conversation with the king at that time immortalizes his famous dictum: "Was there ever . . . such stuff as great part of Shakespeare? only one must not say so! . . . Is there not sad stuff? What?—what?"[49] At her first meeting with the king, when the monarch called upon Mrs. Delany, Frances Burney thought that with everyone standing respectfully at a distance from the king and each other, the party seemed about to play "Puss in the Corner":

> I could hardly help expecting to be beckoned, with a *Puss! Puss! Puss!* to change places with one of my Neighbours.
>
> This idea, afterwards, gave way to another more pompous. It seemed to me we were *acting a Play;* there is something so little like common & real life, in every body's standing, while talking, in a Room full of Chairs, & standing, too, so aloof from each other, that I almost thought myself upon a Stage, assisting in the representation of a Tragedy, in which the King played his own part, of The King; Mrs. Delany that of a venerable confident [*sic*], Mr. Barnard, his respectful attendant; Miss Port, a suppliant virgin, wanting encouragement to bring forward some petition; Miss Dewes, a young Orphan, intended to move the Royal compassion; & myself,—a very solemn, sober, & decent *Mute.*[50]

Burney has an acute sense of role-playing; the king necessitates the theatrical, and King George III, like Sartre's waiter, seems to play his part almost too well. The etiquette which surrounds the part of the king makes everyone behave unnaturally, as in games or theatricals. Frances Burney comically elaborates upon the unnatural constraints of court etiquette (taught her by Mrs. Delany) in a letter to her sister Esther:

> You would never believe . . . the many things to be studied, for appearing with a proper propriety before crowned heads. Heads without crowns are quite other sort of rotundas.
>
> Now, then, to the etiquette. . . . I shall give you those instructions I have received myself, that, should you find yourself in the royal presence, you may know how to comport yourself.
>
> *Directions for coughing, sneezing, or moving, before the King and Queen.*
>
> In the first place, you must not cough. If you find a cough tickling in your throat, you must arrest it from making any sound; if you find yourself choking with the forbearance, you must choke—but not cough.
>
> In the second place, you must not sneeze. If you have a vehement cold, you must take no notice of it . . . if a sneeze still insists upon making its way, you must oppose it, by keeping your teeth grinding together; if the violence of the repulse breaks some blood-vessel, you must break the blood-vessel—but not sneeze.

In the third place, you must not, upon any account, stir either hand or foot. If, by chance, a black pin runs into your head, you must not take it out. If the pain is very great, you must be sure to bear it without wincing; if it brings the tears into your eyes, you must not wipe them off. . . . If the blood should gush from your head by means of the black pin, you must let it gush; if you are uneasy to think of making such a blurred appearance, you must be uneasy, but you must say nothing about it. If, however, the agony is very great, you may, privately, bite the inside of your cheek, or of your lips, for a little relief; taking care, meanwhile, to do it so cautiously as to make no apparent dent outwardly. And, with that precaution, if you even gnaw a piece out, it will not be minded, only be sure either to swallow it, or commit it to a corner of the inside of your mouth till they are gone—for you must not spit.[51]

This fantasia obviously echoes Burney's imagined new etiquette delineated in the joke to Crisp and the ladies in 1774 ("you are never again to *cough*," "whatever is natural . . . is entirely banished from polite circles").[52] But here the comedy is much more violent and energetic, in a crescendo of self-wounding—choking, grinding teeth, breaking a blood vessel, gushing with blood, eating oneself. There are new touches of meaningless pain caused by intense and absurd repression. Enchanted by "proper propriety," the body becomes imprisoned in itself, and self-torturing, the only release being the infliction of further anguish. The disposal of the bitten piece of the cheek is a disturbing image of self-cannibalizing "self-dependence." Julia Epstein quotes this passage to illustrate Burney's general interest in violence and the body, and her particular tendency to relate "decorous propriety and its potential for unexpected explosion."[53]

Burney's court satire is strangely prophetic. Perhaps she had begun, if only unconsciously, to guess what might be in the wind. If only some enemy had been able to forward this satire to the queen! If such impressions and such words had been known to the crowned "rotundas"—or even to Mrs. Delany—Frances Burney might have been spared her forthcoming ordeal.

The royal family was being worked upon with gentle propaganda in Frances Burney's favor. Private inquiries proved her irreproachable in chastity and discreet conduct. (Such inquiries did not reach as far as the anguished journal-letters regarding Mr. Cambridge.) The beneficent trap was at last sprung in June 1786, when the courtier Leonard Smelt told Frances Burney that the queen was prepared to invite her to be deputy keeper of the robes. Her first response was "consternation" so visible that the surprised envoy offered not to mention his commission to her father but to carry her respectful excuse straight back to the queen. Frances Burney could not, however, feel entitled to keep from her father a matter of such significance. She who was now supported by her father would be earning a good salary in the royal service—two hundred pounds a year. She would be provided with an apartment, servants, full board, even some clothes. Mr. Smelt appealed to family feeling, intimating that as the queen's servant she would have "opportunities of serving your particular friends." Even at this flattering picture, Frances Burney made it clear to Mr. Smelt that she felt "no situation of that sort was suited to my own taste, or promising to my own happiness."[54] So she wrote in a frank account of her horrified reaction in a letter to Charlotte Cambridge, sister of the beloved George. She evidently hoped that her imminent fate and her horror of it might arouse the dilatory lover to action. She kept on hoping that her St. George would come and rescue her from the dragon, up to and beyond the eleventh hour.

Burney perhaps also had some slight hope that Charles Burney would say he still needed her (for work on his *History of Music*), and would respond to her own unhappiness by shielding her from this unwanted offer as he had in the case of the insignificant Barlow. Nothing of the sort could happen. Frances let her father decide: "I cast . . . the whole into my father's disposal and pleasure."[55] Dr. Burney was overjoyed, eager to persuade his daughter that this was a wonderful opportunity, a delightful service assuring the happiness of the whole family. Until Frances Burney left her post, Charles Burney continued to hope her situation would lead to a grand promotion for James in the Navy, and a berth for himself as Royal Musician. Unlike her father, Frances Burney was never sanguine about these opportunities, and she had neither her father's talent for charming, nor his taste for flattery and solicitation. She dutifully made herself offer petitions for her brothers James and Charles, in 1790, to no avail; she was sorry at having to disappoint her family, but not herself in the least surprised.[56]

No one outside her family would offer sympathy. The position was almost universally considered an honor. It was, after all, customary for distinguished writers to be given sinecure jobs, but Frances Burney could not be offered a nominal employment in the Post Office or Board of Trade. There was no tradition of patronage for talented females. Frances Burney's post may have been an honor but it was not honorary. She was expected to be on the job from six in the morning until twelve at night, constantly on call. Nobody thought of giving Burney a free annual income, so that she could write in peace and live as she liked—nobody save Burney herself, in a significant joke to her sister Esther:

> You know I told you . . . my various difficulties, what sort of prefer-ment to turn my thoughts to, and concluded with just starting a young budding notion of decision, by suggesting that a handsome pension for nothing at all would be as well as working night and day for a salary.[57]

After all, a handsome pension for nothing at all was what Mrs. Delany got— but she was not only an artist, but a gentlewoman down on her luck, a special case. Middle-class talented males might get pensions "for nothing at all" (as Johnson had been given his three hundred pounds a year), but there was no precedent for regarding a female author in that manner. Indeed, the fact that Burney was an author was now to be forgotten. No one objected that the life for which she was now destined was the least suited to a writer. No one cared about her future novels. The queen cared little for any novels. Frances remarked later, on the occasion of the embarrassing visit of the German novelist Sophie von La Roche (to whom she dared not offer a dinner), "the Queen has a settled aversion to almost all novels and something very near it to almost all novel-writers."[58] Before she met Burney, the queen had been most disagreeably impressed by hearing Mme. de Genlis's remark that "the *charmante auteur de Cécile*" was like the heroine of a novel. The queen kindly told Frances that she herself would interfere "to put a stop to such mistaken panegyric," the character of "the heroine of a romance" being "so unjust and so injurious."[59] Apparently Queen Charlotte expected that novel-writing would naturally be forgotten, like other necessary, if vulgar, habits and activities once appropriate in a lower sphere of life but not now required. Burney's life as a writer was to be suppressed; this was part of the great divorce from life this step meant for her.

In an evil hour of 17 July 1786, the sacrifice took place. A carriage took Frances and her father to Windsor, and to Mrs. Delany: "she was happy we should now be so much united, but . . . she saw the hard conflict within me, and the tenderest pity checked her delight." From Mrs. Delany's dwelling it was only a short walk to the Lodge:

> O, my dear Susan! in what an agony of mind did I obey the summons!
> . . . My father accompanied me. Mrs. Delany . . . gave me her blessing.
> We walked; the Queen's lodge is not fifty yards from Mrs. Delany's door.
> My dear father's own courage all failed him in this little step; for as I was
> now on the point of entering—probably for ever—into an entire new
> way of life, and of foregoing by it all my most favourite schemes, and
> every dear expectation my fancy had ever indulged of happiness adapted
> to its taste—as now all was to be given up—I could disguise my trepida-
> tion no longer—indeed, I never had disguised, I had only forborne pro-
> claiming it. But my dear father now, sweet soul! felt it all, as I held by
> his arm, without power to say one word, but that if he did not hurry
> along I should drop by the way. I heard in his kind voice that he was now
> really alarmed; he would have slackened his pace, or have made me stop
> to breathe; but I could not; my breath seemed gone, and I could only
> hasten with all my might, lest my strength should go too.[60]

This short walk on her father's arm reminds one, as it evidently reminded Frances Burney, of the short journey to the altar and marriage. It certainly re-minded Charles Burney of that ceremonial. In his own letter to Smelt, describing the day with unmixed satisfaction, Charles Burney complacently makes the comparison: "though I have had the good fortune to marry to my own contentment three of my daughters, I never gave one of them away with the pride or the pleasure I experienced in my gift of last Monday."[61] The father is giving the daughter away, forcing her reluctant steps toward a union she abhors—a situation often treated in eighteenth-century literature, and by no means unknown in life. Mrs. Delany in her teens had suffered from a forced marriage to the repulsive Mr. Pendarves, as Frances Burney knew. When in 1789 she visited Longleat, the site of Lord Lansdowne's sacrifice of his niece, Burney remembered with "indignant hatred" the "heartless uncle," and the "sacrifice to tyranny" of young Mary Granville, the victim, "thrown away, as if she, her person, and her existence, were nothing in the scale."[62] Now Frances Burney was sacrificed as if she and her own existence were nothing in the scale.

Mrs. Delany, who had once suffered so unforgivably, was now assisting at a parallel sacrifice, no intuition telling her that Frances Burney ought not to be "thrown away" for apparent advantages. Mary Delany meant well by her friend, whom she praised for "her extreme diffidence of herself, notwithstanding her great genius"; Mrs. Delany told her old friend Frances Hamilton how delighted she was with Miss Burney's new prospects:

> One of the principal ladies that attend the Queen's person as dresser is going to retire . . . being in too bad a state of health to continue her honourable and delightful employment, for such it must be near such a queen; and Miss Burney is to be the happy successor.[63]

It was Mary Delany who brought about the position of the "happy successor." The reward for "genius" so pleasantly tempered with "diffidence" (evidently Mary Delany had not caught Burney's caustic or violent aspects) would be a rise to a higher social level. Mary Delany could not help being conscious of Frances's low origins, which the queen's service would cancel out. King George and Queen Charlotte, in offering a position truly coveted by aristocratic families for their unmarried women, had every reason to believe they were bestowing a most unlooked-for favor upon a fortunate commoner with no claims upon them. Everyone meant so well.

Can Charles Burney be cleared of every charge but meaning well? I think not. Frances Burney's agitation during that sacrificial walk was distressing enough to be noticeable, but whether he was to hurry her along or let her stop to breathe, his only object was to get his daughter within those gates. As Macaulay caustically commented: "Dr. Burney was transported out of himself with delight. Not such are the raptures of a Circassian father who has sold his pretty daughter well to a Turkish slave-merchant."[64] What Frances wanted the "kind voice" to say was that it was not too late to stop the proceedings. With the Burney inability to fight openly, Frances could not combat, could not even make a vigorous appeal to her father. She could not at this instance express "indignant hatred" at a scene of "sacrifice to tyranny." Entries in her journal to Susanna use the word "conflict" repeatedly during ths period, but "conflict" always means *inner* conflict, self-division. "Conflict" in this sense is an important word to Frances Burney—too important for her to allow it to Mrs. Thrale in the solemn advice letter, in which Burney swerves rather strangely into "contrasts" ("when all your contrasts are settled"). Frances Burney is again practicing "the forbearance I recommend": "I could disguise my trepidation no longer—indeed, I never had disguised, I had only forborne proclaiming it." She had forborne protest, open and declared resistance to the court plan. On the fatal walk she still forbears proclaiming anything; she only acts out her trepidation, making physical symptoms of distress manifest. But this silent, correct, irreproachable sort of protest can work only if those around her truly wish to serve her inner wishes, and is splendidly ineffectual when they do not. Even "undisguised" emotion can be ignored or deliberately misread, as long as nothing is really said—and Frances Burney said nothing in her Iphigenia hour. Playing her daughterly role she entered court as "a very solemn, sober, & decent *Mute.*"

After the die was cast, Frances assured her father, "I would from that moment . . . banish all the regret." With proper filiality she reassured him, and had "the fullest success; his hopes and gay expectations were all within call, and they ran back at the first beckoning."[65] Dr. Burney's grateful letter to Smelt describes Frances as "much pleased and flattered by all that had passed during the course of the day," and liking her apartments "extremely."[66] His "hopes and gay expectations" were always within call. They continued to be within call even when his daughter's health was visibly failing. That day, 17 July 1786, marked a great betrayal.

But the deed was done:

> I now took the most vigorous resolutions to observe the promise I had made my dear father. Now all was finally settled . . . it would be foolish, useless, even wicked, not to reconcile myself to my destiny.
>
> . . . I am *married*, my dearest Susan—I look upon it in that light—I was averse to forming the union, and I endeavoured to escape it; but my friends interfered—they prevailed—and the knot is tied.[67]

The entrance into court life continued to seem like a wretched enforced marriage, or alternatively, like that other kind of marriage, entering a convent and taking the veil. The ghastly mock-marriage to the court had also signaled to the world her renunciation of marriage and sex forever—a renunciation not willed by Burney herself. Leading an unnatural "dead and tame life," she was always conscious of the mental and physical sterility of her "monastic destiny."[68] She continued to make bitter resolutions:

> . . . to relinquish, without repining, frequent intercourse with those I love;—
> to settle myself in my monastery, without one idea of ever quitting it;—to

study for the approbation of my lady abbess . . . and to associate more cheerily with my surrounding nuns and monks.[69]

So she determined in the New Year of 1787, in one of a number of such passages of good resolves, echoing the passages of assumed resignation and detachment written during the days of George Cambridge.

However glorified Frances's position, she was still a servant, to be summoned by a bell ("so mortifying a mark of servitude, I always felt myself blush . . . at my own strange degradation"), and to be given a gown by her employer like any housemaid. Queen Charlotte gave Frances a present of "lilac tabby"— evidently she shared Mrs. Thrale's association of ideas.[70] Frances Burney had to master the art of walking backwards "in the true court retrograde motion";[71] an even harder art was that of standing perfectly still in the royal presence (Frances notes that attendants positioned themselves by pillars in order to indulge in furtive leaning). On formal occasions, the physical needs of attendants went unnoticed. During the elaborate royal visit to Oxford in August 1786, the royals banqueted while their entourage went unfed. One of the equerries discovered a little parlor in Christ Church College into which he, Frances Burney, and another lady might retreat, as they were the only ones who had not contrived "a little sitting" during the day; he produced some apricots from his coat pocket. Suddenly, the queen entered:

> Up we all started, myself alone not discountenanced; for I really think it quite respect sufficient never to sit down in the royal presence, without aiming at having it supposed I have stood bolt upright ever since I have been admitted to it.
>
> Quick into our pockets was crammed our bread, and close into our hands was squeezed our fruit; by which I discovered that our appetites were to be supposed annihilated, at the same time that our strength was to be invincible.[72]

Burney's tart observations show her refusal to let go of reality; she is not to be swallowed up in ludicrous rituals and bizarre assumptions, and at least privately maintains her right to her own appetite. Despite loyalty to the king and queen, and real affection for them and the princesses as individuals, she was able to see the absurdity of their way of life. She was able to make allowances for them:

> The Queen had a taste for conversation, and the Princesses a good-humoured love for it. . . . But what will not prejudice and education inculcate? They have been brought up to annex silence to respect and decorum; to talk, therfore, unbid, or to differ from any given opinion even when called upon, are regarded as high improprieties, if not presumptions.

They none of them do justice to their own minds, while they enforce this subjection upon the minds of others.[73]

Burney could make allowances for "prejudice and education," for "prejudice and want of personal experience" in her employers. She could even see the damage they did to themselves by adhering to their idea of propriety. What would the queen have thought had she known that the diffident commoner was making such allowances for her? In her journal-letters Frances Burney succeeded in doing what Elizabeth Montagu fulsomely hoped Burney would accomplish, "delineating the characters of the exalted personages with whom she lived,"[74] though that delineation went unpublished until well into the next century. We have no other such record of court life. Other writers of intimate court memoirs are writing as insiders, like Lord Hervey. Burney's is the only minute record by an *outsider*. And she is honest enough never to pretend to be an insider, never to imagine herself an aristocrat. For this she deserves credit; the temptations to such compensatory vanity lay at hand.

Frances Burney could master the peculiar rules of behavior, and steel herself to bear the physical irksomeness. Queen Charlotte, "the Magnolia" in Burney's code, Frances could love. The queen, only eight years older than her new servant, had spent an exhausting youth bearing fifteen children, of whom Princess Amelia, three years old in 1786, was the last. Queen Charlotte could hardly escape being a mother-figure, to Frances as to the nation. The most dreadful thing about this new life—this horrid marriage, this grimly conventual existence—was something Frances had not imagined beforehand. The worst of her position was her constant subordination not to the queen but to the irascible Mrs. Schwellenberg, first keeper of the queen's robes. Elizabeth Juliana Schwellenberg, middle-aged and plain, was a target of caricaturists of the period. In Thomas Rowlandson's "The Prospect Before Us" (Fig. 22), Pitt manages the queen during the Regency crisis of 1788, while Mrs. Schwellenberg declares her intention of pawning the Crown Jewels: "the name of Schwellenburg [*sic*] shall be trumpeted to the remotest corner of *Rag Fair*!" The queen is depicted as being overfriendly to the Germans (represented by her obese favorite), and indeed, as being prepared to strip England in the German interests. In James Gillray's revolutionary fantasia "The Offering to Liberty" (Fig. 23), Mrs. Schwellenberg appears as a German toad-eater.[75] (Burney must have feared that she too would appear in caricatures of the royal family, but this is one ordeal she was apparently spared.) To political cartoonists, Mrs. Schwellenberg represented the German background of both monarchs, and could be used to hit at the supposed tendency of the court to serve German interests. Mrs. Schwellenberg's devotion to the queen's service meant for her a life in an alien land; she never quite mastered English, and Burney's diary maliciously records her errors in grammar, idiom, and pronunciation. It is possible to feel sorry for Mrs.

Schwellenberg while recognizing that any subordinate would find her detestable. She was given to fits of rage, unreasonable starts of malice. It was her ill treatment that led to the breakdown in health of Frances's predecessor, Mrs. Haggedorn, whose bleeding eyes Mrs. Schwellenberg had observed with composure, insisting that the unfortunate subaltern still endure the cold draft from the open coach window.

Mrs. Schwellenberg ("Cerbera" in Frances's code) observed the second keeper with jealous dislike, which increased when she noticed that the equerries preferred Frances Burney's company to her own. Yet she would not let Frances escape to her own room for free time. Mrs. Schwellenberg insisted that her subordinate ought to endure the long sittings over tea, the dreary evenings at cards. Sometimes Mrs. Schwellenberg insulted her repeatedly; sometimes she would fly into a silent rage, not speaking to "Miss Berner." The irritations created by Mrs. Schwellenberg, the most hideous daily aspect of her wretched situation, counteracted the emotional anaesthesia Frances Burney was cultivating. She explained to Susanna that her plan was "to wean myself from myself— to lessen all my affections—to curb all my wishes—to deaden all my sensations." She had been trying to do this "so long ago as the first day my dear father accepted my offered appointment." The need to deaden feeling became more urgent once Frances found out "the interior of my position . . . when I saw myself expected by Mrs. Schwellenberg, not to be her colleague, but her dependent deputy! . . . her companion, her humble companion, at her own command!" Only a month after entering court service, Frances is recording a revulsion so strong that she is already thinking of "soliciting his [her father's] leave to resign." But she is restrained by "my horror of disappointing, perhaps displeasing, my dearest father . . . indulgent as he is to me, I have not the heart so cruelly to thwart his hopes—his views—his happiness." Her "constant endeavour" must be to bear "the tyranny, the *exigeance*, the *ennui*, and attempted indignities."[76] Burney protests here, as so often, "that struggle is no more"— she must not let herself think of hurting her father. Yet the struggle is not over, she cannot succeed in deadening all sensations, in annihilating herself. She revolts against "tyranny"; a political terminology creeps into her descriptions of her state.

Mrs. Delany, who had promised herself and Frances such pleasure in their new neighborliness, was not much help. Although an approved visitor to the Lodge, Mrs. Delany found evenings with the inescapable Mrs. Schwellenberg too unpleasant, and told Frances "she would positively come no more, unless I would exert and assert myself into a little more consequence."[77] Early in 1787 Burney determined to assert herself by putting into execution a "long-wished project of liberating my evenings from official trammels," by not presiding over the equerries' tea (no part of her official duties). She expected approval from Mrs. Delany: "But how surprised was I to find she totally disapproved it! . . . no innovations ought to be risked."[78] So much for exertion and assertion. Mary

Delany did not want to understand Frances Burney's troubles in her situation—as Frances knew, she could not be asked to understand: "her . . . joy in seeing me situated where we can daily meet would all be . . . destroyed . . . if she read as far into my heart as she suffers me to read into hers.—Our confidence cannot be mutual."[79] Burney was too closely surrounded by people whose feelings she was supposed to consider ahead of her own. At the end of her long life, Mary Delany wanted to tell Burney about her own experiences, not to hear about her young friend's feelings. And then, not unpredictably, Mrs. Delany died in April 1788, leaving Frances alone to bear the worst period of her captivity.

It was a recurrent pattern of Frances Burney's life, the abandonment by the good mother-figures. Esther Sleepe Burney, Hester Thrale, Mary Delany—each left her. And, as in childhood, each time she was deserted by a "mother," Frances was thrown back emotionally upon reliance on her father, and devotion to him and his wishes. If the "good mothers" tended to desert Frances, the "bad mothers" seemed only too hardy. One of the private sources of Frances's extreme stress under the rule of Mrs. Schwellenberg was the fact that (as Hemlow pointed out) Mrs. Schwellenberg reminded her hideously of her stepmother. Burney spells out the resemblance; Mrs. Schwellenberg is the stepmother's "exactest Fellow,—gloomy, dark, suspicious, rude, reproachful." "O Heaven!—how depressing,—how cruel to be fastened thus again on an Associate so Exigeante, so tyrannical, & so ill disposed!"[80] The painful experiences of Frances Burney's teens, when she had had to endure her father's remarriage and her new stepmother's rude sway, were thus psychically revived. Her father's abandonment of the daughter in his remarriage, his betrayal of her by placing her in humiliating subordination to his domineering and detested consort, undoubtedly combined psychologically, in Frances Burney's inner interpretation of experience, with her new abandonment and the new treachery. Yet Frances was blocked from open expression of any hostility toward her father.

In her journal-letters to Susanna, however, Frances Burney allowed herself expression, even if a somewhat censored expression, of the range of her feelings. Enough has been said elsewhere about the historical value of Burney's diary of the court years. Her version of the trial of Warren Hastings is well known; so is her description of the king's madness. My present interest in the diary is in what it tells us about Burney herself, and the way in which it is related to her other writing. A number of important words recur in the diary for 1786–1791: "conflict," "monastic," "captivity," "tyranny," "shackles," "rebel"—also "annihilation," "deadened." These metaphors and their meanings supply plots and actions for the series of plays in which Frances tried to work out her own situation and explore and explain her private hell. The comic mastery is certainly in abeyance in the tragedies written at Windsor and Kew, but that is because the greatest tragedy for Frances Burney was her being there at all. The *Diary* letters still reflect the daylight side of Burney's existence. But daylight and reason do not touch everything. The tragedies were a means of expressing the truth—that her life was a disaster—and a means of rebelling against the heavy reality of imprisonment. Frances Burney never succeeded in her plan of heroic apathy.

> What creatures are we all for liberty and freedom!
> Rebels *partout*!
> "Soon as the life-blood warms the heart,
> The love of liberty awakes!"

Ah, my dear friends! I wrote that with a sigh that might have pierced through royal walls![81]

Frances Burney's comic observation of role-playing in her meeting with the king, "It seemed to me we were *acting a Play* . . . assisting in the representation of a Tragedy," was prophetic. Burney resorted to the tragic mode to describe her own life in the court years; she wrote three tragic plays and a lengthy if fragmentary sketch of a fourth during her royal incarceration. These plays certainly lack the completeness, force, and life of her novels or her comic plays. At times they are, frankly, bad—though it is hard to say what distinguishes a good from a bad tragedy in the 1780s. At times, Burney's tragic dramas are neither unpleasing nor lacking in insight. There is no critical background to draw on in treating them; those students of Burney who have read these manuscript plays (and not many have done so) have dismissed them, relating them neither to her life nor to the drama of her period.[82] The weaknesses of these plays considered as literature (awkwardness, convolution, overstrained emotional reactions and statements) have the same source as the moments of finer insight—in Burney's need to express what she felt, beyond what she was supposed to feel, what was always right to feel.

I am using these plays as evidence in a biographical study, treating them chiefly as psychological documents in Burney's emotional history, but these works are by no means unimportant to her future production as a writer. The matter of, and within, the plays is hard to set before the reader—hard in being both complex and sad. We see here Burney in the middle of the road of her life, lost in the dark wood and savaged by her own terrors. It is difficult for the biographer to enter the most intensely unhappy period of the subject's life—this chapter is a continuous descent into a dark valley. In order to understand the plays it is necessary to get used to reading Burney's symbols and the patterns recurring in the plays, which are primarily private allegories. Each play has a good father-figure, and a bad one who is authoritarian (often a king) and forever unapproachable by the heroine or "suppliant virgin." Each play has a lover for the heroine, but the lover is weakened or under some restraint, finally unable to save or help her. In fantasy manner, the father-figure and the lover-figure may both flicker into the same character in the play; as in dreams, characters shift uneasy symbolic meanings. Each play deals with civil war, and thus symbolically with inner division—with "conflict" in Burney's sense—and each play uses political terms in relation to events safely in the historic past in order to plead for personal liberty. Each of these plays represents a reaction against the wise passiveness, the silent forbearance and accommodation that had served Burney so very ill—and yet the self-anaesthetizing passivity, the elaborate resignation, are here also acted out, but not without countergestures toward rebellion, "liberty and freedom!"

Burney began the first of these tragedies in October 1788, when the king had just entered the worst phase of that illness of 1788–1789 (his great bout with the now-famous porphyria) and was thought mad.[83] With the queen, the princesses, and the other attendants, Burney was boxed up at Kew with the "mad" king and his doctors. Burney wrote that this "composition fit" served to while away time; "societyless, and bookless, and viewless as I am . . . my tragedy goes on, and fills up all vacancies."[84] The tragedy that filled up vacancy in 1788–1789 was *Edwy and Elgiva*. It was then largely "hints and ideas"; after an interval Burney returned to the "long-forgotted tragedy" in April 1790, and began "planning and methodising."[85] The aroused need for writing came from the new period of "conflict" and suspense. Frances had begun to hope for a release. In May 1790, she at last spoke to her father (or he permitted her to catch his private ear), and he seemed to agree that she might leave. But as 1790 dragged on, Frances had reason to fear that her captivity was not to be ended. It is in this period, 1790–1791, that the other tragedies were drafted.

Burney herself recognized to a great degree the therapeutic nature of these compositions. Congratulating herself in August 1790 for finishing the first draft "of her first tragedy," she adds that she does not know "What species of a composition it may prove," but knows that it was "an almost spontaneous work, and soothed the melancholy of imagination for a while," though afterwards it impressed her "with a secret sensation of horror, so like real woe." Merely writing something was a release; "she is pleased to have done something at last, she had so long lived in all ways as nothing."[86] Great unhappiness had at last put an end to the indisposition to writing, the sense of an "empty Brain." This writing was "spontaneous"—irresistible, compulsive. One tragedy led to another; "scarce, however, had this done with imagination . . . when imagination seized upon another subject for another tragedy." It was not so much imagination as a kind of obsession which pushed these writings into the light. The author felt that she was doing something at last, not "living as nothing," not annihilated. Identity returned to the "Nobody" at court as she penned these private anguished dramas.

Frances Burney tried not to overvalue her tragedies, but could not let go of them easily. When she left the court, she still worked on them, and had theatrical hopes for them. She revised *Edwy and Elgiva* again in 1794, when her brother Charles, thinking it stood a chance on stage, gave it to the managers of Drury Lane. It was acted at Drury Lane on 21 March 1795, with Mrs. Siddons as the heroine Elgiva—and it failed ignominiously.[87] It was not acted again, nor published (until 1956). Neither of Burney's other completed tragedies, *Hubert De Vere* and *The Siege of Pevensey*, was ever acted or published. They remain in manuscript, along with the last tragedy, *Elberta*, which exists as fragmentary notes.

Edwy and Elgiva is, like most other eighteenth-century tragedies, a historical play. The title is timely; there was a new nationalist interest in matters Anglo-Saxon, and names like "Edwy" recur in literature of the later eighteenth century.[88] The conflict between young King Edwy and St. Dunstan is a historical fact; as Hemlow points out, Burney adapted Hume's version of the story of the tenth-century king.

The action of the play chiefly concerns the desire of King Edwy to marry Elgiva, his "kinswoman," a choice which his Council claims is contrary to canon law.[89] Even more antagonistic is the monk Dunstan, the self-proclaimed saint. Edwy agrees to postpone the matter until after his coronation, but he and Elgiva are actually (like Mortimer and Cecilia) secretly married. When Elgiva is accused of being his "Concubine," Edwy reveals his secret marriage. Dunstan thunders at his licentiousness, telling him his marriage is not lawful. Confused, Edwy seems fearful of approaching his bride. She is then abducted by Dunstan and "three Ruffians." Edwy claims "The common rights of Equity & Law" (III. iv.41), while Dunstan raves about the authority of the priesthood and need for stricter reforms. Edwy sentences Dunstan to exile, while Elgiva escapes and returns to him. But Dunstan's creature the Archbishop pronounces "the dire sentence of divorce," and Elgiva is again abducted. Aldhelm, Edwy's well-meaning advisor, tells the king he must not search for Elgiva during a constitutional crisis. Dunstan's supporters are rising; civil war is at hand. A sentence of excommunication has been passed on Elgiva, and will be passed on Edwy if he crosses Dunstan.

Elgiva is thus fatally unprotected. At the beginning of Act V, we find Dunstan commending his henchman for stabbing her: "Thou hast done thy duty. / She was but Edwy's Concubine" (V.i.65). Elgiva staggers into view and falls fainting behind a hedge. The king's army passes by, and Edwy at last finds his Elgiva, being reunited with her only in her dying moments. After her death Edwy fights and is killed. Dunstan, though triumphant, is afflicted with remorse, while Aldhelm laments over the fallen king: "See youth untimely fell'd, Virtue oppress'd, / And Guilt victorious" (V.xxii.82). Seeing that matters go so ill on earth, can anyone "retain a doubt / That Retribution waits for all above?"

Edwy is Burney's first king-figure, a weak and good king fated to die (as some believed of good King George III in the autumn and winter of 1788). Edwy is a man of sensibility for whom the pressures of his time prove too strong. He and Elgiva are sexual, emotional creatures, rebelling in the name of private happiness against the decrees of patriarchal power. Aldhelm, the man of moderation, hinders as much as he helps, like an ineffectual Mr. Villars in the wrong situation. The good clergyman of *Evelina* is here oddly reflected in that other celibate cleric and father-substitute, Dunstan. Dunstan, a schemer like Monckton, is all that is repressive—authoritarian, power-hungry, and hard-hearted. He is totally antagonistic to women. When Aldhelm speaks of Edwy's need for friendship and the pleasures of marriage, Dunstan retorts, "Trifles like these a Monarch should disdain." Aldhelm's plea for the importance of marriage arouses Dunstan's incredulous anger, prompting Aldhelm's question, "If woman is our scorn, wedlock our horrour, / Where dwells the virture of our self-denial?" (III.iv.40). For Dunstan, monastic celibacy does rest on a "horrour" of sex and a scorn of women. He is in the line of Burney's woman-hating, strong male characters.

Like her hero and heroine, Burney had suffered under the imposition of authority that denied her desires. Like Elgiva, she had been removed from the scene of pleasure; she too had suffered a "divorce" from love and from living. Like Elgiva, who believes for a while that Edwy regrets the connection and wishes to separate, Burney had had to endure the experience of rejection. During the court period the old hope and desire were still not extinct. A letter written while she was in the court service, describing a chance encounter with George Cambridge, shows how much that still hurt. Seeing the two brothers ahead, Frances Burney would have turned back, but Charles Cambridge recognized her and pushed his brother who "started as if he had seen a Ghost, & with a Face expressive of such a sensation as such a sight might have impressed, he coldly, but very respectfully bowed." They paced together along Bond Street, George not speaking. When they had passed a crossing, "Mr. G. hastily pushed his Brother, saying *come this way*,—& then, taking off his Hat, distantly but with a look of restrained emotion, he just said, 'I wish you good morning Ma'am,' and bowing still more profoundly, hurried off his Brother." In the embarrassing epistle about this short encounter, we can see that Frances is driven still to hope against hope, to read into George Cambridge's coldness some hidden meaning: "the conduct was too unnatural to be the result of real indifference." Later in this confused letter, Frances Burney is even thinking of a possible future, as she had so often thought of it formerly:

> Nothing can make this matter quite clear, but some actual preferment: if then nothing follows, nothing can be intended,—if otherwise . . . how would my whole Heart be grieved & tormented. . . . All this put together, with an obligation so deep for a constancy so extraordinary,—& probably accompanied with palliations & reasons for every future inconsistence,—these are thoughts grievous to my mind,—& would cause scenes of every sort of distress & concern—*except a conflict!*—
> No—nothing could again excite that.[90]

Frances is building castles in the air, still imagining that the clergyman might—must—propose once he has "some actual preferment" and an income. She insists she would feel no *"conflict"* in refusing him—in insisting (against reason) she shows every sign of conflict. The dream of Mr. Cambridge's interest in her was too precious to let go.

Burney's play supplies Edwy with unimpeachable "palliations & reasons for every inconsistence"; he was torn from his love only by circumstances beyond his control. Elgiva in the play feels deserted: "Gone? Can it be?—Without one balmy look / Of fostering tenderness to sooth his absence?" She may wonder, "Has he left me thus? . . . all lost in mystery?" (II.vii.30). But in her fantasy-play Burney can make the lover faithful; Elgiva is at last given assurance of love. If Edwy represents the lover who failed to rescue his lady from a harsh fate, the failure was not his fault. At another level, too, Edwy represents the weak father excused—he is only weak because he is too good. All the blame is heaped on Dunstan, the bad father as an evil—but self-righteous—authoritarian.

Burney's Prologue of 1795 makes an appeal to her eighteenth-century audience in referring to the play's exhibition of "Mystery's gloom and Error's Maze" in an age "Of blind submission and mistaken zeal." References to the bad old days before the Reformation and enlightened Whiggism were thoroughly acceptable. Thus "Gothic" writers could turn to images of the officially bad past in order to express what was wrong with the officially good present—wrongs that could not be readily expressed or understood. By the last two decades of the century, the tropes and metaphors of "Gothic" literature provided the codes in which sexual and social misery might be powerfully but unofficially conveyed. It is noticeable that women and homosexuals make up the greater number of writers who employ these codes, creating genres which have ever since been popular, but have always had to combat patronizing disapproval on the part of the literary and social Establishment. The "codes" were not something that the writers themselves could readily crack and explicate, but were intuitively serviceable as images of unconscious or half-conscious feelings, of knowledge that could not be publicly accommodated. Figures of the bad past, officially despised by enlightened moderns, could be employed covertly and anxiously to question the modernism that still told Woman that the enlightened authority now exercised over her was always benevolent, that social arrangements nowadays worked for her good and required only cheerful submission. Burney had had some tendency toward the "Gothic" in her writings, as can be seen in *Cecilia*. Now in *Edwy*, we can see that the presentation of Dunstan and of the monastic priesthood and of the Church anticipates Ann Radcliffe's portrayal of Schedoni, the monastery, and the Inquisition in *The Italian* (1797), that antipatriarchal novel. Monastic life was Burney's metaphor for the denial of her own sexuality, "her person and her existence." Dunstan's denial or scorn of sexual appetite is presented as an assault upon liberty and identity. Somehow, the evil of Frances Burney's own life should be recognized and cast out, and the king-as-father united with the innocent girl, recognizing her meritorious suffering. Ideally, Dr. Burney should say, as Edwy does, "I feel my wrong—Canst thou forgive it?" (V.xi.75). Even for Elgiva, Frances Burney could contrive so much satisfaction only in death.

In her play, Burney can reject the virtuous plans for self-deadening, the weaning of self from self. Frigid Odo gives such advice to Edwy, who rightly revolts; the soul cannot be remade into tameness:

> Say, must we suffer
> Each human ill, yet spurn each human feeling
> For the vain efforts of presumptuous sophistry,
> That, with no standard or of right or wrong,
> Cavils to err, & errs to cavil on?
> When thou canst fashion to thy Will thy limbs
> Then talk of modelling thy soul at pleasure.
> True piety repels all mask, all mockery.
>
> (IV.vi.56)

Burney had been trying to remodel her soul at command—and found she could not do it. In the Cambridge affair, in the rupture with Hester, and in the acquiescence in the court appointment, she had been guilty of masking and mockery in the name of "right" conduct. She needed to utter this protest to those around her—needed to, but could not. She could manage to say it only to herself. No wonder *Edwy* inspired in her "horror, so like real woe"; it *was* real woe. *Edwy* is a sigh—and a cry—"that might have pierced through royal walls."

So too is *The Siege of Pevensey*, which meant nearly as much to her as *Edwy*, judging from the care taken in making a clean copy (for stage managers?) with the heading (so sad to our eyes) "By the Author of Evelina and Cecilia."[91] Again we have civil war in a remote period, in the quarrel between King William II and his brother Robert, who both lay claim to England. The castle of Pevensey, taken by Robert's forces, is besieged by William's troops. Characters endeavor to pass "through royal walls." At the outset, Adela, daughter of the Earl of Chester, is imprisoned within the starved castle, but escapes with the help of De Belesme, son of the governor of the castle, who is then suspected of collusion with Chester, likewise suspected of treason. Adela offers herself as a pledge, returning a voluntary prisoner to save both her father and her lover. In the castle, De Belesme begs Adela to marry him secretly, for fear she will be forcibly taken in marriage by the rough Norman knight De Warenne, who is trying to ransom her. Adela consents to secret marriage, and is soon racked by guilt which becomes anguish when her father, Chester, coming in disguise to rescue her, finds that she has given herself without his consent. Both father and daughter are saved by De Belesme, but captured by "Tyrant Rufus" (Act IV). In the climactic scene, De Belesme, Chester, and Adela are brought before the king. Adela agrees to marry the hateful De Warenne in order to save her father, though Chester begs her rather to let him die. Adela implores him "render me not a paracide [*sic*]," but proposes a compromise. She will go into a convent instead of marrying De Warenne; the king can have her dowry. Adela begs her father's blessing and is led off, after offering hymnlike praise of her father. She will pass her days in "soft remembrance / Of all his wond'rous goodness, patience, sweetness, / His mild indulgence to her early errors" (Act V). But the ending is abruptly happy; the war ends, and Chester gives Adela to De Belesme.

The central relationship of *The Siege of Pevensey* is quite clearly that of Chester and Adela—father and daughter. The play works out, fantasizes about, and idealizes the relationship between Charles Burney and Frances Burney. It should, however, be emphasized that the mid and late eighteenth-century tragic drama permitted and even invited a kind of enervated psychological expressionism, and that Burney's themes are not much different from those popular with dramatists, audiences, and readers at the time. If the Restoration drama had been largely interested in relations between fathers and sons, eighteenth-century serious dramas were much occupied with relations between fathers and daughters. The late Georgian period seems addicted to the pleasures of the father-daughter relationship. Officially, it is always presented as pure and holy, with the strength of heterosexual love yet delightfully innocent. Under the insistent innocence, however, emotional incest is never far away, though few writers went as far in sexualizing family romance as Horace Walpole, whose drama *The Mysterious Mother* (1768) is the story of a man who has had sexual congress with his mother, and then, years later, falls in love with and marries the young woman who is both his sister and his daughter. Walpole's play, printed but never allowed to be acted, was read aloud by Mr. Smelt and Frances Burney in November 1786. Burney was horrified, professing the work "dreadful! A story of so much atrocious and voluntary guilt," and feeling "indignant aversion . . . against the wilful author of a story so horrible."[92]

Yet Walpole's play may well have been a strong stimulus to her own venture into tragedy. Walpole's play is certainly exceptional (and thus censorable); there was a large cultural investment in insisting on the beautiful purity of father-daughter relations, the daughter becoming a kind of emotional resort for flagging male authority. Filial duty from the female offers reassurance in a blissful uncontaminated relationship that does not remind the father of his brute physicality but vindicates his authority under the guise of tenderness. The father is intense and tender, even when exerting authority in licensed destruction. In the climax of Samuel Crisp's *Virginia* (1754), Lucius Virginius, killing his daughter rather that letting her become the slave of a lustful tyrant, enjoys the submissive approval of his victim: "Yet my soul feels, and owns the deed is noble, / And worthy of my father!"[93] The father can save his daughter from unworthy sexuality and restore her to a pure state. The language of the plays dealing with this theme is not unlike the language of Burney's dramas. In Dodsley's *Cleone* (1758), the heroine, falsely accused of adultery by cunning villains, her child murdered by their order, is discovered by her father in a most affecting state of madness, sitting with the dead child in "a little bower of shrubs and branches . . . picking little sprigs from a bough."[94] Her father Beaufort wonders "if every filial trace in thy poor brain has gone," but the dying daughter comes to, and recognizes him: "My father!—my dear father!—do I wake? / And am I, am I in a father's arms?" Although Cleone does in fact die in her husband's arms, her last thoughts are filial: "where is my father? / Let me but take his blessing up to Heaven, / And I shall go with confidence!"[95]

The existence of such plays points to the cultural sources of some of Burney's problems. The complexities of her relation to her own father were partly caused by the ways in which her era wished to consider the father-daughter relationship. That the daughter in extremity should turn to her father was approved; the father should also be able to rely on the daughter. (Poor King George in a straitjacket called piteously to his youngest daughter, little Amelia, to come and save him.)[96] In her novels Burney had repeatedly denied the wholesomeness of such utter reliance, such soft and self-dissolving gratitudes. But in her deep depressions, she allowed emotional wishes and anxieties to play themselves out. Her fantasies, however, are also protests. In the plays, she could start to observe her own psychic life.

The Siege of Pevensey expresses Frances Burney's sense that she was a victim of tyranny. In her private politics, king had become oppressor. In her heart, Burney was daring to criticize even the benevolent George III, who presided over a court guilty of insane cruelties and starvation. "The King played his own part, of The King" in the tragedy they were all representing. In Act II of *The Siege*, the Earl of Chester valiantly stands up against the tyrant, claiming that no monarch has the right to reduce people to slaves, denied "life's inherent claim, a spirit / That conscious feels equality of Soul, / Bounty divine! the birthright of humanity!" Pleading with the king to view the castle's starving inhabitants not as traitors but as "your Children," Chester makes a long statement about equality. He reminds the king "Man's Earthly Monarch is himself a Man; / And every Subject in his proud domain / Was born his Equal, must his Equal die." It is absurd to abuse the short "term between the Cradle & the Shroud" and to insist on the "brief prerogative" in the face of Death:

> that leveller, who strides
> With hasty steps, to seize thy transient trappings,
> And lay thee, all despoil'd, unfear'd, unenvied,
> To crumble with the Beggar in the Dust!
>
> (Act II)

These lines are not so memorable as Briggs's contemptuous remarks to Mr. Delvile about dust and dustmen, though the sentiments are similar. What stands out is the desire that the father should challenge power and put in a claim for equality—at a time when Burney herself, subjected to the tyrannous Mrs. Schwellenberg, felt at moments, even in the queen's presence, "republican feelings . . . rising in my breast."[97] Chester's sturdy defiance of the tyrant is a piteous extrapolation from Dr. Burney's real behavior as Frances Burney wanted to see it. In her diary Burney goes to great pains to present Charles Burney as unfazed by monarchs and smilingly unaware, in his egalitarian innocence, of court forms: "so regardless or thoughtless of acquiring them, that he moved, spoke, acted, and debated, precisely with the same ease and freedom that he would have used to any other gentleman whom he had accidentally met."[98] Frances Burney wants to believe the impossible—that her father has nothing to do with her bondage, that he moves freely, unaffected by the "trammels" which have somehow or other managed to enmesh his daughter. Charles Burney's behavior (which we can read as awkward display resulting from euphoria, egotism, and *gaucherie*) becomes a sign of the good Doctor's instinctive belief in human equality. Dr. Burney would as soon have gone to court in his nightshirt as mumbled a syllable to any monarch on earth about the short term "between the Cradle & the Shroud," or "equality of Soul, the birthright of humanity." But the vindicated, gentle father-figure who appears in the dreamlike *Siege* as Chester must oppose father-king as tyrant.

The dreamwork becomes difficult, even in the fantasy *Siege*. King William, bad father, sees Adela as a creature to be traded off for money and influence; he does not want her ransomed because of the cost. Chester, good father, can only suffer in sympathy when he realizes his daughter will be starved to death: "She, useless, will the first be left unnourish'd,— / She, captive, will the soonest be abus'd!" (Act I). There are many references to hunger in the tragic plays; Frances was "unnourish'd," mentally and spiritually—and even physically (no chance to eat the bread and apricots at Oxford). Hungry for life, she feared that "provision or relief" was not going to get through the walls of Windsor or Kew, and felt herself, of all the queen's attendants, the most likely to collapse (as her predecessor had done).

In her play, the heroine is confronted by three horrible fates: to remain a prisoner, to marry De Warenne, or to enter a convent. The De Warenne alternative does not indicate a maidenly fear of marriage or of men; in her journals Frances complains of the restrictions put upon her seeing any men at all. The loathsome marriage which appears in the court journals is the forced and unnatural union with Mrs. Schwellenberg: "I had no way to compose my own spirit . . . but by considering myself as *married to her* . . . ! O what reluctant nuptials! . . . Were these chains voluntary, how could I . . . forgive myself that I put them on!"[99] In the play Adela can reject the terrible voluntary chains, but the only alternative, the convent, is just another version of the same grim fate. "I submitted to my monastic destiny from motives my serious thoughts deemed right," Frances Burney writes sadly, recording a reconciliation with Mrs.

Schwellenberg.[100] That particular reconciliation in November 1787 came after Frances had dared to protest about the open coach window, and was given by her father "permission to rebel" about matters affecting her health.[101] This "permission" to let herself be fired if an argument about the state of Miss Burney's eyes led to Mrs. Schwellenberg ordering her expulsion seems half-hearted. Frances was unsure how far she should or could avail herself of "permission to rebel," though conscious of "the rebellion to which this unequalled arrogance and cruelty excited me."[102] "Permission to rebel" is a prize oxymoron, a phrase particularly Burneyesque. In *The Siege of Pevensey* Burney expresses, if she does not at all transcend, the anxieties of working within such dim permission, such needs for restraint, combined with an acute apprehension of forces about to burst out of control.

Burney wished her own self-sacrifice to be at least acknowledged, and that wish itself was, she knew, a division between her father and herself. To state that one is sacrificing oneself is to adhere to a knowledge of one's desires—in itself a form of rebellion. The most puzzling part of *The Siege* is the fifth scene of Act IV when Chester comes to the rescue of an Adela who (with De Belesme's help) has already hit upon another means of rescue. Adela has already felt guilty: "O that my generous Father knew my conflict!" (Act IV). The language in which she addresses her father sounds as if she had been *seduced* during her stay in the castle, but she has merely promised to marry De Belesme. Reduced to incoherent self-reproach, she wishes "that I now could cast me at thy feet; / Trust thee with every thought—expose each wish—." She begs him not to curse her, and he replies with the extravagant assurance "not if thou murder'st me!" But once Adela tells him of her promise to De Belesme, Chester is remorseless in rebuke and threatens her with loss of her father because of "unfilial deeds." Even if she takes back her promise, she has already sinned:

> *Chester.* Say, is it nothing to require forgiveness?—
>
> . . . .
>
> Nothing, to lose the innocent elation
> That, bounding in thy Youthful Breast, till now,
> With virtue's rapture, juvenile & gay,
> Wak'd thee each Morn with this fair filial Hymn,
> And with it closed each Night:
> "My Father's Love is mine, his love deserv'd,
> For I have ne'er offended him—"
>
> . . . .
>
> I blest his latter Days, I sooth'd his cares,
> He call'd me all his joy—"

Any decision Adela makes with a view to her own happiness, without putting his first, must be "self-delusion." Leaving aside the evil, theologically speaking, of the "fair filial Hymn" and the eroticism in the faint flavor of the Song of Songs, we can be struck by the fact that what Adela supposedly owes her father seems to consist in what she has already done for him—and therefore ought to keep on doing. ("I blest his latter Days, I sooth'd his Cares.") The whole scene is one of Burney's big blackmailing scenes—but without the comic novelist as author. Lacking the kind of resistance that characters in Burney novels put up to such extortionate demands, Adela collapses in almost erotic surrender: "take me to thy soft mercy!— / The conflict's o'er,—I yield me to thy guidance—." Adela's mindless collapse into submission brings a happy return to childlike daughterliness, to "My undivided ties! My early confidence! / Primeval blessings! born in tenderness, / Nourish'd in filial joy, unstain'd unmix't.—" (IV.v). We can hear a strange echo of the filial Ode "To ——— ———" prefixed to *Evelina*. Adela's submission is Burney's fantasy dramatization of the decision she had made (and had to keep on making) to endure the life at court because her father wished it. But in trying to subdue her conflict, her active wish for escape, and yield to Charles's guidance, Frances was not compensated by the quasi-erotic possessiveness, the all-in-all relationship Adela expriences. Indeed, the court life the father approved divided her from that father, who was not, like Chester, expressing anxiety about her besieged imprisoned existence. The plot situation is a rickety allegory for the causes of Frances's own "conflict" and guilt. In her dreamlike fantasy, Frances can say that she wants to get out, that this is unbearable, that she is an independent adult and a sexual person who can decide to escape. But even in the fantasy the very thought of such a decision means enormous "conflict," and the tender Chester who actively wanted to rescue his daughter from an unendurable fate is overtaken by the wrathful Chester, a version (one of Frances Burney's many secret versions) of Charles Burney. Permission to rebel really meant delicate cogitations and heartrending sacrifice. Chester-Charles wants Adela-Fanny not only to decide as he would wish, but also not even to acknowledge that there naturally is, and must be, a "conflict." Frances kept on promising that she would deaden her feelings, but could not do so, and it is in that that she was disobeying her father. Adela's mysterious trespass is basically the sin of her own response to her fate; the guilt can be relieved only by complete, if momentary, yielding up of the independent adult mind to infantile dream—but the dramatist, however neurotic, who tries to incorporate the conflict, as well as the infantile dream of union, is not innocent of responding in her own way to her own fate.

The Siege of Pevensey, with all its defects and incoherences, is yet Frances Burney's strongest presentation of the central problems in her life in the court imprisonment. The other two tragedies deal in more extreme forms with abandonment, deprivation, and death.

In *Hubert De Vere,* "A Pastoral Tragedy," the hero de Vere, a supposed traitor, has been harried from the court of the tyrant King John.[103] He believes his betrothed, Geralda, threw him off in order to marry the wealthy Glanville. Living solitary in a remote village, de Vere is admired by Cerulia, a simple village maiden who follows him about everywhere. De Vere's enemy, de Mowbray, in disguise persuades the girl that he is an astrologer who has previsioned her marriage to de Vere. De Mowbray is trying to keep de Vere and Geralda apart. But, after de Vere, touched by Cerulia's devotion, asks her to marry him, Geralda appears, as "an helpless Fugitive" (Act III). Geralda explains that she did not marry Glanville of her own wish; the marriage was a result of blackmail. Glanville betrayed an important conspiracy to King John, who wanted a list of traitors' names. Glanville, knowing that the list included the name of Geralda's uncle, de Mowbray, made his own marriage to Geralda the price of his silence. Thus Geralda was blackmailed into marriage in "that hour, that death-like hour." She had to offer herself as a sacrifice; "Geralda sav'd the Brother of her Father!" (Act III). A similar situation is employed in the plot of Burney's last novel, *The Wanderer*; as we shall see, Geralda's experiences adumbrate those of Juliet, a character for whom she is an earlier sketch, as Cerulia is in some respects for *The Wanderer*'s Elinor Joddrell.

Now released by Glanville's death, Geralda has fled, carrying the fatal list with her as proof of her fidelity. De Mowbray saw to it that de Vere's name was inserted in place of his own, as he wants the political ruin of de Vere; both that and the separation of Geralda from de Vere could be assisted by de Vere's marriage to the "rustic Orphan" Cerulia. De Vere tells Geralda of his promise to the village girl. Geralda nobly says that she is better suited to endure sorrow than is the village maid; de Vere should take care of fragile Cerulia, "this sweet Flow'r a Zephyr might destroy" (Act IV). De Vere argues that he should explain the facts of the case to Cerulia whose "impulsive honour" will make her give him back his freedom. Cerulia enters and sees de Vere at Geralda's feet; she *"wrings her hands with convulsive emotion, and runs wildly off"* (Act IV).

In the last act, "The Scene represents a Country Church Yard." Cerulia has spent a night in the church and has seen a vision telling her she must die. As the other characters collect around her, the girl begs Death to come and bewails her orphaned and loveless state: "No Father's smile foster'd my opening days / . . . / Him who I lov'd—I have lost." De Mowbray breaks into self-accusation and revelation: "I am her Murderer! . . . / Thy Murderer is—thy Father!" (Act V). De Vere will not kill him, but reserves de Mowbray for a traitor's death when the king sends to arrest him. The king has had second thoughts about the conspiracy; de Vere will be restored, united with Geralda, though Geralda speaks almost enviously of the "peace serene" Cerulia found in death.

The hero and the villain seem two aspects of the same nature. De Vere and de Mowbray are brooding, violent, and melancholy—types of the Byronic hero before Byron. The spring of the action is intense emotion arising from dereliction. Identities are unknown, families torn, treachery and betrayal universal.

There is no sweet reunion between father and child. De Mowbray, Geralda's uncle, nearly destroyed her in demanding the sacrificial marriage, and inadvertently destroys his daughter, Cerulia, whose true-blue cerulean faithfulness is not rewarded. Cerulia's only mode of rebellion is death, which frees her from further struggle and at last evokes an acknowledgment of guilt in her parent. The climax of the play is de Mowbray's "Thy Murderer is—thy Father!" De Mowbray, unlike Chester, is the cruel father, the villain who causes sacrifice, and his behavior to his daughter is termed "impious." As an allegory of Frances Burney's feelings about her father, *Hubert De Vere* is much more stark and more accusing than the other plays.

The emotions expressed are almost entirely negative; even love is marked by suspicion and fear, and everyone is both spied upon and alone. The thematic imagery of cold emerges very strongly when Cerulia at her most hopeful thinks about Hubert, "the Star" whose bright radiance "has dispers'd the chill, cold mists, / And mental Snows that flak'd upon my Breast, / To Ice congealing every fond idea" (Act II). Cerulia's Lucy Snowe–like impression that she was "born for Woe" proves quite correct. The whole "pastoral Tragedy" is designed for—and spirals down to—the scene in which Cerulia describes her agony in the churchyard. In the earlier draft, Burney really let herself go in Cerulia's macabre speech describing her vision of Death "Pale, tall, and wan," and the ghastly being's commands:

> "See, see! It cried, the work that thou must do!
> Rise! let me light thee on!—thy Hour is come!"
>
> . . . .
>
> Then, with these Hands, I measur'd out the Ground
> And quick, from Head to foot, I mark'd my Grave.
> Next—so the vision bid—I cast me down
> On the cold Earth, and there I bar'd my Breast,
> And, with the fresh damp mould I strew'd it o'er:
> Thrice then I cried aloud "Bury this first!
> Come! Hubert's Spirit come! thou hast broke my Heart,
> Come, give it Sepulture!"
>
> . . . .
>
> What next I saw I ne'er must tell!—I rose,
> I shriekt—I knelt—I pray'd—for Hubert pray'd!
> Till, all at once the dew of Death crept o'er me
> And Iced me to the Heart: and there, even now,
> Cold, cold it dwells!
>
> (earlier version Act V)

Burney was to use a not dissimilar dream-vision in *Camilla*, but this is a more private indulgence in misery that longs for release. Cerulia really is not a character, but a little nature-spirit, a feminine power of loving that gets crushed into the cold earth. Cerulia's speech picks up strange echoes of the real-life experience and language encountered by Burney. In a Diary manuscript of early 1789, Lemuel Smelt teases Burney with the possibility of her visiting Colonel Stephen Digby (the "Mr. Fairly" of the published *Diary*) and thus ensuring the wrath of the jealous Mrs. Schwellenberg: "'Why do you not go?' . . . cried he, laughing,—'to Dig . . . your own Grave'"; upon her replying, "How do you mean?" he "repeated again, *'To Dig your own Grave!'*"[104] Frances Burney actually had something like a strong crush on Colonel Digby, the queen's vice-chamberlain, in relation to whom she indulged a replay of the emotions and reactions elicited by George Cambridge. She was very distressed at the news of Digby's engagement to the beautiful Miss Gunning in the autumn of 1789. Again she had fallen in love with a pleasant and apparently attentive man above her in station, and again she had been passed over. Like the Cambridge affair, this matter has been censored out of the published *Diary* by Charlotte Barrett's careful editing. Mr. Smelt's teasing remarks about Frances visiting Colonel Digby are a trifle unkind in the circumstances, and might well resonate in a consciousness in which a sense of rejection was being strongly reactivated.

The commonplace but haunting phrase "Go—*To Dig your own Grave*" becomes allegorically dramatized in *Hubert De Vere*, where it is combined with echoes of that major experience of rejection, the unrequited love for George Owen Cambridge. In the letter quoted earlier, describing her meeting with Mr. Cambridge when he "started as if he had seen a Ghost," Burney goes on to analyze her situation:

> I have now, for 2 years & a half, had a firm & encreasing conviction—
> That there is a coldness of Heart which could never accord with Happi-
> ness—& Me. In which case—I clearly foresee,—I must either always feel
> more regard than I could excite,—or be chilled to a coldness myself.[105]

Frances Burney had been chilled by a "coldness of heart," had felt, like Cerulia, "Ice congealing every fond idea." In *Hubert De Vere*, Cerulia's fate presents self-sacrifice from the passive side, in the experience of being rejected, of decaying, of being annihilated. Frances told Susanna, in an expressive phrase, that she feared even Mr. Cambridge senior had forgotten her, that she had been *"oblivionised."*[106] Frances Burney, like Cerulia, became ghostly, her vitality killed off by the sexual rejection and by her father's rejection in consigning her to such a deadly fate. Sweet submission to the father's will and collapse on the paternal bosom, which Adela chooses, are not available; instead, sweet submission means being *oblivionised*, casting oneself into the grave, achieving deadened sensations and annihilated feelings in the one state immune to "conflict."

In *Elberta* (a piece only existing in scraps), the emphasis is on female dereliction combined with responsibility for others.[107] Elberta, daughter of a slain Saxon chieftain, is an orphan but she has ties. She secretly marries the Norman leader Arnulph, against proscription, and lives in a remote place, where she bears his children. They are "happy, in defiance of terror . . . & awaiting an expected general amnesty" (MS scrap #23). Offa pursues her, intending to marry her himself; Elberta cannot acknowledge her secret marriage. She and the children go short of food, and Elberta fears she will see them starve before her eyes. The enemy Offa has the children kidnapped, and Elberta then wanders about seeking the lost children. The plot was evidently to be designed to show Elberta's progressive breakdown into madness under the pain of privation:

> A Female is mentioned, who wild & unknown is seen roaming about— no one is informed whence she comes—woe is in her voice, terror in her aspect;—she never weeps, yet frequently wails, tho' in terms unintelligible from their wildness—
>
> Her interesting appearance—
> Some she affrights,—others derided by—
> Her fierce harangues, though wild, when offended—
> Her gentle supplications to shadows
> Her inattention to pursuit . . . (Scrap #265)

The heroine evidently becomes a mad wanderer, like some of Wordsworth's early characters. The roaming female who has lost her identity is to reappear in *The Wanderer*, but *Elberta* is the only piece in which Burney imagined her heroine as a mother. Responsibility to her offspring means that Elberta must be denied the simple submission available in different ways to Adela and Cerulia. The wildly lamenting heroine, who can allow herself to break out in "fierce harangues," even become "wild" when "offended," is an angrier representation of Frances Burney, whose potential "Children," both biological and literary, have indeed been taken from her.

Was there to be no release from imprisonment and frustration? In May 1790 Frances Burney had at last made an appeal to her father, seizing the chance of speaking to him alone at the performance of Handel's *Messiah* in Westminster Abbey, "the only conference of that length I have had in four years." She told him she was "lost to all private comfort, dead to all domestic endearment." Her health was suffering from fatigue, while she "lived like an orphan—like one who had no natural ties." Dr. Burney told her "if you wish to resign—my house, my purse, my arms, shall be open to receive you back!"[108] This was magnanimous, but after that Dr. Burney did nothing to support his daughter in her attempts to leave. Her royal employer, with gracious incomprehension, promised a doctor's attention and some short holidays. Dr. Burney evidently hoped Frances would change her mind. As 1790 dragged on, Frances became

weaker, suffering from unshakable "languour" so that "the day was a burthen—
or rather, myself a burthen to the day."[109] Her condition aroused the zealous
interest of friends like Mr. Windham. Deciding "it is resolution . . . not inclination, Dr. Burney wants," Windham determined to "set the Literary Club
upon him!" Windham suggested "a petition—an address" from members of
Johnson's old club to Dr. Burney, who—like a king—was to be addressed and
petitioned.[110] The friends who were trying to work upon him became "a confidential cabal," a little set of domestic traitors. ("Treason," "rebellion," and
"conspiracy" had been important terms in the Burney family politics since Dr.
Burney's second marriage.)

While slow endeavors were made to pry Frances loose, she herself became
progressively more ill. But she saw that the queen "concluded me, while life
remained, inevitably hers."[111] That proposes another way out—Frances Burney could die. As can be seen in the diary for 1790, Frances Burney evidently
feared or hoped that she was dying. She had alarming symptoms: loss of weight,
pallor, "cough, pain in the side, weakness, sleeplessness, &c." Yet even after
Charles Burney had been moved to sympathy, the queen was not inclined to
accept Frances's "Memorial" of resignation, proposing a six-weeks' leave of
absence. The letter Frances had sent in did not displease the royal employer,
but "I was grieved to see it was not regarded as final."[112] Such was the situation in December 1790, seven months after the hopeful discussion in the Abbey.
There seemed no change in the dreary progression, "in those months succeeding
months, and years creeping, crawling, after years."[113]

Nearly total debility offered the only way out of the impasse; Frances Burney's subconscious obliged by supplying her with the major symptoms of tubercular consumption. To us it seems startling that anyone with Burney's symptoms was *allowed* to remain among court servants, but eighteenth-century
people, though fearful of the infectiousness of certain "fevers," were extremely
cavalier about tubercular disease. Even if the queen thought Frances's state of
health truly alarming, it would have seemed unkind to cast off a penniless protégée and servant merely for being ill. For most denizens of court, a desire to
leave under any conditions was inconceivable, as Mrs. Schwellenberg showed
in her surprised expostulations: "she offered to save me from it . . . as if life
itself, removed from these walls, would become an evil."[114] Such a desire also
seemed the height of disloyalty, a fact reflected in Mrs. Schwellenberg's displeased reaction: "I am sure she would gladly have confined us both [Frances
and her father] in the Bastile [sic], had England such a misery, as a fit place to
bring us to ourselves, from a daring so outrageous against imperial wishes."[115]
The French Revolution, now in full progress, mingled in the mind of even loyal
Frances Burney with her own efforts to rebel, to get out of captivity, just as her
plays center upon gloomy tyrants and the appeal of liberty, even treason.

Frances's own revolutionary bid for freedom could be accomplished only
subversively, through an increasing ill health that frightened her more than

anyone else. Far from being the obedient "machine" she had earlier flattered herself it was, her body made itself insistently demanding and painful. Pains in her side forced her to creep away to take hartshorn during the ghastly card games ("terrible picquet the catastrophe of every evening"). "And so weak and faint I was become, that I was compelled to put my head out into the air, at all hours, and in all weathers, from time to time, to recover the power of breathing. . . ."[116] The neurotic nature of Frances's sensations is as clear as the meaning of her symptoms. She could not breathe within these walls; she was being stifled, she felt smothered—all those common significant metaphors were literalizing themselves in the allegory of her physical reaction.

But the subconscious does not just put up a clever piece of play-acting. The third alternative to going or staying through those "years crawling after years" was to die—an end to all conflict and treason as well. The plays reveal a truly suicidal streak. Act V of her "Pastoral Tragedy" shows us Frances Burney schooling herself to embrace death, just as her essentially healthy body was being schooled by her unconscious will to get ready to die. That Frances Burney lived to old age does not mean she could not have died in the 1790s if she had had to stay on at court. Even in *Hubert De Vere*, however, the will to live has not quite gone; the energetic Geralda essentially stands for a more life-affirming view, and Cerulia can be taken as representing the submissive and infantile aspect of the author which will indeed have to "die" if her stronger aspects are to be redeemed. With at least part of her nature, Frances wished to cease being gentle, polite, and suppressed—something in her wanted to run wild, like Elberta, wailing and haranguing through the palace, with cries that would pierce through royal walls. In all the tragedies, including the fragmentary *Elberta*, we can also see a fear that Burney never discusses in her diary. I believe—though this is my own supposition—that Frances Burney was afraid of going mad. Compared to madness, death would be a respectable consummation.

After all, it was the madness of the central, *the* royal personage in her present existence that instigated the writing of these "tragedies." She spent long months in 1788 and 1789 immured with a madman in a small world whose daily topics of conversation were symptoms, lunacy, and mad-doctors. When the terrified family and their private attendants decamped hastily to Kew and privacy, Burney commented, "We seemed preparing for captivity, without having committed any offence."[117] The scene of her encounter with King George III in Kew Park, when he ran after her and she fled (as they all had been forbidden to go near him), has often been cited as giving an amusingly vivid glimpse of George III in his derangement. Burney, however, was not amused but terrified as she ran: "I do not think I should have felt the hot lava from Vesuvius . . . had I so run during its eruption."[118] The volcano image is interesting, as if Frances feared some lavalike eruption from within as well as from the exploding king. In the conversation that followed, Frances noticed the king's pleasure in his now-licensed frankness, as he aired his likes and dislikes freely. Himself a captive, he had found a kind of mad mental liberty in breaking through restraints. There is a pleasure in madness which none but madmen know—a pleasure that holds out its own temptations. Something of that release Burney was able to obtain in the presentation of her tragic characters' utterances in extremis.

One lengthy separate section of a draft of *Edwy and Elgiva* headed *"El.'s madness after the Divorce"* consists of a long poem, the ostensible occasion of which is Elgiva's lament for the vanished Edwy whom, in her mad ravings, she imagines dead. The published text of the stage version of *Edwy* conceals some of the private wildness of the original. The attempted ode is really Frances Burney's lament for herself, a wild utterance culminating in another vision of death, or life in death:

> I hear afar
> The cry of War,—
> Guilt and Justice are at Strife:
>
> . . . .
>
> Truth and Justice raise the knife—
> Thing you they Conquer?—no, no, no!
> Oppression cuts their Threads of Life,
> And at a Stroke they both expire.
>
> See yon Infant,—Nature's Child,
> 'Tis Innocence,—of aspect mild!—
>
> . . . .
>
> Wrath, with Cruelty combin'd,
> The infant seize; it's feeble cries
> Reach my Ears,—it bleeds,—it Dies!
>
> The Song of Joy let Treach'ry Sing
> Vice is now to Mirth inclin'd,
> Bring me Myrtle, Lawrels bring,
> Bind their Brows, their Tresses bind.
> Hark I hear of Death the knell;—
> Hist! of Ghosts I hear the Yell
> Murmuring in the Swelling Wind.—
> Mercy now is Deaf & Blind
> She sees no Tears,
> She feels no Woes,
> No sighs she hears,
> No pity knows:—

Now Grief & I must suppliant bend,
And mourn that Mercy is no more our Friend.

He comes! he comes! I see his Steed,
    I know it by its Crest & Mane;
Mark his noble Port!—his Speed!—
    He comes to claim his Wife again.
Many a Day, & many a Night
    Deep in the Clay-cold Earth she laid;
They forc'd her from her Husband's Sight,
While yet she Liv'd they call'd her Dead,
    And Funeral Honours paid.

Low in the Church-yard lies her Head;
    Within the Tomb
    She will consume,—
Worms & Maggots must be fed.

    See! she shivers!—hark! she shrieks!—
Big are the Tears that wet her cheeks,
    Loud & piercing is her cry!—
Ah, know you not the reason why?—
    Lo! behold the Ravens near—
    Quick their flight—their Prey is near—
She lives! she Breaths!—forbear, forbear!
Ah, why so soon her body tear?[119]

Burney's verse, in which one can trace some quite respectable sources (libretti set by Purcell, poems by Blair, Collins, Gray, and Percy) should in charity be set beside that of, for instance, Mason. The mid-eighteenth century had trouble finding ways to express intense emotion in poetry. Burney's lines have a certain hectic memorableness, the pulsation of real pain. More disturbing, in the handwriting of the manuscript these stanzas look like automatic writing; one hates to guess at the internal pressures that found vent in this hectic scrawl. This piece, like Cerulia's death scene, may have been affected by the opium and wine prescribed by the palace doctor in 1790.[120] Wine and opium (the latter given in solution, most usually, as laudanum) were the eighteenth-century version of tranquilizers. Some of the court writings sound like opium visions. Burney may have had more in common with Coleridge and De Quincey than we have imagined; though she did not become an addict, she used the opiate for a while. These verses, like the plays themselves, give us a picture of Frances Burney which is a far cry from that customarily accepted, the cheerful Augustan recorder of chit-chat in drawing-rooms. She did have much in common with the

Romantics—or her experience was making her a Romantic during the early Romantic era. There is a Brontë-like element in her imagination, as in her life. That element becomes increasingly evident here, a desire for the storm that will put an end to life-in-death and the unbearable stifling stillness:

> Aölus!—attend my pray'r—
> Let thy terrors fill the Air,
> Rend the Earth, & storm the Sea!
> Round the Globe thy Whirlwinds spread:
> From North to South, from East to West
> The Atmosphere with Storms infest.[121]

In *Cecilia*, Burney had drawn a heroine gone mad, but now that state of release seemed uncomfortably close. The plays show an attempt to peer over into the abyss, even while she tried to prevent her own fatal approach to that last cliff. The mind has its own cliffs of fall: "Hold them cheap / May who ne'er hung there."

"While yet she liv'd, they call'd her Dead." Frances Burney was recalled to life on 7 July 1791, almost exactly five years after her fatal entrance into death-in-life. There was one good result of her tribulation; the queen with great generosity gave her a pension of one hundred pounds per annum for life. She did at last get "a handsome pension for nothing at all"; the queen could hardly have predicted the enormous span of Frances Burney's future existence. In the autumn and winter after her release, Burney kept writing out her tragedies, "scribbling what will not be repressed." She assured her sisters that in her "present composed and happy state" she could not have thought of "these tales of woe," but she could not bear to leave these "dolorous sketches" unfinished.[122] The themes are "dolorous" but not to be repressed. It is amazing that Charles Burney liked the "pastoral tragedy" *Hubert De Vere*, and even thought it had stage possibilities. (It was *Hubert De Vere*, not *Edwy*, that Burney first offered to Kemble.)[123] Dr. Burney cannot have understood it.

The experience of long drawn-out pain left an enduring mark on Frances Burney. Some fragile Cerulia self had died. Restored to life and liberty, she was not to waste them. Soon, despite all apparent odds, she was to choose a mate for herself, and marry against her father's wishes. She had had enough of the "mental snows" that congealed every fond idea. She was to bear a child and this child would not have to starve, like Elberta's children—Burney herself would provide, through writing a novel. After a gap of about ten years since the publication of *Cecilia*, Burney seriously started novel-writing again.

The Windsor and Kew tragedies were not without importance for Burney's future work as a novelist. In her tragedies, however moribund in themselves, she possessed a clue to her own private language and the deepest levels of feeling. The two later novels, *Camilla* and *The Wanderer*, are a result of Burney's decoding of herself, a translation of the shadow side back into the illumined world of utterance. The later novels combine comic satiric insight with the vision of the depths. The narrative style makes new efforts to accommodate opacities of personality, internal life, and the disjunction of one person from another and of self from self. In her last two novels Burney was trying to invent a new kind of novel. Her efforts have not been entirely appreciated by later generations, particularly since critics have needed her to stand for the late Augustan chatty female writer, sunny if shallow. The private inheritance of the years of dereliction, 1786–1791, made Burney a new kind of writer.

The experience at court was no minor comic frustration but a terrible experience, coloring all her later life. Burney's behavior in not getting out sooner seems weak only if we do not understand her situation. Contemporaries like the Pittite Mr. Batt expressed surprise and admiration at her resigning her post: "I applaud—I honour the step you have taken." Her unusual departure seemed unusually daring. Frances's reply is worth noting: "My conduct . . . all consisted in not pretending, when I found myself sinking, to be swimming."[124] She was always not waving, but drowning. The diaries, at least as Charlotte Barrett edited and published them, exhibit a Frances Burney who is waving; the tragedies show how very near she was to sinking for good. And it should be remembered that she was thirty-four when she entered court service, and thirty-nine when she left. Some of the best years of her life—her active life, her sexual life, her writing life—were gone, never to be recalled.

6

Marriage, "Clarinda," and *Camilla; or, A Picture of Youth*

Frances Burney was past her first youth when her own love story began. In the autumn of 1792 a little colony of French émigrés settled in Mickleham, near Norbury Hall, home of Burney's friends William and Frederica Locke, who offered moral support and hospitality to the aristocratic intelligentsia, constitutionalists who were now fugitives. At Mickleham, Frances met interesting people, including Mme. de Staël, daughter of Necker the finance minister and former hostess of one of Europe's most enlightened salons. Mme. de Staël at twenty-six was a celebrated author and critic, though not yet the novelist of *Corinne;* she admired Burney's novels, and in her Burney found a possible successor to Hester Lynch Thrale. The two women planned to study French and English together. The friendship was broken by Charles Burney's agitated request that his Fanny never spend a night under the same roof as the iniquitous Frenchwoman, who was correctly rumored to be engaged in an adulterous affair.[1] Dr. Burney's maiden daughter should not countenance such immorality, or invite scandal to herself. Besides, Necker and the nobles who moved for change were but begetters of the Revolution. In Dr. Burney's increasingly right-wing opinion, all Frenchmen who had wanted any change were to blame for the plunge into bloody disorder. Commanded, in effect, to sever herself from the brilliant baronne, Frances Burney did so. She sighed as a friend, but obeyed as a daughter, puzzling the offended Mme. de Staël, who complained (as Susanna told her sister): "But is a woman under guardianship all her life in your country? It appears to me that your sister is like a girl of fourteen."[2] Frances herself was not happy about the matter: "I wish The World would take more care of itself and less of its neighbours. I should have been *very safe,* I trust, without such flights, & distances & breaches."[3] But there was another friendship that Frances would not allow "The World" to crush.

At Norbury, she had met another of the émigré colony, M. Alexandre d'Arblay, an officer of the army of Louis XVI who had been on guard at the Tuileries the night the king escaped to Varennes. D'Arblay, adjutant general to Lafayette, was *"constitutionaire"*: he believed that political change in France was necessary and desirable, and he had had great hopes of the National Assembly and its promised constitution. Despite his subsequent losses—of estate, of home, of country, of friends who died in the Revolution—d'Arblay never went back on his original liberal opinions.

The man whom Frances Burney met was no wealthy curled darling but a middle-aged military man (thirty-nine in 1792, a year younger than Burney). (For a rather stiff portrait in later age, see Fig. 24.) Susanna said, "He seems to me a true *militaire, franc et loyal*—open as the day—warmly affectionate to his friends—intelligent, ready, and amusing in conversation, with a great share of *gaîté de cœur*, and, at the same time, of *naïveté* and *bonne foi*."[4] He had experienced hardship and come through misfortune with dignity, even with humor. Frances was attracted almost as soon as she met him. Before the friendship ripened into love acknowledged, they sent each other exercises in the other's language with requests for correction. Many of Frances's first epistles to M. d'Arblay were *"Thèmes"* in admittedly faulty French while he sent back exercises in halting English; she called him *"mon maître"* while d'Arblay referred to her as his "Master in gown" or "Master I.G."[5] Both were masters; the relationship started out as an equal friendship, lightened by the comedy of acknowledged mistakes and sweetened by mutual admiration. Alexandre d'Arblay was gratifyingly able to refer to characters in *Cecilia* by name. Though she made mistakes in her French exercises, Frances Burney in turning to d'Arblay was turning to that other side of her heritage, to her mother's history, to the language of her grandmother. Correspondence was eventually touched with personal affection, then by declarations. Frances may have been the more obedient to her father over Mme. de Staël at the end of February because she did not want to attract attention to or to interrupt her developing friendship with M. d'Arblay. The shock of the execution of the king of France in January 1793 made both Frances and Alexandre more tender, more vulnerable; d'Arblay in particular needed someone to offer emotional support as his world was disappearing. Hesitant because of his lack of means and of all status in England, he began to indicate his feelings in a manner that would allow Frances to withdraw or to ignore them, but, as she told Susanna in April, "to such a Man . . . I could not be so unjust, so ungenerous, so false as to disguise my whole sentiments."[6] The bilingual courtship can now be read in the "Courtship Journal" like a story; it may remind us of the relation between Lucy Snowe and M. Paul in Charlotte Brontë's *Villette*, but this story was to have a happy ending—despite Charles Burney's opposition.

To Charles Burney, a Constitutionalist such as d'Arblay seemed almost personally to blame for all the sanguinary events in France. Dr. Burney did not wish even to meet d'Arblay: "the *Constitutionel* is cruelly in the way! He [i.e., "dear Father"] is all aristocratic!"[7] There were other anxieties and obstacles. D'Arblay was conscious of his lack of money, while Frances confided to Susanna that she wished only that she could give to Alexandre "a *younger Partner*."[8] Yet, in this instance, Frances Burney was able to withstand Dr. Burney's disapproval. Surmounting the obstacles, she entered into a marriage with a penniless French émigré with her eyes open to all the financial and social disadvantages.

It was Frances Burney's income that allowed them to marry at all. Queen Charlotte had awarded her the pension of one hundred pounds per annum (half her former salary), which the queen was kindly willing to continue after her former servant's marriage. The queen in countenancing d'Arblay was less "aristocratic" than Dr. Burney. The dismal court years had brought one good thing in their wake. Frances knew that her friends felt she was throwing herself away on this émigré papist with no status and no prospects. She must have known that enemies and general gossips would say that the foreigner was marrying the withered maid in hopes of English connections and a bit of financial support. People would laugh at or pity the old maid in ripe middle age who was carried away into imprudence by her passions. "How the World would blame me at first, I well know."[9] She should indeed have known, remembering the outcry at the marriage of Mrs. Piozzi—and the cruel jokes. Frances Burney had told Mrs. Thrale that the world would never forgive her "for shewing so great an ascendance of passion over Reason." Now Burney was to exhibit a similar "ascendance of passion over Reason," and she likewise could be accused of giving up *"Religion, Friends, Country"*—if not entirely all *"Character."* She did lose friends' good opinion and even some friends. Anna Ord, formerly a comfortable companion during Frances Burney's restorative tour of the West Country taken after the release from court, now said bitter and sarcastic things about her erstwhile friend, as well as refusing to visit her. Burney commented after the wedding with some bitterness of her own upon so many former friends "caught, or warped, heaven knows how, by Mrs. Ord," who "have taken no steps whatever to shew me the smallest mark of remembrance."[10] In Mrs. Thrale's case Burney had remonstrated as if the world's blame were of the utmost importance; now she would not allow it to stand in her way.

Even a supportive friend like Maria Allen Rishton could joke to Susanna, "I am dying to see the Othello who has drawn her within his spells—for she is quite Desdemona & loved him for the dangers he had passed."[11] Maria wishes for "a description of this Conquering Hero—who has . . . raised 'these Tumults in a Vestal's Veins'."[12] There was further ridicule outside the family and harsher disapproval. Sarah Scott records typical disapprobation in a letter to Mrs. Montagu:

Miss Burney's marriage seems one of the most romantic I ever heard of, a Man who has neither fortune in present or expectancy, no means of livelihood, nor scarcely a Country which he can call his, wanted a much richer Wife than Miss Burney, who has scarcely an independence for herself. If the Lockes encouraged the union they are still more to be wondered at, as they cou'd not be blinded by passion.[13]

The whirligig of time brings in its revenges. Frances Burney, who had once written to Queeney of Mrs. Thrale, "Dear lost, infatuated Soul! . . . My wonder will never cease at her blindness to her own destruction,"[14] was now, nine years later, herself to be considered infatuated, "romantic" (lost to common sense), and "blinded by passion."

Frances Burney and Alexandre d'Arblay were married on 28 July 1793, in the parish church of St. Michael's, Mickleham, and went through a Roman Catholic ceremony two days later in London at the chapel of the Sardinian ambassador, so no question would be raised about valid marriage or inheritance in the husband's native land. (Similarly, Hester Thrale and Gabriel Piozzi had been married first in London by a Roman Catholic chaplain and then in St. James's church in Bath.) Brother James Burney gave the forty-one-year-old bride away. Dr. Charles Burney gave his consent, a "cold acquiescence," but did not attend the wedding, remaining "coldly averse."[15] On the occasion of the wedding of Susanna in 1782 and of Charlotte in 1778, Dr. Burney had composed celebratory verses, "From a Father to a Daughter on her Wedding Day," and he had written a minuet for Susanna. There were no verses and no minuets for his Fanny's wedding day.

Frances and Alexandre were well suited. A real *aristocrate* himself, Alexandre d'Arblay did not possess that obsequiousness, that delighted awe of persons in high life, that had tainted the conduct of Charles Burney. D'Arblay was also a gentle man, who would not take advantage of Frances's own gentleness or force her into passivity. Indeed, their relative circumstances at the beginning of their courtship meant that Frances was stirred into a much more active role than had been her lot in her former relationships with men. It was up to Frances to lead, cherish, and support. Even during the courtship, she was the provider, trying to find tactful ways of lending d'Arblay some money.[16] In the early years of their marriage, she was the one with friends, contacts, some money, and even—if she took up her writing seriously—the one with prospects of earning. D'Arblay was no sponger, no idler; he frequently tried to see if he could take up his French army commission again, hoping to fight his country's enemies while not explicitly swearing allegiance to the new government. When at last in the Napoleonic era he took his little family to France with him, his desire to lead a normal life in all respects, restored to his position as provider as well as to his native land, played a part in his decision. The years of love in a cottage, of literally cultivating his garden in growing cabbages for the family table, must have been hard on him, though he did not complain. But it was very good for the new Mme. d'Arblay to be in a position where she was not to be passive and where she counted for so much. In this relationship, she was treated as an equal. Of all the writing women of her era, she seems to have made the best marriage. She waited a long while, but when she married, she did it well.

The love of Frances Burney and Alexandre d'Arblay can be ascertained by reading their correspondence from their first meetings until d'Arblay's death. He emerges as a kind and sympathetic man, never double-minded, with none of that tendency to emotional blackmail so evident in Crisp and Dr. Burney. (And, one year younger than his partner, he could not be seen as a daddy.) D'Arblay's letters show a strong Catholic faith, a simple and charitable piety which bore him up under many vicissitudes; his religious turn of mind may have made his wife think more about religion than she had done, though she had always been a believing Christian of the Anglican persuasion—and d'Arblay seems never to have tried to convert her. D'Arblay had *"gaité de cœur,"* but some tendency to become gloomy. He lacked Frances's dash of lemon, being really the sweeter-natured of the two. Burney's wit and liveliness charmed him; to a large extent, she was to supply sparks and sparkle in that union. Among the most important facts for Burney the writer was that Alexandre admired her writings enormously. He even copied them for her, sparing her the labor of preparing fine copy for theatrical managers or for printers. Frances Burney had her heart's desire: a dear lover, a fine husband, the good father of her little son Alex who was born 18 December 1794. And, after years of copying her own work and her father's, Frances had acquired an amanuensis of her own.

The first published work of the new Mme. d'Arblay after her marriage was a piece designed to assist other emigrant Frenchmen. She agreed to write a pamphlet for the committee of ladies organized by Mrs. Crewe (née Greville) to help the destitute French clergy who had sought refuge in England. *Brief Reflections Relative to the Emigrant French Clergy: Earnestly Submitted to the Humane Consideration of the Ladies of Britain* (1793) was a charitable work; the title page, announcing the pamphlet as "By the Author of Evelina and Cecilia," ensured sales. Burney in her preliminary "Apology" modestly defends a lady's interfering in public matters. Although women should, because of "prescriptive duties," lead only private lives, "it does not follow that they are exempt from all public claims, or mere passive spectatresses of the moral as well as of the political economy of human life."[17] It is a good sign, and a sign of some powerful fiction-writing to come, that Burney is now able to reprehend "passive" women and passivity of behavior, she who had once tried to be a "passive spectatress" of her own wretched love affair: "I thank Heaven . . . that this is an affair in which I have been merely passive." Here she decorously admits limitations to female activity, but only in addressing some criticism toward the limitations of male activity; feminine "retirement" may be an advantage to women as it "guards them . . . from the heart-rending effects of general worldly commerce."[18] As Burney warms to her charitable theme, however, she speaks proudly of "female tradition" which will "hand down to posterity the formers and protectresses of a plan which, if successful, will exalt for ever the female annals of Great Britain."[19] The pamphlet, though written in a kind of high public style, is a successful and even shrewd piece of argument, covering many points in its twenty-seven pages. The author flatters her readers while arguing them out of national prejudice and English chauvinism ("We are too apt to consider ourselves rather as a distinct race of beings") and appealing to their imaginations with a horrifying description of the massacre of the priests in September 1792. If readers imagine they would then wish to have rescued the helpless victims, why do they not now assist those who escaped?[20] The most Burneyesque point in the pamphlet is the use of the quotation from St. Vincent de Paul, appealing to the charitable as if they were judges: "pronounce, then their fate; do you ordain them to live? do you doom them to die?"[21] Burney's sense of embarrassment and exposure, of the power of pain, the force of the illicit lethal wish, is present in this pamphlet, as in her other writings. Yet, for all its strong appeal to imagination and feeling, the pamphlet shows that the author is practical, too; she reminds potential donors that the money they give will be spent and will circulate in England; the writer is not out of touch with political economy.

The pamphlet shows a sense of history. Burney asks her audience to "anticipate the historians of times to come"; these historians may decide that the French clergy came to the wrong country, an inhospitable and hard-hearted place. Most striking of all here is Burney's sense of these times, and of time:

Already we look back on the past as on a dream . . . wild in its horrors. . . .

Of the present nothing can be said but, *what is it?*—It is gone while I write the question.

The future—the consequences—what judgment can pervade? The scenery is so dark, we fear to look forward. Experience offers no direction, observation no clue; the mystery is so impervious.[22]

The sense of disconnection, of the unpredictable, of mystery colors the novel *Camilla,* although that work does not overtly deal with contemporary public events.

Reflections Relative to the Emigrant French Clergy represents Burney's only entry into public life, into what was, after all, the political arena. It was spoken of in commendation by reviewers as a "charity sermon,"[23] and so it is. However ostensibly modest about female duties, Burney showed that she could preach and teach. Like some other women writers of the decade (including the conservative Hannah More as well as feminists like Wollstonecraft) she makes the line separating male from female duties and works seem harder to draw, even as she pretends to draw it. There was some audacity in her daring to write for this cause, too, conservative as it may seem. The "World" would, as she knew, be still sniggering over Burney's marriage, and the connection between that and a plea for the French would seem evident. It would be thought that Frances Burney herself was getting too soft on Catholicism and might have been perverted to popery. The cause for which she wrote was not altogether a popular one. Many men, even in upper-class circles, sneered at the "Ladies" and their attempt to organize. French Roman Catholic priests were not objects of charity appealing to the population at large. Indeed, outside special circles, the émigrés were disliked and feared. The Burneys' friend Anna Ord thought all these French should be packed off to the place whence they came, and the man who warned Dr. Burney about Mme. de Staël's adultery referred to her as "Diabolical Democrate."[24] Any one of the *bannis* could be suspected of being a French spy, a popular epithet for any Gallic person on the loose in England during and after the Revolution, as well as before (cf. Captain Mirvan's story that Monsieur Dubois is a French spy).[25] Catholic priests were particularly disliked, and the Gordon riots had happened only a decade earlier. Burney did not pursue the beaten track in writing her *Reflections,* and in her personal circumstances (so well-known) it took some courage and independence.

When she was asked to contribute to a truly conservative or right-wing cause, she declined. In early 1797 Mrs. Crewe suggested that she, Dr. Burney, and Frances and some others might conduct a new periodical, a satiric anti-radical magazine (something like the *Anti-Jacobin*). Dr. Burney liked the idea, but Frances evasively protested that she now lived too retired from the world, and that a satiric journalist should have a better idea of what was going on than she did.[26] (A Burney not know what was going on!—a likely story.) It is evident from her polite refusal that she did not wish to commit herself to writing for an anti-*democrate* work; her political views were not the same as her father's.

Burney's major production of the decade was *Camilla*. She had begun it, or one of its original versions, the story of "Betulia," before her marriage; the Lockes and Charles Burney had read part of this in June 1793.[27] But the new novel was essentially written in about two and a half years, undergoing many radical changes and revisions in the writing process. She wrote a major novel despite eventful changes in her life. She was not perturbed by the minor distrac-tion of the production of *Edwy* and its ignominious failure in March 1795, nor was she thrown off course even by the painful abscess in her breast that put an end to nursing little Alex and began the breast trouble which developed into the cancer (if it was cancer) that was later to necessitate a mastectomy. She wrote steadily on. The new novel was advertised a year before it came out. This new fiction was published by subscription, in a determined and businesslike effort to get solid financial returns at last for her writing. There were to be no more contracts arranged by Dr. Burney, like the unsatisfactory agreement about

Cecilia. Burney needed the money for the support of her husband and child—literally to put a roof over their heads; the proceeds of the novel built Camilla Cottage.

Despite Johnson's dictum that no one save a blockhead ever wrote save for money, there is a tendency to look down on anything written with money in mind. The product of a woman writer who takes such a frank look at the profits is particularly suspect. Even Ellen Moers, who praises the production side of *Camilla*, approving Burney's making novel-writing a lucrative female career, condemns the work itself: "Fanny Burney, now Mme. d'Arblay . . . ground out a novel—*Camilla* is her most lifeless production—to support her family. For once in her life, she made the economics of publishing work for her."[28] When even sympathetic feminists damn such an interesting feminist novel, the difficulties in setting the record straight are obviously severe. Far from being "lifeless," *Camilla* possesses vivacity and depth. It is experimental in theme and form. But *Camilla* has constantly been viewed through a haze of expectations and presuppositions. *Camilla; or, A Picture of Youth* seems to be a story about education, particularly female education; at least, that was what contemporary readers expected and wanted to see. The decade was full of works about education, especially of girls.[29] Everyone in the 1790s seems to want some sort of "new woman." All the writers of the period agree that girls should not waste time on dress, parties, and coquetting, but should learn something useful to employ their minds. Liberals and radicals—like Wollstonecraft or Edgeworth—agree with the older Hester Chapone or the pious Sarah Trimmer that self-indulgence and extravagance are bad for the female character and for society at large. In the 1790s the topic of female education was a political arena, for views about women are related to images of the family and of society. *Camilla*, in 1796, arrives in the middle of the decade's interests and controversies and picks up a number of common concerns. The tempting subtitle, *A Picture of Youth,* appears to announce an education book, and the first few chapters even tie the work in with the new children's books, in giving us the events around the heroine's ninth birthday. Readers have always been partly right, indeed, in thinking the novel is an "education book," but to see it only in that light is to see it falsely, especially if there is an entailed assumption that the work must therefore be clearly didactic and that its author makes a simple conservative statement. Our modern reading of the novel has been clouded by the assumption that the author was writing a treatise on female conduct very like late eighteenth-century conduct books. (As soon as the conduct or "courtesy" books were rediscovered, they tended to be offered as an explanation of everything in female literature.) Critics like Hemlow and the Blooms have decided that *Camilla* is a didactic work, albeit with many comic characters, about a girl who errs and learns prudence and "a hero cast in the mould of a tutor-husband."[30]

Some of this mistake—and I think it is one—is understandable, for it is true that Burney originally thought of writing a book rather like that. The unusually voluminous remains of earlier states of *Camilla* show us that it was, as formed in the mind of the author, several different novels. Or more properly, the published novel of 1796 is a book to which several others were sacrificed, including those living and dying in the author's brain or expiring after a brief half-life in sketchy notes. It is probably true that most novels emerge as the result of sacrificed works, of thoughts or ideas that died or were transformed. In the case of *Camilla* we have a tantalizing collection of notes, scraps, and partial drafts; we can glimpse the several novels that were trying to get themselves written.

It seems that at its inception the work ahead was to be about a family that falls on hard times. In our *Camilla*, the severe financial difficulties of the Tyrold family arrive only in the final volume, and do not last very long, yet at the outset the reverses seemed to be the heart of the story.

> A Family brought up in a plain, œconomical, industrious way, all happy, contented, vigourous & affectionate.
> Sudden affluence comes to them—They are exhilarated. Some exult . . .
> Some break out—some gallop on to profusion.
> a sermon on equanimity.
> Some grow indolent—& insolent.
> Suddenly all is lost.
> Reduced to Poverty.
> Some humbly sad—some outrageously repining:—some haughtily hardy—some pettishly impatient—one cheerfully submissive.
> a sermon on Disappointments.[31]

Another scrap is entitled "Every Stage of Poverty" and indicates various characters' responses:

> The suffering from it—Padre—Madre
> Disgrace in Poverty—Harry
> . . . .
> Imprudence in it—Cleora
> Meanness in it—Walter

The brother, Harry (whom we know as metamorphosed into brother Lionel in *Camilla*) seems in these scraps a central character:

> Harry turns out the scourge of his Family.
> commences Infidel
> The Father's grief & shame
>
> ───────────
>
> Harry is in perpetual scrapes—but all end in false alarms—
>
> ───────────

Harry engages in deeper schemes—all concluding in having
a painful suspence & surmize on their nature & design & end.

Harry the very torment—yet delight of his House

————————
. . . .
Unfeeling extravagance of Harry

————————
Harry turns from Profession to Profession in idle futility.

————————
Harry gives bail for a fr[ien]ᵈ improvidently trusted—
. . . .
As soon as the Mother receives her legacy, Harry loses all
controul, & spends at all rates.

The wild Harry would seem, on at least one day of Burney's thought, to be the
central character of her tale. Already the neat schema is giving way under the
pressures of strong interest in extremes. The sedate moral theme quickly generates in the author's mind a number of incidents and even macabre excitements:

Incidents General

A Fire
A dreadful Brawl in the Street
An impassable Mob
Crys of murder
An embroglio of Carriages
A Pickpocket
Losing a servant in the street—fright—adventures—seeming
detections.
Seeing a skeleton unexpectedly
—A Corpse unpreparedly
—One in the agonies of Death
A scuffle
A pursuit without an attack, in the Fields, streets, &c.
with terrifying appearances—
A quarrel in a public place
overturned in a Carriage in the street or Road
Seeking shelter in a low shop
Falling in a Chair in the snow

On the verso of this same piece of paper there is a list of thirty-one settings,
events, or objects to be included as main scenes, including "A spouting Club—
taken to by Harry," "A Trial," "A Foot pad," "A Robbery," "A Mad man,"
"A Highway Man," "Horse Race," "Syllabub under the Cow," "May Day

Chimney Sweepers," "Harvest Home," "A Ballad Singer," "Jack o' the Green," "A mad Dog." The story was apparently to move from country to town and back, with much more emphasis on the particulars of country life than we find in any of Burney's published novels, including *Camilla* ("Long Walks—Hedges—Briars—Styles—Ditches—gates Hay Fields—Hay Stacks—Ponds—Corn Fields"). Perhaps the story of youth brought to Burney's mind recollections of the Norfolk countryside around the small town of King's Lynn.

A neatly regulated and symmetrical moral plan is, in the preliminary scraps, almost at once subverted by the quick-crowding, diverse, and violent incidents, one sparking off another as if the writer could hardly set them down fast enough. Even at its inception, this was not a small neat story—it was a novel that everything in the world was trying to get into. As the work progressed, the daughter Cleora, not scapegrace Harry, became the central character. "The radical failing of Cleora's character an imagination too lively for her judgement," as one of the scraps says. "Cleora" becomes "Ariella" or "Clarinda" in various versions of the novel; Burney always took a while to settle on names for characters. "Cleora" is indeed an erring heroine; she is imprudent during the time of riches and gets into debt. Her brother has got into debt on a much larger scale, so the family will suffer greatly in its plunge to poverty. The heroine cannot endure to tell her parents of her own debts; to escape the financial misery and to help her family, she makes a grave misstep. She agrees to marry Lord Winslow, an elderly and disagreeable (if wealthy) man. In some fragmentary passages from an early version of this story, "Cleora," on the eve of her sacrificial elopement with her rich, elderly suitor, begs her sister "Creusa" to honor her deep repugnance to her prospective husband: "If I die first, they may send to my Spouse to bury me; but be sure, Creusa, He places me not near his own tomb!—Tell him, if he does, I shall break the barrier. . . . My very ashes shall not mingle with his, while a single kind Zephyr will listen to my Prayers to blow them asunder."

In the draft in the British Library, we have a long sequence that must occur toward the end, certainly in the latter part, of this version of the novel (for a page of the draft, see Fig. 25). The sequence shows us the agitation of the heroine on the day before the wedding to old Lord Winslow. The heroine (here sometimes "Ariella" and sometimes "Clarinda") tells a sister (here "Stella") that she cannot endure the prospect of marriage:

"I knew not till this moment the excess of my antipathy. By & bye I thought I might endure him; but I feel now a rooted, fixed abhorrence. Good Heaven! to be his!—irrecoverably his!—to inhabit the same mansion—to bear the same name—to belong to him of right—Impossible! impossible!"

She walked hastily up & down the Room, pushing forward both her hands, with fervant [*sic*] disgust, as if driving away from her the very idea.

Stella sat down, in a consternation too great for words.

Stopping short, at length, & holding up high the offended hand, "Stella, she cried, know you not that this hand, this tainted hand, was once the property of [Edgar Mandlebert crossed out] Leontine! And shall I give it to another?"

In quick, but uncertain paces, she then again paraded her Chamber, exclaiming: "What would he say when he heard of it? How would he disdain his early choice! how triumph in his timely wisdom!"

Stopping then again, & clasping her hands: "O [Edgar crossed out] Leontine she cried, virtuous, noble Leontine methinks I rejoice for you myself! rejoice that you have thus escaped a connection so unworthy your Heart, a Partner so unequal to your virtues!"

She sat down, & softening into Tears of tender recollection, continued:

"Yet, inferior as I was to him, with what patience, what sweetness did he bear with me! with what delicacy instruct, what softness conciliate, what pain remonstrate!"[32]

Clarinda thinks that her friend Mrs. Solmes is helping to break off the engagement, but the worldly-wise lady (an earlier version of *Camilla*'s Mrs. Arlbery) thinks Clarinda's objections are nonsense and has spent her efforts in soothing the rich lord.

Mrs. Solmes now, entering the Room, half laughing, half angrily, said "Well, what are we to do now? I have just composed this poor Man, by a little florid harangue, that neither of us understood, upon the inherent coyness of a Country Vicar's Daughter, & he is again at your service for what ill treatment you next think proper. Only, in the mean time, do give me a hint how long this is to last? For I,—being no Lover,—begin to think we have had nearly enough of it."[33]

The settlements are already drawn up and acknowledged by Clarinda's father; everything is ready for the wedding and the girl tells herself that she must go through with it now. She begs only not to see her father or fiancé until the wedding tomorrow morning:

"I can be silent, but I cannot be false. Save, help me, Mrs. Solmes. Unhappiness will be nothing to the terrour now upon my Senses—I no longer wish to retreat—I feel it too late!—It would be dishonour for me with Lord Winslow, while to my Father, my dear Father I should become but a burthen!"[34]

Clarinda retires, but not to peaceful rest; her "almost delirious sleep" is tormented by visions, and she believes she hears her name being called "in a sound that, to her astonished Ears, seemed hollow" by a "Phantom," an "Image of

Leontine." The repetitive voice proves only that of her sister, who tries to rouse her so she can read a letter from her mother. The letter warns Clarinda against marrying only for money. She is moved by this epistle, but remembers her debts and can see no way out:

> A species of desperation seized Clarinda as she finished this Letter. "In all ways, she cried, then, I am culpable as well as unhappy! in every plan, every effort, & even in every sacrifice I am culpable! . . . I marry but for lucre—the meanest mercenary Wretch is not viler than me!"
> This idea was insupportable; it nearly demolished her; she felt worthless to herself . . . she doubted if what she were about to do were a sacrifice to filial duty or an expedient of cowardice; if it were a self-devotion to spare pain to her Parents, or a miserable feint to spare blame to herself.[35]

Clarinda desperately thinks of getting out of tomorrow's horrid marriage; she begins to dress herself intending at once "to throw herself at the feet of her Father," but the thought of her debts again checks her; she realizes that if she withdraws from the wedding she will have to reveal them, evoking "amazed displeasure" from "the Mother whom she now feared as much as loved."

> "And how, cried she, at this sad period, extricate myself from my debts? how own to my unsuspicious Parents, now denying themselves all comforts to retrieve the misconduct of my Brother, that Bills to such an amount have been incurred by me, for Ball Dresses, for Milliners, for Toys? Impossible! impossible!—I will sooner abide by my first contract. Yes! wretched and culpable Clarinda! pay, by a life of bondage, the forfeiture of thy guilty imprudence!"
> Hastily then, she took off her Cloaths, & returned to her Bed.
> There she dissolved in Tears, till weariness & weakness once more sunk her into Sleep: but Sounds & appearances the most tremendous brought forth by direful Dreams, took from it all its balmy qualities, & made it starting, feverish, & wretched. Integrity appeared to her personified, as shrinking from false vows, Virtue, retreating from broken honour, & Truth, blushing at the Ireton Family in disgrace: while Edgar, rushing forth, as she stood at the Altar with Lord Winslow broke up & finished the Ceremony, with a malediction, instead of a blessing.
> She awaked with a faint scream, while the curse yet vibrated on her Ear, & found herself prostrate upon the floor, though unconscious of having quitted the Bed.
> Her Candle was extinct, but the first faint ray of the living light was breaking into her apartment. She took her Watch, &, though with difficulty, discerning the Figures, saw it was near five o'clock.
> "And in four Hours more, she cried, this miserable hand is to sign away

its liberty,—to sign its own condemnation!" She put her hand to her head; it was burning, almost bursting. She felt nearly distracted. She was upon the point of even flying from the house, without planning or heeding to what refuge.

But the cruelty of such a scheme to her Father, even in this disordered state, stopt its execution. "And from what, she cried, escape? From personal captivity?—Yes! But mental? Whither must be the flight that can now avoid me that? That can say to me I have a right to be free? that my fate is my own? that my honour is inviolate?"

Thus passed the dreadful night. Thus opened upon Clarinda the ill-omened bridal morning.[36]

The girl wretchedly dresses herself in her bridal gown: "In virgin white looked her habit, but her livid, bloodless face, gave to it the semblance rather of a shrowd, herself the white, pale Spectre." Her father enters her room to greet her on the wedding morning. "Her wan face, and the almost wildness of her air, had struck Mr. Tyrold to the Soul. Her bridal habiliment rendered them but the more touching; it seemed the symbol of captivity, rather than the ensignia of new happiness."[37] Fortunately, the father realizes that something is very wrong, and presses the girl until she breaks down and confesses that she cannot bear to go through with the wedding. He has her spirited away in a sedan chair to a house from which she can more calmly write a letter to Lord Winslow retracting her promise. The ceremony does not take place.

The father (sometimes called "Mr. Tyrold" and sometimes "Mr. Ireton") kindly consoles the wretched girl in her misery at dealing such an offensive injury to Lord Winslow (who, however, proudly affected "turning off the whole with a laugh, as a mere light & ridiculous joke").[38] Mr. Ireton (or Tyrold) recognizes her suffering:

> "Compose yourself, however, at present, my dearest Girl. You are greatly changed; & I am not easy to see it. You have suffered, I am sure, from an inward cry against your proceedings, which has frighted away your repose, & reduced you to nearly the shadow of yourself."[39]

It is easy to see in this sequence Frances Burney's vivid recollection of the ill-fated morning of 17 July 1786 that saw her entry on her father's arm along the walk at Windsor and into the Queen's Lodge. The description of "Clarinda's" night of agony before prospective captivity probably gives us the fullest description of Burney's wretchedness on the night of 16 July, when she must have wondered if it were not possible to escape from a "life of bondage," even by getting up and running away, but was checked by the thought of "the cruelty of such a scheme to her Father." She too had doubted "if what she were about to do were a sacrifice of filial duty or an expedient of cowardice." In this story, which we might call *Clarinda,* the father does recognize what is wrong with the sacrifice and intervenes to save the daughter at the last moment before it takes place, even though the sacrifice, the captivity, would be rewarding to him—he does just what Charles Burney did *not* do. The daughter's "inward cry" had to reduce her to a "shadow of herself" over five years before Dr. Burney expressed the kind of sympathy which Frances Burney imagines lavished on the erring Clarinda. As in the tragedies, Burney uses the idea of forced and loveless marriage as a private emblem for her own loss of freedom, as well as for the loss of freedom of women in general. It is noticeable, however, that Burney makes the idea of sexual bondage more immediate than she had done in *The Siege of Pevensey* or *Hubert De Vere;* marriage has given her more courage, as well as more distinct comprehension of the meaning of marital power and possession, both as image and as fact. The comparison of the woman who marries for money with a prostitute was not new, but was currently popular with radical feminist writers. The main point of the sequence is, however, not marriage but captivity, the bondage for which marriage stands. Clarinda's guilt over her debts is a cover for the reasons that had made it possible for Frances Burney to resist her wretched captivity—the sense of unworthiness, of having to make up for inferiority, of owing her father an unpayable devotion (debt) that set up feelings of guilt. The *Clarinda* fragment indicates that Clarinda's debts are quite horrendous, though no sum is here mentioned. In *Camilla* we are invited to calculate Camilla's debts, and to realize that although she was a little extravagant, her money losses were largely the result of her brother's taking her money from her, as well as of his accepting loans in her name from somebody else. If Camilla had not had debts forced on her by her brother, and had been allowed to keep her travel money, she would have been in debt for personal expenditure to the tune of about eighteen pounds—which is the sum her sisters can raise to help her out. The question of Camilla's debts is one of the ironic complications of *Camilla.* In *Clarinda* the heroine seems to be more simply "culpable," in error, an error that she complicates by entering into the unlovely engagement with the old peer. The heroine of the novel that we have does nothing of the kind. Neither is the Tyrold family in *Camilla* exalted into sudden wealth, though they are in fact (because of the misconduct of two family members) driven into temporary poverty.

It can hardly be emphasized too strongly that none of the passages quoted above, none of the events described in that *Clarinda* sequence, occurs in *Camilla.* It is clear to me that Burney in effect wrote two novels between 1793 and 1796; one of them the ur-*Camilla,* or *Clarinda,* the other the novel that we have. The Clarinda novel may be conceived as existing in several states or stages, with varying names for central characters. (It may even be that Burney thought she might salvage that novel somehow and that the names Clarinda, Mr. Ireton, Leontine were actually substituted for Ariella-Camilla, Mr. Tyrold, and Edgar at a late stage, the author trying to revise the earlier manuscript once the real *Camilla* had taken shape.) Whatever the exact chronological sequence, it is clear that *Clarinda* in the fragments in which we have it represents both an *earlier* book and, really, a *different* book. The final novel, our *Camilla*, can be seen as a work that cannibalized that earlier work but did not copy it.

Burney then sacrificed one novel in order to write another. Any novelist will realize the amount of effort and pain involved. Burney "ground out a novel," says Moers. But she did not. Whatever *Camilla* may be, it is not hack work but the result of thought, and of the most costly kind of revision—throwing away whole concepts, in effect a whole novel. No one writing for money alone would do such a thing. Reading the *Clarinda* manuscript, one can see that it was certainly marketable. Excitement, sexual fear, and didacticism are mingled in a way that would appeal to a number of readers. Burney must have got rid of that book because she really found she wanted to write something else. No writer commits such a sacrifice unless there is a greater aesthetic object in view.

In writing the ur-*Camilla*, Burney did try to pursue a tale involving a heroine who commits errors and extravagances and is rescued by her good father—with a worthy and high-minded suitor (Edgar-Leontine) in the offing. This was the didactic frame with which she started out, after conceiving her schematic family and its ups and downs. There is some reason to believe the story was sketched out, if only mentally, during the court years; Frances Burney told the king and queen that "the skeleton" of *Camilla* was "formed" at court.[40] The ur-*Camilla* or *Clarinda* story certainly ran into the emotions and styles of the Windsor and Kew tragedies. *Clarinda* came to involve yet another version of Frances Burney's relation to Charles Burney. The didactic tale came to dissatisfy her; if it had not, she would have persevered, and we would have as the published novel the work whose fragments can be seen in the Berg Collection and the British Library. In writing the final novel, Burney had to get above and away from her most recent preceding works, the Windsor and Kew tragedies, without utterly ignoring what they had to say about captivity, frustration, dereliction. She did rise above them, and above the wishful drama of the girl's relation with her father. Mr. Tyrold in *Camilla* does not provide the most important or most intense relation of his daughter's life—there is none of the heavy breathing about him that there is about Sir John Belmont in *Evelina* or about Chester in *The Siege of Pevensey*.

In writing *Camilla*, Burney evidently saw into the psychological compulsions of her own life—and of her recent writing—and decided to do something about them. Getting away from the simpler drama of *Clarinda*, she refocuses the interest; *Camilla* is a very different novel. It is a skeptical novel about the difficulty not only of making choices but of seeing the truth. The subject, the real center, is the human mind, or, as Burney calls it, "the Heart of man." Burney insisted that she was dealing with a large group and that all her characters were part of the design of a new work "of the same species as Evelina & Cecilia," but

new *modified*, in being more multifarious in the Characters it brings into
action,—but all *wove* into *one*, with a one *Heroine* shining conspicuous
through the Group, & that in . . . *the prose Epic Style*, for so far is the
Work from consisting of detached stories, that there is not, literally, one
Episode in the whole plan.[41]

Charles Burney had expressed his dislike of "detached stories" or narrative
digression, and Burney is probably here recalling also Laclos's criticism that the
comic *"personnages"* of *Cecilia* were *"épisodiques."* An "Episode" is something
aside from the main event; Burney was jokingly to tell the royals that once she
devoted herself wholly to writing *Camilla*, "I had no Episode—but a little
baby!"[42] Aristotle had complained, or at least stated, that most of the action of
the *Odyssey* was episodes; the model for pure plotting, a model upheld by
neo-classical rules, was Greek tragedy, a structure which good epic is expected
to approach. Burney, adapting Cervantes's and Fielding's formula defining the
good novel as a prose epic, tries to explain that the kind of design she has in
mind does not concern only a single character, even the "shining" heroine who
may unify the whole, but is rather a large-scale interweaving, in which diverse
characters are related thematically. The modification of the structural design of
Cecilia is an expansion, making a "more multifarious" novel. Women writers in
general may prefer stories of groups or generations rather than the Aristotelian
unity of one story of one individual hero(ine). Bringing the female aesthetic to
public acceptance and appreciation often poses difficulties for female authors.
Burney wants the reader to see a host of connections, with the focus on the
story of the self-deceiving heart and ironic desire, in an uneasy society where
many different desiring hearts and self-centered imaginations operate. No simple
moral scheme upholds the novel's action. Far from being a novel that justifies
fathers and elders at the expense of a faulty (if teachable) heroine, *Camilla* is a
novel that shows a world of fallible human beings playing mental games and
tricking themselves and each other.

    Camilla was written with energy and enjoyment. Burney told her husband in
March 1796

> I am very careful of myself . . . except in the one article of writing late—
> but—it is so delicious to stride on, when *en vert!* Yet we played a full
> Hour at Where's My Baby? Where's my Baby?—[43]

Since Freud, the game of "Fort/Da!" has been described from the (male) child's
view, illustrating the child's learning symbolic control of his mother's absence,
enduring the separation from the female that makes masculinity, culture, and
symbolic language-systems possible.[44] Recent feminists such as Juliet Mitchell
and Nancy Chodorow have questioned the Freudian myth, pointing out that the

childhood experience of the woman is different, and that the daughter is not required to abandon her mother.[45] The daughter may have a stronger sense of the mother (and of nature) as presence and, as Margaret Homans speculates, may have an uneasy constant access to a literal or presymbolic language that does not require absence. Such matters, feminists agree, are hard to discuss, all the terms, analyses, and myths so far being male; as Homans says, "Had the story of human acculturation been written from the start from the daughter's perspective, it would have been written quite differently."[46] Women writers, however, are constantly engaged in trying to rearrange the androcentric culture in order to make sense for themselves and each other, and Burney is certainly engaged in this operation. She wrote *Camilla* while she had for the first time the experience of becoming a mother and mothering. The pleasure that Frances Burney took in her child is reflected in the enthusiasm with which she notes the silhouettes of the child at play, carefully pasting up the pictures of little Alex given her by a woman friend (Fig. 26). Observing Alex, playing with him, noting his sayings—these were sources of deep pleasure. Burney's letter describes the game that *precedes* Freud's grandson's game, and not from the point of view of the male child but from that of the mother—"Where's My Baby?" Motherhood is power—power in writing, power in narrative playing, in initiating the game, in exhibiting the resourcefulness of the matrix. For Frances Burney personally, the experience of mothering meant a consoling psychic return of the absent mother, now reembodied in herself, and this return was not accompanied by any compensatory enforced reduction in status such as women commonly experience in marriage and mothering. Rather, Burney experienced an entire enhancement of status. During this early period of her marriage, Burney was in the unique position of being cared for while yet being the financial provider. She was also the creator and worker in language, the partner commanding the public resource of print as well as all the resources of the (mother) tongue, as well as many of the resources of the father tongue of her child's father—which is also a language formerly associated with her own mother. Frances Burney could play the game of disappearance with her child, and genuinely "disappear" to write by hours together, carrying on her own independent writing life. Yet as her name for the game ("Where's My Baby?") implies, the mother returns to find *her* baby. Nothing is to be lost. This game, unlike the more dubious games that appear in the novel, fulfills instead of creating antagonisms. The first play of I see/I saw is see-saw without losers, without damage, without the supervision of flawed law. Strong in female and maternal confidence, Burney was in the best psychic position to free herself from the need to placate the daddies. The mother's baby will be found, and all will be well.

The assurance of her motherhood apparently helped to attune Burney to female language and female design, encouraging her in the project of creating the large interwoven texture, the female form of her novel. Every episode, we might paraphrase, is a Baby. Burney also engages in this novel in an increasing, though always characteristic, play with language that serves to deconstruct or disassemble a language system which sometimes seems so male-created, so formidably opposed to women's needs and wants, that feminist theorists have recently presented it as necessitating and built upon the death of the mother, the murder of the feminine.[47] Puns, parodies, and a rich variety of pronunciations and speech patterns abound in *Camilla*, pointing to the "made" quality of language and challenging accepted notions of meaning and authority. Thematically, the novel presents very sharply the different acculturations of male and female, and one of its main and overt subjects is the very discourse about masculine and feminine behavior. The novel's satire looks outward at society's commands while the action focuses upon human feelings, the needs of the individual, and the desires of the human heart.

These needs and desires are "feminine" matters overlooked or overcontrolled by male social laws—like the law that would condemn the poverty-stricken felon to death or transportation for "only one bad action of stealing a leg of mutton" (I:83).[48] This felon's poor ragged wife (an even more wretched descendant of *Cecilia*'s Mrs. Hill) first awakens social conscience in Camilla, who endeavors (successfully) to help rescue the man and nurture his family. This heroine's entrance into the world coincides with the first encounter with the law, and the language of the law of the Fathers—here displaced by the voice of the mother, "a poor woman, nearly in rags, with one child by her side, and another in her arms" (I:82). Burney as satirist points to the inhumane paradox that "the arrival of the Judges of the land, to hear causes which kept life or death suspended, was the signal for entertainment to the surrounding neighbourhood," condemning this "hardening of human feelings against human crimes and human miseries" (*ibid*). Burney hoped to produce some real change in public behavior through "a little hint against dancing around Thieves, Highwaymen, & poor wretches going to the Gallows."[49] There is no need for any woman to dance at the arrival of the Judges; the shade of the phallus is the shade of the Gallows. Within the death-haunted law is starvation, cold, and ritual killing. Outside it is the feminine area of warmth, nurture, and genuine play, represented in the barn where (like a Holy Family) the delivered poor family rests while the mother "was giving nourishment to her baby." Here Camilla joyfully finds them and plays with the three-year-old child; she begins dancing with the little boy, "not less delighted than himself at the festive exercise" (I:110). Camilla is not dancing for the Judges; her "festive exercise" takes place in the abode of the breast.

Camilla; or, A Picture of Youth is, for all its very real seriousness, a festive book. A product of Burney's own revived youthfulness, it was written *"en verf."* The author, reborn after her burial alive at court, had experienced love, marriage, pregnancy, motherhood; *Camilla* is the novel of her fecundity. Burney discarded one set of outworn ideas, and with them really an entire novel, and began another work, using the simple notion of the didactic story of education as an ironic background or weft against which she wove her tale. The resulting novel has always puzzled readers who prefer easy outlines. Some contemporary reviewers of *Camilla* uneasily attempted to slew the book around so it made a simple undisturbing kind of sense, and they have been followed by some modern critics. Essentially, the simplified version (then and now) of the story is this: *Camilla* is the story of a young girl led into errors and indiscretions through departing from the guidance of her Mentor-lover. She comes to self-knowledge and repentance, and is finally united with that lover. For the sake of further comment, and in order to familiarize readers with Burney's novel, it seems proper to give a brief outline of plot and circumstances. *One* way of telling the story of *Camilla* is as follows:

The Reverend Mr. Augustus Tyrold and his wife, Georgiana, have four children: Lionel, Lavinia, Camilla, and Eugenia. Mr. Tyrold's older brother, Sir Hugh, is delighted with Camilla as a little child, and makes her his heir. But when, through a series of misfortunes for which Sir Hugh is to blame, little Eugenia at age seven loses her beauty and is crippled for life, Sir Hugh makes her his sole heir, although he takes a lively interest in all the Tyrold children and in their orphaned cousins, Clermont and Indiana Lynmere, whom he supports. Clermont is sent away to school and then abroad, but the other five children grow up in close association with another child, their neighbor Edgar Mandlebert, orphan ward of Mr. Tyrold and owner of the estate of Beech Park. Edgar's education is supervised by his tutor, the dignified and learned Dr. Marchmont.

All these children display and develop in childhood the qualities that will characterize them later. Lionel from childhood on is joking and thoughtless; Edgar is serious and manly; Indiana is a spoiled beauty; and Clermont is her male counterpart. The three Tyrold sisters resemble each other in good temper and high principles but they have different personalities. Lavinia, the eldest, is serene and patient; the maimed Eugenia is scholarly and heroic. Camilla from her childhood is full of mirth, energetic, and impulsive. Her "radical defect" is "an imagination that submitted to no control" (I:84).

The main body of the novel shows us the characters in youth and the season of courtship exhibiting in their behavior the qualities we have descried in them in childhood. The central story revolves around the relation of Camilla to Edgar Mandlebert. Edgar is rightly determined not to marry a woman who would not make a suitable wife, and, under the wise guidance of Dr. Marchmont, he decides to observe and examine Camilla's behavior and find her true character before committing himself.

Camilla makes a series of mistakes, through indiscretion and lack of prudence. She accepts, against Edgar's advice, the friendship of Mrs. Arlbery, a lively and eccentric wit, and accompanies her to Tunbridge Wells, where Camilla runs into debt. At the instigation of Mrs. Arlbery, Sir Sedley Clarendel, a witty fop, pays attention to Camilla. The heroine, acting on the advice of Mrs. Arlbery, tries to make Edgar jealous of Sir Sedley. This device has delayed repercussions. After a short engagement, Edgar finds out that his fiancée and Clarendel have corresponded, and the engagement is broken off.

Thoroughly miserable, Camilla goes on an expedition to Southampton, under the aegis of another dangerous female friend, the romantic Mrs. Berlinton. Edgar, still attracted, follows Camilla and is disgusted to observe that she encourages the attentions of Hal Westwyn and Lord Valhurst. Though Edgar first intended to renew the engagement, he now accepts the rupture as final and leaves the country. Brokenhearted Camilla has other reasons for misery and regret; she has contracted new debts in Southampton, from foolish expenditure.

Camilla keeps these debts from her father, partly because the family has just received so many severe blows that she does not wish to add to their troubles. Lionel has to flee to the Continent to avoid being cited as co-respondent in a divorce case. His debts fall heavily on his family. Cousin Clermont's hitherto unrevealed debts are enormous and must be met by Sir Hugh; Mr. Tyrold lends his brother his life's savings. Eugenia is captured in a forced elopement and married to a penniless adventurer.

Both uncle and father are severely pressed for money. When the moneylender to whom Camilla has resorted takes out a claim against the father, Mr. Tyrold goes to Winchester Prison for debt. Camilla, confused and full of remorse, cannot face her parents, and her mother's displeasure seems to forbid her to return home. Realizing what troubles she has brought upon her family, she undergoes an intense purgative experience of illness, despair, and repentance. The heroine, an unknown sick lady in a hedge inn, is discovered by Edgar and restored to her forgiving parents. Edgar and Camilla are reconciled, and he marries her.

The foregoing is one way of relating the story of *Camilla*, and there are only two absolutely untrue words in it: "rightly" and "wise" in the third sentence of the third paragraph of the summary. Looked at thus, the novel's thematic and moral structure is very simple. But such a view is a distortion of the novel, just as the plot summary above omits too much and distorts real elements of narrative for the sake of a preconceived pattern. There *is* an eighteenth-century novel about a coquette reformed by a Mentor-lover: Mary Davys's *The Reformed Coquet; or, Memoirs of Amoranda* (1724). It is true that a number of later female novelists draw upon elements of that kind of tale, although, like Elizabeth Inchbald in *A Simple Story* (1791) or Jane Austen in *Emma* (1816), they give it some very strange twists. *Camilla* is one of the strangest manifestations of this theme revised.

The plot summary given above, insofar as it is the story of a girl who errs (through misjudgment, extravagance, coquetry) and is brought to a more sober view of her life through the ministrations of a Mentor, represents the *ironic* model of the story. The real story is played off against it, creating tensions and double meanings which disconcert the reader who wants the story to give a straight rendering of conduct-book maxims. Some early reviewers decided that their puzzlement resulted from inadequate work by the author, her failure to give the heroine's faults a strong enough outline. The *Critical Review* said "her female characters are too *young* to act the part which she assigns them. The errors of Camilla are not errors in one who is almost a child."[50] The *British Critic* decided that "Camilla . . . falls into these inadvertencies rather too frequently, and the consequences of some of them are disproportionately serious."[51] Camilla is not indiscreet enough, her "punishment" is beyond her deserts. Yes. Quite. If we look at Burney's Preface, we find we are actually told her story's "moral"—one that has little to do with avoiding debt or coquetry. The novelist says she is dealing with

> the wilder wonders of the Heart of man; that amazing assemblage of all possible contrarieties, in which one thing alone is steady—the perverseness of spirit which grafts desire on what is denied. . . . In our neighbours we cannot judge, in ourselves we dare not trust it. We lose ere we learn to appreciate, and ere we can comprehend it we must be born again. . . . It lives its own surprise—it ceases to beat—and the void is inscrutable! In one grand and general view, who can display such a portrait?
>
> $(I:7)$[52]

The prefatory paragraph, which opens the book and acts as an epigraph to the whole, explicitly warns us against making easy judgments. The author hopes the novelist may say something true about the human heart. But she expressly says her subject is something unknowable. A stance taken on philosophic ignorance is not that of conduct-books or educational tracts. Burney promises us in her novel an exhibition of "wild wonders," not comfortable certainties, and we would do the author only simple justice if we take a cue from her own statement and forbear to decide in advance that the novel's purpose must be a lecture on female behavior according to received opinion.

If we look afresh at the novel, we can see that many questions raised within it are truly open questions, and that many issues are raised through paradoxes. Paradoxical structures are always teasing. A work of ostensibly realistic fiction constructed around paradoxes tempts in some readers a one-sided reading that eliminates half the terms.

The major instance of paradoxical antithesis and conflict in *Camilla* is the relation between Edgar and Camilla. The plot summary given above (which represents a simple reading) is blind to the other half of the antithesis, the other term of the paradox. It ignores the story of Edgar Mandlebert and ignoring Edgar—or, rather, revising him—involves considerable twisting of the novel (in the attempt to straighten it). The simplified view of Edgar has been used by critics who, like Mary Lascelles, want to point to examples of Mentor-lovers in order to deal with Austen's superior treatment of the type.[53] The love story is more conventional, more "romantic" in the common sense of the word, if Edgar is made an ideal, even if we then can castigate the author for making him such a piece of perfection. The idea that Burney intended a conventional love story is belied by the author herself; she did not want her new book advertised as a "Novel" because of the implications of that word:

> I own I do not like calling it a *Novel:* it gives so simply the notion of a mere love story, that I recoil a little from it. I mean it to be *sketches of Characters & morals, put in action,* not a Romance.[54]

> It is to all intents & purposes a Novel,—but I annex so merely to that title, in a general sense, a staring Love Story, that I hate so to call it.[55]

The novel is not "a staring Love Story." The author is not trying to write one and failing; she is in a sense writing an anti-love-story. If we remember *Cecilia* and the peculiar weaknesses, anxieties, and timidities of Mortimer Delvile, we will be less surprised at the unheroic and antiromantic aspects of Edgar. He certainly does not always act rightly; other characters find fault with him, often very shrewdly and justifiably, although Edgar is, like the heroine and others, subject to misconstruction.

In the story, the orphan Edgar when a boy is attracted to Camilla, though he was briefly caught in childhood by the charms of her cousin Indiana, the official beauty of the family. When he is twenty-one he feels that he is in love with Camilla, and his natural impulses prompt him to declare that love as soon as he feels it. Edgar is, however, proud and shy; having no family of his own, he relies on his tutor Dr. Marchmont as a source of affection and advice and as a model of masculine behavior. Edgar is held in check and his mind is changed by Dr. Marchmont who urges him, with much apparent reason, to study Camilla before he makes her his choice for life.

Edgar's enthusiasm for Camilla is quietly set aside. His tutor substitutes for those feelings vague but unpleasant fears; he turns his pupil's energies in a new direction: "you must study her, from this moment, with new eyes. . . . Whatever she does you must ask yourself this question 'Should I like such behaviour in my wife?' . . . Nothing must escape you . . . even justice is insufficient during this period of probation, and instead of inquiring, 'Is this right in her?' you must simply ask, 'Would it be pleasing to me?'" (I:159–160). This substitution of the ego for the other person is accompanied by urgent commands to think negatively: "But here—to be even scrupulous is not enough; to avoid all danger of repentance, you must become positively distrustful" (I:160). Edgar at first indignantly repudiates acting "a part so ungenerous," but Marchmont attacks him on his weakest side, his lack of self-confidence, suggesting that Camilla might not be able to love Edgar for himself.

The end of this chapter, called "Two Sides of a Question," finds Edgar "filled now with a distrust of himself"; "his confidence was gone . . . a general mist clouded his prospects, and a suspensive discomfort inquieted his mind" (I:161–162). He does indeed become "distrustful" and the only way of relieving his "suspensive discomfort" seems the application of Marchmont's plan—constant critical observation of Camilla. Edgar, at once too proud and too docile, tries to carry out the pseudo-rational program of emotional spying, thus initiating the whole lengthy series of misunderstandings and crosspurposes. Each time he weakens, Dr. Marchmont, like a mad scientist, urges further observation and experiment. Edgar's reliance upon his tutor and the tutor's close advisory in relation to him as he enters adulthood seem to reflect Rousseau's *Emile* (1762), in which the devoted tutor educates the boy to manhood up to the point of his marriage, which he carefully supervises. The story of Book V of *Emile* is a philosopher's courtship story, a paradox in itself, *L'Astrée* in a landscape of schoolmasters. Rousseau and his works were well-known to the Burneys;[56] as a novelist Rousseau's name is among the precursors (or nonprecursors) listed in Burney's Preface to *Evelina*. In the story of Marchmont and Edgar in *Camilla*, Burney seems to be engaging in a parody of *Emile*, questioning its foundations, including the notion of woman presented by Rousseau in his ideally childlike, suitably ignorant and domestic Sophie of Book V—a matter which had already been taken up by Mary Wollstonecraft in chapter five of her *Vindication of the Rights of Woman* (1792). Men are to learn strenuous moral virtues and the reasons of things, Rousseau insisted, while women should never be taught anything complex, should never learn the classics nor even the principles of their own religion, but must remain as nature surely intended—practical, limited, and docile. It is in woman's nature to bear wrong patiently: "Woman is made to yield to man and even to bear his injustice. You would never reduce young boys to the same point; in them inner feeling rises and revolts against injustice; nature does not make them able to tolerate it."[57] This is a comfortable philosophy for the one sex, and does not take long to learn.

Dr. Marchmont is busy marching up the mountain of his male superiority, despising the lowly vale (Duval) of the feminine as much as Captain Mirvan does. (An "M" at the beginning of a male character's name in a Burney novel indicates that the problems of antagonistic masculinity are registered in that character—such as "Mirvan," "Macartney," "Monckton," and even "Mortimer.") The lowly vale of the feminine is in this novel intimated by "the Cleves' estate," or "Cleves," to which first Camilla and then Eugenia, each a member of the cloven sex, is heiress. Marchmont teaches his pupil Edgar Mandlebert, whose first name reflects the outlawed unhappy son of Gloucester in *King Lear,* with a recollection of "Edwy," and whose last name "Mandlebert" (Burney's own invention) is a portmanteau word suggesting "man," "manliness," "manlet," "mangled," "mishandled"—capped with a reminiscence of the "Hu*bert*" in *Hubert De Vere*. Marchmont cultivates Edgar, his pupil and subject, with obsessive enthusiasm, informing his manliness and supervising his sexual coming of age. Yet, unlike the tutor of *Emile*, Dr. Marchmont has not created an ideal young woman, a Sophie, for his charge, but must face the possibility of his pupil's being drawn out of his orbit by someone out of his control entirely—so he must reassert control. The orphan Edgar is only too pliable, as his major source of identity and of all ideas of masculinity is his tutor. Under March-mont's cumulatively negative suggestions, Edgar suffers from repressed feelings; his increasing self-distrust is increasingly projected upon the girl. Dr. March-mont's arguments make distrust almost impossible to remove, as there is no clear way that Camilla could remove the inner obstacles, or provide Mandlebert with assurance that she does love him for himself—no signs she could make are accepted by Marchmont as conveying such meanings. The tutor, with suave vulgarity, has warned Edgar that he is a good catch and that, after all, women are set upon marrying wealth.

Camilla, on her side, has also been warned that her love for Edgar could be construed as mercenary. She goes through several elaborate gyrations just to "prove" to Edgar that she is not mercenary. It occurs to her that if she rejects a wealthier suitor, Edgar will believe her love for him is sincere. But there can be no satisfactory "proof," as the pseudo-logical objections keep moving about. Edgar is at one point sure that he has proof that Camilla is not interested in mere fortune, is not guilty of "the sordid corruption of which you suspected her." Dr. Marchmont, with terrific superiority to logic, waves this away:

> "This does not, necessarily, prove her disinterested; . . . there is com-monly so little stability, so little internal hold, in the female character, that any sudden glare of adventitious lure will draw them, for the moment, from any . . . regular plan of substantial benefit."
>
> (IV:654)

Women are excessively single-minded, steadily pursuing wealth in marriage. Women are excessively unstable, with too little "internal hold" to have any steady objective. This illogical paradox can be true for Marchmont—thus it can also now seem true in the receptive mist he has made of Edgar's mind. "Proofs" are unreal, for something can always be adduced to "prove" the wisdom of distrust. Anything Camilla does can be turned to a proof of her defectiveness. Mr. Tyrold, writing to Camilla about the danger of living in her own wishes, points out that "delusion, while in force, has all the semblance of reality, and takes the same hold upon the faculties as truth." And he adds charitably, "Nor is it till the spell is broken, till the perversion of reason . . . become wilful, that Scorn ought to point 'its finger' . . ." (III:356). Delusions are in force in *Camilla*, and hold sway over the minds of most of the characters, who see hallucinatory semblances of reality.

The constant ironic use throughout the novel of "prove" and "proof" and the delusions resulting from mad searches after shifting proofs can—and should—remind us of *Othello,* to which Tyrold's reference to "Scorn's finger" is an allusion. Perhaps because the *Othello* example had been thrown up at her in her marriage—Frances was "quite Desdemona"—Burney used the play as a major background reference. A happier Desdemona, retired with her heroic general from the intrigue, jealousies, and lonely struggles for reputation, Burney can investigate what causes her world's jealousies, anxieties, and sexual tensions. The novel is extremely rich in allusions to *Othello.* Shakespeare's play is actually performed in one of the most hilarious chapters, "The Disastrous Buskins" (II: chap. 8). The characters (and the readers) see and hear *Othello* enacted by a little ranting group of strolling players, with the wrong costumes, accents, and gestures, and many comic mishaps (Othello's wig catches fire in the last scene). That is, we see *Othello as performed by extremely poor actors.* The novelist could hardly give us a better clue to the novel as a whole. What the circulating-library reader would like to take as "a staring Love Story" is a farcical, deeply absurd rendition of *Othello,* performed by bad actors—that is, by unheroic human beings acting in bad faith. The wretched players, shouting the great lines in heavy accents and making farcical travesty out of the great speeches, provide ironic annotation for Burney's characters' actions, speeches, and internal monologues—particularly Edgar's. Echoes of the play are ironically transposed. "Jealousy is a passion for which my mind is not framed, and which I must not find a torment, but an impossibility!" (II:292). Edgar errs; jealousy is a passion which his mind adapts to very well indeed, although it is a learned emotion taught by Marchmont's "become positively distrustful." Edgar grows to love self-torture; another character calls him "a self-tormentor."

> "Any inevitable evil," he cried, "I could have sustained; any blow of fortune, however severe; any stroke of adversity, however terrible . . . but this . . . this extinction of every feeling I have cherished—"
>
> (IV:572)

Compare Othello's "Had it pleased Heaven / To try me with affliction." There are echoes of the play in Marchmont's speeches, too: "you must either pursue her upon proof, or abandon her at once" (IV:595). On the one startling occasion when he talks about his own emotional life (IV:642–646), Marchmont applies the Othello language to himself: "my peace, my happiness, and my honour, have been torn up by the root, exactly where I thought I had planted them for my whole temporal existence" ("But there, where I have garnered up my heart, / Where either I must live or bear no life").[58]

As in the play, the idea that "to be once in doubt is to be once resolved" is ironically treated. The mind resolves to carry on doubting. Edgar becomes undeniably obsessed. The only excuse he can offer at the end, when he asks for forgiveness, is that he must have been mad:

"Let the past . . . not the present," cried Edgar, "be regarded as the dream! and generously drive it from your mind as a fever of the brain, with which reason had no share, and for which memory must find no place."

(V:897)

An Othello-suitor puts a severe strain on a "Love Story." Almost equally un-nerving is the comparison to the "hero" of Shakespeare's *Measure for Measure*. To Mrs. Arlbery, Edgar seems "that frozen composition of premature wisdom" (III:375). "Ah! . . . look but at that piece of congelation that nothing seems to thaw!" (III:460). So Angelo is referred to, "a man whose blood / Is very snow-broth," he who remains "as marble" to Mariana's tears when he broke off their engagement.[59] Mrs. Arlbery always sees part of the truth. Shakespeare's Angelo is hardly a model Mentor-lover, and neither is Othello.

Dr. Marchmont, in the position of wise Mentor to his Télémaque, acts the part of an Iago. The character in Burney's earlier works whom he most strongly resembles is Dunstan in *Edwy and Elgiva*, the authoritarian monk who divorces the lovers and kills Elgiva. Marchmont is much more complex than Dunstan, or Monckton whom he also slightly resembles. The motives of Marchmont are hidden from himself, and for a long while the reader, like other characters, is tempted to take him at face value. He cannot see what he is doing wrong; he poses successfully even to himself as the disinterested and rational man of the world. It is only after Camilla has broken off the engagement with Edgar that the young man, in a state of unusual emotional shock, asserts any independence from his tutor. For the first time he suspects feelings behind the older man's objectivity:

"Dr Marchmont! how wretchedly ill you think of women!"
"I think of them as they are! I think of them as I have found them. They are artful, though feeble; they are shallow, yet subtle."
"You have been unfortunate in your connexions?"

(IV:642)

Edgar's innocent question elicits from his tutor a torrent of complaining and self-justifying narrative. The author has kept the truth of the polite doctor's inner state from us (and from Edgar) until very late; we have been misjudging Marchmont as a cold and complacent man, like the frigid Dunstan with his overt horror of women, a man who sees women and marriage as "Trifles" to be disdained. But Marchmont has had a sexual life, and disastrous relations with women. He now gives Edgar a bitter account of his two marriages. After his first wife's death, he found her pocketbook, and on the leaves "a gentleman's name . . . charactered in every form, shape, and manner, the wayward, wistful eye could delight to fashion" (IV:643). He realized that his first wife, the one he chose, had been in love with another man and never with him. His second wife, though he was her choice, found him and his way of life uncongenial; "My melancholy returned with a view of our mutual delusion." The wife's "dissipation" ended with "disgrace"; "I just discerned the precipice whence she was falling, in time to avert the dreadful necessity of casting her off for ever." After he prevented his wife from committing adultery, their marriage dragged on through "stifled resentments, and unremitting weariness" until this wife died— and, Marchmont adds with true naïve self-pity, "I am a lonely individual for the rest of my pilgrimage" (IV:643–644).

It does not take a twentieth-century reader to see in this pompous but emotional account the story of a man almost perfectly designed to make a botch of marriage. His narrative puts the blame for matrimonial failure entirely on the wives, but the reader need not accept Marchmont's interpretation in a novel that abounds with warnings against "egotism." Marchmont's failure to "read" situations is seen in the fact that he had literally to *read* his wife's little notebook in order to find out (when it was too late) that she was not happy. Dr. Marchmont's inability to inspire affection, his own unlovingness, rigidity, and vanity are qualities he does not dare think about. In his short narrative, as in Burney's whole novel, the one-sided statement yields a simple moral ("Take warning, my dear young friend, by my experience," IV:645) that the full or stereoscopic statement, provided with the antithesis, the other half of the paradox, would deny. Marchmont's tale has already been parodied earlier in the novel, when the absurd Dubster, the neo-gentleman, descants upon *his* two marriages: "I've known partly enough of the state already" (II:275). Dubster's account provides a risible example of lack of feeling: "very pretty she was, too, if she had not been so puny. But she was always ailing. She cost me a mort of money to the pothecary before she went off" (II:279). Dubster at least obtained money in his two marriages; Marchmont expected another kind of return and feels cheated. Edgar feels "deep concern to have awakened emotions which the absorption of study . . . held generally dormant" (IV:645). Marchmont's dormant—or suppressed—emotions color his actions. He is an Iago because he has also been that paradox, a cold Othello; he is a self-tormentor. His resentment against women for not loving him has found a target in Camilla. Through Edgar he can, vicariously, withhold love from a woman. Furthermore, to Marchmont's secret self, Camilla's main sin or offense lies in her loving Edgar, though the sin he says he suspects is her *not* loving Edgar. His reserves of jealous resentment are agitated by the idea of a desirable woman really loving a man. That would again indict his own failure. Marchmont's rationalized version is that women both good and beautiful do not exist and that those who appear beautiful and amiable never love. His culture creates and accepts the stereotypes that make his woman-hating acceptable. He has every secret reason to wish to "prove" Camilla both unworthy and false.

Dr. Marchmont supplies a major example of "the wilder wonders of the

Heart of man." Like Edgar, he illustrates what Burney claims is the one certain truth of human nature, "the perverseness of spirit which grafts desire on what is denied." He sits in judgment on others, not realizing the elusive strangeness of their hearts and of his own: "in our neighbours we cannot judge, in ourselves we dare not trust it." Within the narrative Burney often warns us of the difficulty of judging motives, and of the self-reflective nature of "those discriminative powers, which dive into their own conceptions to discover . . . the multifarious and contradictory sources of human actions and propensities" (II:271). Within this "multifarious" novel no objective rational standard for judging others or oneself is readily available. Logic is created by the emotions. Motives have hidden sources in elusive and unfixed energies within, as well as in the pressure of difficult commands from without. Everyone is in emotional captivity to both social forces and concealed feelings. In the canceled "Introduction" to *Cecilia* Burney had expressed a sense of her own mysteriousness to herself: "the intricasies of the human Heart are various as innumerable." This sense of the mystery of the psyche and its "wild Mazes" is expressed in the opening of *Camilla* and throughout the novel. The mystery is here applicable to all the characters. A novelist must not say that the characters' intricate feelings "baffle all the power of Language," but she can show how the characters baffle themselves, and she can also indicate the ultimate impossibility of sitting in judgment. Author and reader can go beyond the surface and trace some occulted connections between wild (though rationalized) behavior and concealed "minute & complex" feelings. There are absolute moral principles, Burney believes, but difficulties arise in putting such principles into action. In endeavoring to act rightly the heart may go astray—as the author warns early in the novel: "even the noble principle which impels our love of right, misleads us but into new deviations" (I:9). Mrs. Tyrold and Eugenia—the one an example of "rigid virtue," the other of an heroic standard of honor—supply the novel with examples of the dangers of high standards to human beings, of what happens when "ambition presumes to point at perfection" (*ibid.*). Perfectionism reflects another mode of self-love, another style of fallibility. The course of careful "observation" Marchmont recommends is ridiculous, for the observer is fallible, like the observed.

The center of the novel consists of an enormous spy-story—an absurd yet nerve-racking tale of observation and counterobservation. The action is a satire by hyperbolical extension of the assumption that young women are mainly objects of moral and physical scrutiny. This assumption that women should be observed is shared by conservative conduct-book moralists and by the advanced Rousseau who created the observable Sophie in *Emile*. Part of the entertainment of courtship, according to Rousseau, is that woman must always be dishonest, for "nature" means it so. A man knows better what a woman really means than she can say. Women must be observed; they are voiceless or at least wordless spectacles:

in the true inclinations of their nature, even in lying, they are not false at
all. Why do you consult their mouth, when it is not that which ought to
speak? Consult their eyes, their coloring, their breathing, their timid air,
their soft resistance: there is the language which nature gives them in order
to answer you.[60]

If this is not meant precisely as the rapist's charter to which it can easily be
turned, it is a charter for superior spying. Camilla has less patience than Evelina
at being made a blushing object with "Downcast eye" and "Timid air." Yet she
lives in a world in which women are continually held to be valuable only as they
are spectacular and visible. Consoling Eugenia upon her afflicting discovery that
she is regarded as ugly and deformed, Mr. Tyrold hits upon the expedient of
making her observe another girl. He takes Eugenia and Camilla to look through
an iron fence at a beautiful young female who first stands at the window of a
small house and then enters the garden. There "she sat down upon the grass,
which she plucked up by hands full, and strewed over her fine flowing hair"
(II:308). In this momentarily Edenic scene, which yet conjures up memories of
Ophelia, the girl is visibly "young, fair . . . with features delicately regular." As
the two sisters, under male tuition, watch, the young person astonishes them by
first sobbing aloud, "with violence," then by bursting "into a fit of loud, shrill,
and discordant laughter," then by whirling about and jumping up and down.
Believing her mad, the watching sisters are alarmed, and when the girl comes
over to them, asking for a shilling "while the slaver drivelled unrestrained from
her mouth, rendering utterly disgusting a chin that a statuary might have wished
to model," they are frightened and glad of the iron fence between them. Their
unease continues as the girl seizes the scratching cat and then tears her modest
handkerchief off her neck and puts it over her face, striking her head with her
hands (II:309–310).

The moral lesson Mr. Tyrold wishes to impart is that Eugenia should be
grateful that she has a mind without looks, rather than, like this girl, good looks
but no mind at all. The girl is, as he at length defines her, "born an idiot." The
cure seems nearly as bad as the disease—indeed part of the same disease—in
this curiously intense scene in which the Tyrold daughters are forced to repeat
the intrusive curious behavior with which vulgar gazers had pained Eugenia. It is
Camilla who "fearing they should seem impertinent, would have retreated" and
Mr. Tyrold who makes them remain. Countering the neat moral lesson is the
free-flowing puzzling energy of the young woman, the imbecile or "idiot." Her
behavior is compulsively viewable and yet outside the realm of interpretation
such as Rousseau would offer. She seems both a sexual and a social being, yet
she is not playing the social or sexual game at all; she is not answering anybody.
Though confined behind the iron fence she is free of social confinement to
passivity and the proprieties. Mr. Tyrold forces this unwitting human text to
answer his purposes, but yet the meaning of her tears and laughter can never be

known. Mr. Tyrold is comfortably sure that the "idiot . . . having never known brighter days, is insensible to her terrible state" (II:310), but we may wonder about this. The girl's sobs do not indicate insensibility, and it is after her encounter with her watchers that she attempts to grasp and share the society of the cat and then, in a gesture like shame, covers her face and beats herself. We may be tempted to read her body language, too, and differently from the assumed tutor, Mr. Tyrold. Though she is not incapable of speech—she can say "Good day!" and "Give me a shilling!"—the girl's main communication (in behavior we would label autistic) is with herself, but that does not mean that no communication at all takes place. In ironic affirmation of the Rousseauean scheme, the girl's mouth utters but she does not speak; her body speaks but it is not speaking Jean-Jacques Rousseau's language, and probably not Mr. Tyrold's either. The unlikelihood of Mr. Tyrold's possessing the full explanation is heightened when we consider a much later scene in the book, when Camilla and her vulgar talkative acquaintance Mrs. Mittin, in their progress through the shops at Southampton, are taken for either shoplifters or insane women. They are subjected to pitiless and curious male stares, and the gazers interpret Camilla's face and body language as she was told to interpret the face and gestures of the young woman: "the pensive and absorbed look of Camilla struck him [a haberdasher] as too particular to be natural" (IV:608). When the two take refuge in a bathing hut, they are besieged with impudent gazers making bets on their criminality or insanity; Camilla's silence, as much as Mrs. Mittin's intense loquacity, being taken as support for either position: "when the insinuations of the flippant perfumer had once made her looked at, her beauty, her apparently unprotected situation . . . seemed to render her an object to be stared at without scruple" (IV:613). The word has been spread that "there were two crazy women, one melancholy and one stark wild, that had just, as he supposed, escaped from their keepers" (IV:612). If Camilla's appearance and body language may be misread as signifying her melancholy madness, then the "idiot's" appearance and body language may have been misread by Mr. Tyrold in his diagnosis of insensible want of mind.

Sandra Gilbert and Susan Gubar have taught us to expect and to suspect the figure of the madwoman in women writers' attics, and the scheme that Margaret Homans has taught us can make us see in the girl's strewing her hair with grasses a moment of engagement in the pure feminine, a representation of the return to nature and to the unworded literal, to the presymbolic discourse that Burney as a woman writer both fears and wishes to invoke.[61] Purely feminine— and thus by public definition mad or imbecile—the girl, as Frances Burney (rather than as Mr. Tyrold) presents her, seems a caricature of the female as the male sees her and at the same time a satire upon the endeavors of the masculine to create and define the "feminine." Mr. Tyrold's powerful and simple symbolic scheme, in which the girl figures as an object lesson in his daughter's education, cannot cover the full power of the scene, nor its effect upon his daughters, when they are thus made to gaze with the impudence of male lovers upon a beautiful girl. Eugenia is affected appropriately in Mr. Tyrold's terms, agreeing to bear her affliction without complaint (though it does not make her feel any the less self-conscious). Indeed, the lesson contains a veiled threat of which Mr. Tyrold is supposedly unconscious; if Eugenia goes on lamenting and shutting herself away from society she may well be treated as imbecilic or mad as well as deformed. Eugenia's education here is an education by torture, for the sense of pain in the poor girl makes a deep impression—she is horrified: "I feel your awful lesson! but impress it no further, lest I die in receiving it!" (II:310). Mr. Tyrold does not comprehend the full horror of the situation. He has merely mechanically repeated the turning of the female into the spectacle, a being to be observed, not heard.

Camilla is perpetually in the position of being unheard, but observed—and she hates that position. Her woman's nature is capable of noting injustice, and inner feeling rises and revolts against it. She fights back. Camilla observed becomes an observer in her turn. Aware that she is under surveillance, she begins to take countermeasures, though these are so culturally conditioned as to be of poor service to her. In her novel's structure Burney questions the structure of conventional courtship, displaying the illogicality of the enduringly intricate and rule-bound activity which had supplied so much of the fictional suspense of novels and so much of the misery of real lives, including her own, especially during the George Cambridge episode. She had at last achieved happiness through breaking some of the rules of courtship. She had indiscreetly lent money to a French popish bachelor, she had corresponded with him, she had let her feelings show—and had found a sincere and loving heart on the other side, not an opponent. For the first time in her private life—as distinct from her life as a writer—she had gone counter to the warnings and exhortations of her father. Her experienced happiness gave her the power to cast away the rule-bound and submissive *Clarinda,* and to interrogate authoritative structures and social rules as they claim sovereignty over the feelings. In *Camilla* she defines contemporary propriety and courtship, pointing out the insistently incongruous rules and stressing the paradoxes. The courtship of Camilla and Edgar degenerates into a tense and comic game. They are required to act by parallel and incompatible rules, though the particular strategies change from time to time.

The essential paradox of the central action is to be found in the conduct-book views which constitute the two opposing rules.

A. *Camilla's Rule.* A young woman must never allow her love for a young man to become visible, especially to the object of it, until he has made an unreserved declaration, that is, a proposal of marriage.

Camilla has begun to be aware of this maxim even before her father recommends "the self-command which should dignify every female who would do herself honour" (III:348). Mr. Tyrold elaborates upon this self-command in the letter of advice to Camilla, which takes the whole of the chapter called "A

Sermon" (III: Bk. V, Chap. 5). The clergyman-father explains the precept in terms of an inevitable power struggle. A person of either sex, he says, is always gratified to perceive "a conscious ascendance over the other." But signs of attention from the man she loves may induce a girl to let her unguarded feelings show—a great mistake:

> the female who, upon the softening blandishment of an undisguised prepossession, builds her expectation of its reciprocity, is, in common, most cruelly deceived. . . . The partiality which we feel inspires diffidence; that which we create has a contrary effect. A certainty of success in many destroys, in all weakens, its charm. . . .
> Carefully, then, beyond all other care, shut up every avenue by which a secret which should die untold can further escape you.
>
> (III:360)

Careful to "shut up every avenue" (a sexually loaded phrase), the woman must remain cool or give way to the male sense of power; once she lets her love show, her charm, her own power, departs. The corollary to this proposition is that the woman must inevitably learn a certain kind of hypocrisy, as the father reluctantly acknowledges. The performance of a part is difficult: "In a state of utter constraint, to appear natural is, however, an effort too difficult to be long sustained . . ." (III:361).

Mr. Tyrold's well-meaning essay is so evidently a conduct-book showpiece[62] that some readers overlook the fact that the father's advice provides one of the obstacles between Camilla and Edgar. Dramatically, the advice is questioned over and over again in the novel's action. Tyrold's essay is itself more full of questions about the conventions than conduct-books usually are. He even expresses some doubt about the validity of the custom that allows men free choice in marriage and women only the right of refusal (a feminist issue that will emerge again in *The Wanderer*). There is no ultimate reason why women, as well as men, should not propose: "There cannot, in nature, in theory, nor even in common sense, be a doubt of their equal right" (III:358). The problem lies in contemporary social custom. Mr. Tyrold is sure about what is practicable and prudent for his daughter in the world as it is. Her father's epistle gives Camilla an explicit statement of the major rule by which she must be guided. In the distressing game, this rule generates various temporary modes of behavior to help the player achieve the paradoxical state, "to appear natural."

There remains the other side of the see-saw—Edgar's rule.

B. *Edgar's Rule.* A man must never propose to a woman unless he is sure her heart is now entirely his own. She must also be capable of loving him devotedly and must never have loved another man.

This rule—gain the other's heart before giving anything of yours—is frequently inculcated and explained by Dr. Marchmont. Like Carroll's Alice in remarking upon the dubious worth of the maxim "don't speak until you're spoken to," Edgar uncorrupted recognizes the potential stalemate inherent in his instructions: "how may I inquire into the state of her affections, without acknowledging her mistress of mine?" (I:159). Once corrupted, and no longer thinking in terms of equality, Edgar begins on his own to refine upon the idea. Camilla ought not to betray the slightest interest in any other man, even when Edgar is apparently not interested in her: "It is not alone even her heart that can fully satisfy me; its delicacy must be mine as well as its preference" (II:292).

Each rule can seem reasonable on its own, or, at least, both were supported in real life by persons who seemed reasonable. Rule A, dealt with at length in conduct-books, might be called Richardson's Orthodoxy, in memory of Richardson's *Rambler* 97: "That a young lady should be in love, and the love of the young gentleman undeclared, is an heterodoxy which prudence, and even policy, must not allow."[63] (In Richardson's *Sir Charles Grandison*, however, both the heroines are in this heterodox plight.) The player forced to play by this rule has very limited strategies open to her, and her effort will be spent on concealment. Rule A ought perhaps to be called Viola's Monument, in memory of "she never told her love." Never telling one's love generates another rule (Rule A2), best formulated as "act naturally"—pretend not to feel what you really feel. The player must seem to go in a direction different from that of the secret objective. Rule A2, if followed for any length of time, will inevitably give rise to strategies called "indifference," "levity," or "coquetry." The subtleties of Rule A2 must lead to what might be called the Moving Toyshop Pattern, or zig-zags.

Rule B might proleptically be called Darcy's Act, for it is brought to bear by Darcy in *Pride and Prejudice* against Jane (who has not let her feelings for Bingley show), famously bringing about Bingley's swerve. Rule B offers unlimited opportunity for small moves, and it has its corollary. Rule B2 insists that the woman who is to love the man totally must also be found totally *worthy* of his love, and should prove this to his satisfaction before he commits himself. The refinements of this rule are almost unlimited, and it more than doubles the chance of the opponent's losing the game; the opponent need not even know this rule is in force, while the player (male) is free to rewrite his list of demands, secretly or openly, at any time. This rule, or Mandlebert's Maxim, necessitates constant observation of the possibly unworthy opponent to see if she is acting up to the secret standards. ("I will watch over her unceasingly!") Her attempts at avoidance will lead to errors which may be termed irretrievable.

It will readily be seen that Rule A and Rule B are totally at odds. The only logical result is impasse. The normal result is the breakdown of Player A. But even when B wins the greater number of points, he can still lose by complete loss of his hidden objective (the girl), and such a loss must count as total loss of the game, no matter how brilliantly played. The courtship game can only be truly won by both players in concert breaking the rules *at the same time*. A satisfactory conclusion is not possible without rule collapse. But once play is under way, it is almost impossible for either player to feel the time is right just now for rule-breaking to be permissible.

I have treated the notions that guide Edgar's and Camilla's behavior with unfeeling jocularity, in order to highlight something totally present in the novel. Burney does treat the courtship of Edgar and Camilla as a serious, absurd, and pernicious game, indicating the lack of fit between social controls and the hidden unutterable feelings. Burney had once played the courtship game in deadly earnest, giving herself the kind of advice about "Mr. G: C." that Mr. Tyrold gives Camilla in his "Sermon." Camilla learns to be afraid, as Burney had been afraid, that the man "would be the first . . . to detect the smallest impropriety, & to pay it with its due contempt." Camilla, like Frances Burney in 1783– 1785, must try to force herself to appear, even to herself, as "one who has no *views* whatsoever." Both Edgar and Camilla are taught in such a manner that they must find each other "unaccountable"—a word that recurs in Burney's journals regarding George Cambridge as in *Camilla*. But Burney is no longer at one with a set of precepts, here not internalized but exhibited as coming from the outside. Others (principally the Father) teach Camilla her fears, anxieties, and "feminine" behavior. So, too, Dr. Marchmont teaches Edgar his role and his rights. Both young people are forced into situations which do an injustice to their real nature; *Camilla* is a full-scale illustration of that sad earlier statement by Frances Burney to her sister: "I am sometimes dreadfully afraid for myself, from the *very* different behaviour which Nature calls for on one side, & the World on the other." Now Burney, no longer personally afraid for herself, can show what there is to be feared in this unnecessary and violent antagonism between Nature and the World.

In the novel we see how the two central characters are maneuvered by their advisors (chiefly their clerical seconds) and how, in each case, Nature is subjected to convention, as they each learn what Monckton would have called "the necessity of accommodating [oneself] to such customs as are already received" (*Cecilia*, I:14). They leave their innocence and learn to treat one another as adversaries and opponents, accepting the truisms about male and female. Burney here questions the "rules" which embody whole sets of notions about masculine and feminine nature and behavior. Frances Burney's own courtship and marriage had taught her that the suspicious controls could be dispensed with; she had dared the exaltation of sincere admission, open feeling: "to such a Man . . . I could not be so unjust . . . so false as to disguise my whole sentiments." In *A Picture of Youth* we see the youthful characters being subjected to the process of acculturation; advice and convention redirect the nervous, active, and unstable private emotions, suppressing them or forcing them to choose only approved channels. The result is real craziness, and the world's approved behavior is crazy. In her new novel, Burney certainly wants us to notice the advantages or pseudo-advantages given to men, as she did in *Evelina* in exhibiting the debased language of the ballroom. But the issues are greater, and, as in *Cecilia*, the males, the assumed beneficiaries and designers of the whole system, also feel the costs. Males seem denied the full range of their feelings. Lonely superiority and disdainful suspicion contribute to making men phlegmatic like Dubster, or glacial (as Marchmont has made himself and as Edgar appears to others), or even slightly mad, as Edgar comes to be.

The author also wants us to consider the possibility that whole ranges of behavior labeled female "indiscretion" or female faults such as "coquetry" are the inevitable results of arbitrary conditions for which the individual woman is not to blame. Indeed, blaming others, passing judgment definitively, is an activity vigorously questioned throughout the novel. It is part of the irony of the work that Edgar's strategies are based on Marchmont's command that he keep *judging* Camilla—in a novel that says throughout that we *cannot* judge the heart of another, or trust our own. Female errors may be merely the product of the observer's conditioned interpretation.

Burney has constructed her whole large comic novel out of paradox and antithesis. Camilla's behavior is the product of a miserable paradox: she seems "unworthy" because—and when—she tries to act "discreetly." Even chapter titles make the point and stress the paradoxical theme: "Two Ways of Looking at the Same Thing," "Two Sides of a Question," "A Pro and a Con," "Offs and Ons." Every thesis has its antithesis. Burney has highlighted the absurd and misery-producing rules by placing Dr. Tyrold's well-meant sermon shortly after Marchmont's first lesson to Edgar. We are bound to notice the incompatibility of the hero's and heroine's guiding lights and to understand the inevitable set of crosspurposes that ensues.

The strong element of serious comic game is supported throughout the novel by major metaphoric patterns. Two leading metaphors are (bad) theater and games. The first two chapters, dealing with the young characters' childhood, introduce a wealth of reference to childhood plays, to games and toys, to which a reader more alert than Austen's John Thorpe (disgusted at finding nothing more than "an old man playing at see-saw")[64] must respond. Camilla's memorable ninth birthday party brings out all the toys and games: "cards, trinkets, and blind fidlers" (I:17). It also has its moments of bad theater—mere child's play. Camilla dresses up her uncle, first giving him "whiskers of cork," a powdered wig, and a queue, making him, one might say, into more of a man. The next role is a reversal, the first indication of the sex changes that play metaphorically about the Tyrolds and Lynmeres' family activities: "She metamorphosed him into a female . . . tying the maid's apron round his waist, put a rattle into his hand, and Eugenia's doll upon his lap, which she told him was a baby . . ." (I:18). Sir Hugh, that inadequate male, should perhaps find out if he could play the role of female any better—and femaleness is a role.

The birthday party produces the first example of "desire grafted on what is denied." In an excursion forbidden by Mrs. Tyrold, Sir Hugh cannot refrain from taking seven-year-old Eugenia to the Fair, buying her "as many play-things as she could carry" (I:23). As Mrs. Tyrold had feared, the uninoculated Eugenia catches smallpox. Before her illness is manifest, Sir Hugh makes another day of holiday for all the children. Lionel proposes the amusement of riding upon a plank set upon the trunk of an old oak, and the gardener arranges this improvised see-saw. The older children sit on one end of the plank while Sir Hugh with Eugenia on his lap sits on the other:

> Edgar Mandlebert, who superintended the balance, poised it with great exactness; yet no sooner was Sir Hugh elevated, than, becoming exceedingly giddy, he involuntarily loosened his hold of Eugenia, who fell from his arms to the ground.
>
> (I:27)

Sir Hugh falls, too, but without injury; Eugenia is crippled for life. Male elders can let girls down, and one side of an antithesis is dangerous.

In *Camilla*, everyone engages in games and "play" in all senses, and games and play can be both delightful and dangerous. The see-saw at the beginning of the novel displays danger and delight; it is a visible antithesis. Although Edgar characteristically poised the balance "with great exactness," he cannot prevent the effects of elevation and depression. The see-saw is itself an example of game-paradox; the players can continue the game only while they remain apart, while one side is up and the other is down—just as in the game of prudent courtship. Sir Hugh later refers to Edgar's vacillations in love as "these ups and downs." Cool judges may think they are poising the balance true, but such exactness is unlikely.

References to games and play persist once the characters grow up. Of course they dance and play cards. There are two important raffles. Games become gaming, for adults; several characters run into great debts through gambling. (Lionel is pursued by "debts of honour," Mrs. Berlinton bankrupts herself by "setting up a Faro table"). This kind of exploitative and chancy play is also implicit in Marchmont's view of Edgar's relation to Camilla: "The stake for which you are playing is . . . peace of mind" (IV:594). Everyone plays games of some kind. The witty Sir Sedley Clarendel, an expert in the higher gamesmanship, disconcerts his opponent at chess by his absentmindedness; upon being checkmated he expatiates upon the advantages of not playing while playing. Rather than keeping his faculties "pinioned down to the abstruse vagaries of this brain-besieging game," he allows himself mental excursions to "the four quarters of the globe once, at least, between every move." The pleasure of chess lies in having rules and duties that can be ignored, offering the pleasure of "Those exquisite little moments we steal from any given occupation" (II:249). Sir Sedley, who can be counted on to suggest interesting paradoxes, shows that to lose may be to win, and that play needs to be alleviated by play. What he advocates (noncommitment to the game) ought to be taken seriously by Camilla and Edgar.

The theme of games, or "play," is closely related to the novel's other constant motif of perverse theater. Lionel forces absurd roles on other people in the theatrical games in Mrs. Arlbery's attic, which the young people transform into a makeshift theater:

> Away they sped . . . and in a few minutes reversed the face of everything. Old sofas . . . large family chests, deal boxes, . . . tables with two legs, and chairs without bottoms, were . . . arranged to form a semi-circle, with seats in front, for a pit.
>
> (II:259)

The physical improvisation, the *bricolage,* is itself the chief game; nothing coherent is performed in this ramshackle theater. The gentlemen spout "shreds and scraps of different tragedies" (II:262). Lionel convulses the company by cross-dressing, attiring himself in the maid's clothes, putting the ensign's cocked hat and feather on little Miss Dennel. Theatrical play permits irresponsibility, even the momentary relief of escaping sex roles, if only in caricature, but nothing is properly acted. Within the novel's central narrative nothing is properly acted by anyone—it is all bad acting. As well as seeing the poor actors give their ludicrous performance of *Othello,* Camilla sees several other bad performances, including the nasty and unhappy theater provided by "The accomplish'd Monkies" (III: Bk. VI Chap. 6) and the distressing display of obedience given by "the learned bullfinch" (III: Bk. VI Chap. 13). As the novel progresses, human theater degenerates into animal theater, with exploited, abused creatures made to act parts they do not understand. Burney keeps returning to the monkey theme, in a Swiftian image of mankind—more particularly male mankind; the monkey in *Evelina* mocks and bites Lovel. Monckton in *Cecilia* tells the impudent Morrice that Cecilia has compared him to the orangoutang. In *Camilla* (a wartime book) the monkeys dressed as soldiers exasperate the foolish Ensign Macdersey. If monkey-theater is male, birds in durance are traditionally associated with women. Camilla's sympathy for the poor learned bullfinch is a womanly sympathy, arising from similarities between her own position and that of the bird—a similarity the showman's cruel remarks indicate:

> "O, easy enough, Miss," replied the man, grinning; "everything's the better for a little beating, as I tells my wife. There's nothing so fine set, Miss, but what will bear it, more or less."
>
> (III:492)

Camilla is indignant at the cruelty to a poor creature "who does not understand what you require," but the showman insists "they knows what I wants as well as I do myself; only they're so dead tiresome . . . a little squeak now and then in the intrum does 'em no harm" (III:493).

Training in obedience and the acting of a part have been associated with cruelty to women since the bad performance of *Othello;* the play's wife-murder onstage is connected with wife-beating off, a little squeak in the interim:

> They were detained so long between the first and second act, that Sir Sedley said he feared poor Desdemona had lost the thread-paper from which she was to mend her gown. . . . "Consider," he said, "the trepidation of a fair bride but just entered into her shackles. Who knows but Othello may be giving her a strapping, in private, for wearing out her cloaths so fast! you young ladies think nothing of these little conjugal freedoms."
>
> (II:320)

The novel's enduring association of game-play-cruelty can be found in the fate of Eugenia's scoundrel of a husband, Alphonso Bellamy. He won the fifteen-year-old heiress by a mixture of hypocrisy, blackmail, and force, abducting her to Gretna Green and threatening to commit suicide if she did not consent to marry him. Once her family has reluctantly allowed the marriage to be considered valid, Bellamy shows that, far from being fatally in love with Eugenia, he wanted only her money. He treats his crippled little wife with scorn and hostility, and is interested only in extracting more money from her uncle. When she refuses his demand that she ask her uncle yet again for a large sum, he threatens her in a scene deliberately melodramatic, since Eugenia the heroic has customarily taken heroics at face value:

> He then felt in his waistcoat pocket, whence he took two bullets, telling her, she should have the pleasure of seeing him load the pistol; and that when one bullet had dispatched her, the other should disappoint the executioner. . . . "I must hold the pistol to your ear," cried he, "while you take your oath. See! 'tis loaded—This is no child's play."
>
> (V:887)

The postillion hears this last sentence, which is dramatically repeated, sees Bellamy holding the pistol to his wife's head, and rushes to the rescue. Bellamy is startled, the gun goes off while he tries to hide it, and he shoots himself dead. Eugenia is afterwards "convinced that Bellamy had no real design against either his life or her's." So, ironically, this was "child's play"—and bad play-acting. "Bellamy" the fortune-hunter was play-acting all along. Shortly after his death the family finds out his real name—Nicholas Gwigg. The heroics and even the wickedness of Bellamy are severely diminished if read as the actions only of a Nicholas Gwigg, "son of the master of a great gaming-house" (V:892).

The game Camilla and Edgar play involves oppression and being oppressed, absurdity and bad acting, childishness and exploitativeness. It is a paradox that so non-sensical a game can have such crippling effects. The game-and-play motif within the novel constantly enables the reader to see the connections between various sights, actions, and events, connections occulted from the characters, just as the relation between their unconscious or half-conscious feelings and their actions is obscure to them. *Camilla* may be a long and "multifarious" novel but it is not a series of disconnected episodes. It is constructed of a series of related paradoxes; we see the parallel, even the intimate reciprocal relationship (as in the see-saw) between antitheses. The affair of Nicholas Gwigg shows us how things connect. Child's play and murder, game and suicide, theater and oppression are united at the end, as they are throughout the novel.

Camilla: Mysteries, Clues, and Guilty Characters

Why should not I have my mystery, as well as Udolpho?
(Burney to Charles, 18 June 1795)[1]

"I had rather have lost my ears than that manuscript! . . . it was a clue to a whole section." (Dr. Orkborne in *Camilla*, II:210)

Camilla is the name of a heroine associated with fleetness and airy lightness; she

> Outstrip'd the Winds in speed upon the Plain
> Flew o'er the Fields, nor hurt the bearded Grain:
> She swept the Seas, and as she skim'd along,
> Her flying Feet unbath'd on Billows hung.
> (Dryden, trans., *Aeneid* VII)[2]

"Camilla" is thus an appropriate name for a girl whose airy qualities or even "levity" were initially to be stressed; it is another name for an "Ariella." Camilla is also a name with personal connotations for Frances Burney; Fulke Greville had allotted this pseudonym to his wife in his *Maxims, Characters and Reflections* (1756). Camilla as a name for the godmother Frances Greville, née Macartney, is thus a substitute for "Frances" and carries a private allusion to the name of the author's self. Once she hit upon the name, Burney seems to have felt its full appropriateness. The Camilla of Virgil is an ambiguous heroine;

she is beautiful, but she is a fighter, a woman warrior, "bellatrix"; Dryden uses the term "Virago." She had what would appeal to Frances Burney, a devoted and singular relationship with her father, who, in a phallic gesture of rescue, gives her life and then devotes himself to educating the "little Amazon" in manly arts.[3] Yet, in the end, feminine weakness hastens her death on the battlefield; she is attracted by elaborate arms and accoutrements and thoughtlessly chases her prey beyond the bounds of safety "so greedy was she bent / On Golden Spoils."[4] Female lust for ornament is her undoing—as our Camilla's undoing seems to be her extravagant desire for the "clear lawn and lilac plumes and ornaments" that she thinks will attract Edgar.

That Burney was fully conscious of the Virgilian connotations of her heroine's name is immediately apparent when one sees how she has amplified the Virgilian references. Camilla's prudent elder sister is in some early versions of Burney's story referred to as "Creusa," the name of Aeneas' first wife who perished in the flight from Troy while Aeneas was able to rescue his father and son; Creusa's only speaking appearance in the Aeneid is as a dutiful ghost. In the published version of the novel, Camilla's elder sister is named "Lavinia." That is the name of the exceedingly proper and beautiful daughter of Latinus, betrothed to Turnus but given in marriage to Aeneas, the second wife whose advent the ghostly Creusa foretold. Lavinia, the girl with no speaking part in the epic in which she appears, is simply a conduit of legitimacy, a dutiful representative of the duties of marriage and the founding of the new Roman state in Latium. Lavinia Tyrold is also associated with a dutiful switch of suitors; Sir Harry Westwyn orders his browbeaten son Hal to give over thinking of Camilla and propose to Lavinia; "you'd do the right thing to take her sister; who's pretty near as pretty, and gives herself no airs. . . . I shall never think well of you again as long as ever I live, if you demur so much as a moment" (V:904). Poor Lavina Tyrold is given no love story of her own and is rendered nearly as passive as her classical predecessor; the lot of the dutiful representative of femininity is unenviable. Virgil's Camilla fought against Aeneas and the Roman state. She represented opposition to Roman hegemony, patriarchal control, and the Augustan rule that Virgil has set himself the task of celebrating. In Burney's novel, Camilla's father is *Augustus* Tyrold. Camilla the lovely virago is thus put into a context in which she is, however unwittingly or innocently, in opposition to established or imperial authority. Hers is a dangerous role—the classical Camilla died, and this Camilla nearly does. One of the things the novel is, is a mock-epic, a domestic epic in which the woman who is created by the epic writer only to be defeated becomes the center of her story.

As we have seen, Burney in her teens had been provoked by Homer's depiction of woman in the *Iliad*'s Helen: "Thus has Homer proved his opinion of our poor sex—that the love of beauty is our most prevailing passion . . . But I don't in fact believe it." And she made Lord Orville's "Helen," Evelina, contradict Homer's opinion. If Burney wanted to reverse the epic's picture of womankind even more ambitiously in her third novel, she was undeniably under the handicap of not knowing the original languages in which epics, those culturally defining works, had been written. Knowledge of classical languages and literature was, from the Renaissance to the nineteenth century, the passport to the world of power, sacred to the gentleman's authority. Women's attempts to learn Greek or Latin often aroused deep anger and resentment; ladies were told that such learning defeminized them. According to Mrs. Thrale, Henry Fielding could not bear that his sister Sarah ("Sally") should acquire the classical tongues:

> I have heard Doctor Collier say that Harry Fielding quite doated upon his Sister Sally till she had made herself through his—D^r. Collier's— Assistance, a competent Scholar, & could construe the 6th. Book of Virgil: he then began to joke, & afterwards to *taunt* her, as a literary Lady &c. till she resolved on Study—and became eminent in her Knowledge of the Greek Language, after which her Brother never more could perswade himself to endure her Company with Civility—[5]

The same Dr. Arthur Collier had given young Hester Salusbury (later Mrs. Thrale) regular and solid instruction in Latin. In 1779 Burney, when under Mrs. Thrale's roof, was taught Latin for a little while by Dr. Johnson, who insisted on teaching her and Queeney Thrale. Frances Burney had mixed feelings about devoting "so much time to acquire something I shall always dread to have known."[6] The dread was partly inspired by Charles Burney, who mocked the scheme, thinking Latin grammar "too Masculine for Misses," and eventually forbade Fanny to continue, leading Mrs. Thrale to comment privately that he was a "narrow Souled Goose-Cap."[7] If in 1779 Frances Burney had feared being mocked as a learned lady, by 1796 she appears to have had second thoughts. The issue of women's education and the question of the place of Latin and Greek in life and literature are raised within *Camilla*.

The girls' naïve uncle Sir Hugh first raises the linguistic question when he attributes "every evil of his life" to "his youthful disrespect of Greek and Latin" (I:34). He acquires the tutor Dr. Orkborne to remedy the evil, but possesses "neither quickness to learn, nor memory to retain . . . the elements of a dead language" (I:39). The words mean nothing to him; he refers to it as "all this hard jingle jangle" and, on trying to impress Lionel with some Latin sentences, "he pronounced so ill, and so constantly misapplied that . . . the boy almost rolled upon the floor with convulsive merriment" (I:42). The language of power which Sir Hugh as elder son and landowner should have had is only a magical gibberish. Yet it is something quite different to poor Eugenia; marred by small-pox and crippled for life, she is unable to share in the children's play and needs an engaging sedentary occupation. When Orkborne (to his disdain) is passed on to her as her tutor, she not only does very well but acquires a love of the subject, and reads extensively in classical authors.

The novel offers a cross-section of the kinds of education possible for both males and females. Beautiful Indiana has a few smatterings inculcated by her governess, the stupid and conceited Miss Margland. Lionel has an excellent standard British education (Eton and Oxford), while Clermont is sent to "Leipsic," and Edgar enjoys the private tuition of Dr. Marchmont. There are no ideal modes or results. Lionel, offered the language of power, despises it, and hates reading: "I would as soon be seen trying on a lady's cap at a glass, as poring over a crazy old author when I could help it" (II:240). Young men see an interest in books as effeminate, yet a lady's interest in books makes her unfeminine. Sir Hugh himself, who initiated the education of Eugenia, thinks her "so bookish, I might as well live with an old woman" (I:51) and, when he brought Camilla back to live with him "the first words he spoke upon her arrival were to inform her she must learn no Latin" (I:52). Sir Hugh plans to marry his heiress Eugenia to her cousin Clermont, thus providing for his male ward, whom he expects to be "bookish" likewise. Clermont is dismayed by the pockmarked cripple and still more horrified when he discovers the horrid truth about her learning: "Greek and Latin! why I'd as soon tie myself to a rod. Pretty sort of dinners she'll give!" (IV:579). Eugenia is not a woman at all: "what have I to do with marrying a girl like a boy?" (IV:592).

Eugenia, unlike her sisters, is not given the name of a classical character, though she is given a classical name. "Little Greek and Latin," as her brother calls her, has a Greek name which came into Latin and means "well born." At times she wishes she had not been born at all. Burney makes us realize what it is like to be Eugenia, especially in the sequence that shows the revelation to the girl of her own ugliness. Stuck aloft in an unfinished summerhouse by the side of the road, without a ladder to get down by because Lionel (for a joke) has taken it away, Eugenia is literally exposed to the view of passengers who publicly mock and deride her: "What were you put up there for, Miss? to frighten the crows?" (II:286). Eugenia is inconsolable and thinks of shutting herself up for life; she is irate at her family who, at Sir Hugh's orders, had kept the full extent of her misfortune from her. Mr. Tyrold then attempts to teach her through one of those startling object lessons so dear to post-Rousseauean educators, by presenting her with the "idiot" girl for her edification. As the novel is not some neat moral tale for children, no "proof" can prove that deformity is not difficult to bear. When Clermont arrives, Eugenia "felt as if, even since the morning, the small-pox had renewed its ravages, and she had sunk into being shorter" (IV:577). In all her novels, Burney has shown the effect of attacks upon the body, shame and embarrassment making the person shrink and cringe. Eugenia is in a state of permanent physical embarrassment, always at a disadvantage, always shrunken. "They tell me, ma'am, that ugly little body's a great fortune," says a stranger to Camilla at the girls' first ball (I:77). Eugenia is treated in her youth as old women were treated in *Evelina*.

In the eyes of many around her, Eugenia has a double deformity—her inferior body and her superior education. They are associated; the tittering fashionables of Southampton "were convinced her education had made her such a fright" (V:748). By the 1790s, the reading public, old and young, had been educated into a more liberal view of those whom we now call "the handicapped." Mary Wollstonecraft in *Original Stories* (1788) advocates tact in the treatment of the disabled; Mrs. Pinchard in *The Blind Child* (1793) stresses the necessity of treating little blind Helen as part of the family. Readers whether conservative or radical would accept Burney's attack upon barbarity. But not all readers would have thought it right that any woman should learn what Eugenia knows. In an aggressive, decontaminating reversal of a satiric trope, Burney gives lovable Eugenia the traditional defects of caricatured literary ladies, who squint and have humps and look frightful, like Pope's Phoebe Clinket or Smollett's Narcissa's aunt. Associating the horror at learned ladies with the old vulgar outcry at a crippled body, the author makes us reject both reactions as crude, inhumane, and archaic.

In following Eugenia's career, however, the sympathetic reader of the novel is never in danger of regarding her learning merely as a deformity. We do learn that it has peculiar drawbacks. Eugenia has read little modern literature and no novels. A female Quixote bred on epics, she judges everything in epic terms, expecting nobility and absolute honor of herself and everyone else. She sticks to the Gretna Green marriage to which she was abducted by "Alphonso Bellamy"; she could legally get out of it, but she considers a *vow* as sacred—a view caught from her reading, an heroic view, but perhaps the wrong one. Eugenia is not an epic character but a character who reads epics. She is "well-born"—in the sense of well conceived—the author's representation of woman as reader, the woman who breaks into sacred ground and tries to make sense of it.

After the catastrophe of her disastrous marriage Eugenia becomes a writer, not just a reader. She consoles herself by writing her memoirs, trying to make her own feelings intelligible to the male world which has hitherto been instructing her:

> Ye, too, O lords of the creation, mighty men! impute not to native vanity the repining spirit with which I lament the loss of beauty . . . nor to feminine littleness of soul, a regret of which the true source is to be traced to your own bosoms . . . for the value you yourselves set upon external attractions, your own neglect has taught me to know; and the indifferency with which you consider all else, your own duplicity has instructed me to feel.
>
> (V:905)

This seems a renewal of Burney's response to Homer's treatment of Helen, and the question of women's alleged narcissism. But the young autobiographer, the teenaged widow, is not left to her solemn memoirs. Eugenia marries the bookish Melmond, and he gets "a companion delighting in all his favourite pursuits" (V:912). Their marriage would not suit everyone but it suits themselves; there is no absolute statement as to what is universally recommended or reprehended in the education of either male or female.

Reading is a major theme in *Camilla*. The novel constantly alludes to what people read, and how they read. Sarcastic Mrs. Arlbery (quoting Jonson) describes young Melmond as "melancholy and gentleman-like"; "I know the Melmonds well. They are all half crazy, romantic, love-lorn, studious and sentimental" (III:418). Melmond's sister Mrs. Berlinton bears this out; she reads only books supporting her enthusiastic notions of friendship and imagination: Elizabeth Rowe's *Friendship in Death*, Akenside's *Pleasures of the Imagination*, Hammond's *Elegies*, and Collins's *Odes*.[8] The romantic Melmond is introduced in a bookstore, where his rapturous reading aloud of Thomson's "Spring" has a variety of effects on different hearers. Lionel dismisses the "fogrum stuff," Eugenia is enchanted, and Indiana pays no attention to the words but watches his gestures.

In an earlier manuscript version of the novel (in which the heroine is momentarily "Clarilla") there is an amusing scene in which "Gunniston," the prototype of Melmond, tries to awaken the intellects of his beloved (referred to as both "Cleora" and "Indiana"): "If she were unformed, might he not form her? If she were uninstructed, what bliss to instruct her! what rapture to watch the growth of improvement in so beautiful a disciple!"[9] Here we do have a lover acting as tutor and Mentor—comically and ineffectually. On the first day of his program, a Sunday, he reads one of Blair's sermons to the company (two girls and the governess), and then tries two essays from the *Rambler*, with little success. Cleora sighs, "I'm sure I've counted thirty carriages . . . while you have been reading that last thing."[10] The lover is "unable . . . with all his ardent admiration, to still a secret voice, that began whispering: 'I fear . . . I have tied myself for life to a mere beautiful Machine! without Soul, & without Brains!" while Cleora retires muttering, "I might just as well have engaged myself to a parish Clerk."[11]

Gunniston-Melmond is not too daunted to try again. On Monday he proposes to try some lighter literature, suggesting poems by Beattie, Falconer, and Charlotte Smith.[12] Colonel Digby had read Falconer's *The Shipwreck* (1762) aloud to Burney during her court service, and she had thought that the comic artist Bunbury might make a caricature of them entitled, "the sentimental readers."[13] Cleora refuses to be a sentimental reader, but tries to resign herself.

"O dear, don't count any more. I like one as well as another. I've no choice—if one must always be reading."

"No, my loveliest Cleora, not always—but you know not, if once you will indulge it . . . how a literary taste will grow upon you, nor what you may owe to its resources. Come! what shall I begin with?"

"Dear, I don't care! answered she, pettishly; if you've got nothing to say, but reading Books—I don't think it was much worth while to come to London for that. However, thank Goodness, this is the last Night. So it don't much signify."[14]

This scene does not appear in our *Camilla*; the substance of it is given in two sentences (V:812). One reason for omitting the scene is that it makes Cleora-Indiana oddly sympathetic—as the antiliterary Joyce will be (by authorial intention) in Burney's later play, *The Woman-Hater*. If Indiana is insensible to literature, she is not immune to intoxicating images:

> her ear could not withstand the romantic sound of love and a cottage . . .
> for she considered such a habitation but as a bower of eglantine and roses,
> in which she might repose and be adored all day long.
>
> (V:719)

Melmond falls in love with the beauty because his own egotism leads him to believe she admires him and shares his views. The nature of the human heart is such that no reading matter is completely safe or instructive. Mrs. Berlinton was brought up by a fanatical aunt whose only religion was a fear of hellfire; bred on sensational ideas, she is a ready disciple of sensibility and an easy target for Bellamy's rhetoric and rant about "destiny" that nearly leads her into adultery.

If no literature in the public realm can be guaranteed wholesome in all its effects (including sermons or epic poems), the characters are in even more danger from what might be called "private literature," the works the characters themselves write. Characters in *Camilla* are continually engaged in reading, or re-reading, written pages composed by other characters; they try to interpret the world and themselves through those writings. The clearest example of epistles both absurd and noxious are the anonymous letters Lionel sends his timid uncle Relvil; the first letter promised "he would have his brains blown out" if he did not send money, while the next threatened "if he did not send me double the sum, in the same manner . . . his house was to be burnt to the ground." Lionel also warned his victim not to attempt discovery: "there were spies about him." The fear of incensed laborers, revolutionary gangs, and "incendiary" secret societies was widespread in the troubled 1790s, so it is not wonderful that the victim believed the letters. Lionel's first attempts at extortion were successful: "The good old ass took it all for gospel" (II:225–226). Lionel is, of course, guilty of a serious offense under the law; his mother rightly calls it "A fraud," but Lionel insists on defining his actions as "a joke! a frolic! . . . I am astonished at my mother! I really don't care if I don't hear another syllable" (II:240). The family means to hush the matter up. But chickenhearted Uncle Relvil is not the only character foolish enough to take another character's words "all for gospel."

A number of characters in *Camilla* are tempted to turn the writings of others into sacred scripture. Mrs. Berlinton is first discovered (by Camilla and the reader) perusing by moonlight a letter from her "lovely friend" (a clue that the writer is "*Bell-amy*" (III:387–388). She kisses the paper, puts it in her bosom, treats it as a sacred object. Her romantic absurdity is so patent that it should nudge us into questioning other instances of so ardent re-reading. At an important juncture, Edgar receives a warning letter from Dr. Marchmont (the epistle given in full). This text demands that its readers read it again after coming to the end; "I merely entreat you twice to peruse what I have written" (II:179). We are given the sequence and progress of Edgar's readings. He first runs through the letter impatiently and puts it away, displeased at "these fastidious doubts and causeless difficulties." But he cannot escape: "He was half way down stairs, when the sentence finishing with, 'you cannot excite, you cannot bestow happiness' confusedly recurred to him . . . and, returning to his room, he re-opened the letter to look for the passage." He reads that sentence again, "and presently re-read the whole epistle. . . . The first blight thus borne . . . he yet a third time read the letter." Marchmont has succeeded in instructing his pupil: "'He is right!' he then cried" (II:179–180). Edgar submits, wrongly, to the letter; from dismissing it as a text revealing some defects in the author he turns to accepting it, first as a reasonable statement, then as absolute truth: "'He is right!'" His tutor's letter reads him very well, insinuating itself into the gaps in Edgar's defective sense of worth. Once he starts *re*-reading, he is lost. He transforms the epistle into sacred text, as its author, *Gabriel* Marchmont (a false archangel), wishes him to do. Edgar marks, learns, and inwardly digests the same, which is bad for his health.

Camilla undergoes a similar process in accepting her father's long epistle, called "A Sermon" in the chapter heading. She carries it about with her like a fetish or talisman, reads and re-reads this well-meaning but not very helpful document. Mr. Tyrold's "Sermon" affirms his love for his daughter and expresses some guarded doubts and anxieties about the social code, at the same time binding the daughter to what the epistle itself admits may be an irrational code. Some modern critics have seen in this chapter an authorial statement setting forth an idea of ethical conduct. It is true that (abridged) Tyrold's sermon was reprinted in an anthology of advice to ladies, where it kept company with John Gregory's *A Father's Legacy to His Daughters,* but Burney cannot be blamed for that. As we have seen, Mr. Tyrold's advice is a recipe for stalemate in Camilla's relations with Edgar, bound to be disastrous when combined with the antithetical rules proposed by Marchmont to Edgar. Mr. Tyrold is unaware of these, of course, but his very lack of awareness of the whole context makes his judgment visibly imperfect. With the best of intentions he functions as a false guide and censor. "Tyrold," it should be noted, is a made-up name, not an English surname, although it echoes "Tyrrell," the name of an ogre of the history books, the murderer of the Princes in the Tower. Its syllables suggest "Tyrant-old." *Augustus* Tyrold is the well-meaning representative of brutality, repression, the ancient establishment of wrong—Burney's version of Urizen, the old Nobo-daddy. Camilla errs in making his "sermon" a sacred scripture, reading it every night during her stay in Tunbridge as if it were her Bible. There is nothing in the novel to support such pious readings of another character's writings. The nature of other writings all "taken for gospel" points to a dubious status for the "Sermon." Both hero and heroine are guided by parallel false sacred writings (the two letters), which the young people *re*-read too submissively. The attempts of both "fathers" (both clergymen) to fashion guides to conduct and to imprison present feelings in past experience are ultimately wrong.

Within the novel, the pedantic Dr. Orkborne (born of an ork? or son of Orcus?) comically combines the motifs of reading and writing. In contrast to the subliterary, like Indiana, he is so ultraliterary as not to read the books he uses. Sir Hugh is puzzled when Orkborne refuses to set out on a short coach journey without an enormous supply of books: "you could not get through more than one . . . unless you skip half, which I suppose you solid heads leave to the lower ignoramusses." Orkborne explains, "There are many of them I shall never read in my life, but I shall want them all" (II:189). This paradoxical reply confounds Sir Hugh. But Orkborne's particular study is philology—words in themselves, discrete meanings without connections. He ignores all contexts, as he does when he stops in the field, struck with the scene's "resemblance to a verse in one of Virgil's Eclogues, which he thought might be happily applied to illustrate a passage in his own work." (Orkborne comically extends Burney's Virgilian theme.) He takes out his tablets and ignores the fact that he and Eugenia are menaced by an angry bull: "Dr. Orkborne, intent upon his annotations, calmly wrote on, sensible there was some disturbance . . ." (I:131–132). He evades contexts as much as possible, and his work exists as anthologies of jottings, scraps, broken materials. His only moment of passion occurs when he discovers that Sir Hugh, with the best intentions, has added new bookshelves to his room and had the place tidied in his absence, a comic scene sufficiently striking for Scott to allude to it in *The Antiquary* (1816).[15] Orkborne is as outraged as *The Witlings'* Dabler would be: "If I must have my manuscripts rummaged at pleasure, by every dunce in the house, I would rather lie in the street!" He insists that the maid, in losing the one scrap, has done irreparable harm; "You have ruined me! . . . I had rather you had given me a bowl of poison! you can make me no reparation; it was a clue to a whole section" (II:210). Mary indignantly protests that the "little morsel of paper" was too messy to be any use: "Not a soul could have read it" (II:212). Anyone who has worked with the Burney manuscripts knows Burney's own predilection for writing semi-legibly on "little morsels of paper." Orkborne, even more than Dabler, is a parody of the author, herself engaged in trying to hold on to the clues of the varied sections of her enormous work. Unlike Burney, Orkborne is a slow worker, allergic to interruptions: "he strove vainly to rescue from oblivion the slow ripening fruits of his tardy conceptions" (II:185). Surprisingly, he is successful at last in producing his own slow-ripening fruit, though one imagines the opus of this Orcus must be bound for oblivion. (Was he writing a philological Key to All Mythologies?) He is a comic hidden representative of the author; like his creator, he is engaged in writing a book, and this work occupies his attention from the beginning of the novel to the end, when he (like the author) is just about to see his work through the press.

The single-minded and egotistical pedant who labors to put scraps together and tries to make connections without contexts is a metaphoric center for the novel's main actions. Orkborne acts out what the other characters do as they endeavor to construct a truth out of scraps, hints, and clues. Often they are engaged in literally perusing fragments of manuscript. Sir Sedley Clarendel finds Camilla's pile of scraps, abortive attempts at a letter to Sir Hugh asking for money (really for Lionel and at his request). Sir Sedley collates and interprets the unfinished epistles; he then creates a false solution to the problem by providing Lionel with a bank draft for 200 pounds, putting Camilla in all senses in his debt. The joyful Lionel compounds his sister's problem by writing a letter with the salutation "My dear Lady Clarendel" (III:512–513). Sir Sedley, coming upon this fragment, assumes that Lionel's insolent prolepsis represents Camilla's own ambition. "Rummaging" private papers (the thing that Dabler and Orkborne so greatly dislike) is dangerously apt to lead to misreading.

Edgar is faced with a similar textual problem when he later forces Camilla to hand over the letters she received from Sir Sedley; in effect, he names seeing the letters as his condition for a continuation of his engagement with her. Camilla naïvely believes that the letters will "prove" that there was nothing between herself and the baronet; she is innocent enough to think the letters will tell their own story—that is, the story she knows. But such writings do not "tell their own story"; all depends on the reader. Edgar is incapable of constructing the narrative that Camilla thinks the letters point to; he cannot fill in the blanks. His reading is a blur of cursory anxiety and "misperception": "He then hastily ran over the letters; but by no means hastily could he digest, nor even comprehend their contents" (IV:580). He skims and jumps to a conclusion, and then carries the letters about with him as an unholy scripture of torment. When Camilla nervously asks if he has burned "those foolish letters," he replies angrily, "Their answers are not likely to meet with so violent a death, and it seemed to me that one part of the correspondence should be preserved for the elucidation of the other" (IV:620). Having determined that Camilla does love Sir Sedley, Edgar is stimulated by the invisible half of the correspondence, her letters to the baronet. He will not burn, but preserve, the writings he hates in the antiquarianism of jealousy. He creates a false context and constructs his own story out of the scraps of evidence.

The pattern of reading, re-reading, and misreading is constant throughout the action. The metaphorical language of authorial narration consistently uses words like "prepossession," "hypothesis," "misconstrue." At the end Camilla says she has suffered from "continual misconstruction" (V:896). Characters try to read other people's behavior the way they read scraps of writing. That is, they tend to ignore or re-create contexts in order to come out with some simple interpretation. Through much of the novel, Edgar, under the stimulus of Marchmont, is miserably determined to freeze Camilla into the simple definition "a coquette." He forces all kinds of evidence into his dismal hypothesis. For instance, having engaged Camilla for the first country dance at the ball at Southampton, he is confounded when he sees her standing up with another man; he does not wait long enough to discover that this dance is a cotillon, not the country dance. He is detecting from a distance, watching people talk without hearing their words: "He had *gathered* the subject was dancing, and he *saw* the Major most earnest with Camilla. He was *sure* it was for her hand, and *concluded* it was for a country dance . . ." (III:445 [italics mine]). If he had not "quitted the ballroom" under the pressure of an imagined event, the matter would have been truly clear to him as soon as the dance itself began. But he takes signs for substance and reads a few gestures as a whole story, a whole text instead of a fragment. The characters in *Camilla*, Edgar probably most of all, go through intellectual processes of observing, conjecturing, concluding—and these intellectual processes of decoding and construction lead them to absurdity.

Most of the characters in *Camilla* thus seem like mad detectives. Their observation and conjecture are driven by anxieties, and their relation to each other is suspicious: Camilla is Edgar's suspect. Like philologists they try to find some deep original meaning, a simple significance that ignores the current context and the interactive, illogical effects of relationships. Edgar immediately defines Mrs. Arlbery as a dangerous friend for Camilla, though he can hardly say why, admitting "she is undoubtedly a woman of character. . . . Her reputation is without taint" (I:155). Edgar of course needs some sign of his power over Camilla, and the arbitrary imposition as law of his wish that she not visit the lady will do. Indiana and Miss Margland read Camilla's acquiescence in Edgar's prohibitions as a sign that she is trying to entrap Edgar and take him from Indiana; to acquit herself of this accusation Camilla must disobey him. Camilla does visit Mrs. Arlbery, as Frances herself perhaps wished she could have gone on seeing Mme. de Staël. ("I wish The World would take more care of itself, and less of its neighbours.") What right has Edgar to assume authority over a girl who has a full complement of parents? Mr. Tyrold in fact approves the friendship and later sends Camilla to be cheered up by Mrs. Arlbery.

Burney family members reading the new novel saw in Edgar a reflection of William Locke the younger (b. 1767), heir to Norbury Park. Something of the plot situation may be related to William's youthful attraction in 1787 to Mrs. Delany's great-grandniece, the lovely Mary Ann Port, whom friends thought too flighty for him (and who, in any case, was infatuated with a Colonel Goldsworthy). The identification of Edgar with young William did not mean approval of the character. Dr. Burney thought that "Edgar is a handsome likeness of William Locke, & sufficiently punished for his too fastidious system of ideal perfection."[16] (If William Locke the younger were the model for Edgar, he had his revenge in 1814 when he reappropriated Camilla Cottage.) Yet perhaps the portrait of Edgar is also and more deeply affected by the character of the elder William Locke, whose "Lecture" to his wife had "lessoned her with great earnestness" about subduing her impulses and emotions. The madness that threatens Camilla because of her association with Edgar seems not unrelated to the madness that had menaced Frederica. In her strange position between the Lockes, Frances had been cast in something of the position of a Mrs. Arlbery, a dangerous friend for another woman to know, at least until an ardent nature and enthusiasm could be satisfactorily controlled. The world encourages male manipulation of female friendship, but such interference is, as Burney shows, sometimes dangerous and almost inevitably absurd.

Edgar's motives include resentment of Mrs. Arlbery's power: "I saw she had charmed you" (I:155). He has reason to distrust the lady's wit, for he has none himself. Mrs. Arlbery deals in paradoxes and is not simply the victim of them. Far from being an undesirable acquaintance from the reader's point of view, Mrs. Arlbery supplies much of the novel's liveliness; Burney's sister Esther expressed a reaction that must have entertained the author:

> M^rs. Arlbery (whom we are apt to call *d'Arblay*) entertains me extremely & with all her Caprices, she has so much wit & sense that it is impossible not to like & almost love her. . . . M^rs. Arlbery is never gross.—in short I admire her—& think she must have been bewitching amongst Men.[17]

A member of the Burney family (all adept at word-play) spotted the concealed pun or anagram in the character's name; the intelligent older woman stands in for the author herself. In his ambitious prejudice against Mrs. Arlbery, Edgar is repudiating any acquaintance with Mme. d'Arblay, turning against his own author. If Edgar is, as Mrs. Arlbery says, "a watcher" (III:482), there are things he cannot bear to see.

The very earliest notes for the new novel that became *Camilla* emphasize suspicion and watching, in the manner of the story of mystery. Among the manuscript scraps in the Berg Collection, one dated "Feb. 1790" outlines a story or play based on detection (this four years before the appearance of *Caleb Williams*).

> *Conquest of Enmity*   Incidents
>   *Drama*
> A Man set to watch an Enemy, or ill-suspected, finds in him such candour, such freedom of [sic] artifice, that, abandoning his employment, he

owns his office, takes part with the suspected, & generously vindicates & befriends him.

A later undated scrap suggests another idea of mystery (to be picked up in *The Wanderer*):

A carried on disguise, from virtuous motives, producing a mystery which the audience themselves cannot pierce. Exciting alternatively blame & pity.

Another undated scrap notes another point of suspicion:

A good Man has appearances agst. him of committing some dreadful crime: every thing corroborates—he is on the point of suffering,—when his innocency is wonderfully cleared.

The short section of *Camilla* in which Mr. Tyrold is in Winchester Prison for debt (the reader does not see him there) may well replace some scenes earlier imagined, with the father imprisoned on a more serious charge. The ideas of crime and violence, detection and mystery, haunt the notes that began what was to be *Camilla* ("seeming detections. Seeing a skeleton unexpectedly—A Corpse unpreparedly"). Burney could have said of her novel as Godwin did of *Caleb Williams*, that it was "a general review of the modes of domestic and unrecorded despotism" and even "a series of adventures of flight and pursuit . . . the pursuer, by his ingenuity . . . keeping his victim in a state of the most fearful alarm."[18] Novels of the 1790s tend to deal in a story of "mystery" related to an idea of guilt, both individual and collective—what Wordsworth in an early work called "Guilt and Sorrow." Authors of all sorts are concerned with what separates the individual from his fellows as well as what unites him to them. Novelists found new and expressive images and modes for conveying guilt, anger, breakdown, isolation. It is not only in *The Mysteries of Udolpho* (1794) that characters approach death and guilt circuitously, working upon hypotheses, inferences, and clues. Burney, an early reader of Radcliffe's novel, presents similar activities in her five "*Udolphoish* volumes" of *Camilla*.

The central mystery of the novel is the mystery of man's ways with woman, man's meaning in relation to woman. At one point Camilla bitterly tells her sister

"if you would avoid deceit and treachery, look at a man as at a picture, which tells you only the present moment! Rely upon nothing of time to come! They are not like us, Lavinia. They think themselves free, if they have made no verbal profession; though they may have pledged themselves by looks, by actions, by attentions, and by manners, a thousand, and a thousand times!"

(IV:538)

The mystery at its simplest definition is what men mean by their gestures toward women in the realm we call "love." Camilla's resentful statement sums up much of the experience of Frances Burney, who had had to realize that Mr. George Cambridge thought himself free, even when his "attentions" to her had persuaded friends (and newspapers) that they represented intentions. His "actions" and "attentions" had set Burney on the futile but frantic endeavor to detect his true inner meaning by observing and interpreting looks and gestures: "If you had seen with how irresolute an air he followed me in my retreat with his Eye . . . you *must* have concluded he was provoked at my departing. . . ."; "it was a look of such unaccountable consciousness as I cannot easily, if ever, forget." Burney had at length been forced to realize that, although a woman is to be looked at, judged, her body language closely observed and assigned a meaning, men do not consider their own gestures as subject to such scrutiny or open to similar significant reading. In Rousseau's terms, with males it is only the mouth that is supposed to speak. When speaking a physical language, men do not regard themselves as speaking a real language. Looks, actions, attentions do not commit them—they are to be committed only by the word, by "verbal profession." With a Whiggish preference for contract over custom in personal relationship, men can disregard all but the contract which only themselves can initiate and verify. Yet they still hold to their right to watch woman, to interpret her looks and manners, her downcast eye and timid air, and all the rest. Camilla's angry statement tries to turn the tables by transforming the unpromising male into a static voiceless object made only to be looked at, "a picture." But this retaliatory metamorphosis gives her no pleasure, and she must always acknowledge that men define woman's right to speak or not to speak—she has no right to make her own verbal profession. She is to be interpreted without that excrescence—a woman who has made no "verbal profession" can be accused of coquetry as a crime.

Camilla's story centers on a courtship, a manageable though culturally central topic with wide implications. Such unequal structuring of power and significance inevitably entails men's and women's being mysterious to each other. The men conceal a large part of their actions, feelings, and meanings, relegating them to a realm of nonmeaning; thus they become uninterpretable by women and unintelligible even to themselves. The male insistence that only certain behaviors are truly meaningful on woman's part ensures that a man misses a large part of woman's life and misinterprets her actions and reactions. As in *Cecilia*, the assumed beneficiary of the whole social and philosophical system, the first-born male, the heir as represented in the hero, is weakened by that system, which is now capable of driving him as well as the woman into melancholy and craziness. Most of the characters are always on the edge of harming another person, themselves, or both. The "modes of unrecorded despotism" operate mysteriously and powerfully to injure the individual and the community. The sense of mystery and even of "dreadful crime" hangs about this comic novel. The characters are uneasy with each other, fear each other's detection. As Mrs. Arlbery tells Camilla, "It is not speech, my dear Miss Tyrold, that makes detections: It only proclaims them" (III:454). To be told one is found out is dreadful; to be found out and not told, more dreadful still. Each character fears others, and the narrative itself bustles with overdetermined anxiety, as if it too is trying to stave off confronting the frightful through observing the trivial. The story of Camilla's debts does exactly that. Through her point of view, we adopt anxious guilt about petty sums, while her brother and cousin owe combined debts of over two thousand pounds. They rook, extort, and squander. While the pseudo-priggish schoolroom narrative that masquerades at times as *Camilla* pretends that Camilla's behavior with money is what matters, the big narrative that ironically enforces the other one lets us see that is not so. Camilla's little debts are not the crime the novel is busy detecting.

There is a great deal of actual crime in *Camilla*. Mrs. Mittin, who lives on commission from shopkeepers and on requested presents, is an extortionist and semi-swindler. Lionel commits not just emotional blackmail, like Mr. Harrell, but literally criminal extortion, for which he could be severely punished by law. He is also guilty of adulterous fornication and is legally answerable for alienation of a wife's affections. Bellamy is guilty of not only the abduction of a minor; he proceeds to threats of murder, ending in accidental self-murder. The idea of murdering Eugenia is, however, hinted at early in the novel by the most apparently good-natured character. Sir Hugh says to the girl's grieving parent, "if she had died, you might all have had the comfort to say 'twas I murdered her" (I:32–33). In fact, Sir Hugh is as culpable as anyone in the novel, and wreaks a good deal of havoc. The violence that enters the novel very early in the midst of the children's games and country pleasures tells us that there is no pastoral escape—any more than Virgil's Eclogues will be respected by the bull. *Camilla* is not a pastoral, but an epic mock-epic tale in which building, founding, putting together, take place amidst conflict and chaos ("multa quoque et bello passus, dum conderet urbem").

The language of most of the characters at some point reflects the violence that is ready to burst out anywhere. Dr. Orkborne in his passion at the loss of a scrap of paper raves, "I had rather have lost my ears than that manuscript! I wish with all my heart you had been at the bottom of the sea . . . !" (II:210). Characters frequently explode into fantasies of violence to others and themselves. After his mother rebukes him and commands him to spend his summer in study, Lionel forcefully objects: "But as to study . . . if my mother had but exacted any thing else . . . If she had ordered me to be horse-ponded, I do protest to you, I would not have demurred" (II:243). "Study" in Lionel's mind represents an endless blank nothing from which he flies in preference to ideas of unexpected pain. Lionel's preference of pain over barren normality is reflected also in the speech of the enthusiastic Irish ensign Macdersey, as when he is insulted by the former shopkeeper Dubster: "it's a thing I can't bear from a mean person, to be talked to. I had a hundred thousand times rather stand to be shot at" (III:433). Macdersey lives a mental life of richly violent alternatives:

> "there is nothing upon the face of the earth so insipid as a medium! Give me love or hate! a friend that will go to jail for me, or an enemy that will run me through the body! Riches to chuck guineas about like halfpence, or poverty to beg in a ditch! . . . Every thing has some gratification, except a medium. 'Tis a poor little soul that is satisfied between happiness and despair."
>
> (II:251–252)

The Irishman's statement can be seen as Burney's parodic retort to Irishman Edmund Burke's criticism of the ending of *Cecilia*: "in a work of imagination there is no medium." The idea of a medium horrifies most of the characters in this novel; the silly and the intelligent alike are repelled by limitation. Sir Sedley's complaint to Mrs. Arlbery is really a compliment:

> "How you navigate my sensations from cold to heat at pleasure! Cooke was a mere river water-man to you. My blood chills or boils at your command. Every sentence is a new climate. You waft me from extreme to extreme, with a rapidity absolutely dizzying."
>
> (III:368)

In this postrevolutionary world of sensationalism, no one wishes to stay in one mental clime for more than a few minutes. Dizziness in going from extreme to extreme is courted by all the characters, and first indicated in that play at see-saw, when Sir Hugh was no sooner "elevated" than he became "exceedingly giddy" (I:27). Characters prefer to risk giddiness and to pass above or below the still point of equilibrium. Marchmont passes himself off as the extreme example of the rational, but he is a passionate extremist. Burney shows there is no possibility of living a life of open-eyed realism, prudence, and sense. Society creates pressures which weigh heavily upon the individual, making free rational behavior impossible. At the same time, there is an equal and opposite pressure from within the individual, pushing against society with the force created by psychic stress, wishes, and secrets. Each character lives a life of fantasy that spills over into the external world, into processes of living as well as of speech. The debate set up at the beginning of *Cecilia* as to the merits of conformity against the claims of originality is now felt to be passé, for there is no such choice possible. Like the earlier two novels *Camilla* deals with embarrassment, but it is a more pervasive embarrassment. We do not focus on moments of exquisite discomfort, but on a constant sense of dislocation. The immediate impediments to living are not introduced by the presence of a few vulgarians—although those certainly exist; rather, we are shown how the self can embarrass the self, tying it into irrational knots. Moments of privacy now have the same vulnerability as public moments in *Evelina* or *Cecilia*.

In the texture of *Camilla*'s text, private thought and public action, speech and behavior, flow into one another without the break of big set scenes that characterized the earlier novels. In *Evelina*, we saw the comic flux of power in Madame Duval's drawing room when she vanquished Sir Clement. In *Cecilia*, we were given the more serious case of Mrs. Delvile's power mania, and watched her growing frustration as her sway over Cecilia and her own son began to wane, culminating in the big "conflict scene." We do not have the equivalent of these large set scenes in *Camilla*—or rather, what happens in major scenes is so like what the characters are doing all the time that we do not sense a special heightening. Major scenes of power interchange occur here, surprisingly, in interviews between hero and heroine, with no one else present.

In *Camilla*, the hero and heroine are themselves contaminated by the desire for power, which is no longer only a matter of snobbery or social oppression, but an activity of the human heart itself, a grasping at what is denied. The burden and the guilt of power-seeking and fantasy-making must be taken up by the lovers, with no scapegoats. Their conversations are erratic, secretive, strategic, and disorderly. In a long sequence in the fourth volume, for instance, Camilla, realizing her fiancé's suspicion of her connection with Sir Sedley, feels she must release Edgar from his engagement—and one of the feelings going into this half-decision is anger. Edgar is nervous because he has his own plans of "expostulation" but finds it hard to start to scold. Camilla has an initial advantage which she lets fall. Edgar gains strength. "Nothing gives so much strength to an adversary as the view of timidity in his opponent" (IV:617). Throughout the course of this conversation, however, as Camilla becomes more spirited, power becomes equal. Edgar summons his forces again when they are interrupted.

The scene is continued in a subsequent interview for which both have plans. Camilla, having heard Edgar's half-muttered remarks at the end of the previous interview, has intuited her power over him and believes the conversation will lead to "an ultimately happy conclusion" while Edgar on his side expects "a clearance of all mystery" (IV:640). Each has a secret agenda and a design for the interview's structure. Camilla, however, uses the very worst words she could choose to discuss the correspondence with Sir Sedley: "And, indeed, I acknowledge myself, in that affair, a most egregious dupe!" Suddenly she loses all power over Edgar: "the idea of Camilla duped by any man, seemed, in one blow, to detach him from her person, by a sudden dissolution of all charm to his mind in the connection" (*ibid*). She regains power only when she makes the inevitable subsequent move, and with some real anger and increasing dignity genuinely breaks off the engagement: "we Both are Free!" Earlier, she had thought of breaking-off as a potential strategy; it is when she employs it seriously that Edgar is "confounded by a stroke so utterly and in every way unexpected"

(IV:641). Camilla has generated more power than she had previously lost. But the reaction that leads to reconciliation is interrupted by the arrival of others. Edgar goes off to reassert his fallen power and regroup his forces. Their emotional states at the next meeting need not be anything like those in the previous one. ("Of the present nothing can be said but, *what is it?*")

The action no longer centers, as in Burney's earlier novels, on outward displays of gain or loss. Characters still blush and stammer and so on, but these things are less significant in themselves than previously. The real work of defining the inner life focuses elsewhere. Characters in the novel often make the mistake of thinking they can read personality and motive easily through body language, but we are shown that it is often impossible for the human body to give utterance to the quick succession of feelings and reactions which run through the psyche in a moment. Gesture is an inadequate language. Burney in her new novel not only uses a greater variety of language than ever before (including slang, dialect, scholarly terms, and a multitude of idioms) but also creates an *internal* language. She is no longer quite satisfied with her earlier techniques; there are matters that dramatic method, letters, and character sketches cannot fully represent. Some of the awkwardness of which the novel has been (not altogether unjustly) accused arises from the author's endeavor to try a new kind of mimesis, an imitation of the mind in flux.

For an example, the sentence quoted above describing Edgar's reaction to Camilla's use of the word "dupe" is awkward, but not as a result of carelessness; the language is trying to do a considerable job. The author makes us follow the recoil of Edgar's feelings, a sudden effect which is the result of complex invisible causes not fully known by him. Edgar does not *think* connections through, does not *decide* anything. As the passive mode indicates, his response is an involuntary twitch. He just feels, abruptly as a blow, the sense of being "detached from her person"—disconnected, withdrawn. The action takes place in his mind: "a sudden dissolution of all charm." The drama of disintegration is outside his control; he feels like the recipient of his own changes. Edgar's blush is not at all sufficient to indicate the process; the author has to give us the process itself by reflecting Edgar's mind. If the author were to use strong simple moral words ("disgust") or rational words ("Edgar thought"), she would be rendering something different. Here she has to avoid a number of normal descriptive terms as if they were clichés. In *Cecilia*, as we have seen, Burney developed an authorial voice. In *Camilla* she develops beyond that kind of authorial voice, creating more flexible and subtle techniques.

The novel itself becomes multivoiced. To a far greater extent than in *Cecilia*, Burney uses characters to comment on and interpret one another. Every character as commentator is partly right and partly in error because of limited knowledge. The heroine is not, as in *Cecilia*, surrounded by a *cordon sanitaire* of authorial preference but like the rest is subject to unflattering and comic comment. When Mrs. Arlbery tells Sir Sedley that Camilla suffers from "that common girlish disease, an hopeless passion," he replies, "'Twould be odious to cure her. . . . I shall now look at her with most prodigious softness. Ought one not to sigh as she approaches?" (III:366).

Camilla's characters take up room not only in dialogue but in passages without quotations marks, in indirect speech. And indirect speech is carried further into *style indirect libre*. Edgar's voice, in particular, is often ironically invited to take over the narrative job: "Yet why had she so striven to deny all regard, all connection? what a unaccountable want of frankness! what a miserable dereliction of truth!" (III:446). Critics too eager to see Edgar as Mentor have perhaps taken the *style indirect libre* passages unironically, as authorial reflection. That Burney has this narrative technique constantly in mind in writing her new novel is evident in its use in the discarded drafts. In the scene where Gunniston-Melmond decides to educate Cleora-Indiana, we find the young man's thoughts represented: "If she were unformed, might he not form her? . . . what rapture to watch the growth of improvement in so beautiful a disciple!" *Style indirect* is a device of irony, but also of sympathy. There is mock complicity in characters' illusions, while at the same time their attempt to cover what they do not wish to see is exhibited. Characters about whom *style indirect libre* is employed become less heroic and more fallible.

In all the devices of narrative language reflecting the characters, Burney in *Camilla* shows the relation of public to private as disturbing. Shakespeare's *Othello* is the play above all others in which private emotion and domestic life are transformed into the public and the spectacular. (And to some critics, like Rymer, it has always seemed suspiciously near comedy on that account.)[19] The introduction of this domestic play of jealousy into *Camilla* reminds us of the potential dangers of the pressure of private feeling and misconstruction, while the play as enactment reminds us of an art that makes emotions appear artless. In this instance, the lack of art on the part of the players becomes the occasion for a more skilled art on the part of Sir Sedley Clarendel, who transforms the play back into farcical comedy. He achieves this by decontextualizing the play, deliberately confounding presenter (actor as human being) with the presented (character):

> Desdemona, either from the effect of a bad cold, or to give more of nature to her repose, breathed so hard, as to raise a general laugh in the audience; Sir Sedley, stopping his ears, exclaimed, "O, if she snores I shall plead for her no more, if she tear her gown to tatters! Suffocation is much too lenient for her. She's an immense horrid personage! nasal to alarm!"
>
> Othello then entered, with a tallow candle in his hand, staring and dropping grease at every step; and having just declared he would not
>
> Scar that vhiter skin of hers than snow,

perceived a thief in the candle, which made it run down so fast over his hand, and the sleeve of his coat, that, the moment not being yet arrived for extinguishing it, he was forced to lay down his sword, and, for want of better means, snuff it with his fingers.

Sir Sedley now protested himself completely disordered: "I must be gone," cried he, "incontinently; this exceeds resistance. . . . If I did not build upon the pleasure of seeing him stop up those distressing nostrils of the gentle Desdemona, I could not breathe here another instant."

(II:321–322)

Gesture is inadequate to convey meaning, as it is throughout the performance of the "disastrous Buskins," whose "outrageous" gestures make the male actors look, in Sir Sedley's opinion, as if "they were giving challenges for a boxing match," while the actresses "took so much exercise in their action, that they tore out the sleeves of their gowns," and raise their arms so high that the baronet fears they will "finish by pulling caps" (II:318–319). Gesture is always over- or under-determined, and spontaneous action (snuffing the candle) interrupts intended effects. Sir Sedley's fun includes the lethal wish. He persuades us that his imagined world in which the snoring female would be murdered is preferable to the real one in which actors will only mimic murder. He fantasizes a world without controls, which is also a world of licensed cruelty—though he points out in the process some elements of real cruelty in the dramatist's treatment of Desdemona. Sir Sedley in his fantasy is momentarily liberated by resisting controls: he resists the controlling forces of Shakespeare as an author, as an object of cultural reverence, and he dismisses the decorum which conventionally demands that we separate actor from character. His wit indulges in new transformations—as the players themselves unwittingly do, when for instance Desdemona unintentionally appears in her own clothes, "a dirty red and white linen gown," and "an old blue stuff quilted coat," which she had on beneath the character's "white satin bedgown" (II:322).

The novel at large exhibits superimpositions and transformations, the melting together of identities supposedly distinct, or the artificial separation of same from same. Two of the grotesque types, cunning Mrs. Mittin and ugly Mr. Dubster, illustrate the superimpositions and transformations that the other characters express most often in speech. Mrs. Mittin is first seen in "a large black bonnet, and a blue checked apron" but dramatically reveals herself ("I'm a gentlewoman!") and displays her good clothes underneath (III:423–424). At the most distant remove from the story's true Desdemona, Camilla (on whom the vulgarian preys), Mrs. Mittin yet reflects her in reflecting the bad actress who played Shakespeare's heroine. Like that Desdemona in reverse, she wears her good clothes for a higher appearance beneath the everyday wear; she convinces herself that she has these alternate identities, and her existence as a "gentlewoman" is a piece of play-acting. Mr. Dubster thinks he has erased his previous self; he says "since I became a gentleman." This is a nonsensical utterance; a gentleman knows no time in his life when he was not one. Dubster casually muddles up his different identities, with no inhibitions about living in the "old dirty cloaths" when at home as long as he knows his new self is available: "my best coat is at this very minute at Tom Hicks's, nicely packed and papered up" (II:277). When we first meet Dubster he is concerned with the missing gloves that would complete his appearance as a gentleman. He finds Mrs. Mittin unduly discriminating: "when I was not dressed out quite in my best becomes, she made as if she did not know me. Not as it signifies. It's pretty much of a muchness to me" (IV:601).

Dubster's former occupation involved the creation of multiple selves: he kept a shop for ready-made wigs. Burney always found *wigs* irresistibly funny—*vide* Briggs. The only complete anecdote of Burney's childhood relates to wigs. Charles Burney told the story in his fragmentary memoirs:

> There lived next door to me in Poland Street a hair Merchant, who furnished peruques to the Judges, and Gentlemen of the Law. The Merchant's Children & mine used to play together in the little garden behind the House—and unluckily, one day the door of the Wig Magazine being left open, they each of them put on one of these dignified ornaments of the head, & danced and jumped about in a thousand antics, laughing till they screamed at their ridiculous figures; unluckily, in their vagaries one of the Flaxen Wigs, said by the proprietor, to be worth ten guineas fell into a tub of water, lost all its Gorgon Buckle, and was said by the owner to be totally spoiled. He was extremely angry with the whole Party, and chid very severely his own Children, when my little daughter, the old lady, says, with great gravity & composure—"What signifies making such a work about an accident?—The Wig was a good Wig to be sure; but what's done can't be undone." Whether these stoical Sentiments appeased the enraged Peruqier I know not; but the younkers were stript of their honours and much dignity.[20]

In writing up this tale for its published form in the *Memoirs,* Burney elaborated and changed her own childish speech: "What signifies talking so much about an accident? The wig is wet, to be sure; and the wig was a good wig, to be sure; but it's of no use to speak of it any more." Charles Burney says, and his daughter repeats, that the incident illustrated his little Fanny's "excellent heart," "natural simplicity & probity," and "straightforward morality," but it seems rather to exhibit the pert toughness of the child. (The probity or morality of the Burneys may have been invisible to the injured "hair Merchant"; there is no indication that Charles Burney thought of offering to pay for the expensive commodity ruined.) The anecdote shows up sharply the young Frances Burney's sense of the absurd pomposity of the adult male world. Wigs pertain to

"Judges" and "Gentlemen of the Law"; these may be mimicked and made into "ridiculous figures." The wig itself, especially the club or tie-wig, is a reference to and an illustration of the male member, a phallic badge awarded to those who belong to the ruling gender and class. The novel that opens its social scene with "the arrival of the Judges of the land" features a ridiculous wig-maker as a central comic character. Dubster seems an instance of comic revenge, not only upon the "enraged Peruqier" of Frances Burney's childhood, but also upon all symbolic wig-makers, the power brokers who arrange and decorate the social order.

Dubster the would-be gentleman serves different purposes from the old satiric types like Burney's Branghtons or Johnson's Ned Druggett.[21] Dubster with his villa and grounds provides a comic fantasia extremely like something out of Lewis Carroll—indeed, it is probable that Carroll knew this work. Dubster is a Carrollian character altogether; at his first appearance he resembles the White Rabbit in his anxious sending for gloves; he uses the phrase "much of a much-ness"; and the visit of Eugenia, Camilla, and Lionel to Dubster is a mad party, if not a mad tea-party. Dubster's new small house is a mad little place, uselessly if significantly ornamented:

> on the first story, a little balcony, decorated in the middle and at each corner with leaden images of Cupids; and, in the attic story, a very small venetian window, partly formed with minute panes of glass, and partly with glazed tiles, representing, in blue and white, various devices of dogs and cats, mice and birds, rats and ferrets, as emblems of the conjugal state.
>
> (II:274)

The antifemale, antimatrimonial decorations are partly drawn from Chessington, home of "Daddy" Crisp, bachelor and recluse. We know from Burney's account that a chimneypiece at Chessington was ornamented with "blue and white tiles, representing, *vis-à-vis*, a dog and a cat, as symbols of married life and harmony."[22] Dubster, complacently twice widowed, represents a comic extreme of masculinity, and his abode is a home of Nonsense—male Nonsense. Dubster's actions are parodies of the great Augustan male activities of imposing order on Nature by imitation of divine fiat. It is men who are the busy builders of the Augustan age, undertaking "To rear the Column, or the Arch to bend, / To swell the Terras, or to sink the Grot."[23] Dubster is creating his own wonderful works; the journey over his house and grounds is a journey through a Wonderland.[24] The house has ornaments but no steps, the grounds are entered through an incongruous "small Chinese gate, painted of a deep blue," and the "lake" is, as Eugenia says, "nothing but a very dirty little pond, with a mass of rubbish in the middle" (II:275). Dubster is very proud of this body of water, and the "mass of rubbish" is to him an "island." He has his own way with Nature, finding the imitation preferable to the real thing. He boasts: "I shall have a swan. . . . It will only be made of wood, painted over in white. There's no end of feeding them things, if one has 'em alive. Besides it will look just as pretty; and won't bite" (II:278).

Dubster takes his visitors to his "grotto": "a little square hole, dug into a chalky soil, down into which, no steps being yet made, he slid as well as he could, to the no small whitening of his old brown coat." At his insistence, Camilla, "without waiting for help, slid down into the intended grotto" (II: 280). All there is to see are the places where the grotto's ornaments *will* be when Dubster picks up shells from the seashore. The party are then conducted through "what he called his labyrinth, which was a little walk he was cutting, zig-zag, through some brushwood, so low that no person above three foot height could be hid by it" (II:281).

Dubster's villa is a piece of egotistical transforming play ("child's play" like the Burney children trying on the wig-maker's wigs). A piece of painted wood will be a swan, a dirty pond is a lake, brushwood is a maze or labyrinth, a hole in the ground is a grotto. Gaps or blank spaces are covered over by the work of the mind, as Dubster already sees the chalky walls of his "grotto" covered over with blue-painted cockle-shells and bits of coal. The pleasure grounds and house exist as scraps, pieces, and plans, like Orkborne's work on philology—or like *Camilla* itself. The images provided by Dubster's retreat are images for the novel and its actions in general—ups without downs, downs without ups, dead-end holes, zig-zags, elaborate promises, and reversals. The place makes a concrete locus and reflection for the nonsense-strain in the novel at large, as all the characters, in their language, work at transformations. " 'Contrive to hate you!' repeated Macdersey; 'I could as soon contrive to turn the world into a potato' " (III:479). Unfettered by reality, the mind makes a home for desire. Yet the mental play is disconnected, makes for discontinuity. Everywhere in Dubster's place we see an indicative problem with *steps*. There are no logical or convenient means of moving continuously from place to place. The summerhouse has no steps—only a ladder, which Lionel takes away as a practical joke, leaving his host and his sisters no way down—a succinct image of disconnection. Eugenia is unfairly exposed to misery because there is no orderly way out. Characters take no progressive or continuous steps in their speeches and actions; they make abrupt moves, up and down or zig-zag. "Only Connect," says Goethe encouragingly, but Burney is skeptical about the possibility of connection.

Characters in *Camilla* do not connect. Each lives a life of private fantasy that spills over into the external world. There is always a blank, a gap at the center of what they see and what they say. Edgar psychologically "forgets" former confidence in *Camilla*, though he does this under the tutelage of Marchmont, who "forgets" that there could be a connection between his own past and his reaction to Edgar's love. The most salient and self-proclaimed forgetter is Lionel, who protests heatedly that he loves his parents and sisters: "I would cut off my left arm for Lavinia and Eugenia; and for thee, Camilla, I would lop off my right!" Despite—or perhaps because of—the intensity of his feelings, he adds, "yet, when some frolic or gambol comes into my way, I forget you all! clear out of my memory you all walk, as if I had never beheld you!" (V:739). Memory and love are connected with ideas of violent pain, loss of parts of the body. Forgetting provides relief, particularly when responsibility for it can be thrown upon the images of those who should be recollected: "clear out of my memory you all walk." This augurs ill for Coleridge's "every home born feeling, by which [Philanthropy] is produced and nurtured," or for Wordsworth's developing confidence in memory and love.[25]

Burney's concerns are similar to those of Wordsworth and Coleridge, but she approaches them from a different direction. Her characters find introspection almost impossible. Childlike characters, like Sir Hugh, are deformed, if attractive; we can see Sir Hugh, in his language, defeating any incipient adulthood. Memory may be a sacred power, but most of us have means of shutting it off. Like Johnson, Burney felt the connection between memory and guilt, but, like her contemporaries of the 1790s, she was interested in examining both the social and psychological processes of guilt and the experience of inner pain. Burney knows the characters' blank spaces, the dead center of their lives and minds which they do not dare quite to look at. She has the confidence to investigate the gaps and chasms, the differences between what is thought and what the speaker presumes he or she has thought, between one moment's reaction and that of the next. Burney's writing in *Camilla* explores cavities and craters, holes in the ground of rationality like Dubster's hold in the chalk.

Like other works of the 1790s *Camilla* is concerned with creating a new language, a language both social and nonrational. When, for instance, Edmund Burke argues in *Reflections on the Revolution in France* (1790) that a society is held together by emotion and imagination, his own language—sharp, musing, emotional—stands for the internal language of England itself, a language too great (so Burke would have us believe) for the formalities of academic discourse or the artifices of external structure. His antagonist Mary Wollstonecraft is like him in that; her *Vindication of the Rights of Woman* (1792) reaches toward moral truth through a personal language of thought, musing, digression. Godwin's *Caleb Williams* is all internal language delineating the irrationality of authority and rebel, or pursuer and pursued. What claims precedence over all for writers and readers of the 1790s is the peculiar movement of the human mind. Writers must catch not only thought and feeling, but the thought thinking itself, the feeling feeling itself. One of the most typical titles of the period is "Reflections on . . ." something or other (a title form Burney herself had used in her tract about the émigré clergy). One of the typical images of the period is reflection (of stars in a lake or in ice, for instance). Everything is capable of reflecting. The mind in itself meets mind reflecting itself. To express this insight, authors adopt the old satiric or moral imagery of mirrors or portraiture. Portraits seem to alter with different viewings (like that of the hero in Mary Hays's

Emma Courtney [1796]).²⁶ Edgar makes a "degenerate portrait" of Camilla. The contents of the mind change in different moments under different lights. It is a telling coincidence of history that among the popular new sights of the time were the Panorama (where, as if inside a huge head, viewers could see a whole scene around them) and the Eidophusikon (which offered changing scenes in changing lights).²⁷

Writers had to find a language to accommodate the personal, reflective, and emotive mind—a language, too, that would both reflect the "energy" that all sides appealed to as a value and negotiate with the irrational truths. Burney's *Camilla* is a novel of the 1790s, written by an author who had already taught many of her younger contemporaries (like Radcliffe, Godwin, and Wollstonecraft) what could be done in fictional re-creation of a society haunted by its own destructive forces. This author was now ready to undertake the task of delineating more closely the work of inner life. Like all the other works of the decade *Camilla* is an experimental work, and seems to be pushing against its own boundaries, shifting with the shiftingness it tries to make us feel. This novel is willing to express the disintegration and incoherence that exist not only without, in the social structure (as in *Cecilia*), but also within the psyche, which is bound to respond to the contradictory messages issuing from society, and to respond in a variety of ways. Very much like Godwin, in fact, Burney sees the interaction of traditional society and the nervously active individual mind as likely to issue in disaster. The main story of this novel (in which lovers fear they will lose each other while taking courses which would almost assure that loss) is a suitable "objective correlative" just within the bounds of comedy for expressing anxiety, and exhibiting the perverse activities evoked by pain and fear. *Camilla* is from the outset full of pain and loss; Sir Hugh's regret for his own wasted years leads perversely to Eugenia's premature loss of strength and beauty. The world of *Camilla* is a world of dis-integrations; the frame of realism is employed in a manner that allows sur-real effects, reflecting the irrationality of the world Burney describes. The novel itself seems to be looking for a point to break down, a point where all the vain, ingenious languages will find themselves at a loss, and the narrative will run into some kind of hole or large gap.

In effect, this is what happens in the climax of the novel, which exhibits the most powerful expression of disintegration and incoherence. Breakdown can of course always be anticipated for any heroine who follows such "rules" as Mr. Tyrold's, but at the point where this heroine comes to grief the novel itself appears to share in the breakdown. The disintegrative fantasies conjured up at times in the speech of most characters seem to have come to stay. In Camilla's horrific nightmare in Book X, the internal life is lived at maximum pressure, with no ready escape into social expressions of the rational kind.

Camilla's dream-vision or hallucination occurs after she has endured a series of shocks. Her father has been imprisoned; when she returns to Cleves, her childhood home, she finds her uncle gone and the place a labyrinth of emptiness and silence. Believing that her mother in displeasure has forbidden her return home, Camilla takes refuge in a small wayside inn, whence she sends messages that receive no reply. Incapable of eating or sleeping, in her misery she begins to wish for death. A corpse is brought into the inn; Camilla catches sight of the figure stretched on the bier in the room next to hers. She compels herself to go and look at it. In horrified fascination, she removes the cloth from the face; it is the body of her sister's husband. She turns her head away, but still cannot avoid seeing the corpse and the "large splashes of blood." Overtaken by horror, she is also smitten with guilt. Her wish to die was wrong, she now sees, rejecting "the cruelty of this egotism" that created the wish. She "feared she had been presumptuous" and now "called back her wish" (V:872–873). She tries to pray, tries to rest, but sees the corpse "still bleeding in full view," whether her eyes are closed or open. Hallucination slides into dream.

When the dream happens, Camilla knows that she does not wish to die. In her dream, she *is* dead:

> Death, in a visible figure, ghastly, pallid, severe, appeared before her, and with its hand, sharp and forked, struck abruptly upon her breast. [. . .] She trembled; she shrunk from its touch; but it had iced her heart-strings. Every vein was congealed; every stiffened limb stretched to its full length, was hard as marble; and when again she made a feeble effort to rid her oppressed lungs of the dire weight that had fallen upon them, a voice hollow, deep, and distant, dreadfully pierced her ear, calling out 'Thou hast but thy own wish! Rejoice thou murmurer, for thou diest!' Clearer, shriller, another voice quick vibrated in the air: 'Whither goest thou,' it cried, 'and whence comest thou?' [In quotations from this sequence, my own marks of omission are in brackets, to leave Burney's ellipses distinct.]

Camilla's mind is dividing into separate voices, some felt as external, while the image of her body "hard as marble" freezes away from identity. Her body itself then acquires a voice not her own, as if she were becoming her own ventriloquist:

> A voice from within, over which she thought she had no controul, though it seemed issuing from her vitals, low, hoarse, and tremulous, answered, 'Whither I go, let me rest! Whence I come from let me not look back! Those who gave me birth, I have deserted; my life, my vital powers I have rejected.'
>
> (V:874–875)

Camilla is being summoned to a judgment of herself by herself, but she is diffused over the universe, scattered—no longer able to make any claim to a right to exist, to any identity before or beyond death.

Quick then another voice assailed her, so near, so loud, so terrible . . . she shrieked at its horrible sound. 'Prematurely,' it cried, 'thou art come, uncalled, unbidden; thy task unfulfilled, thy peace unearned. Follow, follow me! the Records of Eternity are opened. Come! write with thy own hand thy claims, thy merits to mercy!' [. . .] 'O, no! no! no!' she exclaimed, 'let me not sign my own miserable insufficiency!' In vain was her appeal. A force unseen, yet irresistible, impelled her forward. She saw the immense volumes of Eternity, and her own hand involuntarily grasped a pen of iron, and with a velocity uncontroulable wrote these words: 'Without resignation, I have prayed for death; from impatience of displeasure I have desired annihilation.' [. . .] Her head would have sunk upon the guilty characters; but her eyelids refused to close, and kept them glaring before her. They became, then, illuminated with burning sulphur. She looked another way; but they partook of the same motion; she cast her eyes upwards, but she saw the characters still [. . .]. Loud again sounded the same direful voice: 'These are thy deserts; write now thy claims:—and next,—and quick,—turn over the immortal leaves, and read thy doom.' . . . 'Oh, no!' she cried, 'Oh, no! . . . O, let me yet return! O, Earth, with all thy sorrows, take, take me once again, that better I may learn to work my way to that last harbour. [. . .]' In vain again she called;—pleaded, knelt, wept in vain. The time she found, was past [. . .] and a thousand voices at once, with awful vibration, answered aloud to every prayer, 'Death was thy own desire!' Again, unlicensed by her will, her hand seized the iron instrument. The book was open that demanded her claims. She wrote with difficulty . . . but saw that her pen made no mark! She looked upon the page, when she thought she had finished, . . . but the paper was blank! . . . Voices then, by hundreds, by thousands, by millions, from side to side, above, below, around, called out, echoed and re-echoed, 'Turn over, turn over . . . and read thy eternal doom!' In the same instant, the leaf, untouched, burst open . . . and . . . she awoke.

(V:875–876)

Nothing Camilla does in the dream is by her own will. She seems to be taken over by Otherness, and yet that Otherness is herself divided from herself. Unable to gather up her identity she is now fragmented, unreadable even to herself. Or rather, she has nothing worth reading, no good existence worth recording. Language fails absolutely. The words will not come, "her pen made no mark." The idea of trying to write and making no mark is especially terrifying to a writer; it is of course an author's complete idea of hell.

The imagery in Camilla's dream is derived from the Bible with its many references, both in the Old Testament and the New, to angelic prophetic books and the book of life; see, for example, Psalm 40:7; Psalm 69:28; Psalm 139:16;

Ezekiel 2:9–10. Jeremiah supplies an important verse: "The sin of Judah *is* written with a pen of iron . . . *it is* graven upon the table of their heart" (KJV, Jeremiah 17:1). The sense of guilt in the light of imminent mortality is related to feelings expressed in many of the Psalms, for instance Psalm 90:

Thou hast set our iniquities before thee, our secret *sins* in the light of thy countenance.

For all our days are passed away in thy wrath: we spend our years as a tale *that is told.*

(vv. 8–9)

This Psalm is recited at the Anglican service for the Burial of the Dead according to the Book of Common Prayer that Frances Burney knew. Before the Burial of the Dead comes the Visitation of the Sick, a service of contrition and comfort at which is said Psalm 71, a hymn that affirms the value and worth of God-given life, even in suffering: "thou art he that took me out of my mother's womb. . . . I am become as it were a monster unto many: but my sure trust is in thee. . . . Thou O God, hast taught me from my youth up until now . . ." (BCP version, vv. 5–15). As her agony approaches, Camilla "desired to hear the service for the sick," but nobody at the hedge inn has leisure or literacy enough to help. "She then begged they would procure her a prayer-book, that she might try to read herself; but her eyes, heavy, aching, and dim, glared upon the paper, without distinguishing the print from the margin" (V:873). Later Edgar, substituting for the clergyman, comes to read to the sick lady, and begins at her request "the prayer for those of whom there is but small hope of recovery" (V:876). He no sooner begins with the phrase "O Father of mercies" than the two recognize each other; the return to the Book of Common Prayer as readable breaks the spell.

Camilla's dereliction is seriously treated as an important experience, and it is a feminine Agony or Dark Night. Among the other Biblical echoes in the passage might be adduced Psalm 116, "The sorrows of death compassed me, and the pains of hell gat hold upon me: I found trouble and sorrow" (v. 3). Psalm 116 was said by the new mother at the service of Thanksgiving of Women after Child-birth (commonly called the Churching of Women), a service which Mme. D'Arblay had had reason to think of when Alex was born in December 1794. Indeed, the whole experience undergone by Camilla is reminiscent of childbirth, with the body being torn apart, the vitals alienated by uncontrollable forces, and the emergence of another being. The experience of the "marginalized" (to borrow from the jargon of our own day) is made central, and the blankness of the margin becomes the story and the crisis.

The nightmare vision of Camilla represents a new kind of intensity in Burney's work. It replaces Clarinda's night of tension before the dreaded wedding, but in the manuscript, Clarinda's bad dreams, for all the surrounding excitement, seem curiously tame: "Integrity appeared to her personified . . . Virtue, retreating from broken honour . . . while Edgar, rushing forth . . . broke up & finished the Ceremony, with a malediction, instead of a blessing." In *Camilla* the heroine's nightmare is not framed, nor is it composed of abstractions. The reader is forced to share the heroine's experience with her.

Not only Biblical language is recalled here. The near-death of Burney's Camilla, "pallid, weak, and shaken by nervous tremors" (V:866), seems related to the death of Virgil's Camilla. This heroine was also struck upon the breast:

> She wrench'd the Jav'lin with her dying Hands;
> But wedg'd within her Breast the Weapon stands;
>
> . . . .
>
> (A gath'ring Mist o'reclouds her cheerful Eyes,
> And from her Cheeks the rosie Colour flies.
>
> . . . .
>
> *Acca,* 'tis past! He swims before my sight,
> Inexorable Death; and claims his right.
>
> . . . .
>
> Short, and more short, she pants: By slow degrees
> Her Mind the Passage from her Body frees.
>
> . . . .
>
> In the last Sigh her strugling Soul expires;
> And murm'ring with Disdain, to *Stygian* Sounds retires.
> (Dryden, trans., *Aeneid* XI)[28]

Burney has reminded us of Camilla's literary origins at the beginning of this long sequence of fear and dereliction when Camilla anxiously runs through the empty grounds of Cleves at twilight: "she '*skimmed,*' like her celebrated namesake, the turf" (V:849). It is the destiny of a swift Camilla to be shot down—the novel asks whether a Camilla can avoid that destiny. If she does, it is only by going through all but the real "last Sigh." Visible Death appearing before the sight (Dryden's Miltonic elaboration of Virgil) must appear to a Camilla, and the heroine must know herself as dying, however reluctantly "murm'ring with Disdain" ("vitaque cum gemitu fugit indignata sub umbras"). Mind and body are separated, struggling, felt as distinct. The sense of dissipation of the self seems related to images and concepts surrounding another important female of the *Aeneid*, the Sibyl of Cumae. Her cave, like her body, is an echo chamber for the god; through its hundred floors "As many Voices issue, and the sound / Of Sibyl's Words as many times rebound." The Sibyl's passive endurance under inspiration resembles the feminine role in sexual congress, but the suffering is that of childbirth or death:

> Her Colour chang'd, her Face was not the same,
> And hollow Groans from her deep Spirit came.
> . . . .
> Strugling in vain, impatient of her Load,
> And lab'ring underneath the pond'rous God,
> The more she strove to shake him from her Breast,
> With more, and far superior Force he press'd:
> Commands his Entrance, and without Controul
> Usurps her Organs, and inspires her Soul.
>
> (Dryden, trans., *Aeneid* VI)[29]

Burney makes her heroine undergo similar throes, but there is no identifiable god. Death himself at the beginning presses on her breast and weighs upon her, but this Power seems to give place to all the various powers of the voices from within and from without. Enduring this agony, plumbing the depths of dereliction, is in a terrifying fashion inspiring, and makes the heroine prophetic. At first, prophecy seems to affect only the heroine; her judging voices, like the rest of her ordeal, are aspects of herself addressing herself. But in the texture of the novel as a whole, Camilla's ordeal is prophetically expressive of what is going wrong. The blank spaces which cannot be expressed, blanks lurking in all the characters' utterances, are brought to the fore. The motifs of writing, reading, and being misread (or miswritten) that play through the novel are brought together here, where we also see the failure of language (in a language-conscious, not to say philological, age) to sustain the life wish. To endure this agony, to plumb these depths of dereliction, is to be inspirited and inspiring. The heroine is prophetic—but what does her prophetic experience mean?

At a simple level, Camilla is merely suffering for her errors in order to be restored, chastened, to happiness—but, as we have seen, her sufferings are always recognizably disproportionate to her venial errors. The pain here far outweighs the gravity of wearing lilac plumes and getting slightly into debt. The tension and intensity are unmistakable; we recognize here the same qualities as are to be found in Burney's tragic dramas. Here, however, the novelist has not lost control. The scene teases us as a kind of sliding allegory. The nightmare vision is very visibly Gothic, containing "the bare elements of Gothic fiction . . . sleep, dreams, live burial, the unspeakable, the sublime of privation."[30] Camilla's lonely agony, bearing some resemblance to the opium dream of Romantic literature, is strongly reminiscent of Burney's sickness at the end of the court years, when she felt weak, oppressed, unable to breathe. In terms of Burney's own literary history, the scene recovers the suffering of Elgiva: "See! she shivers!—hark! she shrieks!— . . . She lives, she Breaths!—forbear, forbear! / Ah, why so soon her body tear?" It is also a return to the cold agony of Cerulia in *Hubert De Vere:* "all at once the dew of Death crept o'er me / And iced me to the Heart." Undoubtedly the autobiographical elements that went into the plays went into the whole of *Camilla* (which is in a sense a thoughtful replay of the George Cambridge experience), but by 1796 Burney was much more daring about plumbing the sources of distress and deliverance and opening them to the daylight world of the novel, not leaving them in the psychic shadows of her tragedies.

Yet the author confronts us with a riddle rather than a solution. Camilla, who has already looked upon the "idiot" girl and has been in turn gazed upon as a curious example of melancholy madness, now looks upon a corpse, and is soon in a corpselike state, which is also a state of agonized life-in-death. Her motionless, unobserved body is the scene of frantic inner activity—she here leads only the interior life. The nightmare scene ironically recalls two previous "spectacular" women, the "idiot" girl and the "Desdemona." Both of these were introduced as female figures only to be gazed upon by the story's central characters (and the reader), yet both were examples of what is not supposed to be seen (or heard), as well as of what is to be officially seen. The beautiful "idiot" undergoes emotion which no one else can reach or understand; the parts of her body responding under immense yet invisible pressure, she utters noises which cannot speak her deep inarticulate pain. The "Desdemona," whose nostrils Sir Sedley so sadistically builds upon seeing stopped, is cast in the role of a woman asleep, who is soon passively to accept her own death, yet this "Desdemona" enacts passivity and insensibility while being very much alive and sentient—her stertorous breathing speaks for her when she is to be silent, her body is ready to spring up and move unbidden. These women, who were formerly illustrative figures outside of and quite distinct from the heroine, merge with her in a sleight of narrative combining the spectacular victims with the heroine, who has ceased to be a spectacle to all the other characters and even to the reader—for Camilla's experience is presented in terms of what it feels like, not what she looks like.

The sequence seems to call for interpretation from the reader, and modern (or postmodern) modes of allegorical reading seem legitimately applicable. One kind of reading, derived from feminist post-Lacanian theory, springs to the eye almost at once. According to such a reading, Camilla, like the Sibyl in Virgil, undergoes the unrewarding pangs of bearing the word emanating from the male deity (exhibited in all the scriptural references) by which she herself must be condemned, because the deity's word upholds the masculine order, according to which she is unimportant and even dispensable—a Nobody who cannot make her mark. Camilla represents the female in the Oedipal phase of separation from the mother; her predecessor, Clarinda, was also separated from her mother on the night of dreadful dreams. Like her author, Camilla has suffered acutely over an arbitrary separation from the mother, in her case temporary, caused by her mother's misunderstanding and disapproval. Near the beginning of the entire sequence, Mrs. Tyrold's rejection causes Camilla's first loud wishes for death: "She will not see me then! . . . she cannot bear my sight! O Death! let me not pray to thee also in vain!" (V:862). Forcibly separated from the Mother, the heroine tries to acquire identity and power through language, but language rebukes her, and written language of her own is denied her. Her grasping at the phallic pen is an absurdity, for she will not be able to do anything with it. The pen being reserved for male authority, she cannot properly be said to have any "claim" to it—and no amount of personal "merit" as a woman could give her any right. Camilla can only regress into the infantile, the wailing unspeaking bundle, thus inwardly repeating the anguish of the idiot girl while, like Desdemona, waiting for death. She is a Nobody indeed.

At some level such an interpretation must be "true." Who can doubt that the sequence reflects some of Burney's deepest fears and frustrations about being a writer, about having a right to speak, or being able to make any impression? Camilla's hour of dereliction dramatizes the agony of female helplessness in the culture as a whole.

Yet, feminist criticism teaches one not to take hold of one side of a dichotomy and to prefer the fluid and multiple over the monolithic and fixed. The novel itself keeps displaying "Two Sides of a Question," showing that both sides in an antithesis or paradox may be right. Thus, even if the above-offered interpretation is "true," it is possible to re-read the passage with another (and more optimistic) interpretation. If we look back at the whole context of the deathly vision, it comes just after Camilla has looked on the body of death. But it is not the death of the Mother, which Freud's myth predicates as the basis of culture, upon which Camilla must gaze and which she must mourn. She intrudes her forbidden gaze on what one might call the opposite scene—the Death of the Male. Masculine narratives very commonly have a female character who dies and whose sacrifice does good in some way to the hero—we are less well trained in accepting the counterpart, but Burney has sacrificed a male character for her heroine's edification. Instead of urging us to contemplate the death of the Mother, the absence of Nature, the story shows us the death of the male, of the death-dealing Father associated early in the book with the arriving Judges of the Northwick assizes. Burney does not, of course, offer up Augustus Tyrold on her altar, nor his Sternean brother, the androgynous and self-reversing Sir Hugh, but she finds a surrogate for both, and for Marchmont, in the woman-abusing Alphonso Bellamy. Bellamy's (adopted) name itself, like his pistol, reminds us of the organ which masquerades as the "lovely friend" of woman. "Alphonso" is really "Nicholas" (Old Nick, Father of Lies), and

"Bellamy" is really "Gwigg," one of Burney's made-up names, rich in sexual suggestion, including "Gigg" (slang for nose, snout, i.e., male member); "niggle" (to copulate), and, once again, the phallic "wig." "The wig is wet": the wig lies bleeding, prostrate, dead. Bellamy has destroyed himself. Camilla lifts the veil. She does not wish to remove the linen cloth covering the corpse's face, but she steadily advances toward the body, then toward the cloth, and makes herself lift it "with enthusiastic self-compulsion" (V:871). She feels guilt, fascination, and horror, and, like Ann Radcliffe's shocked heroine in *The Mysteries of Udolpho*, lets the veil drop at once, but what she has seen, she has seen. The horror has some touch of guilt about it, as if she were committing some female version of the sin of Noah's son who gazed upon his father's nakedness, but there is also terrific excitement present in the scene. Of course we know on the plot level that the death of Bellamy means deliverance for Eugenia; it was either his life or hers. The woman-hater, the woman-destroyer, is dead.

Gazing on the corpse of the Male, Camilla gazes at dead law, absence of authority, abstraction, and false names, the (temporary) end of the Law of the Father. She enters a short space and time of freedom, signified also in the absence or unreadability of the Book of Common Prayer. Burney seems to be trying to create a mythic opposite to the psychoanalytic theorists' death or "killing" of the Mother in exhibiting the death of the Father. At such a point, the woman must face herself alone, a self veiled hitherto in proscriptions, exhortations, sermons, and codes. That such a self-confrontation would not be pleasurable is easy to believe. "Clarinda" in delirious doze saw the image of Leontine and heard his voice in that of her sister rousing her. Image and hollow voice were externalized others, and "Clarinda" was haunted by her lover and his masculine authority. Even in hallucination "Clarinda" could not confront herself. The voice Camilla hears, in contrast, is certainly not Edgar's, and sister and mother are far away. Reborn without the decorative systematic trappings, unobserved by the usually reliable persecutors, the constant watchers, Camilla in the void becomes her own Mother, giving birth to herself—or her selves— while her body speaks in the various parts usually hidden. Camilla is in the throes of parturition of herself, a Sibyl who goes through the ordeal for no Aeneas but for herself and for womankind. She delivers multiple selves in her condition of agonized self-knowledge. She faces the death-turning nature of much of her life, for under the laws and customs she has been living a death-in-life already. Burney had had that experience vividly brought home to herself in her pain over "Mr. G: C.," in her agony over her obedient incarceration at court, and in her deathly weakness in the later court years. Camilla needs to be reborn, to start again. The novel consoles us with her reunion with her parents, and her emotive reconciliation with her mother, but in the nightmare agony she is her own mother. "Where's My Baby?" For the first time in her mature fiction, Burney could deal with such charged material as the separation from her mother, personally such a deep source of pain in her early life, a pain repeated each time she was "deserted" by a mother-figure such as Mrs. Thrale, Mrs. Delany, or even her formerly "truly maternal Friend"[31] Anna Ord. In a new enlightenment of reassurance, love, and daring, she could recognize that a woman may talk to herself, mother herself, and pull herself back from death in the absence of the Father's imperial, august, and death-dealing Law. The "*very different behaviour which Nature calls for on one side, & the World on the other*" had once caused her to write, "I am sometimes dreadfully afraid for myself." There is much to be afraid of, for the World tries to erase female nature and female desire, in effect wishing the woman to die decorously like Desdemona ("I don't know what a woman lives for after thirty"). The woman must fight back, must cherish her own existence (*am*-ella) unlike the sad anti-heroine of Virgil, who is delivered to death in the necessary production of history and epic. This other "Amazon," Burney's Camilla, is a fighter and a cherisher, and she manages to survive. If Virgil's Camilla's deathly fate is part of a legal imperial plot, to change her fate is to change the plot. This interpretation is surely also in some sense "true," and Camilla as prophet speaks with multiple voices.

Less grandly, Camilla's prophetically expressive ordeal makes startlingly manifest the pain and fragmentation present throughout the novel. The blank spaces which cannot be expressed, blanks lurking in all the characters' utterances, are brought to the fore, and the motifs of writing, reading, and being misread converge on her in the failure of language. All the characters are implicated in Camilla's ordeal.

In a novel that includes so much crime, damage, and unhappiness, it is natural to look for a villain. Many readers have probably agreed with Jane Austen, who caustically recorded her opinion of the good Doctor in a note she scribbled at the end of her copy of *Camilla:* "Since this work went to the press a circumstance of some assistance to the happiness of Camilla has taken place, namely that Dr. Marchmont has at last died."[32] He does seem to be Camilla's archenemy, "the unrighteous and cruel man" from which the petitioner in Psalm 71 prays to be delivered. His desire to undo the heroine is a version of the desire of Aruns, slayer of Virgil's Camilla, who prays, "Let me, by stealth, this Female Plague o'recome."[33] More than the more obvious but less interesting Bellamy (Nicholas Gwigg), Marchmont has been a destroyer, a death-wisher. But, after all, Marchmont stands as only an extreme example of the sin that all in the novel are guilty of: setting up oneself as judge over others. From the novel's outset, with its attack on the heartless conduct of the assizes, we are urged to be uneasy at the human rush to judgment—particularly when judgment becomes protected by a carapace of orders, blueprints, and self-righteousness. The last words of the novel are a clear expression of its moral: "What, at last, so diversified as man? What so little to be judged by his fellow?" (V:913).

If the crime of which all are guilty is misjudging others, the sin which the novel finally speaks out against is the wish for self-destruction, the desire to cease being misconstrued at last by ceasing to exist. Camilla in her death wish (and her fear of that wish) is not unique in the novel any more than she is unique in her egotism. Whereas Macartney and Harrel were special cases in *Evelina* and *Cecilia*, respectively, here in *Camilla* there is something suicidal in the life of every character. The characters' own actions constantly endanger them, and there is a violence, a desire to destroy the self of another, evident in the most apparently playful speeches ("This is no child's play!"). The novel, working with great energy through the perverse energies of its characters, brings the hidden desires to light and makes us contemplate "the wilder wonders of the Heart of man."

The whole novel is a scene of wild wonders. *Cecilia* had suggested that social values force a weird life on individuals. *Camilla* also says this, but is concerned to show as well the ways in which the weird inner life, struggling into expression and achieving momentary impressions, inevitably makes the community life bizarre. The "real life" of *Camilla*, though at one level realistic enough, is constantly fantastic. The story gives us a world of small squires, country towns, military officers, shopkeepers, and holiday resorts, with London occasionally glimpsed. In short, it shows us the normal English social landscape of the 1790s, the landscape also of *Pride and Prejudice*, whose first version was written in the same decade. But the imagery of the story gives us violence and strange meta-morphosing figures: an old man on a see-saw, an Othello dressed like Richard III and a Desdemona on fire, a wig-seller sliding down a burrow in the chalk, a mysterious woman in white in the moonlight. The imagery in the characters' language gives us men with arms lopped off, hearts torn into a hundred thousand millions of atoms, the world turning into a potato, memories walking out of the mind. The effects of all these, combined with the characters' deep inner disregard for logic, give us an unreasoning and irrational world, a world in which dislocated voices and an iron pen that makes no mark seem appropriate.

The whole of *Camilla* is a phantasmagoria of the mind's playing—sometimes desperately playing—with what it does. Individuals and societies are those wild minds—or hearts. The Heart is "that amazing assemblage of all possible contra-rieties" which "lives its own surprise." *Camilla* gives us, with surreal accuracy, the contrarieties and the surprise, while telling the not altogether happy story of its "little Amazon," the girl noted for vivacity and playful good humor. If *Camilla* is in some sense the last Augustan novel, it is also one of the early Gothic novels. If it is a Gothic novel, its Gothic elements interpenetrate a family saga, a story of provincial life. It is a Romantic novel of the '90s, which looks like one of the original "loose baggy monsters" and marks a new departure in fiction. In its affinity for "magic realism" rather than strict realism, and in its play with the mythic and the violent, it points ahead not so much to Jane Austen's novels as to *Jane Eyre* and *Bleak House*, and to modern and post-modern novels of our own times.

8

Incest, Bereavement, and the Late Comic Plays

The latter part of the last decade of the old century was to be a troubled time for the Burney family. For Frances Burney, the mid-1790s were good years, perhaps the best ones. She nursed and educated her little son, about whom she recounts fond anecdotes in her letters. She and her husband enjoyed each other's company, and the pleasures of rural life, with shared amusement at their initial blunders in gardening: "I must not omit that we have had for one week Cabbages from our own cultivation—every Day! . . . We had them for too short a time to grow tired of them, because . . . they were beginning to run to Seed before we knew they were eatable."[1]

After the publication of *Camilla*, Alexandre d'Arblay designed Camilla Cottage, which he also helped to build. The drawing of it (Fig. 27) is presumably his. In November 1797 the little family was able to move into the new house and cultivate a garden on what they thought of as their own land.

> M. d'A is Gardening all day long, with a laborious perseverance that procures us Cabbages, potatoes, & soupe meagre every Day. What can the times do to people *revelling* in such luxuries? If they will but leave us our Field, & our Cottage, & *de quoi* to buy bread & small beer, we almost defy them.[2]

The "self-dependence," "self-sufficiency," advocated in *The Witlings* and always sought by Frances Burney seemed at last to have been achieved. She and her husband paid rent for their land, and when they could not afford something, they did without it. Frances firmly told Queeney Thrale that she had "an inherent dislike to all sort of presents," and that one of the problems in the friendship with Mrs. Thrale was that she "loaded me with obligations . . . oppressive to me, dearly as I loved her."[3] The d'Arblays were not to accept serious presents or labor under financial obligations. When an anonymous donor sent them five pounds, Burney recognized that "it is certainly done in great kindness, by some One who Knows £5. is not so small a matter to Us as to most others," but the recipients grandly donated the gift to the war effort: "we determined to devote it to our *Country!*—There's Patriotism!"[4] "Patriotism" was a handy resource for uncontaminated "self-sufficiency." Happy and proud in her new independent life, Burney looked forward to a future of the same manner of living, improved by ultimate purchase of the land with money to be gained by her own efforts in writing. William Locke always said he intended to give the d'Arblays a ninety-nine-year lease of the land, and his intentions were amiable. But he signed no document of gift or of lease and made no disposition in his will; his death left the d'Arblays with no security of tenure at all, and the house and land disappeared when his heir sold Norbury Park in 1814.[5] The fate of Camilla Cottage provides another ironic example of the difference between "attentions" and contract. Burney's projected small estate and inheritance disappeared as rapidly as Cecilia Beverley's grander possessions.

In the mid-1790s, however, life seemed secure, and living in Norbury Park meant the companionship of William and Frederica Locke. Frances had hoped to settle near Susanna, who formerly lived nearby, but Susanna had been forced to accompany her husband to Ireland in September 1796, and that change was the first of a series of disruptions experienced by the Burney family. Another change in the same period was the death of the second Mrs. Burney, after a long illness. The shock plunged Charles Burney into a grief nearly as acute as that experienced thirty-four years earlier, at the death of his first wife. Indeed, the second widowhood revived memories of the first, and sad remembrances of things past. "As yet only one subject occupies me—reminiscence of past times & present privations," he wrote to his son Charles, adding, "Everything else is insipid."[6] His daughter Frances was keenly aware of Dr. Burney's tendency to fall into fits of gloom, a tendency which had threatened him especially since an illness of 1792, "casting him into a state the least natural to his vigorous character, of wasteful depression," as she wrote in the *Memoirs*.[7] Dr. Burney always needed other people to attend to him and restore him to the character that he regarded as natural to himself. Frances now did her best to restore cheerfulness, suggesting many projects to her father, including looking over his old poems. This suggestion (a repetition of his wife Esther's deathbed advice to him) took effect, and Charles soon discovered an old fragmentary poem on astronomy (in his usual tetrameters) which he revived. Astronomical research and conversations with Herschel kept him busy. Frances was surprised to find, many years later, that he had burned "Astronomy," but, as she says in the *Memoirs,* her motive for suggesting the piece had been "to draw him from . . . melancholy inertness," and she knew that "for many years, this Poem had answered all the purposes for which it had been suggested."[8]

Perhaps the therapy was too successful. Energetically recovering from mourning, Dr. Burney had little sympathy to spare for others. His daughter Charlotte (now the widowed Mrs. Francis) was nervous enough of him to feel obliged to use Frances as her envoy to ask her father's consent to her second marriage[9]—an embassy that had but indifferent success. Charlotte's choice was Ralph Broome, formerly a judge advocate in India, and an emphatic defender, through journalism, of Warren Hastings. Broome had brought back with him from India a natural daughter by an Indian woman "of high rank."[10] Charlotte agreed that the girl should live with them. Dr. Burney was not sympathetic to Charlotte's desire to marry again, and objected, not to Broome's natural daughter but to his unnatural politics, telling Frances "he was in *horrour* of the plan, as he was now convinced Mr. B. was a Democrat, if not a Jacobin."[11] Charles Burney disapproved of the wedding, which took place without him on 1 March 1798, and he punished his daughter Charlotte by not seeing her for some time afterwards. Reporting her father's refusal to visit, or to listen to her own representations against such a public breach, Frances commented to Susanna in May, "*why* so much anger, & wherefore its blaze to the World, it is difficult to explain: except upon the terrible score of *politics,* in which he has no mercy for a dissentient opinion."[12]

Dr. Burney's political views were certainly pronounced. His family suspected that he was the author of an article in the reactionary periodical *The Anti-Jacobin,* in December 1797.[13] The piece is a (fictitious) letter from "Letitia Sourby," who complains that her father has accepted the new radical ideas and disturbed the family's "domestic Felicity," so that "our House . . . is become gloomy and disconsolate to us all." Mr. Sourby shuts himself away with wicked books and pamphlets and declaims against marriage, quarrels with his former benefactor because he cannot bear "the weight of an obligation," and forces his daughter to be his companion in long walks instead of going to church. "The greatest grievance of all" is that he has now "put a stop to" his daughter's marriage; because Letitia's fiancé joined the "Yeomanry Cavalry," Mr. Sourby has "downright quarreled with him . . . and turned him out of the house."[14] In short, "Mr. Sourby" acts remarkably like Dr. Burney with the political views reversed. It is interesting that the Burneys thought it possible that Charles Burney could write in the persona of a daughter. Certainly, no daughter of Charles Burney had any cause to complain that her father was too radical.

Frances worried about her sister's new marriage on grounds other than political. Broome seemed to her too pompous and arrogant: "he wanted adulation, not sociality"; "I see he does not believe the human being was ever created who equalled himself in knowledge or parts."[15] The success of the union would depend too much on Charlotte's offering a constant supply of adoration and unquestioning obedience. Frances's misgivings (and thus her father's antagonism also) were justified in the event by the unhappiness of the marriage, as Broome subjected Charlotte to his irrational fits of rage.

Susanna Burney was no happier in her partner. The Phillipses' move to Ireland, undertaken in order to guard the Irish estate, in a time of danger and incipient invasion and rebellion, meant for Susanna a move into danger in the domestic arena as well as the national. As we shall see, Burney had acute anxieties about Susanna and knew before her removal to Ireland that much was terribly wrong with Susanna's marriage. At the same time, Burney was also the confidante of her stepsister, Maria Rishton. Maria, whose elopement with Martin Rishton had so electrified the family in Frances's youth, was now trying to break free, having long found her husband's character "austere, haughty, irascible, & impracticable."[16] Frances encouraged her as she struggled toward "an AMICABLE PUBLIC SEPARATION."[17] Marriages were not faring too well in the Burney family.

The strangest case of trouble, separation, and misalliance was about to manifest itself. James Burney, the seafaring brother, had married at Chessington, in 1785, Sarah (Sally) Payne, daughter of the bookseller who had published *Cecilia*. Mrs. James Burney had a temper; Charles Lamb is supposed to have portrayed her, in her whist-playing aspect, as "Mrs. Battle."[18] By 1798, James had already left his wife twice, even though they had two children living. Even when not in a state of declared separation, he tended to hang about his father's house in Chelsea, or go off visiting his relatives, often in company with his half-sister. When he had no ship, he was at a loose end, although he contributed to public welfare by writing two pamphlets, one a *Plan of Defence against Invasion* (1797), the other, the same year, on the support of public monetary credit. Anxieties about imminent invasion, or imminent fiscal collapse, made a number of English people uneasy, and the national nervousness in the depth of the war years had an effect on personal lives. At the beginning of September 1798, James Burney asked his father to take him in, as he wished to leave his home and wife; Dr. Burney refused. There is no more dramatic case of marital breakdown—or of elopement—among the Burneys than that of James, who both left his spouse and made the most scandalous possible elopement.

On 2 September 1798, Captain James Burney (Fig. 28) eloped with his half-sister Sarah Harriet ("Sally") Burney (Fig. 29). Incest, like some invoked demon, haunts the eighteenth century, and not only in the pages of novels or of plays like Walpole's *Mysterious Mother*. Incest hovers over the heads, not just of fictional characters like Evelina and Macartney, but over Queeney and Crutchley, over Hester Thrale and her fantasy "Brother" Piozzi. Incest was now fully realized in the public action of James Burney and his sister. The September elopements did not come upon the family as a bolt from the blue. The late Mrs. Burney had issued by no means uncertain warnings about the relationship between the two. She had forbidden James the house. Her warnings were apparently too little regarded, although, just before the "fatal Step," Maria Rishton was told by Dr. Burney "all his *dreadful* Apprehensions about their uncommon Intimacy."[19] Stephen Allen, like Maria, had heard some hints from their mother, but could not believe there were grounds for such horrid ideas. After Mrs. Burney died, Dr. Burney had invited his son back as a visitor to the house in Chelsea—and then complained about James's and Sally's neglect of him. The new household arrangements, with young Sally (already a published novelist) cast as the stay-at-home daughter caring for her widowed father, had at first filled Maria with the happiest prognostications, as she told Frances in December 1796:

> God Bless your dear Father . . . I always loved him . . . like one of *his primitive Children* . . . nothing gives me so much pleasure as the charming manner in which my dear Sister Sally writes and speaks of him I am sure she will be all *we* can wish her her temper and Character will be softened down by his kind Indulgence—her Manners will acquire a Polish by being his Companion—she will lose that eccentricity she had indulged herself in, and I am sure will be an Ornament to her Family . . . her *Temper* and *Manner* woud have been totally ruind if she had long continued to have lived in a perpetual State of Warfare. She was violent and often took up things too warmly—and Certainly my poor Mother did irritate and try her temper to the Utmost.[20]

Yet the death of her mother, however ill-tempered she had been, was a real bereavement for Sally, and it cannot have been pleasant to her to find herself regarded as an eccentric savage in need of good influences. Her father's influence had none of the softening and polishing effect Maria expected. Unlike Maria, Sally did not adore Charles Burney or look up to him "as to one of the first of Men."[21] The week before the elopement, Maria was surprised, as she told Frances, to hear a great outburst from Sally against Dr. Burney:

> she complaind bitterly of her Father's Severity and Coldness towards her—that they pass'd days without speaking—and that if he did address or answer her it was with *bitter raillery*—or Harshness—and that he treated James worse than Ever . . . I have been so wretchedly uncomfortable for some time at being a Witness of such constant unhappiness—so unlike what I remember when I was a girl—and if I have attempted to conciliate Sally—I have been accused of joining the D^r: and when I have mentioned the Unaminaty [*sic*] that used to Subsist, and how happy his Children always were at the very Sound of his Voice—I have been told nothing but *Servile Flattery* and *Fear* kept him in good humour.[22]

Sarah Harriet's love for her brother can be traced in her first novel, *Clarentine* (1796), in which the heroine loves a sailor guardian. But the elopement with James can be seen as Sally's working out of her relationship with her father—

another version, rendered by another daughter, of the struggle that occupied Frances Burney and found expression (though not resolution) in *The Siege* and *Hubert De Vere*. Sarah, little "Queerness,"[23] her mother's companion, had not been able to fly, as her older half-sisters did, from unreasonable fits; thus she had lived in a "perpetual State of Warfare." She evidently wished to please her father by imitating or joining the elder children, the members of his first and more real family—to be, in Maria's striking phrase, "one of *his primitive Children*." In Sarah's becoming a novelist, we can see the influence of her sister Fanny's success—but *Clarentine* did not achieve the success of *Evelina*, and the place of daughter novelist had long been filled.

James Burney also felt a need to claim a place in his family. The eldest male, he had not been the one on whom education or care was expended; he had been banished to sea in childhood. Now, in taking one of his father's daughters he opposed his father. James, one of the punning Burneys, who had delighted the natives of Tahiti by making a pun in their language,[24] perpetrated a practical pun when he replaced one "Sally" by another; he took his father's woman, reasserting his claim to the mother who had been thrust out of the world when he was away at sea as a boy. Sarah's unfortunate love can be read as an attempt both to defy the father and to unite herself with him by taking the son-brother (himself a father) in his stead. The advanced age of this incestuous pair in 1798 (when James was forty-eight and Sarah twenty-six) indicates a long emotional involvement, though no one seems to know when it began. The affair indicates Sally's craving for love; her anger at being denied her father's love seems also to have played a part in her imprudent flight. The letter left for her father on that occasion has not survived, but Sally's note to the maid Molly exhibits anger disguised as flippancy: "Do not hear me more abused than you can help—I trust I am gone to be happy & Comfortable."[25]

Maria Rishton may have unwittingly influenced Sally's decision. It was after her mother's death that depression and sickness had, as Maria said, "opend [*sic*] my Eyes to my true Situation"; she had decided to leave her husband, as she had admitted, "only because she was not happy."[26] James was helping Maria with financial arrangements with Rishton up to the point of James's and Sally's elopement. If Sally's sister could separate from her husband, why should James not separate from his wife, and why should Sally herself, since she was unhappy, not make a bid for being "happy & Comfortable"?

The family tried desperately (and with considerable success) to keep this most shameful liaison a secret. The situation did not, as first hoped, resolve itself quickly. The couple refused to come to their senses or to hide in the depth of the country. After a quick dash to Bristol they returned to London lodgings, where the maid Molly visited them and gave an account of their "Style of Living," as Maria in turn reported to Frances:

> she said she never saw Sarah look so well or in such good Spirits—that at present they had a little Lodging near Kentish Town—where the Woman

of the House emptied *their Slops for them* once or twice a day when Sally had deposited them in a tin pail she had bought that they Cookd their own dinners—and went to Market—and the Woman Washd for them —but they meant to get a Lodging near London. . . . Mentiond the distemper Sally had felt for want of her Cloaths—for she did not take even a Night[cap]—and as I fancy they set out for Bristol the very Night they left Chelsea and travelld all Night she bought a Man's Cotton Cap and tied it under her Chin—and had bought a ready made gown—Molly says she never saw her Face so Clear from Humour and her Nose has not lookd so well for some years—I suppose the Active Life she leads, agrees with her.[27]

A little while later the couple had changed lodgings, but not, in Maria's opinion, for the better:

they are living in the most grovling mean Style, Making their own Beds Cooking their Food—and have taken a dirty Lodging in a Suspicious House in Totenham [*sic*] Court Road where they have found out that the Womans Daughter is a Common prostitute who brings home a different Visitor every Night—and they dare not both leave their Apartments together lest they shoud be rob'd.[28]

Maria's list of the low details the maid was able to ascertain, the emphasis on mean lodgings and sordid arrangements, encodes the suspicion that such mean privations would not have been endured without the compensation of sexual pleasure. Certainly James and Sarah had undergone a dramatic change of environment, associating themselves with the poor and the licentious, as neighbors to "a Common prostitute." The brothers and sisters of the strange couple were perforce becoming acquainted with low life, with the "grovling mean Style" which Dr. Burney had spent his life in trying to avoid. Sally was evidently happy in her new domesticity, "in such good Spirits" despite the stinking tin pail or prostitute neighbor. Maria, Frances, Esther, and the rest tried hard to believe that the case was not one of "unnatural Intimacy," kept reassuring one another that fraternal moral principles could be relied on, even when the codes of their statements admitted the other possibility. Molly's observation, as transmitted by Maria, that Sally's face was "Clear from Humour" refers not to the young woman's temper but her complexion. There is a folk belief that marriage (or its equivalent) clears up adolescent skin trouble. Such a sudden clearing of Sally's skin would indicate to Maria and Frances that there was more to Sally's new "Active Life" than cooking dinners in cramped rooms. It is extremely doubtful that the Allen and Burney children, for all their stated assurances, ever really believed that the liaison was not sexual.

The couple lived together for nearly five years. In May 1803 Sarah Harriet wrote to her cousin Charlotte explaining that she was leaving James, since he wanted to have his little girl with him and it would be too cruel of her to take his wife's child: "I have therefore made up my mind, to shift my quarters." With an overdone flippancy she inquires if her Aunt Broome knows "any worthy soul in them there parts she abides in, who would like to give me a good fat salary as governess to her brats?"[29] The splitting-up of this strange household took place just before the publication of James's new book; volume one of his *A Chronological History of the Discoveries in the South Seas or Pacific Ocean* came out in June 1803. James went home to his wife and children. He was to write four more volumes of his history, which eventually won him promotion to rear-admiral, and to make new literary friends like Charles Lamb; he and his wife were to live fairly happily in later years, as Frances was pleased to discover in 1812.[30] His elopement had given James a long holiday from his marriage, an interval in which, evidently with his lover-sister's encouragement, he developed an idea for his history and seriously set to work.

The relationship with James did not give Sally very much in the long run. She produced no book during their time together. She never married, and she had no children—belying the prophecy of a fortuneteller in Gower Street, who, as she records, told her in 1793 that she would have *"seven children!!!"*[31] She was left to struggle along as a governess. She produced several novels, but always ran the risk of their being unfavorably compared to her sister's, though her novels have their own interest. Sarah Harriet Burney deserves a biographical study to herself.

During the five-year interval, the family had to create an acceptable story for the outside world, saying only that "J[ames] had parted from his wife, & S[arah] was gone to keep his house."[32] Charles Burney was extremely upset, though he worked hardest at trying to believe that no "unnatural Intimacy" could be involved. He coped with the horrifying situation largely by ignoring it: "He would speak of it but once—he desired to allude to it in no manner any more.—He struggled only, he said, to forget it!—"[33] He insisted he was not interested in a reconciliation: "he wishes never more to see or hear of them!" At times Frances herself struggled to do "as my dearest F. does himself—strive with my utmost power to drive—force them from my thoughts!" To her credit, however, Frances Burney was not successful in forcing the errant couple from her thoughts.[34] Encouraged by d'Arblay, she kept up a correspondence with James, and although her disgust with Sally is particularly evident, in her notes to James she inquired after Sally.

Charles Burney, on the other hand, was much more successful in driving his son and daughter from his thoughts, or at least suppressing reference to them. He translated his feelings on the subject into a sense of justified grievance at unwarranted injury to himself; as his daughter noted, "Resentment is a powerful diminisher of sorrow, in diminishing the feelings that first excited it, of wounded esteem, & disappointed expectations,"[35] and he was therefore entitled to resent and to forget. Almost comically, he lowers the situation to a manageable level, speaking at times as if the essence of the trouble were his being left in the lurch by his housekeeper, Sarah Harriet, who had been supposed to take care of him. His other daughters should sympathize, and supply the loss:

> Dear—Dear Susey!—I know well how she will wish to come to me— especially now she knows how I have been abandonned![sic]—[36]

The effectiveness of Charles Burney's mechanism for translating all potential guilt into grievance (for which others should console him) had not diminished with advancing years.

Susanna, "Dear Susey," was more in need of consolation than her father, and might more properly have complained of being "abandoned." Her sorrows had increased when Phillips, now unfaithful, tyrannical, and cruel, took complete possession of their son, sending him away to school and preventing Susanna from seeing him. Early in the decade, the Burney family had begun to hope that Phillips could be tacitly bought off. Dr. Burney advanced a large sum (two thousand pounds) as a mortgage on Phillips's property in Ireland, a mortgage whose payments the son-in-law did not bother to keep up.[37] Such an arrangement often signified the private management of an extralegal separation. If the Burneys in 1796 expected Molesworth Phillips to return to his estate in Ireland, leaving Susanna with the Lockes at Mickleham, they had been disappointed. Susanna, against her wishes and in the face of all her fears, had been forced to go to the kingdom across the water, far from family and friends, in complete control of her husband. Phillips had the law on his side; a husband had the legal right to compel the companionship of his wife. Divorce was out of the question; ladies did not divorce their husbands, even for adultery or cruelty, although a legal separation might be arranged on those grounds. The process of seeking a legal separation would have been protracted and expensive, and would have provided gossip-mongers with material; moreover, Susanna might have condemned herself to complete separation from her children. Any endeavors to remonstrate with Phillips seemed to make matters worse. Charles Burney said in 1796, "I had no hope of working upon his wrong-headed & tyrannical spirit . . . and there was great reason to fear the making bad worse, by putting him out of humour, since we *must*, circumstanced as we are, submit."[38] Submission was the order of the day, though Susanna wished to rebel, to refuse to go to Ireland, and to precipitate a true separation. Frances Burney, the happily married Mme. d'Arblay, took part in persuading Susanna to take up her wifely duties, unfortunately pushing her dearest sister toward the meek resolution of a conflict in the style of meekness she herself had attempted in trying to endure court service. Susanna's words of unhappy resignation in a letter to Frances of September 1796 are oddly similar to Frances's earlier sad resolves:

I have now been much calmer since, my heart's dear Sister—& now that the terrible struggle is over—I think I shall be capable of submitting as you would have me—not from *mere* despondence—but from something better.—That despondence may not *at times* seize me I do not presume to hope my Fanny,—but I intend to subdue it when I can, & to make such efforts as I am able to support myself for the sake of those who w^d. make every effort for me—

She added even more somber words of submission:

I see what now befalls me as my Fate—& as I once before said to my Fanny, can only hope it may be an expiation of my Sins—my Fanny will smile perhaps—but I am very serious—.[39]

Susanna was compelled—even by her Fanny—toward a "Fate" which coul have been prevented. But Susanna had not been given her father's "permissio to rebel." It was practically impossible for a respectable lady to leave her hus band if a parent would not shelter her, or a strong male relative give her hi countenance. Susanna needed to be, as Frances said about a different occasion *"called"* to the paternal home. Despite her great and visible misery, the call dic not come. The unhappy couple departed for Ireland on 14 October 1796; "struggle" and "despondence" were to continue.

One source of shock was a new acquaintance, Jane Brabazon, who Susanna's son Norbury (who called her "Janey Paney") told his mother was "the person I should best love in Ireland." On attending church Susanna felt herself "viewed in stolen glances with something like particular interest" by a young lady whom Susanna describes in detail, as "tall—with perhaps something more than the right degree of embonpoint, & I think rather too large—but well made," possessing a fair complexion, "fine fair hair," and "blue eyes to which I did not at first do justice but wch. I have since found capable of conveying the sweetest expression." Young Jane Brabazon, Molesworth Phillips's second cousin, at once treated Susanna like *"a bosom Friend,"* writing letters and giving bouquets: "finding I loved flowers, she continually brought or sent me such regales as I was least proof against." Susanna thought Jane possessed "Sensibility," "a very lively understanding, self improved," and "a nature at once open & modest—her principles pure, & even strict." Having lulled her sister Frances with this picture of an ideal new friend, Susanna then dramatically let the cat out of the bag:

Her [Jane's] modest firmness I am convinced has awed the M [Major Molesworth Phillips] from anything like open declarations . . . but this can certainly be known only by themselves, & in the meanwhile his pursuit of her is flagrant & his assiduities unceasing—I am but too well persuaded these have been very generally remarked . . . I am far enough removed from a Jealous Wife by my nature, & circumstances have rendered any tendencies of that kind for many years impossible—yet it w^d. be as repugnant to my feelings as to every idea I have of rectitude to submit to being considered as *la complaisante de mon Mari* in such a situation.[40]

This is one of the murky situations in which Burneys were to be involved in the 1790s. Susanna's statement that jealousy has been for her "for many years impossible" is a bitter way of stating that she had long ceased to feel any love for Phillips, and thus could not care what he did. Nevertheless, his "flagrant" pursuit of Jane was at the very best an embarrassment and irritant. Susanna stedfastly refused to believe "Janey Paney" guilty of a liaison with her husband—yet the physical description of the young woman shows how conscious she is of Jane's physical presence, and of the attractions of a woman fair like herself, but robust—tall, fat, even "too large"—unlike short and thin Susanna. Jane offered valuable companionship; without her, Susanna would have been more catastrophically lonely in an alien environment; she could compare "Janey Paney" with Hetty Burney, Frederica Locke, or even Frances herself. Soon Susanna became "an object of Jealousy" for taking Miss Brabzon's attention from the major: "the acquaintance between us, wch. at first was desired, is become a cause of Suspicion, & every means employed to interrupt it." Jane Brabazon must have been a flirt, at the very least, for she did not remove herself from the society of a married man who was visibly pursuing her; she seems in some fashion to have been flirting with both Molesworth and Susanna. (Jane's getting talked about did not prevent her marrying a clergyman, the Reverend Robert Disney, in November 1798, after which she is not a feature of the Phillipses' marriage.) Despite Susanna's initial revulsion at being "*la complaisante,*" the complaisant wife conniving at her husband's affair with his mistress, Susanna would not be the first or the last woman who has in daily life put up with that situation, and has even felt some friendship for the mistress. Frances took the hint from Susanna in treating "Janey Paney" as her sister's agreeable friend. Yet the puzzle remained, and Frances Burney knew about it—she was not living a sheltered life. She knew much about the ugliness and distortion of Susanna's marriage, and the sorrows of what Susanna in 1798 termed "*ma triste vie.*"

Susanna's life in Ireland became increasingly lonely and more miserable, as she was subjected to Phillips's harsh temper and perhaps even to physical violence. Susanna's health declined, and it was at last clear that she was very seriously ill and not likely to improve under Molesworth Phillips's control. Charles Burney at last consented (how many echoes there are of Frances's release from court!) to receive Susanna in his own home. Still the prudent Burneys hoped to avoid open separation and defiance of the husband's wishes.

Valuable time was lost in tact, as Phillips, enjoying his power, prevaricated and hesitated. By October 1799, Frances was anxious enough about her sister to contemplate going to Ireland herself to nurse Susanna and bring her back no matter what the obstacles:

> My wretchedness at the thoughts of her consuming away to a lingering death in *that* prison with *that* geoler [sic] conquers every obstacle of cowardice & of expence that oppose my voyage. I should never be happy again not to make this *attempt* to save her.[41]

But it was not easy to remove a wife from her husband's control. Phillips might legally have pursued the fugitives, and he certainly could have taken the matter up in the law courts and made himself disagreeable. The Burneys had, however, the advantages in England of an impressive network of friends and advisors, and once they got Susanna home to England, her husband might have become more reasonable about accepting a separation. But Phillips put the Burneys off with frequent promises to bring Susanna over to England for a visit, while making difficulties about the expense of the journey. By late autumn 1799, they had moved to Dublin; Susanna was barely able to travel. Her brother Charles went to Holyhead to receive her; after many delays the yacht bearing Mr. and Mrs. Phillips reached harbor. Susanna trod English ground again on 30 December 1799. The married couple (the major still boisterously carrying on the charade of normal relations, journeying, and family reunion) lodged with Charles at the White Lion at Chester. Phillips wrote, "We are all very merry in a comfortable little Lodging."[42] On 6 January 1800, Susanna died at Chester. The news reached the d'Arblays on 9 January of the new year.

The whole sad episode has an ironic resemblance to Frances's imprisonment and final escape through ill health from unendurable circumstances. But in this case salvation came too late. There had been too much caution, too many endeavors not to alienate Phillips. If in 1799 some member of Susanna's family had dashed over to Ireland and removed her abruptly, she might have had a better chance of life, or, at least, the opportunity of dying in peace surrounded by the family she adored. It is true that we usually do not know that the time is ripe for heroic action until the opportunity is gone. One can, however, wish for Frances Burney's own sake that she had expiated her fatal persuasion of Susanna into doing her duty (as she had once tried to persuade Mrs. Thrale to do hers). Her guilt for her own complicity in Susanna's terrible fate would have been alleviated if she had taken the rescue trip to Ireland.

Frances Burney paid terribly for whatever faults she had committed in her good intentions. After October 1796 she never saw her sister, alive or dead. Even the funeral happened too quickly for her to be present; it took place on 10 January (the anniversary of Susanna's wedding in 1782). It is strange that the ceremony could not be postponed until some more of the family could get to

Chester; Major Phillips was presumably, as he was legally entitled to be, in charge of all such arrangements. Frances's reaction was great agony. Unable at first to shed a tear, she screamed "for some vent to the weighty oppression upon my soul."[43] She had lost her twin self:

> From our earliest moments . . . we *wanted nothing but each other*. . . . She was the soul of my soul—& tis wonderful to me . . . that the first shock did not join them immediately by the flight of mine—but that over—that dreadful—harrowing—never to be forgotten moment of horrour that made me wish to be mad—over—the ties that after that first endearing period have shared with her my Heart come to my aid—Yet I was long incredulous—& still sometimes I think it is not—& that she will come.[44]

Once Frances had feared going mad; in this most intense agony of mental pain she knew a "moment of horrour that made me wish to be mad." There was no such relief from the steady knowledge of an absolute loss. This was the greatest bereavement Burney had known hitherto. She never got over it. She kept the sixth of January as a sorrowful anniversary for ever after, even when her father rebuked her for the practice. The grief for the lost sister endured through the rest of her life.

At the end of the old century and the beginning of the new one, the Burney family sustained many changes, losses, and shocks. Yet the period from 1797 to 1802 saw the production of the greatest concentration of Burney's comic works. Burney began her next novel, *The Wanderer*, as she tell us in the preface, "before the end of the last century"—presumably around 1798—"but the bitter . . . affliction with which this new era opened to our family . . . cast it from my thoughts, and even from my powers, for many years."[45] Yet the gap between *Camilla* and *The Wanderer* is partly filled by work on three dramatic pieces; anxieties and bitter affliction did not cast the writing of plays out of Burney's power. As she tried to explain to Dr. Burney,

> My imagination is not at my own controll [sic], or I would always have continued in the walk you approuved [sic]. The combinations for another long work did not occur to me. Incidents & effects for a Dramma did. I thought the field more than open—inviting to me.[46]

She again endeavored to become a dramatist because the urge seemed irresistible, even though she knew her father preferred her novel-writing. In this new period of worry and sorrow, the dramatic *œuvre* was not to consist of dismal tragedies, but of "laughing comedies," written with stage production in mind. Yet Burney's new stage comedies resemble the tragedies in that they involve the use of psychological material, a translation of inner experience.

In January 1798 Burney was writing a play, showing that the failure of *Edwy* (in her father's eyes an important failure) had not depressed her unduly. She now took up "a scribbling business that fills all my scribbling ideas," giving to it all the time she could spare "from my little occupying Alec."[47] Financial reward from playwriting would benefit little occupying Alec, too. The scribbling business produced the comedy *Love and Fashion,* which the author's brother Charles offered to Thomas Harris, manager of Covent Garden Theatre, in October 1799. Her brother told her, "H. is surprised that you never turned your thoughts to this kind of writing before; as you appear to have really a genius for it!—There now!"[48] Harris had evidently not heard of *The Witlings,* buried twenty years before. Burney was offered a handsome 400 pounds, and the play was to be produced, after some alterations, in March 1800. The play was even unofficially advertised in the papers, possibly through judicious puffing by Harris. The advertisements mentioned the author by name, wrecking Burney's hopes of secrecy and spilling the news to Charles Burney, inducing in him all the old nervous pudency about his daughter's writing comic plays for the public stage. It was after the *Morning Chronicle* announcement of 29 January 1800 that he began to raise objections. Burney withdrew her *Love and Fashion* from the Covent Garden management in early February.

By January 1800, the family had been shattered by the death of Susanna; the presentation of a lighthearted comedy might have seemed callous, and postponement of production seems normal under the circumstances. But it seems evident that Burney did not intend to withdraw the piece until Charles Burney forced her hand. Susanna's death provided the excuse, but the real battle is over the puzzling obscure old issues, the objections on Charles's part really stemming from the same feelings which had put an end to *The Witlings.* This time, Frances dared voice her puzzlement:

> to combat your—to me—unaccountable but most afflicting displeasure, in the midst of my own panics & disturbance, would have been ample punishment to me, had I been guilty of a crime in doing what I have all my life been urged to, & all my life intended, writing a Comedy.

She tried to argue by drawing a genial parallel between them:

> I hope, therefore, my dearest Father, in thinking this over, you will cease to nourish such terrors & disgust at an essay so natural, & rather say to yourself with an internal smile 'After all—'tis but *like Father like Child* . . . She took my example in writing—She takes it in ranging . . . Come on then, poor Fan . . . & I will *disencourage* you no more.'[49]

But Charles Burney could not truly acknowledge his daughter's right to range, and he never ceased to *"disencourage"* her attempts at comic drama. His displeasure was "unaccountable" but still "most afflicting" to his daughter—the comedy invoked the old permission issue all over again. But she shows that she knows his "terrors" are causeless. This time, as not in the case of *The Witlings,* she does not bind herself to his judgment. Her argument, however hurt and affectionate, does not sound the old note of submission. It is perhaps significant that Burney's little diary of "Consolatory Extracts Daily collected or read in my extremity of Grief at the sudden & tragical loss of my beloved Susan on the instant of her liberation & safe arrival in England" contains much less of religious musings on death and immortality than one might expect, and a surprisingly large proportion of thoughts on anger. Extracts culled from the work of women writers (Mme. de Staël, Miss Talbot, Mrs. Chapone) are found under headings like *"Duty of bearing the failures of others,"* "A road to Truth in Anger." The general trend of these extracts is constant self-reminding not to be impatient, not to be irritated at others, not to be angry at a reproach.[50] Evidently, Burney found that anger and resentment were among her problems in 1800, and one suspects that one of the causes of anger was Charles Burney's attitude to her writing.

Burney signed no capitulation. She did not withdraw from the project, but still hoped to have her play produced in the future. And she followed the writing of *Love and Fashion* almost defiantly with two more comic plays, *A Busy Day* (1800–1801) and *The Woman-Hater* (1801). The last two plays perhaps represent an attempt to avoid exile. General d'Arblay, his name at last removed from the proscribed list of émigrés, thought that he and his wife ought to go to France to recover some of his lost property and to look after the affairs of his family. Burney tried to persuade him that she could earn money by her pen to support them in their English "Hermitage"—and play-writing could make money more quickly than novel-writing. She was working industriously on her comedies while d'Arblay was visiting France from November 1801 to January 1802. He took up his commission in the French army, but his stipulation that he never be required to bear arms against his wife's native land was unacceptable to the first consul, Napoleon himself, who complained that d'Arblay had written him the devil of a letter. He forgave the preposterous request for the sake of the novelist who had given him pleasure: "with a smile half gay, half cynical, he said: 'However, I ought only to regard in it the husband of Cecilia.'" D'Arblay's commission was annulled, and he was advised that "he could not quit France without seeming to have gained his wish in losing his appointment. He determined, therefore, to remain a twelvemonth in Paris, to shew himself at hand in case of any change of orders."[51] As he wanted his wife and child with him in this semienforced residence in France (and without compliance he might lose residency for good), Frances and her son had to pack up and go. Frances Burney left England in a quick and chaotic removal in April 1802. The tenuous peace between the two nations was soon to be broken, and return to England proved impossible. The family remained in France; General d'Arblay worked in a respectable but not highly paid post in the Ministère de l'Intérieur.[52] The proposed year abroad extended to ten years. The exile Burney had tried to avert had come upon her. Events, even international affairs, seemed to conspire against her getting a comedy on the London stage. But the comedies she wrote in those three years would have been worth producing.

Love and Fashion, the first of the sequence, seems the least good of the three, but it is a stageable play (as Harris thought), with many good things in it. Burney here uses the circumstances she had once sketched as the ground plan of the novel that became Camilla—the story of a family plunged into poverty, and the different members' reactions to the change. Lord Exbury, his daughter, and his younger son Valentine are impoverished because of the extravagance of his elder son, Mordaunt Exbury. The family is forced to move to a humble dwelling in the country. Lord Exbury's ward, Hilaria Dalton, good-hearted but volatile, flippant, and worldly, has doubts about life in the country, and is torn between Love (for Valentine) and Fashion, in the prospects offered by marriage with the wealthy if unpleasant Lord Ardville. Hilaria, who seems more like the original "Ariella" than does the ultimate heroine of Camilla, goes very near making the same mistake "Clarinda" almost makes, marrying a disagreeable old peer for his money. But Hilaria has little capacity for sentiment or self-reproach and a very strong sense of what she wants. When the fop Sir Archy Fineer woos her for old Lord Ardville, her mind runs on the attractions of the life Ardville can offer:

> *Hilaria.* Is it not provoking one can't marry a man's fortune, without marrying himself? that one can't take a fancy to his mansions, his parks, his establishment,—but one must have his odious society into the bargain?
> *Sir Archy.* But think how soon you'll be free.
> *Hilaria.* No; I hate to think about people's dying.
> *Sir Archy.* But you don't hate to think about people's being comfortably wrapt in fleecy hosiery,—reclined on an easy chair, & unable, by the month together, to hop after & torment their fair Mates?
> *Hilaria.* Why no—that is not quite so disagreeable. But, really, poor Women are cruelly off: 'tis so prodigious a temptation to be made mistress in a moment of mansions, carriages, domestics—to have Time, Power, & Pleasure cast at once at their disposal—
> *Sir Archy.* And where is the cruelty of all this?
> *Hilaria.* It's [*sic*] accompaniment is so often discordant! If the regard of Lord Ardville be sincere—why can he not settle half his wealth upon me at once, without making me a prisoner for life in return?
>
> (IV.iii.182–183)[53]

One recognizes in Hilaria the tone of the Frances Burney who had thought that "a handsome pension for nothing at all would be as well as working night and day for a salary." Hilaria, analyzing the situation in which marriage is a lady's only way to come at mansion, establishment, power, and pleasure, mocks and (with the help of Sir Archy) caricatures the powerful but strangely impotent and unnecessary male who can command all this. She is the other side, the aggressive side, of Clarinda, and she has the same desire for choice that other Burney heroines have. She carries forward the theme of woman's choice—of libido, if you will—so marked in Burney since Evelina first laughed in the fop's face, and refused to dance with the man she found unattractive, intending to choose one she liked. Hilaria, of course, has to come about. When she hears that Valentine has been ruined at play and is being pursued by a bailiff who wants to arrest him, she accepts Lord Ardville's present of jewels, in order to free her true love, even though that means she must accept Lord Ardville. Her act of self-sacrifice is misinterpreted by Valentine, though she is persuaded to break off with Lord Ardville by Valentine's homily: "You wish . . . to unite Love with Fashion? . . . The happiness of true Love is domestic life: the very existence of Fashion is public admiration" (V.i.204–205). Lord Arville, in order to get out of the embarrassment of being considered "a disappointed Man," will not take back the jewels, pretending they were a free gift and that he had no particular interest in Hilaria. She gives the jewels to Lord Exbury, and from them, presumably, the family debts may be paid—a dubious transaction, sorting ill with the moral that ends the play: "What is there of Fortune or distinction unattainable in Britain by Talents, probity, & Courage? . . . Has a Man hands, & shall he fear to work for the Wife of his choice?" (V.iv.233).

Independence achieved through work—this moral is similar to that of *The Witlings*. Burney is not quite as forceful about independence and work as she might have allowed herself to be; she could have asked "Has a Woman hands, & shall she fear to work for the Husband of her choice?" It is undoubtedly true, as Hemlow notes, that *Love and Fashion* reflects Burney's own pride in the choice she had earlier made of "love in rural poverty" with General d'Arblay, and a *"retort courteous"* to those who mocked and cut her.[54] But the play also peculiarly validates the choice of Sally and James in 1798, for they had chosen love, poverty, and "domestic life," if not in a cottage then in a slum up Totten-ham Court Road. Sally and James act like distorting reflectors of Burney's own values.

If the play had gone into serious rehearsal, Harris would probably have helped the author achieve a clearer plot outline and some tightening. Valentine (one of Burney's weak *jeunes premiers*) needs more part in the action. Some of the notes for revision (probably originating from criticism by Harris) indicate as much.[55] The strength of the piece lies in Hilaria and in some of the minor characters and subordinate episodes. Silly Miss Exbury, setting her cap for Sir Archy, is a good if conventional comic type. Davis is a typical comic servant, but there is something new in his mixed humor, combining a love of exaggeration with a conscientiousness that leads him to persistent self-correction: "And his face turned all blue . . . that is, a sort of a blue green" (III.ii.104).

Mordaunt Exbury, laconic, cool, and heartless, is one of the very best comic characters in the play. Mordaunt, unscathed by all consequences and all lectures, is moved to any flicker of reaction only by strictures on the taste of his waistcoat or hat. In a world of overreactors, he happily underreacts. A subplot or running theme of the comedy involves a supposed ghost. That the country house is reputedly haunted frightens Miss Exbury and her maid: "she's been seen walking in the very same cloaths she wore alive!" says Innis impressively and Miss Exbury responds, "How horrid!" but Mordaunt keeps cool: "You think, perhaps, she ought to have set you some new Fashion?" (III.ii.106–107).

The ghost motif in the play is a joking allusion to Monk Lewis's highly successful play *The Castle Spectre* (1797), which Burney had seen in February or March of 1798, in a period when she undertook some brisk theater-going, catching up with the new actors and the new dramatists such as Lewis, Hannah Cowley, Thomas Holcroft, and Frederic Reynolds.[56] She was determined to write a professional and actable modern comedy, and the effects can be seen in all these works. The "ghost" motif in *Love and Fashion* is a good comic theatrical idea, leading to short bursts of farcical action, as when Valentine and Sir Archy blunder about a dark chamber, each hitting out at the other's invisible presence (IV.i). Such a scene of blundering activity in stage darkness is uncommon in eighteenth-century theater, and Burney has made clever and actable use of a good device.

Another good comic idea in the play is the running mystery provided by the character named in the Dramatis Personae simply as "Strange Man." His identity and purpose are obscure to the other characters; he gives nothing away; only at the end do we find that he is a London bailiff. His Cockney streetwise manner and gift of understatement resemble the attributes of Sam Weller, and his refusal to fall for social gambits and local authority is dramatically attractive. In one scene the obsequious Litchburn, acting for Lord Ardville, respectively and timidly tries to rid the area of the vulgar stranger:

> *Litchburn.* I mean no harm, Sir; only my lord has condescendsion [*sic*] to command me to say, that he is rather of the particular, in not being over complaisant about any Gentleman's walking much at random just without his Park pales.
> *Strange Man.* Why then let un ax 'em to walk within 'em.
> *Litchburn.* . . . It's pretty lucky his lordship does not hear you—craving your pardon for the remark. . . . Sir, I hope you'll favour me to excuse my not over-caring to stay in this sharp air, the Wind being rather a detriment than otherwise to my Cough; for last Thursday Evening, walking out pretty nigh upon twilight, I caught a great cold. Good day, Sir. *Exit.*

Strange Man. Did ye? Make much on't then; it's well to catch any thing these hard times.

(II.ii.68—70)

Litchburn, the fragile and humbly explanatory toady, supplies one of the play's moral themes. Burney is always interested in, and resentful of, snobbery and condescension, and keenly observes what different effects social tyrannies have on different people. The willingness of some of her own family to humble themselves before the glamor of position was always a source of deep if obscure unease. The reward of such earnest humility is seen here in the fate of Litchburn who, after years of earnest service, is cast off by Lord Ardville in a fit of pique, and remarks in distress, "So here I've been trampled upon all these Years for nothing—except just the Honour!" (V.v.231). Burney has sympathy for the abused sycophant, and a sense of the horror of the position. Her interest in the matter is first manifested in her presentation of Evelina, whom malice presents as "a kind of toad-eater" (*Evelina*, III:294), and the interest had deepened over the years, with her own experience of the exigencies of life, including court life. (The title of the play *The Triumphant Toadeater* offers the only temptation for believing this manuscript piece in an unidentified hand to be Burney's; it has sometimes been attributed to her but the evidence is all against it.)[57] In *The Wanderer* her own heroine becomes perforce a "toad-eater," a humble companion subjected to the whims and cruelties of her patroness, the "toad-eater-maker." Toadying is itself the opposite of self-sufficiency and love of independence, and it brings its own unhappy psychic penalties. Litchburn had been "trampled upon all these Years for nothing," but his little personality has been so warped that he still must regard being thus treated by a lord as an "Honour." Once cheered (by the assurance of a new patron) he plucks up spirit—his version of spirit:

Why then, the next time I see my good Lord Ardville, I'll pluck up courage to tell him—at least to give a little—sort of a—kind of a—hint,— respectfully! *bowing*—that I begin to think—*smiling*—I know—almost—black from white!—humbly craving pardon for the liberty.

(V.iv.234—235)

There is pathos in the comic picture of someone whose humility has become ingrained, for whom even rebellion must be obsequious. Litchburn is a monument to the worst of the Burney obsequiousness and a comic portrayal of the inability of the Burney family members to express anger.

The deeper meanings of the play are conveyed through the characters who cannot reach adequate emotion. Burney was working on *Love and Fashion* during the period of Charlotte's marriage, when Dr. Burney refused to see his daughter, and she continued work on the play after the elopement of James and

Sarah, in a period when inadequate emotional response to human disaster was evident in the Burneys' family life and most particularly in Dr. Burney's reaction. Charles Burney, as Frances reported, would not even talk about the matter:

> I frequently started the subject, at first,—but found it would not bear discussion. . . . If I persevered, in the hopes of leading to something satisfactory, he cut me short himself, with much displeased emotion, saying 'For God's sake don't let us talk upon this subject!—'[58]

The best of Burney's late comic drama is founded on imperfect responses to situations, the way to "something satisfactory" being "cut short." The author keeps a close eye on those who bungle human relations because of timidity, prudence, or coldness. Her most effective original characters in *Love and Fashion* are those whose responses to life arise not from exaggeration, from plenitude, but from deficiency. Mordaunt Exbury is an excellent creation precisely because he is so far from the conventional spendthrift rake. He seems to have depleted the family coffers without, like Charles Surface, feeding his own sense of life. He is a Meadows at a more serious level of ennui. He is never flamboyant, for his light burns too low; he is exhausted by his own negativity. He cannot be reformed; he hasn't got the energy. He is given, in the end, the play's best speech (in the eyes of the modern reader): "I have been the ruin of you all,—& I feel cursed queer. I'll go and lie down again" (V.iv.224). Lurking in Burney's comic play-writing were Chekhovian possibilities.

Burney's next comedy, *A Busy Day or, An Arrival from India*, exhibits smoother plotting than *Love and Fashion*, while carrying on the investigation of inadequate emotional responses. The plot of *A Busy Day* (the title a favorite phrase in Burney's journals) is more firmly fastened round the heroine than is the case with the preceding play. Eliza Watts has what Hilaria Dalton wished for—money and power without a disagreeable husband. Eliza has long been in India, with her adoptive father, Mr. Alderson, who on dying has left her a fortune of eighty thousand pounds. This heroine is thus an heiress, like Cecilia Stanley and Cecilia Beverley. She has just returned to England with her fiancé Cleveland, whom she met in India. Cleveland has now been recalled home by his family, and presumes it is because his uncle wants to make him his heir. Neither Eliza's nor Cleveland's family knows of their engagement.

Cleveland's impudent younger brother, Frank, hearing by accident of the fortune of the heiress from India, decides to woo this "city Gentoo" (i.e., "city Hindoo") as he needs the money. Cleveland's uncle, Sir Marmaduke, and his aunt, Lady Wilhelmina, after frigidly receiving him, inform him he must marry rich Miss Percival or lose hope of inheriting his uncle's estate. The right opportunity to announce Cleveland's and Eliza's engagement does not seem to arrive. Affairs are complicated by Frank's pursuit of Eliza and by the fond Miss Percival's attentions to Cleveland, whom she takes for granted as her fiancé. Both

Cleveland and Eliza are embarrassed by the behavior of Eliza's vulgar family. The play's recent editor, Tara Ghoshal Wallace, points out that none of the misunderstandings could cause any problems for the heroine and hero "if each were not so ready to misconstrue the actions of the other."[59] Eliza believes Cleveland is utterly repelled by her crude relations, while he believes she is acting distant because she minds his losing the estate. The comedy of misconstruction parallels that of *Camilla,* though on a lighter level, because both hero and heroine really know what they want, although they are somewhat hampered by fine feeling and obligations.

At length, Cleveland bursts out with the truth to Frank and Miss Percival, astonishing and angering both, and wounding Miss Percival by a public rejection. Determined to get revenge, Frank and Miss Percival invite the Watts family and Sir Marmaduke and Lady Wilhelmina to a party, planning to humiliate Eliza and Cleveland by the mixture of the two groups and thus to make it harder for Cleveland to announce or to keep his engagement. The party is a festival of vulgarity, snobbishness, and mortification. Sir Marmaduke, when he realizes that any arrangement with Miss Percival is off, announces that Cleveland will lose the Lincolnshire estate and calmly suggests his immediate return to India. But once the basic misunderstandings between Cleveland and Eliza are cleared up, the heroine, who has a large inheritance of her own, is willing to take up the financial arrangements that Sir Marmaduke had desired as part of Miss Percival's dowry. As long as his mortgage is paid, Sir Marmaduke does not mind what niece-in-law pays it; the still-horrified gentility of Lady Wilhelmina goes for nothing. As in *Love and Fashion,* the generous heroine solves the hero's financial problem by coming up with the money, though her possession of the means ultimately depends on a gift made by some powerful male. Cleveland is reinstated:

> *Sir Marmaduke.* . . . Since the young lady's so generous—what a happy young rascal thou art!—since she's so generous, I say, why—sooner than lose sight of thee again,—I'll . . . Accept her proposition . . . and make over to thee my Lincolnshire Estate.
>
> (V.145).[60]

Frank then blackmails Miss Percival into marrying him (lest it be thought she should "wear the Willow" for Cleveland), and all ends happily, leaving Cleveland to enunciate the official "moral" at the end: respect is due to the merchant class, and we should feel

> a cool superiority to resentment against those who, forgetting that Merit is limited to no spot, and confined to no Class, affect to despise and degrade the natives of that noble Metropolis, which is the source of our Splendour,

the seat of integrity, the foster-Mother of Benevolence and Charity, and the Pride of the British Empire.

(V.148)

The cause of merchants against aristocrats had long been taken up, and this sort of point had very emphatically been made in English comic plays since the 1770s—though the concept of "the British Empire" is relatively new. But the plays (such as Cumberland's *The West Indian*) that stress the virtues of the middle classes and rich colonials present at least one patently virtuous male middle-class character on stage—some banker, merchant, lawyer who is a man of sensibility, benevolent and far-seeing. There is no such character in *A Busy Day*. Indeed, in all of Burney's works the avuncular man who sets all to rights, such a popular type in late eighteenth-century fiction, is conspicuously absent. Even in *Evelina* it is a woman, Mrs. Selwyn, who takes an active part in bringing the girl and her father together; in the dramatic development of the plot she takes over the role one might expect the passive Villars to act. In *A Busy Day,* no character who claims authority or is in a superior position has any claim to anyone's real respect. As for the benevolent nabob—Eliza herself is the returning nabob. At some remove, the plot situation is derived not just from other dramas but from real life—from the combined stories of Richard Owen Cambridge and George Cambridge. Cleveland in England finds that he must go to the Indies because he has no income on which to marry the girl he loves; that is, he is in just the position Richard Owen Cambridge had once occupied, and is to be rescued, as Richard Cambridge was rescued, by an uncle's settling an estate on him. Richard Owen Cambridge had not at first been able to become engaged to Miss Trenchard, and similarly "Mr. G: C." did not become engaged to Frances Burney. In the play, Eliza Watts can bring enough money to allow her lover to have what he wants—the estate and herself. Just so, Frances Burney had surely wished in 1783 that she could bring sufficient dowry to settle all Cambridge's financial worries. And in later life she had really been the partner whose money (a far cry from Eliza's great fortune) had enabled the desired union with d'Arblay to take place. The union with George Cambridge had of course not taken place, and indeed Cambridge did not marry until late, in 1795, after Burney herself had married. It is probable that news of George Cambridge's marriage stimulated recollections in Burney and had some effect in the shaping of her new dramatic courtship stories. Tara Ghoshal Wallace points out that *A Busy Day* exhibits a conflict "between Eliza's sense of independence and her desire to be an unexceptionable sentimental heroine." Long separated from her family, and well-bred and wealthy without their help, "Eliza quite understandably feels independent of them,"[61] while a sense of duty prescribes that her parents should have some control over her actions, and that she should feel what are taken to be appropriate emotions. But the essence of the comedy is that Eliza cannot live up to her prescribed task of being a proper lady and a dutiful daughter. When this heroine discovers her natural family, she discovers alienation.

On her return from India, Eliza is reverentially emotional about being restored to her family: "A Father,—a Mother—my dear Cleveland! what sacred ties! even though my memory scarcely retains their figures, my heart acknowledges their rights, and palpitates with impatience to shew its instinctive duty" (I.34). But her parents do not merit, and indeed do not have any idea of, all this reverence and hallowed feeling. The reunion is entirely anticlimactic:

> *Eliza.* . . . My Father! my dear Father!
> *She runs to* MR WATTS, *takes his hand, and drops upon one knee to him.*
> *Mr Watts.* How do do, my dear? You're welcome home again. Well! I should never have known you!
>
> (I.45)

And a little later he enquires after the really important matter,—the money: "Pray, my dear Darter, what was it took old Alderson off? Did he leave much over your fourscore?" (I.46). Mr. Watts does not know what to do with Eliza's displays; comically, she is acting in one style, kneeling and making elaborate utterances, and he responds in a different style altogether. Vulgar Mr. Watts is the opposite pole from Chester of *The Siege of Pevensey*. He is incapable of making or responding to warm emotional demands; cosy filiality is rejected, leaving the girl curiously liberated. This is the first time that Burney has made a mock of a heroine's father; daddying is coming unraveled.

The reunion with the Mother is no warmer:

> *Eliza.* Is that my Mother?—my dear Mother!—
> *Runs to* MRS. WATTS *with open arms.*
> *Mrs Watts.* Take care, my dear, take a little care, or you'll squeeze my poor new Handkerchief till it won't be fit to be seen. And it cost me sich a sight of money—
> *Miss Watts.* La', Ma', what signifies? I hope you can buy another. (*whispers her*) What do you talk so mean for before those two smart Gentlemen?
> *Mrs Watts.* Nay, my dear, I don't do it to find fault, for I think it very pretty of your Sister to be in sich a hurry; only there's no need to spoil one's things. Come, my dear Betsey— . . . Pray, my dear, have you got over much Indy muslin? I ha'n't bought a morsel since I knew you was coming.
>
> (I.45–46)

The mother sends the daughter from her breast, valuing the "poor new Hand-kerchief" over the poor new daughter, the baby she used to nurse at that breast. The maternal fund has dried up. It is not that the vulgar Wattses have no appre-ciation of the girl they still want to call "Betsey"; the appreciation is tepid, and they see her as acting nicely, "very pretty." They have no understanding of her weeping for the dead Mr. Alderson, who interests them (as he does us) only as a source of money and stuffs. Eliza will have to get along with the family she has, keeping a distance between herself and them; they cannot fulfill her fantasies of warmth and dependence. It is as if Burney had asked herself what would have happened had the Tyrold parents been Branghtons. Eliza has to face her own adulthood. The break with the family has really happened, and there is no reason why these persons who happen to be related to her should control her. The moral at the end of the play, which is ostensibly that time-honored theme, the proper honoring of the middle class, is really asserting that "merit is limited to no spot, and confined to no Class," including the position of parent. Throughout the play, no one shows that he or she has any claim to veneration and obedience, even though there are some who make that claim.

Cleveland's family, with the exception of his sister, is more hardhearted than Eliza's and much more authoritarian. In examining these vulgarians of high class, we see another set of underreactors. Sir Marmaduke Tylney represents "total apathy . . . toward everything and everybody where he has no personal interest" (I.38). He hears unmoved of a fire in the village near Tylney Hall, and cares nothing for the losses and accidents suffered by his unfortunate neighbors, but is seriously upset when he hears that he himself has lost a little hayrick in the conflagration. Lady Wilhelmina, his sister, cares only for pure caste, and can sympathize only with her own kind. She is shocked to hear that a lord has "nearly lost all his Hair" in this fire and dismayed to hear her niece exclaim that "poor old Walters," who broke both his legs, is a subject of more concern. She explains that not only was Lord Garman's hair "deservedly admired" but he is the true sufferer:

> A man of rank is peculiarly susceptible of evil, because not brought up to vulgar vicissitudes; but a low person has so little leisure to reflect or refine, that a few disagreeable accidents can make but little impression upon him.
>
> (II.55)

This ungentle gentle class, claiming as its own right the freedom from "vicissi-tudes," is more than willing to take what it can from the vulgarians with the new money. Frank Cleveland inherits his elder relatives' greed, snobbery, and callousness, combining these with the cheerful spirit he shares with his friend, the stupid Lord John. Frank, the manipulator, deserves that other manipulator, Miss Percival. A more attractive successor to the Lady Louisa Larpent of

Evelina, Miss Percival indulges in affected hysteria as proof of her superior sensitivity. Her excuse for running away from the coach and throwing herself into Cleveland's arms—that she was running away from a fainting fit—is certainly novel. So, too, is her proclaimed peculiar phobia: "I have the infirmity of a terrour about old men's wigs not to be expressed" (III.89). Sighting Mr. Watts and his friend Mr. Tibbs, Miss Percival screams, "The monsters! The monsters! Wigs! The very Wigs!" (III.91), as if the male wig engulfed the person underneath, taking him over and making him monstrous. She explains that she has a "serious aversion" to wigs "for old men . . . Young men have a pretty air enough in them" (III.89). Miss Percival's odd phobia seems a reflection of Burney's sense of the import of male wigs. Miss Percival seems to object to the assumption of phallic power by old men, when they are past the fully physical virility that makes young men seriously and literally potent. The assumption of such power is monstrous and ugly. Miss Percival screams at the sight of the heroine's father, the only *father* on stage, and her reactions contribute thematically to the rejection of daddying and filiality that runs through the play.

Hardheartedness, combined with a claim to position of authority, is everywhere mocked. At the very opening, Eliza asks the hotel waiter to look after the Indian servant, and the waiter merely keeps repeating, "What, the Black?" His opinion that a "Black" is beneath notice, not quite human, is shared by Eliza's maid, Deborah, and by her sister, Peg Watts:

> La, nasty black things! I can't abide the Indins. *(sic)* I'm sure I should do nothing but squeal if I was among 'em.
>
> (I.47)

The acquaintance with Ralph Broome had given Burney, perforce, an education about India, and in his daughter Miriam she encountered a (half) Indian woman, now in some sense a member of her own family. Racial prejudice is presented at the outset of *A Busy Day* as a major example of the dominant vice examined in the play, the vice of looking down on and cutting off individuals and whole groups. Almost everyone is guilty. The vulgar Watts family is trying to rise in the world and looks down in its turn; Peg Watts tries to cut her rough kinsman Mr. Tibbs. Miss Percival, with a harshness animated by jealousy, enjoys quizzing the Watts family: "Admirable! I was sure the Father was some Tavern keeper! And the carissma sposina elect—was she educated at the Bar?" (IV.113). Burney presents radical prejudice as a natural outgrowth of English ignorance and apathy, intimately connected with the prevalent snobberies about class. The servant Deborah complacently remarks, "after all, a Black's but a Black; and let him hurt himself never so much, it won't shew. It in't like hurting us whites, with our fine skins" (I.32–33). Her notions are reflected in Lady Wilhelmina's view of the physical superiority of an upper-class person like Lord Garman to the poor laboring man whose injuries are unimportant. Frank equates an "inferior" race with membership of an "inferior" class, as is seen in his constant reference to Eliza (whom he woos for wealth) as the "little Gentoo." In *The Wanderer*, a novel apparently begun before *A Busy Day* although not finished until many years later, the heroine, when we first meet her, is disguised as a black woman, and all the objects of English contempt—racial and national otherness, poverty and femaleness—seem united in her. At least one of Burney's heroines did (temporarily) get under the other skin.

In *A Busy Day*, the dramatist's sympathy moves toward any character who is being thrust into a subordinate and inferior position. Mr. Tibbs's heavy forthrightness to his kinswomen is disagreeable enough to render him not a simply sympathetic victim of their snobbery, but when he is placed among the upperclass snobs we cheer him on as he takes revenge for the whole Watts party, who have been invited to Miss Percival's only to be derided. Joel Tibbs mimics the manners of Lady Wilhelmina's aristocratic male peers by swearing to her face, nodding familarly, throwing himself *"full length"* upon her sofa in a consummate display of exemplary bad manners. One of the themes of *Evelina*, that vulgarity is found in all classes, who reflect each other's crudities, is here rendered inescapably clear in a dramatic scene; Miss Watt's appreciative "He! He!" resembles the Branghtonian laughter at the discomfiture of Sir Clement Willoughby. The play's unstable comic sympathy, shifting to those who suffer at any time from unjust power, makes us feel with the efforts of snobs abused to counteract snobbery in control. We can even feel for Peg Watts, at a loss among the rude members of the quality: "They look as if they thought we were just a set of nobodys. Let's talk of our Coach" (V.128). Her fear of being one of a "set of nobodys" connects Peg Watts with Evelina, Cecilia, and Camilla, and with the creator of them all.

A Busy Day has been declared Burney's best play;[62] it is the lightest, most sheerly and evenly funny of her comedies, although I think *The Witlings* and *The Woman-Hater* more inventive. It may seem strange that Burney wrote her most purely comic piece in a period of deep mourning. The loss of Susanna meant a cutoff point. Frances Burney was now sundered from the member of her original family closest to her in affection. The nature of the family was radically changed for her. The temptation to sink overwhelmed into agitation and shame over James and Sarah, and into deep sorrow over Susanna, represented a danger. "Ne succombons pas" Burney wrote in her "Extracts," quoting Mme. de Staël, under the heading "The necessity to dissipate sadness." The plays show her not succumbing. The alternative to sinking in affliction was to rise to an examination of all the original problems of the old *"primitive Children,"* and the primitive family, and the codes and dictates that had bound them. The resented stepmother, the target of anger (often displaced from the father) had gone. Some real wrongs had been done to (as well as by) James and Sarah, and a great injury to Susanna in urging her to stick to her duty. *A Busy Day* offers a corrective to filial reverence, to the awe of what Eliza initially and conventionally calls "sacred ties." Sentiment meets a sharp check; strong, self-subduing filial piety is out of place, and emotional filiality is an absurd overreaction. Hardheartedness and apathy, the dangerous underreactions within the play, seem a reflection of Charles Burney's valuation of apathy in relation to the plight or disgrace of James and Sally: "he struggled only, he said, to forget." Sir Marmaduke's absurd self-pity over his little hayrick when others have lost their possessions and health is not unlike Dr. Burney's egotistical self-pity in relation to Susanna ("now she knows how I have been abandoned"). In the play, such sluggish sympathies and quick self-attention are connected with the aristocrats and their snobbery that shrugs off groups and individuals. "I feel always *democrate* where I think Power abused,"[63] Burney once wrote, and *A Busy Day* is oddly *democrate,* its ostensibly Whiggish moral tag the least important of its moral points. Charles Burney was of the *aristocrate* party, perhaps capable of writing of poor "Letitia Sourby" for the *Anti-Jacobin,* and he was a devout snob. The more pressing question in the Burneys' lives was not national politics but whether the wicked James and Sally were to be totally disdained and utterly repudiated. Charles Burney's response, as also in a lesser degree his response to Charlotte's second marriage, opened cold vistas and gave Frances Burney a glimpse of what she had always known and feared—her father's power to reject. In her creative comic work she was able to criticize such a capacity for anaesthetizing feelings, for creating partitions and hiding behind them. In *The Wanderer,* Burney was to show English society suffering (as in *A Busy Day*) from debased hierarchies, stupid snobberies, and ignorant prejudices, and from an exhaustion resulting from the application of too many negative controls. *The Wanderer* shows that keeping other people beyond the pale has high psychic, social, and moral costs, whereas in *A Busy Day* we are invited to laugh more lightly at the absurdity of individual callous characters.

The last of Burney's three late comedies is strongly related to her first comedy, *The Witlings,* whose suppression had illustrated the powers of rejection. Burney had perhaps never quite given over *The Witlings.* An examination of the packet of manuscript notes, now bound up with *The Woman-Hater* in the Berg Collection, suggests that perhaps all these late comedies grew out of earlier efforts to rewrite and salvage the first play. There are fragments of a play containing some characters whose names are the same as names found in *Love and Fashion* and *A Busy Day* (Dawson, Sir Marmaduke), although other characters in this fragmentary piece are our old friends from *The Witlings,* such as Lady Smatter, Jack, Codger, and Censor. As in the first play, Cecilia Stanley is in love with Beaufort, but comes to believe him false. The really new character is Sir Marmaduke, Cecilia's uncle and guardian, who treats her badly. Unlike the apathetic personage of the same name in *A Busy Day,* the Sir Marmaduke of the post-*Witlings* fragment is outrageously choleric. This Sir Marmaduke, a misogynist, is (like Samuel Crisp?) somewhat reclusive and misanthropic. He lets his unwanted guests, who are trying to find out what happened to Cecilia, know exactly what he thinks of them:

> S^r. Marm[aduke]. My visitors may all go to New York, & I wish they were there already! What the D——I, are people to force themselves into my House, & to take possession of my Rooms . . . & then to teach me how to behave to them into the Bargain? Why at this rate a Man that has Mansion [sic] of his own must be a Slave to all the World. . . .
> If I c^d. but find out what you all want, I might give ye an Answer; but I begin to think you come for nothing on Earth but just to put me out of my way. . . .
> Cen[sor]. Favour me, then, with a specimen of y^r. manners when *not* put out of y^r. way. I am really curious to see the Workings of Nature upon y^r. Mind, when you do not, as at present, hold y^r. self to be fettered by the niceties of punctilio, or restrained by the daintiness of decorum.
> S^r. Marm. I have no more notion, now, where that little Fool can be gone—
> Cen. Than you have Solicitude, if I may judge by the severity with which you drove her from y^r. House.
> S^r. Marm. Severity? pray what do you call severity? I suppose I must not speak to my own Niece next! Why I have talked to the Girl 100 Times; & she Minded it no more than if I had Whistled; but now she's got among these Readers & Writers they've given her such a cursed Set of new-fangled notions, that she's off at a Word. I drive her from my House indeed!—why I don't believe she's out of it now, unless my Scoundrel Servants have let her go.[64]

Sir Marmaduke, the absurd blusterer who misuses his paternal position, here replaces *The Witlings*'s Lady Smatter as the dominant character in opposition to the heroine. His contradictory fondness for driving a person away and at the same time keeping a tight hold over her (the servants would be scoundrels to let her go) is reminiscent of some behavior well-known to Burney in real life. By the end of the century, three of the Burney daughters (Charlotte, Susanna, and Sarah Harriet) had all been in some measure and some sense "driven away" by the parent who could boast of striving with his "utmost power" to "drive—force them [Sarah and James] from my thought!" The new play, with its blustering Sir Marmaduke at the center, replaces the action of *The Witlings* (which has no family ties except the relation of a nephew to his aunt) with a central conflict between a father-figure and a surrogate daughter who has acquired "new-fangled notions" of feminine literacy and even, apparently, of rights and independence.

These efforts to revise *The Witlings* (a play metaphorically driven out of the house) eventually bore fruit in *The Woman-Hater*. Except for Lady Smatter, the characters from the first comedy have by now disappeared. The Sir Marmaduke of the fragment has changed into Sir Roderick, the bad-tempered misogynist. The last of these comic dramas goes back to much earlier works, *Evelina* and *The Witlings*, transforming them and subjecting them to a new analysis. Drama was always for Burney a means of dealing with new experience. Even *The Witlings* was the result of its author's being introduced to new groups, and of her taking a new kind of place within her society. The Windsor and Kew tragedies had assisted Burney in coping with the terrifying experience of incarceration and privation. She turned to drama again in a period when life again battered her, altered her circumstances, and violently forced her to change her emotional outlook. *Love and Fashion*, begun after the death of Burney's stepmother, was completed during the era of the first shock over the incestuous affair of Sarah and James. That situation by no means resolved itself during this period of comedy writing (the errant pair were still together when Burney moved to France). *A Busy Day* succeeded the shattering death of Susanna. Amid all this pain and turmoil, Burney refused to turn again to tragedy as an outlet; evidently tragedies were to her sacred to *inner* conflict. As Burney herself felt more assured, less fragmented than in the years at court, she was no longer the accomplice of external demands, no longer the self-divided victim of rules and duties. In her new comedies, she questions the systems of social behavior and prescribed responses, as well as exhibiting in various characters a number of well-observed modes of deficient response to other human beings. The first two of these late comedies are determinedly light and conventional in plot, tone, and character type. Burney is not yet willing to reach the mythic level as she had done in her most recent novel, *Camilla*. The last of these three comedies, however, shows a blending of some of the concerns of the tragedies, and of themes and images of *Camilla*, with the interests and manners of the preceding two comedies. *The Woman-Hater* is a nodal work, taking account of a great deal of Burney's earlier fiction, narrative and mimetic, and trying to resolve issues in these other works and in the author's life.

The Woman-Hater, offspring of the suppressed play, crowns a trilogy of comedies that examine injustice, separation, and inadequate or inappropriate responses. In *The Woman-Hater*, Burney explored the Burney "Family Romance," and began to work more clearly and overtly than before with some of the complexities of parental, filial, and sexual relations. *The Woman-Hater*, of all Burney's works, most fully expresses discontent at the daughterly relationship, and most openly asks whether something has not gone grievously wrong.

When *The Woman-Hater* opens, we find that the bachelor Sir Roderick has named a distant relative, Young Waverley, as his heir, on condition that he forswear women and matrimony forever. Young Waverley, already interested in the beautiful daughter of a widow living nearby, finds the condition hard, but is warned by his father that he must accept it. Old Waverley is a natural toady:

"it's all for your sake that I pocket being treated so like a dog by him, & that I am so contented to see you treated like a puppy" (I.i.4–5).[65] Sir Roderick is a woman-hater because the former Miss Wilmot, now the widow Lady Smatter, jilted him in former years. Sir Roderick then disowned his own sister Eleanora because she married Lady Smatter's brother, Mr. Wilmot. Eleanora, so they have heard, ran away from her husband years ago, leaving her baby daughter with its father. Mr. Wilmot is now returning from the West Indies with his nearly grown-up daughter. Old Waverly fears that the arriving niece might succeed in winning her uncle over, despite his misogyny: "Girls are very apt to be wheedling" (I.i.7).

Sir Roderick's bad temper is thoroughly exhibited in many outbursts. Lady Smatter (*rediviva*, but not as amusing as in *The Witlings,* and now deprived of her town circle) is foolishly literary, complacent, and very susceptible to flattery. Sir Roderick's Steward (who has designs of his own on his employer's estate) encourages Young Waverley to make up to the mature Lady Smatter, for the sake of her "noble mansion & jointure" (I.iii.13), as he knows any hint of his heir's connection with his former love will guarantee Sir Roderick's wrath and immediate disinheritance. Young Waverley's advances have some effect on Lady Smatter, though she waits for some sign of returning affection from Sir Roderick.

Mr. Wilmot, newly arrived from the West Indies, hopes to bring his daughter to the favorable attention of her aunt. When we first see father and daughter in the room at an inn, Wilmot is gloomy and preoccupied. He has recently discovered that his wife, Eleanora, was innocent of the infidelity for which he drove her from him, and he feels private remorse. His daughter, Miss Wilmot, has been strictly brought up; she seems quiet, docile, and stiff, under the influence of improving books. But when her father goes out, and she is left on her own with the Nurse and Bob and Jenny Sapling, Miss Wilmot shows her true nature—she is a perfect hoyden.

The vanished mother, Eleanora, supposed a runaway, independently comes to Lady Smatter to plead her own cause. Lady Smatter is a long time in recognizing "the hapless, persecuted, fugitive Eleanora" (II.viii.26), and when she does at last know her, utters strictures on "the confidence of Vice" (II.viii.28). Eleanora explains that it is Lady Smatter's brother who should be penitent for his insane and causeless jealousy on the voyage out. When Lady Smatter tells her that Wilmot has arrived, his wife fears he comes with "confirmed hate." Lady Smatter's reactions to these revelations is inappropriately sedate.

At the beginning of Act III, Eleanora in her cottage is revealed to be the widow to whose beautiful daughter Young Waverley has been attracted. Eleanora tells her daughter, Sophia, the story of her separation from Mr. Wilmot, and reveals that the mother has her daughter against the father's express command: "when I begged thee of him, his refusal was so peremptory, so disgraceful, & so heart-breaking, I could not submit to it" (III.ii.4). Eleanora persuaded the Nurse to give her the baby, in effect stealing her own daughter from its father, the legal guardian. Eleanora has always been puzzled that there was no pursuit and no endeavor to retake the child. After her failure to win Lady Smatter, she feels separated irrevocably from her family and her husband. Sophia suggests that she herself go to her Uncle Roderick and plead for recognition.

Another claimant for notice, Mr. Wilmot's child, is introduced to Lady Smatter. In her father's presence, Miss Wilmot is silent, only curtseying when spoken to. Her father explains that she is "simple & unpolished, fearful as the Hare . . . invincibly shy, pensive, & nearly mute" (III.viii.24). Lady Smatter agrees to take the timid girl under her roof, but as soon as Mr. Wilmot leaves she is dumbfounded by the abrupt disappearance of all the girl's bashfulness. Miss Wilmot's good-natured impudence and loquacity drive her aunt out of the room. Miss Wilmot happily regales herself with her aunt's "classics"—which she takes to be the bonbons in the cupboard—until interrupted by her tearful Nurse. Nurse tells the girl the dreadful truth: she is not Mr. Wilmot's daughter, but the child of Nurse and "a journeyman Shoe-maker." Her real name is not Sophia Wilmot but Joyce. The former Miss Wilmot begins rapidly to see the cheerful side of this news.

Hearing of his wife's presence in the neighborhood, Mr. Wilmot intends to try for a reconciliation, but when he finds Eleanora has a daughter living with her, he decides this is a love-child, and anger flares again. Rival visits by Old and Young Waverley, both pursuing Sophia, complicate scenes at Eleanora's cottage. Sir Roderick, having caught sight of some verses Young Waverley was sending to Lady Smatter, decides to disinherit him. The steward puts in a good word for his own nephew, Bob Sapling's heir, but even Bob has plans for sharing his hoped-for fortune with a female (Joyce), to Sir Roderick's intense disgust.

A young woman who says (ambiguously) that she's been told she's his niece tries to coax a few thousand pounds out of Sir Roderick. Joyce assures him that she will spend all the money on tarts and dances and plays—and almost succeeds in her object when she promises to make "a large, huge, gigantic bonfire of all Aunt Smatter's Books" (V.iv.8). Sophia, arriving shortly afterwards to plead her cause, is taken for an imposter. Sir Roderick tells Young Waverley he may marry the real niece (Joyce) but not the imposter (Sophia). The Nurse is glad that Joyce has escaped detection, but when Joyce understands that there is a real Miss Wilmot, she insists on revealing the truth.

Joyce interrupts an angry scene between Eleanora and Mr. Wilmot, the husband threatening to shut his wife away and take her child of lawless love (Sophia) from her. Joyce brings about a clarification and reconciliation by explaining all she knows. She tells all with a splendid, though not selfless, generosity. She wants to lead her own kind of life. She will marry Bob Sapling. Young Waverley will marry Sophia. Mr. and Mrs. Wilmot are reunited at last, as are Lady Smatter and Sir Roderick.

The story is a variant version of *A Winter's Tale,* from the daughter's point of view. The Father is reunited with the Daughter whom he last saw as an infant, after years of separation caused by his jealousy. But in this case the Father also casts off the Daughter he has been trying to shape and mold, allowing her to go her own way. The plot focuses on an event in the past—the breakdown of a marriage. Mr. Wilmot's version is that his wife abandoned him. Miss Wilmot (Joyce) is brought up to believe that she has been an abandoned child, that her mother left her: "My Mamma ran away" (IV.viii.13). Burney was evidently digging quite deep into her own past when she wrote this play. Eleanora, who as a persecuted fugitive seems a revision of Elberta, is the only character in any of Burney's completed writings who seems clearly to represent Esther Sleepe Burney, the mother who departed so long ago. In her dramatic fable, Burney can provide a consolation: the mother did not die, and did not run away from her daughter. The daughter was never left to the care of the Father; Mother and Daughter have always been together. (This is true in the case of Nurse and Joyce as well as of Eleanora and Sophia.) In the story of Eleanora, too, we can see Burney dimly and unconsciously making amends to Mrs. Thrale, whom she had long ago accused of heartlessly abandoning her daughters. Once the true story is known, the woman is justified, and the aspersions cast on her character are both false and irrelevant. It is the conduct of the Father, though rigidly upright and "moral," that is mistaken, and the law promulgated by the Father, a law of decree and exclusions, is serving only to fragment the family. Matters will get worse unless the Daughter can help—but she can only help by proving she is not the Daughter. Paradoxically, she must get outside the situation, as Joyce can, before she can help, as Joyce does.

The play really divides the role of the Daughter into two characters. There is the shadowy, if lovely and ideally good daughter, Sophia, and the awkward, physical, un-ideal Joyce. Joyce, the most appealing character in the play, is hearty and life-affirming. It is pleasant to see her burst through the folly and negativity and exclusiveness around her. She horrifies her "aunt," Lady Smatter, by telling her "what I'd do, if I had no Children, & was as old as you are." She would pick up some poor beggar's brat and clean it and "bring it up for my own." "You can't think," Joyce says frankly, "how I hate a house without Children." Her aunt inquires coldly, "Perhaps you hate every thing?" and brings upon herself the torrential list of Joyce's enthusiastic likings:

> *Miss Wilmot.* O no, I don't. I like a great many things, but my first best favourite of all is dancing. It makes one so light, & so blyth, & so gaysome, & so skipping! . . . Well, & the second next best thing that I like is singing. Can you sing, Aunt? . . . I sing, sometimes, do you know, Aunt, from Morning to Night? O, it makes the house all alive! But that's only when Papa's out.
>
> *Lady Smatter.* I am glad, at least, you are so considerate to his nerves.
> . . .
> *Miss Wilmot.* Perhaps you think I've told you all? Why there's an

hundred things besides! There's walking—& there's running,—& there's jumping— ... And then, when one's famished, & empty,—how delightful are minced veal, and Pancakes!—

(III.x.30–34)

Lively and physical Joyce, who can sing "only when Papa's out," knows she is a disappointment to her "father" but she cannot understand him. Natural rebellion comes to the fore, as when Mr. Wilmot leaves the inn room in Act II and she jumps up and sings, flinging away the improving books:

> So march off, Mr. Thompson! decamp, Mrs. Chapone! . . . & off! off! with a hop, skip, & a jump, ye Ramblers, spectators, & Adventurers! . . . Why Nurse, Papa's so dismal dull! always setting one to study! I wonder what's the use of Books, Nurse? If Papa had as many words of his own as I have, he would not be always wanting to be poring over other people's so. I can find enough to say of myself. And I'm sure that's cleverer.

(II.iii.10–13)

Mr. Wilmot may be urging books upon a young lady, but his notion of the young lady's reading suspiciously resembles that of Mr. Compton Delville, who discourages any female reading outside the proper bounds: "The Spectator, Tatler, and Guardian would make library sufficient for any female in the kingdom" (*Cecilia*, II:186). As we have seen, in the ur-*Camilla* Burney had attempted to create a scene in which a young woman ("Cleora") proves herself ill-conditioned and unworthy by not responding to the books with which her suitor ("Gunniston") enthusiastically tries to educate her. But however appropriate a true love of reading might be to a really sympathetic heroine, Burney could never bring herself to produce the scene in which a woman is seriously put down by a man for her lack of interest in reading what interests him. Something subversive in Burney always showed her the danger of the male indoctrination of the female. Reading urged by the male has too much of power and the Law about it. In *The Woman-Hater*, that is definitely so; Mr. Wilmot is using his culture to browbeat and tame his resisting daughter, who has health of mind enough to reject the dutiful essays and good conduct-books. "Decamp, Mrs. Chapone!" Burney might recollect not only Mrs. Chapone's *Letters on the Improvement of the Mind*, but Mrs. Chapone herself, and the evening when Frances Burney and George Cambridge had been "in too high spirits for her *seriousity*, & rattled away without minding her."[66] Burney herself had had "words of her own," though she had not been able to say them all, in the conflict between Nature and the World. Joyce has little allegiance to the "World." When she is told by her mother, the Nurse, that if the truth comes out, Joyce will have to be a kitchenmaid or a ballad singer, the girl is at first shocked, but rapidly adjusts to the new prospects:

Miss Wilmot. O Nurse! Nurse! *bursting into Tears,* How could you serve me so? Setting me up for a lady, only to be made Game of! What must I do?—what will become of me?—I can't scrub rooms—& I won't scrub rooms! *sobbing* And I can't turn ballad singer, &—yes, I can, though! *suddenly brightening* That I can, Nurse! & if I must be something—I had rather be a ballad singer than any thing else. . . .

Nurse. O, don't play tricks now, Miss! but let's see what we can get from Sir Roderick before we're discovered.

Miss Wilmot. Lend me your handkerchief, Nurse. There! that's to be tied under my Chin. Now lend me your apron . . . There! that's to be tied so, & then swung up round me, so. There! Now I must stuff up my Nose as if I were snuffy.

Miss Wilmot. Now for my ballad.

Takes a ballad from her Pocket.

(IV.viii.16–17)

The energetic and physical Joyce strongly resembles the "idiot" girl whom Mr. Tyrold made his daughters observe. Like that unnamed girl in *Camilla* fond of physical motion and gesture, she, too, runs, jumps, dances, sobs, laughs. Joyce, like the "idiot," ties her head up in a handkerchief in order to make her own noise. The false Miss Wilmot of *The Woman-Hater* is of course not imbecilic, and not mad; she is really the "idiot" re-read, or seen the right way. Joyce insists that women have physical urges, bodies to be satisfied, appetites— all the things that Mr. Wilmot and Lady Smatter try to suppress. They try to quench in her the natural enjoyment of life. For Joyce, everything is bearable, everything is fun, except the life her father wants her to lead. The one truly unendurable prospect is being left alone with Mr. Wilmot:

O, la, Nurse, I won't be left to live with Papa, when he knows he i'n't Papa! read, read, reading!—I'd sooner be off with you [. . .] I'd sooner . . . marry Bob!— . . . I shall like that a great deal better than always studying Books; & sitting with my hands before me, & making Courtsies; & never eating half as much as I like,—except in the Pantry!—

(V.xii.21–22)

Appetite thwarted figures in the tragedies, in the fear that Adela will be the first to go "unnourished," in Elberta's fear that her children will starve. Joyce will not be a good starving child; she will find independence and eat as much as she likes, not a ladylike allowance. She will also make her own choice in sex and marriage; she decides briskly upon Bob, thus exerting the right to choose what all Burney's heroines wish for.

The unmasking of Joyce as false daughter is her way to freedom. Her "father" does not detect her as a cheat; she detects herself. It will readily be seen that the central situation in *The Woman-Hater* is strongly similar to that in *Evelina*, in which the true daughter's place has been taken by an imposter, the "bantling of Dame Green, wash-woman and wet nurse" (*Evelina*, III:378). But in the play of 1801, it is the imposter who really interests, and whose fortunes we are to follow, whereas the "real" daughter is a relatively dull and shadowy character. It is as if Burney rewrote *Evelina* from the view of "the little usurper," "poor Polly Green" (*Ibid.*). In the novel, the real daughter convinces her father of her identity and thus, in company with the father, detects the imposter. In the play, the father is unmoved by his real daughter even when he sees her, until the "usurper" spontaneously brings them together, frankly giving up a position which is not only uncoveted by her but truly disliked. Sir John Belmont, metamorphosed into another rigid and rejecting parent, Mr. Wilmot, is *not* a desirable father. The play defies the conventions of the novel's "serious" plot. Evelina is at last in a position to acquire her paternal name and a father. Joyce recovers her real name (a maternal name, a first name only) by losing the (false) paternal name. The audience is, of course, to be misled as to the name and identity of the character whom we know at the beginning as "Miss Wilmot." Sophia is referred to only by her first name, Mr. Wilmot's supposed child only by her last name. The two cross over, change positions, Sophia acquiring her tribal last name and the false "Miss Wilmot" a lively first name. In *The Wanderer* Burney will keep us in the dark as to the heroine's real name until halfway through the novel; the device is first explored in *The Woman-Hater*.

Joyce is in an enviable position in that she can *generously* and of her own accord cast off the Father. With the dissolution of the inhibiting old bond, Joyce has a new freedom. There is a special poignancy in her recognition of that freedom: "why I a'n't afraid to speak to him now he i'n't Papa!" (V.xvi.31). *The Woman-Hater* exhibits a rebellious desire to cast off the trammels of the father-daughter relationship—or of that relationship as it had been—for the good of both father and daughter. Burney seems to be suggesting that the Father should reexamine his own sexual life, his relations with his wife (or both wives), and with his children in order to see them in proper perspective and to recover the vital relationship. He also needs to recapture true joy and spontaneity (represented in the play by rejoicing Joyce). But the recovery of true joy can come about only through the acknowledgment of the truth. Something in the Father's real self has been concealed from him, and he must find it. Only then can the sexual and emotional misery which threatens all those connected to him be removed.

In the titular "woman-hater," the "foamy & stormy" Sir Roderick, Burney portrayed the extreme forms of comic masculine anger at and disparagement of women. The misogynist's views, though in some ways patently absurd, are not entirely out of step with those of the rest of the world:

Why, what does a woman spend her life in? D'ye know? Doing nothing but mischief; talking nothing but nonsense [*sic*], & listening to nothing but flattery! Sitting, with her two hands before her, all day long, to be waited on; & sighing & moping, because her noodle pate can't hit upon things to give trouble fast enough!

(IV.xvi.40)

Have not you heard me tell him, an hundred times, the whole Sex was good for nothing? A poor feeble, puling, useless Race! changing their minds every half hour; with more freaks in their composition than blood, or bones; fit for nothing but making faces at bad dinners, & squalling at bad roads; & so helpless, if they fall into a ditch they are drowned,—& if you don't put the meat into their Mouths, they are starved!

(IV.iii.5)

What Sir Roderick says, many men thought. The weak-bodied, complaining middle-class woman had been strongly attacked by Mary Wollstonecraft, though she sees this type as the result of a certain kind of bad education.[67] There is something to be said for Sir Roderick's antipathy to such feeble creatures, though his remedy would simply be the imposition of greater ignorance ("Women writing Letters! What can they have to say?" [I.ix.25]). The feeble indolent creature is what Mr. Wilmot is really trying to rear. What Sir Roderick (or Mary Wollstonecraft, or Frances Burney) detests is what Joyce is trying to escape: "always studying Books; & sitting with my hands before me, & making Courtsies." Joyce's antipathy to the limited stylized behavior recalls Burney's own parodic sense of an etiquette that forbids one to sneeze and her horrified amusement at the court etiquette which requires immobility and self-mutilation. Joyce has no intention of becoming the proper, limited, bored and boring personage. She will rather work as a ballad singer, or as a housewife married to Bob Sapling, than be such a lady. Her version of housewifery includes feeding herself; in energy and appetite is eternal rejoicing.

Sir Roderick would like women, even ladies, to be only housewives, dutifully to clothe themselves and humbly to feed others:

Women ought to be ashamed of talking much jargon; what can their little heads make out of such matters? What do they know? And what ought they to know? Except to sew a Gown, & make a Pudding?

Old Waverley. Two very good things, Sir Roderick; very very good things; serving outside & inside.

(I.ix.25–26)

The traditional phrase "makes a Pudding" is old shorthand for woman knowing her place in the domestic spere. It is no endorsement of woman's own appetite. Burney ridicules the phrase, with its halo of meaning, connecting it with the patronizing view of women's "little heads" and showing the whole structure of male superiority and the attitudes of condescending denigration as ludicrous. Sir Roderick's prejudices against women are, as the play points out, the result of personal rejection and fear of sexual failure. Sir Roderick is a Dr. Marchmont made laughable. The most clearly defined misogynist in Burney's works, Sir Roderick is the most harmless, the one most readily to be laughed at and reformed. He belongs in a long line of Burney's "woman-haters" beginning with Captain Mirvan, Mr. Smith and the fops of *Evelina*, and continuing in *Cecilia*'s Mr. Delville and Mr. Hobson, through St. Dunstan and King William (in the tragedies), to Clermont Lynmere and Dr. Marchmont. "Woman-hating" is central to all Burney's works. In her next novel, *The Wanderer*, Burney was to show another array of "woman-haters" who increase the difficulties of the heroine at the very time she is trying *not* to be helpless, and is endeavoring to put meat into her own mouth, to do seriously what Joyce more lightly considers—to earn her own living in preference to starving.

Who is the real "woman-hater" in *The Woman-Hater*? Comic Sir Roderick is overtly intolerant of women, an outrageous misogynist, though his attitudes are partly endorsed by society. In the light cast by Sir Roderick, we can see the more dangerous Mr. Wilmot, who seriously mistreats several women. The "serious" character is an unconscious "woman-hater," whose responses, like those of his boisterous counterpart, are rooted in psychological pain and confusion.[68] Wilmot's repressive responses are, however, considered respectable and, unlike Sir Roderick's, may pass without notice. Mr. Wilmot represents the more normal forms of woman-hating in the world Frances Burney knew: disapproval of feminine wishes; dictatorship over feminine conduct; censorship of female utterance; fraternal, filial, and marital coldness. Mr. Wilmot's conduct is essentially banal, even though he has his Gothic moments, as when (like the bad husband in Mary Wollstonecraft's *The Wrongs of Woman*) he wants to shut his wife away and take her child. He wants his women to shut up. He is pleased at the fact that his supposed daughter is "invincibly shy, pensive, & nearly mute." Mr. Wilmot is not alone in his preference: Burney had marked long before men's Rosseauean interest in the female's "Timid air," the downcast eye, blushing cheek, and silence. Mr. Wilmot prefers this version of his girl-child, the shy dumb creature, just as Dr. Burney unconsciously cultivated the shyness of "little Fan." The child Fanny Burney was shy in the presence of her elders. It was with her playmates, her contemporaries, that she was "so merry, so gay, so droll, & had such imagination in making plays"[69]—that is, she was like Joyce once the inhibiting presence of Mr. Wilmot is removed.

The Woman-Hater proposes that the barriers of shyness, silence, and misunderstanding should be broken down. But the process would have to start with the father. The daughter could assist by being her real self to him—though that is a self the father would find a cheat, a false changeling, because it would not accord with his idealized version of his daughter and her filial feelings. At one level of private meaning in the play, the mournful mother Eleanora and her daughter are shadows of an ideal, as well as shades of the past, the shades of

Dr. Burney's lost loves, his wife Esther and his daughter Susanna. In the play, as not in the *Memoirs*, Burney admits that the departed sister, not herself (though her other self) was the favored daughter. There is guilt involved in the recognition, for Frances (like the bouncy Joyce) was a survivor, and survived her sister, in that sense usurping her place. Beyond either jealousy or guilt, there is the generous impulse to set free the living and the dead by asking that the real relationships be examined and taken for what they are. Burney herself is tired of being prudent wisdom (Sophia) and wants to be joyfulness (Joyce), living her own life, unafraid of her capacity for enduring and rejoicing. The task of familial restoration lies at hand. The insistence on isolating offenders, "forgetting" and rejecting, as well as the sustained silence about important things and the endeavors to drive those once loved from thought, only institute confusion and add to the general familial pain and separation.

The three comedies, actable plays in the way the tragedies are not, fulfill a function of private allegory as well as of public comic statement. Each of these three plays shows the rupture of some bond, and the opportunity to escape from some oppressive or irrelevant demands. Hilaria Dalton of *Love and Fashion* has the easiest conditions of any of the heroines, for beyond the very cool relation to her guardian she has no filial attachment; she helps her lover Valentine escape from bearing all the sins of his elder brother, though she first attempts this by a sexual sacrifice of herself in a marriage to the lord. Hilaria, whose name means "laughter," is witty and sophisticated, and acts with her eyes open. She is a little like the Lady Honoria of *Cecilia* combined with the spritely idea of an "Ariella," a mercurial, airy, spontaneous heroine that Burney always wanted to create and never quite brought into being. Eliza Watts, though wealthy and thus independent, is neither witty nor sophisticated, though she is decisive. Eliza has the burden of both her idealized (and culturally derived) notion of filial duty and her very unideal embarrassment at her actual family. She has to free herself from both the ideal and the embarrassment, and she can then free her lover from the absurd demands of his family. In each successive play, the ties binding the heroine become more important, and the breaks more serious. Joyce is in the hardest position of confinement and obligation, and springs farthest in order to get free. Joyce has none of the detachment of Hilaria, none of the financial independence of Eliza. The youngest of the three heroines, with no position in the world at all, she is set the most difficult task.

All of these three comedies examine the curious truths concealed in underreaction, coldness, prejudice, rejection. *Love and Fashion* has its "ghost", but all three plays are haunted by specters of the past. *The Woman-Hater* exhibits less emphasis than the other two plays on social snobberies and pretensions for their own comic sake, and more interest in the disturbances that create the defense mechanism of hatred, snobbery, and prejudice. The relation of *The Woman-Hater* to its immediate predecessor, *A Busy Day*, seems parallel to the relation of *Camilla* to the more outer-directed *Cecilia*.

It is sad that none of these comedies was staged. Burney seems to have hoped that Harris would initiate a new production of *Love and Fashion* in the spring of 1801. She wrote to her sister Esther, "even yet I know not what is purposed as to *time,* or even whether at ANY it will be heard of!" She adds that her "Agent" (brother Charles) is *"dead silent"* and her own "wishes & desires about it" nearly "in the same insensible state." The numbing of desire "keeps me patient in an ignorance that—15 months ago, would have kept me on the rack." She adds that she has insisted that the play should not be given under her name, with "a renewed insistance on *incog,* if any trial is made."[70] She is clearly prepared for the play to go forward, if only somebody else would do something about it. But Harris needed some pushing and reminding, presumably some enthusiasm from the Burney side—the author had, after all, let him down once before. Burney takes too passive and negative a line. Part of the numbness of desire was caused by going over all Susanna's old papers, and recovering from continuing grief and fresh recollections. But it is evident also that the insistence upon *"incog."* related to Dr. Burney's attitude to Burney's engagement in the theater. There was no reason to believe that his "unaccountable and most afflicting displeasure" at his daughter's writing comedies had abated. If in 1800 he made Burney feel that he saw her as "guilty of a crime" for coming out with a comedy, it would still be hard for her to have a play produced in 1801. It is a sad irony that her outspoken and rebellious comedies should still be subject to internal suppression and parental censorship. It was to be easier to smuggle anti-Revolutionary manuscripts past Napoleon's soldiers than to smuggle a comic play out to the public past Dr. Burney's barriers. Yet Frances Burney still did intend to have a play produced; she kept writing her comedies, and it was the removal to France that put out of the question any further negotiation with the theater managers.

The meaning of her comedies was not forgotten by Burney in her last great novel, *The Wanderer: or Female Difficulties,* for which the plays were in some measure a preparation. The novel shows us a woman-hating and a woman-suppressing society in which "Female Difficulties" abound. Earning a living and making a choice in love (satisfying the appetites) are not easily to be done with Joyce's naïve assertiveness, but the issues of independence, choice, and freedom, so prominent in the comedies (and particularly in the last) are everywhere in evidence. In the last novel, barriers, coldness, rejections, inadequate responses have national and international consequences in an era of revolution and war.

The Wanderer; or, Female Difficulties:
Revolution, the Rights
of Woman, and "The Wild Edifice"

During the dire reign of the terrific Robespierre, and in the dead of night, braving the cold, the darkness and the damps of December, some English passengers, in a small vessel, were preparing to glide silently from the coast of France, when a voice of keen distress resounded from the shore, imploring, in the French language, pity and admission.[1]

This is the first sentence of *The Wanderer*, and a strong opening to a tale, plunging us into the middle of an adventure and a historical crisis. The manuscript itself had, like its heroine, made an escape from France. As Burney says in the prefatory dedication, "the early part" of the work had "already twice traversed the ocean in manuscript"; its origins were both French and English. Burney explains to her public that her novel was begun "before the end of the last century" but that "bitter . . . affliction" (the death of Susanna) "cast it from my thoughts . . . for many years." She took the manuscript with her to France "where, ultimately . . . I sketched the whole work; which, in the year 1812, accompanied me back to my native land."[2] Her emphasis on the work's history shows how intimately she connected it with her own history.

Frances Burney ardently desired to be able to return to her "native land" and to the family from whom war had separated her. She suffered the pain of exile during her residence in France; she was later to say, "my forced absence from my dear Country, & all to which I was natively & tenderly attached was a constant worm that eat . . . into my peace of mind."[3] She felt at first strange and shy in the new country, and her husband's enforced daily absences at the office were an unwelcome novelty. She had much to occupy her in becoming acquainted with d'Arblay's relations and managing her small household on a small income. She also had to help to oversee Alex's education. At first, the child's health was delicate and he worked at home, tutored by his parents; he then attended a village school. In 1805 the d'Arblays moved to Paris, to the rue du Faubourg St. Honoré; in Paris Alex had to attend a large school. Here his coming first in his class won some unfavorable attention from other boys. (Perhaps Alex later, in his Cambridge days, felt he had done too much prize-winning in these early schooldays in France, in order to please his ambitious parents.) Alex, winning his crowns of laurel and volumes of Racine at prize-giving, was now becoming a French schoolboy. He wrote verses for his mother in proper French hexameters (with classical names thrown in), as we can see in the birthday greetings he fashioned for her when he was twelve years old (Fig. 30).

Burney's life was brightened by new friends, and no one more valued than Mme. de Maisonneuve, sister of d'Arblay's closest friend, Victor de Latour-Maubourg. The aristocratic Marie-Françoise-Elizabeth Bidault de Maisonneuve, whom Burney first admired for "native dignity" and "highly principled mind," was another poverty-stricken royalist in Napoleonic France; she lived in tiny quarters with her son, Maxime, Alex's playfellow. Burney later said their relationship was immediately "frank & friendly" and gave rise to "the tenderest & most unreserved affection on both sides. The obligations I owe to her are countless—Countless! . . . A more devoted friendship can hardly be imagined."[4] The editors of Burney's Journals think she was not aware that Mme. de Maisonneuve was divorced,[5] but, even if she did not know this in 1802, there is no reason to believe that such a devoted friendship ultimately excluded the truth about the absent emigrant husband. After the experiences of Maria, Charlotte, and Susanna, Burney had no need to look harshly upon full legal separation of unhappy spouses. Divorce, such as modern France offered, did not entail the wife's adultery. Pious Mme. de Maisonneuve led an exemplary life, and had something of the sweetness of Susanna. "How I love to love her!"[6] Burney exclaimed in 1804. With affection and friendship, the pleasures of attending the theater and reading works of French literature such as Gil Blas aloud at home, life was more than bearable. Burney began to write industriously. A diary section entitled "Scribleration" shows that in 1806 she was well advanced in the first draft of The Wanderer;[7] cryptic notes such as "Humours of a Milliner's Shop" and "Introduction to Toad Eating" show that she was working on the sections in the middle of the book in which the heroine earns her own living.

Pain and danger interrupted the writing. Burney developed swelling in the breast, for which both her husband and her friend Mme. de Maisonneuve urged her to seek medical assistance. She was diagnosed as having cancer in the right breast. On 30 September 1811, she underwent a radical mastectomy. The operation took place in her own home; she did not inform her husband at the time, and cheated him into going out. Mme. de Maisonneuve humbly waited *"in the Kitchen!* & there, dissolved in tears, she spent the whole time of my agony, & afterwards nearly the rest of the day, in case female assistance . . . should be wanted."[8] The courage involved in daring to endure such an operation as Burney underwent can hardly be exaggerated; the ordeal is a testimony to her desire to hold onto life. The twenty-minute operation was performed without an anaesthetic. When the knife went in, "cutting through veins — arteries — flesh — nerves — . . . I began a scream that lasted unintermittingly during the whole time of the incision — & I almost marvel that it rings not in my Ears still!" Although she fainted twice during the process ("two total chasms in my memory"), she was agonizingly conscious during most of the procedure, feeling "the instrument — describing a curve — cutting against the grain, if I may so say, while the flesh resisted in a manner so forcible as to oppose & tire the hand of the operator."[9] Burney wrote a complete account addressed to her sister Esther, though she heroically wished the matter kept secret from the newly widowed Frederica Locke, and from her father. As soon as the slow process of recovery had fairly begun, the desire to see home and family again increased. The terrible episode reminded her of mortality, not only her own but of those she loved. In the shadow of mortality *The Wanderer* was completed.

There were practical reasons for a trip to England. Camilla Cottage, the land of which now belonged to William Locke the younger, had to be seen to. (The d'Arblays eventually had to sell the cottage to William Locke for less than it had cost to build). The payments of the queen's pension had to be inquired after; it proved that Dr. Burney had got these entangled with his own financial transactions. Even more pressing was the fate of young Alex, now nearing the age of conscription; neither parent wished him to fight against his mother's country. But a visit to England required permission — and that seemed impossible to obtain. The departure of Napoleon for Russia led, oddly, to some easing of restrictions, or more likely to mere confusion on the part of the bureaucracy. The d'Arblays were able to get permission for both Frances and Alex to depart, after softening the acting chief of police, M. de Saulnier, with the *douceur* of a signed copy of *Evelina*, which de Saulnier indicated would make an acceptable present for his daughter.[10] The police chief knew that Mme. d'Arblay and her son wished to go to England, but the fact was not admissible; the pretense was that they were to visit the United States. Frances had to take a passage on a ship flying the American flag, although the captain intended to land a number of passengers privately at Dover.

Frances and Alex waited at Dunkirk for weeks while their vessel, the prosaically named *Mary Anne,* signed up passengers and waited for clearance from French officials. During this period of inactivity, Frances thought of her novel which, surprisingly, she had not planned to take with her. She wrote her "PARTNER IN ALL" to send the manuscript, and that again required permission. M. d'Arblay again waited on de Saulnier at the Police Office and asked that the manuscript might be sent, and might be taken on board the ship. De Saulnier "on being assured, upon his [d'Arblay's] Honour, that the Work had nothing in it political, nor even National, nor possibly offensive to the Government . . . invested him with the power to send me what papers he pleased." The manuscript papers already "filled a small portmanteau, in which M. d'Arblay packed them up with as much delicacy of care as if every page had been a Bank note."[11] D'Arblay always appreciated her writing, and saw her work as valuable, as Burney happily expresses in her imagery of treasure. It was something of a smuggled treasure, too; the return of both Frances Burney and the incomplete manuscript novel to her native land was fraught with difficulty, excitement, and even danger.

The manuscript was a treasure still subjected to question, even to possible confiscation. The officer at the customhouse at Dunkirk was not prepared for the sight of all those papers fresh from Paris, and harbored the worst suspicions. The "little portmanteau" was opened in Frances's presence and the police officer "began a rant of indignation & amazement at a sight so unexpected & prohibited. . . . He sputtered at the Mouth, & stamped with his feet." The tirade continued, the officer making accusations of "traitorous designs" while the author of the manuscript, finding her explanations went unheard, "stood before him with calm taciturnity." Eventually he calmed a little, but "this Fourth Child of my Brain had undoubtedly been destroyed ere it was Born, had I not had recourse to an English Merchant."[12] The merchant vouched for Burney's identity, and the license from de Saulnier was allowed. The Burney family had often engaged in "talking Treason," but on this occasion the treason was national.

Frances had already been taken for a spy during her sojourn at Dunkirk. She had been sympathetically attracted to the melancholy Spanish prisoners of war in their work gangs in the harbor; she had offered them money and had tried to communicate with them. One day she had been talking to the Spanish "Chief," and trying to give some "small money, to distribute to my new & completely dilapidated Friends," when "I beheld an Officer of the Police, in full gold trappings, & wearing his Badge of authority, & his head covered, & half a yard beyond it, with an enormous Gold Laced cocked Hat, furiously darting forward from a small house at the entrance upon the Quay."[13] Frances was interrogated at the police office on suspicion of espionage (and perhaps, too, of sabotage), though she was eventually allowed to depart. The "uninteresting Leisure" of the Dunkirk delay was not without incident. The episodes as Burney describes them show a mingling of the dreary and the exotic, the calm and the brutal (the sluggish town, the melancholy Spanish prisoners), the whole ruled by wild outbursts from authoritarian males, comically aggrandized (in half a yard of "Gold Laced cocked Hat"). Similar elements appear in *The Wanderer*: the suspicion of espionage and interrogations of Burney's "Dunkirk Journal" reflect the unease, suspicion, random convictions, and abrupt events that characterize the novel.

Random adventure did not end with embarkation. After a slow journey, the vessel arrived in sight of the English shore only to be captured by a British ship, "not as French, but American booty, War having been declared against America the preceding Week." Frances had been so seasick that she had not known when the vessel was taken: "I had become a Prisoner without any suspicion of my captivity."[14] She was at once recognized and treated with flattering attention by Lieutenant Harford, though Alex was thought to be French and hence a real prisoner; his mother had to explain (as she and Alex were to do repeatedly) that he had been born in England. Frances and her papers were allowed to disembark at Deal on 15 August, and she was soon reunited with her family after a Channel crossing almost as strange as the one which opens her fourth novel.

The manuscript which had such an adventurous arrival became a major project during Burney's new residence in England. She worked at it diligently for over a year, despite the pain in her mutilated right side which made writing laborious. The novel was completed in full draft by August 1813, then revised and copied (with no Alexandre to help). A financially promising agreement was worked out with Longman, Hurst, Rees, Orme and Brown.[15] Burney remembered the unlucrative profusion of editions of the earlier novels, which she had sold outright; this time she hoped to benefit the d'Arblay family with each new edition. The book set in the "terrific reign of Robespierre" was published on 28 March 1814, shortly before the Allies' victory; the allied armies marched on Paris and on 31 March Paris capitulated. Napoleon's forced abdication and imprisonment on Elba soon followed, and the spring months were full of self—congratulatory celebrations of the new peace.

In *The Wanderer*'s prefatory dedication to her father, Burney indicates her affections for both warring nations, and says that she is proud of both of her countries' behavior over the manuscript of the book:

> And, to the honour and liberality of both nations, let me mention, that at the Custom-house on either—alas!—hostile shore, upon my given word that the papers contained neither letters, not political writings; but simply a work of invention and observation; the voluminous manuscript was suffered to pass, without demur, comment, or the smallest examination.
>
> A conduct so generous on one side, so trusting on the other, in time of war . . . cannot but be read with satisfaction by every friend of humanity.
>
> (*The Wanderer*, I,viii)

She hoped to serve to unite the unfortunately hostile countries, herself serving as a "friend of humanity" by presenting both France and England in her novel; in her preface she unites them in generosity to herself, in candor, in unwillingness to engage in censorship. But she here omits any references to the difficulties of getting her manuscripts through, or to her use of "pull," or to her surmise that such permission "would never . . . have been obtained during the residence in Paris of Buonaparte."[16] And if those local Dunkirk officials had read—or been able to read—the first sentence of her new novel, would they have allowed it to pass? Alexandre d'Arblay swore that "the Work had nothing in it political, nor even National." But Frances must have known that the new novel which she had, in effect, smuggled over to England was both "political" and "National." *The Wanderer* is Burney's most political novel, and the one in which she deals most consistently with public and national issues.

The Wanderer; or, Female Difficulties deals with the French Revolution and the Rights—or Wrongs—of Woman. Begun in the 1790s, it is in a sense a novel of the '90s. It belongs to a new genre of that decade, the English novel set during the French Revolution, in which characters are in various ways affected by historical events, trends, and ideas. The modern historical novel, as Scott was to develop it, is really an offspring of those novels of the French Revolution and of the Revolutionary era. Charlotte Smith's *Desmond* (1792) had dealt with the early Revolution and liberal-radical enthusiasm, while her later *The Banished Man* (1794) had looked more sadly on later developments in France, in following the life and trials of an émigré. Conservative novelists like Jane West in *A Tale of the Times* (1799) illustrated the horrific effects of seductive revolutionaries on middle-class female English life, as did Elizabeth Hamilton in her largely satiric novel *Memoirs of Modern Philosophers* (1800) with its heroine Julia, seduced by a philosophe-valet, and its antiheroine, the comic Bridgetina Botherim, a vulgar believer in female rights. Some novelists took a wider scope of historical action, as Jane Porter did in her *Thaddeus of Warsaw* (1803), which treats the life of a Polish exile, victim of his country's invasion by Russia. All such novels are to some extent "democratic" in tendency, whether the authors are explicitly liberal or conservative in their message. They all exhibit the pathos and perplexity of ordinary people thrown into the uncontrollable current of historical events. Until Scott, women writers were the major practitioners of this new genre. To this modern development, whereby the bourgeois novel becomes overtly an epic of the individual fate in history, Frances Burney was a contributor. Her earlier novels, like *Cecilia,* which affected most novels of the '90s, question society but they are not conscious representations of a period as a period. *The Wanderer* is very definitely set in a particularized recent past: "in the reign of the terrific Robespierre"; the death of Robespierre (28 July 1794) coincides with the dénouement of the novel. That the years 1793–1794 had been of the utmost importance in Burney's personal life, a period of dynamic change, revolt, and fulfilment, may have had something to do with her choice of a time.

The heroine of *Evelina* is embarrassed by warring individuals in a society (apparently accepted by the narrative) that functions on greed and hostility. The next heroine enters a more explicitly delineated society, the corruption and limitation of which the narrative makes us overtly conscious; *Cecilia* is based upon a debate on ideological grounds. In *Camilla*, the heroine is enmeshed in conflicting rules and perverse structures in a society that seems quiet but is, under its provincial placidities, turbulent and threatening. Published in 1796, that novel of the '90s had avoided all overt reference to the greatest public event of the time. *The Wanderer*, however, is determined not to evade history. The heroine of *The Wanderer* makes an entrance into English life, and the life she discovers is, like that which Camilla encounters, very largely provincial English society. But this heroine is, in all senses, an alien. Much lonelier than Burney's other heroines, this young woman has a fate determined by historical events and conditions to which she may respond, even energetically, but over which she has no control.

Once the world is seen in terms of historical movements and historically conditioned social and economic structures, then the conduct-book morality of advice to young ladies ceases to operate as an intelligent guide to anything. That message, submerged in the ironic and paradoxical *Camilla*, is more open here. The novel itself is, like *Cecilia*, a more extroverted and analytical novel than *Camilla*. Instead of making us see the young woman's behavior as the foreground, with an adventitious background of circumstantial events, the novelist wishes us to keep focused upon what is more usually thought of as background, so that we see the conditions that make for "female difficulties" and for other difficulties. For the first time in Burney's works, society itself is presented as an historical phenomenon. Remote and violent causes of wrongs and perversities cannot be simply detected and cast out, while particular communities are not readily subject to either sentimental or satiric reformation. Living in history means living in dread. Life in history is life in a mystery.

The unusual structure of *The Wanderer* means that the reader must participate in mystery, must consent to be mystified. The novel does not open its facts to the reader. The reader is not even let in on the heroine's central anxieties, but must give allegiance to the character before knowing what she conceals. If *Camilla* is in some sense a mystery story and a spy story, *The Wanderer* is literally a spy story. It is in part a working-out of the idea suggested in the earlier draft scrap: "A carried on disguise, from virtuous motives, producing a mystery which the audience themselves cannot pierce. Exciting alternatively blame & pity." *The Wanderer* is not well known. The summary given in the next few pages concentrates on the heroine's story as the novel's reader is made to follow it. There are many more characters and incidents in the five-volume work than such a description can include, and some subordinate characters and incidents will be brought in later in this chapter.

We first see the heroine on the shore of France, a solitary figure asking for passage on a boat fleeing away on a December night in 1793. The woman, first a voice, then an indecipherable figure, is an object of amused curiosity once she gets on board, as she is dark-skinned, apparently "Creole" (i.e., black), and heavily bandaged. Save for the profane French pilot, the others on board are very English. There is the bluff admiral; the sardonic Mr. Riley; fussy Mrs. Maple with her niece, the volatile and witty Elinor; kind young Mr. Albert Harleigh; and sharp-tongued Mrs. Ireton with her spoiled son. (These characters are all to recur throughout the novel's action.) The foreign female, who speaks English with a French accent, refuses to give any name. After the pilot tells them they are halfway over the Channel, the strange young woman, suddenly casting something into the sea, cries out "Sink, and be as nothing!" (I:8). But she will not tell what she has cast overboard.

On arrival at Dover, the stranger is visibly depressed when she finds no letters have been left for "L. S." On the journey to London, the dark color of "that black girl" gradually fades, and she is metamorphosed into a beautiful young European woman. When repeatedly asked her name, the "Incognita" replies riddlingly, "I hardly know it myself!" (I:116). Elinor determines to take the stranger in as an interesting protégée; Mrs. Maple dislikes harboring "a french-ified swindler" (I:114) but, finding the girl is useful in sewing, allows her to travel with them to their home in Lewes. Anxious, for reasons unknown, to live near Brighton, the émigrée resides in Mrs. Maple's house, assisting Elinor in her projects. She even takes part in an amateur production of The Provok'd Hus-band directed by Elinor (an episode adapted from an early version of Camilla). This heroine (like the "Ariella" of the draft) discovers that acting calls forth talents she enjoys exercising, but this event brings her to the notice of Brighton and Lewes society. The girl has now acquired a pseudonym from the mysterious initials "L. S." As "Miss Ellis," she attracts the admiration of young Lady Aurora Granville and her brother Lord Melbury, but is driven from their home on the order of their uncle and guardian, Lord Denmeath. Before she can leave the house, the girl is distressed by Lord Melbury's advances to her. The penniless "Ellis" determines to find an independent way of life.

Love complicates the heroine's life, however; Albert Harleigh (one of Burney's well-intentioned and rather weak young men) is attracted to the stranger, despite his very proper dislike of mystery in relation to a woman's character. Elinor Joddrel becomes jealous of Harleigh's interest in her protégée, as Elinor, formerly engaged to Harleigh's younger brother, now decides that she wants Albert Harleigh instead. Elinor makes "Ellis" her confidante and her messenger in carrying a proclamation of her love to Albert. When Harleigh refuses Elinor's offer of herself, Elinor blackmails "Ellis" through a suicide threat, extorting from "Ellis" (but not from Harleigh) a promise that Ellis and Harleigh will never become attached.

The heroine endeavors to become self-supporting. Through the middle of the novel we find her in a variety of employments. At last, she meets in Bright-helmstone the friend for whom she was searching, Gabriella, another émigrée. Gabriella's marriage is unsatisfactory; now her little son has died, and she has fallen on hard times. At the meeting of Gabriella and "Ellis," we find out at last the heroine's first name—Juliet—but are told nothing else about her. Even her old friend Gabriella does not fully understand Juliet's reasons for concealing her identity. Lord Denmeath threatens Juliet in a manner which indicates that he has knowledge about her and her situation that the reader does not. We wonder what are "those old claims so long ago vainly canvassed" to which Denmeath refers? Who is Juliet's "champion, the Bishop" (IV:130)? Why does Lord Denmeath insist that she return to France voluntarily, or be transported there by force? The heroine seeks the anonymity of London, where she works with Gabriella in a small haberdasher's shop in Soho. She is apparently pursued and spied upon.

Gabriella at last tells Juliet's old friend of Brighton days, the elderly crippled Sir Jaspar Herrington, the secret of Juliet's birth. She is the daughter of the Earl of Melbury's only son, Lord Granville, who had married the orphaned and destitute Miss Power, and had kept the marriage secret for fear of his father. Juliet Granville was brought up by her grandmother on the banks of the Tyne for her first seven years. The widower then took the daughter of his first marriage to France, where Juliet was educated in a convent, with Gabriella, niece of Granville's friend, the bishop. Granville married again, and before he could bring himself to reveal his first marriage and its offspring, he died suddenly. Juliet's guardian, the bishop, told Lord Denmeath, brother of Granville's second wife, of the existence of the legitimate elder child. Lord Denmeath, interested in obtaining the whole of the inheritance for his sister and her heirs, repudiated the connection, but offered to buy Juliet off if she married and promised to remain in France. The bishop was about to accompany Juliet to England to make her claim, when the Revolution broke out. In a fire at the château, all the relevant documents were destroyed, except Lord Denmeath's promissory note. Sir Jaspar and the reader now know the reasons for Lord Denmeath's blackmail and persecution of Juliet, but the reason for her total secrecy has not been explained. Other agents, French ones, seem to be acting against her as well as those of Lord Denmeath.

Fearfully, the heroine takes flight. In the last quarter of the novel she is a wanderer indeed. Knowing that she has been advertised for in the newspapers, she fears each new acquaintance and is overshadowed by some inexplicable terror. At last she is trapped in the galleries of an inn. Just as Albert Harleigh, one of the inn's lodgers, begins to recognize her, Juliet is seized by a man "dressed with disgusting negligence, yet wearing an air of ferocious authority," who commands her *"viens, citoyenne, viens; suis moi."* Harleigh tries to protect her, expostulating, and asking by what right the man acts: "One claim alone can annul my interference. Are you her father?" The rough man laughs, answering, "Non! . . . *mais il y'a d'autres droits! . . . n'est ce pas ma femme? Ne suis-je pas son mari?"* Juliet refuses to deny the claim that she is this man's wife, and will not utter the "syllable" that would permit Harleigh to "secure your liberty"; Harleigh will not help her (V:39–46). Just as this horrible husband is about to take Juliet away in a coach, a peace officer arrives with orders to deport the Frenchman, and Sir Jaspar Herrington drives up in the nick of time to help Juliet escape.

Juliet tells her story to Sir Jaspar, and at last we know what that story is. The strange "husband" is a commissary of the Convention—that is, one of the commissioners first sent out by the Convention in March 1793 to quell insurrectionary movements, particularly after the antirevolutionary revolt in La Vendée. This commissary arrested the bishop and found Lord Denmeath's promissory note offering Juliet a large dowry (6,000 pounds) if she would marry and settle in France. The commissary made a hideous bargain with Juliet: if she would marry him, he would save the bishop from the guillotine. The bishop commanded her not to agree, but the commissary forced Juliet and the marchioness (Gabriella's mother) to watch the guillotine at work in the public square (V:78). Juliet agreed to the condition, the bishop was released, and the commissary took Juliet to the *mairie* where she was rushed through a civil ceremony. Her new "husband" was compelled to leave at once, to quell an insurrection in a neighboring town, so the marriage was not consummated. The marchioness planned Juliet's escape in disguise, and warned her that she must never, under any circumstances, reveal her name until assured of the bishop's safe arrival in England. As long as Juliet is supposed to be in France, her "husband" (who has already applied for the money) will be more likely to keep the bishop alive; if the bishop were to be captured, he would be "detained as an hostage for my [Juliet's] future concession" (V:96).

These circumstances explain Juliet's secrecy. A life has depended on her silence. The object she threw into the Channel was her wedding ring. Letters from both the marchioness and Gabriella were to be directed under the initials "L. S.," and Juliet waited impatiently near the seacoast for news that the bishop was safe. Juliet's dangers have been multiplied because Lord Denmeath, knowing of the "marriage," has been working with the commissary and his agents to have the troublesome relative and inheritrix sent back to France and out of the way.

Still uncertain about the fate of the bishop, Juliet makes her way to Teignemouth, where Lady Aurora and Lord Melbury defy Lord Denmeath and acknowledge her as their sister. Juliet's earlier extreme distress at Lord Melbury's sexual offers is now fully explained; not only did Lord Melbury mistake her character and insult her, but the attraction itself was incestuous. A former French servant brings news that Juliet's "husband," the commissary, has now captured the bishop and imprisoned him. The bishop will be executed if Juliet does not return to France. She determines to return, and to face public and private horrors in order to save her guardian's life. But before she makes the journey, while she is waiting on Teignemouth sands for the boat that will take her to France, she hears happier news. Passengers from France bring word that the commissary himself has just been executed for conspiracy (a fate that parallels Robespierre's). And the bishop himself, it turns out, is one of the boat's passengers. Secrecy and wandering are over.

As Elinor has some while ago revoked her threat of suicide and released Ellis-Juliet from the promise, Harleigh and Juliet are free to marry. The bluff admiral proves to be Admiral Powel, her uncle on her mother's side, so Juliet is reunited with her maternal line and Welsh inheritance. Juliet has profited from her tribulations, as one of her admirers exclaims; the Revolution, through the suffering it inflicted, has taught its victims "to strengthen the mind with the body"; "it has animated the exercise of reason, the exertion of the faculties, activity in labour, . . . and cheerfulness under every privation." Juliet herself has benefited, the admiral is told, by the Revolution, which "has formed . . . in the trials, perils and hardships of a struggling existence, your courageous, though so gentle niece!" (V:386). In short, the French Revolution has had the invigorating effect on its surviving victims that the pro-Revolutionary theorists designed for themselves. And the heroine has had the opportunity of strengthening her mind, exercising her faculties, and proving her courage.

Juliet Granville ("Ellis") is the most active of all Burney's heroines, the most energetic and self-sustaining, and the most lonely. A number of themes from Burney's earlier works unite in her story. Like Evelina, the heroine suffers from a blank last name, her legitimate name and birth denied. Like Cecilia, she is persecuted for her inheritance, and like Cecilia Stanley of *The Witlings,* she is abused by those who sheltered her and must consider earning her own living (and unlike Cecilia Stanley, Juliet does much more than consider). Like Adela in *The Siege of Pevensey,* she is called upon to make a sacrifice of herself in a forced and hateful marriage in order to save a father-figure. Her situation is indeed very close to that of Geralda in *Hubert De Vere;* Geralda saved her father's brother by sacrificing herself in marriage, an action originally misunderstood by her lover de Vere, just as Harleigh does not understand the nature of Juliet's union with the *"mari"* who claims her. (The similarity in the characters' names, Geralda Glanville/Juliet Granville, indicates a reworking of the situation.) The pressures of conscience that lead to a horrible wedding parallel those in Clarinda's story, and like Camilla, the heroine is spied upon. This novel is, however, freer than most of Burney's other works from the influential presence of the Father. In the background there is one weak absconding father, Lord Granville, who, unlike Evelina's father, never acknowledges his daughter, and one villainous father, the rejecting and blackmailing Lord Denmeath. The valued Father is the pious but passive bishop, always invisible in the course of the narrative; he represents something that has to be saved and protected, not something that can protect and save. Very little overt emotion is expressed by any character for any father-figure. The patrilinear and patriarchal are questioned in the lack of emphasis given to Juliet's last name. Indeed, once we have got to know her by her own made-up name "Ellis" (which will do either as a first or last name) the system of identifications becomes questionable. There is a kind of romanticism in the structure of the tale, as we are asked to set aside the rules of society, which require us always to inspect the background and social standing of our acquaintance and to admit them into our lives only if they have the correct social passport.

"Incognita" Ellis is a disconcerting puzzle. Bad-tempered Mrs. Ireton early mocks the girl's changeability, her fluctuating being:

> "O, I am diving too deeply into the secrets of your trade, am I? Nay, I ought to be contented, I own. . . . You have been bruised and beaten; and dirty and clean; and ragged and whole; and wounded and healed; and a European and a Creole, in less than a week. I suppose, next, you will dwindle into a dwarf; and then, perhaps, find some surprising contrivance to shoot up into a giantess. There is nothing that can be too much to expect from so great an adept in metamorphoses."
>
> (I:85)

Metamorphosis is a theme of the novel. (In a passage such as this, as in some parts of *Camilla*, we can see a resemblance to *Alice in Wonderland*). Juliet does not become a dwarf or shoot up into a giantess, but she moves with great rapidity from one guise, place, condition, occupation to another. She resides in ambiguity, representing to the view of others incompatible identities, the union of logical contraries. Her fellow passengers find it impossible at first to be sure whether she is a white or a black woman (it is a disappointment to the modern reader that Burney did not give us a black heroine). Then it is impossible to say whether she is French or English—and, indeed, Juliet is in a sense both. She is both gentlewoman and plebeian, both very rich and very poor. She is neither single nor married, yet both of these at once. Juliet the riddle is Womankind in various metamorphoses. The union of various contradictions within Juliet should make us wary of accepting too readily the existence of plain opposites in other circumstances of the story. We may remember the play with opposition and paradox in *Camilla*, with its many instances of "Two Ways of looking at the same Thing," or "Two Sides of a Question."

The Wanderer, like *Cecilia*, begins with a debate, and there are two sides to a question. *Cecilia*'s first conversation scene was an argument between the supporter of Originality and the supporter of Conformity. The first debate in *The Wanderer* involves similar issues, but now localized and complicated by the unignorable historical fact of the French Revolution. Elinor Joddrel, the romantic radical, opposes Albert Harleigh, the rational conservative. Elinor proclaims, like Wordsworth, a bliss in the new dawn: a new "happiness in going forth into the world at this sublime juncture. . . . I feel as if I had never awaked into life, till I had opened my eyes on that side of the channel." Harleigh objects to the French excesses, which Elinor claims are "only the first froth of the cauldron";

she accuses him of not enjoying "as you ought, this glorious epoch, that lifts our minds from slavery and from nothingness, into play and vigour; and leaves us no longer . . . merely making believe that we are thinking beings." Harleigh insists that unbridled liberty "suddenly unshackled" brings barbarism; "safety demands control, from the baby to the despot." Elinor asks heatedly, "must the world in a mass alone stand still, because its amelioration would be costly? Can any thing be so absurd, so preposterous, as to seek to improve mankind individually, yet bid it stand still collectively?" If education is valuable, she argues, then alteration and improvement must likewise be available for "states, nations, and bodies of society." Harleigh argues on the other hand that effective change, like education, must be gradual: "If you shew the planetary system to the child who has not yet trundled his hoop, do you believe that you will form a mathematician?" (I:18–21).

Elinor, here and in her actions throughout *The Wanderer,* may seem simply another manifestation of a stock character type found in most conservative novels of the '90s with the propaganda purpose of counteracting radical views. Novelists wishing to counteract the spread of "Jacobinical" or radical-democratic ideas emphasized the damage these could do on the home front—indeed the nature, status, and treatment of women was one of the arenas of ideological war. The naïve or stupid woman seduced by radical thought into beliefs incompatible with her happiness is a character insistently introduced by both male and female "anti-Jacobin" authors. Most novels of the 1790s or of the first decade of the next century can indeed be readily categorized politically; Claudia L. Johnson has recently given us an excellent survey of "The Novel of Crisis," pointing out the political implications of elements in novels of the last decade of the eighteenth century and the first decade of the nineteenth. Certain characters and situations are consistently employed by writers of certain ideologies. Certain types of scenes and characters predictably appear in novels of the right, including a guillotine scene, a vulgar male revolutionary seducer or sexual assailant attacking an innocent female, as well as the mistaken petticoat radical. As *The Wanderer* has all of these, it can readily be classified as a right-wing novel—at first glance. Novelists of the left (liberal or radical) tend to exhibit the Bastille, a brutal husband, an aristocratic seducer of a lower-class innocent, and poor working women, as well as satirically displaying middle-class respectable persons with crassly stupid attitudes, especially callousness toward the poor and to women.[17] Except for the Bastille, all of these can also be found in *The Wanderer.* Burney deliberately mixes ideological elements—knowing that the plot situations themselves are ideological elements.

Elinor speaks for "all that snatches us from mere inert existence" and gives birth to "our passions, our energies, our noblest conceptions." Without such potential for intense experience and an "idea of mental enlargement," human nature is of little worth: "without it, I regard and treat the whole of my race as the mere dramatis personae of a farce; of which I am myself, when performing with such fellow-actors, a principal buffoon" (I:347). Elinor resembles that earlier spokesman for the Romantic view, the sympathetic Belfield. The author herself in her novels presents many of the human race as "mere dramatis personae of a farce," stunted in growth and repetitive in action. Elinor is no straw woman set up only to be knocked down. If she is wrong in that first debate, she can be only partly wrong; she has a case, well put, and Harleigh's many hesitations, unfinished sentences, and ponderous analogies do not give great strength to his side of the debate. Elinor's touches of self-irony ("myself a principal buffoon") set her above the stupidity of the anti-Jacobins' caricature Revolutionary female.

Elinor's views are indirectly supported by the presentation of the middle-class English characters aboard the boat. They are snobbish, callous, and prejudiced. Mrs. Maple and Mrs. Ireton complain about the pilot's having taken such an outlandish passenger aboard their chartered vessel; private boats are not for picking up refugees. Riley laughs at her bandages: "Why, Mistress, have you been trying your skill at fisty cuffs for the good of your nation?" (I:23). Provoked by the stranger's not giving her name, Riley declares, "They are clever beings, those French . . . always playing fools' tricks . . . yet always landing right upon their feet, like so many cats!" (I:16–17). Any émigré—or émigrée—may be ignorantly hated, confounded with the revolutionaries, and suspected of spying for the French government, or working in some way to bring the guillotine and Revolution to England. The kind of insults made to Madame Duval and M. Dubois in *Evelina* are now political issues and central topics in *The Wanderer*. The heroine—not her painted old grandmother or her grandmother's cicisbeo—is suspected and insulted because she is French.

During the decade of the 1790s, as Burney could well remember, anti-Gallicism and xenophobia increased in England. Under the pressure of the threat of invasion from France toward the end of the century, antipathies had strengthened. Any radical or even liberal ideas were seen as direct encouragement to the French to come and subject the English to slavery under the banner of "Liberty." Gillray's caricature of 1798, "The Storm rising;—or the Republican FLOTILLA in danger," shows blasts from Pitt keeping back the invading French and their revolutionary principles, while treacherous liberals like Charles James Fox and Richard Brinsley Sheridan winch the French invaders to the shore. On the French coast, a devil dances and plays the fiddle atop the guillotine (Fig. 31). The print conveys general notions about the undesirability of anything savoring of the French, notions that were current from 1792 onward. The good English should have nothing to do with French diabolical fashions, and only those who would undo England could find any fault with the present English system of things.

Throughout the novel, the English characters are complacent, politically obtuse, and xenophobic. They carry their prejudices about with them while thinking that they have happily avoided history. Many share the attitude to the

Revolution of the merchant Tedman: "I never enquire into all that . . . one wastes a deal of time in idle curiosity, about things that don't concern one" (III:205). Young Gooch the farmer's son, however, regards the Revolution with a childlike curiosity, and is fascinated by an impression of blurred but exciting horrors, and by "Bob Spear, as we call him at our club" (III:204). New, if hazy, notions and old prejudices jostle in his shallow mind: he wonders how the French can "go on acting, and piping, and jiggetting about, and such like, if they know they are so soon to have their heads cut off. . . . You could not get we English now to do so." Old Farmer Gooch treats the horrors as mere travelers' tales, tolerating his son's credulity in believing "such a pack of staring lies." His own opinions of the French are the comfortable prejudices of the last two hundred years: "as to roast beef and plum pudding, I do hear that they do no' know the taste of such a thing. So that they be but a poor stinted race" (III:205). Mr. Stubbs the steward can think only that now would be a good time to buy land in France, and that the French have "no great head" for business. At a higher social level, the gentleman Mr. Scope, "self-dubbed a deep politician" and termed by Elinor one of the "famous formal quizzes" of Lewes, is calmly antagonistic to the Revolution:

> "I have no very high notion, I own, of the morals of those foreigners at this period. A man's wife and daughters belong to any man who has a taste to them, as I am informed. Nothing is very strict. Mr. Robertspierre, as I am told, is not very exact in his dealings."
>
> (I:167)

Scope, a comic understater like some of the characters in Burney's late comic plays, presents the emotional aridity of a flaccidly conservative temper. "Moral" means sexually moral, and respectful of property—and the two are the same. It is evident to him that "a man's wife and daughters" are property. He is one of Burney's woman-haters. Although Juliet has just escaped from Revolutionary France, he cannot demean himself to discuss political affairs with her:

> "And, if there were any gentlemen of your family, with you, Ma'am, in foreign parts," said Mr. Scope, "I should be glad to have their opinion of this Convention, now set up in France: for as to ladies, though they are certainly very pleasing, they are but indifferent judges in the political line, not having, ordinarily, heads of that sort. I speak without offence, inferiority of understanding being no defect in a female."
>
> (I:201)

Mr. Scope, whose myopic vision allows him no scope at all, insists on a view of history and current affairs (in which he is not very current) that ignores the female as participant in history. As Juliet is a political nobody, one of the "ladies" whom politics cannot affect, he cannot see that she understands affairs in her adoptive country better than he, or that she is no sheltered lady living under the protection of males but a person battling life on her own. The facts of the plot show that the safety of one of "the gentlemen of her family" (or adoptive family) depends on her courage, intelligence, and discretion, while the "gentleman of her family" who should be her protector is actively trying to get rid of her. Pompous Mr. Scope provides a deal of justification for Elinor's rebellious views.

If in *Cecilia* we saw a fully developed society uneasily tottering at the edge of change, perhaps of a crash, in *The Wanderer* we see a static society that has refused to admit any change. The heroine enters an English society in semi-urban coastal Sussex that seems much more provincial than Camilla's provincial world in Hampshire. By the time Burney published her novel, Brighton had been made fashionable by the Prince of Wales's choosing it as the site of his pleasure palace, the Brighton Pavilion, and we might expect Brighton to be presented as a glamorous, even decadent, scene. In a rather subtle anti-Tory turn Burney has made it a scene of old dead conservatism. The novel's tight middle-class society of Brighton and Lewes, largely composed of widows, spinsters, and bachelors on private incomes, is a small-town world, mean, barren, and unlovely. The people occupy themselves with small snobberies and petty amusements, ignoring the poor around them as well as events happening in the outside world. They are on a coast facing France, but they do not look seaward.

Through that group of provincials England is presented as an affluent society turned in upon itself and withering away. The conspicuous absence of marriage and of families, the preponderance of the unmarried, seems to signify a lack of future. It is no wonder that Elinor wants to let in a breath of fresh air. There is no safe conservative model of living to turn to. It would be damaging just to exist on the terms of Lady Kendover: "the circle in which she moved, was bounded by the hereditary habits, and imitative customs, which had always limited the proceedings of her ladyship's." Lady Kendover can patronize only "those who had already been elevated by patronage." To discover talent and give money to an artist who needs it is beyond her, the work of a character "of a superiour species, a character that had learnt to act for himself, by thinking for himself and feeling for others" (II:84−85). The author here repeats in her authorial voice the phrases associated with Belfield; all of her works inculcate self-dependence, acting and thinking for oneself. A world based on "heriditary habits, and imitative customs" is moribund.

That all is not well with England is felt through the experience of the heroine, who is caught between various worlds and belongs nowhere (until the novel reaches a convenient closure). Juliet, not the rich dilettante Elinor, is the truly Romantic figure, "The Wanderer"—the very phrase is in the Romantic mode. Romantic literature is full of lonely wanderers, from Rousseau's "Solitary Walker" to Wordsworth's poetic population of "wanderers," like the Old

Cumberland Beggar, the Female Vagrant, the Leech Gatherer. It is, incidentally, highly probably that Burney knew the *Lyrical Ballads,* which Dr. Burney had reviewed for the *Monthly Review* of June 1799. Dr. Burney's review was not entirely unfavorable, though he disliked the political and social implications of some pieces; even "Tintern Abbey" is the product of a mind "poetical" but "tinctured with gloomy, narrow and unsociable ideas."[18] Burney's novel might likewise be accused of being "tinctured with gloomy and unsociable ideas." The heroine is occasionally gloomy, and seems "unsociable" in her very lack of that basic social sign, a name. She has at first instead of a name only that unstable arbitrary composition of syllabic sounds, "Ellis," always ready to dissolve again into the strange initial letters "L. S." In the plot of the novel, "L. S." stands for nothing at all, a riddle without an answer.

Why L. S.? The initials are, interestingly, the same as those of "Letitia Sourby," the fictitious, conservative daughter perhaps invented by Dr. Burney. But "L. S." has a wider frame of reference. Until the 1970s, L. S. had for English people a basic meaning as the first two symbols of the signification of money: l.s.d. The heroine in her false riddling denomination represents a means of exchange—as indeed she does, for Ellis-Juliet is a token of currency between the bishop and the commissary. Women in our culture (and others) are a medium of exchange between men—as anthropologists, psychologists, and feminist critics have told us.[19] A culture based upon the ownership and exchange of women may seem agreeable and normal to Claude Lévi-Strauss, or to men like Burney's Mr. Scope or Admiral Powel, who assume women to be property. The incest taboo ensures that men keep the women in circulation and create the symbolic order. But the Burney family members had denied the symbolic order and the appropriate male circulation of women in an incestuous relationship of the fraternal kind adumbrated in Burney's earliest novel. Fraternal incest (in *The Wanderer* suggested by Lord Melbury's attraction to Juliet) is one mode of breaking into society's version of the use of women. So, too, is a woman's undertaking, in a "masculine" way, financial charge of herself. To men, it seems proper that women should be currency and property. But for a woman this position (once even dimly realized) is a false position, which can be acquiesced in only as a penance and which demands to be seen ironically—as it is in the punning initials "L. S." Juliet has a double and paradoxical objective: to sacrifice herself as a medium of exchange, if duty demands, and on the other hand to resist with all her power everything that threatens her independence. Juliet, like Joyce, is determined to make honest money through labor, rather than sitting by idly in a ladylike way to represent that which is passively exchanged. But earning money demands the bourgeois stability that causes Lewes to stagnate. Juliet is a Wanderer, like a beggar, like a Romantic poet, or—in a woman's case—like a prostitute. (Burney herself in Dunkirk in 1812 feared to be "remarked as a Female Wanderer.")[20]

The heroine, nameless and penniless, wanders about England, very like

Wordsworth's vagrants of a lower social class—and on the mother's side the girl *is* of a lower social class. The reference to kind grandmother Powel makes amends at last to old Mrs. Sleepe for the portrait of that other grandmother, Madame Duval. "Ellis," the heroine's pseudonym, is the name of Frances Burney's grandfather's first wife, Rebecca Ellis, the dancer, while the heroine's "real name" is "Granville," which not only echoes the "Anville" of Evelina's anagram but again echoes the name of Burney's godmother Frances Greville, while picking up the maiden name of Mary Granville, later Mrs. Delany. About Ellis-Juliet, Burney has assembled the alienated and rootless or unhappy women, including the poor, the socially unacceptable (Ellis the performer), the victim of forced marriage (Mary Granville). Burney has symbolically made peace here with all the mothers. The maternal inheritance is always the true private inheritance in her novels. By a sleight of fiction, here she gives the maternal inheritance final precedence over the unsatisfactory paternal authority.

Female friendship is also enshrined in this novel. Juliet is reunited with Gabriella, after first seeing her only as a lonely female figure moving through Brighton streets at dawn with "quick, but staggering steps." Concerned, Juliet follows "the foreigner" to the top of a hill, where "stopping, she extended her arms, seeming to hail the full view of the wide spreading ocean; or rather, Ellis imagined, the idea of her native land." Gabriella—and "Ellis"—look seaward; this is one of the few points in the narrative where we are made aware of Brighton's cliffs and shore and the beauty of "the expansive view, impressive though calm, of the sea." The moment of oceanic feeling is associated with both love and death. Gabriella has come to mourn over the grave of her infant son, a grave that she has been able to mark only by natural things: "a small elevation of earth, encircled by short sticks, intersected with rushes" (III:5–9). Gabriella is mourning over the grave of her only baby, like some poor woman in a lyrical ballad, when the heroine recognizes her: "Ah, mon amie! . . . T'ai-jè chercheè . . . t'ai-je si ardemment desirée, pour te retrouver ainsi? pleurant sur un tombeau?" (III:10 [accent marks *sic*]). The ensuing conversation is held in French (translated in footnotes). *The British Critic* was to call Gabriella "a true French character . . . in the school of M. Cottin" and to declare the conversation over the grave "French, not English pathos," adding "we can therefore readily excuse our authoress from a violation of a rule of taste, in cloathing it in French garb."[21] Burney associates emotional openness with the French language. She wants a "true French character" to impress upon the English reader that there are real French people, with their own feelings and way of putting things. She was willing to break "a rule of taste" in giving such an extensive scene in a foreign language, because she wished to bring home to the reader the concept of another culture. Burney's marriage to a Frenchman and long residence in his country had made her aware of the value of another country, and of a dual heritage. Juliet is technically English by strict line of birth, but she speaks English with a French accent, and her life is divided—those who accuse her of

Frenchness are not wrong. The scene in French offers a welcome exchange of the affections, of sympathy, in contrast to the abrasive and callous utterance of so many English characters, including Gabriella's landlady, whose harsh voice was heard just before this sequence. Frances Burney has recognized her own doubleness, her dual identity (as Frances Burney/Mme. d'Arblay) and the double identity which is hers by birth as the descendant of French immigrants into England. But just as many—nay, more—characters insult Juliet on the grounds of her nationality as insulted Madame Duval on her (assumed) French origin. Mrs. Maple repeatedly calls Juliet "a frenchified swindler," as if her Frenchness were an aggravation of her supposed swindling propensities. Even Sir Jaspar, who likes Gabriella, cannot resist calling her "my dulcet frog!" (IV:210).

French-speaking Gabriella is an important character; though she makes but few appearances in the novel, those appearances are important. In a scene in her shop, Gabriella endorses Juliet's concern for independence, sustaining the theme that has marked Burney's writing since *The Witlings*: "Self-exertion can alone mark nobility of soul and self-dependence only can sustain honour in adversity" (IV:187). She is a dignified and gentle aristocrat, married perforce "before the Revolution, from a convent, and while yet a child." Burney has taken to heart d'Arblay's remonstrances when he thought her too hard on Mme. de Staël, and explained that among French aristocrats arranged marriages were unhappy sacrifices of which women were always the victims.[22] Gabriella suffered in a union with an elderly and coldhearted husband, now an emigrant on the Continent. In Gabriella we can see Burney's tribute to affectionate and dignified Mme. de Maisonneuve and her devoted friendship. Gabriella, who stands in for the sister (the half-sister Aurora) from whom Juliet is artificially separated, functions as the true sister. At another level, she is another aspect of the heroine—she is Woman as grieving Madonna and woman as true Friend. The novel as a whole has at its symbolic heart a kind of tripartite female being composed of *Eli*nor—*Ell*is-Juliet—Gabri*ella*. We can hear in their names the ring of *elle . . . elle*. Elle is.

One of the moral themes of *The Wanderer* is the need for wider sympathies. The author makes a play for mutual appreciation, for understanding and respect between two hostile nations. Her work is itself a voice from the coast of France, imploring (sometimes in the French language) pity and admission. It was not a voice very likely to be favorably heard at the time. In her prefatory remarks, which aroused some reviewers' ire, Burney defends her subject, saying that, though she is not "venturing upon the stormy sea of politics," it is impossible to avoid the French Revolution:

> to attempt to delineate, in whatever form, any picture of actual human life, without reference to the French Revolution, would be as little possible, as to give an idea of the English government without reference to our own [i.e., the "Glorious Revolution" of 1688]: for not more unavoidably

is the last blended with the history of our nation, than the first, with every intellectual survey of the present times.

(I:xiii)

But many readers in 1814 did not want to think of the Revolution as a world-historical event that had changed the face of things; they wanted to see it as an unfortunate episode, and to get back to normal. The facts of Burney's life were well known and her allusion to them in her autobiographical dedication, with its praise of France, did something to sabotage the novel. The author had married a Frenchman, resided in France—and now failed to criticize Napoleon. Readers would have enjoyed reading a novel displaying the evils of France under the Corsican tyrant and evoking patriotic enthusiasm for simple English virtues. The Wanderer is scarcely patriotic at all, in that sense; it says England ought to change. It offers a somber view of deep-rooted wrongs in the structure of English social, economic, and sexual life. Such an analysis, and the plea against social cruelty, did not fit too well with Lord Liverpool's and Castlereagh's England. Government and the middle classes had been taking a firmer conservative line while the nation was involved in the expensive Napoleonic wars. The lot of the poorer classes in England in 1814 was in many ways worse than it had been at the beginning of the 1790s. Had the novel been published between 1798 and 1800 (about the time Burney first started working on it), it would have fitted in with contemporary fictional debate; the Revolution was still unignorable. But The Wanderer appeared in 1814. Its date of publication worked against it—it appeared just after the defeat of Napoleon. By the time the reviewers got to it, the Allied leaders were assembling to discuss what could be taken from France and how Europe was to be disposed of. It was a good time for right-wing triumph and a bad time either for pleas for more social justice or appeals for a better understanding of France.

Certainly, most of the reviewers wanted to forget the bad old days of radical thought, and to make sure that their readers were not taken in. There has been a rather hazy impression that The Wanderer was a failure from the outset, but that is not so. The first edition sold out at once, and a second edition had to be run off at the time of publication; 3,500 copies were sold almost instantly—an extremely large issue of a novel for the time.[23] It is interesting that the reviewers were stimulated into dealing with the novel almost at once. With unusual rapidity for the time (by the next month), they extinguished it. It was the reviewers who very authoritatively expressed the view that the work was an utter failure, unendurable to persons of taste. Almost to a man (and the reviewers were all male), the critics insisted that the topics were passés—revolutionary ideas were of course a forgotten fad. As the Gentleman's Magazine said, "Had this Novel appeared when the infatuation alluded to [i.e., Elinor's] reigned in full force, it must have made a much stronger impression upon the public mind than it will at present; but as there are juvenile readers . . . 'The Wanderer' will . . . serve as an historical antidote to any lurking remains of poisonous doctrines."[24]

(That was the most favorable review.) The *Quarterly Review* raked Burney fore and aft for having had the effrontery to refer favorably in her dedication to her life in France and to French acquaintances, instead of showing up "the gigantic despotism, the ferocious cruelty, the restless and desolating tyranny of Buonaparte."[25] Burney had sworn to the customhouse officers that her papers contained no "political writings," but the book really was political, and of course the reviewers noticed it. The novel was subversively Romantic and democratic, praising where it ought to condemn and censuring where it ought to praise. It was more than unsatisfactory—it was an affront, especially to public guardians of the Right, like John Wilson Croker of the *Quarterly*, who was to write a notoriously scathing review of Keat's *Endymion* four years later, largely because of the low-class young poet's sympathy with the Cockney radicals. The first reviewers of Burney's novel were not simply enlightened persons of taste, appealing disinterestedly to universal standards. They had axes to grind.

Their axes were to be the sharper and more ruthless because the novelist explicitly developed questions of woman's rights and woman's wrongs. The persistent theme in all of Burney's novels—the struggle to survive, the conflict between the urge to rebel and the urge to conform—are in her last novel oriented to the issues of woman's social and sexual destiny. The novel contains one apparently doctrinaire feminist of the Wollstonecraft school in Elinor Joddrel. Croker cites her character as an example of the novel's "monstrous absurdities":

> if, where all is monstrous, we should select any individual instance . . . a certain Miss Elinor Joddrel [*sic*], who after appearing as a gay trifling pleasant sort of young gentlewoman, breaks out, of a sudden, as a Jacobin, philosopher and atheist.[26]

But Elinor's first speeches on board the boat show that she is a pleasant young Jacobin. Croker evidently objected to any woman who possesses such views being presented as an interesting and entertaining character—there ought to be an absolute split between a witty well-bred woman and a woman with horrid opinions. He was not the only critic to feel a strong objection to the issue of the rights of woman being raised at all, still less as a living concern in the lives of the central female characters. Indeed, female characters airing their problems create a disgusting spectacle. William Hazlitt, who was a radical democrat in some respects but not all, and most definitely not in relation to women, uses his review of *The Wanderer* to disparage all of Burney's works, united as they are by certain common principles which the new subtitle gives away: "The difficulties in which she involves her heroines are indeed 'Female Difficulties,'—they are difficulties created out of nothing." In this same article in the *Edinburgh Review*, Hazlitt attacks womankind in general as an inferior species, and all women writers:

The surface of their minds, like that of their bodies, seems of a finer texture than ours; more soft, and susceptible of immediate impression. They have less muscular power,—less power of continued voluntary attention,—or reason—passion and imagination: But they are more easily impressed with whatever appeals to their senses or habitual prejudices. The intuitive perception of their minds is less disturbed by any general reasonings on causes or consequences. They learn the idiom of character and manner, as they acquire that of language, by rote merely, without troubling themselves about the principles.[27]

Women are quick, shallow, and prejudiced, capable of noting manners and "alive to every absurdity which arises from . . . a deviation from established custom." As writers, they can convey a few scattered impressions, but they cannot reason. "There is little other power in Miss Burney's novels, than that of immediate observation"; the author is "a very woman."[28] This retrospective damning review of all Burney's novels states that women are doomed to be shallow writers of transitory fiction. Hazlitt is not annoyed at the silly novelists but at a female novelist who forsakes her humble place as prattling entertainer and tries to talk about female experience as if it mattered. He is, of course, right in seeing that *all* of Burney's novels were really about "Female Difficulties," though, as we have seen, these difficulties were not "created out of nothing," but have historical and social "causes or consequences." These causes and consequences Hazlitt denies, as he denies women's ability to deal with any such connections. He not only damns, he tries to disconnect. There is no sense in any of it; like Mr. Scope, he is certain there is no sense in observing England at the present time through the experience of a woman.

The Wanderer shows that Burney had at least been listening, seriously listening, to the feminists of the '90s, to writers like Mary Hays and Mary Wollstonecraft. Critics wanted to say that her heroine Juliet's experiences were just silly (as Hazlitt does), while pouncing on the radical Elinor as an anachronistic example of an outmoded folly. It is an ironic entertainment to read the remarks in *The British Critic:*

> The revolutionary spirit, which displays itself in the sentiments and actions of Miss Elinor Joddrel, is fortunately for a bleeding world, now no longer in existence; few of our female readers can remember the *egalité* mania which once infested the bosoms of their sex.[29]

Things have gone back to normal. The "*égalité* mania"—the outcry about the rights of woman—has now happily past. So the reviewers ardently wished and believed. It belonged to the bad old days of the decade of the Revolution; they evidently thought of that period rather in the way some people have thought of the Sixties in our Eighties. The reviewers, holding the line, were not going to be grateful to any novelist who should remind other women about the plague of desire for equality. The sixty-two-year-old novelist was not to escape the sharpest personal attack as a punishment for her mistake. Croker attacks her gloatingly in specifically sexual terms; her books are merely a reflection of her body:

> The Wanderer has the identical features of Evelina—but of Evelina grown old; the vivacity, the bloom, the elegance, 'the purple light of love' are vanished; the eyes are there, but they are dim; the cheek, but it is fur-rowed, the lips, but they are withered.[30]

Crisp's prophecy of 1778 had indeed come to pass: "Years and wrinkles in their due season . . . will succeed. You will then be no longer the same Fanny of 1778, feasted, caressed, admired. . . ."[31] *The Wanderer* was not the work of a winsome young Fanny, offering the voice of a naïve Evelina in order to charm; the work of the aging Madame d'Arblay must be rejected, as a man would reject the claim for his sexual attention made by an aged hag. To like *The Wanderer* is to sympathize with the unpatriotic, the passé, the foolish—and for a woman reader, to identify herself with the unlovely, the graceless, the withered.

A book that attracts so very much heated abuse must have some life in it, of some kind. A novel that brings down such thunder from the Right cannot itself be a simple support of conservatism. Unfortunately, until recently the few critics who have dealt with the novel have generally been intimidated by its poor reputation (without inspecting the sources of that reputation), and many are disappointed to find that Burney does not endorse feminist views as we would have her do.[32] The problem, for feminist readers in the late twentieth century as for male conservatives in the Regency era, is chiefly definable in terms of the distressing role of Elinor Joddrel. We will not understand the novel if we do not get a good view of Elinor, and see the various uses to which the novelist puts her.

From the outset, the reader is drawn into feeling a good deal of sympathy with Elinor. Her desire to make life more dramatic is understandable; she hates "stagnation" and middle-class life in Lewes, and Brighton is certainly stagnant. She has the difficulty of the intelligent woman of finding a suitable mate. With great frankness she confesses to "Ellis" how she came to be engaged to the wrong man. The rising lawyer, Dennis Harleigh, let her argue against him when he was practicing his "causes": "I always took the opposite side . . . in order to try his powers, and prove my own." She then began to argue other subjects with him, "canvassing . . . the Rights of Man," and enjoyed his presence because she associated him with "the display of my own talents" (I:344–345). Elinor might have made a good wife for a lawyer; if life were different, she might have been a good lawyer herself. Elinor breaks the engagement with a glee that is partly a cover for guilt. She knows that she and Dennis are not really suited: "The truth is, our mutual vanity mutually deceived us." But she has fallen in love with another man, and determines to engage in a grand revolutionary experiment. Albert Harleigh, her Dennis's older brother, has not shown any interest in her, but, she reasons, that is merely because of the proprieties of the former connection. Elinor, like Mary Hays and like Mary Hays's fictional heroine Emma Courtney, will assert the new rights of woman to make the choice and take the sexual initiative. Elinor feels, as she tells "Ellis," inspired, reborn "as if just created, and ushered into the world" and the world is made new: "Every thing now is upon a new scale, and man appears to be worthy of his faculties" (I:355–356). Elinor rejoices in "throwing off the trammels of unmeaning custom, and acting, as well as thinking, for myself" (I:342). These are some of Burney's own favorite phrases, and she does not give them lightly to Elinor. The novel does endorse acting for oneself, and many customs and forms are shown to be unmeaningful. Yet the problem is how, when, and in what manner a woman should act for herself. Elinor's action, after all, involves other people, including the hapless Ellis-Juliet whom she uses as unwilling messenger to Harleigh, partly because she wants to find out if Harleigh has, as her jealousy hints, fallen in love with the foreign stranger. "Ellis" tries to fulfill the task faithfully, and brings Harleigh's response, which she words as tactfully as she can. The answer, in short, to the female wooer is "no."

Elinor's mistake seems not her making the declaration, but her unwillingness, for which persevering males have set a precedent, to take "no" for an answer. In her fantasies, the daring superwoman must achieve the supernal reward. She cannot let herself think that the grand trammel-breaking inauguration of freedom can sink into the commonplace daily world of embarrassment and unhappiness. She confronts Harleigh and Ellis in the summerhouse, and tries to argue him into changing his mind and feelings. She wants to assure him that her motives are worthy,

> "though they may lead you to a subject which you have long since, in common with every man that breathes, wished exploded, the Rights of woman: Rights, however, which all your sex, with all its arbitrary assumption of superiority, can never disprove, for they are the Rights of human nature; to which the two sexes equally and unalienably belong."

She knows, and he acknowledges, that he does not wish "to look down upon the wife . . . and upon the mother, of whose nature you must so largely partake; as upon mere sleepy, slavish, uninteresting automatons." Harleigh's "noble, liberal nature," which does not look down on women, accords the basis of her defense "in allowing me the use of my faculties." She then argues for woman's use of her faculties:

"Why, for so many centuries, has man, alone, been supposed to possess, not only force and power for action and defence, but even all the rights of taste . . . in the choice of our life's partners? Why, not alone, is woman to be excluded from the exertions of courage, . . . not alone to be denied deliberating upon the safety of the state of which she is a member, and the utility of the laws by which she must be governed;—must even her heart be circumscribed by boundaries as narrow as her sphere of action in life? Must she be taught to subdue all its native emotions? To hide them as sin, and to deny them as shame? Must her affections be bestowed but as the recompence of flattery received; not of merit discriminated? . . . Must nothing that is spontaneous, generous, intuitive, spring from her soul to her lips?"

(I:399–405)

Elinor makes a strong rhetorical argument, and she seizes upon her right to use rhetoric. One of the reasons reviewers criticized Burney's language in *The Wanderer*, finding it guilty of "bombast and awkwardness,"[33] may have been that they disapproved of the concerns expressed in the language. Nobody in the novel takes Elinor on or answers her back, nobody argues—let alone argues well—that woman ought for good reasons to be denied any part in the government of the state in which she lives, or participation in framing laws by which she must be governed, or articulation of her own sexuality. Burney wishes Elinor's questions to ring in the mind, and her statements to arouse some sympathy in the reader. This in itself marks a wide difference between Burney's Jacobin Elinor and the parodic female new thinkers of the anti-Jacobin works, such as Bridgetina Botherim in Elizabeth Hamilton's *Modern Philosophers* (1800). In a scene that is at once similar and very different, Hamilton shows vulgar Bridgetina determining to declare her love to the hero, Henry Sydney. Bridgetina goes over the heads of her speech, which she has written out: "*Moral sensibility . . . congenial sympathy, congenial sentiment . . . delicious emotions . . . tender feeling, energetic feeling . . . the germ, the bud and the full-grown fruits of general utility, &c. &c.*" When rejected, Bridgetina can complacently retort, "You do not at present see my preferableness, but you may not always be blind to a truth so obvious."[34] The ultimate source for both scenes is Mary Hays's ardent but unrequited love of William Frend, mathematician and philosophe, as examined in Hays's own novel *Emma Courtney* (1796). In that novel the heroine Emma pursues with lovelorn philosophy her Augustus Harley, as Elinor does her Albert Harleigh—the similarity of names seems scarcely coincidental. Mary Hays had reason to complain that her novel was misinterpreted. She had stated in her "Preface" that Emma was not exemplary, not one of literature's "fantastic models," but "a human being, loving virtue while enslaved by passion." Emma's emotional activities exemplify sensibility gone wrong, but women's energies, repressed from seeking other outlets, tend to go in the direction of love. True sexual liberation must entail the liberation of woman from repressions and false education that make her regard sexual sensibility as all-important while she is yet taught to conceal it—a view that Wollstonecraft shared. Burney does not seem entirely to disagree with Hays's ultimate intention, and what Hays said of Emma Courtney could be (and in effect is) said of Elinor: "light and shade are more powerfully contrasted in minds rising above the common level . . . vigorous powers not unfrequently produce fatal mistakes and pernicious exertions."[35] The scene in which Elinor woos Harleigh is carried out sympathetically, very much in the style of Hays, and not at all in the manner of the broad satire which distinguishes Hamilton's portrait of the stupid feminist Bridgetina. In a review of *The Wanderer,* however, *The British Critic* pointed out Hamilton's work as a preferable model: "were we disposed to recommend a portrait of a female revolutionist, we should certainly advise them [female readers] to seek it in the chaste and animated pages of 'Modern Philosophers,' and not in the overdrawn caricature of Miss Elinor Joddrel."[36] This is disingenuous. Bridgetina is obviously the caricature, and Elinor the character of the genuine "female revolutionist." She is too convincing and appealing a female revolutionist—she might win susceptible female readers to her side, which Bridgetina could never do.

Elinor takes the initiative that even Camilla's father had hesitantly admitted must be allowed to women in reason and nature, although custom and delicacy go against it. Elinor goes wrong in her refusal to accept a negative answer. Having begun in the heroic she must continue. She came to the summerhouse, intending, she says, to commit suicide at the end of the interview if Harleigh did not change his mind. Unlike Harrel, or Lionel, or Bellamy, she does not use the suicide threat as a deliberate weapon, but it is a weapon. In the summerhouse scene, she wants to punish and redeem herself, to punish Ellis and Harleigh, and to exalt herself at their expense. She extorts the promise from Ellis, not from Harleigh, but gives no credit to her friend for any renunciation; she has to think the stranger is "cold" and pretend to herself that Harleigh is undergoing a rejection similar to her own.

Like Edgar Mandelbert, Elinor becomes a watcher, tormentingly suspicious of any connection between Ellis and Albert Harleigh. When Ellis-Juliet must appear as a performer in a public concert, Harleigh is to be in the audience. Elinor hates being upstaged by Ellis at any time. She comes to the concert disguised in masculine apparel. As the concert begins, she reveals herself with a dramatic gesture and—in full view of the Brighton assembly—stabs herself (II: chap. 38). This puts an end to the concert, and Elinor is anticlimatically restored by medical treatment. The doctor who attends her finds her something of a joke; any English gentleman must "demur at venturing upon a treaty for life, with a lady so expert in foreign politics, as to make an experiment, in her own proper person, of the new atheistical and suicidal doctrines," even if "our kind-hearted young ladies of Sussex" are scandalized at Harleigh's "insensibility" (II:434). Elinor becomes a sick joke even to herself:

> Laughing, now, though with bitterness . . . "What does the world say," she cried, "to find that I still live, after the pompous funeral orations, declaimed by myself, upon my death? Does it suspect that I found second thoughts best, and that I delayed my execution, thinking, like the man in the song,
>
> > That for sure I could die whenever I would,
> > But that I could live but as long as I could?
>
> Well, ye that laugh, laugh on! for I, when not sick of myself, laugh too! But, to escape mockery, we must all be guided one by another; all do, and all say, the very same thing. Yet why? Are we alike in our thoughts?"
>
> (III:37)

Elinor has a restless, self-conscious mind, quick to catch sight of her own exhibitionism at work, mocking herself with a Romantic irony that also mocks the world that mocks and judges. She tells "Ellis" that an appearance in a concert would now be more popular than ever: "You may make your own terms, now, with the managers, for the subscription will fill, merely to get a stare at you. If I were poor myself, I would engage to acquire a large fortune, in less than a week, by advertising, at two-pence a head, a sight of the lady that stabbed herself" (III:43). Unlike the other suicidal egotists in Burney's novels, Elinor has an unsentimental view of the communal reaction. She knows what Burney has always known, the secret desire of the group to watch one of its members being destroyed. Elinor is Burney's most interesting blackmailer and most complicated suicidal character. Like Mrs. Delvile, she is a mixed character, a frustrated woman of many talents. Like Mrs. Delvile, she has some wrong beliefs—though the kind of wrong beliefs are different.[37]

In Elinor, Burney deliberately created a character who is strongly and consciously theatrical. Elinor produces, directs, and acts in a play, Vanbrugh and Cibber's *The Provoked Husband*. When her leading actress drops out, Elinor persuades Ellis to act. As she proceeds, Ellis, though at first embarrassed, finds she enjoys acting: "her evident success produced ease . . . her performance . . . seemed the essence of gay intelligence . . . and of lively variety" (I:204). Both heroines, then, are given to the theatrical, as was Burney herself. The staging of *The Provoked Husband*, adapted and reshaped from a sequence in the ur-*Camilla* where the witty Mrs. Solea (a predecessor of Mrs. Arlbery) acts in and directs the same play,[38] is partly based on recollections of the performance of scenes of Cibber's *The Careless Husband* at Chessington in 1771. Burney had played Lady Easy and her half-sister Maria Allen had played Sir Charles, dressed in old Mr. Featherstone's clothes and making a "most dapper, ill-shaped, ridiculous figure."[39] The stage performance in *The Wanderer* (unlike that in the ur-*Camilla*) has no transvestite acting, but when Elinor comes to the concert at which Ellis is to perform she comes as a deaf-and-dumb man in men's clothes: a scarlet coat, "a brilliant waistcoat," a slouched hat, and "a cravat of enormous bulk" (II:400). Like Maria Allen, Elinor parodies the masculine role in taking it on. It is not maleness but masculine freedom, especially freedom of sexual choice, that she wants. Hitherto there has been much cross-dressing in Burney's fiction, but none of it female as male; jokes in her letters, however, show her acutely conscious of the gender implications of the language she uses, which forces mock transvestism upon her: "a little chear-up from you, my dearest Madam, always new *Mans* me"; "I . . . determined to *behave like a man—*being my first appearance in that Character."[40] Elinor, like the rejected wife Eleonora of *The Woman-Hater,* finds it difficult to be a woman in a woman-hating world. She gets momentary freedom in the gaudy masculine attire, but at the price of concealing her female self in appearing "deaf and dumb." When she both speaks and acts on this occasion, the male clothes have "rapidly been thrown aside" and rising in the audience "Elinor appeared in deep mourning; her long hair . . . hanging loosely down her shoulders" (II:404). In the female clothes of sorrow, she plunges a dagger into her breast.

In her later suicide attempt Elinor is equally aware of the theatricality of the event she is staging—which does not mean that she is not in earnest. She inveigles both Juliet (who expects to meet Gabriella) and Harleigh (who expects to meet Juliet) to the churchyard at dawn. Juliet, seeing a female figure gliding through the churchyard, thinks it is Gabriella come to mourn over her child's grave. But, as in a cinematic dissolve, Gabriella mourning becomes Elinor mourning over herself and her lost desires. Juliet perceives "a form in white; whose dress appeared to be made in the shape, and of the materials, used for our last mortal covering, a shroud. A veil of the same stuff fell over the face of the figure" (IV:40). The figure summons them both into the church

> where she threw her left hand over a tablet of white stone, cut in the shape of a coffin, with the action of embracing it; yet in a position to leave evident the following inscription:
>
> > "This Stone
> > Is destined by herself to be the last kind covering
> > of all that remains of
> > ELINOR JODDREL:
> > Who, sick of Life, of Love, and of Despair,
> > Dies to moulder, and be forgotten."
>
> (IV:41)

Exclaiming "Here stands the alter for the happy;—here the tomb for the hopeless!" Elinor points a pistol to her temple, though Harleigh is able to seize her arm before it goes off. The report of the pistol "let off by her own hand, operated upon her deranged imagination." Elinor believes she has fulfiled her purpose and is dying. In a moment, however, she has to realize there was no need for her to fall down like an actor "killed" in a stage play. She has to undergo the extreme embarrassment of realizing she is alive, "recovering . . . to conscious failure, and conscious existence." The irony of the anticlimax impresses especially herself: "I am food, for fools,—when I meant to be food only for worms!" (IV:43).[41] The slight parodic echo of Hotspur's dying words impresses us with Elinor's capacity to rise above her situation while yet still remaining helplessly embedded in it. The theater of her consciousness torments her and she can find no relief from it. Always to a large extent aware of the absurdities of her actions, Elinor can even recognize her own responsibilities, but without seeing any world order which would make such accountability helpful and significant. As she at length tells the woman she knows only as "Ellis": "With my own precipitate hand, I have dug the gulph into which I am fallen!" (V:208).

Elinor is not necessarily wrong in what she sees or feels; she acts out theatrically roles which are socially proffered, and literalizes what is usually left metaphorical (girls may have wounded hearts, one would rather shoot oneself, love is a dagger to the breast). Clarinda's wedding dress evokes a somewhat conventional simile: "In virgin white looked her habit, but her livid, bloodless face, gave to it the semblance rather of a shrowd, herself the white, pale Spectre."[42] Elinor, waiting for Harleigh's answer, asks Juliet, "How am I to be arrayed? . . . Is it a wedding garment? . . . or . . . a shroud?" (I:382). But Elinor will not remain in the realm of figures of speech; she insists upon wearing the shroud and observing the reactions of others to her significant costume. If Elinor is an actress *en costume,* so, after all, is Juliet, who is decidedly in costume when we first see her, and whose whole progress through England is a sort of unwilling masquerade. Juliet adopts the roles of women who are socially lower and weaker than she "really" is (poor Creole, seamstress, teacher in a dame-school). Elinor adopts the male role, which is much stronger than her own, and then, almost in parody of Gabriella, the humble role of the mourning woman—woman in weakness and misery. Like Camilla, she comes close to death; like Elberta she wants to disturb the peace with shrieks and "fierce harangues." Eve in a veil (a veil that can become a shroud), she keeps trying to unveil the mystery of who or what woman can or may be.

Suicide is a reflex of extreme distaste for reality—and sometimes reality is distasteful. Yet Elinor's kind of suicide is a learned response, a mediated reaction instructed by Bolingbroke, Hume, and young Werther. The suicide threat is a testimonial to Elinor's allegiance to heroic dogma and Romantic modernism. In her suicide attempt she is very visibly a disciple of Mary Wollstonecraft. After

Godwin published his own "Memoir" of his wife in her *Posthumous Works* (1798), the whole world knew of Mary Wollstonecraft's unsuccessful attempts at suicide, especially her leap from Putney Bridge in October 1795, in despair over rejection by her lover, Gilbert Imlay. Elinor is one of the suicidal feminists, then—those paradoxical strong-minded martyrs to sensibility, whose revolutionary principles bid them ignore the canon 'gainst self-slaughter.

But Burney had more immediate sources than accounts of the life of Mary Wollstonecraft for any study of obsessive loving and female self-destructiveness. When Godwin's biography of his wife appeared in 1798 (not a year in which Burneys could feel smug about their own sexual arrangements), Burney must have been struck by the resemblances between herself and Wollstonecraft. True, Burney had lived a sexually regular, moral, and chaste life—but she had known nonetheless what it is to be in the grip of an obsession. Her tormented account, in letter after letter, of her unrequited love for George Owen Cambridge, shows her knowledge of those depths. And in the court years (rejected, again, by Colonel Digby), she had come to feel suicidal. Several years before Wollstonecraft's plunge from Putney Bridge, Burney had been penning scenes of suicidal misery. Burney was not looking upon Elinor Joddrel from a high vantage point of safety. In Elinor, Burney examines her own sensibility and her own capacities for both protest and self-destruction—a self-destruction which she had nearly literalized in the court years, in determinedly pining and being consumed away. Elinor's passion in the churchyard and church is a revisiting of Cerulia in the churchyard in the last act of *Hubert De Vere:*

And quick, from Head to foot, I mark'd my Grave,
Next—so the vision bid—I cast me down
On the cold Earth, and there I bar'd my Breast,
And, with the fresh damp mould I strew'd it o'er:
Thrice then I cried aloud "Bury this first!
Come! Hubert's Spirit come! thou hast broke my Heart,
Come, give it Sepulture!"[43]

"Go—*To Dig your own Grave*"; "With my own precipitate hand," says Elinor, "I have dug the gulph into which I am fallen" (V:208). Cerulia, in the play, wins not censure but admiration from the other characters, including Geralda, who envies her calm response.

Yet the female suicidal gesture, though it seems defiant, original, and liberating, is an obedience to social commands, in the perverse way that Mr. Harrel's suicide is a homage to social commands regarding wealth. The customary command for woman is that she be unobtrusive, slender, and quiet. In Albany's inset tale in *Cecilia*, this is angrily parodied by Albany's girl, who seemed "deaf, mute, insensible," who looked at him with "dove-like softness and compliance" while refusing to speak, and eating only a little dry bread, until she expires (IV:707–708). Joyce in *The Woman-Hater* reacts against the inanimate personality her father wishes on her, "shy, pensive, & nearly mute"; Joyce rejects the value of ladylike behavior, "sitting with my hands before me . . . & never eating half as much as I like." There is no better way to be unobtrusive, slender, and mute than to be dead—which is perhaps woman's ideal condition ("I don't know what the devil a woman lives for after thirty"). In turning her sexual feeling and her anger against herself, Elinor is not helping other women but betraying them. She is willing, for the price of one brilliant theatrical display, to act as accomplice in despising and destroying a body which she does not enjoy. She is very physically insistent on her desire "to moulder" in a manner reminiscent of Elgiva ("Within the Tomb / She will consume,— / Worms & Maggots must be fed").[44] Juliet treats her own body with more respect, and notices when it is being mistreated by others, like employers who wish to fatigue her mercilessly. Yet Juliet first appears in bandages, as if she conceals wounds; her fellow passengers discuss possible causes, ranging from "playing with kittens" to "scrambling from some prison" (I:23), but Juliet gives no explanation for a false woundedness which seems to accompany the concept of a female.

In Elinor we see represented the problem of woman's body, which our culture says is a problem, something to mourn for. The debate on the soul between Elinor and Harleigh in the last volume of the novel is a debate about the nature and future of Elinor's body. Harleigh's propositions for the immortality of the soul offer an imperfect consolation. What impresses and scares Elinor is the alternative suggestion that every particle of the dust to which the body returns may retain some portion of consciousness. This macabre speculation turns the earth into an abode of horror indeed, a permanent ground of unspeaking embarrassment, every part of it a mute but sensitive body of life-in-death engaged in a silent scream. Elinor's own body is at the center of the argument, a fact which may have aroused unconscious unease and disgust in the reviewers, women's dying bodies not being easy matters for contemplation.

Elinor is insistently physical. In the concert hall, she "plunged a dagger into her breast. The blood gushed out in torrents" (II:404). The ladies hide their faces while "the men, though all eagerly crowding to the spot of this tremendous event" approach "rather as spectators of some public exhibition, than as actors in a scene of humanity" (II:405). Harleigh heroically calls for a surgeon and a chair for "the bleeding Elinor," and the surgeon declares she cannot be removed "till he should have stopt the effusion of blood" (II:406). Her wound, her blood, are incessantly referred to—though woman's blood is properly something to be hidden. Elinor refuses to have the wound dressed, but when she faints the surgeon, at Harleigh's bidding, is able to "snatch this opportunity for examining and . . . dressing the wound" (II:410) while modest Harleigh refrains from looking. This whole scene has echoes in it of Burney's mastectomy, when a knife was indeed plunged into her breast and she bled profusely; denied female company, she was hemmed in by doctors, "surrounded by the 7 men" as spectators at her theater of pain.[45] Lightly veiled in a cambric handkerchief thrown over her face, she had been the central figure at a species of execution, a macabre sort of theater. Julia Epstein comments on the way Burney's account of her mastectomy "depicts and metonymizes a dynamic of male-female power relations, a play of professional authority against female autonomy as symbolized by the sacrosanct female body here to be defiled."[46] A similar play of male and professional authority against female autonomy is here enacted in *The Wanderer,* with Harleigh's and the surgeon's (beneficent) control over Elinor's body. Elinor has, however, tried to take all the power literally into her own hands by taking up the male instrument and preempting the power to wound herself.

In Elinor, relations between female mind and body, social personality and physical self, are literalized. Metaphors become realities, as they had done for Burney. In her heartbreak over Mr. Cambridge, she had suffered a metaphorical pain in the breast, complaining to Susanna of "the depth of the Wound which has so long been kept open, & the unmerciful heedlessness with which it has so often been probed."[47] She lived to experience a most literal, deep wound of the breast. Elinor combines the metaphorical and the literal, defining the region of pain and restlessness that is woman's body and her sensibility under new regime and old. The mind-body problem is very real for Elinor. Like Camilla in her terrifying vision, Elinor renders the woman's body as felt from within. She experiences the mind-body problem in a female way, and there is sense in her personal theater. But to a man like Mr. Naird, the doctor, she is only a mad scientist, "a lady . . . to make an experiment, in her own proper person, of the new atheistical and suicidical [*sic*] doctrines" (II:434). For a lady to make an experiment is in itself a kind of absurdity or impertinence, and Mr. Naird agrees with the "prudent mammas" and not with the "kind-hearted young ladies of Sussex" who think Mr. Harleigh should not "resist love so heroic."

Elinor seems, however, in some way justified in trying to make a stand for sexual passion in the tepid and cautious social environment where sexual energy burns very low. The world of England (or at least of representative Sussex) seems nearly sexless, as if the "prudent mammas" have done too much already. There is no rival to Harleigh for the role of *jeune premier,* but he is noticeably weak and hesitant, and even more notably absent from most of the action. When he is present, dutifulness makes him hesitate from any kind of intervention; once the commissary swears he is Juliet's *"mari,"* Harleigh is rendered helpless. He is ironically all decorum and no passion; the least interesting of all of Burney's love-story heroes on one level, on another he seems a satiric creation.

Harleigh seems to participate in a general blight of males. Young Lord Melbury is puppyish. Sir Lyall Sycamore is a stock seducer, an example of vulgarity and mean oppression in the upper ranks of society—he will cautiously pursue a simple-minded shopgirl. Mrs. Ireton's son has the reputation of a "male jilt," having been engaged many times. He has been taken over Europe by his mother, in order to find the perfect wife (in mockery of such *Cœlebs*-like searches).[48] This silly young fellow, an upper middle-class Mr. Smith, tells Juliet, in a comic interview, that she is not the kind of girl he likes: "Don't take it ill, my love, for you are a devilish fine girl. I own that. But I want . . . something . . . frisky, flighty, fantastic,—yet panting, blushing, dying with love for me!" (III:360).

Young Ireton uses Juliet as his confidante in a conceited discussion of his love troubles: "of all the females with whom I have had these little engagements, there is not one whom I have seriously thought of marrying, after the first half hour" (III:365). But Elinor's public demonstration has shown him what he wants: "O that noble stroke! That inimitable girl! Happy, happy, Harleigh! . . . If I could meet with one who would have taken such a measure for my sake, and before such an assembly,—I really think I should worship her!" (III:368). Neither Juliet nor the reader would have connected silly Ireton with intelligent Elinor. But the fatuous young man wishes to be loved for himself alone, with grand passion, and when he has once seen what could be done in the passionate line he greedily wants to collect it. He toys with images of feminine sexual submission, of self-sacrificing adoration, yet wishes at the same time to be somehow overpowered into matrimony. His wish for a woman to attempt suicide publicly for his sake is of course a form of woman-hating, and reminds us of the ironic consequences of Elinor's sensibilist romanticism. Her heroic demonstration might, in fact, be digested all too readily by a culture which believes that women should be submissive, wounded, and appropriated. Elinor's error lies in thinking she could mark her claim to Harleigh by her action; a man would not, however, mind marking his claim to a woman by her volunteering such a noble stroke for his sake. The admiration or, rather, fantasies of Ireton would be one of the most humiliating penalties Elinor could undergo for her action.

The comic male juniors are flighty and mean (perhaps not even Harleigh can be utterly exonerated on these counts). The comic male elders are much stronger characters, though no more reassuring. Admiral Powel, to whom events in France signify only the opportunity for the advancement of naval men, tries to interest his niece in matrimony with a young sea captain who "had had the luck . . . to see his two senior officers drop by his side." He will soon be a commodore: "And then, my dear . . . think what would have been your pride to have read all o' the sudden, news of him in the Gazette!" (V:375–376). The admiral may not have much interest in marriage as union (the wife's pleasure is to be in reading news about her husband), but he has a dogmatic belief in marriage. He is disconcerted by the complications of Juliet's first marriage, and scandalized at her relief in hearing of the commissary's death: "a husband's a husband . . . if a woman may mutiny against her husband, there's an end of all discipline" (V:354–355). (He sounds a little like the judge in *The Wrongs of Woman* responding to the wife's plea with a statement on "the fallacy of letting women plead their feelings, as an excuse for the violation of the marriage-vow . . . he had always determined to oppose all innovation, and the new-fangled notions which incroached on the good old rules of conduct.")[49] To Admiral Powel, institutions are institutions; wives are but wives.

Powel is one of the many old bachelors who crowd the novel. Mr. Riley is obviously unattracted by women except when they are objects for his thirsty curiosity; this curiosity leads him to become a spy for the French. Giles Arbe, a more sympathetic old bachelor, has a strong and innocent sense of fair play, and often functions in the novel as the voice of social justice. But he is always committing little acts of destruction, as when he destroys Juliet's note to Miss Arbe, using it as a spill for his lamp. He describes other instances of his absent-minded violence, as if giving an account of curious natural phenomena. He once burned a gentleman's stick, "a mighty curious sort of cane," by using it to poke the fire; and once struck a lady in the face, trying to kill a gnat: the lady was "quite angry" and "I ran away as fast as I could" (II:,236–237). Emotionally, he is a permanent child.

The novel's extreme example of the childish man is Sir Jaspar Herrington, the gouty old bachelor of seventy-five. The bitter flavor of Burney's sexual comedy in *The Woman-Hater* is recalled in the presentation of Sir Jasper. He eventually tells Juliet his story. In youth, determined to be scrupulous and exacting in his choice of a wife, he undertook a search for the perfect wife, misguided by the same principles as those of Edgar Mandlebert and Dr. Marchmont in *Camilla*. He overzealously applied Rule B of the courtship game—"modestly persuaded that I ought to find a companion without a blot!" (IV:168). He found no one good enough; now he is paying for "youthful severity" by falling somewhat in love with every young woman: "I never see a lovely young creature, but my heart calls out what a delicious wife she would make me! were I younger (IV:170). Sir Jaspar lavishes compliments upon Juliet, and fills his discourse with references (derived from *The Rape of the Lock*) to fairies, elves, sylphs. Some of his dialect may be recalled from Dr. Charles Burney's language of compliment and badinage in addressing a lady such as Mrs. Thrale ("there are . . . mischievous Sylphs & Gnomes that successfully forge Fetters for Resolution . . . I seem surrounded with an army of them, that prevent me from doing every thing I wish & intend").[50] The florid language of Sir Jaspar is the result of his uneasy half-knowledge of himself and his sexuality, which he can at moments play off as merely charming fantasy. He is, like Dr. Johnson, tormented by solitary thoughts: "An hundred little imps of darkness scrambled up my pillow." He is tortured by his own sexual waste, and by his present unattractiveness; his imps "encircled my eye-balls, holding mirrors in each hand. . . . You think, they expressed, of a young girl? Behold here what a young girl must think of you!" (IV:157). Yet he has a title, money, and lands to offer; he does propose to Juliet.

Burney, strongly aware of the male attitude to older women (vividly illustrated in *Evelina*), had long wished to deal with the complementary distaste of young women for older men. In her unpublished works, this issue had been frequently raised. "Clarinda" is petrified at the ugly thought of marriage to old Lord Winslow; Miss Percival derides the "Monsters," "The Wigs!" and runs from them; Hilaria Dalton loathes the thought of Lord Ardville's "odious society"; and Sir Archy joins her in mocking crippled old husbands "wrapt in fleecy hosiery,—reclined on an easy chair, & unable, by the month together, to hop after & torment their fair Mates." Sir Jaspar is this crippled, ugly old man. If Elinor represents the problem of woman's body as woman sees it and is made to feel it, Sir Jaspar represents the problem of the male's body as woman sees it—a body given to age and weakness, disease and death, yet culturally assertive of mastery. Sir Jaspar's position gives him power; the visibly impotent body can still doggedly express sexual and social aggressiveness. This unusual emphasis by a woman author upon male physicality in its grotesque and piteous aspects proved a shock for Burney's readers, and the effect on some of these readers may be gauged by the need Croker felt to heap physical abuse upon the author.

Sir Jaspar's feelings for Juliet are undeniably sexual; he begins a proposal to her, holding her by grotesquely "fastening her gown to the grass by his two crutches" (III:399–400). This gesture is deeply unpleasant, representing the masculine aggression, impotence, and uncertainty combined that we find throughout the novel. Sir Jaspar's abuse of sex has recoiled upon him, adding to the choleric irritability of his disposition, as was the case with the original "Woman-Hater," Sir Roderick. But Sir Jaspar is a much stranger figure than Sir Roderick, at once appealing and repulsive, naïve and possessive. In the latter part of the novel's action, he acts the part of the love-story hero—finding Juliet in London, following her, rescuing her in the nick of time from abduction by the villain—all of which activities Harleigh, who *should* be the hero, refrains from with his own kind of impotence. But Sir Jaspar only "rescues" Juliet because he wants her to join him in his fantasy games.

The male characters in *The Wanderer* are all weak men with decided ideas as to their strengths in dealing with women, and all have some designs of their own for the women's roles. Elinor rebukes Ellis-Juliet when the latter comes to her sickbed after the suicide debacle:

"Ellis, Ellis! You only fear to alarm, or offend the men—who would keep us from every office, but making puddings and pies for their own precious palates!"

(III:40)

Burney herself had mocked the view and the cliché image in her portrait of Sir Roderick, who believes women have no business reading: "what can their little heads make out of such matters? . . . And what ought they to know? Except to sew a Gown, & make a Pudding?" Elinor may be unjust to Juliet, but not to her world, as she attacks the causes and grounds of woman-hating and female inferiority in her society:

> "By the oppressions of their own statutes and institutions, they render us insignificant; and then speak of us as if we were so born! . . . They assert not that one man has more brains than another, because he is taller. . . . They judge him not to be less ably formed for haranguing in the senate; for administering justice in the courts of law; for teaching science at the universities, because he could ill resist a bully, or conquer a footpad! No!—Woman is left out in the scales of human merit, only because they dare not weigh her!"
>
> (III:41–42)

Hazlitt connects woman's lesser muscular strength with lack of mental strength; his review is, indirectly, an indignant reply to Elinor's claims, which he seems (rightly) to have felt that Elinor's author supports. Like Wollstonecraft and others, Elinor sees the injury involved in the elevation of woman on a pedestal which is really just a jail: "They require from her, in defiance of their examples!—in defiance of their lures!—angelical perfection. She must be mistress of her passions . . . she must always be guided by reason, though they deny her understanding!" (III:42–43). This is a complaint implicit in *Camilla*, here made explicit, and not denied or refuted by either the heroine or the narrator. Throughout the novel the stupidities and restrictions that lead Elinor to rebellion are constantly placed before our eyes. The reader is induced to feel some stirrings of rebellion, too, from time to time, as when hearing the complacent rumblings of the obtuse Mr. Scope, who wonders why the French have "so many females being called Goddesses of Reason": "I cannot much commend their sagacity . . . in putting the female head, which is very well in its proper sphere, upon coping, if I may use such an expression, with the male" (II:182–183).

Such attitudes are both causes and byproducts of the unjust and absurd conditions that make life so difficult for women. These conditions are clearly set out—they are the given. The question is, what can or should a woman do in such a world of things as they are? Elinor makes what Burney sees as the customary error of ideologues of all sorts, of mistaking wish for reality. She is not really democratic, for she expresses contempt for the common herd; she views radicalism as the opportunity for self-fulfilment, which she associates only with the liberation of her emotional and sexual sensibility. In some respects, love-longing is only too traditional an occupation for women. Elinor confuses her radical chic and personal intensity with dynamic concern; she pays too little attention to the freedom needed by others. Janet Todd criticizes Burney for not showing true friendship between Elinor and Juliet: "the most promising tie of Juliet with Elinor is rejected in ridicule, although their union might have released the androgynous power Wollstonecraft described." But Burney is not particularly interested in portraying "such a union as a psychic model."[51] The novel as a whole exhibits different aspects of femininity against the background of those rather weak men.

Any strong thematic relationship in a Burney novel is a relationship of conflict and complement together. Elinor may be Cerulia to Juliet's Geralda, but they have, in their situations during the action, changed social classes. Juliet is poor. Elinor does not realize that her own financial security is part of the picture—in some ways she is not revolutionary enough. Burney seems to be taking a hint from *The Wrongs of Woman* as well as from her own *Hubert De Vere*: in Wollstonecraft's unfinished novel, the middle-class woman is concerned with love and the restrictions of sexual freedom while the poor working woman, Jemima, is concerned with earning her own living, and the economic restrictions placed on the woman who enters the marketplace. Elinor is free from the basic constraints of economic life. One of the really comic things in her presentation is the pompous way she exhorts her émigrée friend. Juliet complains that the choice of work is very limited,

> but when she lamented the severe DIFFICULTIES of a FEMALE, who, without fortune or protection, had her way to make in the world, Elinor, with strong derision, called out, "Debility and folly! Put aside your prejudices, and forget that you are a dawdling woman, to remember that you are a active human being, and your FEMALE DIFFICULTIES will vanish into the vapour of which they are formed. Misery has taught me to conquer mine!"
>
> (III:36–37)

Elinor is at this moment lying down recovering from her self-made wound and addressing the friend who has taken valuable time off from laborious and ill-paid work to come and see her. Later, when Juliet tries to explain what her life is like, Elinor cannot grasp the hard facts of seeking financial independence: "Nay, 'twas your own choice, you know, to live in a garret, and hem pocket-handkerchiefs." Juliet has to explain that there is little real choice, that independence is in some sense a chimera: "how imaginary is the independence, that hangs for support upon . . . daily exertions!" We may call such situations independent without considering "the difficulty of obtaining employment, the irregularity of pay, the dread of want." Independence and freedom are fine-sounding words unless they are seen in their real and somber relation to hard economic facts: "ah! what is freedom but a name, for those who have not an hour at command from the subjection of fearful penury and distress?" (III: 222–223). Burney shows that any desire to make people free rests on a fallacious dream if it does not consider the economic conditions of employment, wages, and poverty. The freedom of woman is but a hazy fantasy if its middle-class adherents on private incomes can do nothing but declaim and look for

more sexual liberty. Elinor cannot see that it is she, despite her emotional restlessness, who is really the "dawdling woman." Ellis-Juliet has to find out what it
means to be an "active human being" in the harsh outside world. Elinor tends
to think of "freedom" as a mental sensation. Juliet finds that her "freedom,"
like that of so many human beings, male or female, is the liberty to starve or to
work if she can find work.

Juliet's experiences offer a feminist and social view complementary to the
theories of Elinor. They are "Two Ways of looking at the same Thing," "Two
Sides of a Question." The organization of The Wanderer around Juliet means
that the question of the rights and wrongs of woman are everywhere apparent
in the novel, and everywhere connected with questions about the economic
order itself. The questions posed by Juliet's working experience still seem perti-
nent not only to the rights of woman but to the organization of our society in its
economic functions. Burney had been interested in the case and life of working
women in The Witlings, where she gave so much attention to the milliners, and
in Cecilia, where she delineated at some length the life and circumstances of the
carpenter's wife who works in a haberdasher's shop and the pew-opener who
finds work as a clear-starcher. But in Cecilia, the heroine is able to give her
bounty to these poor women, and they are humble adjuncts to her. Now the
heroine is no Lady Bountiful, but herself one of the poor women who must earn
her own living. If "self-dependence" is desirable—as Burney has always believed—and "mental freedom" something human beings naturally seek, then
independence must be defined by relations to material independence, the capacity of the individual to ensure survival and some degree of pleasure through the
economic exchange of his or her own labor and talents.

At the end of her novel Burney explains the position she had designed for
her heroine, as "a being who had been cast upon herself; a female Robinson
Crusoe, as unaided and unprotected, though in the midst of the world, as
that imaginary hero in his uninhabited island" (V:394). "A female Robinson
Crusoe"—a phrase both plangent in its suggestion of loneliness, and satiric. For
the poor woman who tries to earn her own living, contemporary England is
a desert island.[52] In writing about a heroine who takes jobs and becomes
involved in the working world, Burney is following a minor tradition established
by English women novelists of the eighteenth century. Sarah Scott and Charlotte
Lennox had experimented in showing their heroines working for a living,
sometimes in a variety of successive employments. Juliet's life as a paid companion to Mrs. Ireton may owe something to the situation of Lennox's heroine, a
paid companion to Mrs. Autumn in Henrietta (1754). Mary Wollstonecraft's
The Wrongs of Woman follows poor Jemima's progress through a variety of
employments, giving us a cross-section of economic life in England as seen from
the woman's point of view. Burney may also have been influenced by Mary
Hays's The Victim of Prejudice (1799), in which the supposedly illegitimate
heroine is hampered by employers' supercilious doubts as to her morals, as well

as by the designs of gentlemen who can easily think of the method by which a beautiful and unprotected girl should be supported. The detailed presentation of the life of the working woman was at the end of the century associated with liberal or radical women writers such as Inchbald, Hays, and Wollstonecraft. In undertaking the subject, Burney was, as her contemporaries knew, entering the domain of the radical women and in effect allying herself with them.

Ellis-Juliet's working life begins on a fairly high level, though not a comfortable one. Initially, she resides with Mrs. Maple and Elinor as protégée and servant, expected to do needlework. Unable to continue in this awkward position, Juliet moves to cheap lodgings and takes up the suggestion made by Miss Arbe that she should offer lessons on the harp. Miss Arbe, an old young lady of thirty-one, wishes for free lessons for herself. She begins to organize Ellis's affairs as officiously as if her financial patronage were responsible for the musician's career. The section dealing with Ellis's career as a music teacher offers an amusing gallery of students, almost all without talent—Burney was drawing on the lifelong experience of Dr. Burney as a music teacher, as well as on the teaching experiences of her musical brother-in-law, Charles Rousseau Burney, and her sister Hester. Well-to-do ladies refuse to pay their accounts on time, though they join willingly with Miss Arbe in the bustle of getting up a private benefit concert for the reluctant musician at which the amateurs of fashion can perform. Lady Aurora (the Incognita's half-sister, though neither of them knows it) sends fifty pounds to assist the émigrée harpist. Without telling Ellis, whom a languorous connoisseur calls "The Ellis," Miss Arbe lays the money out in buying dress material, "a sarcenet of a bright rose-colour." The other young women exclaim at this choice: "The Ellis will be The rose! . . . but I should sooner take her for my wax-doll, when she's all so pinky winky." Haughty Miss Sycamore explains, "As our uniform is fixed to be white, with violet-ornaments, it was my thought to beg Miss Arbe would order something of this shewy sort for Miss Ellis; to distinguish us *Dilettanti* from the artists" (II:291–293). The whole point of the bright pink gown is to show that Ellis is not a lady. She cannot waste money in buying an elaborate violet and white outfit (as Camilla did), but the money must be wasted for her on bright stuffs that signal the real artist as social inferior. Miss Sycamore casts scorn on the word "artists," a scorn comparable to Compton Delvile's for "writers and that sort of people." The common view of artists as déclassés, and of female artists as degraded, makes Juliet hesitate before assenting to Miss Arbe's concert scheme, but she is rebuked by brusque Giles Arbe, who, knowing her bills, presents her choice not as between dignity and indelicacy, but between dishonesty and honesty: "Better sing those songs, my dear! much better sing those songs!" (II:268). Juliet plays her harp and sings her songs. On the same principle of honesty, she unhappily agrees to take on the role of full professional performer and to sing at a benefit, even though Harleigh urges her, emotively, not to go through with this dreadful scheme, not to transgress the "hitherto acknowledged boundaries of elegant life," not to deviate "from the long-beaten track of female timidity" (II:364–365). By "timidity" he means, as she knows, "modesty." Harleigh is too delicate, too conventional, too considerate to enunciate the word "modesty" itself in telling Juliet she is breaking a kind of by-law of chastity. Performing women lose their chaste bloom. (Burney may have been thinking of Mme. de Staël's *Corinne*, published in 1807.) A woman immodest enough to perform in public unfits herself for the station of a lady, and is making herself unfit to be considered as the potential wife of a gentleman. But Harleigh also does mean *timidity*. We have seen how timidity is valued: Macartney, who was rescued by Evelina, pays her back by praising her downcast eye and timid air. Rousseau and others praise timidity *("leur air craintif")* in a female, the timidity Camilla sometimes spontaneously forgets and that Joyce wants to get rid of. Timidity keeps woman in the beaten track—the track Elinor, like Belfield, decries; there is no reason to believe the "long-beaten track" is not dangerous for women. Juliet is divided; she partly wants to be the kind of lady Harleigh would have her be—but she has already left the beaten track in being the heroic savior, the explorer and wanderer, the female Robinson Crusoe. In the end, she cannot and does not take Harleigh's advice. She must transgress against gentility and female delicacy, in choosing public performance over living on handouts. On the plot level, Juliet's exhibition of herself in public, even under a false name, entails a danger of the revelation of her identity, and a threat of extinction to the distant father-figure—a recurring psychological motif in relation to Burney's feelings about her own writing, and especially relevant to the antagonism expressed by her father to her work's appearance on stage.

Burney defiantly takes the opportunity to speak up for the despised artists, trying to teach her reader how much labor and strain is involved in their work. The ladies of Brighton make the convenient assumption that Juliet's work in both teaching and performing music is trifling and pleasant. Giles Arbe points out with a frankness disagreeable to them the difficulty of being obliged "to fag at teaching people who are too dull to learn" (II:313). Knowing that Juliet is beset by bills she cannot meet, he assails the ladies for not paying their music teacher. Miss Bydel exclaims, "Why are you calling all the ladies to account for not paying this young music-mistress, just as if she were a butcher or a baker; or some useful tradesman," and Mr. Scope ponderously presumes "you do not hold it to be as essential to the morals of a state, to encourage luxuries, as to provide for necessaries?" Giles Arbe tries to explain that the musician, dancer, or actor may be called "an artist of luxury" but " 'tis of your luxury, not his" (II:314–316). Everyone has a right to fair pay and decent treatment, including those who labor with their talents:

> "And because you . . . lounge in your box at operas and concerts . . . do
> you imagine he who sings, or who dances, must be a voluptuary? No! all
> he does is pain and toil to himself; learnt with labour, and exhibited with

difficulty. The better he performs, the harder he has worked. All the ease, and all the luxury are yours. . . . He sings, perhaps, when he may be ready to cry; he plays upon those harps and fiddles, when he is half dying with hunger; and he skips those gavots, and fandangos, when he would rather go to bed!"

(II:320–321)

Through Giles Arbe, Frances Burney speaks up not just for her heroine but for all creative and interpretive artists. Herself the daughter of a musician, and friend of musicians, singers, dancers, actors, she speaks as their advocate, and not just for the great stars but for all. In the earlier novels, characters attend an opera or concert, some appreciating the artists and some disdaining them and treating their work lightly. In this novel, we are taken down among the performers, as the novelist tries to make us see what they see and feel what they feel. Once she is a professional, for instance, Juliet dreads getting a cold and becomes hypochondriacal about her health—her body is an exhibit and an instrument that may let her down.

The Wanderer as a whole is concerned with the *cost*—the human cost—of many things, from the French Revolution (which provides mental luxury and stimulus to some spectators) to the concerts the middle-class gentry see and the clothes they wear. People do not wish to live according to Mr. Arbe's suggested standards of equity. They like to get bargains, as Miss Arbe gets free instruction from Juliet by assuming patronage. "Nobody is born to be trampled on," says Giles Arbe, innocently making his own statement of the rights of man. But his hearers do not agree:

"I hope, too, soon," said Mrs. Ireton, scoffingly, "nobody will be born to be poor!"

"Good! true!" returned he, nodding his head. "Nobody should be poor! That is very well said."

(III:341)

Only Giles Arbe desires that "nobody should be poor." On the contrary, most people need to feel that someone is there to be trampled upon. Like Mr. Harrel, the well-off both exploit the poor and ignore them.

Juliet has to forsake the semi-genteel mode of existence as a music teacher, since it demands capital (the rent of the harp) and brings in returns too slowly. After her meeting with Gabriella, the two émigrées live together in hired lodgings and take orders for embroidery. This is the sort of work more usually available to women, and they have the pleasure of each other's society, though this is severely restricted by the hardships of their task—they cannot even look at each other while talking. They are always working, "though they limited themselves to five hours for sleep; though their meals were rather swallowed than eaten;

and though they allowed not a moment for any kind of recreation, of rest, or of exercise" (III:47). It is an unhealthy life, and brings in too little income for Juliet to continue on her own once Gabriella leaves. The ladies again will not pay their debts. Labor, worry, and loneliness begin to tell upon her spirits: "With an ardent love of elegant social intercourse, she was doomed to pass her lonely days in a room that no sound of kindness ever cheered; with enthusiastic admiration of the beauties of Nature, she was denied all prospect, but of the coarse red tilings of opposite attics" (III:59–60).

Juliet is forced to take a further step downwards from both gentility and independence by seeking employment in Miss Matson's milliner's shop: "Thus . . . concluded her fruitless effort to attain a self-dependence which, however subject to toil, might be free, at least, from controul" (III:104). Now she is no longer to be "self-dependent" as self-employed; she is an employee. In Miss Matson's shop as temporary assistant, Ellis-Juliet is under someone else's control, ordered about, and supervised the whole time. From deadly solitude she is plunged into "a whirl of hurry, bustle, loquacity, and interruptions" (III:105). Mrs. Wheedle's shop in *The Witlings* is here presented from another point of view. Miss Matson turns Juliet's recent escape from France to banal advantage, as she can advertise the latest modes from Paris. The genteel customers are thoughtless, rude, and vain. The milliner and her girls overcharge the humbler customers, and make up for losses on credit by asking exorbitant prices for old or shoddy goods. Juliet's moral sense is offended by the fact that she has no say in the conduct of the business. One of the first casualties of the life of an employee is independent morality; individual responsibility is lost in collective operations.

The atmosphere of the shop is tainted with a flavor of prostitution. The pretty girls sit where they are visible through the window, purposely, so starers will be attracted. The beautiful foreigner with her mysterious history is used as a draw. The other girls entertain themselves with gossip and the hopes of catching some of the many military officers billetted in Brighton, each holding "the fond persuasion of proving an exception to those who had ended in misery and disgrace, by finishing, herself, with marriage and promotion" (III: 111). Sixteen-year-old Flora Pierson, with her "round, plump, rosy cheeks" and "bright, though unmeaning eyes" (III:115) is in particular danger from the attempts of Sir Lyall Sycamore. It does not require much to seduce Flora—a few earrings serve very well. True innocence is extremely dangerous to women; in her nubile naïveté, Flora seems almost a parody of Evelina.[53] Juliet intervenes to try to save Flora because the girl, unlike the others, really has no notion of what she is doing. She is genuinely stupid—so that even her seducer is annoyed by her from time to time, as Flora frankly admits: "Sometimes he'll say I am the greatest simpleton that ever he knew in his life; for all he calls me his angel! He don't make much ceremony with me, when I don't understand his signs" (III:136). Flora is hurt at being cut off from a source of presents, but nothing affects her for very long: "papa says, if the world were all to tumble down, it would not hinder me of my smiling" (III:133).

Anxious to avoid Sir Lyall, who transfers his attentions to her, and suffering the other girls' annoyance at her having (as they see it) enticed away another girl's sweetheart, Juliet leaves Miss Matson (who has underpaid her). Her next employment is at the establishment of Mrs. Hart the mantua-maker. As Juliet cannot bind herself to an apprenticeship, it is agreed that she is "at liberty to continue, or to renounce her engagement, from day to day" (III:168). Juliet is naïvely pleased; the arrangement seems "an approach to the self-dependence, that she had so earnestly coveted." With grateful zeal, she works with extreme diligence at the outset, winning elaborate praise from Mrs. Hart who holds her up as "a pattern to the rest of the sewing sisterhood" (III:169)—thus ensuring this "pattern" worker the resentment of all her workmates. Juliet finds that she cannot keep up this first spurt, and must revert to a more natural pace. Mrs. Hart grumbles at the difference, and Juliet understands the ill will she had excited in the other seamstresses: "she was soon taught to forgive the displeasure which, so inadvertently, she had excited, when she saw the claims to which she had made herself liable" (III:172).

This is an extraordinary point to come upon in a novel of this date. One would expect such an insight only much later—in the work-conscious fiction of the 1830s and '40s. No other author of the eighteenth century or the Regency quite dared to say that a working person's diligence could be overdone, particularly when the work concerned is a perpetual monotonous labor. Burney transcended the customary middle-class attitudes to work as something for which members of lower classes should be grateful, as she escaped from the condescending view of workers as given to idleness. More fully than any other writer of her time, even a radical like Wollstonecraft, Burney examines the sheer *drudgery* involved in such labor. The novel's working scenes are a credit to Burney's imagination, as well as to her heart and her moral sense; after all, she had not herself worked as a milliner or seamstress—she had to *imagine* what such a life would be like. Other writers, like Lennox or even Hays, had shown their young lady workers as pitiable because put in false situations or doing work which is beneath them. Burney examines the nature of the work itself, asking not if her *heroine* is to be pitied for having so to descend, but whether the *work* as at present organized is something which it is right to ask of other human beings.

The seamstress in the mantua-maker's establishment is required to perform only mechanical tasks. In this deadly boredom, Juliet misses the variety of the milliner's shop and the work in which her own "taste and fancy" could play some part, rendering it "at least, less irksome, than the wearying sameness of perpetual basting, running, and hemming" (III:174). She is now selling not her talents but mere mechanical capacity. "Yet what is the labour that never requires respite? What the mind, that never demands a few poor unshackled instants to itself?" (III:172). Frances Burney, who had experienced the labor of employment at court, and knew the need of such "unshackled instants," could extend her experience and the sympathy that arose from it to the life of the nameless worker of low estate. It is all very well to say, as Wollstonecraft does, that a virtuous woman should have sufficient "energy of character" not to shrink even from the occupation of a milliner or mantua-maker if this is the only situation "in which you can be the mistress of your own actions."[54] But such economic independence is so hard won, so costly in human terms, and so restricted that it is questionable whether it can be called independence. Burney seems to be the first novelist to investigate at any depth the phenomenon now known to us as "alienation," the state in which the worker feels no personal participation in the labor by which he—or she—earns a livelihood but is simply a devitalized functionary performing perpetual routine tasks, enduring the "wearying sameness." We often forget that this condition existed before the advent of the great factories, and that much of all labor in affluent societies subjects the worker to the same kind of repetitiveness and mental inertia as the production line. Juliet, an alien in so many senses, discovers the alienation of work.

Ironically, as Juliet discovers, even a situation of drudgery is not secure. Eventually "the particular business for which Mrs. Hart had wanted an *odd hand* was finished; and Juliet . . . abruptly found that her occupation was at an end" (III:177, italics mine). Juliet's self-congratulation at her imaginary liberty in being employed by the day was the effect of her ignorance of the labor market. She now realizes it meant "she was a stranger to security, subject to dismission, at the mercy of accident, and at the will of caprice" (III:178). She was not seen as a human being with whom any relationship was entered into—she was a convenient "odd hand."

Left with her empty freedom of unemployment, the "female Robinson Crusoe" again searches for means to support herself. She is forced to fall back on one of the most traditional genteel employments, as a paid companion to a lady of leisure. That employment and its indignities Frances Burney knew only too well—her grief at entering court had been exacerbated by the shock of horror at discovering "the interior of my position . . . expected by Mrs. Schwellenberg, not to be her colleague, but . . . her companion, her humble companion, at her own command!" Mrs. Ireton requires a "humble companion" for the same purposes; she needs to have someone about her whom she can abuse. She can be indulgent to those whom she favors. Juliet, arriving to take up her post as "an humble companion" (III:252), enters upon a scene of crowded squalor. Mrs. Ireton lies on a sofa; beside her, her nephew teases her lapdog with a greasy chicken bone, while a nurserymaid works with a duster and a hearth-broom, "evidently incensed beyond her pittance of patience" (III:234). Mrs. Ireton can spoil her cur and her nephew while enjoying the trouble they give to others. The trouble provides fresh opportunities for outbursts on Mrs. Ireton's part; Juliet hears the lady berate the nurserymaid, her negro page, and a little charity-girl. Mrs. Ireton, like "Cerbera" Schwellenberg and "Precious" Mrs. Burney the second, enjoys treating those about her to her bad temper. Her flow of invective gives her a kind of poetic pleasure. In that first job interview, she treats Juliet to some sarcastic barbs when the applicant fails to express sufficiently humble solicitation:

> "I should hardly imagine you would take the trouble to present yourself merely to afford me the pleasure of seeing you?—Not but that I ought to be extremely flattered. . . . Who knows but you may propose to make an actress of me?—Or perhaps to instruct me how to become an adept in your own favourite art of face-daubing?"
>
> At least, thought Juliet, I need not give you any lessons in the *art of ingeniously tormenting!* There you are perfect!
>
> (III:252–253)

The phrase that comes to Juliet's mind is the title of a strange eighteenth-century treatise of one-upmanship. *An Essay on the Art of Ingeniously Tormenting; with Proper Rules for the Exercise of that Pleasant Art* (1753) was written by Jane Collier, a friend of Sarah Fielding. Little is known of Collier, but the chapter addressed "To the Patroness of an humble Companion" may have been written out of the experience of working as such a "humble Companion." The author, whose device is to recommend the methods most effectively employed to create misery in all relationships, indicates that this relationship of "Patroness" and "Companion" offers delicious opportunities for cruelty. "From the dejection that is so often seen in the countenance of those that live dependent . . . may we not infer that there are many patronesses, who have true relish for this sport . . . ?"[55] Pointing out the superiority of a companion over a servant as a victim, Collier gives detailed instructions. "Furious scolding and abuse is no bad method . . . but insulting taunts, I think, will do rather better."[56] As examples of taunting ridicule of a young woman of sense and talents, Collier suggests "Begin most requests, or rather commands, with these sort of phrases. . . . 'Can a lady of your *fine parts* condescend to darn this apron? Would it not be too great a condescension for a WIT, to submit to look over my housekeeper's accounts?'"[57] This method is employed by Mrs. Ireton. Scolding Juliet for not attending to her troublesome nephew, Mrs. Ireton asks, "Do you design to let him break his neck down the stone steps? . . . It may be necessary, perhaps, to some of your plans, to see a tragedy in real life? You may have some work in agitation, that may require that sort of study" (III:279). These actually sound rather like taunts that could have been made by Mrs. Burney or Mrs. Schwellenberg to Burney the writer, who might have (literary) work in agitation.[58]

Mrs. Ireton explains to Giles Arbe what she meant by a companion: "I thought . . . I had engaged a young person, who would never think of taking such a liberty as to give her opinion; but who would do, as she ought, with respect and submission, whatever I should indicate" (III:345–346). She is not prepared for Giles Arbe's retort: "Why that would be leading the life of a slave! And that I suppose, is what they meant . . . by a toad-eater." He is amazed that anyone would want such a commodity: "What can rich people be thinking of, to lay out their money in buying their fellow-creatures' liberty of speech and thought!" (III:346). From the time of her sojourn at court, Burney could never acquiesce in the right of anyone to command the submission of others, to control "their fellow-creatures' liberty of speech and thought." In *The Siege of Pevensey* she had made an historical-political point of a personal issue. "Chearless the mightiest Monarch over Slaves, / Mere finely form'd Machines"; such slaves are denied their natural birthright, "a spirit / That conscious feels equality of Soul" (*The Siege of Pevensey*, Act II). The experience of private slavery and banal tyranny is transmuted in the novel into a means of making a social and political point—and with no pretense that slavery and tyranny existed in bad old medieval days and have been solved by the Whig settlement. Modern slavery and tyranny exist within and are promoted by the economic structure. Juliet's employment with Mrs. Ireton is not just an individual accident. The paucity of decent jobs for well-bred women was filling the drawing rooms of England with miserable single ladies tyrannized over by their patronesses. And Juliet's previous experience has shown her and ourselves how much of a human being's liberty (even a white human being's liberty) may be bought and sold. It should be pointed out that Mrs. Ireton is a slaveowner. She threatens her black page, "her favourite young negro," with having him "shipped back to the West Indies," and adds, "there, that your joy may be complete, I shall issue orders that you may be striped till you jump, and that you may jump.—you little black imp!—between every stripe!" (III:241).

Juliet is deeply shocked by "her new patroness" and embarrassed by Giles Arbe's accusation that she is "a toad-eater." As we have seen, Burney was annoyed when, in 1781, the newspapers falsely proclaimed that she was "now domesticated with Mrs. Thrale" as, in effect, a dependent companion. Juliet's reactions reflect some of Burney's own feelings against being patronized, even by Mrs. Thrale. However "respectable" Juliet's employment may seem, it can become a terrible abuse. To sell one's personality seems worse than to sell machinelike labor. The heroine is glad to escape to London and to Gabriella, where she takes on a rank and position despised by persons of fashion. Juliet is in trade—not like an Evelina or an Eliza Watts who can feel degraded merely by her association with members of her family in trade.

By showing her two émigrées keeping a haberdasher's shop, Burney deliberately divests them of some of the glamor that could still hang about a heroine doing embroidery. Trade may be respectable, but it is neither genteel nor picturesque. The haberdasher's shop is an eligible position for Mrs. Hill, the carpenter's widow in *Cecilia*—but here it is the refuge of the heroine herself. Burney emphasizes the practical problems of keeping a business, including the work of bookkeeping, the problems over repairs, and the worry of paying taxes. To enter the masculine business world is to grapple with practicalities of the kind that escape theoretical-minded Elinor's notice. The liberation of women into "masculine" affairs of business (many of which are not very liberating) does not entail soaring into realms of power.

Thus far, Juliet's occupations belong to town life. In the last section of the novel, when she has to fly from London, the heroine plunges into a rawer world. Like Belfield in his survey, she enters the life of the rural laborer. Her hurried travels take her into remote areas; she is lost for a while in the New Forest. The people whom she now meets are the "low," unsophisticated by the standards not only of the fashionable but also of milliners and seamstresses. Some of the women, like Dame Margery, are kinder to her in their fashion than were the working women in town. The old ballad-singing grandmother rebukes the children in her care when they try to push the stranger away; she lives not by prejudice but by the Golden Rule. But the rural world is often rough and violent, and the people all to some degree deprived. Juliet's appearance on the road attracts coarse comment, unwelcome attention, and attack. Two young louts set their dog on her. The poacher who frightens Juliet lives in brutal fashion. The heroine has some moments of pure horror in the poacher's house when she imagines the track of blood must indicate a human corpse—a kind of parody of a scene in a Gothic novel.[59]

When she lodges with Farmer Simmers, Juliet sees another level of life, not without prosperity, but mentally impoverished. The farmer considers "A woman . . . as every way an inferiour being: and, like the savages of uncivilised nature, he would scarcely have allowed a female a place at his board, but for the mitigation given to his contempt, from regarding her as the mother of man" (IV:325–326). The women who live under the shadow of such coarse contempt are mentally inert and limited. Without contact with poetry and ideas the notion of enjoying natural beauty is not born. Finding the women's company depressing and monotonous, Juliet takes lodgings with a laborer's family in a "beautifully picturesque cotteage." She has high expectations because "The dwelling of the shepherd, or husbandman, had already in its favour the imagery of Poesy, and the ardent predilection of juvenile ideas" (IV:332). But although the laborer and his sons and their wives are "as worthy as they were industrious," they are dull, like their lives. Like one of Dr. Johnson's seekers after happiness, including Belfield in his retreat to rural life, Burney's heroine discovers the vanity of imaginings and the fallacies of pastoral poetry. The poet may praise the lot of the peasant, but the peasant has no voice in the matter. "Does he write of his own joys? Does he boast of his own contentment? Does he praise his own lot? No! 'tis the writer, who has never tried it, and the man of the world who . . . would not change with it, that gave it celebrity" (IV:335). Poets display the vanity and lack of moral imagination that Burney criticizes in her society as a whole.

Burney views the landscape which the connoisseur sees, and the writer of idylls describes, through the eyes of a heroine who knows the paintings and the poems. Using the stylized language of canonical poetic tradition, Burney wonders what the peasant, the figure *in* the landscape, can see:

> The verdure of the flower-motleyed meadow; the variegated foliage of the wood . . . and the wide spreading beauties of the landscape, charm not the labourer. They charm only the enlightened rambler, or affluent possessor. Those who toil, heed them not. . . . If the vivid field captures their view, it is but to present to them the image of the scythe, with which their labour must mow it; if they look at the shady tree, it is only with the foresight of the ax, with which their strength must fell it; and while the body pants but for rest, which of the senses can surrounding scenery . . . enchant or enliven?
>
> (IV:336–337)

Burney asks very pointedly whether there has not been too great a disparity between the vision of the "affluent possessor" and that of the laborer. Thomson, in the georgic *Seasons*, took it for granted that laboring thousands should ply the oar of the national ship, directed by the rich and educated—but do we have a right to condemn any fellow being to the dullness of labor, so that the body is wearied and the faculties not developed? Is there not a heavy price attached to idyllic rural views and the self-congratulating love of Nature? Perhaps affluent England costs too much, in human terms. Burney definitely does not take the view that the inferiority of the laborers is a happy dispensation of Nature or Providence. The inferiority, the dullness, have been *made,* and we are responsible for it.

The life of Juliet in her many alienating and monotonous jobs has been designed to lead the reader to understand what drudgery, monotony, and lack of stimulation are, and what they do to people. Taking a haughty attitude to others, condemning individuals and groups to inferiority, has been the cardinal sin of society in *The Wanderer*. In her late comic plays, Burney had shown the ill effects of boundaries and separations, the sterile misery caused by putting up partitions through snobbery or fear. Now in *The Wanderer* the heroine herself is on the other side of the barriers, sharing the lot of the low, the outcast, the forgotten.

Even the question of woman's rights—and woman's economic needs—important as these questions remain, become part of larger questions about the rights of human beings. At the end, we see Burney is focusing not only on the wrongs and rights of woman, but on the wrongs of all. The weary drudgery and unjust circumstances of most women's work reflect drudgery and injustice elsewhere. Elinor's own thinking is still too class-bound (she compares herself to the gentleman M.P. as distinguished from the digger or porter). Juliet's experience has shown us that both men and women suffer from overtasked monotony in a world which cares little or nothing for the physical and mental health and development of either the agricultural laborer who digs and ploughs or of the seamstress who sews. Juliet looks beyond her own experience to what it has shown her, and contemplates the suffering of others with melancholy awe. If we want "equality" as Elinor claims, we begin to find it when we take up our labors. It is not Elinor but Juliet who feels the weight of the burden placed on so many, Juliet who rises to passionate exclamation against unjust oppression which need not be manifested in grim tyrant or bloody guillotine to destroy lives. As Mrs. Hill had said, if you only knew "what the poor go through." Juliet wishes passionately that people would know:

> O ye, she cried, who view them through your imaginations! were ye to toil with them but one week! to rise as they rise, feed as they feed, and work as they work! like mine, then, your eyes would open; you would no longer judge of their pleasures and luxuries, by those of which they are the instruments for yourselves! you would feel and remark, that yours are all prepared for you; and that they, the preparers, are sufferers, not partakers!
>
> (IV:337–338)

This cry for enlightenment of the moral imagination is accompanied by despair that moral imagination can even be evoked in the mass of the well-to-do. The very order which Hannah More was laboring to create or maintain in her *Cheap Repository Tracts* of the '90s, written to scold the poor of England into good behavior, is a hierarchical order that here looks like cruelty stuffed out of sight by condescension.[60] The society that Juliet finds in good old true-blue nonrevolutionary commonsense England presents not a pattern of cheerful order, but a complex structure of pain. There is a wildness in the novel itself that questions all complacent views of order, good sense, and trustworthy custom.

This is nowhere more apparent than in the strange setting which provides a major image for the novel: Stonehenge. Juliet gets to Stonehenge in a wild comic sequence combining many disparate elements. Old Sir Jaspar Herrington, having rescued her from her repulsive mysterious *"mari,"* insists on taking her on a weird party of pleasure. They travel through the landscape that figured in two important journeys in Burney's life, once during her and the Thrales' escape from the Gordon Riots, again when she was recovering from her royal confinement. At Wilton, Sir Jaspar wants to imagine himself inside a painting by Salvator Rosa. At Stonehenge, he tries to realize his private dream of love with a picnic amid the gigantic ruins. He showers his companion with gifts; his wild talk about dallying with a nymph attended by fays and elves oppresses her.

Juliet begins to wonder if the old baronet is mad; Sir Jaspar's life of rational respectability has left unsatisfied desires that now emerge in euphoric near-insanity.

Under the circumstances, Juliet cannot admire the fine things at Wilton, although shown "marbles, alabasters, spars, and lavers of all colours . . . pictures glowing into life and statues appearing to command their beholders" (V:119). The world of luxurious art fails her, becoming a chaos of history which she cannot contemplate, a mere multicolored show. Juliet finds relief from that clutter of images in the complete contrast, the severe loneliness of Salisbury Plain and the gigantic monument:

> Glad to breathe a few minutes alone, she . . . walked forward . . . with eyes bent upon the turf; till she was struck by the appearance of a wide ditch . . . and perceived that she was approaching the scattered remains of some ancient building, vast, irregular, strange, and in ruins.
>
> Excited by sympathy in what seemed lonely and undone, rather than by curiosity, she now went on more willingly, though not less sadly; till she arrived at a stupendous assemblage of enormous stones. . . . Yet, though each of them, taken separately, might seem, from its astonishing height and breadth, there, like some rock, to have been placed from "the beginning of things;" and though not even the rudest sculpture denoted any vestige of human art, still the whole was clearly no phenomenon of nature. The form, that might still be traced, of an antique structure, was evidently circular and artificial; and here and there, supported by gigantic posts, or pillars, immense slabs of flat stone were raised horizontally, that could only by manual art and labour have been elevated to such a height. Many were fallen; many, with grim menace, looked nodding; but many, still sustaining their upright direction, were so ponderous that they appeared to have resisted all the wars of the elements, in this high and bleak situation, for ages.
>
> Struck with solemn wonder, Juliet for some time wandered amidst these massy ruins, grand and awful, though terrific rather than attractive. Mounting, then, upon a fragment of the pile, she saw that the view all around was in perfect local harmony with the wild edifice, or rather remains of an edifice, into which she had pierced. She discerned, to a vast extent, a boundless plain, that, like the ocean, seemed to have no term but the horizon; but which, also like the ocean, looked as desert as it was unlimited. Here and there flew a bustard, or a wheat-ear; all else seemed unpeopled air, and uncultivated waste.
>
> In a state of mind so utterly deplorable as that of Juliet, this grand, uncouth monument of ancient days had a certain sad, indefinable attraction, more congenial to her distress, than all the polish, taste, and delicacy of modern skill. The beauties of Wilton seemed appendages of luxury, as

well as of refinement; and appeared to require not only sentiment, but happiness for their complete enjoyment: while the nearly savage, however wonderful work of antiquity, in which she was now rambling; placed in this abandoned spot, far from the intercourse, or even view of mankind, with no prospect but of heath and sky; blunted, for the moment, her sensibility, by removing her wide from all the objects with which it was in contact; and insensibly calmed her spirits; though not by dissipating her reverie.

(V:132–135)

Burney is not often associated with Thomas Hardy, but here she is in Hardy country, and her Juliet anticipates Hardy's Tess in finding refuge in Stonehenge. This sequence of strange imagery has in *The Wanderer* the same sort of position and importance that Camilla's dream had in *Camilla*. The narrative here seeks some images of the mind itself. Sophisticated civilization represented by Wilton is pretty and brittle; it demands the attention of social personality, of "sentiment," and there are layers of being which it cannot reach. There is a gap, a "wide ditch," between the outward personality in the social world and the inner self which finds its semblance in what is grand, strange, and primitive. Feeling, as Juliet does, a permanent alien, a stranger in the world, she finds solace and rests upon the strangeness of the world.

Burney's Wanderer—literally here a Wanderer of Salisbury Plain—is a Romantic figure, but the romanticism of the narrative in this whole episode (as in the entire novel) is the romanticism of the second generation. The novel displays the characteristics of Regency art and poetry, in fantastic play and mock-fantasy (as in the Prince Regent's Pavilion, or Keats's "Cap and Bells"), in dissolving surfaces and subjective illusion. In Regency narratives the reader can be plunged into untranslatable worlds that seem symbolic but do not yield up their significance readily on request, as in Coleridge's "Christabel" or even in the novels of Scott, with their dreamlike characters such as Meg Merrilies or Madge Wildfire. Many Regency works have a slightly decadent quality which is an aspect of their fascination. They deal with colorful strange dreams, fantasies amid shifting perspectives, and they are fascinated by dissolution and decay. Burney's *The Wanderer* shares all these characteristics; its base may be in the earnest '90s, but the finished version belongs, in its stylistic combinations, to the era in which it was published. *The Wanderer* gives us odd perspectives in offering the view and feelings of a heroine who has not told her secret. It is a work of disintegration and reintegration, with odd shapes appearing and disappearing. Elinor's suicidal obsession has a nightmarish "sick" quality, as does Sir Jaspar's valetudinarian love-making amid his riot of obsessive references to his elves and fays (a perverse use of *A Midsummer Night's Dream* as well as Pope's *Rape*). Sir Jaspar's crazy picnic is a Regency fantasy by itself. The surface of Burney's story is ornamented by repeated references to tales (that favorite device of Regency writers), especially to fairy tales (like the Sleeping Beauty), to nursery rhyme ("the maiden all forlorn"), to ballads like "The Babes in the Wood" (III:292; III:320; IV:265). By the end of the story, we realize that this historical novel is also a kind of fairy tale, with Juliet the unknown (the Incognita, "Mrs. Thing-ami") representing a mythic lost princess, as well as the "fair Aenigma" that cannot readily be solved.

The tendency of many Romantic narratives of the Regency period is to draw the reader through a narrative which at some point breaks its own framework and questions its own structure by an encounter with ruin. Ends and beginnings not covered by the ostensible story are suggested by a new vision of things ancient—by ruins and death. The story is thus itself brought into question, its structure visibly posed as only a construction, only a tale. What came before the ruinous vision has to be reconsidered. In Keats's *Endymion,* for instance, the hero comes upon the new world of the sea-floor, where the first things he sees are fragments of vast antiquity, "things / More dead than Morpheus' imaginings" and he feels "A cold leaden awe" when contemplating "sculptures rude / In ponderous stone . . . / Of ancient Nox."[61] Later, Keats was to write of the fallen Titans that they lay "like a dismal cirque / Of Druid stones upon a forlorn moor."[62] The hero is invited within Moneta's temple of utmost age:

> So old the place was, I remembered none
> The like upon the earth: what I had seen
> Of gray cathedrals, buttressed walls, rent towers,
> The superannuations of sunk realms,
> Of Nature's rocks toiled hard in waves and winds,
> Seemed but the faulture of decrepit things
> To that eternal domèd monument.[63]

In invoking Stonehenge, Burney, like Keats, desires to get beyond the readily accessible history, seen in the chatter and the spoils of Wilton, and into the realm of deep time, of measureless antiquity. She reminds us that our story and our history are fragments of a time not readily measured, that the beginning of everything, and of everything human, lies outside of the sphere of plain knowledge. All history, even Juliet's humble story, is attached ultimately to myth, and the roots of all story, even of the true story of the French Revolution, lie in mythological time.

In its context in this novel about history—and about the *pain* of history— Stonehenge is a release from history, or at least from the business of interpreting history. Wilton with its spars and its statues represents art and science, the man-made and historical as masculine, the objects requiring knowledge not fully open to women. Rather like Dorothea Brooke in her flights from undecipherable Rome to the quiet ruinous spaces of the Campagna,[64] Juliet finds relief in the "boundless plain" and in the "savage and wonderful" work of antiquity. When

Frances Burney herself first visited Stonehenge, she was, as she records, "prodigiously disappointed, at first, by the little shape, or intelligence, of the huge masses of stone." (For an eighteenth-century representation, see Fig. 32.) Once she got out of the carriage and walked among the stones, "the more augmented my Wonder, & diminished my disappointment."[65] But Juliet, in contrast, feels no "disappointment" because Juliet has no cultural expectations—only a sense of release.

When she (temporarily) escapes the ridiculous father-lover, hobbling old Sir Jaspar, Juliet, like an Eurydice reversed, flees into an open labyrinth, an awe-ful place. Juliet, that wandering adventurer, momentarily crosses or unites gender. Impinging upon the authority of the male, she "pierced into" the circle; standing erect upon "a fragment of the pile," she commands the view. The young lady's entrance into the place of "massy ruins" symbolizes, as Camilla's vision symbolizes, the (momentary) death of the law, of culture, of names. Sir Jaspar, who has "toiled after his fair charge" (V:135) is soon to tell Juliet what the place is named: "learn, fair fugitive, you ramble now within the holy precincts of . . . Stonehenge" (V:136). In telling her what the place is named, he puts her in her place, a fair fugitive and intruder upon a holy precinct. Juliet (herself nameless) has attached no name to the place, although in "any other frame of mind, Juliet . . . would not have required any nomenclator to have told her where she was." Sir Jaspar, as "nomenclator," the one who announces names, also begins filling in the authority of the place, its religious and ritual significance: "behold in each stony spectre, now staring you in the face, a petrified old Druid!" and he sees in the stones a reflection of himself, "so fast ossifying to resemble" them (V:141). Sir Jaspar revives the "stone spectre" of historical masculinity, of law and authority. Once Sir Jaspar has entered the circle with his information, his love-talk to the "lovely nymph," and his plans for a picnic, the nature of the place is altered for the heroine, and her serenity is lost: "the heart-oppressed Juliet relieved her struggling feelings by weeping without controul" (V:138). But the place makes its impact on the novel and the reader because of the "few minutes alone" that Juliet spends in the "stupendous assemblage of enormous stones."

In the little time in which Juliet is alone in the "wild edifice," she is free. The Law and the culture for which the place once stood are unknown—they are vanished, leaving only phallic remnants behind. It was prophesied of Delvile Castle that a "fair structure" might die through "latent injury" working its way "into the very *heart* of the edifice, where it . . . laid waste its powers" (*Cecilia*, IV:598). Here we see that such prophesies may indeed come to pass. That which was once culturally closed, significant, and authoritative has become an openness without closure, a place beyond significance, not interpretive of Nature but at one with her. The female's desire for the transcendent, treated elsewhere in this last volume in the debate about the fate of Elinor's soul, is here expressed as a desire not to depart from nature for the sake of some abstraction but to include Nature, here invoked as "unpeopled air" and "uncultivated waste," in the vision of justice, peace, and life.

Burney contrives to make Stonehenge, which might at first seem suitable only to masculine phallic statement and symbolism, into a feminine place. That which is purely phallic is (like Sir Jaspar) crippled and decayed—although valiantly decayed. But Burney emphasizes the circle. The shape of Stonehenge has been anticipated in another figure in the novel. Gabriella had marked as best she could the grave of her baby son, "a small elevation of earth, encircled by short sticks, intersected with rushes." Again, as in *Camilla* with the corpse of Bellamy, we look upon the site of the death of the male, which is associated here with the site of the circle, of the female power. The circle is a place of the Mother.

Gabriella's little circle is a woman-made inarticulate monument, a miniature and more transitory Stonehenge. Once she has gone, there will be no one to explain this fragile but not meaningless construction. Gabriella's monument (all she can afford) is both feminine and "prehistoric" for she has no access to the proper historic symbols and materials of the stone-mason's yard. The poor and the helpless have a kinship with the inhabitants of the land in its prehistory. The countless numbers of women and men who have no place in the privileged culture (like the Earl of Pembroke's Wilton) are outside of history. Juliet in this scene is glad to get outside of history, if momentarily. Yet the stone circle is, it is emphasized, a human, if a mysterious, scene. The stone circle testifies that it has been made by "manual art and labour." Juliet, who has participated in "manual toil" (IV:151) is but part of that endless process of human work, and the struggle of making. Human beings are always creating, yet whatever is man-made (or human-made) is fragmentary, "vast, irregular, strange, and in ruins." What human beings make is destined to incompleteness. Man-made things attempt to resist the "wars of the elements" and in their resistance suggest perpetual suffering and conflict. A little later in the novel, Harleigh is to ask Elinor if her belief that soul is only body does not commit her to other possible beliefs. "May we not apprehend that . . . the worms which are formed from the human frame, may partake of and retain human consciousness?" Perhaps these reptiles are "tortured by their degradation?" And even this dust "to which . . . all will be mouldered or crumbled;—fear you not that its every particle may possess some sensitive quality?" (V:184). There is something deeply terrifying about the vision of a world in which every worm and every mote of dust is a shrinking sentient fragment of the human soul. The possibility of being rocked round in earth's diurnal course thus is truly painful. The whole creation groaneth and travaileth indeed. The vision of embarrassment that began with the comedy of *Evelina* now embraces the possibility of a sensitive universe—Sterne's sensorium with a vengeance—a combination of helpless consciousness that shrinks and suffers.

Harleigh's gruesome fantasy blends with the description of Stonehenge to overshadow the more cheerful historical hopes of reunion, reconciliation, and peace expressed in the novel's necessary ending. The fears that the novel deals with are also the substance of the novel's truest judgments. The world is mysterious. There is mystery at its heart—represented by Salisbury Plain and Stonehenge. That the heroine is an alien, never really at home, expresses something beyond the historical position of émigrées in 1794. We are not at home in the universe, *The Wanderer* says. We are not known to ourselves or each other. The only key to a true understanding of self and others in the world is the sense of pain. History can be understood, if at all, only in relation to the sense of pain. Human pain, past and present, is something that history has to answer for. When we look backwards and around us, we see a panorama of suffering ending in death. The terror of the past is irredeemable on this earth. The cost of history is too terrible to be redeemed in history—for how can we compensate anyone, how render justice to the dying and the dead? So Juliet thinks as she stands on a hill near the end of the novel—not Adam getting answers from an angel on a mountain, just Eve in a veil with anguished questions:

> Who can reflect, yet doubt, that Man, placed at the head of these stupenduous [*sic*] operations, lord of the earthly sphere, can fail to be destined for Immortality? Yet more, who can examine and meditate upon the uncertain existence of thy creatures,—see failure without fault; success without virtue; sickness without relief; oppression in the very face of liberty; labour without sustenance; and suffering without crime;—and not see, and not feel that all call aloud for resurrection and retribution! that annihilation and injustice would be one!
>
> (IV:338–339)

This sense of the unrighteousness of human affairs and of earthly conclusions denies in advance the restorative ending of the novel itself—just as the giant ruin of Stonehenge ridicules any neatness in the survey that has preceded its appearance, and casts a proleptic shadow of future suffering and disintegration. The sight of what man is enduring and has endured is so disturbing that the heart cries out for Immortality because otherwise all is too absurd to bear. Revolution is too small, and too unjust. Political convulsions are too humanly unjust to let justice roll down. The dealings of eternal Justice alone would be great enough to touch the depth of crying need. It is not wonderful that conservative patriotic reviewers were affronted by a book which showed that man— and English man (and woman)—continues to deal out "oppression in the very face of liberty." The "wild edifice" of the novel (which itself seems made of massy parts and strange intersections) reflects the wild edifice of human history, crazily contradictory, always being constructed at great cost, and yet always tending toward ruin. The heroine in the broadest sense of this novel is Elinor-

Ellis, the double-faced entity of two fighting the battle of womankind, in conjunction with, and sometimes in opposition to, each other. The story can close, but for the real heroine there can be no conclusion. History is the constant story of the nameless "I" in the unintelligible world, whose form, like that of mysterious Stonehenge, "might still be traced" but whose meaning and true name can never be known.

End of Story

Out of sight? What of that?
See the Bird—reach it!
Curve by Curve—Sweep by Sweep—
Round the Steep Air—
Danger! What is that to Her?
Better 'tis to fail—there—
Than debate—here—

Blue is Blue—the World through—
Amber—Amber—Dew—Dew—
Seek—Friend—and see—
Heaven is shy of Earth—that's all—
Bashful Heaven—thy Lovers small—
Hide—too—from thee—

(Emily Dickinson)

The eyes of a familiar compound ghost
Both intimate and unidentifiable.

(T. S. Eliot)

The publication of *The Wanderer* preceded by a very few days the death of Dr. Charles Burney on 12 April 1814. It is not even certain that he ever read this last novel, with its dedication to him that is Burney's one published critical work, a manifesto vindicating not only Burney's own writing career, but the status of the novel and the value of the practice of fiction. The shame once felt at appearing "a votary to a species of writing that by you, Sir, liberal as I knew you to be, I though condemned" is cast aside (I:xxi–xxii). The dedicatory essay itself dramatizes the overcoming of daddying, and exhibits escape from the condemnation of the powerful "Sir," the keeper of the canon, into the exercise of the true talents. But it is doubtful if Charles Burney ever literally read this message. And it is hardly a matter of doubt that he would have understood this novel no better than its predecessors. Frances Burney's novels were all messages that Charles Burney could not accept, however pleased he might be at the praise and publicity. With his sensitivity to public opinion, he would have been lacerated indeed at the harsh criticism lavished on *The Wanderer;* he was spared having to feel that his daughter had disgraced him by failing "in the Novel way."

The first public literary work that Burney produced after that sad time was an epitaph (written in 1816) for Charles Burney's memorial stone in Westminster Abbey. That epitaph, the "Sepulchral Character" that she gives of her father, describes him as "the unrivalled Chief and Scientific HISTORIAN of his Tuneful Art," and lays particular emphasis on the virtues of his private character, including his "Fame Unblemished," "High Principles, and Pure Benevolence" in the usual monumental manner. But she individualizes him by attributing to him some qualities less often found, at least on tombstones. The original epitaph praised Dr. Burney's "self-acquired Accomplishments"; at the insistence of the family, "self-acquired" was struck out. Burney, however, restores it in her version of the *Memoirs;* she recognized the effort and honored the self-dependence of her father's intellectual achievements. Her epitaph for Dr. Burney is even more unconventional in referring to "the Genial Hilarity of his Airy Spirits."[1] This is ambiguous praise. It is not, in the end, supposedly erring heroines like Camilla-Ariella or Hilaria who are "airy" but the spirit of the father. The more conventional version of the epitaph is inscribed in stone in Westminster Abbey.

The death of her father was too severe a blow to allow Burney to follow the fortunes of *The Wanderer* with the same eagerness—and thus the same pain —that she might have felt otherwise. She decided not to fret over the reviews, or even to read them "till my spirits & my time are in harmony for preparing a corrected Edition." As she seems to have worked on correcting for a new edition, she probably did read all the reviews eventually. Her attitude to what she knew was very negative criticism was reasonable: "I think the public has its full right to criticise—& never have had the folly & vanity to set my heart upon escaping its . . . severity." Yet she could not help believing that as the other novels had pleased readers, so, too, *The Wanderer* must please eventually, once temporary feeling over Napoleon had died down: "if the others were worthy of good opinion, THIS, when read fresh, & free from local circumstances of a mischievous tendency, will by no means be found lowest in the scale."[2] It is a very rational judgment, but she—or rather, her novel—was to wait a very long time indeed before anyone else would publicly agree with her. Even her devoted niece, Charlotte Barrett, first editor of Burney's *Diary,* closes the seven volumes with a short eulogy of her aunt of which the last sentence praises her as "the Author of EVELINA, CECILIA, and CAMILLA."[3]

In February 1814 Burney had been annoyed to find that the booksellers, in search of advance publicity, were circulating the first volume of *The Wanderer* to Sir James Macintosh, Mme. de Staël, and others (including Lord Byron and William Godwin). But she was to take comfort later, when stung by Hazlitt's review, in the fact that these early readers had responded favorably to the book at their first glimpse of it: "The first Volume . . . was received by the reigning Critical Judges, with almost unbounded applause . . . M^c. de Staël, Sir S. Romily, Lord Byron, Mr. Godwin,—& others whose names I do not recollect, sung its panegyric." But, she admits, first readers could still hope that the novel's "scene would change to The Continent, & bring the Reader into the midst of the political bustle." Yet, some valuable readers had liked the first volume, and "nobody, impartially, will pronounce The First Volume to be the Best—Ergo—."[4] Hope was slow to yield.

Life in this period was sad and somewhat tense. The death of Dr. Burney had caused not only sorrow but bitterness in his family. James Burney was seriously hurt and offended by his father's will, which seemed to ignore him altogether, and made Dr. Burney's daughters Esther and Frances chief legatees and executors. James felt that he had been disinherited, that his father had never recognized his position as eldest son and was now withholding love and punishing him for his elopement of 1798. Esther and Frances offered to share their legacy with James, but Charles objected, and the money was not the major issue. Sarah Harriet thought James ill-treated and took his part. So, too, did Maria Allen Rishton, who about this time was reunited with the husband from whom she had separated some years before; she and Martin Rishton were to die within a few months of each other in 1820.

The d'Arblays' own scene was to change to the Continent. Napoleon's endeavor to return to power entailed the active service of Alexandre d'Arblay, who was sent to Trèves to attempt to recruit deserters to serve in the army against Napoleon—an activity not without its dangers. Frances was left in Brussels during the tense days before and during the battle of Waterloo. Hearing that Napoleon's army was advancing upon the city, Frances with her English acquaintances the Boyds tried to make an escape, but "every chaise had been taken, & every Diligence secured; the cabriolets, nay, the Waggons & the carts, & every species of caravan, had been seized for military service."[5] Burney knew personal fear: "the horrible apprehension of being in the midst of a City that was taken, Sword in hand, by an Enemy."[6] The aftermath of victory was alarming and terrible in itself, with cartloads of the wounded and dying brought back into Brussels: "Maimed, wounded, bleeding, mutilated, tortured victims of this exterminating contest, passed by every minute:—the fainting, the sick, the dying & the Dead, on Brancards, in Carts, in Waggons, succeeded one another without intermission. There seemed to be a whole, & a large Army of disabled—or lifeless soldiers!"[7] She worked at making bandages and nursing the English wounded. Burney's account of Brussels at the time of Waterloo is impressively vivid and detailed; as published in the *Diary and Letters*, it appears to have served Thackeray as a source for a memorable section of *Vanity Fair*.[8]

The service of General d'Arblay was rewarded by Louis XVIII with the title of Comte d'Arblay. Frances Burney was now a French *comtesse*. The title meant little to her (though it pleased her royal friends, the princesses). The d'Arblays decided not to use it in England, to which they returned. As Burney realistically pointed out, it would be a liability in England without money to support it, and rather an embarrassment than a help to their son. The d'Arblays' service to the French crown was not rewarded financially; in fact, they sustained financial losses during the campaign in which General d'Arblay lost his health. Crippled by a kick from a horse, the aging general was threatened by gangrene; his wife rushed across Europe to Trèves to attend him. He seemed to improve by the time they went to England, but was soon the victim of a long and agonizing illness (apparently cancer of the intestine). Alexandre d'Arblay died in Bath, 3 May 1818.

Burney has left a moving account of his last days, including the especially terrible day when, realizing that he was dying, Alexandre wrestled with death and would not speak, and forbade her to speak to him. After he accepted his death, he was able to speak to his son and his wife, as a dying man, making last affectionate bequests and exhortations. He told his son, young Alex, to marry a woman like his mother: "Be There the Model thou seekest!"[9] Apparently he had no idea how daunting this command might be. Alexandre d'Arblay received the sacrament from a Roman Catholic priest, and told his wife a few hours before he died, "Je ne sais si ce sera le dernier mot—mais, ce sera la derniere pensee—Notre Reunion!"[10]

Her husband's death left Frances in deep mourning. She felt, as the widowed tend to do, that she was going to die also, very soon, so that all activities and plans seemed provisional and unreal. Concern for her son kept her tied to earth and to daily life. She sometimes wished for a more supportive companion: "I have often—often regretted I had not also a *Daughter* . . . a *male* rarely gives; he always *wants* aid."[11] For two years after her husband's death, she could take little interest in reading and writing. Books became blank pages before her eyes, conveying no ideas to her mind. She sought consolation from her family, although she already had to endure the loss of her favorite brother, Charles, who had died of a stroke in December 1817. Her sister Charlotte, widowed again since 1805 when Ralph Broome (prematurely senile and still bad-tempered) had died, was a constant friend and resource. So, too, was her older sister Esther, but Frances had to console Hetty in turn when Esther's husband of many years, Charles Rousseau Burney, died after a long illness in 1819. Frances began to harbor hopes of the kind that she and Susanna cherished in the old days, when they planned to live together as "2 loving Maiden Cats"; the sisters would be free once their sons had married: "Charlotte & I always *mean* to approximate our Dwellings, when our Males are well *Fe*maled—If, then, it might be so arranged as to form a *Trio* by my dear Hetty!"[12]

Burney had renewed another old acquaintance from whom, in her earliest days of widowhood, she hoped for some comfort. She and Hester Lynch Piozzi, formerly Mrs. Thrale, were both living in Bath after the d'Arblays' return to England in 1815. Burney made the first advances, calling and leaving cards. There was no longer any danger of meeting the Italian for whose sake Hester had enticed herself from her duty; Mrs. Piozzi was now a widow in mourning. Mrs. Piozzi admitted Burney as a caller on 16 December 1815. Burney, "strongly moved at her sight, by the remembrance of all her former fondness," felt a surge of affection, "but though my first impulse was ready to throw me into her arms, her frigid mein [sic] & manner soon chilled every feeling."[13] Inimical feelings had not vanished, and there were limits to the placability of either. Mrs. Piozzi noted in her diary, "Madame D'Arblaye [sic] came!!!" and added, "Madame D'Arblay's Visit must be returned—Amicitiae Sempiterniae; Inimicitiae placabiles."[14] At another visit, in November 1816, as Burney told Queeney, the two women talked well, but "entirely as two strangers." They exchanged anecdotes of their lives, "yet was all far more like a dialogue, in some old Grammar between una Italiana & une françoise, than like the talk of two old friends." Even so, Mrs. Piozzi's "old gaiety & fertility & originality" made Frances forget her dinner hour, and Mrs. Piozzi was moved to say impulsively at parting "God bless you!"[15] Yet Hester evidently felt in some way taken in, seduced by the lively charm Burney, the "wonderful Girl," used to have for her in the old days. After one such meeting Mrs. Piozzi recorded drily in her diary

> Madame d'Arblay—always smooth always alluring;—pass'd two or Three Hours with me to day—My perfect Forgiveness of l'aimable Traitresse, was not the act of Duty, but the impulsion of Pleasure rationally sought for . . . In her Conversation. I will however not assist her Reception in the World a *Second* Time—'else She'll betray more Men' as Shakespear says . . . .[16]

The *Othello* theme revives. Chaste Frances, who in her own eyes is the defender of the Thrale girls against their wicked deserting mother, becomes, in Hester's eyes, the seductress, the dishonest woman that Desdemona was not—the lovable traitress. Queeney Thrale had married, at the mature age of forty-four, the sixty-year-old widower Admiral Keith, to her financial and social advantage (thus proving the perfect subjection of all *her* passions to cool reason). Queeney monitored the meetings between Burney and her mother, always afraid that her mother would disgrace her, and always evidently careful to see that the friendship did not become too warm. Burney, in her accounts to Queeney of her meetings with Lady Keith's mother, seems partly to be asking for permission to love Hester again without feeling she has betrayed Queeney. Queeney's comments on her own mother in reply are neither kind nor filial: "What a strange compound she is! . . . being so sunk, she cannot now as formerly choose her society & must be thankful to whoever shews her any attention."[17]

Since Burney had never taken any kind interest in Mr. Piozzi and showed by her calls that she could value Mrs. Piozzi only once she was sundered from her husband, Mrs. Piozzi hardened her heart against offering Burney any sympathy in her bereavement when General d'Arblay died. Frances evidently came to Mrs. Piozzi at that point as if she were still Mrs. Thrale, and expected maternal help. "Madame D'Arblay writes and comes, and cries," Mrs. Piozzi noted in her journal for 15 October 1818, adding "She is very charming: she always was; but I will never trust her more."[18] When Burney moved to London (to Bolton Street, Piccadilly) soon afterwards, Hester refused to send her any expressions of regret at her departure, or any written word of sympathy or condolence. She wrote with irritating sprightliness, and talked about *Frankenstein,* wounding Burney who wanted to talk about her own sorrows.[19] There was a long gap before a reply. After a time, there was a more cautious growth of something like friendship, though a specter of a friendship rather than the thing itself. Yet, in one of her last letters to Hester Piozzi, in February 1821, Burney referred to Susanna and then to a particular keepsake: "that sister you so well, Dear Madam, know to have been my Heart's earliest darling—& with whose Hair you so kindly wove your own for me in a Locket that travels with me whithersoever I go."[20] It is something of a shock to realize that during all the years since 1784 Burney had been carrying about with her a lock of Hester's hair— and she really wanted Hester to know that. Hester Lynch Piozzi died on 2 May 1821, aged eighty-one. Burney, as survivor, had the last word on this strong and troubled friendship. She wrote in her memorandum book a statement on the character of her friend:

> I have lost now, just lost, my once most dear, intimate, and admired friend, Mrs. Thrale Piozzi, who preserved her fine faculties, her imagination, her intelligence, her powers of allusion and citation, her extraordinary memory, and her almost unexampled vivacity, to the last of her existence. . . . She was, in truth, a most wonderful character for talents and eccentricity, for wit, genius, generosity, spirit, and powers of entertainment.

Burney goes on to compare Mrs. Piozzi with Madame de Staël:

> They had the same sort of highly superior intellect . . . the same ardent love of literature, the same thirst for universal knowledge, and the same

buoyant animal spirits. . . . Their conversation was equally luminous. . . .
Both were zealous to serve, liberal to bestow, and graceful to oblige; and
both were truly high-minded in prizing and praising whatever was admirable that came in their way.[21]

This quotation is taken from the account printed by Charlotte Barrett in the
Diary and Letters. The original is missing, but Barrett's written transcript shows
what was suppressed. Burney put in the dark colors with a firm hand. Hester's
wit, genius, etc., "would have rendered her a phenomenon had not want of
judgment, carelessness of veracity, & passions unguarded & uncontrolled,
perversely & ruinously sunk her from the fair height to which she was elevated
by her charming qualities." If Madame de Staël was more faulty in her morality,
she had at least the excuse of a licentious society, which could not be called in to
explain Mrs. Piozzi's exhibition of passion. If Madame de Staël licentiously
"betrayed her conjugal duty for an adored lover," then Hester "literally took
out a licence to desert her maternal duties for a similar indulgence of passion."[22] That is always the charge—that Hester Thrale had been a deserting
mother. Burney could never admit any parallels between her own marriage and
Hester's, never go back on her old judgment, never admit that she was to the
slightest degree in the wrong over the rupture of the friendship. Yet, as Piozzi's
latest biographer William McCarthy points out, Burney's "moving eulogy"
speaks of Hester Piozzi (and Madame de Staël) in terms of strong praise: "The
terms of this eulogy are indeed essentially heroic. They are such as might be used
in eulogizing a great man: 'Highly superior intellect,' 'ardent love of literature,'
'thirst for universal knowledge.'"[23] McCarthy, relying on the *Diary,* does not
know about the intermixture of negative views in the original, but he is not
wrong. Burney did have a sense of the heroic in the female. She is generous
enough at the last to attribute great qualities to Hester. Their friendship is a
moving record of human abilities and human fragilities.

The remainder of Burney's life was troubled by the loss of friends and
relatives. James Burney died in 1821, shortly after he had been given the title of
admiral and pension to match. Already long retired, he was only "Admiral of
the Yellow,"[24] as such a noncombatant officer was jokingly referred to, yet he
rejoiced at the honor of his promotion as a vindication of his life, his service,
and his writings. Knowing how hurt James had felt about his father's will,
Frances Burney was stirred to a rare form of exertion; she brought herself to
speak to Princess Augusta and to Princess Mary (now Duchess of Gloucester)
about James.[25] That was the only time she ever truly and spontaneously used
her position at court to attempt to obtain the kind of patronage that Dr. Burney
had so sanguinely hoped for in 1786. James Burney died shortly after. The loss
of her eldest brother saddened Burney, and she sympathized with those most
affected, with Sarah Harriet very much in mind; "I hear poor Sarah Harriet is
very unwell—her grief must be very great!"[26] James Burney's will and his
funeral (planned by himself) gave rise to familial indignation. At James's express

wish, Molesworth Phillips was one of the only four persons to attend him to the grave on 23 November 1821. Frances and her sisters were hurt "that the hard-hearted, & impenitent Author of our first dread Family calamity should have been one out of only Four selected for the last personal tribute!"[27] What was known of Phillips's behavior since Susanna's death was disgusting: "a 2^d. wife deserted—Children by a 2^d. Bed abandoned—a mistress openly kept —."[28] But Molesworth Phillips was valued by James as an old close friend (James's "Tyo"), his shipmate in the Cook expedition. Phillips arranged for a death mask to be taken in order to create a bust of Admiral James Burney. At his own death in 1832, Molesworth Phillips was buried, as he had earnestly requested, in the grave of his friend James Burney.[29] Perhaps Susanna had always been only the substitute, and the Tyo the one truly loved.

In those sad latter years of constant bereavements, Burney began a new and large task. She and Esther were the inheritors of their father's papers, but Esther was too busy at home, and too inexperienced in literary matters, to do anything with them. The family expected Frances to deal with them and to produce a biography of their father, with collected letters to and from interesting people. Once Burney recovered from the death of her husband, she set to work—not celebrating the loved husband, as widows commonly do, but celebrating the loved father, and fulfilling the spirit of his last wishes. The task of reading all the papers was itself considerable. The emotional as well as physical and mental work involved was sometimes very taxing—there were all of Susanna's papers to go through. When she returned to the practicalities of editing and publishing, Burney found that living letter-writers and the heirs of dead ones got very nervous upon getting wind of any publication plans. Mary Delany's niece, Mary Ann Waddington (née Port), asked for all her letters to be sent back to her at once. And it was represented to Burney that letters belonged to their writers. The material available to her dwindled, and she found that of the remaining letters even those from the famous were often too trifling, or too involved in technical details regarding music, to be of interest to the general polite audience the Burneys had in mind.

Frances Burney had thought that Charles Burney had written his autobiography more completely than he actually had done. When she read his *Memoirs*, she found them incomplete, and she was sadly disappointed at the quality of what was there: "they really were so unlike all that their honoured writer had ever produced to the Publick, that not only they would not have kept up his Credit & fair Name in the literary World, if brought to light, but would certainly have left a cloud upon its parting ray." The father's description of his childhood, for instance, contained either merely "*literal* Nurse's tales . . . trivial to poverty, & dull to sleepiness," or very unhappy accounts of his family:

> What respected his family, mean while, was utterly unpleasant—& quite useless to be kept alive. The dissipated facility & negligence of his Witty

& accomplished, but careless Father; the niggardly unfeelingness of his
nearly unnatural Mother; the parsimonious authority & exactions of his
Eldest half Brother; the lordly tyranny of his elder own Brother; the selfish
assumingness of his Eldest sister,—& the unaffectionate & Worldly total
indifference of every other branch of the numerous race to even the
existence of each other . . . all these furnish matter of detail long, tedious,
unnecessary,—& opening to the publick view a species of Family degradation to which the Name of Burney Now gives no similitude.[30]

Burney has been severely dealt with by scholars of the Burney family,
especially, and naturally, by her father's later biographers, for the fact that she
was willing not only to cut most of Charles Burney's writing out of the printed
account, but also to destroy material: "all that I thought utterly irrelevant, or
any way mischievous, I have committed to the Flames."[31] Burney herself has
been accused of priggishness and snobbery. But if we read the horrified passage
on the family quoted above we must remember that she is talking about her
father's account of that family—it is really that *account* that is "unpleasant—&
quite useless to be kept alive." We find that we are watching Burney register her
horror at being asked to accept her father's view of his own family, while being
told what that view is. After all, some of these relatives were known to her (and
to the other children), including Uncle Richard Burney of Worcester and eldest
sister Aunt Anne, "good Aunt Nanny . . . the best nurse in England," who, with
her sister Rebecca, was an early reader of *Evelina*.[32] Burney must have felt there
was a discrepancy between the people she knew and her father's view of them.
It was a shock for her, following Dr. Burney's account of his personal life, to
find out how many grudges he harbored and how angry he still was at nearly
everybody. With filial piety having to accept or pretend to accept her father's
version of his family's sins, Burney also knew there would be a further "degradation" in store for her father himself if she produced all his complaints and
self-pity before the public.

Burney's concern, above all, was to create a favorable picture of her father, to
keep up "his Credit & fair Name." It is obvious that she did not think her
father had cooperated well enough in creating a favorable picture of himself. She
labored in her biography to produce a father cheerful, generous, and sophisticated—the man she believed he had really always wanted to be. He did not
always see how he let himself down (in sponging, for instance, in egotism, in
self-pity—"when she sees how I have been abandoned"). But Burney would not
let Charles Burney let himself down; she censored him—committing his
writings (or large parts of them) "to the flames" in revenge of the old bonfire in
Poland Street, recently recalled in the Dedication of *The Wanderer*. Her censorship was all in the good cause of re-creating Dr. Burney as he would really like
to be—becoming Author of the Author of her being. In the *Memoirs* of 1832
she is determined to prove that he is a great man—as great as Johnson (about

whom so many biographical works were written) but more perfect. Her biography is partly a riposte to Piozzi's *Anecdotes of Johnson,* proving that Burney, too, can write from intimate knowledge of a great man, and thus is great herself. She adjusts the account here, putting herself forever at her father's side, as his favorite child, for does she not tell his story? In her biography of him she can write her own autobiography, in which the young Frances Burney can stand forth cleansed of all filial disobedience, triumphant and vindicated.

The *Memoirs* did not win critical acclaim. The book and its author were attacked viciously by the implacable Croker of the *Quarterly Review.* The book also lost Burney a friend—or more truly, made her an enemy. Mary Ann Waddington, Mary Delany's niece, was seriously angry at a section of the *Memoirs* which indicated that the Duchess of Portland's death was a financial as well as emotional blow to Mrs. Delany: "Her condition in life . . . as well as her heart, was assailed . . . unnumbered were the little auxiliaries to domestic economy which her Grace found easy to convey to St. James's Place."[33] It was a little unkind of Burney, who herself so disliked any suggestion of patronage— and who had certainly not mentioned the "little auxiliaries to domestic economy" which had found their way from Mrs. Thrale's house at Streatham to Dr. Burney's hungry family. Mrs. Waddington protested against the presentation of her aunt as in any way a dependant of the duchess; Burney was able to show that she had manuscript proof that Mary Delany did indeed get presents from the Dowager Duchess of Portland.[34] The insult was not forgotten. Mrs. Waddington stipulated that her name should not appear in Charlotte Barrett's *Diary and Letters,* and when Waddington's daughter Lady Llanover produced *The Autobiography and Correspondence of Mary Granville, Mrs. Delany* in 1862, she included unkind remarks about Frances Burney, going back to Croker's *Quarterly Review* article on the *Memoirs* for ammunition. The association with Mary Delany was never thoroughly lucky for Burney. Lady Llanover was to revive Croker's false and ridiculous charge that Burney had lied about her age—she had never, in fact, pretended to be the same age as Evelina when *Evelina* appeared. Though she would not respond to the *Quarterly's* attack at the time, in the last months of her life Burney recalled Croker's "Defamation" and told Charlotte that she ought to have mounted a defense of her own veracity: "I poignantly regret that I did not at once answer it or let my dearest Alex—who could not even Name my wanton calumniator but with trembling emotion."[35]

"Dearest Alex" himself was, however, the greatest source of anxiety and sorrow to Burney in her latter years. As a child, he seems to have been happy and bright, perhaps forced a little toward precocity by his fond and elderly parents. The removal to Paris had been in many ways for him an unhappy change. He did not adapt well to the French schools, and was the odd man out. The return to England in 1812 served him little better, for he then confronted the British university and the system of preparing for it, and the English teachers told him he was backward and ill-prepared. He required coaching and intense preparation before entering Cambridge. Alex d'Arblay manifested an interest in mathematics (reflected in his constant absorption in chess); this interest promised well, but the mathematical philosophies of France and England differed, and he was caught in the middle. He went to Cambridge with a weight of family expectations on his shoulders. He did not apply himself, and he did not distinguish himself as Burneys were accustomed to do. Frances complained that he seemed able to do nothing without someone to keep him at it, and that she had to act "in the character of Flapper to Alexander"[36]—an allusion comparing Alex to one of the abstracted mathematical philosophers of Swift's Laputa. All the combined efforts got him through creditably enough; he was listed as Tenth Wrangler, a respectable position—but the Burneys were accustomed to being at the top. Alex did not gain a college fellowship, and his moody and abstracted ways and unpunctual habits were not well suited to teaching. He had mathematical ability but was not a true mathematician, although among his friends he counted those who decidedly were, such as Charles Babbage. His interest in mathematics may have been in part the result of an attempt to separate himself from his mother, his Uncle Charles, and the other literary Burneys.

Had Alex been a young Newton, all his fits of apathy, all his eccentricities and lack of attention to the niceties (including letter-writing) would have been forgiven. But he did not distinguish himself, and did not seem to be growing up into a sensible man. General d'Arblay had worried much about his son. At one point, in a fit of impatience, he had declared the only way to make a man of Alex was to marry him off in an arranged match—a notion which his wife declared against in horror: "Est-ce Vous—bien vous—who return thus to l'ancien regime in a point upon which I have so often heard you condemn it?"[37] But when Alex reached and then passed the age of thirty, the widowed mother also became increasingly anxious that he should marry, as well as take an interest in his profession.

Steadiness was what Alex could not supply. He was nudged into the only profession relatives and friends could think of for him—the church. He was ordained a priest of the Church of England on 11 April 1819. In this matter Burney had the assistance of her old friend George Cambridge, childless himself, who took a friendly interest in Alex, and whose friendship Burney enjoyed; her letters of later years are full of references to "my dear Archd[n]. and Mrs. C." Alex ran away from his work whenever he could; he treated himself to a long holiday with Babbage and others, rambling about the Alps; the party was to make scientific observations, but Alex separated from his companions and— instead of making scientific observations—began writing religious poetry on the sublime scenery. He would never do the right thing at the right time. He published one poem and some sermons, thus joining the writing Burneys and winning his mother's esteem. His love for his mother is clear in his letters and his dialogic responses as she records them, but it is also clear that he found her at times exasperating, at times intimidating. This is not an unusual reaction to a parent, but Alex lacked any compensating world of business in which he felt competent and confident; neither did he have a sexual or domestic life in which to take his ease. Near the end of his life he began cautiously to court a girl named Mary Anne Smith; Frances loved Mary Anne as a daughter, and perhaps the young woman was introduced into the picture for the mother's sake rather than for the son's.

Alexander reminded Frances Burney, at times, of her cousin Edward Francesco Burney. Edward Francesco had made a place for himself (although not a great one) among English artists, whereas Alex made no real place for himself at all, but both men were sweet-tempered, slightly depressive, and erratic— eccentric to unsympathetic eyes and even to their own. Both men may have been homosexual without quite knowing it. The fact that a man is not married by the time he is forty need not indicate any such thing, of course—both George Cambridge and Alexandre d'Arblay senior had waited until that time before taking the plunge. But Alex showed little interest beyond the familial in women, even though his mother was quite delighted at any suggestion that a girl was interested in him, or vice versa. He took an interest in Amelia Angerstein, but it was when he thought she would die. It is hard not to believe that the prospect of marriage frightened young Alex very much indeed. Perhaps marriage frightened him because it meant settling down, assuming the power and solidity which he feared he would never know how to achieve. He was never strong, and his languor and depression in the last years may have been caused by some then-undiagnosable medical condition, such as a disease of the blood or bone marrow.

Alex seems almost to have welcomed death when he became ill with influenza after Christmas 1836. That he harbored some grudge against his mother may be suspected from the fact that he expressly wished and commanded that she not come to his bedside. But perhaps he feared that his officious "Flapper" would work too successfully at keeping him alive. He died on 19 January 1837, and was buried beside his father, in Wolcot Churchyard, Bath. After Alex's death, his fiancée, Mary Anne Smith, at her own suggestion (and at Alex's wish) came to live with the woman who might have been her mother-in-law. The son had left his mother a last valued gift—not without a certain irony. She had sometimes wished for a daughter; now she had a daughter but no son. There were no descendants of Frances Burney; descendants of some of her siblings are living now. She had endured the greatest grief that can befall a parent. She had outlived her child. Alex was the only child, the much-loved son.

The short remainder of Burney's life was to be largely a series of farewells. Esther had died in 1832. In 1838 laughter-loving warm-hearted Charlotte left her. The loss of Charlotte was the sundering of "that last original tie to active original affections."

Of all her siblings, only Sarah Harriet outlived her. Frances Burney had a long slow walk through the valley of the shadow, remembering and learning as she went. In the spring of 1839, she wrote to Charlotte's daughter, Charlotte Barrett:

> My spirits have been dreadfully saddened of late by whole days—nay weeks—of helplessness for *any* employment. They have but just revived: How merciful a Reprieve!
> How merciful is All we *know! The ways of Heaven* are not *dark* and *intricate* but *unknown* & unimagined till the great Teacher, Death, developes them.[38]

We hear again the echo of the verse from Addison that found its way into the canceled introduction of *Cecilia*. Addison's Portius said: "Remember what our Father oft has told us; / The Ways of Heav'n are dark and intricate." Burney contradicts the paternal lore as well as the paganism, in favor of exploration through personal experience and spiritual education. By the end, she made a friend of Death.

Frances Burney, Madame d'Arblay (still the comtesse d'Arblay to the French government offices that sent her a tiny residual pension) survived to see the new queen come to the throne; she lived to see the dawn of the Victorian Age. Among the last of her friends of the old days was the faithful archdeacon, who gave her Holy Communion at home and tried to see her in her last days. Perhaps no love is ever really lost. Her dear Mary Anne and her niece Charlotte attended her. Upon her niece's saying, when Burney said she had slept, "you wanted rest," Burney replied, "I shall have it soon, my dear."[39] Yet she waited, as if to clarify the ways of Heaven and fulfil one of Heaven's plots—not dark and intricate, but surprising. She died in the month of January, that month fatal to Susanna and Alex. She seems almost to have chosen to depart on the anniversary of Susanna's death, the anniversary kept for so many years. She died in London on 6 January 1840. Her body was conveyed to Bath, to be buried in the graveyard of Wolcot Church, beside her husband and son. A tombstone put up by the Burney family in 1906 still stands in Wolcot churchyard, although it was removed from the burial site in 1955 and the actual position of the remains is now unmarked and unknown.[40] A tourist may make the pilgrimage (though few do) to look at the large stone that commemorates Alexander d'Arblay and Frances d'Arblay. Wolcot Church was not and is not in the fashionable area of Bath; the district, in her days slightly rowdy, and now certainly not well-to-do, is in a fringe area or social borderland. The other memorial is a street called d'Arblay Street in Soho, London, near the site of the old Burney residence in Poland Street. Wolcot and Soho—Burney did not in death make an entrance into the fashionable world.

Frances Burney may be found in Westminster Abbey, but only in her father's monument, in words glorifying him. She deserves her own memorial, commemorating the writer. She produced an impressive œuvre. Her works published to date number many volumes: twenty volumes of diaries and letters, one biography, two plays, four novels. If we include the works unpublished but completed by her (three tragedies, two comedies) we see what a rate of production she really had. The fertility of her mind, her constant activity as a writer, can be attested if one "rummages" (like Mrs. Wheedle through Dabler's *"Miniscripts"*) among her papers. The surviving manuscripts of short notes and sketches show there was still much unused material in her mental storeroom. These scraps give us a tantalizing glimpse of the author's workshop; one comes upon ideas and conversations never realized in whole pieces. These entertaining scraps revive afresh the admiration for Burney's talents as a writer, and tantalize with the possibilities of other works that never came into being:

> Well—I hope you have made a good dinner?
> O, I can hardly move—
> Well, you eat pretty heartily—
> O—I'll never touch a mushroom again
> as long as I live—I'm so sick!—

> Miss Megrim calls upon a Set of ordinary people, breaks in upon them, & distresses them by comments upon their Dress, which she advises them to improve; tells them she shall stay & dine with them; they run out, one after another, making preparations, & whisper each other. . . . She sees a Goose pass the Window, & over hears them plan a rich plumb Pudding: soon after, when they are a little quiet, she begs them to hasten Dinner, as she is hungry; they run about again, & make apologies for giving her nothing but *pot-luck;* she declares she can Eat any thing in the World, except Goose & Plumb Pudding.

Badino

> A magnificent House, a numerous retinue, a splendid Equipage, & a beautiful wife, were the 4 articles of anticipated luxury to which his toils, in the few moments which accident bestowed upon reflection, looked decidedly forward. The very day, therefore, on which he found himself worth a Plumb, that stated pinnacle of his desires whence his happiness was to begin, he set vigorously about putting into practice the Theory of his wishes; & went to work in as business-like a manner to procure himself the enjoyment of his wealth, as he had hitherto observed for attaining it's [sic] possession . . . the Land, the attendants, the conveyance, & the lady were all to be looked out: but he considered, with great complacency, the whole World was now before him to chuse, & he resolved to obtain these ingredients for his future bliss one by one, so as to

have every thing complete as he proceeded. In this order, therefore, the
mansion, the Servants & the Carriage, were purchased, hired, & built, &
then, he said, he looked upon his difficulties to be over, the 4th article
being so much the easiest. . . .

She's turned complete democrate—
I'm glad of it.
Finds fault with Government.
It's a sign of her sense. I do it myself.
Thinks not one thing right in ten.
No more do I
Says the world is beginning.
I like her spirit.
. . . .
Says Jack is an owl . . . you are an ass, & Simon a Parrot.
Says what?
Says everyone is to blame
But . . . did not you name me?
O, she spares no one.
What was that you said she said of me?
You're an ass; that's all.
Me?
Yes. Why not?

Sir Chrystal Astrakhan

Sir Chrystal Astrakhan possessed a character free from all shadow of evil.
. . . He thought of Mankind neither as of his friends or his Enemies; he
thought not of them at all, but as they presented themselves before him;
& then . . . he received or neglected them, according to his own immediate impulse. All this was no effect of insensibility; it resulted simply from
absence: he unaffectedly honoured merit . . . he would indignantly have
hated vice, could its idea have entered his mind.[41]

There are literally hundreds of scraps such as these. Few novelists, certainly no
other of Burney's period, have left us with such a view of working ingredients,
nor such intimations of the ideas that pass through the mind, glimmerings of
works not realized. The multitude of scraps testifies to the author's fertility of
invention. When *The Wanderer* was published, she had material on hand
sufficient to serve as the basis for several plays and one or two novels. The death
of the father to whom she wanted to say so much seems important in explaining
the rather sudden end of Burney's fiction-writing life. The author of her being
had disappeared and had left her without authorship; the secret addressee had

vanished. This would seem a major reason why Burney published no more fiction after 1814. Yet a few of these scraps may have been written after that date, and Burney did return briefly to *Elberta* after her father's death; a session of play-writing might have helped her to recover. Her abrupt travels on the Continent, her husband's illness and death, and her grief explain why there is no writing save journalizing from 1815 to 1820. And after that she immersed herself in the unshared filial task.

Conclusion

If we put up a monument to Frances Burney the author in Westminster Abbey, who is this author we should celebrate and commemorate? Fortunately, there now seems less chance of such a memorial commemorating "Fanny Burney," the cute, ever-girlish, unalarming little lady who wrote one attractive and charming little novel in *Evelina*. John Wilson Croker, in his lengthy and vitriolic review of *The Wanderer* in the *Quarterly Review*, accused Burney of being "a *mannerist*"; that is, "she has given over painting from the life and has employed herself, in copying from her own copies." Worse, she is "a mannerist who is *épuisée*":

> The Wanderer has the identical features of Evelina—but of Evelina grown old; the vivacity, the bloom, the elegance, "the purple light of love" are vanished; the eyes are there, but they are dim; the cheek, but it is furrowed; the lips, but they are withered. And when to this description we add that Madame D'Arblay endeavours to make up for the want of originality in her characters by the most absurd mysteries, the most extravagant incidents, and the most violent events, we have completed the portrait of an old coquette who endeavours, by the wild tawdriness and laborious gaiety of her attire, to compensate for the loss of the natural charms of freshness, novelty, and youth.[1]

To read such insults, such physical insults, of a kind which would never be deployed against a male novelist, is to realize the pressures and constraints under which Burney produced her work. It was her duty to be youthful and charming. "You please, and the world smiles upon you—this is your time," said Crisp.

"Years and wrinkles in their due season . . . will succeed."[2] The confusion between a woman's writing and the feminine duty of pleasing, between an entertaining smoothness of style and the attractive smoothness of female skin, is evident in reactions to Burney from the beginning of her career to the end. To move out of the modest blushing Evelina persona, the timid, sweet, engaging voice, was to risk having it said that she was an old hag—an old coquette who had lied about her age in pretending to be seventeen when she produced *Evelina*. An elderly female novelist who wants to say what she means is ugly and should be told that she cannot please any longer, and has no right to make an appearance, physical or literary. It is to Burney's credit that she had not as a writer submitted to the pressures upon her, that she did not keep to the role of pleasant entertainer and turn out novel after novel narrated by a charming girl whose naïveté assures us that the author knows her place. Burney in her major work, as not in her life, was truly "self-dependent."

Croker accuses Burney of being a "mannerist," guilty of self-imitation—a particular sin in a woman, who should not have the assurance to think of having a self to refer to. There is some truth in his claim, though he means it only as an accusation. Burney returns to the matter that haunts her, finding varied expression for familiar themes, and carrying matters forward both in insight and technique in each novel; the plays help her to develop and understand her themes more clearly.

In *Evelina* Burney's central subject is woman's desire to find out who she is by entering her world, and her embarrassment and resentment at finding out how woman is treated in this world. Burney discovered her powers of rendering comic scene and dialogue to exhibit the continual flux of power, the plays of social aggression. In *The Witlings* she began to embody a middle-class society's reluctance to be moved to moral or intellectual action, and discovered the structural value of pseudo-climax and anticlimax. In *Cecilia* Burney again moves through pseudo-climax and anticlimax to harsher and more significant effect, and the meaning of social aggression becomes larger and more complex. The third-person authorial voice is developed in order to examine a society in its basic operations of Class and Money. Women of good will must contend against a very powerful structure which also subjugates and controls good men. In this novel, Burney truly discovers her powers in creating the macabre and grotesque in persons and scenes. Blackmail becomes a major subject, as does suicide—material that carries over into the tragedies, which give voice to inner suffering.

In the tragedies, Burney first reaches for the mythic world, for psychological symbolism. In *Camilla,* that Janus-faced novel, she places historical realism and the comfortable assurances of moral intent against surrealism, develops myth amid questioning. This novel, investigating the workings of the mind as a practical joker upon itself, displays the operations of the psyche as cause and effect of social absurdities and tyrannies. This long and complex novel tends to be the

Burney novel that the author's younger contemporaries in fiction-writing—Edgeworth, Scott, and Austen—wish to quote.

The comic plays that follow investigate private affairs and personal sources of unhappiness through the public mode of dramatic comedy. The plays represent a turn outward to the external world, after the inwardness of the last part of *Camilla*, but the comic action expresses social and psychological divisions. The last of these comedies, *The Woman-Hater*, dramatizes psychological obsession and emotional fear, turning us again to the mythic world as Burney, reversing the plot of *Evelina*, examines in a new way what has gone wrong with her family and her culture.

In *The Wanderer*, the central character, the "female Robinson Crusoe," experiences not only the loneliness which has been more and more characteristic of successive Burney heroines, but alienation. Each of Burney's heroines makes an "entrance into the world," and the world she enters becomes increasingly more problematic with each novel. Juliet endeavors to enter society not in order to make a debut but to earn her own living. The society she enters is arid and apathetic, given to division and rejection, and apparently possessing no power to heal itself. The strange inner world presented through the characters of *Camilla* is now the world of the novel itself—fantastic, shifting, with abrupt transitions and dreamlike images, especially the image of Stonehenge. *The Wanderer* is a tragicomedy about disjunction and disintegration, looking at history in the light of human suffering, the pain that no novelist can bring to a closure. If all the novels show young ladies making entrances into the world, and the world as hazardous, in *The Wanderer* it is no longer certain that any entry can be truly achieved, that a place in the world can be found. England can be entered (even desperately), but still it remains closed. English society is not accessible to a woman who craves "self-dependence." Beyond that truth is another even starker truth. The world is forever alien. We all—men and women—must remain partly strangers in it and to it. The individual identity cannot be recognized by the world, cannot fit into the world; neither can the dark outer world swallow up and incorporate the troubling identity. There remains self alone, woman alone: Elle is / Ellis. Burney had given us a wonderful gallery of comic characters from Mr. Smith and Madame Duval to Sir Jaspar Herrington and Mrs. Ireton. Yet all these gain their significance from their place in the story of a heroine who is trying to comprehend the world of which these comic characters are expressions. They represent the hard edges of the intractable world, as well as illustrating in themselves the struggle for identity and control.

Undoubtedly, some readers will be shocked at having the nice little comic writer taken away. Some will feel horrified at what they will regard as a changeling-substitution of a mad Gothic feminist for the cheerful little Augustan chatterbox. It is, of course, my contention that the comic, the grotesque, and the macabre elements in Burney's writings are all united, and that the themes and insights of *The Wanderer* are already adumbrated in the violence of *Evelina*, where old women are thown into a ditch or forced to run a footrace. Hazlitt said *The Wanderer* exhibited not a decay of Burney's talent but "the perversion" of it.³ It is neither a decay nor a perversion; *The Wanderer* is a culmination, saying clearly what readers could have found in the earlier works.

In her various works Burney was trying to develop not only her own themes but also—inseparable from these—her own language. The language of all her works after *Evelina* is often charged with clumsiness and false expression, but it should be realized that it represents her attempt to mold language and obtain the meaning she wants. Recent research on the new edition of the *OED* has shown to what an extent Burney contributed to English language and usage.⁴ She is not only an early recorder of words in modern usages, but also a word-coiner. One of the pleasures of reading the letters is the light play of nonce-words, "un-Julyish"; "that unsniggered him."⁵ In her fiction Burney takes the liberty of trying to form a language suited to her purposes. Her devices include the incorporation of slang and vulgarism: "fine jemmy tye"; "smart as a carrot" (*Cecilia*); the introduction of portmanteau words: "stroamed" (*Camilla*); the play with a character's abuse of words: "a little squeak in the intrum" (*Camilla*), "she's music-learner to my darter . . . she tudles upon them wires the prettiest of any thing" (*The Wanderer*). Burney's authorial language includes the unusual use of verbal functions to express the surges of astonishment and pain in human life: "It lives its own surprise" (*Camilla*); "Where the dominion of the character falls chiefly upon the heart, life, without sympathy, is a blank" (*The Wanderer*); "Who can . . . see . . . oppression in the very face of liberty . . . and not see, and not feel that all call aloud for resurrection and retribution!" (*The Wanderer*). The abstract and the concrete, the literal and the symbolic are mingled in subtle twists of personification. The rhythms are decided, sometimes operating in long sequences of pulsation, often to capture the effect of suspense or pain: "but that over—that dreadful—harrowing—never to be forgotten moment of horrour that made me wish to be mad—over" (*Journals*). The combination of unhyphenated words in connective adjectival ideas is a characteristic of Burney's later style, a habit upon which some critics pounced.⁶

It is, of course, hard for women writers to hear that they must strictly obey the rules of a masculine definitive language. The man who varies from the beaten path may be termed a strong stylist, but a woman who does so is merely mistaken and ignorant. Yet to defer utterly to the superior language is to render oneself incapable of writing—the iron pen will indeed make no mark. The masculine-defined ordered language may truly not say or do everything that a woman wishes it to do. Burney presumably used inverted structures a great deal (to instance one mannerism that critics found a detestable "gallicism") because she thought many things were back-to-front. Burney's use of language reminds me both of Charlotte Brontë and Emily Dickinson—very different stylists, who were both experimenters in language, and who were both cited by critics for insufficient command of what everyone knows is the proper way of writing.

Like Brontë and Dickinson, Burney can sometimes be abstract, rhetorical, distant, tangential, or crowded; like them, she can use to full effect the force of strong or complex words. Burney is to be classified among those writers who experiment with style. If she sometimes failed, she sometimes succeeded, and succeeded on her own terms—but to succeed in one's own terms is to show an audacity that tempts the Guardians of the canon to put the female "mannerist" in her place.

Embarrassed as she was, Burney was in her own way heroic. She was encumbered and constrained (as we all are) by her circumstances, including her era and its mores, her family history, and her personal emotional needs. Those constraints shape every individual. But Burney had courage and intelligence. Had she written timid, blushing, pleasing novels, she might have met with even more contemporary approval, but she might not have attained even that peculiar position she has occupied hitherto: if never quite in the canon, always on the border of it. She remains to delight and disturb us. She is not a writer who induces cultural contentment. Unlike, for instance, Maria Edgeworth, she does not lay reassuring moral cards on the table. She really fulfilled Belfield's prophetic description and, in defiance of the maxims of the world, intended to be "guided by the light of her own understanding."

To maintain the integrity of one's own understanding is hard for any human being to do. Burney is admirable in her gallant intelligence. If I have sounded at times critical of her, of her family, of her era, it is not because I think that I have no comparable faults, or that we in the twentieth century live in a wonderfully healthy and moral era, or are free from constraints and cultural neuroses parallel to those that bound Burney and her family. "A Woman's life should be a perpetual allegory." Burney's life seems immense and helpful. It was a real life and she lived it very fully, and sometimes splendidly. I admire her as a person. She was a woman of integrity, independence, and generosity, with a genius for friendship. As far as I know, although she made some mistakes, as we all must, she did only one really wrong thing in her life—something I could not say for most other poeple I know, including myself. But Burney achieved not only her life but her works, works in which she was able to utter something of what life had shown her. It does not matter if we do not crown her with laurels, but we do ourselves a disservice if we nudge her novels back to the periphery instead of giving them their due by reading them—the only honor that can truly reward the labors and achievement of a writer.

Notes

Introduction

1. Austin Dobson, *Fanny Burney* (London: Macmillan & Co. Ltd., 1903), p. 205.

2. It is anticipated that *The Early Journals and Letters of Fanny Burney* will cover the period from 1768 to mid-1791; that is, the new work will offer a corrected and greatly amplified replacement of the *Early Diary* and the *Diary and Letters*.

3. Edward A. Bloom, "Introduction" to *Evelina*, p. xxi.

4. See my article, "George Eliot and the Eighteenth-Century Novel," *Nineteenth-Century Fiction* 35 (December 1980):260–291.

5. Patricia Spacks, "Dynamics of Fear: Fanny Burney," chap. 6 of *Imagining a Self: Autobiography and Novel in Eighteenth-Century England* (Cambridge, Mass. and London: Harvard University Press, 1976), pp. 158–192; Janet Todd, *Women's Friendship in Literature* (New York: Columbia University Press, 1980), pp. 312–319; Jan Fergus, *Jane Austen and the Didactic Novel* (Totowa, N.J.: Barnes and Noble Books, 1983), pp. 62–72; Julia Epstein, "Writing the Unspeakable: Fanny Burney's Mastectomy and the Fictive Body," *Representations* 16 (Fall 1986):131–166. Other articles of interest include Edward W. Copeland, "Money in the Novels of Fanny Burney," *Studies in the Novel* 8 (Spring 1976):24–37; Rose Marie Cutting, "A Wreath for Fanny Burney's Last Novel: *The Wanderer*'s Contribution to Women's Studies," *College Language Association Journal* 20 (September 1976):57–67; the same author's "Defiant Women: The Growth of Feminism in Fanny Burney's Novels," *Studies in English Literature* 17 (Summer 1977):519–530. Copeland treats an important topic, but his discussion is hampered by condescending attitudes which preclude his noticing the novels' deliberate ironies. Cutting is one of the first published critics to treat Burney as a feminist; she points out, for instance, that Burney's four heroines have financial difficulties in common. Susan Staves develops some similar points in "Evelina, or Female Difficulties," *Modern Philology* 73 (May 1976):368–381. Martha G. Brown argues, against Staves and Cutting, that Burney was a writer in the romance tradition and therefore (strange implication!) not touched by

"feminism," at least until *The Wanderer;* see "Fanny Burney's 'Feminism': Gender or Genre?" in *Fetter'd or Free? British Women Novelists 1670–1815,* ed. Mary Anne Schofield and Cecilia Macheski (Athens, Ohio: Ohio University Press, 1986), pp. 29–39.

6. John J. Richetti, "Voice and Gender in Eighteenth-Century Fiction: Haywood to Burney," *Studies in the Novel* 19 (Fall 1987):263–272; J. N. Waddell, "Fanny Burney's Contribution to English Vocabulary," *Neuphilologische Mitteilungen* 81 (1980):260–263; the same author's "Additions to *OED* from the Writings of Fanny Burney," *Notes & Queries* 225 (1980):27–32.

7. Judy Simons, *Fanny Burney* (Totowa, N.J.: Barnes and Noble Books, 1987) in Women Writers series, ed. Eva Figes and Adele King; D. D. Devlin, *The Novels and Journals of Fanny Burney and the Feminine Strategy* (Lexington, Ky.: University of Kentucky Press, 1987); Kristina Straub, *Divided Fictions: Fanny Burney and the Feminine Strategy* (Athens, Ga.: University of Georgia Press, 1987).

8. Peter Sabor and Margaret Anne Doody have undertaken to edit *The Wanderer* for World's Classics. Pandora also promises an edition of this novel. The Virago text of *Cecilia,* aside from the new introduction by Judy Simons, is a photocopy of a text edited by Annie Raine Ellis, originally issued a hundred years previously; the name of the editor (whose footnotes are used) is expunged from the Virago text. Annie Raine Ellis is an important Victorian editor and the first real Burney scholar aside from the novelist's immediate family.

9. See below, chap. 4, p. 143 and n. 63.

10. *D&L,* I:36.

1. Frances; or, A Young Lady's Entrance into Life

1. Edward A. Bloom, Introduction to *Evelina,* p. xxiv.

2. Lonsdale, p. 481.

3. *Memoirs,* III:434.

4. "Introduction Copied from a manuscript memoir in the Doctor's own handwriting," *Memoirs,* I:xiv–xv. Burney destroyed most of her father's autobiographical account of his life, and allows Charles only a few pages in his own words in the *Memoirs.* See Lonsdale, pp. 432–455 for a detailed and hostile account of Frances's treatment of her father's papers; see also chap. 10, below, pp. 376–378.

5. *Memoirs,* I:3.

6. FB to her sister Hester, 20 November 1829, *J&L,* XI:188–189.

7. Charles Burney, "Fragmentary Memoir," BL Addington MS. 48345; quoted by Lonsdale, p. 7.

8. "Preface, or Apology," *Memoirs,* I:ix.

9. Dr. Burney repeatedly arranged that his books should be reviewed by his friends William Bewley (in the *Monthly Review*) and Samuel Crisp and Thomas Twining (in the *Critical Review*). He also made sure his rival Hawkins's *History of Music* would be thoroughly and extensively attacked in a three-part review by Bewley. According to one report (which came through his son-in-law Molesworth Phillips), Dr. Burney spent two hundred pounds in buying up copies of a parody of his *Travels;* the prospect of any

adverse criticism seems always to have terrified him unduly. (See Lonsdale, pp. 106–111, 120–123, 153–157, 209–219, 268–270, 311–312.)

10. Dr. Charles Burney (hereafter CB) to Hester Lynch Thrale (hereafter HLT), 1 November 1777, Rylands MS 545, no. 1.

11. *Memoirs*, I:26, 30.

12. Later, unpleasantly and most unreasonably, Greville—when feeling financially hard pressed—was to try to recover the three hundred pounds from Charles Burney.

13. CB to Frances Crewe, 5 July 1794, quoted in Lonsdale, p. 21.

14. *Memoirs*, I:69–70.

15. *Ibid.*, p. 81.

16. *Ibid.*, p. 71.

17. *Ibid.*, pp. 77–78.

18. "Fragmentary Memoir," quoted by Lonsdale, p. 21.

19. See Hemlow, p. 6; Lonsdale, p. 22.

20. *Memoirs*, I:63.

21. The heroine of Defoe's *Roxana* (1724), for instance, states the belief that her Dutch lover ought not to have any idea of marrying her once he had slept with her: "where is the Man that cares to marry a whore, tho' of his own making?" (*Roxana the Fortunate Mistress*, ed. Jane Jack [London: Oxford University Press, 1969], p. 145). Fielding's young Nightingale protests against marrying the girl whom he seduced under promise of marriage, even though he desires to do so: "was I to marry a Whore, though my own, I should be ashamed of ever shewing my Face again." (*The History of Tom Jones, a Foundling*, ed. Sheridan Baker [New York, N.Y.: Norton, 1973], bk. XIV, chap. 7, p. 589).

22. Lonsdale, p. 447.

23. The first of Dr. Burney's important literary works was *The Present State of Music in France and Italy; or, The Journal of a Tour through those Countries, undertaken to collect Materials for a general History of Music. By Charles Burney, Mus. D.* (London: T. Becket & Co., 1771). This was followed by *The present State of Music in Germany, the Netherlands and the United Provinces; or, The Journal of a Tour through these Countries, undertaken to collect Materials for a General History of Music. By Charles Burney, Mus. D., F.R.S.* Honors accumulated; Burney's *Tours*, as accounts of men and manners, won the admiration and interest of readers like Dr. Johnson who did not care for music.

The great work designed to ensure its author a firm place in the world of belles lettres as well as of music is entitled *A General History of Music, from the Earliest Ages to the Present Period*. The first volume came out in 1776; the second volume appeared in 1782, and the third and fourth volumes in 1789. The entire labor took about twenty years, and is a monument to love of the subject as well as to Dr. Burney's perseverance. Save for the times of journeying, he was working full-time as a music teacher throughout this period, giving over fifty lessons a week, to the amazement of Dr. Johnson; research and writing were done at night.

For an account of Charles Burney's writing, see Percy Scholes's editions of Dr. Burney's works, and Scholes's biography, *The Great Doctor Burney, His Life, His Travels, His Works, His Family and His Friends*, 2 vols. (London: Oxford University Press, 1948). For a discussion of the musicologist's contribution to the learned world, see

Lawrence Lipking, *The Ordering of the Arts in Eighteenth-Century England* (Princeton, N.J.: Princeton University Press, 1970), chap. 10, pp. 269–324.

24. Thomas Babington Macaulay, *Edinburgh Review* 76 (January 1843):545. Macaulay was the first writer publicly to express a sense of the striking awfulness of Burney's incarceration at court; as an ardent Whig, however, with an interest in deploring the court of George III, Macaulay had a political axe to grind.

25. *Memoirs*, III:287–288.

26. FB to her brother Charles's son, Charles Parr Burney, 26 February 1818, *J&L*, X:795. Charles also had the plea that his allowance was "scanty," and he had actually sold some of the stolen books to London booksellers. Frances's nephew Charles Parr was shocked to learn soon after his revered father's death of this early disgrace, and Burney wrote a candid and consoling letter of explanation. In the event, her brother had completed his undergraduate education at Aberdeen, and had gone on to become one of the most admired Greek scholars of his age.

27. Poor Richard, sent to India, lived a pious and laborious life as the headmaster of the orphan school at Kidderpore and died in Rangoon in 1808, without ever having returned to his native land or seeing his original family again. He had married abroad, and Burney expressed a wish "to know more of his numerous family & poor widow," *J&L*, VI:589, and note 9; see also Lonsdale, p. 333. One of Richard's sons acted as the executor of Frances Burney, Madame D'Arblay, and accompanied her corpse to the grave. This nephew, evidently proud of his aunt, named his son Alexander d'Arblay Burney, after her husband and son.

28. *Thraliana*, I:399.

29. *Memoirs*, II:168.

30. *Ibid.*, p. 123.

31. *J&L*, XI:286.

32. It has been suggested by Kathryn Kris that what Kris sees as Burney's lifelong tendency to feel shame and to resort to regressive behavior can be attributed to Burney's "childhood learning disability." This is portentous and vague; in fact, Burney shows no symptoms of any particular learning disability—dyslexia, for instance, would be incessantly evident in the writings of one who left such a trail of handwritten papers as Burney. See Kris, "A 70-Year Follow-up of a Childhood Learning Disability: The Case of Fanny Burney," *Psychoanalytic Study of the Child* 38 (1983):637–652.

33. *The Woman-Hater*, Berg MS, II:iii.13.

34. *Memoirs*, II:124.

35. FB, "Juvenile Journal," April 1775, Berg Diary MS (out of order, in packet labeled "Suppressed 1783," in box labeled Volume II part ii—hereafter II ii); cf. Lars Troide, Introduction to *Early Journals,* I:ii; Hemlow, p. 11; *ED,* I:xlv–xlvi.

36. *J&L*, XI:98–99.

37. This faded sampler can now be seen at Parham Park, Sussex.

38. *ED,* I:102, 151–152. Burney may have been shy of speaking French for fear of betraying a provincial accent or lower-class grammatical irregularities caught from her French relatives. She studied Italian in 1771, again largely self-taught, but the Burney household was frequently visited by musicians and singers from abroad, speaking in French or Italian, and Burney was more conversant with foreign languages than many a young lady who went to school.

39. Hemlow, p. 15.

40. See Erna Furman, *A Child's Parent Dies: Studies in Childhood Bereavement* (New Haven, Conn.: Yale University Press, 1974).

41. See Jean H. Hagstrum, *Sex and Sensibility: Ideal and Erotic Love from Milton to Mozart* (Chicago, Ill.: University of Chicago Press, 1980). The idea of any such "feminization" must for males be accompanied by a certain uneasiness. The recently idealized "androgyny" is likely to be as culture-bound as the component notions of "feminine" and "masculine," and thus to raise as many problems as it solves.

42. Mary Shelley, journal entry for 21 October 1838; see *Mary Shelley's Journal*, ed. Frederick L. Jones (Norman, Okla.: University of Oklahoma Press, 1947), p. 205.

43. *The Wanderer*, V:394.

44. Lonsdale, p. 75.

45. *Memoirs*, I:196, 190.

46. "To Sue on her recovery From the Jaundice," in Scrapbook labeled "Fanny Burney and the Burneys," Berg MS.

47. Charlotte Burney to FB, 4 July (?1778), BL Egerton MS, 3700B, pp. 169–170. Cf. expurgated version, *ED*, II:288.

Crisp engaged in what he called "treasonable Correspondence" with Charlotte, which he relayed to his sister Sophia Gast, passing on Charlotte's vexed statements about her stepmother: " 'As to Precious (her nick-name) I really think she is just now more intolerable than ever—Nothing is said that she does not fly into a Passion at and contradict!' " (*Burford Papers, being Letters of Samuel Crisp to his Sister at Burford*, ed. William Holden Hutton [London: Archibald Constable & Co. Ltd., 1905], p. 82).

48. FBd'A, "Memorandum Book" for 29 September 1806, Berg MS; *J&L*, VI:778.

49. *ED*, I:181.

50. FBd'A, French exercise book, 1804, *J&L*, VII:524.

51. FB to Queeney Thrale, 13 June 1784, in *The Queeney Letters*, ed. the Marquis of Lansdowne (London: Cassell & Co. Ltd., 1934), p. 99.

52. Charles Burney made flippant remarks upon Mrs. Piozzi and her husband even at a time (1808) when the Burneys hoped to reestablish the friendship. Dr. Burney wrote to his daughter on 12 November 1808 on his seeing Hester and Gabriel Piozzi again:

> The old rancour, or ill-will, excited by our desire to impede the marriage, is totally worn away. Indeed, it never could have existed, but from *her* imprudence in betraying to him that proof of our friendship for *her*, which ought never to have been regarded as spleen against him, who, certainly, nobody could blame for accepting a gay rich widow.—What could a man do better? (*Memoirs*, III:380–381).

Charles Burney's mean joke exhibits a wilful determination to ignore the fact that in his courtship of Mrs. Allen he, himself, was open to the charge of taking "a gay rich widow." The extra dig (obviously a standing joke repeated) that Piozzi *accepted* Hester Thrale (i.e., that *she* proposed) is gratuitously insulting. In printing this letter his daughter colludes in the insult and in Dr. Burney's techniques of self-insulation.

53. *Evelina*, I:1.

54. Mrs. Agnew, formerly housekeeper to Mrs. Delaney, in *The Autobiography and Correspondence of Mrs. Delany*, ed. Lady Llanover, 2nd ser., 3 vols. (London: R. Bentley, 1863), III:318.

55. Hemlow, pp. 158–159, 166.

56. *Ibid.*, pp. 164–167. The *camera obscura* comparison was first made by Hester Lynch Thrale.

2. *Evelina; or, A Young Lady's Entrance into the World*

1. *D&L*, II:317.

2. "To Doctor Burney, F.R.S. and Correspondent to the Institute of France," in *The Wanderer*, I:xx–xxi. In a later account (*Memoirs*, II:125), Burney seems to think that her father and Mrs. Allen were married at the time, though they were not married on Frances's fifteenth birthday.

3. Letters to and from Dr. Burney indicate that he was conversant with Continental and English fiction, and one of his last letters suggests that he may have had novels other than *Amelia* in what he regarded as his library: "I have no desire to part with the remnant of life . . . as long as I can amuse & divert thought from *self* when pain is not intolerable by the most silly books . . . in my miscellaneous Lib^y" (Lonsdale, p. 474).

4. *ED*, I:49.

5. *Ibid.*, e.g., pp. 7–8, 15. "I never pretend to be so superior a being as to be above having and indulging a *Hobby Horse,* and while I keep mine within due bounds and limits, nobody, I flatter myself, would wish to deprive me of the poor animal; to be sure, he is not form'd for labour, and is rather lame and weak, but then the dear creature is faithful . . . and tho' he sometimes prances, would not kick anyone into the mire . . . and I would not part with him for one who could win the greatest prize that ever *was* won at any Races" (p. 15). Burney's Sternean *"Hobby Horse"* is her writing.

6. In 1768, Burney read in rapid succession Elizabeth and Richard Griffith's *A Series of Genuine Letters between Henry and Frances* (1757), a work based on the authors' real-life courtship; Oliver Goldsmith's *The Vicar of Wakefield* (1766); and Samuel Johnson's *Rasselas* (1759). Her novel-reading stimulates Burney's comments upon such various matters as love and marriage, the death penalty, and the pursuit of happiness.

7. In her teens Burney was tackling on her own such works as Plutarch's *Lives* (in translation), Pope's *Iliad*, and, later, all the works of Pope, including the *Letters;* Hume's *History of England;* Hooke's *Roman History;* and Conyers Middleton's *Life of Cicero.* (See *ED*, I:22–26, 29–30; 144–46, 135.) She also learned Italian, and studied music theory in Diderot's treatise (*ED*, I:134, 144). Burney's niece Charlotte Barrett was to make a point of Burney's self-education; in drawing up a defense of the author against Croker, Barrett pointed out the intellectual powers which triumphed over disadvantages (Barrett, BL Egerton MS 3702 B; see Hemlow, pp. 18–19). Another woman, such as the bright Charlotte Barrett, could recognize what the disadvantages were.

8. BL Egerton MS 3696, pp. 74r–74v.

9. *Memoirs*, II:130–131.

10. *Ibid.*, p. 131.

11. *Ibid.*, II:126–127. The Pierpont Morgan Library has a sample of the final draft

in the "feigned hand"; the 208 pages of draft of *Evelina* in the Berg Collection are written in Burney's ordinary hand.

12. CB, Fragmentary Memoir, Berg MS, "Collection of Miscellaneous Holographs," folder 3, "Memoranda No. 5"; cf. Hemlow, p. 99. For Frances Burney's account of their tearful reunion, her father's approbation, and her relief and "amazement," see *Memoirs*, II:144–145.

13. See, e.g., Patricia Spacks, *The Female Imagination* (New York, N.Y.: Alfred A. Knopf, Inc., 1975), pp. 103–104; Emily H. Patterson, "Unearned Irony in Fanny Burney's *Evelina*," *Durham University Journal* 36 (June 1975):200–204. The charge of snobbery, leveled against both the author and her Evelina, is a cliché of Burney criticism; it is repeatedly made in Michael Adelstein's *Fanny Burney* in the Twayne Authors Series (New York, N.Y.: Twayne Publishers, Inc., 1968), while Ronald Paulson makes a more sophisticated commentary on Evelina's social ascent in *Satire and the Novel in Eighteenth-Century England* (New Haven, Conn.: Yale University Press, 1967), pp. 283–292. More recent writers, especially women, treat Evelina's "snobbishness" and what Judith Lowder Newton calls her "positive response to Sir Clement's courtly fictions" more sympathetically, as indexes of a social and economic condition which Burney explores even while capitulating to it; see Newton, *Women, Power, and Subversion: Social Strategies in British Fiction 1778–1860* (Athens, Ga.: University of Georgia Press, 1981), pp. 23–54. Patricia Spacks, in her later *Imagining a Self: Autobiography and Novel in Eighteenth-Century England*, gives a more favorable account of *Evelina* than that in Spacks's earlier book, though maintaining that the heroine chooses passivity and "assumes the utter propriety of remaining as much as possible a child: ignorant, innocent, fearful, and irresponsible" ([Cambridge, Mass.: Harvard University Press, 1976], p. 178). Katharine M. Rogers follows Spacks in her view of the novel, its author, and its heroine; see "Fanny Burney: The Private Self and the Published Self," *International Journal of Women's Studies* 7 (March–April 1984):110–117. Many of the new feminist critics see Evelina as sly out of necessity, her actions or non-actions a dramatized set of strategies for dealing with her world; Spacks says Evelina's and Burney's "insistent withdrawals" represent "not true timidity but a socially acceptable device of self-protection" (*Imagining a Self*, p. 181). Kristina Straub and Julia Epstein, while critical of the heroine, see some positive and subtle meanings in what Evelina's artful acquiescence displays, as does Judy Simons, for whom *Evelina* "mirrors Burney's dilemma as a woman writer by taking and using the idea of subterfuge as a defence" (*Fanny Burney* [Totowa, N.J.: Barnes and Noble Books, 1987], p. 60), although Simons's case is weakened by her presentation of Burney as "an unsophisticated artist" (p. 59). D. D. Devlin takes a strongly masculinist no-nonsense line, disagreeing abruptly with Spacks and all other feminists; Evelina is simply a nice young girl, and there is no need to see anything more in the novel than what Burney's antagonist John Wilson Croker saw in it: vivacious descriptions, "natural though rather too broad humour," and portrayal of the different classes (*The Novels and Journals of Fanny Burney and the Feminine Strategy*, p. 88). Even if there were any truth in the readings that find sharp satire, symbolism, or feminist ironies, "it is not worth the trouble to find out" (p. 90).

14. Patricia Spacks says, "Evelina chooses dependency and fear, a choice no less significant for being thrust upon her. . . . The identity she cares about most is given her from without by husband and father" (*Imagining a Self*, p. 179). Mary Poovey writes

interestingly about Evelina's relation to her two fathers, and points out that by "narrative sleight of hand," the heroine is made to suffer no conflict. The hero-as-husband seems, Poovey thinks, just another version of the father. Yet, in confronting her abandoning father, Evelina is given a fantasy position of revenge, and "indirectly retaliates for the male's crimes against both her mother and herself" ("Fathers and Daughters: The Traumas of Growing Up Female," *Women and Literature* 2[1982]:39–58.

15. *ED*, I:5–6.

16. Anthea Zeman, *Presumptuous Girls: Women and Their World in the Serious Woman's Novel* (London: Weidenfeld and Nicolson, 1977), p. 13.

17. Newton, *Women, Power, and Subversion*, pp. 24–28.

18. *ED*, II:54.

19. *Ibid.*, p. 69.

20. *Ibid.*, p. 70.

21. *Ibid.*, p. 49.

22. *Ibid.*, pp. 66–68.

23. *Ibid.*, pp. 74–75.

24. *Ibid.*, I:17.

25. See, e.g., Hemlow, p. 94; Bloom, "Introduction" to *Evelina*, p. xxiii. Jane Spencer, in a chapter on "Reformed Heroines," in *The Rise of the Woman Novelist from Aphra Behn to Jane Austen* (Oxford: Basil Blackwell Ltd., 1986), sees Orville as "a lover-mentor like [Haywood's] Trueworth or [Davys's] Formator" (p. 156). Spencer believes that Burney bridges satire and cultural acquiescence by creating Lord Orville: "the rules of society encourage men to treat women badly, but by introducing Orville she manages to attack only the bad behaviour, not the rules themselves." Harsh truths about male control of society "can be evaded through the fantasy of the perfect gentleman" (p. 155).

26. Draft of *Evelina*, Berg MS, fragment number 103.

27. *ED*, I:30.

28. *Ibid.*, p. 134.

29. See Austin Dobson, *Fanny Burney* (London: Macmillan & Co. Ltd., 1903), pp. 74–75.

30. *ED*, I:325–326. Miss Notable is a character in Swift's *Polite Conversation* (1738); Burney picks up Crisp's allusion at once. Swift's treatise is a florilegium of hackneyed smart remarks, a set of dramas in which every character speaks in clichés.

31. Samuel Foote, *The Minor* (London: J. Coote, T. Davies et al., 1760), Act I, p. 14.

32. *D&L*, V:31.

33. Samuel Foote, *Taste* (London: R. Francklin, 1752), Act I, pp. 8–10.

34. Simon Trefman, *Sam Foote, Comedian, 1720–1777* (New York, N.Y.: New York University Press, 1971), p. 58.

35. *ED*, II:175–176.

36. Susanna Burney (hereafter SB or SBP) to FB, 25 August 1779, BL Egerton MS 3691, p. 14r.

37. Draft of *Evelina*, Berg MS, fragment dated "April 13th."

38. Samuel Foote, *The Englishman in Paris* (London: Paul Vaillant, 1753), Act I, pp. 14–15.

39. "'Oh, Mr. Smith, Mr. Smith is the man!' cried he, laughing violently. 'Harry

Fielding never drew so good a character!—such a fine varnish of low politeness!—such a struggle to appear a gentleman!'" *D&L*, I:63.

40. Germaine Greer, *The Female Eunuch* (New York, N.Y.: McGraw-Hill, 1971), p. 245.

41. Kristina Straub, *Divided Fictions: Fanny Burney and the Feminine Strategy* (Athens, Ga.: University of Georgia Press, 1987), p. 50.

42. See Fielding, *Tom Jones*, bk. XI, chap. 2, pp. 438–440.

43. The drawing, from which a print ("Tricks upon Travelers") was published in 1810, is later than Burney's novel; I do not argue for influence either way, but for spiritual kinship. See dissertation by Patricia Dahlman Crown, "Edward F. Burney: An Historical Study in the English Romantic Art" (Ph.D. diss., UCLA, 1977) for a valuable study of the art of Burney's cousin, the shy eccentric who made a career out of book illustration but showed ability as a caricaturist. Edward Francesco shares his cousin Frances's belief that life is more absurd and painful than conventional realism would have it.

44. *Thraliana*, I:368.

45. Christopher Ricks, *Keats and Embarrassment* (Oxford: Oxford University Press, 1974), p. 4.

46. Male novelists in the eighteenth century tend to transform the Oedipal encounter between father and son into an episode in which the estranged and disinherited son rescues the father from some other assailants; revenge is taken and the father beaten and humiliated without the son's deviating from propriety, as in the case of the Man of the Hill in *Tom Jones* (bk. VIII, chap. 13). Henry Brooke in *The Fool of Quality* (1760–1772) portrays a young man unjustly cast off who turns robber; in one of his nocturnal excursions, armed with a pistol, he rescues a man from street thieves and finds that the stunned and bloody victim is his father. Murderous desire for revenge on the father is apparent, but the bad deeds are transferred to anonymous actors. Gushes of feeling and tears follow each filial reunion with the male parent; Burney's heroine is no more emotional about her father than Brooke's Hammel Clement is about his. Clement seems a source for Macartney, though his name is given to Sir Clement Willoughby. Burney reverses the customary pattern in making her heroine rescue a man from suicide and vicious courses, a benevolent act appropriate to heroes such as the Man of the Hill who saves a gambler from suicide, or a Tom Jones who saves other men from vice, or Brooke's virtuous Henry Moreland who rescues everybody from evils. Evelina is given a *manly* deed of active virtue.

47. *Thraliana*, I:360.

48. See young Charles Burney's long and gloomy autobiographical poem of 1777–1778 (Osborn Collection, Yale University Library); see Hemlow, pp. 73–74. Charles was banished and disgraced: "Torn from my Father, Brothers, Sisters, Friend, / Can my anxiety e'er know an end?"

3. *The Witlings:* The Finished Comedy

1. Frances Burney wrote a description of Mrs. Thrale in her diary after meeting her and Dr. Johnson for the first time when (on 20 March 1777) they visited Dr. Burney's

house (ED, II:152–158). Mrs. Thrale, however, made no corresponding diary entry about Frances Burney, and does not appear to have noticed her; see Mary Hyde, *The Thrales of Streatham Park* (Cambridge, Mass.: Harvard University Press, 1977), pp. 177–178.

2. CB to HLT, 8 March 1771, Rylands MS 545, no. 4.

3. *Thraliana*, I:470.

4. *Ibid.*, pp. 347–348, 367, 414.

5. *Thraliana*, I:375; fragments of "The Flasher's" editorial, including the sentence quoted here, are to be found among the "Camilla scraps," Berg MS. Even this mock paper shows the concerns that run through *The Witlings;* the subject is the dignity of work.

6. FB, August 1781, Berg MS, Diary; cf. Hemlow, pp. 114–115. Hemlow quotes this piece in full, but reverses the order of third and fourth stanzas. It seems that the first stanza is Johnson's, the second Hester Thrale's, and the third Frances Burney's.

7. *D&L*, I:114.

8. *Ibid.*, p. 111.

9. *Ibid.*, pp. 115–116.

10. *Ibid.*, p. 213.

11. *Ibid.*, pp. 158–159.

12. *Ibid.*, p. 126.

13. *Ibid.*, pp. 135, 137–138.

14. J. Paul Hunter, "'Peace' and the Augustans: Some Implications of Didactic Method and Literary Form," in *Studies in Change and Revolution: Aspects of English Intellectual History 1640–1800*, ed. Paul J. Korshin (Menston, Yorks.: The Scolar Press Ltd., 1972), pp. 161–189.

15. Hugh Kelly, *The School for Wives* (1774), 3rd ed. (London: T. Becket, 1774), IV.i.72.

16. Kelly, *The School for Wives,* I.i.10; Colman and Garrick, *The Clandestine Marriage* (1776) (London: John Bell, 1792), I.i.12.

17. Hannah Cowley, *The Runaway* (London: Printed for the Author; And sold by Mr. Dodsley . . . Mr. Becket . . . Mr. Cadell et al., 1776), I.i.1.

18. It has been customary to agree with Oliver Goldsmith who in his "Essay on the Theatre" (1773) decried sentimental or "crying" comedies and praised "laughing" comedies, but as Robert D. Hume points out there was in fact very little difference, and Goldsmith praises Cibber's works as "laughing" comedy though they are generally viewed as marking the advent of the "sentimental" drama (Robert D. Hume, "Goldsmith and Sheridan and the Supposed Revolution of 'Laughing' against 'Sentimental' Comedy," in *Studies in Change and Revolution*, pp. 237–276). The ideal comedy of the period combined the laugh-provoking with the pathetic or serious and moral, in a manner very like that of our moral situation comedies.

19. David Garrick, "Prologue" to Hannah More's *Percy*, in *The Works of Hannah More*, 6 vols. (London: H. Fisher, R. Fisher & P. Jackson, 1833–1834), V:109–110.

20. Garrick, "Epilogue" for More's *The Inflexible Captive, ibid.*, p. 101.

21. Harriet Lee, "Advertisement" prefixed to *The New Peerage; or, Our Eyes may deceive us* (London: C.G. J. & J. Robinson, 1787), p. 3.

22. *The Witlings*, Berg MS, 126 pages. This is a clean manuscript, evidently prepared for theater managers, copied in a fair hand with a few light crossings-out indicating

minor revisions, mainly to shorten. See also Hemlow, p. 135. There is no pagination after the second act; references will be made to the act numbers, with no further annotation.

23. Lady Smatter alludes to the opening lines of the second of Pope's *Moral Essays*, the "Epistle to a Lady of the Characters of Women" (1735). The meaning of the line is explained by the ensuing couplet: "Nothing so true as what you once let fall, / 'Most Women have no Characters at all.' / Matter too soft a lasting mark to bear, / And best distinguish'd by black, brown, or fair" (ll.1–4). Lady Smatter misquotes and misunderstands. Pope's view of feminine lack of identity is treated ironically by Burney.

24. Frances Burney acted the part of the unhappy wife, Mrs. Lovemore, in a family production of Murphy's *The Way to Keep Him*, in Worcester in 1777. She was nervous (she disliked the role), but a little cousin was delighted with her opening business, taking tea on stage: "'Ay, cousin Fanny, I saw your drinking your tea by yourself, before all the company! did you think they would not see you?'" (*ED*, II:173).

25. In Murphy's *All in the Wrong*, based on Molière's *Le Cocu Imaginaire*, Sir John and Lady Restless are jealous of each other. When Lady Restless accuses her husband of concealing an inamorata in the closet, the closet at length opened reveals Mr. Beverley, the man whom Sir John suspects of cuckolding him. The audience of course has known who is concealed where, and why.

26. "Sacharissa" (Lady Dorothy Sidney) was the object of Waller's love poems and his inspiration; Sappho, the Greek lyric poet who is the first female author recorded in Western literary tradition, was always invoked in relation to women writers of the eighteenth century. Literary or artistic Englishwomen of the time were referred to as new Muses. See the composite portrait (entitled *The Nine Living Muses of Great Britain*) of celebrated ladies including Charlotte Lennox, Elizabeth Montagu, and Hannah More in vaguely classical garb (reproduced in Robert Halsband's "'The Female Fan': Women and Literature in Eighteenth-Century England," *History Today* 24 (October 1974):702–709.

27. *D&L*, I:211.

28. *Ibid.*, p. 208.

29. Susanna Burney to FB, 3 August 1779, BL Egerton MS 3690, ff. 9r–10r.

30. *D&L*, I:210.

31. *Memoirs*, II:271.

32. *D&L*, I:178.

33. Journal entry of 1 May 1779, *Thraliana*, I:381.

34. *Ibid.*, pp. 386–388; Act I of her unfinished comedy *The Humourist* (adapted from Philippe Destouches's *L'Homme Singulier*) can be found in Rylands MS 650.

35. *D&L*, I:209.

36. Samuel Crisp to FB, 21 July 1779, BL Egerton MS 3694, pp. 104–105.

37. *D&L*, I:170.

38. CB to FB, BL Egerton MS 3690, pp. 4–5. The letter is dated only "Sunday Night" and is evidently written from Chessington; the weather is still hot. Alvaro Ribeiro in correspondence has suggested 29 August 1779.

39. *D&L*, I:209.

40. *Memoirs*, I:198–199.

41. *D&L*, I:214.

42. Hester Lynch Thrale approved of Burney's virtue in giving up the piece "for fear it may bear hard upon some Respectable Characters" but thought her friend gave up "a Play likely to succeed" (journal entry of 18 August 1779, *Thraliana*, I:401). Hester knew

that Murphy liked it (*ibid.*, p. 381). Friends outside the family had not doubted *The Witlings'* prospects. Apparently, Burney represented her giving up the play as a decision of her own, and did not tell Hester Thrale the full extent of Dr. Burney's interference and her chagrin.

43. See Lonsdale, pp. 57–60.

44. *D&L*, I:208.

45. *Ibid.*, p. 209.

4. *Cecilia; or, Memoirs of an Heiress*

1. Lonsdale, p. 262.

2. FB to SB, January–February 1781, Berg MS, A 141.

3. *D&L*, II:8.

4. [George Huddlesford], *Warley: A Satire*, Part II "Containing a Curious Detail of the Operations of the Grand Army during a Royal Review: and interspersed with a Variety of Fresh Characters Addressed to the First Artist in Europe" (London: D. Brown, 1778). The author asks if his "scurrilous dogg'rel" will do him any good:

> Will your Metre a Council engage or Attorney
> Or gain approbation from dear little Burney?
>
> (p. 28)

There is no need for dragging in Burney (who is noted at the bottom of the page as "The Authoress of Evelina") unless the author thought the allusion would please Joshua Reynolds, the addressee. For Burney's annoyance, see *D&L*, I:136, 138–139.

5. *D&L*, II:105. Charlotte Barrett comments upon the discovery of the manuscript copy of these verses in Dr. Burney's own papers "with so many erasures, interlineations, and changes as to give the most direct internal evidence that they were the doctor's own composition." Burney discovered the true authorship when she went through her father's papers.

6. FB to SB, 15 December 1781, Berg MS, A 143.

7. *D&L*, I:345.

8. *Ibid.*, p. 347; see also James Clifford, *Hester Lynch Piozzi* (New York, N.Y.: Columbia University Press, 1986), p. 185.

9. Joyce Hemlow first discovered Frances Burney's complaints about her father's eagerness for the work to be done and her own sense of pressure; see Hemlow, pp. 139–140, 142–147. This information has been treated superficially by some critics, with no attention to complex circumstances: see, for example, Judy Simons in her introduction to the Virago edition of *Cecilia*, pp. viii–ix, and in her *Fanny Burney* (Totowa, N.J.: Barnes and Noble Books, 1987), pp. 61–62.

10. Hester Lynch (Thrale) Piozzi's autobiography, the "Biographical Anecdotes" she wrote in 1815, show her lifelong resentment and horror of the sacrifice made of her at the age of twenty-two, when she was given by her uncle and mother to the unloving Henry Thrale, to whom she was "a *plain Girl* who had not one Attraction in his Eyes" (Firestone Library, Princeton, N.J., MS 3891.9.313, p. 22).

11. *D&L*, I:35.

12. HLT, Rylands MS 629, no. 10r–10v. The lines related to Burney come from Romeo's description of Rosaline in *Romeo and Juliet*, I.i.214–219.

13. HLT to FB, n.d. [February 1781], BL Egerton MS 3695, f. 37v.

14. FB to HLT, n.d. [February 1781], *ibid.*, f. 39r–39v.

15. *Ibid.*, f. 40r.

16. HLT to FB, 7 February [1781], BL Egerton MS 3695.

17. For *Morning Herald* account, see Clifford, *Hester Lynch Piozzi*, p. 194. Susanna Burney's account of the dress is given in *ED*, II:265–266. She and Mrs. Burney had a private view: Mrs. Thrale sent a note "to say that the *Owyhee savage* was to be seen at Mrs. Davenant's, Red Lyon Square, before two."

18. FB to HLT, 22 January 1781, BL Egerton MS 3695, f. 35v.

19. See Barrett's note, *D&L*, II:25.

20. HLT to FB, 20 February [1781], BL Egerton MS 3695, f. 43r.

21. FB to HLT, n.d. [February 1781], Rylands MS 545, no. 22, ff. 1v–2r.

22. *D&L*, II:8.

23. HLT to FB, 20 [March] 1781, BL Egerton MS 3695, f. 45v.

24. *Thraliana*, I:489; see Clifford, *Hester Lynch Piozzi*, p. 198; Lonsdale, p. 263.

25. *Gentleman's Magazine* 51 (1781):134.

26. FB to HLT, 17 February [1781], Rylands MS 545, no. 25, 1v–2r. Lars Troide suggests that Jenny Barsanti, actress and singer, who left London for Dublin and married the manager of Dublin Theatre, may have had something to do with Burney's mysterious Irish Prologue.

27. William McCarthy, *Hester Thrale Piozzi: Portrait of a Literary Woman* (Chapel Hill, N.C.: University of North Carolina Press, 1985), p. 46.

28. HLT to FB, 20 February 1781, BL Egerton MS 3695, f. 43v.

29. *Thraliana*, I:502.

30. *D&L*, II:26.

31. HLT to FB, n.d. [1782], BL Egerton MS 3695, f. 66v.

32. FB to HLT, n.d. [1782], Rylands MS 545, no. 18.

33. *D&L*, II:110.

34. *Ibid.*, pp. 111–112.

35. FB to HLT, 25 November [1781], BL Egerton MS 3695, f. 61v.

36. FB to SB, n.d. [January–February 1781], Berg MS, A 141.

37. FB to SB, 3 February 1781, Berg MS, A 141.

38. FB to SB, 3 October 1781, Berg MS, A 142, folder 3.

39. FB to HLT, 16 December [1781], BL Egerton MS 3695, f. 63v.

40. For correct publication date (since Dobson, misrepresented as 12 June), see Alvaro Ribeiro, *Notes and Queries* 225 (October 1980):415–416.

41. All references are to *Cecilia; or, Memoirs of an Heiress*, ed. Peter Sabor and Margaret Anne Doody, 5 vols. in 1 (London: Oxford University Press, 1988). Volume and page numbers will be given after each quotation.

42. *The Merchant of Venice*, I.ii.25–26.

43. *ED*, I:134.

44. *Memoirs*, II:172.

45. Jonathan Swift, *Gulliver's Travels*, bk. III, chap. 10.

46. Pope, *Epistle to Burlington* (1731), ll. 203–204.

47. John Dryden, *The Works of Virgil: Containing His Pastorals, Georgics and Æneis* (London: Jacob Tonson, 1697); translation of *Æneid* bk. VI, ll. 1175–1178, p. 397.

48. Samuel Richardson, *Clarissa; or, The History of a Young Lady* (London: J. F. and C. Rivington et al., 1785), I:231.

49. *ED*, I:133; cf. pp. 28, 66.

50. For Smart's "Epilogue" see Katrina Williamson, ed., *Miscellaneous Poems,* vol. IV of Smart's *Poetical Works* (Oxford: Oxford University Press, 1987), p. 264 and note. See also Betty Rizzo, "Enter the Epilogue on an Ass—by Christopher Smart," *The Papers of the Bibliographical Society of America* 73, no. 3 (1979):340–344. Burney elsewhere quotes Smart's "Soliloquy of Princess Periwinkle," a fragment of a comedy that appeared in *The Old Woman's Magazine* (1750): *J&L*, I:80.

51. Samuel Crisp to FB, 27 April 1780, *D&L*, I:277.

52. *Memoirs,* II:88.

53. Originally, as we can see in the manuscript draft, Burney wrote that the castle was surrounded by "Fortifications of long standing," a phrase which she crossed out, inserting "a Moat" (Draft of *Cecilia,* Berg MS, section III, f. 129v). The Berg Collection has 547 pages of holograph manuscript of *Cecilia,* portions of different parts of the novel in different stages.

54. Sarah Scott, *The History of Cornelia* (Dublin: John Smith, 1750), p. 188. Sarah Scott was known to Burney, but not as well as her more famous and imposing sister, Elizabeth Montagu.

55. Lonsdale, p. 280.

56. Draft of *Cecilia,* Berg MS, III, f. 92r.

57. Terry Castle, *Masquerade and Civilization: The Carnivalesque in Eighteenth-Century English Culture and Fiction* (Stanford, Calif.: Stanford University Press, 1986), p. 263.

58. Draft of *Cecilia,* Berg MS, III, f. 84r, crossed out.

59. *Ibid.,* IV, f. 214r, crossed out.

60. *D&L,* II:213.

61. Choderlos de Laclos, review of *Cecilia ou les Mémoires d'une Héritière* in *Mercure de France* (17 April, 24 April, 15 May, 1784), reprinted in Laclos's *Oeuvres complètes* (Paris: Editions Gallimard, 1979), pp. 449–469. Laclos describes in some detail the "moment où Cécile a l'heureux malheur d'instruire Delvile de tout l'amour dont elle brûle pour lui" and compares it with the scene of the Princess of Clèves looking at the portrait of Nemours and not knowing she is observed—a scene in Mme. de Lafayette's novel (1678) that may have influenced Burney's (pp. 462–463). See Pat Rogers, review of Virago reprint of *Cecilia:* "One episode in a summer-house where Delvile surprises Cecilia as she sits brooding has the air of a Schubert song," "Puellilia," *The London Review of Books* 8 (7 August 1986):12.

62. SC to Sophia Gast, *Burford Papers, being Letters of Samuel Crisp to his Sister at Burford,* ed. William Holden Hutton (London: Archibald Constable and Co. Ltd., 1905), p. 74.

63. Samuel Hoole, *Aurelia; or, The Contest,* An Heroi-Comic Poem in Four Cantos (London: J. Dodsley, 1783), pp. 62–63. Cf. *D&L,* II:227.

64. *Gentleman's Magazine* 52 (October 1782):485.

65. *London Magazine* 52 (January 1783):40.

66. *Critical Review* 54 (December 1782):414. The approving review in this periodical may have been written by Charles Burney's old friend Thomas Twining; Dr. Burney was accustomed to making careful arrangements that his own books should be reviewed only by friends; see Lonsdale, pp. 109–110, 121–122.

67. *English Review* 1 (January 1783):14.

68. *Ibid.*, pp. 15–16.

69. *Critical Review* 54 (December 1782):420.

70. *D&L*, II:159.

71. *Ibid.*, pp. 107–108.

72. *Ibid.*, p. 145.

73. *Thraliana*, I:555.

74. Laclos, review of *Cecilia, ou les Mémoires d'une Héritière*, as cited above n. 61, pp. 461, 453, 457.

75. [William Godwin], *The Herald of Literature; or, A Review of the most Considerable Publications that will be made in the Course of the Ensuing Winter; with Extracts* (London: John Murray, 1784). "Article IV. Louisa, or Memoirs of a Lady of Quality. By the Author of Evelina and Cecilia. 3 vols. 12 mo.," pp. 63–64.

76. *Ibid.*, pp. 65, 66, 75.

77. See Burton R. Pollin, introduction to his edition of Godwin's *Italian Letters; or, The History of the Count de St. Julian* (Lincoln, Neb.: University of Nebraska Press, 1965), p. x.

78. See Gary Kelly, *The English Jacobin Novel 1780–1805* (Oxford: Clarendon Press, 1976), pp. 191–192.

79. Mary Wollstonecraft to her sister Everina, 4 March 1787, in *Collected Letters of Mary Wollstonecraft*, ed. Ralph M. Wardle (Ithaca, N.Y.: Cornell University Press, 1979), p. 141.

80. Burney's draft of an introduction to *Cecilia*, BL Egerton MS 3696, ff. 1–3.

81. The lines are slightly misquoted from Portius' speech in Joseph Addison's *Cato* (1713):

> Remember what our Father oft has told us;
> The Ways of Heav'n are dark and intricate,
> Puzzled in Mazes, and perplext with Errors;
> Our Understanding traces 'em in vain,
> Lost and bewilder'd in the fruitless Search;
> Nor sees with how much art the Windings run,
> Nor where the regular Confusion ends.
> (London: J. Tonson, 1713), I.i.2.

5. Love, Loss, and Imprisonment: The Windsor and Kew Tragedies

1. FB, Brighton journal to SBP, 12 November 1782, Berg MS, Diary, II, pt. i.

2. FB to SBP, 28 October 1782, Berg MS, A 145, folder 6.

3. FB to SBP, Brighton journal, 28 October, Berg MS, Diary, II, pt. i.

4. FB to SBP, Brighton journal, November, Berg MS, Diary, II, pt. i.

5. FB to SBP, 31 August 1782, British Library.

6. FB to SBP, journal to Susanna, 26 December 1782, Berg MS, Diary, II, pt. i.

7. FB to SBP, 11 January 1783, Berg MS, Diary, II, pt. i.

8. FB to SBP, 22 February 1783, Berg MS, Diary, II, pt. i.

9. FB to SBP, February 1783, Berg MS, Diary, II, pt. i.

10. FB to SBP, 5 April 1783, Berg MS, A 145, folder 6.

11. FB to SBP, letter marked as received 12 April 1783, Berg MS, A 145, folder 6.

12. FB to SBP, April 1783, Berg MS, A 146, folder 7.

13. FB to SBP, letter received 12 April 1783, as above, n. 11.

14. FB to SBP, 23 February 1783, Berg MS, A 145, folder 6.

15. FB to SBP, 28 June 1783, Berg MS, A 145, folder 6.

16. FB to SBP, 25 November 1783, Berg MS, Diary, II, pt. ii.

17. FB to SBP, 30 December 1783, Berg MS, A 146, folder 8.

18. Samuel Richardson, *Sir Charles Grandison,* ed. Jocelyn Harris, 3 vols. (Oxford: Oxford University Press), II:418, 429.

19. FB to SBP, 30 December 1783, as above, n. 17.

20. FB to SBP, 25 January 1784, Berg MS, Diary, II, pt. ii.

21. FB to SBP, 23 January 1784, Berg MS, Diary, II, pt. ii.

22. Samuel Richardson to Lady Bradshaigh, 8 December [1753], in *Selected Letters of Samuel Richardson,* ed. John Carroll (Oxford: Oxford University Press, 1964), p. 255.

23. *Sir Charles Grandison,* I:66.

24. FB to SBP, 23 January 1783, as above, n. 21. The word "Nature" has been crossed out, presumably deleted in FB's later editing of her papers rather than at the time.

25. FB to SBP, 23 May 1784, Berg MS, A 146, folder 8.

26. *Ibid.*

27. FB to Frances Brooke, October 1783, Berg MS, "Scrapbook," "Fanny Burney and Family," section 26; this is a draft of letter presumably sent.

28. FB to SBP, 3 February 1781, Berg MS, A 141.

29. "I am sorry you are *disinclined* to writing at present, but I have that opinion of your sincerity, that I do not believe you wou'd have given that reason if it had not been a true one; therefore I can only say, *the more's the pity* . . . I cou'd wish Apollo had made you one of his visits just now." Frances Brooke to FB, 31 October 1783, Berg MS, "Scrapbook," p. 228. Cf. Lorraine McMullen, *An Odd Attempt in a Woman: The Literary Life of Frances Brooke* (Vancouver, B.C.: University of British Columbia Press, 1983), pp. 204–205.

30. SC to FB, July 1782, Berg MS, Diary, II, pt. i. Cf. *D&L,* II:123.

31. *Ibid.*

32. HLT to FB, Monday 21 [September] 1782, Berg MS, A 779, folder 4.

33. HLT to FB, 28 September, Berg MS, A 779, folder 4.

34. FB to SBP, 24 November 1783, Berg MS, Diary, II, pt. ii.

35. HLT to FB, 13 August 1782, Berg MS, A 779, folder 3.

36. FB to SBP, Brighton journal, 4 November 1782, Berg MS, Diary, II, pt. ii.

37. Annotation of letter of HLT to FB from Streatham [?1781], Berg MS, A 779, folder 1.

38. FB to HLT [?26 January 1783], Berg MS, in separate hardbound blue folder labeled "Autograph Letters to Mrs. Thrale & Fanny Burney," 166667B. Burney writes

her later explanatory remarks in the margins and on the back. Cf. also Hemlow, pp. 171–172. For Hester Lynch (Thrale) Piozzi's story during this period, see James Clifford, *Hester Lynch Piozzi* (New York, N.Y.: Columbia University Press, 1986), chap. x, pp. 203–231.

39. See the Marquis of Lansdowne (Henry William Edmund Petty-FitzMaurice), ed., *The Queeney Letters* (London: Cassell & Co. Ltd., 1934).

40. She was later to say that she kept of Hester Thrale's letters of that troubled time those that would prove her friend had at least fought against her unworthy passion.

41. FB to Hester Maria Thrale (Queeney), June 1784, *The Queeney Letters*, p. 99; cf. Lonsdale, p. 284.

42. HLP diary entry, 3 September 1784, *Thraliana*, II:612.

43. Clifford, *Hester Lynch Piozzi*, pp. 330, 414.

44. FB thus annotates a letter from HLT of 20 February 1781:

This dear—& at this period most fervently attached of Friends, as well as most agreeable, lively, spirited, & entertaining of Women, no sooner heard I was really ill at Chesington than she drove over the Worst cross roads of those times, to visit me in the mist of a severe Frost! Ah! how I loved her! (BL Egerton MS 3695.)

45. FB to SBP, 10 August 1784, Berg MS, A 146, folder 8.

46. *D&L*, II:282.

47. See *Mrs. Delany's Flower Collages from the British Museum*, catalogue of exhibition of Mrs. Delany's flower collages at the Pierpont Morgan Library, New York City, 2 September–2 November 1986. For Frances Burney's description of Mary Delany's flower collages, see *D&L*, II:209.

48. *D&L*, II:307.

49. *Ibid.*, p. 338.

50. FB to SBP, 16 December 1785, Berg MS, Diary, II, pt. ii; cf. *D&L*, II:316.

51. *D&L*, II:345–346.

52. *ED*, I:325–327; Annie Raine Ellis notes a resemblance between the two passages (*ibid.*, p. 325, n. 1); see above, pp. 48–49.

53. Julia L. Epstein, "Writing the Unspeakable: Fanny Burney's Mastectomy and the Fictive Body." *Representations* 16 (Fall 1986):131–166; remark quoted is on p. 133.

54. *D&L*, II:353–354.

55. *Ibid.*, p. 355.

56. Hemlow, pp. 213–215.

57. *D&L*, II:345 (letter of 17 December 1785).

58. *Ibid.*, p. 123. Sophie von La Roche's own account of her visit to Windsor indicates that she was delighted with everything and particularly with Miss Burney: "all noble-minded rational beings would delight in her acquaintance and feel at home with her." Burney struck her as "the ideal English Miss: quick-witted, gentle, sensitive, virtuous, and with great human insight . . . and all these qualities . . . only appear like delicious sprites just at the right time and for a fleeting moment," *Sophie in London, 1786*, trans. Claire Williams (London: Jonathan Cape, 1933), pp. 186, 197.

59. *D&L,*, III:266–267.

60. *Ibid.*, pp. 4–5.

61. *Memoirs*, III:96.

62. *D&L*, V:50.

63. *Letters from Mrs. Delany to Mrs. Frances Hamilton, from the Year 1779 to the Year 1788; comprising Many Unpublished and Interesting Anecdotes of their Late Majesties and the Royal Family*, 2nd ed. (London: Longman, Hurst, Rees, Orme, and Brown, 1820), pp. 68–70.

64. Thomas Babington Macaulay, *Edinburgh Review* 76 (January 1843):545.

65. *D&L*, III:6–7.

66. *Memoirs*, III:94.

67. *D&L*, III:7.

68. *Ibid.*, pp. 342, 367.

69. *Ibid.*, p. 238.

70. *Ibid.*, pp. 23, 55–56, 135. In Mrs. Thrale's associative game, Frances had been associated with lilac and with tabby (watered silk); see above, chap. 3, p. 68.

71. *D&L*, III:88.

72. *Ibid.*, p. 90.

73. *D&L*, V:79.

74. *D&L*, III:188. The passage paraphrases a letter from Mrs. Montagu to Mrs. Delany, which the queen of the Blues obviously wanted passed on to Burney and, indeed, to the queen; Burney thought some expressions "meant for the royal eye."

75. See M. Dorothy George, *Catalogue of Prints and Drawings in the British Museum: Political and Personal Satires* (London: British Museum, 1870–1954), Vol. 6, nos. 7383 and 7548.

76. *D&L*, III:102–103.

77. *Ibid.*, p. 113.

78. *Ibid.*, pp. 234–235.

79. *Ibid.*, p. 113.

80. Hemlow, p. 36; FB to SBP, (?20) June 1787, Berg MS, Diary, III.

81. *D&L*, IV:135.

82. The fullest account of the tragedies until now has been that given by Hemlow, pp. 216–221, an account on which subsequent critics have relied. For similar dismissive judgments, see Wallace's one-paragraph summary, "Fanny Burney and the Theater," *A Busy Day*, pp. 157–158. See also Judy Simons, "*Edwy and Elgiva* survived one disastrous performance only and we should perhaps be grateful for the natural demise of the rest," *Fanny Burney* (Totowa, N.J.: Barnes and Noble Books, 1987), p. 133.

83. See Ida Macalpine and Richard Hunter, *The King and the Mad-Business* (London: Allen Lane: The Penguin Press, 1969).

84. *D&L*, IV:225.

85. *D&L*, V:81.

86. *Ibid.*, p. 120.

87. For the fate of *Edwy and Elgiva* on its one night, see Burney's own account, *J&L*, III:97–100. She saw its defects:

> it was not written with any idea of the stage, & my illness & weakness & constant *absorbment* in the time of its preparation [just after the birth of her child], occasioned it to appear with so many *undramatic* [ef]fects, from my inexperience of Theatrical requisites & demands, that when I saw it, I perceived myself a

thousand things I wished to *change*. The Performers, too, were cruelly imperfect, & made blunders I blush to have pass for mine,—added to what belong to me—

See also Appendix A, "Reviews of Edwy and Elgiva," *ibid.*, pp. 366–367.

88. In 1780 Burney had read "a tale called 'Edwy and Edilda'" by a sentimental male author "and unreadably soft, and tender, and senseless it is" (*D&L*, I:273).

89. Unless otherwise noted, all references to *Edwy and Elgiva* (giving numbers of act, scene, and page) will refer to the published text edited by Miriam J. Benkovitz (Saratoga Springs, N.Y.: Skidmore College, 1956), based on the manuscript in the Library of Emmanuel College, Cambridge. That fair text (copied out by Alexandre d'Arblay) is presumably close to the acted version; an earlier manuscript exists in the Berg Collection.

90. FB to SBP, undated, [?January–March, 1787], Berg MS. Although found in Diary, II, pt. ii (1783–1786), in packet labeled "Suppressed 1783," this letter certainly is not of 1783, as FB mentions being at court; she has just had "a snap Dinner with Mrs. Ord," her first "opportunity" since her "residence under the Royal Roof," and she seized the chance, since the royal family was dining at Kew.

91. All quotations from *The Siege of Pevensey* are taken from this very finished manuscript copy in the Berg Collection. Burney supplies no page numeration, and scene division is vague. Act numbers only will be given after quotations.

92. *D&L*, III:201.

93. Samuel Crisp, *Virginia: A Tragedy*. As it is acted at the Theatre Royal in Drury-Lane (London: J. and R. Tonson and S. Draper, 1754), V.i.70. Crisp's plot is taken from the old story of Appius and Virginia, repeated in Chaucer and formerly dramatized by Webster.

94. Robert Dodsley, *Cleone: A Tragedy* (London: John Bell, 1792), IV.i.55.

95. *Ibid.*, V.i.57, 62–63.

96. See Macalpine and Hunter, *The King and the Mad-Business*, p. 65.

97. *D&L*, III:182.

98. *Ibid.*, p. 224.

99. *Ibid.*, p. 374.

100. *Ibid.*, p. 367.

101. *Ibid.*, p. 364.

102. *Ibid.*.

103. *Hubert De Vere* exists in two manuscript versions, both in the Berg Collection. The earlier draft is in fragments of paper held together by (rather dangerous) old pins. Quotation is from the later and clearer draft unless otherwise specified; this draft consists of five *cahiers*, one for each act, and Burney has numbered by folds, save in Act IV, which is paginated. Act numbers will be given after quotation.

104. FB to SBP, [?January 1789], Berg MS, Diary, III.

105. FB to SBP, undated manuscript of 1786–1787, as quoted above, p. 181.

106. *D&L*, V:108.

107. *Elberta*, never written out as a drama, is a heap of disconnected scraps, 303 in the Berg Collection. The Berg scraps have been numbered but with no reference to the plot or the chronology of the writing, and some of these scraps are not *Elberta*. Quotations will be followed by scrap number.

108. *D&L*, V:105–107.

109. *Ibid.*, p. 132.

110. *Ibid.*, pp. 134–135.

111. *Ibid.*, p. 141.

112. *Ibid.*, p. 148.

113. *Ibid.*, p. 170.

114. *Ibid.*, p. 146.

115. *Ibid.*, p. 149.

116. *Ibid.*, p. 140.

117. *D&L*, IV:286.

118. *Ibid.*, p. 334.

119. "*El.'s madness after the divorce,*" draft of poem in manuscript with the draft of *Edwy and Elgiva* in the Berg Collection; the quotation here represents only a portion of this "Ode."

120. Dr. Gisborne ordered Burney "opium and three glasses of wine in the day," *D&L*, V:147; he also recommended rest and freedom from anxiety.

121. "*El.'s madness*" as above, n. 119, first stanza.

122. *D&L*, V:221–222; cf. *J&L*, I:73–74.

123. *J&L*, III:258.

124. *D&L*, V:228.

6. Marriage, "Clarinda," and *Camilla*

1. Anne-Louise-Germaine, baronne de Staël-Holstein (1766–1817), had long taken as her lover Louis-Marie Amalric, comte de Narbonne Lara, by whom she had two children. M. d'Arblay, a friend of Narbonne, the former minister of war, was forced to confirm Dr. Burney's suspicions when Frances Burney anxiously made inquiries. D'Arblay is generously concerned that Frances and other English people should do justice to Mme. de Staël: "On l'a calomniée si on n'a pas rendu justice aux eminentes qualités de son cœur, comme de son esprit." He explains, "Nos mœurs . . . sont si peu en mesure avec celles de ce Pays . . . qu'en verité il serait non seulement injuste mais barbare d'y puiser les raisons de juger—nos mariages par exemple. Tous, pour ainsi dire, n'etaient qu'autant de sacrifices . . . à des convenances dont les femmes ont toujours été les victimes." *J&L*, II:31–32. French spelling and accents as in the original, here and in all other quotations.

2. *D&L*, V:348; for remark in original French, see *J&L*, II:123, n. 2.

3. *J&L*, II:123.

4. *D&L*, V:302.

5. For *Thèmes*, see Appendix II, *J&L*, II:188–205; see especially pp. 197, 200–201.

6. *J&L*, II:42.

7. *Ibid.*, p. 65.

8. *Ibid.*, p. 41.

9. *Ibid.*, p. 50.

10. *J&L*, IV:105–106.

11. Maria Allen Rishton to SBP, 14 August 1793, Berg MS; see Hemlow, p. 239.

12. *Ibid.*, cf. Maria's letter of 12 August to FBd'A, *J&L*, II:184–186, where she also wishes "to see the Hero who has raised 'these Tumults in a Vestals Veins'"—the reference is to Pope's "What means this tumult in a Vestal's veins?" in *Eloisa to Abelard;* l. 4.

13. Sarah Scott to Elizabeth Montagu, 16 December 1793, Huntington Library, San Marino, Calif., MS MO 5497.

14. The Marquis of Lansdowne, ed., *The Queeney Letters* (London: Cassell & Co. Ltd., 1934), p. 76.

15. *J&L*, II:182, 175.

16. Frances Burney wrote to M. d'Arblay in March 1793 offering money: "puis-je vous demander—si, malheureusement—une telle petite somme vous pourra être, ou incessament, ou à l'avenir, du moindre commodité, d'être votre première *Banquiere?*" (*J&L*, II:36). She sent him a ten-pound banknote and some gold, and offered to lend him one hundred pounds without interest (which must have represented about all the savings to which she had access). D'Arblay was surprised and touched, but insisted on sending the money back straightaway. Frances Burney's offer was entirely outside the bounds prescribed by the conduct-books.

17. *Brief Reflections Relative to the Emigrant French Clergy: Earnestly Submitted to the Humane Consideration of the Ladies of Great Britain.* By the Author of Evelina and Cecilia (London: T. Davidson, for Thomas Cadell, 1793), p. iii.

18. *Ibid.*, p. iv.

19. *Ibid.*, pp. 5–6.

20. *Ibid.*, pp. 22–26.

21. *Ibid.*, p. 8.

22. *Ibid.*, p. 11.

23. *Monthly Review* 12 (December 1793):475; see also Hemlow, pp. 244–245.

24. *J&L*, II:25.

25. M. d'Arblay told Burney of an unpleasant incident: a party of soldiers refused to drink beer in the kitchen of Juniper Hall, where he and the other émigrés were living, for fear that the French living there would poison their drink. "Vous jugez bien que si je desire rester en Angleterre, ce n'est pas pour cette sorte de gens" (*J&L*, II:40).

26. *J&L*, III:277–278.

27. *J&L*, II:153.

28. Ellen Moers, *Literary Women* (New York: Doubleday Anchor Books, 1977), p. 180.

29. Older treatises such as Mrs. Chapone's *Letters* (1773) and James Fordyce's *Sermons to Young Women* (1766) were reprinted during the period, but were surpassed in popularity by new fictional treatises dealing with education, such as Mme. de Genlis's *Adelaide* and *Theodore* (1779) and *Tales of the Castle* (1784) (translations of her *Adèle et Théodore and Veillées du Château*), Sarah Trimmer's *Story of the Robins* (1786), and Anna Laetitia Barbauld's *Evenings at Home* (1792–1796). Mary Wollstonecraft's *Vindication of the Rights of Women* (1792) was preceded by her fictional book on the education of girls, *Original Stories from Real Life* (1788). Maria Edgeworth and Richard Lovell Edgeworth published *Letters to Literary Ladies* in 1795, to be followed by Maria's two volumes on *Practical Education* (1798). Little storybooks were written especially for young girls, such as Mrs. Pinchard's *The Blind Child* (1791) and *The Two Cousins* (1794), heralding a mode of didactic realistic juvenile fiction soon taken up by Maria Edgeworth, Barbara Hofland, and others.

30. Edward A. Bloom and Lillian D. Bloom, introduction to *Camilla*, p. xv.

31. This and the following six quotations are taken from manuscript scraps in the Berg Collection, all now filed under "Draft of *Camilla*." Such scraps on separate and very small pieces of paper do not represent a continuous draft of a story, but a jotting-down of ideas.

32. From "Draft of *Camilla*," in Barrett Collection, now in the British Library, Egerton MS 3696. This is an extensive draft (49 folio leaves) containing continuous narrative, though there are many lacunae and we have nothing approaching a whole novel. The passages here quoted come from late in the draft of a novel; p. 59 (recto) begins "Book X Chapter 20," and page 67 (recto) begins "Book XI Chapter 1." Pagination (not original) in this section is continuous. The passage quoted comes from "Book X Chapter 19," pp. 44r–44v.

33. *Ibid.*, p. 45r.

34. *Ibid.*, p. 47r.

35. *Ibid.*, pp. 50v–51r, 56v.

36. *Ibid.*, pp. 57r–58r.

37. *Ibid.*, Book X, Chapter 20, pp. 59v, 60v.

38. *Ibid.*, Book XI, Chapter 1, p. 72r.

39. *Ibid.*, p. 70v.

40. *J&L*, III:176.

41. *Ibid.*, pp. 128–129.

42. *Ibid.*, p. 176.

43. *Ibid.*, p. 157.

44. Freud discusses the game of Fort/Da! in *Beyond the Pleasure Principle* (1920); Freud watched his grandson throw a toy away and retrieve it, exclaiming "Fort!" (gone!) and "Da!" (there!). Freud treats this as the (male) child's own invention, mastering its mother's absence. As Terry Eagleton says, the infant's symbolic game "can also be read as the first glimmerings of narrative" (*Literary Theory, An Introduction* [Minneapolis, Minn.: University of Minnesota Press, 1983], p. 185). Jacques Lacan has refined Freudian Oedipal theory in the interest of language and culture, and sees in the (male) child's symbolic mastery of the absence of its mother its entry into the symbolic world of language, which depends on absence. To be liberated from the mother and the literal is to be initiated into the world of language and mental constructs, into metaphor and thus (for Lacan) into the Law of the Father and the phallic power which so richly consoles the (male) child for the absence of the mother and the deadness of the material world. See his *Ecrits* (1964), trans. (New York, N.Y.: Norton, 1977).

45. Juliet Mitchell, *Psychoanalysis and Feminism* (New York, N.Y.: Pantheon Books, 1974); Nancy Chodorow, *The Reproduction of Mothering: Psychoanalysis and the Sociology of Gender* (Berkeley and Los Angeles: University of California Press, 1978).

46. Margaret Homans, *Bearing the Word: Language and Female Experience in Nineteenth-Century Women's Writing* (Chicago and London: University of Chicago Press, 1986), p. 14.

47. French feminist theorists, looking gloomily at what Lacan contemplates so cheerfully, a culture built on the idea of the absence of the mother, her symbolic "death," tend to see language as so deeply implicated in the plot of male mother-murder as to be inimical to women's needs. According to the psychoanalytical-structuralist theory, all figuration and structure is under phallic rule. Jacques Derrida coins the portmanteau

word "phallogocentric" to describe our culture. To accept such a myth would seem very dangerous for women, although French feminist criticism has produced some beautiful and powerful works discussing the point. See Hélène Cixous, "The Laugh of the Medusa," *Signs* 1, no. 4 (1976), and Luce Irigaray, *Ce sexe qui n'est pas un* (1977). Julia Kristeva in *La révolution du langue poétique* (1974) and *Desire in Language* (New York, N.Y.: Columbia University Press, 1980) has proposed a "semiotic" process which retains contact with the pre-Oedipal phase and enters linguistic works as rhythm, silences, plays upon sound and the "meaningless." Pope's Goddess of Nonsense in *The Dunciad* thus can be taken as a "phallogocentric" and hostile figuration of the maternal refusing to be absent and emerging into the "semiotic," while James Joyce and Virginia Woolf (and Lewis Carroll) challenge "phallogocentric," fixed and meaningful, culture in resorting to this feminine language/nonlanguage. "The semiotic is fluid and plural, a kind of pleasurable creative excess over precise meaning, and it takes a sadistic delight in destroying or negating such signs," says Eagleton—though sadistic (a phallic word) may be questioned. See *Literary Theory*, pp. 188–189.

48. *Camilla; or, A Picture of Youth*, ed. Edward A. Bloom and Lillian D. Bloom (London: Oxford University Press, 1972). Each quotation will be followed by a reference in parentheses indicating volume and page numbers.

49. *J&L*, IV:134.

50. *Critical Review* 18 (November 1796):40.

51. *British Critic* 8 (November 1796):535.

52. This prologue to *Camilla* was sufficiently well known to be parodied by William Beckford:

> The narrator of the adventures of juvenile humanity finds less of labyrinthine involutions in the eccentricities of accumulated improbabilities, less of indescribability in . . . the revolutionary scenery of planetary evolution, than dismaying-incomprehensibility in the enfoldings and vicissitudes of the involucrums of the pericardiac region. The wildest wonders of imagination . . . fade into imperceptible invisibility, when opposed to the prevaricating pertinacity, which inoculates perspective projects on what is prohibited. ("Exordium Extraordinary" to *Azemia*, 1797; see *"Modern Novel Writing" and "Azemia,"* facsimiles with an introduction by Herman Mittle Levy, Jr. [Gainesville, Fla.: Scholars' Facsimiles and Reprints, 1970], pp. 136–137)

53. Mary Lascelles, *Jane Austen and Her Art* (Oxford: Clarendon Press, 1939), pp. 66–68.

54. *J&L*, III:117.

55. *Ibid.*, p. 136.

56. Charles Burney translated and produced an English adaptation of Rousseau's comic opera, *Le Devin du Village*, translated by Dr. Burney as *The Cunning Man*, in 1776, and during Rousseau's English sojourn, Dr. Burney tried to help him get a pension; the memory of Rousseau's praise lingered pleasantly in his mind at the end of his life; see Lonsdale, pp. 70–73, 101–103, 436.

57. Jean-Jacques Rousseau, *Emile ou de l'éducation* (Paris: Garnier-Flammarion, 1966), bk. V, "Sophie ou la Femme":

La femme est fait pour céder à l'homme et pour supporter même son injustice. Vous ne réduirez jamais les jeunes garçons au même point; le sentiment intérieur s'élève et se révolte en eux contre l'injustice; la nature ne les fit pas pour la tolérer. (p. 520)

58. *Othello* IV.ii.47–48, 57–58.
59. *Measure for Measure* I.iv.57–58; III.ii.238–239.
60. Rousseau, *Emile*, bk. V:

dans les vrais penchants de leur sexe, même en mentant, elles ne sont point fausses. Pourquoi consultez-vous leur bouche, quand ce n'est pas elle qui doit parler? Consultez leurs yeux, leur teint, leur respiration, leur air craintif, leur molle résistance: voilà le langage que la nature leur donne pour vous répondre. (p. 505)

61. See Sandra M. Gilbert and Susan Gubar, *The Madwoman in the Attic: The Woman Writer and the Nineteenth-Century Literary Imagination* (New Haven, Conn.: Yale University Press, 1979), and Homans, *Bearing the Word*.

62. Mr. Tyrold's "Sermon," quoted in full by the *Critical Review* and highly praised by the *Monthly Review* and the *British Critic*, was later included in a conduct-book, being republished separately in 1809 with a new issue of Dr. John Gregory's *A Father's Legacy to his Daughters* (first published 1774). Dr. Charles Burney also liked Tyrold's "Sermon," urging critics to praise it, but Mr. Tyrold's epistle keeps odd company with Gregory's work, which opposes female education and takes views which are satirized in *Camilla* itself.

63. Samuel Richardson, *Rambler* 97 (19 February 1751); see Samuel Johnson, *Works* (New Haven, Conn.: Yale University Press, 1969), V:164–171.

64. Jane Austen, *Northanger Abbey*, ed. R. W. Chapman (London: Oxford University Press, 1969), I:49.

7. *Camilla:* Mysteries, Clues, and Guilty Characters

1. *J&L*, III:117.
2. John Dryden, translation of *Aeneid* in *The Works of Virgil: Containing His Pastorals, Georgics, and Aeneis* (London: Jacob Tonson, 1697), bk. VII, ll. 1200–1203, p. 433.
3. *Ibid.*, l. 1198, p. 433; bk. XI, l. 838, p. 563.
4. *Ibid.*, bk. XI, ll. 1153–1154, p. 573.
5. Hester Lynch Piozzi, undated letter, salutation missing, Rylands MS 533, no. 16.
6. *D&L*, I:204.
7. *Thraliana*, I:502.
8. Mrs. Berlinton likes rhapsodic or introspective literature that broods on the workings of the mind. Elizabeth Rowe's *Friendship in Death* (1728) is a collection of narrative fictions illustrating the love of the dead for still-living friends; Mark Akenside's *Pleasures of the Imagination* (1744) is a speculative and rapturous poem on the powers of the mind; James Hammond's *Love Elegies* (1743), though dismissed by Johnson as

"frigid pedantry," appealed to a number of readers, as did the better-known *Odes* (1747) of William Collins. James Thomson's *The Seasons* (1726–1730), which Melmond loves, was praised alike by Johnson and Wordsworth for its observation of Nature and its sublimity.

9. "Draft of Camilla," BL Egerton MS 3696, p. 27r; these scenes are evidently from an earlier sequence of the scrapped novel than the "Clarinda" scenes quoted in the previous chapter.

10. *Ibid.*, p. 29v.

11. *Ibid.*, p. 30r.

12. James Beattie wrote *The Minstrel* (1771–1774), tracing the growth of a poet's mind in an imagined primitive age; William Falconer's *The Shipwreck* (1762) is an impressive work by a sailor-poet treating the sublime of nature, danger, love, and death; Charlotte Smith's *Elegiac Sonnets* (1784), one of the best-known recent volumes of poems by a woman, treated melancholy themes of loss and deprivation amid natural scenes. Some of Smith's poems are included in her novels; she was a contemporary novelist, and the influence of Burney's *Cecilia* can be felt in her first novel, *Emmeline* (1788).

13. *D&L*, IV:143–146, 178–180.

14. "Draft of Camilla," BL Egerton MS 3696, pp. 30v–31r.

15. "Mr. Oldbuck hated *'putting to rights'* as much as Dr. Orkborne, or any other professed student." Sir Walter Scott, *The Antiquary*, chap. iii, in *The Waverley Novels*, 28 vols. (Edinburgh: T. and A. Constable for T. C. and E. C. Jack Causewayside, 1901), V:31.

16. CB to Charles Burney the younger, as quoted by SBP in letter to FBd'A, 19 July 1796, Berg MS, Phillips folder 9. For young William Locke's interest in Mary Ann Port, see Hemlow, pp. 257–259. Married off in an arranged marriage to plain, middle-aged Benjamin Waddington in 1789, Mary Ann nevertheless cherished a lifelong infatuation for Colonel Goldsworthy, as even her daughters knew; see *J&L*, I:61–62 and n. 10; IV:231; VII:55–56 and n. 3.

17. EBB to FBd'A, 1796, BL Egerton MS 3690, f. 114–115.

18. William Godwin, Preface to *Things as They Are; or, The Adventures of Caleb Williams,* ed. David McCracken (London: Oxford University Press, 1970), p. 1. This preface was withdrawn from the original 1794 edition and not published until 1795. Burney does not appear to have read the novel until November 1796, when she notes that William Locke "avers that one little word is omitted in its title, which should be thus—or Things as they are NOT" (*J&L*, III:245). Burney did know *The Mysteries of Udolpho;* her reference to her own "*Udolphoish* volumes" (*ibid.*, p. 137) comments chiefly upon her book's length, but the number of references to Radcliffe's novel in letters of the period indicates that it was on her mind in the last stages of writing her new work.

19. Thomas Rymer in his *A Short View of Tragedy* (1692) had mocked *Othello* for its presentation of a love between a white lady and a black man and for its concern with domestic matters, its plot hinging on a ridiculous handkerchief; he condemns the play at last as "a bloody farce."

20. Charles Burney, Fragmentary Memoir, Berg MS, "Collection of Miscellaneous Holographs," folder 3; cf. *Memoirs*, II:170–171; cf. Hemlow, p. 14. Charles Burney's account recollects Pope's *Epistle to Bathurst:* "That live-long wig which Gorgon's self might own, / Eternal buckle takes in Parian stone," ll. 295–296.

21. For the holiday enjoyments of Ned Druggett, a City haberdasher who hires a

lodging in the country, and counts the carriages passing by on the road, see Johnson's *Idler* 16 (29 July 1758).

22. *Memoirs*, II:170–171.

23. Pope, *Epistle to Burlington*, ll. 48–49.

24. I must believe that the author of *Alice* knew Dubster—with his gloves, his nonbiting birds, and his hole in the ground, as well as his "much of a muchness."

25. Samuel Taylor Coleridge, "Conciones ad Populum," lectures given in 1795, quoted by Mary Jacobus in *Tradition and Experiment in Wordsworth's Lyrical Ballads 1798* (Oxford: Clarendon Press, 1976), p. 35, in connection with Wordsworth's "Lines left upon a Seat in a Yew-tree," a contemporary poem which speaks of the dignity of both suspecting and revering oneself, matters not unrelated to *Camilla*.

26. Mary Hays, one of the circle of radical writers and thinkers around Joseph Johnson the publisher, a friend of Godwin and Wollstonecraft, based her first novel, *Memoirs of Emma Courtney*, on her own experience of unrequited love for the philosopher William Frend. The novel tracing the course of obsessive love has more in common with *Camilla* than merely the year of publication, although Hays is overtly a radical and supporter of the rights of woman in a way that Burney is not. The influence of *Emma Courtney* can be felt in Burney's last novel, *The Wanderer* (see below, chap. 9).

27. See Richard D. Altick, *The Shows of London* (Cambridge, Mass.: Harvard University Press, The Belknap Press, 1978), pp. 121–139. Burney's sister Sarah Harriet Burney describes a visit to the Panorama in her novel *Traits of Nature* (1812); see 3rd ed., 4 vols. (London: Henry Colburn, 1813), II:179–184.

28. Dryden, *Aeneid*, bk. XI, ll. 1169–1190, pp. 573–574; cf. Virgil, bk. XI, ll. 816–831.

29. *Ibid.*, bk. VI, ll. 66–67, p. 364; ll. 70–125, pp. 364–366.

30. Eve Kosofsky Sedgwick, *The Coherence of Gothic Conventions* (New York and London: Methuen, 1986), p. 40.

31. FB to SBP, Court Journal, 29 November 1786, Berg MS, Diary, II, pt. ii.

32. Austen's penciled note at the end of vol. V of her copy of the first edition of *Camilla* (for which she was a subscriber), now in the Bodleian Library. The writing is exceedingly faint, and the infra-red photograph should be consulted.

33. Dryden, *Aeneid*, bk. XI, l. 1143, p. 572.

8. Incest, Bereavement, and the Late Comic Plays

1. *J&L*, III:49.

2. *J&L*, IV:129.

3. *Ibid.*, p. 155.

4. *Ibid.*, p. 111.

5. See *J&L*, III:48, n. 14; J&L, IV:16.

6. Charles Burney to his son Charles, November 1796, quoted in Lonsdale, p. 383.

7. *Memoirs*, III:175.

8. *Ibid.*, pp. 415–416.

9. *J&L*, IV:29–30.

10. *Ibid.*, p. 123.

11. *Ibid.*, p. 120.

12. *Ibid.*, p. 139.

13. *Ibid.*, p. 65.

14. William Gifford, ed., *The Anti-Jacobin; or, Weekly Examiner*, 4th ed., 2 vols. (London: Printed for J. Wright, 1799), I:197–199.

15. *J&L*, IV:44, 138.

16. *Ibid.*, p. 75.

17. *Ibid.*, p. 87.

18. G. E. Manwaring, *My Friend the Admiral: The Life, Letters, and Journals of Rear-Admiral James Burney*, F.R.S. (London: George Routledge & Sons Ltd., 1931), pp. 226–228.

19. Maria Rishton to FBd'A, 3 September 1798, BL Egerton MS 3697, f. 276v.

20. Maria Rishton to FBd'A, 24 December 1796, BL Egerton MS 3697, f. 237r–v.

21. *Ibid.*

22. Maria Rishton to FBd'A, 3 September 1798, BL Egerton MS 3697, f. 276v.

23. Thomas Twining's phrase for Sarah Harriet as a small child, quoted in Hemlow, p. 47.

24. "I supped last night with Rickman, and met a merry *natural* captain, who pleases himself vastly with once having made a pun at Otaheite in the O. language," Charles Lamb wrote on his first acquaintance with James Burney in February 1803; quoted in Manwaring, *My Friend the Admiral*, p. 216. Manwaring, James's biographer, avoids all mention of the incest affair and skips over the five years concerned; more surprisingly, Margaret Patterson, in her account of Sarah Harriet Burney in Janet Todd's *Dictionary of British and American Women Writers 1660–1800* (Totowa, N.J.: Rowman & Littlefield, Inc., 1985), p. 67, likewise avoids any reference to the episode.

25. Maria Rishton to FBd'A, 3 September 1798, BL Egerton MS 3697, f. 276r.

26. Maria Rishton to FBd'A, 24 December 1796, BL Egerton MS 3697, ff. 240r; 239v.

27. Maria Rishton to FBd'A, November 1798, BL Egerton MS 3697, f. 286r–v.

28. *Ibid.*, f. 289r.

29. *J&L*, VI:521, n. 10.

30. *J&L*, VII:17–18.

31. Sarah Harriet Burney to Martha Young (née Allen), June 1793, BL Egerton MS 3700A, f. 213v.

32. *J&L*, IV:244.

33. *Ibid.*, p. 192.

34. *Ibid.*, pp. 217, 219–220. Burney records that in November 1784 she asked the dying Johnson if he ever heard from the former Mrs. Thrale:

> "No," cried he, "nor write to her. I drive her quite from my mind . . . I never speak of her, and I desire never to hear of her more. I drive her, as I said, wholly from my mind." (*D&L*, II:274)

The eighteenth century evidently did see active forgetting as an attractive and vengeful duty (cf. the Harlowe family), but the phrasing in this remark attributed to Johnson is so typical of an idiom passed from Charles Burney to his daughter that we may ask if Frances Burney has not retranslated Johnson into the home idiom.

35. *J&L*, IV:297.

36. *Ibid.*, p. 220.

37. The mortgage loan was made in 1795; see Hemlow, p. 276.

38. Letter of September 1796; *J&L*, III:201, n. 1.

39. Letter of Susanna Phillips to FBd'A, begun Sunday, 15 September 1796, and continued Wednesday and Thursday; Berg MS, Phillips, folder 9.

40. SBP to FBd'A, 18 January 1797; also June 1798, 9 October 1798, Berg MS, Phillips, folder 10. See also *J&L*, III:268, n. 20; for Frances's treatment of "Janey Paney" as a friend to Susanna and a "sweet Creature," see *J&L*, IV:200.

41. *J&L*, IV:348.

42. Hemlow, p. 288.

43. *J&L*, IV:387.

44. *Ibid.*, p. 386.

45. Dedication to *The Wanderer*, I:vii.

46. *J&L*, IV:395.

47. *Ibid.*, 65–66.

48. *Ibid.*, p. 361, n. 4.

49. FBd'A to Dr. Charles Burney, 11 February 1800, *J&L*, IV:394–395.

50. The extracts are in a very small notebook now in the Huntington Library, San Marino, Calif. Burney's handwriting is small and not very shapely in this little notebook; its appearance communicates agitation and distress, and the writings, though largely quotation, seem very private.

51. *Memoirs*, III:317–318. See d'Arblay's letter quoting this account given by La-fayette, who was the intercessor undertaking this interview with Napoleon on d'Arblay's behalf; neither of the d'Arblays was there (*J&L*, V:173).

52. See Hemlow, p. 317. The d'Arblays' financial position was not much improved during this period. The salary plus d'Arblay's recovered military pension came to about one hundred sixty pounds per annum; Burney's pension from the queen could not be sent to France. D'Arblay's job kept him at the office between 9:30 A.M. and 4:30 P.M. daily, and he had a long walk to and from Passy, where they first settled.

53. *Love and Fashion* exists as a holograph manuscript of 235 pages in the Berg Collection. As Hemlow notes, this manuscript looks like the final draft of the play (Hem-low, p. 273); it is presumably what Harris saw. The play is divided into acts and scenes, and has running pagination from the beginning. Act, scene, and page numbers will be given after each quotation.

54. Hemlow, p. 273.

55. E.g., FB's note "A[ct] 3 Long & unmeaning no interest but the momentary

Valentine! Hilaria!—and Valentine's plan."

Burney's notes to herself about revision are found in a memorandum book of 1801 in the Berg Collection, indicating that in 1801 (or later) Burney was still thinking of provid-ing an improved version of *Love and Fashion* for the theater.

56. *J&L*, IV:129; also November 1797, *ibid.*, p. 29.

57. "The Triumphant Toad-eater," manuscript in an unidentified hand among Bur-ney papers in the Berg Collection, is described on the title page as "A Musical Entertain-ment in Two Acts." The plot concerns the efforts of Mrs. Torment to marry off her sullen niece Miss Roundabout to Sir Nat Nonsuch, whom Mrs. Torment herself loves,

despite her being a married woman: "My first husband Mr. Torment still lives to plague me. Where he is, let those enquire who wish to know—as for me I have something else to think of than where he's kicking up his heels" (Act I). Sir Nat plays the flirtation game with Mrs. Torment; finding Miss Roundabout too ungracious, he is easily snapped up by the two-faced Jenny Backfriend, Mrs. Torment's companion and "toad-eater." As Miss Roundabout and the fop Mr. Mawkin have already secretly made "our little journey to Gretna Green," Mrs. Torment makes Jenny her heir. The mockery of the sexual feeling of an older woman is harsher than anything found in Burney's work, and none of Burney's constant themes (such as the value of work) are found. The language is coarser than Burney's in the plays and seems more based on dialect; Miss Roundabout is called "a horse godmother." Sentence rhythms are also not typical of Burney. The play is, however, evidently a piece by a woman, and probably by a Burney, or one of their circle; tone and manner remind me of Charlotte Burney more than other members of the family.

58. *J&L*, IV:243.

59. Fanny Burney, *A Busy Day*, ed. Tara Ghoshal Wallace (New Brunswick, N.J.: Rutgers University Press, 1984), introduction, p. 13.

60. Quotations from the play are made from Wallace's edition, with act and page numbers given after quotation. The manuscript exists in the Berg Collection, in five *cahiers*, one for each act; there is no consistent scene division, and the numeration is by folios. The manuscript is in the hand of General d'Arblay, who acted an amanuensis for this work. See Wallace, "Description of the Manuscript," *A Busy Day*, pp. 173–174.

61. Wallace, introduction to *A Busy Day*, p. 5.

62. Hemlow, 298–306; see also note regarding *Love and Fashion*, *J&L*, IV:395: "Her best comedy 'A Busy Day' she was yet to write." See also Hemlow, "Fanny Burney, Playwright," *University of Texas Quarterly* 19 (1949–1950):170–189. This is the line implicitly adopted by Tara Ghoshal Wallace in editing *A Busy Day*, although Wallace gives *The Woman-Hater* credit for "a much more complex plot" than any of Burney's other comedies, and thinks the audience would be more concerned in the fate of its characters; see Wallace, "Fanny Burney and the Theatre," *A Busy Day*, p. 159.

63. FB to Susanna, November 1791 (apropos of Mrs. Schwellenberg): "'Tis dreadful that Power thus often leads to every abuse!—I grow *Democrate* at once upon these occasions! Indeed, I feel always *democrate* where I think Power abused,—whether by the Great or the Little." *J&L*, I:89.

64. Fragmentary scene of untitled play, to be found in packet marked "suggestions for Plots & Dialogues" now boxed with the second version of *The Woman-Hater* in the Berg Collection.

65. *The Woman-Hater* exists as two manuscripts in the Berg Collection. The earlier version is written on scrap paper; the later version is a neat holograph of 202 pages, in five *cahiers*, one for each act. Quotations are taken from this second version, following original act and scene division, which is very clear, and original pagination, which starts anew with every act.

66. See above, chap. 5, p. 154. Burney was grateful for Mrs. Chapone's countenance and continued friendship after her marriage to d'Arblay, when so many former friends fell off; she may not have been utterly pleased to have Mrs. Chapone tell her she had detected "some *gallicisms*" in *Camilla*, some of which she pointed out (*J&L*, IV:105–106).

67. "Fragile in every sense of the word, they are obliged to look up to man for every comfort. In the most trifling dangers they cling to their support, with parasitical tenacity . . . and their *natural* protector extends his arm, or lifts up his voice, to guard the lovely trembler—from what? Perhaps the frown of an old cow, or the jump of a mouse; a rat would be a serious danger. In the name of reason, and even common sense, what can save such beings from contempt . . . ?" (Mary Wollstonecraft, *A Vindication of the Rights of Woman,* ed. Carol H. Poston [New York, N.Y.: Norton, 1975], p. 62).

68. Wallace also points out that Sir Roderick "is in some ways the obverse, comic side of Wilmot"; see "Fanny Burney and the Theatre," p. 160.

69. *J&L,* VI:778; see above, chap. 1, p. 29.

70. *J&L,* IV:477.

9. The Wanderer; or, Female Difficulties

1. *The Wanderer; or, Female Difficulties,* By the Author of Evelina; Cecilia; and Camilla, 5 vols. (London: Longman, Hurst, Rees, Orme and Brown, 1814), I:1. All references are to this edition, and quotations from the novel will be followed by citations of volume and page numbers.

2. Dedication, "To Doctor Burney, F.R.S. and Correspondent to the Institute of France," I:vii–viii.

3. *J&L,* XI:71.

4. *Ibid.,* p. 84.

5. *J&L,* V:xlvii.

6. *J&L,* VI:510.

7. *Ibid.,* p. 785.

8. *J&L,* XI:85.

9. *J&L,* VI:612–613.

10. *Ibid.,* p. 709.

11. *Ibid.,* pp. 715–716.

12. *Ibid.,* pp. 716–717.

13. *Ibid.,* pp. 720–721.

14. *Ibid.,* pp. 726–727.

15. It was agreed that the author was to be paid 500 pounds on delivery of the manuscript, 500 pounds six months after publication, and another 500 pounds a year after publication; there was to be a payment of 500 pounds for the second edition, and 250 pounds each for each subsequent edition through the sixth. *J&L,* VII:157, n. 5.

16. *J&L,* VI:717.

17. Claudia L. Johnson, "The Novel of Crisis," in her *Jane Austen: Women, Politics, and the Novel* (Chicago: University of Chicago Press, 1988), pp. 1–27. It occurs to me that many of the major topics of the contemporary novel of the French Revolution by both radical and conservative writers of the 1790s are picked up by Dickens in *A Tale of Two Cities.* Probably his source material included some of the English fiction written during or just after the Revolution. The fury of aristocratic driving in the Paris streets under the *ancien régime* is discussed in Smith's *Desmond,* 3 vols. (London: G.G.J. and J. Robinson, 1792), I:108–109. But Dickens is unwilling to include a central Revolutionary

issue (a major point in *Desmond*) of the woman's suffering under a bad marriage, treated sympathetically by women writers, including Burney.

18. Dr. Charles Burney, unsigned review, *Monthly Review* 39 (June 1799):210.

19. See Luce Irigaray, "Le marché des femmes," in *Ce Sexe qui n'en est pas un,* translated as "Women on the Market," trans. Catherine Porter with Carolyn Burke, *This Sex Which Is Not One* (Ithaca, N.Y.: Cornell University Press, 1985), pp. 170–191.

The society we know, our own culture, is based upon the exchange of women. Without the exchange of women, we are told, we would fall back into the anarchy (?) of the natural world, the randomness (?) of the animal kingdom. . . .
Are men all equally desirable? Do women have no tendency toward polygamy? The good anthropologist does not raise such questions. *A fortiori:* why are men not objects of exchange among women? It is because women's bodies—through their use, consumption, and circulation—provide for the condition making social life and culture possible, although they remain an unknown "infrastructure" of the elaboration of that social life and culture. (pp. 170–171)

20. *J&L*, VI:719.

21. *The British Critic*, n.s. 1 (April 1814):381.

22. "Nos mœurs . . . sont si peu en mesure avec celles de ce Pays . . . qu'en verité il serait non seulement injuste mais barbare d'y puiser les raisons de juger—nos mariages par exemple. Tous, pour ainsi dire, n'etaient qu'autant de sacrifices, plus ou moins douloureux, à des convenances dont les femmes ont toujourrs été les victimes, sur tout dans la classe de la societé jusqu'à present la plus relevée." Alexandre d'Arblay to FB, March 1793, *J&L*, II:32. See above, chap. 6, n. 1.

23. See *J&L*, VII:267 and n. 1; *J&L*, X:631 and n. 1; Hemlow, p. 337.

24. *Gentleman's Magazine* 84 (June 1814):381.

25. [John Wilson Croker], *Quarterly Review* 11 (April 1814):130.

26. *Ibid.*, p. 129.

27. William Hazlitt, *Edinburgh Review* 24 (February 1815):337.

28. *Ibid.*, pp. 337, 336.

29. *The British Critic*, n.s. 1 (April 1814):385.

30. Croker, *Quarterly Review* 11 (April 1814):125–126.

31. See above, chap. 3, page 70.

32. See, e.g., articles by Rose Marie Cutting, "Defiant Women: The Growth of Feminism in Fanny Burney's Novels," *Studies in English Literature* 17 (Summer 1977): 519–530, and her "A Wreath for Fanny Burney's Last Novel: *The Wanderer*'s Contribution to Women's Studies," *College Language Association Journal* 20 (September 1976):57–67. The latter article at least called attention to the novel and its feminist issues, as did Spacks in her remarks on *The Wanderer* in *Imagining a Self: Autobiography and Novel in Eighteenth-Century England* (Cambridge, Mass.: Harvard University Press, 1976), pp. 183–188. Spacks, however, does not contradict Adelstein's summary judgment (which she quotes), "There is no doubt but that *The Wanderer* is Fanny Burney's poorest novel" (p. 187), and sees the novel as endorsing only female strategies of weakness and passivity in a clumsy plot: "Fanny Burney was unable to integrate her deep perceptions of the female condition into a believable fiction . . ." (p. 188). Janet Todd found that of all Burney's novels, *The Wanderer* "presents her most

ambiguous and complex portrait of female relationships" but criticizes Burney for not showing a true friendship between Elinor and Juliet; see *Women's Friendship in Literature* (New York, N.Y.: Columbia University Press, 1980), pp. 314–315. More recent critics now tend to show symptoms of (cautious) approval of *The Wanderer;* following Spacks and Todd in preferring Elinor of the two heroines, new critics see her as to some considerable extent endorsed by her author. "Elinor cannot be laughed off or ignored. She is voluble, forceful and stimulating," says Judy Simons (*Fanny Burney* [Totowa, N.J.: Barnes and Noble Books, 1987], p. 108), while D. D. Devlin remarks, "Elinor's language is . . . never refuted. . . . She loses her lover but not the argument" (*Novels and Journals,* p. 108).

33. *The British Critic,* n.s. 1 (April 1814):376.

34. Elizabeth Hamilton, *Memoirs of Modern Philosophers,* 4th ed., 3 vols. (Bath: R. Cruttwell for G. and J. Robinson, 1805), III:100, 103.

35. Mary Hays, "Preface," *Memoirs of Emma Courtney,* 2 vols. (New York & London: Garland Publishing, Inc., 1974) [facsimile of 1796 edition], I:8.

36. *The British Critic,* n.s. 1 (April 1814):385–386.

37. Some elements of Elinor's characterization may have grown from Burney's encounter with a "young and agreeable infidel" in Bath in 1780; this girl announced her intention of committing suicide if she were to find and then lose the perfect bosom friend of either sex: "I should not hesitate a moment." Burney pondered on this character, romantic and unguarded, "with ideas so loose of religion, and so enthusiastic of love," yet with "strong and lively parts." (The real young lady may simply have been showing off to the famous author.) See *D&L,* I:320–325, 339–340.

38. *The Provoked Husband* (1728) by Colley Cibber, based on Sir John Vanbrugh's unfinished *The Journey to London,* concerns the frivolous Lady Townly, whose husband endeavors to reclaim her by the threat of divorce; the more farcical comic action deals with the fate of Sir Francis Wronghead, the blundering bumpkin cheated by Count Bassete. This play was evidently a favorite of Burney's; she quotes from it in *Cecilia,* and in the British Library draft of the ur-*Camilla* the characters' casting and rehearsing of this play takes up a number of pages, evidently part of a considerable sequence. Tybalt (prototype of Lionel) is cast as Lady Wronghead; there is a brief reference to this vanished idea in *Camilla,* when the heroine "pulled off the maid's cap from her brother's head, and put on the wig in its place, saying—'There, Lionel, you have played the part of *Lady Wrong Head* long enough; be so good now as to perform that of *Sir Francis*" (II:265). In *The Wanderer,* Elinor performs the part of Lady Wronghead, and Ellis-Juliet takes the role of Lady Townly, which in the ur-*Camilla* falls to the lot of the heroine, here "Ariella." Although both are shy about acting, "Ellis" and "Ariella" (how unlike Fanny Price!) find they enjoy it once they get into it. Ariella, melancholy at estrangement from the man she loves, does not expect to enjoy her task, but is surprised:

> She next took her part, which she read, for the first time, with a desire to render interesting; & she soon found, both in that & in herself, powers of which she had formed no idea. She studied every speech attentively, tried various modes both of delivery & of action, & gave effect to every word.
>
> The success which she could not but feel attended her labours, imperceptibly rendered them less irksome, & what at first she undertook in mere desperation . . . she soon continued to put in force from that pleasure which arises from the first

discovery & first use of faculties, which, uncalled upon, had been unknown. (BL Egerton MS 3696, f. 41v.)

39. *ED*, I:129.

40. FB to HLT [1782], Rylands MS 545, no. 18; to EBB, 3 September 1821, *J&L*, XI:269.

41. "But thought's the slave of life, and life Time's fool, / . . . No, Percy, thou art dust and food for—"

Prince. For worms, brave Percy.

(*Henry IV, Part I*, V.iv.81–86)

42. BL Egerton MS 3696, f. 59v.; see above, chap. 6, p. 212.

43. *Hubert De Vere*, earlier draft, Act V; see above, chap. 5, p. 190.

44. "*El.'s madness.*"; see above, chap. 5, p. 196.

45. *J&L*, VI:611.

46. Julia Epstein, "Writing the Unspeakable: Fanny Burney's Mastectomy and the Fictive Body," *Representations* 16 (Fall 1986):146.

47. FB to SBP, 22 January 1785, Berg MS, Diary, II, pt. ii.

48. Hannah More, seriously taking to heart Marchmont's kind of rules for men looking for perfect women, produced a novel—or, rather, a fictional tract—called *Cœlebs in Search of a Wife* (1809). The young bachelor Cœlebs, inspecting and rejecting various young ladies for various faults, at last finds the model wife in reward of his search. Jane Austen decided in advance that she would not like it (see *Letters of Jane Austen*, ed. R. W. Chapman, 2nd ed. [Oxford: Clarendon Press, 1979], pp. 256, 259). Burney's last novel repeatedly argues against the notions advocated in *Cœlebs*, especially in the portrayal of young Ireton and Sir Jaspar Herrington.

49. Wollstonecraft, *The Wrongs of Woman*, ed. Gary Kelly (Oxford: Oxford University Press, 1976), pp. 198–199.

50. CB to HLT, 1 November 1777, Rylands MS 545, no. 1.

51. Todd, *Women's Friendship in Literature*, p. 318.

52. An anonymous novel of the 1790s entitled *The Female Crusoe* mocks the portrayal, particularly by radical women writers, of resourceful working women, and of downtrodden women of the lower classes. Work for women was a concern of writers of the 1790s. Mary Anne Radcliffe in *The Female Advocate: or, An Attempt to Recover the Rights of Women from Male Usurpation* (London: Vernor and Hood, 1799) points out the very small number of jobs available at all to female workers; like Evelina, the author notices the service of "effeminate tradesmen" serving ladies in dry-goods shops (cf. *Evelina*, I:27). Radcliffe sees such usurpation of service jobs as an economic affliction to women, and suggests that women boycott "these authors of female destruction" (p. 59). Burney in her fiction had made a point of settling women in occupations suited to them, especially shopkeeping but also chair-seat weaving and clear-starching. Radcliffe points out that an able-bodied woman is not eligible for relief under the law, and the Vagrant Act offers a reward to anyone who should apprehend her begging; thus a virtuous woman, taken to the house of correction and classed as a criminal, might well be driven to prostitution. The legal dangers confronting Juliet in her wandering search for employment would have been understood by contemporary readers.

53. Flora resembles Hetty Sorrel in George Eliot's *Adam Bede* (1859)—or rather, she is like a mentally retarded Hetty.

54. Wollstonecraft, *The Wrongs of Woman*, p. 149.

55. Jane Collier, *An Essay on the Art of Ingeniously Tormenting with Proper Rules for the Exercise of that Pleasant Art* (London: A. Millar, 1753), pp. 41–42.

56. *Ibid.*, p. 49.

57. *Ibid.*, p. 57.

58. The resemblance of Mrs. Ireton to both Mrs. Burney and Mrs. Schwellenberg was first noted by Joyce Hemlow (Hemlow, pp. 341–342).

59. Burney had read both *The Mysteries of Udolpho* and *The Italian* when they first came out, preferring the latter; see *J&L*, III:337. The influence of Radcliffe's earlier *The Romance of the Forest* may be traced in *The Wanderer;* the scene in which Juliet is captured before the eyes of her lover seems a reversal of the scene in *The Romance of the Forest* (1791) in which a party of soldiers enters the inn and seizes the hero, Theodore, before the eyes of his anguished Adeline. In keeping Adeline's identity a secret until the end of the story, and having the de la Motte family take her in without knowing who she is, Ann Radcliffe is an obvious precursor of the Burney of *The Wanderer.*

60. Hannah More's tract *Village Politics* (1792), an exhortation to the poorer classes in England to abhor all the doctrines of the French Revolution and stick to personal moral "reform," was such a success that, with the encouragement of influential persons who saw her as a forceful propagandist, More issues a series called *Cheap Repository Tracts,* subsidized pamphlets sent all over the kingdom. The moral of these works is that piety, industry, and respect for the hierarchy of classes are rewarded (materially and spiritually), whereas the reverse qualities (especially an interest in pleasure, or in rising above one's station, or in any democratic notions) must be punished by moral and material decline. The success of this venture led to the formation, in 1799, of the Religious Tract Society. The eighteenth century saw the full development of techniques for writing *down*—to young ladies, to children, to the poor. Burney never writes down (though some had thought that was her intention in *Camilla*). Part of Burney's intention in *The Wanderer* is to confute both the Hannah More of *Cœlebs* and the Hannah More of the *Cheap Repository Tracts.*

61. John Keats, *Endymion: A Poetic Romance* in *The Poems of John Keats*, ed. Miriam Allott (London: Longman Group Ltd., 1970), Canto II, ll. 121–137, pp. 211–212.

62. Keats, *Hyperion*, in *Poems*, bk. II, ll. 34–35, p. 419.

63. Keats, *The Fall of Hyperion*, in *Poems*, bk. I, ll. 65–71, p. 661.

64. "She had been led through the best galleries . . . and she had ended by oftenest choosing to drive out to the Campagna where she could feel alone with the earth and sky, away from the oppressive masquerade of ages, in which her own life too seemed to become a masque with enigmatical costumes." (George Eliot, *Middlemarch* [1872], bk. II, chap. 20 [New York, N.Y.: Norton, 1977], p. 134).

65. *J&L*, I:21.

10. End of Story

1. *Memoirs*, III:435–436.

2. *J&L*, VII:484.

3. *D&L*, VII:302.

4. *J&L*, VIII:317–318.

5. *Ibid.*, p. 435.

6. *Ibid.*, p. 440.

7. *Ibid.*, p. 447.

8. We know that William Makepeace Thackeray owned a copy of Burney's *Diary and Letters;* his daughter, Anne Thackeray (later Ritchie), discovered the book in her father's library and felt inspired to become a diarist and novelist; see Winifred Gérin, *Anne Thackeray Ritchie: A Biography* (Oxford: Oxford University Press, 1981), p. 100.

9. *J&L*, X:898.

10. *Ibid.*, p. 907.

11. *J&L*, XI:134–135.

12. *Ibid.*, p. 184.

13. *J&L*, IX:40.

14. James Clifford, *Hester Lynch Piozzi* (New York, N.Y.: Columbia University Press, 1986), p. 447.

15. *J&L*, IX:277–278.

16. Clifford, *Hester Lynch Piozzi*, p. 447. See *Othello*, V.ii.6.

17. *J&L*, IX:278, n. 13.

18. Abraham Hayward, *Autobiography, Letters and Literary Remains of Mrs. Piozzi [Thrale]*, 2nd ed., 2 vols. (London: Longman, 1861), II:253; see *J&L*, X:918, n. 2; *J&L*, XI:11, n. 1.

19. *D&L*, VII:275–276.

20. *J&L*, XI:206.

21. *D&L*, VII:284–285.

22. *J&L*, XI:208–209.

23. William McCarthy, *Hester Thrale Piozzi; Portrait of a Literary Woman* (Chapel Hill, N.C.: University of North Carolina Press, 1985), p. 265.

24. *J&L*, XI:276.

25. See *J&L*, XI:227, n. 3, and G. E. Manwaring, *My Friend the Admiral: The Life, Letters, and Journals of Rear-Admiral James Burney, F.R.S.* (London: George Routledge & Sons Ltd., 1931), pp. 284–285.

26. *J&L*, XI:309.

27. *Ibid.*, p. 313.

28. *Ibid.*, p. 384.

29. *Ibid.*, p. 298, n. 6; cf. Manwaring, *My Friend the Admiral*, p. 282, n. 2.

30. FBd'A to EBB, 25–28 November 1820, *J&L*, XI:188–189.

31. *Ibid.*, p. 191.

32. *ED*, I:41; *D&L*, I:29.

33. *Memoirs*, III:50.

34. Hemlow, pp. 461–462.

35. *J&L*, XII:969.

36. *J&L*, IX:231; cf. Swift, *Gulliver's Travels*, bk. III.

37. *J&L*, IX:247.

38. *J&L*, XII:964.

39. *D&L*, VI:300.

40. For the distressing story of Burney's grave, see *J&L*, XII:982–989.

41. This and the preceding four quotations are taken from various scraps in the Berg

Collection; there are five folders of them catalogued as "Miscellaneous." The fourth of these examples is dated "November 1796"; the others are undated. None of these seems to be associated with any of the completed works, though there is some resemblance between Badino, Lord Winslow (in *Clarinda*), and Sir Jaspar Herrington. The name "Badino" was perhaps suggested by the French saying, *on ne badine pas avec l'amour,* "one does not trifle with love."

Conclusion

1. [John Wilson Croker], *Quarterly Review* 11 (April 1814):124, 125–126.

2. *D&L,* I:116.

3. William Hazlitt, *Edinburgh Review* 24 (February 1815):338.

4. See articles by J. N. Waddell, "Fanny Burney's Contribution to English Vocabulary," *Neuphilologische Mitteilungen* 81 (1980):260–263; "Additions to *OED* from the Writings of Fanny Burney," *Notes & Queries* 225 (1980):27–32.

5. *J&L,* IV:312, cited by Waddell; unpublished letter to SBP, 23 May 1784, Berg MS, A 146, folder 8.

6. See, e.g., Croker's review of *Memoirs, Quarterly Review* 49 (April 1833):97–125.

Index

Addison, Joseph, 82, 306, 381; *Cato,*
    149, 381, 405
Adelstein, Michael, 397, 421
"Advice to the Herald," 99–100, 143,
    152
Agnew, Anne, 33, 395
Akenside, Mark, *Pleasures of the
    Imagination,* 244, 414
Allen, Elizabeth, later Meeke,
    ("Bessy"; stepsister), 29, 30
Allen, Maria, later Rishton (stepsister),
    29, 47, 113, 161, 201, 277–280, 314,
    340; marriage of, 29–30; separation
    from husband, 277, 314; death of,
    371
Allen, Stephen (stepbrother), 29, 278
Amelia, Princess, 185
Andrews, Miles, 150
Angerstein, Amelia, 380
anti-Gallicism, 205, 326, 411
Anti-Jacobin, The, 205, 276, 300, 329,
    417
Arblay, Alexander Charles Louis
    Piochard d', the Rev. (son), 160, 205,
    216, 274, 287, 372; birth of, 203,
    266; childhood, 216, 314;
    education, 314, 378–379; life in
    France, 314, 378; life back in England,
    315–317, 378–379; maturity,
    378–380; ordination, 379; relations

with parents, 216, 274, 372,
    378–379; reluctance to marry, 379,
    380; death of, 380–381
Arblay, Alexandre-Jean-Baptiste
    Piochard d' (husband), 23, 200–203,
    275, 288–289, 290, 331, 379–380,
    418; character, 200, 202–203,
    274–275; courtship of FB, 200–203,
    230, 410; defense of Mme. de Staël,
    331, 410, 421; design of Camilla
    Cottage, 274; English life of,
    202–203, 274–275; life in France,
    202–203, 288–289, 418; appeal to
    Napoleon, 288; political views, 200,
    288; religious views, 203; service in
    royalist army in 1815, 371–372; title
    of comte awarded by Louis XVIII,
    372; worries about son, 379; attitude
    toward FB's writing, 200, 203, 419;
    assistance in releasing *The Wanderer*
    from customs, 316, 318; death of, 372
Aristotle, and the unities, 215
Arne, Thomas, 13–14, 16
Augusta, Princess, 375
Austen, Jane, 2–3, 45, 49, 219, 221,
    232, 234, 273, 423; comments on
    Camilla, 272, 416; *Emma,* 81, 219;
    Mansfield Park, 6; *Northanger Abbey,*
    234, 414; *Pride and Prejudice,* 232,
    273

Babbage, Charles, 379
Barbauld, Anna Laetitia, 411
Barlow, Thomas, 42–43, 153, 170
Barrett, Charlotte, née Francis (niece), 1,
    158, 191, 198, 371, 375, 378, 381,
    396, 402
Barsanti, Jenny, 403
Bath, 19, 100, 372–373, 380–381, 422
Batt, John Thomas, 198
Beattie, James, 244, 415
Beckford, William, *Azemia*, 413
Benkovitz, Miriam J., 409
Bentinck, William Henry Cavendish,
    Duke of Portland, 18
Berg Collection, the (NYPL), 98, 250,
    300
Bewley, William, 392
Bible, the, 265–267, 271
Blair, Hugh, the Rev., sermons of, 244
Blair, Robert, 196
Bloom, Edward A., 206, 391, 392, 398,
    412
Bloom, Lillian D., 203, 412
Bogle, John, 153
Bolingbroke, *see* Saint-John
Bonaparte, Napoléon, Emperor, 288,
    312, 315, 317, 318, 332, 370, 371,
    418
Book of Common Prayer, the, 118, 266,
    271
Boswell, James, 6, 31, 66, 82
Brabazon, Jane, later Disney, 283–284
Brighton (Brighthelmstone), 100–101,
    150, 159–161, 328
Bristol Hot Wells, 19, 46, 62
British Critic, The, 220, 330, 334, 337,
    414, 421, 422
British Library, 209
Brontë, Charlotte, 197, 388, 389; *Jane
    Eyre*, 137, 273; *Villette*, 90, 200
Brooke, Frances, 75, 158–159, 406
Brooke, Henry, *The Fool of Quality*, 399
Broome, Miriam, 276, 298
Broome, Ralph, 29, 153, 202, 276–277,
    292, 298, 300
Brown, Martha G., 391
Bunbury, Henry William, 244

Burke, Edmund, 39, 67, 145, 254;
    *Reflections on the Revolution in
    France*, 262
Burney, Anne ("Aunt Nanny"), 50, 377
Burney, Dr. Charles, 5, 10–33, 131,
    148, 215, 259, 329, 413, 417;
    biography of, 5, 10–11, 376–378;
    birth of, 11; childhood, 11–12, 17,
    259–260, 376–377; death of twin,
    11–12; character, 12–14, 18–20,
    96–97, 165, 172, 186, 275–276,
    281–282; life with Grevilles, 14–16,
    38; marriage to Esther Sleepe, 15–18,
    19, 38, 275, 311; marriage to
    Elizabeth Allen, 25–27, 30, 36,
    96–97, 177, 396; as musician and
    music teacher, 18, 97, 110, 351, 393;
    as member of Streatham circle, 39,
    67–68; attitudes toward Mrs. Thrale
    (later Piozzi), 67–68, 163–165, 395;
    political views of, 199, 201, 205, 276,
    300; position of FB at court and,
    167–173, 192–193; love of favorable
    and fear of adverse publicity, 12–13,
    99, 100, 392–393; reaction to
    daughter Charlotte's marriage to
    Broome, 276, 292; reaction to FB's
    marriage to d'Arblay, 200–202;
    reaction to Elizabeth Burney's death,
    275–276; reaction to James Burney's
    elopement with Sarah Harriet,
    277–278, 280, 281–282, 292–293;
    relations with Susanna, 11, 282,
    284–285; relations with sons, 20, 30,
    394, 399; tendency to depression, 19,
    275; death of, 165, 369, 372,
    383–384; Westminster Abbey
    memorial for, 370. *See also* family
    relationships; father-daughter
    relationships
—attitudes toward FB's works:
    approves *Evelina*, 39–40;
    suppresses *The Witlings*, 92–96;
    response to tragedies, 96, 197;
    sustained objections to dramatic
    comedies, 96–97, 287–288; presses
    FB to complete *Cecilia*, 99–100,

107; response to *Cecilia*, 145; reads early version of *Camilla*, 250; approves Tyrold's sermon, 414 —works: "Memoirs," 10, 259, 376–377, 392, 415; *History of Music*, 13, 18, 20, 27, 39, 42, 99, 393–394; review of *Lyrical Ballads*, 329, 421; *Tours*, 27, 393; verses by, 76–77, 99–100, 275–276

Burney, Charles (brother), 18, 22 , 170, 275, 379; acts as FB's agent, 38, 287, 312; expulsion from Cambridge, 20, 61, 394, 399

Burney, Charles Parr (nephew), 394

Burney, Charles Rousseau (brother-in-law), 26, 351, 372

Burney, Charlotte Ann, later Francis, later Broome (sister), 18, 22, 92, 281, 372, 395, 419; marriage to Francis, 153, 202; marriage to Broome, 29, 276–277, 292, 300, 314, 372, 378; death of, 380

Burney, Edward Francesco (cousin), 56–57, 128, 150, 153, 380, 399

Burney, Elizabeth Allen (stepmother), 25–30, 36, 55, 96–97, 109, 163, 165, 177, 277–278, 357, 395, 396, 424; warns of relationship between James and Sarah Harriet, 277–278; death of, 275, 278, 299, 302. *See also* family relationships

Burney, Esther, née Sleepe (mother), 21, 153; marriage to CB, 15–18; death of, 19, 22–24, 177, 271–272, 275, 305, 311. *See also* family relationships

Burney, Esther ("Hetty"; sister), 16, 21, 22, 51, 109, 200, 250, 280, 284, 351, 372–373; FB's letters to, 168–169, 170, 312, 315, 376–377; marriage of, 26–27, 109, 161; recognizes Mme. d'Arblay in character Mrs. Arlbery, 250; will of CB and, 371, 376; death of, 380

Burney, Frances, later d'Arblay: birth, 18–19; childhood, 19–23, 29, 259, 310; death of mother, 22–23, 30, 271–272; destruction of early works, 35–37, 377; as father's amanuensis, 39,

42; courtship by Barlow, 42–43, 170; *Evelina*, publication and responses, 25, 33, 37–40; in Streatham circle, 66–70, 100–110, 241; Latin lessons from Johnson, 241; *The Witlings* suppressed, 92–98; *Cecilia*, publication and responses, 111, 143–147; love for George Owen Cambridge, 151–158, 160, 164; portraits painted, 150, 153; service in Royal Court, 169–198, 212–213; hatred of Mrs. Schwellenberg, 176–177, 356; love of Stephen Digby, 191; king's madness and FB's fear of madness, 194–197; laudanum, use of, 196; leaves queen's service, 193–198; pension from queen, 193, 197, 201; courtship of Alexandre d'Arblay, 200–202, 411; marriage, 23, 202–203; motherhood, 216–217; production of *Edwy*, 179–180, 205, 287, 408–409; *Camilla*, publication and responses, 205–206, 213–214, 220, 413; death of Susanna, 285–286, 311, 381; exile in France, 288–289, 313–315; mastectomy, 205, 314–315, 343–344; return to England, 313, 315–317; *The Wanderer*, publication and responses, 317, 330, 332–335, 369–371, 385–386; residence in Brussels during battle of Waterloo, 371–372; title of comtesse, 372, 381; death of husband in Bath, 372; removal to London, 374; *Memoirs*, publication and responses, 33, 378; death of son, 380; death of FB, 381; memorial to, 381, 385, 425. *See also* family relationships; friendships —views and attitudes: early attitudes toward marriage and position of women, 42–43, 54, 105, 164; French heritage, need to explore, 23, 330–331; "permission" as an issue, 16, 38, 126, 163, 187; political views, 205, 300, 338, 419; religious views, 203, 366–367, 381; responses to publicity and criticism, 59, 88–90, 94, 99–100, 156–157, 205, 287,

Burney, Frances (*continued*)
371; urge to write, 35–37, 148–149, 179, 369–370
—works. *See separate works index*
Burney, James, Captain, later Admiral (brother), 18, 23–24, 109, 170; incestuous elopement with Sarah Harriet Burney, 23–24, 29, 30, 277–281, 290, 292–293, 299, 302; marriage, 153; performance in *Tom Thumb*, 50; voyage to the Pacific, 104; reaction to CB's will, 371; late promotion to Admiral, 375; death of, 375–376; funeral, 375–376; *Plan of Defence against Invasion*, 277; *History of Discoveries in the South Seas*, 281. *See also* family relationships
Burney, Rebecca (aunt), 377
Burney, Richard (half brother), 20, 30, 394
Burney, Richard (uncle), 377
Burney, Sarah Harriet (half sister), 23–24, 30, 380; incestuous elopement with James Burney, 23–24, 277–281, 290, 292–293, 299, 302; reaction to CB's will, 371; reaction to James Burney's death, 375; *Clarentine*, 278, 279; *Traits of Nature*, 416. *See also* family relationships
Burney, Susanna Elizabeth, later Phillips (sister), 11, 18, 19, 20, 22, 153–156, 165, 172, 176–177, 202, 285; FB's journal-letters to, 99, 100, 151, 153–156, 172–173, 176–177; jaundice, recovery from and FB's poem on, 26; on reading of *The Witlings*, 92–93, 97; marriage to Molesworth Phillips, 29, 109–110, 161, 202, 275, 282–285, 314; on Phillips's flirtation with Jane Brabazon, 283–284; and son Norbury, 282, 283; death of, 19, 285–286, 287, 288, 299, 302, 311, 313, 376, 381. *See also* family relationships
Byron, George Gordon, Lord, 189, 371
Bysshe, Edward, *Art of Poetry*, 83

Cambridge, Charles, 181
Cambridge, Charlotte, 151, 170
Cambridge, George Owen, the Rev., later Archdeacon, 151–158, 160, 164, 167, 174, 183, 191, 306, 344; assists FB in finding position for son, 160, 379; marriage, 295, 380; relationship with FB in old age, 379, 381; and the content of *Edwy and Elgiva*, 181–182; and the content of *Hubert De Vere*, 191, 342; and the content of *Camilla*, 158, 230, 233, 252, 269; and the content of *A Busy Day*, 295; and the content of *The Woman-Hater*, 306; and the content of *The Wanderer*, 342, 344
Cambridge, Richard Owen, 151, 152, 154, 158, 191, 295
Camilla Cottage, 206, 250, 274, 275, 315
Carroll, Lewis, *Alice in Wonderland*, 231–232, 260, 324, 413, 416
Carter, Elizabeth, 100, 107
Castle, Terry, 134, 404
Catholicism, 17, 23, 100, 203, 205, 361
Catholic Relief Act, 100
Centlivre, Susanna: *A Bold Stroke for a Wife*, 122; *The Busy-Body*, 64
Cervantes, Miguel de, *Don Quixote*, 130, 215
Chapone, Hester, 154, 206, 288, 306, 411, 419
Charlotte, Queen, 16, 167, 171, 172, 174–175, 214; provision of FB's pension, 193, 197, 201, 315
Chodorow, Nancy, 215
Churching of Women, the, 266
Cibber, Colley: *The Careless Husband*, 339–340; and Vanbrugh, *The Provoked Husband*, 320, 339–340, 422
Cixous, Hélène, 413
Clifford, James, 402, 407
Coleridge, Samuel Taylor, 196, 262, 363, 416; *The Rime of the Ancient Mariner*, 129; *Christabel*, 363
Collier, Dr. Arthur, 241
Collier, Jane, *The Art of Ingeniously Tormenting*, 357, 424

Collins, William, 196, 244, 415

Colman, George: *The Deuce Is in Him*, 49; *The English Merchant*, 81; *The Man of Business*, 73, 75

comedy, dramatic, 48–50, 73–77, 80–87, 91, 96; contemporary view of female dramatists in eighteenth century, 72–73, 76–77

conduct-books, 231–232

Congreve, William, 118; *The Double-Dealer*, 81

Cook, Captain James, 104, 109, 376

Cooper, Anne, 11

Covent Garden Theatre, 287

Cowley, Hannah, 75, 291; *Albina, Countess Raimond*, 120; *The Runaway*, 74, 400

Crewe, Frances Anne, née Greville, 14, 61, 203, 205, 239, 330

Crisp, Samuel, 27–28, 31, 42, 43, 48–49, 51, 55, 99, 103, 109, 260, 392, 395; advice to FB about writing, 70–71, 73, 145, 159, 335, 385–386; Chessington home of, 27, 31, 100, 109, 159, 160, 260; death of, 160; *Virginia*, 71, 72, 184, 409. *See also* friendships, of FB

Critical Review, The, 144, 220, 405

Croker, John Wilson, 18, 333, 334, 347, 378, 385, 386, 396, 397, 414, 421, 426

Crown, Patricia Dahlman, 399

Crutchley, Jeremiah, 105, 277

Cumberland, Richard, 74, 99, 122; *The Fashionable Lover*, 74, 75, 122; *The West Indian*, 75, 295

Cutting, Rose Marie, 391, 421

Davys, Mary, *The Reform'd Coquet*, 219

Defoe, Daniel, *Roxana*, 393

Delany, Mary, née Granville, 23, 30, 167–168, 172, 249, 330, 378, 407; and FB's position at court, 168–172, 176–177; death of, 177, 272. *See also* friendships, of FB

Delap, John, 106, 107

De Quincey, Thomas, 196

Derrida, Jacques, 412–413

Devlin, D. D., 4, 397, 422

Dickens, Charles, 2, 3, 9, 17, 63, 127, 273, 291, 304; *Our Mutual Friend*, 63; *A Tale of Two Cities*, 420–421

Dickinson, Emily, 369, 388, 389

Diderot, Denis, 146, 396

Digby, the Hon. Stephen, 191, 244, 342

Dobson, Austin, 1, 6, 48, 391, 403

Dodsley, Robert, *Cleone*, 185, 409

Drury Lane Theatre, 106, 107, 180

Dryden, John, translation of Virgil's *Aeneid*, 117–118, 239–240, 267–268, 272, 404, 414, 416

Dublin Theatre, 106, 403

Eagleton, Terry, 412, 413

Edgeworth, Maria, 206, 387, 389, 411

Edgeworth, Richard Lovell, 411

Edinburgh Review, The, 333–334, 408, 421, 426

Edwy and Edilda [by Thomas Sedgwick Whalley], 409

Eliot, George, 9; *Adam Bede*, 424; *Middlemarch*, 248, 364, 424

Ellis, Annie Raine, 6, 392, 407

embarrassment and social identity, 33, 34, 59–60, 65, 85, 122, 124, 139, 242, 254–255

English Review, The, 144, 405

Epstein, Julia, 3, 4, 169, 344, 391

Falconer, William, *The Shipwreck*, 244, 415

family relationships
—Charles Burney and FB, 10–11, 30–33, 59, 186, 205, 369–371, 383–384; and publication of *Evelina*, 36–39, 66, 397; and suppression of *The Witlings*, 80–81, 91, 93, 94–99, 287–288; FB's achievement of independence from, 230, 288, 308, 312, 370. *See also* father-daughter relationships
—Elizabeth Allen Burney, FB's hatred of, 25–30, 36, 165, 177
—Esther Burney, née Sleepe, and FB:

family relationships (*continued*)
love for, 21–23, 177, 271–272, 305; keeps sampler of, 23; FB's need for mother-figures, 55, 177, 192, 273, 305, 330
—James Burney and Sarah Harriet Burney, FB's attitude toward incestuous elopement of, 279–281, 299, 302
—Susanna Burney, later Phillips, and FB; 18–22, 26, 99, 100, 151, 153–156, 165, 172, 176–177, 202, 285; FB as confidente over SBP's unhappy marriage, 282–284; FB's reaction to SBP's death, 285–289, 302, 312, 313
—*See also* Allen, Maria, later Rishton; Arblay, Alexander d'; Arblay, Alexandre d', Burney, Charles (brother); Burney, Charlotte Ann; Burney, Esther (sister); Burney, Richard (half brother)
father-daughter relationships, 24–25, 139, 184–185, 213; in *Evelina*, 31–33, 37–38, 61–62, 64, 308; in *Cecilia*, 122, 139, 141; in *Edwy and Elgiva*, 181, 182; in *The Siege of Pevensey*, 184–185, 187–188; in *Hubert De Vere*, 190–191; in *Clarinda* fragment, 212–213; in *Camilla*, 228–230, 231, 240, 246–247; in *A Busy Day*, 296, 298; in *The Woman-Hater*, 301–302, 304–308; in *The Wanderer*, 323, 346, 352, 365
Female Crusoe, The, 423
Fielding, Henry, 2, 9, 145–146, 150, 215, 241; *Amelia*, 36, 396, 398–399; *Tom Jones*, 56, 118, 146, 393, 398, 399; *Tom Thumb*, 50
Fielding, Sarah, 241, 357
"Flasher, The," 69, 400
Foote, Samuel: *The Commissary*, 49; *The Englishman in Paris*, 52; *The Minor*, 49, 398; *Taste*, 50
Fordyce, James, 411
Fox, Charles James, 326
French Revolution, the, 16, 112, 193, 199, 200, 420; in *The Wanderer*, 57, 318, 323, 324, 326, 331–332, 334, 353, 364
Frend, William, 337, 416
Freud, Sigmund, 61, 215–216, 270, 412
friendships, of FB
—Samuel Crisp, 27–28, 31; Chessington as refuge to write in, 100; encourages writing, 27–28, 159; mocks FB's stepmother, 27–28, 109; suppresses *The Witlings*, 91–95; death of, 160
—Mary Delany, 166–168, 176–177, 378; as grandmother-substitute, 167; instrumental in securing FB's position at court, 167–169; death of, 177
—Samuel Johnson, 66, 69–70, 94, 101, 163, 241, 400; praise of FB's writing, 53–54, 145–146, 398–399; death of, 166–167, 417
—William and Frederica Locke, 165–167, 199, 202, 205; and fear for Frederica's sanity, 165–166; land for Camilla Cottage and later complications, 206, 250, 275
—Marie-Françoise-Elizabeth Bidault de Maisonneuve, 314; offers assistance during FB's mastectomy, 315
—Hester Lynch Thrale, later Piozzi, 66–70, 100–110, 159–165, 201, 358, 373–375, 407; FB's descriptions of, 14–15, 115, 202, 374–375, 399–400, 407; rupture of friendship over marriage to Piozzi, 163–165, 305, 395; reunion, 373–374

Garrick, David, 71, 76, 97, 400
Gast, Sophia, 92, 93, 395, 404
Gay, John, *Three Hours after Marriage*, 81
Genlis, Stéphanie-Félicité Brulart, née Ducrest de Sainte-Aubin, comtesse de, 171, 411
Gentleman's Magazine, The, 106, 143, 332, 404, 421
George III, King, 4, 35, 73, 167–168, 172, 180, 214; illness and madness of, 179–180, 185, 194–195
George IV, King. *See* Prince Regent

Gilbert, Sandra, 229, 414
Gillray, James, 175, 326
Gisborne, Dr. Thomas, 196, 410
Godwin, William, 25, 139, 146–147, 263, 342, 371; *Caleb Williams*, 147, 250, 251, 262, 415; *The Herald of Literature*, 146–147, 405; *Political Justice*, 139
Goethe, Johann Wolfgang von, 261; *The Sorrows of Young Werther*, 341
Goldsmith, Oliver, 74, 77, 94, 396; "Essay on the Theatre," 74, 400; *She Stoops to Conquer*, 74; *The Vicar of Wakefield*, 396
Goldsworthy, Col. Philip, 249–250
Gordon riots, 100, 205, 361
Gothic elements in literature, 147–148, 182, 268, 273, 359
Granville, George, Baron Lansdowne, 172
Gray, Thomas, 196
Greer, Germaine, 54, 399
Gregory, John, *A Father's Legacy to His Daughters*, 246, 414
Greville, Frances, née Macartney, 14, 61, 239
Greville, Fulke, 13–16, 38, 131, 239, 393
Griffith, Elizabeth, 75; and Richard Griffith, 396
Gubar, Susan, 229, 414

Hagstrum, Jean, 24, 395
Hall, Augusta, née Waddington, Baroness Llanover, 378; *The Autobiography and Correspondence of Mrs. Delany*, 33, 378, 395
Halsband, Robert, 401
Hamilton, Elizabeth, *Memoirs of Modern Philosophers*, 318, 337–338, 422
Hamilton, Frances, 172, 408
Hammond, James, *Love Elegies*, 244, 414–415
Hardy, Thomas, *Tess of the Durbervilles*, 363
Harley, Margaret Cavendish, Duchess of Portland, 139, 167, 378
Harris, Thomas, 287, 289, 290, 312
Hastings, Warren, 177, 276

Hawkins, Sir John, 13, 392
Hays, Mary, 147, 334; *Emma Courtney*, 262–263, 336, 337–338, 416, 422; *The Victim of Prejudice*, 350–351, 355
Haywood, Eliza, 45, 398
Hazlitt, William, 333–334, 348, 371, 388
Hemlow, Joyce, 1, 9–10, 16, 33, 34, 44, 177, 180, 206, 290, 396, 398, 400, 407, 408, 411, 417, 424
Herschel, William, 275
Hervey, John, Baron Hervey of Ickworth, *Memoirs of the Reign of George the Second*, 175
Hill, Dr. John, 119
Hobart, Albinia, 150
Hofland, Barbara, 411
Homans, Margaret, 216, 229, 412
Homer, 37; Helen in the *Iliad*, 45, 215, 240, 243; the *Odyssey*, 215
Hooke, Nathaniel, *Roman History*, 396, 404
Hoole, Samuel, *Aurelia*, 6, 143, 404
Huddlesford, George, *Warley*, 99, 143, 402
Hume, David, 180, 341
Hunter, J. Paul, 73, 400
Hunter, Richard, 408, 409
Hyde, Mary, 399–400

Imlay, Gilbert, 342
incest, 20, 23–24, 61–62, 161, 184, 277–281, 329. *See also* Burney, James; Burney, Sarah Harriet; family relationships
Inchbald, Elizabeth, 75, 351; *A Simple Story*, 219
India, 20, 276, 293, 296, 298–299
Irigaray, Luce, 413, 421

James, Henry, *The Sacred Fount*, 59
Johnson, Claudia, 325, 420
Johnson, Dr. Samuel, 9, 12, 31, 39, 53–54, 66, 69–70, 94, 101, 105, 115, 145–146, 160, 163, 166–167, 170, 193, 241, 262, 346, 359, 377–378, 393, 400, 415, 417; *Dictionary*, 48; *The Idler*, 260, 415–416; *The Rambler*,

Johnson, Dr. Samuel (*continued*)
66, 244; *Rasselas*, 66, 396. *See also*
friendships, of FB
Jonson, Ben, *Every Man in His Humour*,
43, 244
Joyce, James, 3, 413
Juvenal, Decimus Junius, 54, 63

Keats, John, 333, 364, 424; *Endymion*,
333, 364; *The Fall of Hyperion*,
Hyperion, 364
Keith, Admiral George, Viscount
Elphinstone, marriage to Queeney
Thrale, 373
Kelly, Hugh, 74; *The School for Wives*,
73–74, 81, 400
King's Lynn, Norfolk, 18–19, 209
Kirkman, Jacob, 13–14
Kris, Kathryn, 394
Kristeva, Julia, 413

Lacan, Jacques, 45, 269, 412
Laclos, Choderlos de, 141, 146, 215, 404
Lafayette, Marie-Joseph-Paul-Yves-Roche-
Gilbert du Motier, marquis de, 200, 418
La Fayette, Marie-Madeleine de la Vergue,
comtesse de, *La Princesse de Clèves*,
404
Lamb, Charles, 277, 279, 281
Lansdowne, Baron, *see* Granville
La Roche, Sophie von, 171, 407
Lascelles, Mary, 220–221, 413
Latour-Maurbourg, Victor de, 314
Leavis, F. R., 1
Lee, Harriet, 75; *The New Peerage*, 76,
400
Lennox, Charlotte, 45, 48, 401; *Henrietta*,
350, 355
Le Sage, Alain, *Gil Blas*, 314
Lévi-Strauss, Claude, 329
Lewis, Matthew G. ("Monk"), *The Castle
Spectre*, 291
Lipking, Lawrence, 393–394
Llanover, Lady, *see* Hall
Locke, Frederica, 165–167, 199, 202,
205, 250, 275, 315. *See also* friendships,
of FB

Locke, William, 165–167, 199, 202, 205,
275, 415; character of, reflected in
Camilla, 250. *See also* friendships, of FB
Locke, William (son of above), 275, 315,
415; character of, reflected in *Camilla*,
249–250
London Magazine, The, 144, 404
Lonsdale, Roger, 10–11, 12, 18, 392, 394
Louis XVI, King, 200
Louis XVIII, King, 372
Lowndes, Thomas, 38, 70

MacAlpine, Ida, 408, 409
Macartney, Frances, 14, 61, 100
Macaulay, Thomas Babington, 1, 9, 18,
172, 394
Macburney, Anne, née Cooper, 11
Macburney, James, 11
McCarthy, William, 107, 375, 403
Macintosh, Sir James, 371
madness, 119, 166; FB's fear of, 194, 286
Magnificat, the, 118
Maisonneuve, Marie-Françoise-Elizabeth
Bidault de, 314, 315. *See also* friend-
ships, of FB
Marxism, 118, 141
Mary, Princess (Duchess of Gloucester),
375
Mason, William, 196
Meeke, Samuel, 30
Mercure de France, 146, 404
Mickleham, 199–200, 202, 282
Middleton, Conyers, *Life of Cicero*, 396
Mitchell, Juliet, 215
Moers, Ellen, 206, 214, 411
Molière, Jean-Baptiste Poquelin de, 80-81,
93, 146, 401
Montagu, Barbara, 127
Montagu, Elizabeth, 70, 107, 152, 155,
175, 401, 404, 408; and *The Witlings*,
93, 96, 97, 100
Monthly Review, The, 204, 329, 411, 414,
421
More, Hannah, 77, 96, 100, 107, 204,
401; *Cheap Repository Tracts*, 361,
424; *Cœlebs in Search of a Wife*, 345,

423; *The Inflexible Captive*, 76; *Percy*, 75–76

Morning Herald, The, 99, 104

Mortimer, John Hamilton, 32, 53

Murphy, Arthur, 67, 70–71; and *The Witlings*, 91, 93, 94, 97, 98, 402; *All in the Wrong*, 88, 401; *The Way to Keep Him*, 87, 401

Napoleon, *see* Bonaparte

Newton, Judith Lowder, 42, 397, 398

Norfolk Ladies' Pocket Book, 128

Ord, Anna, 157, 201, 205, 272, 409

Oxford, royal visit to, 174, 186

Oxford English Dictionary, 388, 426

Pacchierotti, Gasparo, 153

Patterson, Emily, 397

Paulson, Ronald, 397

Pepys, William Weller, 152

Percy, Thomas, bishop of Dromore, 196

Phillips, Molesworth, 29, 109–110, 282–286, 376, 392

Phillips, Norbury (FB's nephew), 283

Pinchard, Elizabeth, 243, 411

Piozzi, Gabriel, 17, 30, 106, 108, 131, 161–165, 373, 374, 378, 395

Piozzi, Hester Lynch, *see* Thrale, Hester Lynch

Pitt, William, 175, 326

Plutarch, *Lives*, 396

Poovey, Mary, 397–398

Pope, Alexander, 9, 21, 37, 81, 117, 243, 363, 396; *Dunciad*, 413; *Eloisa to Abelard*, 201, 411; *Epistle to a Lady*, 84–85, 401; *Epistle to Bathurst*, 415; *Epistle to Burlington*, 117, 260, 416; *Iliad*, 396; *Rape of the Lock*, 346, 363; *Three Hours after Marriage*, 81, 243

Port, Georgiana Mary Ann, later Waddington, 168, 249–250, 376, 378, 415

Porter, Jane, *Thaddeus of Warsaw*, 318

Portland, Duchess of, *see* Harley

Portland, Duke of, *see* Bentinck

Prince Regent, later George IV, 328, 363

Pringle, Veronica, 22

Purcell, Henry, 196

Quarterly Review, The, 333, 378, 385, 421, 426

Radcliffe, Ann, 3, 137, 263; *The Italian*, 137, 182, 424; *The Mysteries of Udolpho*, 147, 239, 251, 271, 415, 424; *The Romance of the Forest*, 424

Radcliffe, Mary Anne, *The Female Advocate*, 423

Regency crisis of 1788, the, 175

Regency period, 355, 363, 364

Reynolds, Frederic, 291

Reynolds, Sir Joshua, 12, 39, 72

Ribeiro, Alvaro, 401, 403

Richardson, Samuel, 9, 42, 48, 108, 127, 150; *Clarissa*, 118, 120, 127, 142, 146, 404, 417; *Rambler 97*, 232, 414; *Sir Charles Grandison*, 42, 64, 154–155, 157, 232, 406

Richetti, John J., 3, 392

Ricks, Christopher, 60, 399

Rishton, Martin Folkes, 29, 161, 201

Robespierre, Maximilien-Marie-Isidore de, 313, 317, 318, 323

Rochester, Earl of, *see* Wilmot

Rogers, Katharine M., 397

Rogers, Pat, 141, 404

Romanticism, 140, 197, 268–269, 273, 328–329, 363

Romilly, Sir Samuel, 371

Rousseau, Jean-Jacques, 146, 228, 229, 242, 252, 328, 413; *Emile*, 222–223, 227–228, 229, 310, 352, 413–414; *La Nouvelle Héloïse*, 146

Rowe, Elizabeth, *Friendship in Death*, 244, 414

Rowlandson, Thomas, 175

Rymer, Thomas, 257, 415

Sabor, Peter, 392

Saint-John, Henry, Viscount Bolingbroke, 341

Saint Margaret's Church, King's Lynn, 10–19, 25

Saint Vincent de Paul, 204
Sappho, 89, 401
Scholes, Percy, 393
Schwellenberg, Elizabeth Juliana, 29,
  175–177, 186–187, 191, 193,
  356–357, 419, 424
Scott, Sarah, 127, 350; letter regarding
  FB's marriage, 201–202, 411; *The
  History of Cornelia*, 127, 404; *Millen-
  nium Hall*, 127, 137
Scott, Sir Walter, 118, 247, 318, 363, 387;
  The Antiquary, 247, 415; *Guy
  Mannering*, 363; *The Heart of
  Midlothian*, 363
Sedgwick, Eve Kosofsky, 268, 416
Shakespeare, William, 60, 62, 168, 258;
  All's Well That Ends Well, 121;
  Hamlet, 62, 228; *Henry IV, Part I*, 341,
  423; *King Lear*, 222; *Measure for
  Measure*, 225, 414; *The Merchant of
  Venice*, 111, 403; *A Midsummer
  Night's Dream*, 97, 363; *Othello*, 201,
  224–225, 226, 236, 237, 257–258,
  269, 272, 273, 373, 414; *Romeo and
  Juliet*, 102, 403; *Twelfth Night*, 232;
  A Winter's Tale, 304–305
Sheeles, Anne Elizabeth, 22
Shelley, Mary, 25, 295; *Frankenstein*, 146,
  374
Shelley, Percy Bysshe, 146
Sheridan, Frances, 45, 75
Sheridan, Richard Brinsley, 67, 72, 77, 94,
  118, 326; *The School for Scandal*,
  74–75, 79, 82, 88, 118, 293
Siddons, Sarah, 180
Sidney, Lady Dorothy, 401
Simmons, Judy, 4, 392, 397, 402, 408,
  422
Sleepe, Esther. *See* Burney, Esther (mother)
Sleepe, Frances, née Dubois (grandmother),
  23, 30; FB's love for, 23, 51; Catholi-
  cism of, 23, 100; French heritage,
  importance of, 23, 200; relation to
  characters in *Evelina*, 51, 55, 330
Sleepe, James, 17
Smart, Christopher, 119–120, 134, 404

Smelt, Leonard, 169, 170, 171, 173, 184,
  191
Smith, Charlotte, 3, 244; *The Banished
  Man*, 318; *Desmond*, 318, 420–421;
  Elegiac Sonnets, 244, 415; *Emmeline*,
  415
Smith, Henry, 105
Smith, Mary Anne, 380, 381
Smollett, Tobias, 2, 3, 9, 48, 147;
  Roderick Random, 243
Song of Songs, the, 188
Spacks, Patricia, 3, 391, 397, 421–422
Spencer, Gervase, 153
Spencer, Jane, 398
Staël-Holstein, Anne-Louise-Germaine (née
  Necker), baronne de, 199, 200, 205,
  249, 288, 331, 371, 410; FB's compari-
  son of Hester (Thrale) Piozzi with,
  374–375; *Corinne*, 352
Staves, Susan, 391
Sterne, Laurence, 36–37; *Sentimental
  Journey*, 36–37; *Tristram Shandy*,
  36–37, 270, 396
Stonehenge, 361, 364–365, 366–368
Straub, Kristina, 4, 56, 392, 397, 399
Streatham circle, the, 39, 66–70, 101
style indirect libre, 3, 124, 257
suicide, 3, 9, 60–61, 194, 238, 342–343,
  386
Swift, Jonathan, 9, 82, 117; *Gulliver's
  Travels*, 117, 379, 403, 425; *Polite
  Conversation*, 48–49, 87, 398

Tahiti, 104, 279, 417
Talbot, Catherine, 288
Thackeray, William Makepeace, 425;
  Vanity Fair, 372
Thomson, James, *The Seasons*, 244, 306,
  360, 415
Thrale, Harry, 101
Thrale, Henry, 66–70, 100, 361; illness
  of, 102–103, 105; death of, 106, 107,
  139, 140
Thrale, Hester Lynch, later Piozzi, 13, 16,
  20–21, 25, 152, 183, 199, 272, 304,

344, 361, 374, 400, 403, 407; and character of Mrs. Delville in *Cecilia*, 114–115, 140, 164; descriptions of CB, 59, 164–165; descriptions of FB, 59-61, 102, 151, 373, 374, 396; education, 241; FB's descriptions of, 14–15, 115, 202, 373, 374–375, 407; encouragement of *The Witlings*, 70, 93–94, 106, 401–402; gift of lock of hair, 374; gift of silhouette, 110; marriage to Thrale, 102–103, 105–107, 140, 402, 407; mature marriage to Piozzi, 16, 30, 106–108, 161–165, 173, 177, 201, 202, 305, 395, 417; Polynesian dress, 104, 403; death of, 374. *See also* friendships, of FB
—works: *Anecdotes of Johnson*, 378; "Biographical Anecdotes," 402; *The Humourist*, 94, 401; Prologue to *The Royal Suppliants*, 106, 107, 403
Thrale, Queeney, later Lady Keith, 105–106, 108, 161, 163, 202, 241, 274–275, 277, 373–374; FB's letters to, 163–164, 202, 275, 373–374, 395
Todd, Janet, 3, 348–349, 391, 421–422
transvestism, 50, 110, 120, 340
Trefman, Simon, 50, 398
Trimmer, Sarah, 206, 411
"Triumphant Toadeater, The," 292, 418–419
Troide, Lars, 1, 391, 403
Twining, Thomas, 279, 392, 417
Tyrrell, Sir James, 246

United States, 94, 95, 315, 317
Urfé, Honoré d', *L'Astrée*, 222

Vanbrugh, Sir John, and Colley Cibber, *The Provoked Husband*, 320, 339–340, 422
Victoria, Queen, 381
Virgil: *Eclogues*, 247, 253; *Aeneid*, 117–118, 239–240, 267–268, 269, 272, 404, 414, 416

Waddell, J. N., 3–4, 388, 392, 426
Walker, James, 32, 53
Wallace, Tara Ghoshal, 4, 294, 295, 408, 419, 420
Waller, Edmund, 89, 401
Walpole, Horace, *The Mysterious Mother*, 184, 277
Waterloo, Battle of, 371–372
West, Jane, *A Tale of the Times*, 318
Westminster Abbey, 381, 385
Wilmot, John, Earl of Rochester, 64
Wilton, 100, 361, 362, 364, 366
Windham, William, 145, 193
Wollstonecraft, Mary, 25, 146, 204, 206, 263, 309, 333, 334, 338, 341–342, 348, 355–356, 405, 420; *Original Stories*, 243, 411; *A Vindication of the Rights of Women*, 147, 222, 262, 309, 411, 420; *The Wrongs of Women*, 310, 346, 348, 349, 350–351, 356
Woolf, Virginia, 413
Wordsworth, William, 146, 192, 251, 262, 324, 330, 360, 415, 416; *Guilt and Sorrow*, 251; *Lyrical Ballads*, 328–330

Young, Martha, née Allen, 417

Zeman, Anthea, 42, 398

Index of Works

Brief Reflections Relative to the Emigrant French Clergy: Earnestly Submitted to the Humane Consideration of the Ladies of Britain, 100, 203–205, 256, 262; publication of, 203; contemporary responses and reviews, 204–205

Busy Day; or, An Arrival from India, A, 4, 288, 293–300, 302, 311–312, 347, 358; publication of, 419; manuscript of, 419
—compared with: *Evelina*, 297, 299; *The Witlings*, 299, 300; *The Siege of Pevensey*, 296; *Camilla*, 297; *Love and Fashion*, 293, 294; *The Woman-Hater*, 299, 300–302, 311; *The Wanderer*, 299, 300, 347, 358

Camilla; or, A Picture of Youth, 3, 4, 158, 191, 197, 199–238, 239–273, 274, 286, 302, 311, 363, 386–387, 424; Mrs. Arlbery and Mme. d'Arblay compared by EBB, 250; Camilla's dream-vision in, 263–271, 363; courtship, absurd 'rules' of, 230–233; crime in, 252–254; Dubster's villa, 260–261; education as an issue in, 206, 241–244; hero, position and problems of, 221–223; "idiot" girl in, 228–229, 269, 307; language in, 388, 419; significance of Marchmont in, 221–223, 225–227, 272; money earned from, 205–206, 214, 274; mystery and detection in, 249–251, 319, 323, 338; *Othello* in, 224–225, 236, 257–258, 269, 273; paradox and antithesis as structural principles of, 220–221, 234–235, 319, 324; playing and games as motifs in, 235–238, 346; publication of, 4, 205–206, 248, 274; reading and re-reading in, 244–249, 268; Tyrold's "Sermon" in, 246–247; Virgil in, 209, 239–240, 247, 267–268, 272
—*Clarinda* fragment, 209–214, 230, 270, 290, 323, 341, 347, 412, 415, 426; compared with *The Siege of Pevensey*, 213; *Hubert De Vere*, 213; *The Woman-Hater*, 306; *The Wanderer*, 340, 341, 347
—compared with: *Evelina*, 214, 233, 242, 255, 273, 297; *Cecilia*, 215, 217, 233–234, 236, 252, 254–255, 256, 263, 273, 311; *Edwy and Elgiva*, 225, 269; *The Siege of Pevensey*, 213, 214; *Hubert De Vere*, 213, 269; *Love and Fashion*, 289–290; *A Busy Day*, 297; *The Woman-Hater*, 245, 302, 306,

307; *The Wanderer*, 231, 319, 323, 324, 338, 340, 341, 346, 347, 352, 363
—contemporary responses and reviews, 220, 250, 413, 414, 415, 419
—manuscripts of, 207–209, 244–245, 257, 412
Cecilia; or, Memoirs of an Heiress, 2, 3, 31, 33, 99–148, 158, 180, 197, 200, 217, 233–234, 255, 275, 277, 293, 311, 318, 319, 323, 324, 359, 365, 386; "conflict scene" in, 138–139, 255; debate on conformity vs. originality in, 112–113, 119, 233, 254, 324, 389; Delviles' marriage in, 114–116, 137–138, 140–141; ending of novel and criticism of ending, 143–145, 254; guardians in, 111, 122–126, 259, 306, 351; hero, position and problems of, 134–136, 139, 221, 252; cancelled "Introduction" to, 148–149, 227, 381, 405; mixed characters in, 145–146, 339; money earned from, 143, 159; money in, 119, 122, 124, 126, 133, 141, 350; name as issue in, 111, 135, 139, 142, 145; narrator and narrative manner in, 124, 256; publication of, 111, 143, 148; working women in, 127, 128, 350
—compared with: *Evelina*, 99, 101, 111, 112, 116, 143, 146; *The Witlings*, 102, 113, 323; *Edwy and Elgiva*, 180, 181, 185, 197; *Camilla*, 215, 217, 233–234, 236, 252, 254–255, 256, 263, 273, 311; *Love and Fashion*, 293, 311; *The Woman-Hater*, 306, 310; *The Wanderer*, 318, 319, 323, 324, 328, 342, 350, 352, 358, 365
—contemporary responses and reviews, 143–147, 150, 171, 404–405
—manuscript of, 123, 132, 137–139, 404
"Consolatory Extracts," 288, 299, 417

Diary and Letters, The: Charlotte Barrett as editor of, 1, 158, 191, 193, 198, 371, 375, 378; Barrett's suppression of material in journal mss., 158, 191, 375; journal-writing of FB, general comments, 26, 36, 41, 177–178. *See also Early Diary; Early Journals and Letters; Journals and Letters*

Early Diary of Frances Burney, The, Ellis as editor of, 1, 6
Early Journals and Letters, Troide as editor of, 1, 391, 394
Edwy and Elgiva, 179–183, 197, 205, 225, 408–409; production of, 179–180, 205, 287, 408–409; 1795 Prologue to, 182; unpublished section entitled *"El.'s madness after Divorce,"* 195–196, 197, 269, 343, 410
—compared with: *Evelina*, 181; *Cecilia*, 180, 181, 185, 197; *The Siege of Pevensey*, 183; *Camilla*, 225, 269; *The Wanderer*, 343
—manuscripts of, 195, 196, 409, 410
Elberta, 180, 191–192, 194, 197, 305, 341, 384; manuscript fragments of, 191, 409; compared with *The Woman-Hater*, 305; *The Wanderer*, 92, 341
Evelina; or, The History of a Young Lady's Entrance into the World, 2, 3, 18, 23, 35–65, 84, 116, 158, 205, 214, 233, 255, 260, 273, 277, 292, 295, 297, 302, 358, 377, 378, 385, 386, 396–397, 398, 423; "Dedication" of, 47–48; Dedicatory verses ("To —— ——") prefixed to, 31–32, 37–38, 86, 188; father-daughter relationship in, 61, 64, 308; father-son relationship in, 61–62; hero, status and significance of, 44–45, 63–64; male characters in, 42, 45, 53–54, 61–65, 82, 112, 181, 214; mother-figures in, 46–47, 49–51, 53–55; name as issue in, 40–41, 45, 64; narrative form of, 59, 62, 72; practical joking in, 56–57; publication of, 4, 25, 26, 37–40, 70, 158; theatrical

Evelina (*continued*)
  comedy and, 48–51, 52–53; treatment
  of old women in, 56–57, 87, 163, 242,
  326, 347, 350, 387–388
  —compared with: *The Witlings*, 82, 84,
  87, 89; *Cecilia*, 99, 101, 111, 112,
  116, 143, 146; *Edwy and Elgiva*,
  181; *The Siege of Pevensey*, 188;
  Camilla, 214, 233, 242, 255, 273,
  297; *Love and Fashion*, 289; *A Busy
  Day*, 295, 297; *The Woman-Hater*,
  297, 299, 307–308, 310, 387; *The
  Wanderer*, 40, 318–319, 323, 326,
  330, 347, 352, 358, 385, 387–388
  —contemporary responses and reviews,
  39–40, 51, 66, 99
  —manuscripts of, 44, 51, 396–397,
  398
"extempore Elegy" ("Here's a Woman of
  the Town"), 69–70, 129

"Flasher, The," 69, 400

History of Caroline Evelyn, The, 35–36,
  38, 40, 42; destruction of the
  manuscript, 35–36, 38, 377; influence
  of, on *Evelina*, 38, 40
Hubert De Vere, 180, 188–191, 197, 213,
  222, 279; agony of Cerulia in,
  189–191, 194, 269, 342; compared
  with *Camilla*, 213, 269; *The Wanderer*,
  189, 323, 342–343, 349; manuscripts
  of, 409

Journals and Letters, Hemlow et al. as
  editors of, 1, 314

Love and Fashion, 287–293, 294, 300,
  302, 311, 312, 347; withdrawn from
  production, 287; compared with *The
  Witlings*, 290; *Clarinda* fragment,
  290; *Camilla*, 289; *A Busy Day*,
  293–294; *The Wanderer*, 292, 299,
  347; manuscript of, 418

Memoirs of Doctor Burney, 10–11, 15,
  25–26, 33, 38, 96, 115, 131, 259,

275–276, 311, 376–378; censorship of
  CB's manuscripts by FB, 10–11,
  376–378; FB's epitaph for CB, 370;
  Greville episode in, 15, 131; second
  marriage of CB in, 25–26, and death of
  second wife, 275–276; Susanna's death
  in, 311; wig story in, 259–260; publication, 376–378
  —contemporary responses and reviews,
  33, 378
miscellaneous manuscript scraps,
  207–209, 250–251, 300–301, 319,
  382–383, 425–426

Prologue, "spoken upon the Dublin
  theatre" (unknown), 106, 403

Siege of Pevensey, The, 180, 183–188,
  213, 214, 279, 296; compared with
  Evelina, 188; *Edwy and Elgiva*, 183;
  Camilla, 213, 214; *Clarinda* fragment,
  213; *A Busy Day*, 296; *The Wanderer*,
  189, 323, 358

"To Sue on her recovery from the
  Jaundice," 26, 395

Wanderer; or, Female Difficulties, The, 3,
  23, 25, 35, 37, 40, 77, 100, 189, 192,
  197, 231, 286, 318–368, 383,
  387–388; "Dedication" to, 35–36,
  317–318, 369–370, 377, 420;
  England, condition of as presented in,
  328–329, 332, 344, 360–361; fairy-
  tales in, 364; French Revolution in, 57,
  318, 323, 324–325, 331–332, 353,
  364; historical context of, 318–319,
  332, 364–365, 423, 424; human suffering as presented in, 349–350,
  355–356; language in, 330–331, 337,
  388; male characters in, 344–348, 426;
  mystery in, 319, 359, 367; name as
  issue in, 319–320, 329; publication of,
  4, 317, 332, 369, 383, 420; race and
  racial prejudice in, 299, 320, 324, 356,
  358; rights of women in, 231,
  337–338, 360–361; Romanticism of,

333, 363–364; self-dependence in, 331, 358; slavery in, 358; Stonehenge as image in, 3, 361–365, 366–368, 387; "toad-eating" in, 358; unrighteousness of human affairs, 366–368; work and suffering of men and women, 352–353, 355–356, 358, 359–361; working women in, 320–321, 349–359
—compared with: Evelina, 40, 318–319, 323, 326, 330, 347, 352, 358, 387–388; The Witlings, 323, 331, 350, 354, 358; Cecilia, 318, 319, 323, 324, 328, 342, 350, 352, 358, 365; Edwy and Elgiva, 343; The Siege of Pevensey, 189, 323, 358; Hubert De Vere, 189, 323, 342–343, 349; Elberta, 92, 341; Clarinda fragment, 340, 341, 347; Camilla, 231, 319, 323, 324, 338, 340, 341, 346, 347, 352, 363; Love and Fashion, 292, 299, 347; A Busy Day, 299, 300, 347, 358; The Woman-Hater, 308, 340, 343, 347, 352
—contemporary responses and reviews, 332–335, 337, 338, 370–371
Witlings, The, 66–98, 113, 158, 274, 287, 290, 299, 300, 323, 331, 358, 382, 386; "self-dependence" as theme of, 90, 113, 118, 274, 290, 331, 358; play-reading at Chessington, 91–95; suppression of, 80–81, 91, 92–98, 99, 100, 103, 113, 287–288; later revision of, 300–302
—compared with: Evelina, 82, 84, 87, 89; Cecilia, 102, 113, 323; Love and Fashion, 290; A Busy Day, 293, 299, 300, 301–302; The Woman-Hater, 300–303; The Wanderer, 323, 331, 350, 354, 358
—manuscripts of, 77, 300–301, 400–401, 419
Woman-Hater, The, 21, 245, 288, 299, 300–311, 341–343, 346, 387; character of Joyce in, 304, 305–308, 310, and FB, 305, 310
—compared with: Evelina, 297, 299, 307–308, 310, 387; The Witlings, 300–303; Cecilia, 306, 310; Clarinda fragment, 306; Camilla, 245, 302, 306, 307, 310, 311; A Busy Day, 299, 300–303, 311; The Wanderer, 308, 340, 343, 347, 352
—manuscripts of, 300–301, 419